A History of Japanese Religion

A History of Japanese Religion

edited by

Kazuo Kasahara

translated by

Paul McCarthy
and
Gaynor Sekimori

Kosei Publishing Co. • Tokyo

This book was originally published by Yamakawa-Shuppan-Sha in Japanese in two volumes under the title *Nihon Shūkyō Shi* (A History of Japanese Religion) in the *Sekai Shūkyō Shi Sōsho* (History of World Religions Series).

The photograph on the title pages shows part of the temple Enryaku-ji on Mount Hiei near Kyoto, which was originally established in 785 by Saichō, the founder of Japanese Tendai Buddhism. Since the later founders of major Japanese Buddhist sects studied and practiced their faith on the mountain, it has been called the mother of Japanese Buddhism.

Cover design by NOBU. The text of this book is set in a computer version of Monotype Baskerville with a computer version of Optima for display.

First English edition, 2001
Fourth printing, 2004

Published by Kosei Publishing Co., 2-7-1 Wada, Suginami-ku, Tokyo 166-8535, Japan.
Copyright © 2001 by Kosei Publishing Co.; all rights reserved.

ISBN 4-333-01917-6   Printed in Japan

Contents

11. Women and Buddhism

12. Shintō and Shugendō

13. The Tokugawa Shogunate and Religion

21. Buddhism and Modern Society   545

22. The Growth of New Religious Movements   561

23. The Established Religions Today   585

Maps

13

Preface

The Japanese today are free to choose the philosophy or religion that will be the foundation of their lives, and a tremendous variety of worldviews compete for their allegiance. Those Japanese who, from amid a welter of conflicting intellectual systems and values, elect to follow the teachings of a religion are said to constitute about twenty percent of the population. The majority are committed to Buddhism as a system of belief for addressing the problems of living and dying.

The history of religion in Japan, particularly that of Buddhism, coincides with the two-thousand-year history of the Japanese as a people. The investigation of such questions as what the Japanese have sought in religion and how religion has responded to their needs is one of the major tasks of the scholarly study of religion in Japan. The history of doctrines has been studied ever since the arrival of the Buddhist religion, challenging the intellectual resources of the various schools, sects, and subsects; and those efforts have been fruitful. In contrast, the study of the history of religious communities and groups began rather late, gaining recognition only with the development of modern historiography in Japan. It has been only about three-quarters of a century since the history of religion came to be seen as a facet of the intellectual and spiritual history of the Japanese people—rather than simply as the tracing of the evolution of a particular sect—and studied with a view toward learning from the past so as to better plan for the future.

In that time, the methodical study of the history of religions has yielded much information, yet only since the end of World War II have Japanese historians begun to study the history of religious organizations and doctrinal systems in the context of their historical backgrounds. Since the war, a number of histories of Japanese religion and of Japanese Buddhism have appeared as a result of these new scholarly directions.

A History of Japanese Religion originally appeared as volumes 11 and 12 in the History of World Religions series published by Yamakawa Shuppan-sha, Tokyo. The authors and editor have tried to approach their subject from a fresh perspective, incorporating new information on the history of religious devotion, on the relation between religion and political power, on the connection between ethics and religion, and on Japanese folklore and folkways, all of which have been relatively neglected in earlier histories of Japanese religion. Given the growth of knowledge in various areas of religious studies and the important differences in doctrine, organization, political power, and so forth, among various schools and sects, it is too much to expect a single scholar to be able to elucidate the entire spectrum of Japanese religion. Therefore, the editor solicited the cooperation of a number of scholars, each expert in a specific area, so as to be able to include in the present work the fruits of the latest research and the most acute scholarly insights. As a result, some chapters are the work of more than one author, and some authors are responsible for more than one chapter. The authors' contributions are detailed in the List of Contributors. To achieve consensus on our approach to various problems that arose in the course of our work, all the authors participated in a number of discussion meetings; and the editor is most grateful for their generous cooperation.

It should be noted that with the exception of the names of the authors and editor, the names of all Japanese in this book are given in the Japanese style, surname first. The few Chinese terms appearing in this book are transliterated according to the Wade-Giles system.

Finally, if the present work contributes to greater knowledge of the history and characteristics of the spiritual life of the Japanese people over the past two thousand years, as well as to determination of the direction in which Japanese religion should develop, the authors and the editor will feel that their work has been worthwhile.

KAZUO KASAHARA

Introduction
Religion and the Japanese

RELIGION IN JAPAN TODAY

Japan is deluged with philosophies and ideologies. There is tremendous diversity of mental and spiritual attitudes and value systems. The various systems of thought and belief evolved by the world's peoples in the course of their historical development are now proffered to the Japanese people. Proffer may be too weak a word—in a sense, a choice is demanded of them. Moreover, Japanese today may freely choose the worldview that appeals to them and live by its dictates, without much concern for the opinions of others or for political and social pressure. Not only are they free to believe what they wish, but also they may freely propagate that view, attempting to convince others of its correctness. Article 20 of the postwar Japanese Constitution guarantees freedom of religion, and Article 89, forbidding the use of public moneys for religious purposes, strengthens that provision. In no other period in the nearly two thousand years of Japanese history have the people enjoyed such freedom of thought and religious belief. But what position does religious thought, especially Buddhist thought, occupy in the spiritual life of contemporary Japanese?

The value of religious thought in Japan today in comparison with other systems of thought can be viewed both qualitatively, that is, in terms of its content, and quantitatively, in terms of the number of Japanese who subscribe to a religion and try to live by its teachings. With regard to quality, I believe we can say that the teachings of the religions historically regarded as somehow characteristically Japanese are consistent with the modern

17

spirit of democracy, compassionate concern for others, universal love, and humanism. In that sense, I think we can affirm that most of the religions in contemporary Japan have a significant function in today's world and will continue to have one. With regard to quantity, there are over one hundred and eighty thousand temples, shrines, and churches in Japan. The numerous Japanese who seek strength for their lives in religion look to these institutions for fellowship and instruction. There are various estimates of the religious population of Japan, but it is probably safe to say that approximately twenty percent of the total population of one hundred and twenty-four million believe in some deity and are affiliated with some religious organization.

If one in five Japanese is a believer, then quantitatively, too, religion is a significant factor in contemporary Japan. The actual figures are of course open to question. For example, according to the 2000 Annual Directory of Religion, compiled by Japan's Agency for Cultural Affairs on the basis of statistics supplied by religious organizations, the total number of religious adherents in Japan exceeds two hundred million. Since the figures supplied by each organization are accepted without question, it is certain that the actual number of adherents is much lower. On the other hand, if we look only at the new religions, which have been especially active in the post–World War II period, it is clear that they have succeeded in winning an enormous number of adherents in the short space of four or five decades. When we consider that one religious organization has been able to advance into the political realm through its influence on its members and wield significant power as a result, we gain a clearer idea of the size and potential power of religious organizations in Japan today.

If the immense religious population of Japan were affiliated with a single religious organization, it would not be difficult for a kind of theocratic government to emerge. But in fact, the religions that claim the loyalties of one-fifth of the nation's population are almost countless. The "eighty-four thousand buddhas" of Buddhism and "eight million gods" of Shintō all have their place in the hearts of the Japanese. Indeed all the world's religions are represented in Japan today. Shintō (the indigenous religion of the Japanese people), the foreign faith of Buddhism (which began to wield enormous influence in the mid-sixth century C.E.), Christianity, and a wealth of other faiths coexist. The religions of Japan are extremely varied, not only in doctrine but also in age. Each faith insists that it fulfills the functions and mission proper to religion. Those functions are variously defined, but surely one of the most important is to teach people how to live and die, to offer them support. By that measure, one may well ask how many of the multitude of religions have fulfilled their mission, both in the past and in the present.

In discussing the tremendous variety of contemporary Japanese religions, several categorizations suggest themselves, but the most common are "established religions" and "new religions." Yet these terms are not precise, in that there are various classifications of the established religions and the new religions, based on their origin and age. In this book, the term established religions refers to those groups that originated and developed prior to Japan's early modern period (that is, the late nineteenth century), and the term new religions refers to those groups that originated and developed in the modern period. Thus the various forms of Buddhism that emerged during the Nara, Heian, and Kamakura periods (between the seventh and early fourteenth centuries) constitute the core of the established religions. The new religions include both the thirteen groups constituting so-called Sectarian, or Religious, Shintō, which emerged in the late nineteenth century and developed within early modern society, and the groups generally known as new religions, namely, those that emerged in the pre– and post–World War II periods and have burgeoned in contemporary Japan.

Our first question must be: What are the functions of the established Buddhist sects in contemporary Japanese society? Major functions include conducting funeral and memorial services for deceased votaries and maintaining cemeteries. Another major function, quantitatively at least, is the touristic or cultural one of displaying the Buddhist artifacts of earlier ages, such as sacred images, for the appreciation of the general public. At the same time, a considerable number of Japanese have a strong interest in Buddhist thought, though not all of them are believers or people seeking a faith by which to live. Perhaps the interest of the majority might be described as academic or cultural. Thus in considering the ties of the contemporary Japanese to established Buddhism, it seems likely that the number of those who are actually believers is far smaller than the number of adherents claimed by each group.

Given the current state of the established Buddhist sects in Japan, it is no wonder that an increasing number of people feel that "the deities have left Japan" or that "the buddhas have passed away." In response to this criticism, many sensitive Buddhist leaders have begun to reflect on their religion's proper role in the modern age. A kind of Buddhist revival movement has developed in postwar society, urging a return to the vital, living spirit of the various sects' founders. However, the effectiveness of this movement is questionable.

On the other hand, looking at the new religions in the context of contemporary society, we appear to be witnessing a kind of springtime for religion in Japan. In the last four or five decades the new religions have been remarkably active. The majority have succeeded in winning the devotion of a vast number of followers and incorporating them into strong, tightly knit organizational structures. The conducting of funerals and memorial services and maintaining of cemeteries (all activities connected with the dead) are not the basis of the ties between the new religions and their followers. Neither do the new religions attract mass followings because of the purely artistic or historical interest of their sacred images and monuments. Nor do the philosophies of the new religions appeal primarily on the academic or cultural level. The attraction of these groups is based on factors quite different from those that pertain in the case of the established sects. The new religions' appeal rests on their ability to provide a sense of meaning in life, spiritual aid in the business of living and dying. They provide individual believers with a feeling of joy in having been "saved" and a zeal to spread that joy to others. It is this that accounts for the extraordinary development of the new religions in the postwar period.

In view of the growth of the new religions, then, we can say that religion is indeed alive and well in Japan. In short, the age is a good one for religion. People have the right to believe in the religion of their choice without interference and to spread that faith to others. For the first time in Japanese history, religion is truly independent. Under the present democratic political system, it is possible for a religion to enter the political arena, unseating existing political power groups and exercising power to benefit people in accordance with its own tenets. This is a new phenomenon in the two millennia of Japanese history.

Yet the place of religion in contemporary Japan is in many ways puzzling. For example, why are there so many kinds of religion in Japan today? Religions have multiplied throughout Japanese history, to an extent greater than one might think necessary. Are Japanese incapable of transmitting a religion unchanged from generation to generation? Without exception, large numbers of religions, especially popular religions, have come into being in every major age of transition in Japan's history. Let us next look at religion in the context of these transitional periods.

RELIGION IN PERIODS OF CHANGE

Japanese history can be divided into four broad periods: ancient, feudal, early modern and prewar, and postwar. Though each of the four major periods can be subdivided, these subdivisions do not represent the basic, essential changes of the larger divisions. The ancient period includes the Nara (646–794) and Heian (794–1185) periods; and the latter can be subdivided into the periods of direct imperial rule, the rule of ministers of state and regents, the rule of cloistered emperors, and the rule of the Heike (or Taira) clan. The feudal period can be divided into the Kamakura (1185–1336), Muromachi (1336–1568), Momoyama (1568–1603), and Edo (1603–1868) periods. Each of these smaller periods within the ancient and feudal ages shared a common value system, in that a single class (the aristocratic or the warrior class) held power. However, periods of major change are accompanied by shifts in the power-holding classes and the accepted value systems. Thus there have been three major transitions in Japanese history: from the ancient to the feudal period (that is, from the Heian to the Kamakura period), from the feudal period to the early modern period (that is, from the Edo period to the Meiji period [1868–1912]), and from the early modern and prewar period to the postwar period. These three transitions demarcate the four major periods first mentioned above.

In each of the three periods of great change, new popular religious movements emerged and developed rapidly in the crucible of the new age. For instance, during the Kamakura period six great Buddhist priests (Hōnen, Eisai, Shinran, Dōgen, Nichiren, and Ippen) founded new religious movements in the space of about seventy years. Of all the available means of salvation, Hōnen, Shinran, and Ippen preached *senju nembutsu*, or exclusive reliance on recitation of the sacred name of Amida (Amitābha) Buddha. Thus the Jōdo (Pure Land) sect, regarding Hōnen as its founder, the Jōdo Shin (True Pure Land) sect, regarding Shinran as its founder, and the Ji (Timely) sect, regarding Ippen as its founder, developed from similar teachings. The Rinzai sect, founded by Eisai, and the Sōtō sect, founded by Dōgen, chose zazen, or *shikan taza* (seated meditation), as the means of attaining enlightenment as taught by the historical Buddha, Shakyamuni. Finally, Nichiren, founder of the sect that bears his name, preached the recitation of the sacred title of the Lotus Sutra, or the *daimoku*—*Namu-myōhō-renge-kyō*—as the sole means of salvation.

The new sects did not simply deny the means to salvation and enlightenment preached by the older schools; their emphasis on salvation through *senjaku* (selection), *senju* (sole practice), and *igyō* (easy practice) denied the essentially polytheistic nature of Nara- and Heian-period Buddhism. This denial of the characteristic features of the older forms of Buddhism resulted in the oppression and persecution of the new Kamakura sects. Yet these groups continued to win the support of the masses, preaching their new messages in the country's lanes and alleys.

The development of the new sects paralleled that of the feudal system, and by the Edo period they were all more or less tightly linked to the holders of political power, having become established religions that cooperated with the government in controlling the populace. With the shift from the Edo period to the Meiji period of the early modern period, the Japanese people again produced numerous new popular faiths: the thirteen sects of Sectarian Shintō, among them Tenrikyō, Konkōkyō, and Kurozumikyō. These groups were able to develop under the Meiji Constitution (though not without interference from government, society, and the established Buddhist sects), and they gave many people at the lowest social level a sense of meaning in life and death.

Once again, in the transition from the prewar to the postwar period (with August 15, 1945, the day of Japan's surrender, as a convenient demarcation), numerous new popular religions emerged. There are said to be one to two thousand of these new religions, including such large and influential groups as Risshō Kōsei-kai and Sōka Gakkai. In the postwar period, these groups have won immense followings. Thus a host of religions, both traditional and new, coexist in Japan today. The question is: Why have the Japanese produced so many popular faiths in periods of major change?

Each of the three major transition periods mentioned above ushered in a new age in the wake of civil or foreign war. The Kamakura period was born out of the wars between the Taira and Minamoto clans; the early modern period was the fruit of the conflicts of the late Edo period and early Meiji period; and the postwar period was born out of World War II. In each period of conflict, the entire nation's wealth and energy were poured into the struggle for political supremacy. The birth pangs of each new age forced people to an awareness of the poverty and emptiness of the existing political structures. The effect on the populace of the political developments attending the birth of the postwar period clearly reveals how much people living in a time of great change suffer as the result of the poverty of politics.

On August 16, 1945, postwar Japanese democracy took its first steps, both in theory and in practice. Yet one may question how many politicians really acted out of concern for the people's welfare, despite the postwar political system, under which they were elected by direct popular ballot. The Japanese people in fact had to rely on their own inner strength to survive amid the poverty and emptiness of politics. History shows how intensely the majority of the people suffered as a result of the bankruptcy of politics in an age in which political power could be gained and held through military might alone, without popular support.

An age of transition forces people to experience the emptiness and poverty of the economic order, as well. The Japanese living through the transition from the prewar to the postwar period lacked even the necessities of life. Inevitably, a new age—born from a period of internal strife or foreign war—emerges only after the people's resources have been all but exhausted. Whichever side wins, the new age is born in economic ruin. The people, thrust into an age of change, must deal with both the poverty of politics and the ruin of the economic order.

Those who live in a period of major change must deal with yet another problem—a radical shift in accepted values. Each age has its own value system, created by the political powers of the time and forced upon the common people, which gives rise to the popular ideal of the age. The ancient, feudal, and early modern and prewar periods all had their own ideal or model image. Of course, the source of the values that foster the ideal image differs from age to age. In the ancient period the degree of consanguinity to the imperial family had great value; in the feudal period loyalty to one's lord (especially to the "supreme lords"—the shōgun and daimyō) was important; and in the early modern and prewar period loyalty to the emperor was of supreme value. The prewar model image was born at great cost in sweat, blood, and lives sacrificed for the sake of such ideals as "loyalty to the emperor and love of country" and "the whole world under a single roof—Asia united under the Japanese emperor." The symbol of this sort of model figure was the official decoration awarded by the government. Indeed, the idea that a person's worth can be measured by the number of decorations he or she has received may be peculiar to the modern period.

If the value system of a particular period is the creation of the political powers of the period, then it is natural that this value system should disappear in the next age, following the collapse of the previous power structure: that which was most highly prized yesterday is now least valued. This kind of turnabout in values regularly occurs in periods of major change. Thus with the dawn of a new era on August 15, 1945, the image of the ideal Japanese underwent a total change. Prewar official decorations became worthless—more, they became a liability, to be borne by each recipient. One manifestation of this liability was the categorization of people as class A, B, or C war criminals. Naturally, people were bewildered by such a dramatic reversal of values during the transition to the postwar age.

Similar phenomena occurred in earlier periods of change, from the ancient period to the feudal period and from the feudal period to the early modern period. In every transitional period, the people had to learn to survive on their own, in a political, economic, and spiritual vacuum. The masses sought salvation from the deities and the buddhas, but the existing religions had been born in the dawn of the previous age, had developed together with it, and ultimately had become the servants of the political establishment. In most cases, the established faiths were not able to respond to the spiritual needs of people seeking to cope with the problems of a new age. The people usually found it necessary to look elsewhere for the help they needed. Though they could not find what they required in the established faiths, the people continued to seek religious succor. And in each period of major change, in response to popular need, there arose numerous new faiths that vigorously propagated their beliefs. Since so many people sought relief in religion, these new groups were able to grow and develop with amazing speed.

Some of the distinctive characteristics of the history of Japanese religion can be seen in the birth and development of the six sects of Kamakura-period Buddhism during the transition from the ancient period to the feudal period, of the thirteen sects of Sectarian Shintō during the transition from the feudal period to the early modern period, and of the myriad new religions that have emerged since the end of World War II. Let us, then, examine that history, bearing in mind what has been said about the Japanese people's ties to religion, as evidenced in both contemporary Japan and the periods of major change mentioned above.

A History of Japanese Religion

1. Religion in Primitive Japanese Society

RELIGION IN THE JŌMON PERIOD

It is by no means clear when human beings first began to inhabit the Japanese archipelago. Today, it is said that there is a possibility of human habitation dating back to the early period of the Former Stone Age, but what is now generally accepted is from the late period of the Former Stone Age. However, the number of artifacts recovered is too small to suggest a date for the earliest religious phenomena, which are expressions common to all human societies.

Approximately fifteen thousand years ago, earthenware began to be produced alongside stone objects, which had originated in an earlier period. To the modern eye, these earthenware artifacts seem to be far more expressive than the earlier stone artifacts. Even the earliest earthenware has incised patterns, which some experts see as expressions of religious feeling. Excavation level nine at the Kamikuroiwa rock-shelter site in Ehime Prefecture, Shikoku, has yielded linear-relief pottery, pointed implements, scrapers, and tanged points, as well as small flat stones (chlorite schists), some of which are engraved. The stones are very small—only four to five centimeters long—and the engraved lines represent human females with full breasts and short skirts or loincloths.

The figurative artifacts from the Kamikuroiwa site are made of stone, but earthenware figurines are found throughout sites dated to the Jōmon period (ca. 10,000–300 B.C.E.). Almost all the figurines represent human females, some with clearly depicted breasts; some holding children; some

27

obviously pregnant, with enlarged abdomens; and some with beads, possibly representing unborn children, inside their hollow bodies. Virtually none are intact, which is true of most earthenware of that period.

The number of earthenware pieces found at sites varies from age to age, from area to area. In the case of the Shaka-dō (Śākyamuni hall) in Yamanashi Prefecture, more than a thousand pieces were discovered at a single site.

In some cases, the earthenware figurines appear to have been accorded special care. They were set on a small earthen platform or a stone base and surrounded by a fence of pottery shards or small rocks, or set inside a circle of stones that was roofed over with a larger stone. Most, however, have been found without any attendant structures. These figurines seem to have had little connection with graves. While some late-Jōmon-period figurines contain the bones of newborn infants, in general the figurines do not appear to have been used in conjunction with burials.

A great many Jōmon-period graves have been discovered, usually grouped together not far from prehistoric settlements. Most are simply holes in the ground large enough to accommodate the bodies. A substantial number of human skeletons have been preserved in graves in shell mounds, though those graves are no more than pits or trenches. While there are some instances of full-length burial, in this period most bodies were flexed, with the knees drawn up, and were buried face up, face down, lying on one side, or sitting upright. In other cases, the limbs were more loosely arranged, approximating full-length burial.

Various explanations for the flexed postures of the bodies have been offered. Some suggest the limbs were flexed so that the grave could be smaller; others theorize that the knees were drawn up in an attempt to make the body resemble an unborn child; still others hold that the arrangement of the limbs was intended to prevent the spirit of the deceased from escaping into the outer world. Since the bodies were generally not arranged in an extreme or unnatural posture, however, the intent may simply have been to represent an instinctive, natural posture, like that of a person huddling to keep warm in the cold. Skeletons hugging stones to their chests and others with the head covered with an earthenware jar have also been found.

Graves in shell mounds, where human remains are exceptionally well preserved, yield evidence of various types of multiple burial. Examples include graves in the Ōta shell mound in Hiroshima Prefecture, where a mother-and-child pair is buried; the Tsukumo shell mound in Okayama

Prefecture, where several people are buried together; the Satohama shell mound in Miyagi Prefecture, where an old man-and-child pair is found; and instances of later burials in old graves, with the earlier remains pushed to one side. Several thousand skeletons have been recovered from shell mounds throughout Japan, including 340 skeletons from the Yoshigo shell mound in Aichi Prefecture, 232 from the Tsukumo shell mound, and 191 from the Ikawazu shell mound in Aichi Prefecture.

Jōmon-period graves have also yielded large earthenware burial jars containing the bones of infants, burial jars provided with stone stoppers, and multiple burial jars—for example, two jars joined mouth-to-mouth to accommodate a body. In some cases, stones were piled on top of the burial jars, and in others the jars were surrounded with stones. Numerous small burial jars appear to have been used for the secondary burial of bones rather than for original interment.

Burials in stone chambers have been discovered, in addition to those in simple pits dug in the earth. There are also graves whose openings are covered with stones, and some graves include a stone on which the body's head was rested, as on a pillow. Furthermore, groups of trench graves have been discovered in association with stone circles. It seems possible that some groupings of stones, either piled up or set in the ground, were intended as grave markers for trench graves beneath them.

There were, thus, three basic types of burial: in pits, in jars, and in stone chambers. There were also several types of burial practices: interment of the body, secondary burial (reburial of the bones after the body had decomposed), and, perhaps, cremation. The possible connections with the burial practices of later ages are intriguing.

Grave goods in the Jōmon period seem to consist principally of ornaments, which were either used by the deceased during life or put on the body at the time of death. Bands of shells on the arm, amulets and charms made of animal bone or horn hung around the neck, and loose stone beads are most frequently encountered. Tools and weapons are less frequently found.

In spite of their female form, the earthenware figurines of the Jōmon period were not necessarily connected with rites performed by women. Though many rites may have been carried out by individuals or small groups, surviving stone circles seem to be evidence of communal religious observances.

The best-known stone circles are those at the Ōyu site in Akita Prefec-

Jōmon Sites

SEA OF JAPAN

Ōta   Tsukumo

Kamikuroiwa
SHIKOKU

KYUSHU

HOKKAIDO

Ōyu

Satohama

HONSHU

Teraji

Shaka-dō

Wappara

Tokyo

Shimoyato

Mt. Fuji▲

Yoshigo
shell mound

Kyoto

Tōshōin

Ikawazu
shell mound

PACIFIC OCEAN

ture, where stones are arranged to form circles, rectangles, and ovals. Some of the stones stand upright, and others are laid flat. Thousands of stones are arranged in two pairs of concentric circles. The diameter of the outer circle of the southeastern pair, which are known as the Nonakadō, is roughly forty meters. In the open space between the inner and outer circles, there is an upright stone surrounded by flat stones radiating from its base. Some have suggested that this arrangement may represent a sundial. The diameter of the outer circle of the northwestern pair, the Manza, is well over forty meters. A few artifacts have been recovered from the Ōyu stone circles, among them stone axes, staffs, and plates, as well as a few earthenware shards. Beneath some of the stone groups at Ōyu are pits that were probably used as graves. Dozens of similar stone circles are scattered throughout eastern Japan.

Numerous charred bones have been found at the Shimoyato site in Isehara and the Tōshōin site in Kamakura, both in Kanagawa Prefecture. At Shimoyato there are stone-floored dwellings, chamberlike pits or shafts lined with stone, and rough groupings of stones. In one area, flat river boulders are laid in a fan-shaped pattern, with a row of three large stones set upright across the breadth of the fan. A long, narrow paved "path" extends from the "fan" to a hearth, and charred bone fragments have been found in the hearth area. Small stones are laid to outline a square, centering on the hearth. The whole structure appears to have been the site of large-scale bird and animal sacrifices.

At the Wappara site in Nagano Prefecture pillar-shaped river boulders are set up at regular intervals to form several circles, and large amounts of charcoal have been unearthed at this site. At the Teraji site in Niigata Prefecture an arrangement of flat river boulders and thick wooden posts surrounded by a row of riverbed stones appears to have been a ceremonial site.

While the various sites mentioned thus far display different features, all of them consist of fairly complex structures occupying a considerable area. In the latter part of the Jōmon period, the variety of site types increased. Although it is possible that there are collective graves near these sites, they can also be viewed as the sites of communal religious ceremonies unrelated to burial practices.

The communal structures of the Jōmon period are still not adequately understood. There appears to be little continuity between these structures and cultural phenomena of the following Yayoi period, which increases the difficulty of developing a systematic explanation of Jōmon-period communal religious activities. But the large pit dwellings—over twenty meters in diameter—are thought by some scholars to have been used for communal meetings. At any rate, it seems certain that communal religious ceremonies were conducted on a fairly large scale. Moreover, there appear to have been special ritualists or shamans, identified by the extraction of certain teeth, who participated in numerous magical ceremonies, in some of which masks were employed.

RELIGION IN THE YAYOI AND KOFUN PERIODS

Yayoi Burials

Excavations suggest that religious phenomena grew more complex during the Yayoi period (ca. 300 B.C.E.–C.E. 300). *Dōtaku* (bronze ritual bells) and bones used for divination give clues to the characteristics of the religion of this period. There were no fundamental changes in burial practices, but in addition to burial jars and dolmens, burial mounds bounded by rectangular ditches began to appear throughout the land. On Kyushu, burial jars and dolmens are especially characteristic of the Yayoi period. Grave goods are found in Jōmon-period graves, but in Yayoi-period burials grave goods begin to appear not simply at isolated sites but also throughout specific regions, and patterns begin to emerge.

In the Yayoi period, bodies were buried either full-length or flexed in earthen pits, earthenware jars, or stone chambers. In addition to simple pits dug in the earth, dolmens were favored. Many Yayoi-period stone chambers resemble coffins, in that they were built with huge slabs of stone. Both single and paired earthenware jars were used in jar burials. Several thousand large-jar burials have been discovered on northern Kyushu. The jar burials fall into two groups: those that include grave goods and those that do not.

Bronze objects from continental Asia are found in some Yayoi-period graves. These objects are evidence that by this time certain groups had acquired sufficient power and wealth to amass foreign objects and inter them with particular individuals, perhaps leaders of the groups. However, even at the sites where grave goods have been found, the majority of individual graves do not contain such objects. It appears that only a small

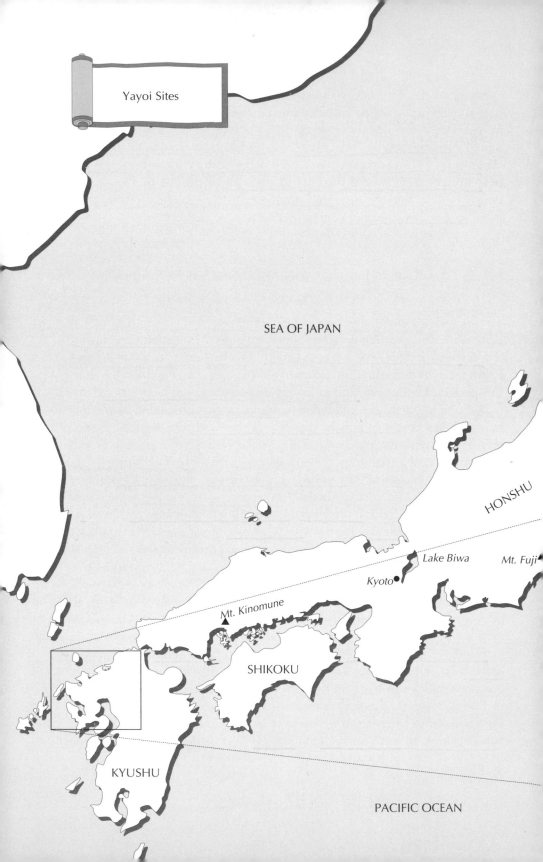

Yayoi Sites

SEA OF JAPAN

HONSHU

Lake Biwa

Mt. Fuji

Kyoto

Mt. Kinomune

SHIKOKU

KYUSHU

PACIFIC OCEAN

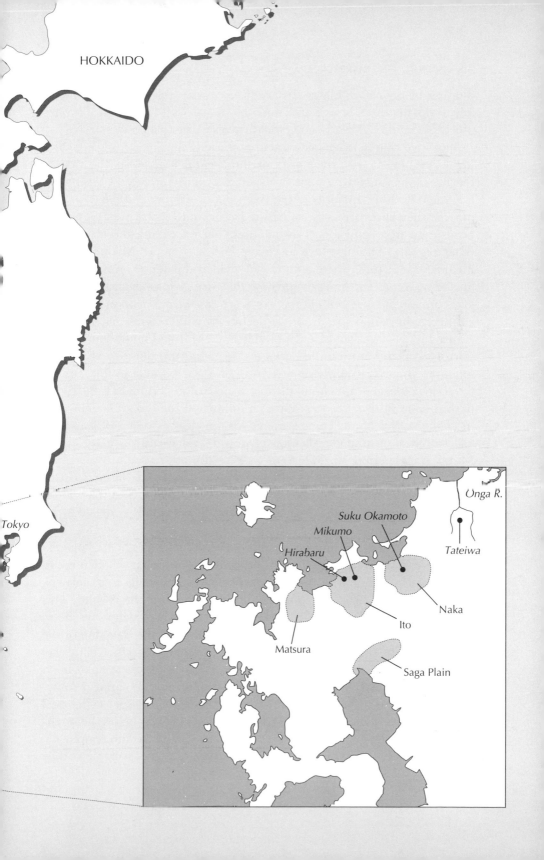

HOKKAIDO

Tokyo

Ōnga R.

Suku Okamoto

Mikumo

Hirabaru

Tateiwa

Naka

Ito

Matsura

Saga Plain

number of people within restricted groups were able to provide themselves with imported bronze and iron objects—or with locally made bronze objects, ornamental beads, and other articles—as grave goods.

Imported objects have been found at various sites on Kyushu, including Matsuura, Ito, Naka, a part of the Saga Plain, along the middle reaches of the Onga River, and in the area around Tateiwa. In this region are found both the majority of the Former Han–dynasty (206 B.C.–A.D. 8) mirrors that have been discovered in Japan and bronze weapons, glass beads, and iron implements in quantities far exceeding those found in other regions. The most extraordinary find was at the Mikumo site in Fukuoka Prefecture, where a jar burial yielded thirty-five bronze mirrors (including some that appear to predate the Former Han dynasty), annular glass ornaments, the comma-shaped beads known as *magatama*, cylindrical beads, imported metal objects decorated with bronze gilt, a bronze sword, bronze spearheads, and a bronze halberd. In addition, four broken mirrors were set around the burial jar, bringing the number of mirrors found at Mikumo to thirty-nine. This total is comparable to the number found in the largest tumulus of the following Kofun period, as is the figure of thirty-odd mirrors recovered from a dolmen at the Suku Okamoto site in Fukuoka Prefecture. These grave goods are clear evidence of major social stratification and the division of power and wealth as early as the Middle Yayoi period (ca. 200 B.C.E.–ca. C.E. 20).

These jar-burial sites also yield earthenware, including large earthenware jar-stands, which were used for religious rites at the graves. The stands are further evidence of the gradual formalization of rituals associated with burial mounds.

The burial mound discovered at Hirabaru in Maebaru in Fukuoka Prefecture has a rectangular pit in the center, in which a wooden coffin was placed together with forty-two broken mirrors at its four corners. Beads have been recovered from the ditch surrounding the mound. This ditch also contains a number of pit graves that are plainly auxiliary graves. Probably there was a religious significance to the breaking of the mirrors, which were clearly valuable, hard-to-obtain objects. Cylindrical beads made of jasper found in Yayoi-period large-jar graves in Fukushima Prefecture, in the Tōhoku region of northern Honshu, also appear sometimes to have been shattered before burial. Graves with jasper cylindrical beads and glass beads that appear to have been broken before being interred have also been found in Chiba Prefecture, in the Kantō region.

The burial mound at Hirabaru is an example of a grave surrounded by a ditch. This sort of grave spread throughout Japan during the Yayoi period and seems to be related to the large mounded tombs of the following Kofun period. Several hundred Yayoi-period burial mounds have been discovered, and research is gradually clarifying their connection with population centers. The rectangular ditches that surround most of these low burial mounds measure from several to twenty meters in length. Pit graves were dug in the center of each mound.

Many beads appear as grave goods, and there are also iron and bronze implements; but most of the graves contain no human remains. Only earthenware vessels are found in the surrounding ditches. These include high-footed bowls and wide-mouthed jars, but small-mouthed jars are most numerous, and the bottoms of many of these jars appear to have been broken deliberately.

Holes left by posts have been found in some ditches, and other ditches appear to have been covered over shortly after they were dug. It seems likely that a fence of tree branches was built at the ditch and that earthenware utensils were placed at the base of the fence in connection with funerary rites. Rectangular altars were erected on top of the round section of large early-period keyhole-shaped burial mounds. The altar constituted the focal point of the site. Rows of *haniwa* (earthenware funerary sculptures) were set up along the altar's four sides, and it is likely that there was a brushwood fence, as well.

Dōtaku *and Oracle Bones*

The bell-shaped bronze *dōtaku*, found mainly in the Kinki region, stand out among Yayoi-period ceremonial objects that appear to be unrelated to grave sites. Though their shape is said to derive from the small harness bells of the Korean peninsula, the *dōtaku* appear to have been used for ceremonial and religious purposes from earliest times. In recent years, molds for *dōtaku* have been found in Osaka, Nara, and Fukuoka prefectures, and their distribution patterns are currently being studied. The majority of *dōtaku* molds have been unearthed by chance, however.

Some *dōtaku* are quite large—over one meter in height—but they suddenly disappear as we move from the Yayoi to the Kofun period. This is one of the discontinuities between the two periods. It is impossible to know what kind of ritual observances the five hundred *dōtaku* thus far discovered were used for. The *dōtaku* found on Mount Kinomune in Hiroshima Prefecture, unassociated with any structures, was unearthed together with a bronze sword and a halberd at the base of a great crag that stands halfway up the mountain. Probably the artifacts were buried after use in rites conducted at the crag.

In addition to *dōtaku*, evidence of divination employing animal bones has been found at Yayoi-period sites. The shoulder blades and ribs of deer were heated over a fire, and good or bad fortune was predicted on the basis of the lines, cracks, and holes that appeared on the bones. From remains found in Kanagawa Prefecture, it appears that tortoise shells were also used in divination rites. While *dōtaku* did not survive the Yayoi period, the practice of divination did continue in the next period.

Kofun Burials

The beginning of the Kofun, or Tumulus, period (C.E. 300–646) is marked by the sudden emergence in the Yamato Basin, in the heart of the Kinai region, of the practice of building large tumuli, or *kofun*. The most typical of these tumuli are some two hundred meters in length and shaped like a keyhole, being composed of a circular mound connected to a rectangular mound. In fact, however, Kofun-period burial sites range from monumental tumuli (in a variety of shapes) to simple pit graves of the sort favored earlier. Though not numerous, jar burials are found, and large cylindrical earthenware coffins and other styles of earthenware coffins seem to have been widespread in some areas. Wooden coffins appear throughout the period, and the shapes of stone coffins become more varied, with many large sarcophagi carved in the shapes of split bamboo (resembling halves of a hollow tree trunk), boats, chests, and houses, among other shapes. Large-scale tumuli contain stone burial chambers.

Research on the siting of tomb mounds reveals that they are by no means limited to the topographic pattern most commonly seen, stretching from a mountaintop down to level ground. The shapes of tumuli include keyhole, squared keyhole (with a square mound replacing the round mound of the usual keyhole tumulus), round, square, rectangular, and round with two square mounds on opposite sides of the central mound. We do not know whether the particular shape was chosen by the person to be entombed or by his or her community, or whether it was determined by other factors. Assuming that it was chosen freely, the shape of a tumulus might tell us something about the person or community that built it. On the other hand, if we assume that the shape of a tumulus was determined by some external factor, we might conclude that there was a connection between tumulus shape and the social status of the person interred. We find that there were different situations, depending on the age and area, for the three hundred years from the third through the sixth century.

Typically, an early tumulus incorporated a vertical pit, which was lined with stone, clay, or pebbles. Such tumuli were used for individual interment, which predominated in the first half of the Kofun period. Horizontal corridor-style stone chambers were employed on Kyushu in the fifth century, becoming the principal form of tomb in the latter half of the Kofun period. This type of tomb could be reused simply by unsealing the entrance. It seems probable that corridor-style chambers that opened on the slopes of mounds were used as family tombs.

When it would be difficult to reuse a chamber (as in the case of vertical-pit stone chambers, whose only access was through the ceiling), the construction was completed in such a way that the crest of the mound could accommodate subsequent burials. At the same time, corridor-style stone chambers were usually intended to accommodate a single body and were not originally used for multiple burials. Thus the shift from vertical-pit to corridor-style stone chambers seems to be related more to changes in taste than to changes in burial customs and the religious mentality associated with them, as has sometimes been suggested.

The grave goods in the tumuli differ greatly in both quantity and type from site to site, but clothing, personal ornaments, weapons, armor, and ritual objects are found throughout the Kofun period. It is not clear whether bodies were dressed for burial or were simply interred with clothing laid over them. Skulls wearing crowns have been found. The use of beads and mirrors as grave goods characterizes the entire period. Weapons and armor tend to be the most up-to-date type available at the time, and utilitarian horse trappings also seem to have been buried when available. Highly decorated weapons, armor, and horse trappings, obviously ceremonial in character, were also interred with some frequency. Ritual objects include mirrors, beads, and, early in the period, objects made of jasper. Later in the period the jasper objects are superseded by earthenware utensils. Occasionally small iron or stone replicas of various articles and large, decorated ceremonial swords are found, as well.

Since the early-period tumuli in which these grave goods are found also contain many mirrors and stone artifacts of a sacred character, some scholars view them as the tombs of the shamanic elite that had existed since the Yayoi period or, in the case of tombs that contain many weapons and pieces of armor, as the tombs of a warrior elite. Yet it seems more

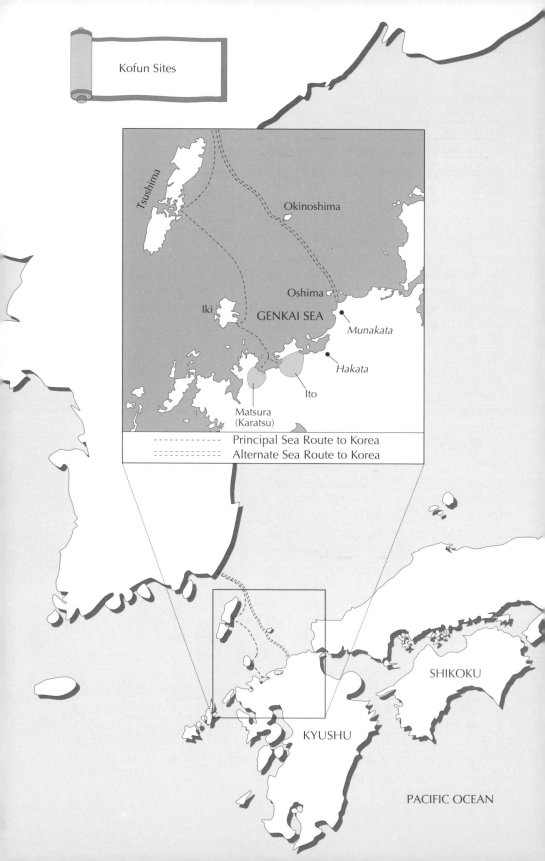

Kofun Sites

Tsushima

Okinoshima

Oshima

Iki

GENKAI SEA

Munakata

Hakata

Ito

Matsura
(Karatsu)

- - - - - - - - - - Principal Sea Route to Korea
- - - - - - - - - - Alternate Sea Route to Korea

SHIKOKU

KYUSHU

PACIFIC OCEAN

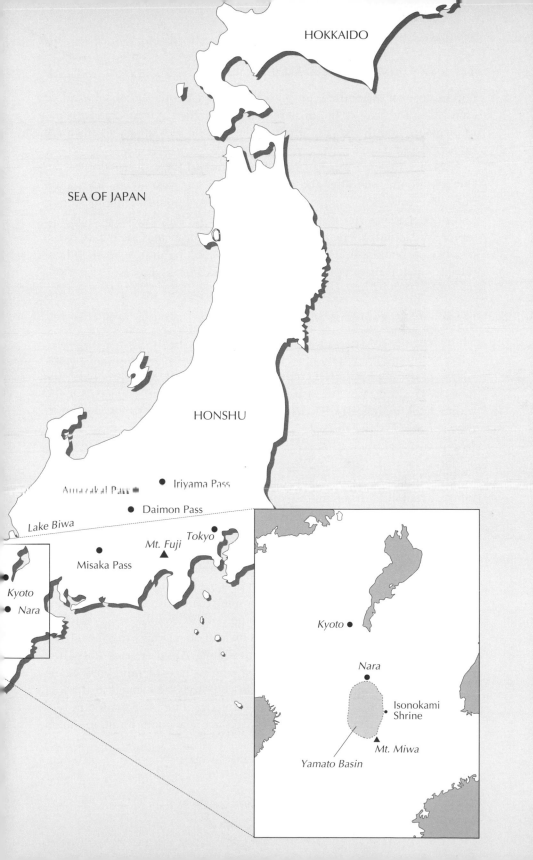

HOKKAIDO

SEA OF JAPAN

HONSHU

● Iriyama Pass

Amazakal Pass

● Daimon Pass

Lake Biwa

● Misaka Pass

Mt. Fuji ▲

Tokyo ●

Kyoto
● *Nara*

Kyoto ●

Nara ●

● Isonokami
Shrine

Yamato Basin

▲ Mt. Miwa

natural to view the variety in grave goods as a manifestation of gradual changes in the way of life of hereditary local elites. Grave goods, ritual implements, and the ways in which bodies were interred vary significantly by period and region.

Evidence of funerary rites conducted prior to the construction of the earthen mound and after the interment also survives: altars, *haniwa* figures, stone images of humans and horses, traces of bonfires, piles of stones, and stone markers. In the late Kofun period, even the remains of Buddhist temples are found. Yet many points are still unclear, such as the nature of the practice of the temporary interment of high-ranking people prior to final burial, which is mentioned in historical records of the late Kofun period.

Deities of Sea and Mountain

Many religious artifacts and sites dating from the Kofun period are unrelated to tumuli. Mountaintops and lowlands, plateaus, mountain passes, rivers, springs, the seashore, promontories, islands—any space where people have lived—and even the seabed can yield significant artifacts. Of the several hundred religious sites discovered thus far, those from the late fourth through the sixth century are the most noteworthy. The areas around Isonokami Shrine and Mount Miwa in Nara Prefecture have yielded many artifacts.

The Munakata site on Okinoshima, Fukuoka Prefecture, has been particularly rich in finds. Okinoshima is an isolated island in the Genkai Sea, off Kyushu. The location of one of the three principal Munakata shrines, each dedicated to a female sea deity, this island has been regarded as sacred since ancient times. Because of the stringent religious regulations governing Okinoshima and because it lies more than fifty kilometers from the nearest inhabited islands, evidence of ancient religious rites has been preserved there, with beads, horse trappings, and mirrors found undisturbed many centuries after the completion of the rites.

The Munakata Okitsumiya Shrine is located on a craggy marine terrace in the middle of the south side of Okinoshima. An altar from about the end of the fourth century stands atop a crag with a splendid view of the sea, while altars from the fifth and sixth centuries are located at the foot of the rock, in the shadow of the immense crag. The objects used in religious rites here are virtually identical with the grave goods found in tumuli of the same period.

Rites of the seventh and eighth centuries were performed at rectangular stone altars somewhat removed from the crag and employed a large number of pottery vessels, including the highest quality ceramics available, such as tricolored jars from T'ang China or of domestic manufacture. Even in earlier periods, most of the ritual items appear to have been of the highest quality: round mirrors decorated with engravings of arcs and of gods and beasts; hoe-shaped stones, of which only a few examples have been found on Kyushu; dragons' heads of gilt bronze that look as if they are of Northern Wei manufacture; carefully crafted looms of gilt bronze; faceted glass bowls; and superb horse trappings. Surely such valuable objects were brought here in such quantities because of this island's significant location.

The usual route to the Korean peninsula passed from Hakata (present-day Fukuoka), Ito, and Matsura, on the northwestern coast of Kyushu, via the islands of Iki and Tsushima. However, in time of urgency or military expeditions, the route from Munakata via Ōshima and Okinoshima was taken as the shortest sea route. This route must have been especially important to the rulers of the Kinai region, because they could travel directly to the Korean peninsula without passing through northern Kyushu. It is not surprising that this area should be safeguarded by a national religious center, for it was the gateway to the peninsula, through which the newest cultural developments—as well as dangerous epidemic diseases—might enter Japan.

Just as the gods of Okinoshima were worshiped as guardians of the boundary between Japan and Korea, so, too, were many guardian deities worshiped at another sort of boundary, mountain passes throughout the country—for example, Misaka, Iriyama, Daimon, and Amazakai passes in Nagano Prefecture. At all these sites there is evidence of religious observances conducted continually from about the end of the fourth century onward, although these observances were not so large in scale as those at Okinoshima.

Mirrors, iron objects, beads, and ritual implements of stone have been found, together with large quantities of earthenware. Rites were conducted wherever a steep mountain path ends in a narrow pass—the gateway to unknown territory. The pass was thought to be inhabited by a boundary deity who might prevent access to the land beyond; and rites were conducted there in an atmosphere compounded of religious awe and physical fatigue, the result of the effort of attaining the mountain's heights.

The distribution pattern of these religious sites shows that they spread widely throughout Japan in a relatively short time, during the fifth century.

A number of interesting hypotheses are suggested by the distribution pattern. The areas of western Japan where ancient religious artifacts are found are also the sites of later major local shrines, which implies continuity. The religious sites on seacoasts and islands from the Inland Sea region to the Munakata area were also stops on the sea route through the Inland Sea. They were religious focal points not only for local communities but also for seafarers. Thus it is quite possible that these areas were under the direct control of the rulers of the central Kinai area. By the same token, the principal religious sites in eastern Japan may have been focal points for rulers of that region in their effort to control the Kantō region and extend their control into the Tōhoku region.

The above conjectures presuppose that the religious observances at these sites were primarily group rituals. Still, the main ceremonial artifacts of this period—stone copies of functional objects—seem also to have been used in individual worship in the southern part of the Tōhoku region and in the Kantō and Chūbu regions. Their use continued into considerably later times. There are also earthenware and wooden implements, but those of stone are the most numerous.

Site-by-site classification of the stone artifacts reveals both regional differences between eastern and western Japan and differences between purely religious sites and sites connected with burials. For example, most of the stone artifacts recovered from Kofun burial sites are copies of utilitarian objects, such as swords of a type that was in use at the time. By contrast, copies of the type of sword that had prevailed in the earlier Yayoi period are found at the purely religious sites. Differences in the objects used in religious rites may signify differences in the nature of the rites themselves.

On the basis of artifacts alone, however, it is extremely difficult to identify the specific deities worshiped in Kofun-period religious rituals. This contrasts greatly with the situation in the following Nara and Heian periods, in which offerings to specific deities clearly identify the character and function of the deity. The deity of water or the sea, for example, was offered imported goods, such as horses, combs, and looms, indicating that this deity was regarded as a transmitter of continental culture.

In contrast to the difficulty of establishing a direct relation between Yayoi or pre-Yayoi ceremonial sites and later shrines and sacred precincts on the same sites, the sacred character of the religious sites that have yielded artifacts from the latter half of the fourth century onward has generally been recognized continuously; and these sites eventually became the seats of shrine worship. This indicates a certain continuity at the root of the Japanese religious consciousness, a chain whose links can be traced back archaeologically to the era of the great tumuli. Now that the artifacts of the Kofun period at last permit us to distinguish clearly between the general religious consciousness manifested in burial rites and purely religious rites addressed to the deities of nature, it is necessary to carefully investigate whether rites connected with so-called ancestor worship developed from rituals of the Kofun agrarian society or whether other factors were involved.

The element of continuity in religious rites—conspicuously lacking in the Yayoi period, as evidenced by the disappearance of the *dōtaku*—seems to have developed in the Kofun period, in tandem with a growing sense of territorial and economic security. It was against this religious background that Buddhism first appeared in Japan.

2. Buddhism
and the Nara Schools

BUDDHISM IN ANCIENT JAPAN

State Buddhism

The Japanese had seen and felt the presence of divinities everywhere in their natural surroundings. In the middle of the sixth century, foreign "deities" appeared in Japan, together with a profound, complex philosophical system. When Buddhism entered Japan, its "eighty-four thousand buddhas" were conveyed from the Korean peninsula and the Chinese mainland to the Japanese archipelago. Among the Japanese, it was especially the powerful members of the imperial court who actively encouraged the acceptance and indigenization of Buddhism, bringing its "deities" into the world of the Japanese divinities. It was not that these people fully understood the spiritual essence of Buddhism or its elaborate philosophy. Rather, they looked on Buddhism as a facet of continental civilization that had contributed to the cultural advancement of China and Korea and that, moreover, promised direct, practical benefits to its believers and practitioners. Thus Buddhism was first understood more in terms of form than of content.

Buddhism greatly impressed the Japanese with its beautiful rituals, elegantly inscribed sutras, monumental temples and pagodas, and splendid statues. Nonetheless, some—a very few—Japanese managed to comprehend the tenets of Buddhism rather than be blinded by its forms alone. Representative of this select group is Prince Shōtoku (574–622), who wrote: "The world is vain and illusory, and the Buddha's realm alone is true."

The Japanese understanding of Buddhism deepened over time, even as the effort to master its forms was energetically pursued.

In the Nara period (646–794) the central government gave Buddhism unstinting support and protection but at the same time instituted a comprehensive system for regulating and controlling the new religion. The Nara-period rulers decided to make full use of Buddhism as a spiritual buttress for the new continental-style, centralized nation-state that they were building, complete with a legal code and administrative regulations. The establishment of a state-supported monastery (*kokubunji*) and nunnery (*kokubunniji*) in each province and the construction of the temple Tōdai-ji and its colossal Buddha image in Nara, the capital, were manifestations of the government's policy.

With this firm foundation of government support, the Nara schools of Buddhism worked to deepen understanding of Buddhism through scholarly study and religious practice. The distinguishing characteristic of Nara Buddhism is the emphasis on comprehensive study of all the Buddhist traditions that had been transmitted to Japan—an emphasis summed up at that time in the phrase "simultaneous study of all six schools." Priests of the Nara schools were expected to study the outer form and inner spirit of the various traditions within Buddhism: this was their principal duty as state appointees. Their way of life was dictated by the *Sōni Ryō* (Regulations for Priests and Nuns), included in the legal code of the new nation-state promulgated in 701. These regulations enjoined priests to stay in monasteries and develop themselves through religious study and practice, and forbade them to go out among the common people to guide and help them directly. Any priest who violated these regulations was to be expelled from his monastery; the celebrated itinerant priest Gyōki (668–749) appears to have suffered this punishment.

Ironically, the Nara government's expenditure of vast sums of money for the construction of temples and monasteries, which were intended to support the new legal and governmental system, hastened the downfall of that very system. The Nara rulers eventually realized that to preserve and strengthen both the state and their own power it would be necessary to break free of the influence of the increasingly corrupt and decadent Nara schools. Thus the rulers decided to abandon both the six Buddhist schools and Nara, their power base, and move the capital to Heian-kyō (present-day Kyoto).

Though disillusioned by the corruption of the Nara schools, the nobility had by no means lost their devotion to Buddhism. It was no longer possible for the Japanese to live and grow culturally or spiritually without Buddhism. Having decided to move to Heian-kyō, the nobility also conceived the idea of importing new forms of Buddhism from the fountainhead—China. The task of introducing these new forms, appropriate to a new age, fell to Saichō (767–822) and Kūkai (774–835), the most eminent Japanese priests of their day. They did not have the time to spend years studying in China, examining and selecting teachings in the light of long experience. On the contrary, they had to accomplish their task in less than two years. Yet they succeeded magnificently: the Tendai sect, founded by Saichō, and the Shingon sect, founded by Kūkai, became the foundation of Heian Buddhism.

Heian Buddhism

Buddhism of the Heian period (794–1185) was similar to Nara-period Buddhism in that priests sought to realize the essence of Buddhism through study and practice and to serve the nation by chanting incantations to secure its protection. For the Japanese of that time, the ideal relation between politics and Buddhism was expressed in the statement "The imperial law and the Buddhist Law are like the two wheels of a cart": the mutual support of these two well-balanced forces would assure the power and prosperity of both. Through prayer to the eighty-four thousand buddhas, various forms of Buddhist practice, and earnest study of the sutras, the priests of the Nara and Heian schools of Buddhism sought to attain the deepest spiritual insight. Their emphasis was ascetic, and their faith had a polytheistic slant. Since polytheism is perhaps the most distinctive feature of Japanese religion, it is hardly surprising that Buddhism, too, came to be accepted in a polytheized form.

The ascetic nature of Heian Buddhist practice is clearly seen in the rules for religious training on Mount Hiei, on the outskirts of Kyoto. When Saichō established the temple Enryaku-ji there as a religious training center, he had already spent twelve years in seclusion on the mountain. In Saichō's *Sange Gakushō Shiki* (Regulations for Student Priests of Mount Hiei), twelve years of seclusion on the mountain, including one thousand days of the stringently ascetic "pilgrimage to the peaks," are stipulated as a requirement for becoming a spiritually mature priest—a severe regimen involving not only intense study of difficult scriptural texts but also rigorous ascetic practices.

By no means were all priests able to endure such strict ascetic training;

the majority failed. As the number of mediocre priests grew, so did the potential for the monasteries of Nara and Heian Buddhism to become more corrupt than "the vain world" outside. Hastening the process of corruption was the tendency for the imperial family and the noble elite to regard temple offices as sinecures for their offspring. Most of these clerics were interested not in spiritual attainment but in maintaining their privileged lifestyle. For in fact, family connections and social status in the secular world counted for a great deal in the Buddhist world, as well.

As high positions and important offices in the Buddhist establishment were increasingly monopolized by a hereditary elite, Japanese Buddhism sank further and further into stagnation and decadence. Eventually, those who truly sought to follow the way of buddhahood often found it necessary to leave the great monastic centers and live as recluses. Having abandoned the world to enter monasteries, they were forced to abandon the monastic world, as well. Thus, it was only rare individuals who were able to comprehend the essence of Buddhism and attain enlightenment within the world of Nara- and Heian-period Buddhism. Many failed student priests left the monasteries to seek their livelihood in the secular world once again or, alternatively, remained in the great monasteries as warrior-priests, or *sōhei*. At any rate, throughout the Heian period Buddhism generally failed to address the needs of ordinary people in their everyday lives. It was left to the Buddhists of the Kamakura period (1185–1336) to accomplish that important task. Let us now take a closer look at Nara- and Heian-period Buddhism.

THE JAPANESE RESPONSE TO BUDDHISM

Paths of Transmission

The Buddhism that spread to China during the Later Han dynasty (C.E. 25–220) was in turn introduced into the northern Korean kingdom of Koguryŏ from northern China in the latter half of the fourth century and into the southwestern Korean kingdom of Paekche from southern China around the middle of the fifth century. Buddhism was transmitted to Japan from Paekche in the mid-sixth century, at approximately the same time that it entered the southeastern Korean kingdom of Silla from Koguryŏ.

The precise date of the introduction of Buddhism into Japan is debated. One view, relying on the *Nihon Shoki* (Chronicles of Japan; 720), gives a date corresponding to the year 552 of the Western calendar. Another proposes 538, on the basis of the following passage from the *Gangō-ji Garan Engi Narabi ni Ruki Shizai Chō* (History of the Gangō-ji Monastery and Record of the Temple's Assets; 747): "The Buddhism of our land of Yamato begins with its transmission in the twelfth month of the seventh year* of the reign of Emperor Amekuni-oshiharuki-hironiwa [Kimmei; r. 531–71] in the palace of Shikishima at the time when the great minister Soga no Iname no Sukune [d. 570] was serving his majesty. King Syŏngmyŏng of Paekche presented the court with an image of Prince [Siddhārtha, i.e., Śākyamuni] and a set of ritual vessels for bathing the Buddha image, as well as a box of scrolls recounting the life of [Śākyamuni] Buddha."

The 538 date, based on the Gangō-ji record, is now generally accepted as correct because the *Nihon Shoki* account includes among its rhetorical embellishments expressions from the *Konkōmyō Saishōō-kyō* (Golden Light Sutra; in Sanskrit, *Suvarṇaprabhāsottama-rāja-sūtra*), which was first taken to Japan by the priest Dōji (d. 744) when he returned from China in 718. Moreover, the 552 date corresponds exactly to the first year of the period of the Decay of the Law, or *Mappō*, in the Buddhist eschatological system that was ascendant in China at the time that the *Nihon Shoki* was compiled.

Buddhism is, to be sure, only one of several foreign religions that have entered Japan in the course of the nation's history. Still, it would be wrong to assume that the Japanese of that time regarded Buddhism as just one among many religions, as present-day Japanese generally do. Buddhism (and Confucianism, as well) not only was a personal faith or moral guide but also, as bearer of a richly developed culture, brought with it a supreme political concept and practical policies. In modern terms, Buddhism encompassed the arts, humanities, social sciences, and natural sciences, in addition to its purely religious culture complex.

Thus the transmission of Buddhism implied far more than the arrival of a single foreign faith. It meant the introduction of the latest developments of a highly organized continental culture, and as a result the transmission of Buddhism to Japan was of great historical significance. It would have been impossible for such a culture system to take root and flower had it been transmitted only privately or haphazardly, or on only one occasion. It was essential that the process of transmission be systematic and continue over a fairly long period. Furthermore, the Buddhist religion

---

* Because the first year of the reign is counted as the first year in this figure, by Western reckoning the transmission of Buddhism began in 538.

and cultural tradition had to be transmitted from the ruling class of a foreign country to the ruling class of Japan, for only in that way could it attain official recognition. This is why official transmission—to the Japanese court—was so important.

Beginning with its account of Emperor Kimmei's reign, the *Nihon Shoki* mentions Buddhist matters frequently. For example, entries for the years 554, 577, and 588 relate that priests sent to the Yamato court by the king of Paekche were replaced every three to six years and that the Koreans sent to Japan sutras and commentaries, Buddhist relics, a nun, a Buddhist sculptor, a temple architect, a painter, a tile maker, a metal founder, and experts in Buddhist monastic law, meditation, and spells and exorcisms. These references indicate that the transmission of Buddhism to Japan was indeed the result of organized, official contacts between the ruling classes of Japan and of foreign states over a long period. This lends support to the view of Professor Nakai Shinkō of Bukkyo University that the existence of two alternative dates for the official introduction of Buddhism may represent not an error in the dating of a single historical event but the recording of two separate, independent transmissions of Buddhism from the Korean peninsula.

There is also a recorded instance of private transmission of Buddhism prior to the religion's official introduction. The *Fusō Ryakki* (Abridged Annals of Japan; late eleventh century) states that the Chinese craftsman Shiba Tatto (Ssu-ma Ta-teng, in Chinese) arrived in Japan in 522, erected a small temple in Sakatanohara, in the Takechi district of Yamato, installed a Buddha image, and paid reverence to it. The chronicles of the temple Hisodera in the Yoshino district of Yamato Province, as recorded in the *Nihon Ryōiki* (Miracle Stories of Japan; ca. 822), clearly suggest that there were instances of Buddhism being transmitted directly by immigrants. Yet even though we find cases of private transmission, there are hardly any instances of Buddhism thriving without the patronage of the Yamato court. This is evident from the fact that the Buddhist sculptors Kuratsukuri no Tasuna and Kuratsukuri no Tori, the son and grandson of Shiba Tatto, worked directly for the court. Thus, while certain transmissions may have been private in origin, they tended to take on an official character in the course of their development.

At this point there is no documentary evidence for private transmission in the sense of the introduction of the religion to a Japanese individual or community by a foreign priest or lay believer. However, certain artifacts that have been discovered suggest that this did happen. A *haniwa* funerary figure of a woman unearthed from the Ozakata Tumulus in Ibaraki Prefecture has a white tuft of hair on its forehead that resembles that characteristic iconographic feature of depictions of the historical Buddha. Another *haniwa* figure, found in the Dōyama Tumulus in Atsugi, Kanagawa Prefecture, bears a close resemblance to an itinerant Buddhist priest. Research has now reached the stage at which we can begin to investigate the factual evidence for possible instances of the transmission of Buddhism directly to the Japanese populace.

Pro-Buddhist and Anti-Buddhist Factions

King Syŏngmyŏng's presentation of an image of the historical Buddha and Buddhist ritual implements to Emperor Kimmei meant that the Japanese court had to decide whether to include this alien "deity" in the indigenous pantheon. The emperor seems to have been quite affected by his first encounter with Buddhism and Buddhist images. He is recorded as saying: "Never have I seen so solemn and serene a countenance." Yet he could not make so fundamental a decision alone. The power and authority of the imperial family—and of the Yamato court itself—were maintained by a hereditary priestly hierarchy controlled by the Nakatomi and Imbe clans. It was only natural that as court ritualists the heads of these clans should strongly oppose the introduction of foreign "gods" into the pantheon of the indigenous religion. In the end, the emperor gave King Syŏngmyŏng's Buddhist image to Soga no Iname, who held the imposing rank of *ōomi*, or great minister.

The Soga clan came from Kawachi Province, where large numbers of foreign families had settled since the early fifth century and where the civilization imported from Korea flourished. Of all the aristocratic clans, the Soga clan, which had alliances with some of the foreign families, was the best informed about conditions on the Korean peninsula. Evidence of Soga connections with Korea is seen in the names of Iname's father and grandfather, Koma and Karako, respectively, which appear to derive from the Japanese words for Koguryŏ and Han. Thus it was not coincidental that the emperor gave the image of Śākyamuni Buddha to Iname, nor odd that Iname accepted it despite the opposition of the priestly clans. Iname purified one of his residences (which later became the temple Toyura-dera, according to traditional accounts) and enshrined the image there.

That was not the end of the matter, however. As noted earlier, the introduction of Buddhism meant the advent not simply of a new foreign religion but also of a new, highly advanced civilization. The acceptance or rejection of Buddhism, therefore, was directly linked to the acceptance or rejection of that continental culture, and control of these new cultural forces directly influenced the fortunes of the ruling classes. Even the determined opposition of the priestly clans at court could not stem the new cultural tide. Nevertheless, the Yamato court was divided into two clearly defined camps, one supporting the introduction of Buddhism and one opposing it. The opposition was led by the Mononobe clan, which had become extremely powerful after the beginning of the sixth century and had displaced the rival Ōtomo clan in the wake of that clan's failure to protect Japan's enclave on the Korean peninsula. Mononobe no Okoshi, who held the rank of ōmuraji, or great minister, was the leader of the group opposed to the introduction of Buddhism, and he was in direct conflict with Soga no Iname.

Iname died in 570. His son and successor, Soga no Umako (d. 626), built a Buddha hall in 584 to enshrine a stone image of Miroku (the future buddha Maitreya) that had been brought from Paekche. He had three nuns, including Zenshinni, the daughter of Shiba Tatto, make offerings to the image. In this and other ways, Umako endeavored to propagate the Buddhist faith.

The anti-Buddhist faction redoubled its efforts. The reaction against the new religion peaked when a plague suddenly broke out in Yamato Province, claiming many lives. The anti-Buddhists argued that the epidemic was caused by the indigenous deities, angered by the encroachment of the new religion. The ōmuraji Mononobe no Moriya (d. 587), Okoshi's son and successor, burned Umako's Buddha hall to the ground and cast the image into a canal in Naniwa (present-day Osaka), according to the *Nihon Shoki* entry for 585. The entry for 552 tells a virtually identical story, except that the protagonists are Iname and Okoshi.

No doubt Moriya's extreme actions were prompted by the belief that the only way to stop the epidemic was to send the alien image back across the seas. Yet it is important to note how little this anti-Buddhist reaction differed from practices associated with the cult of the deity of epidemics, which suggests that the Mononobe clan did not oppose Buddhism solely on religious grounds. This conclusion is supported by the intimate involvement of the Nakatomi clan—which headed the indigenous priestly organization—with Buddhism during the next fifty years.

Emperor Yōmei, who was a patron of both Buddhism and the indigenous religion, fell ill and died in 587, after only two years on the throne.

The court was soon embroiled in a fierce power struggle over the imperial succession between the great ministers Soga no Umako and Mononobe no Moriya. Eventually both sides resorted to military force. Umako's army attacked the Mononobe stronghold, and Moriya was killed. The Soga clan thus succeeded in destroying its greatest political rival and ensured its own supremacy. The anti-Buddhist faction had lost its principal support, and the way for the propagation and growth of Buddhism in Japan lay open. In 588, the year after the defeat of the Mononobe, the Soga began building Hōkō-ji (popularly known as Asuka-dera), completing it about nine years later, in 596. Located across the Asuka River from Amakashi no Oka, site of the Soga clan seat, Hōkō-ji was the first full-fledged Buddhist temple complex in Japan. With its lofty pagoda and central hall enshrining a large gilt-bronze image of Śākyamuni Buddha, flanked by two lesser halls to the east and the west, Hōkō-ji clearly demonstrated the great power of the Soga clan, which supported and controlled the bearer of the new, high civilization—Buddhism.

Acceptance of the New Religion

According to the *Nihon Shoki* account of Empress Suiko's reign (593–628), there were forty-six Buddhist temples in Japan in 623. The remains of over fifty temples from the Asuka period (552–646) have been discovered through excavation in the past several decades, suggesting that this figure is reasonable. Most remains are concentrated in the heart of the Kinai region (in Yamato, Kawachi, Izumi, and Yamashiro provinces), but a fair number of sites are found in Settsu, Harima, Bitchū, Iyo, and Bizen provinces, along the Inland Sea. There are also several in Ōmi, Iga, and Owari provinces, northeast of the Kinai region. Considering that the Mononobe clan, which formed the backbone of the anti-Buddhist faction at court, was annihilated only in 587, it is obvious that Buddhism had made tremendous strides in the space of just thirty-six years.

That the temples of this period were all major edifices with tiled roofs is clear from the roof tiles and foundation stones that have been unearthed. In that age even the imperial palaces normally were thatched; Empress Kōgyoku's palace built in Asuka in 643 was the first to be roofed with wooden planks instead of thatch and was called the Asuka Plank-roofed Palace in recognition of this novel feature. Even during the period of Sinicization of laws and government administration, most dwellings and administrative buildings were very simply constructed, their wooden posts

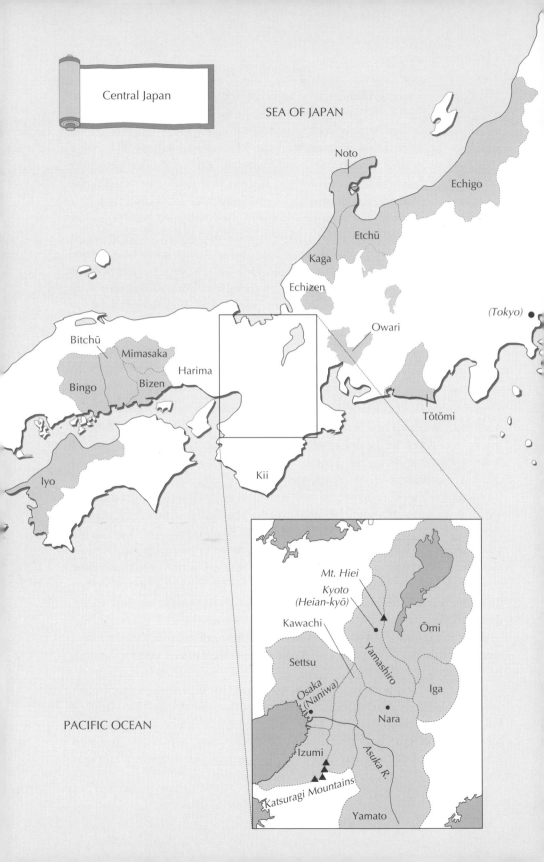

Central Japan

SEA OF JAPAN

Noto

Echigo

Etchū

Kaga

Echizen

(Tokyo)

Owari

Bitchū

Mimasaka

Harima

Bingo

Bizen

Tōtōmi

Iyo

Kii

PACIFIC OCEAN

Mt. Hiei

Kyoto
(Heian-kyō)

Kawachi

Ōmi

Settsu

Yamashiro

Iga

Osaka
(Naniwa)

Nara

Izumi

Asuka R.

Katsuragi Mountains

Yamato

THE JAPANESE RESPONSE TO BUDDHISM   57

set directly into the ground, without a stone foundation. With their multistory pagodas set on massive stone bases and grand Buddha halls roofed with a variety of ornamental tiles, the Buddhist temples stood as towering monuments to civilization. Within the temple halls were beautiful gilded images that dazzled worshipers. It must be remembered that temples were not built in the Asuka area alone. Though concentrated in Yamato and Kawachi provinces, they were scattered across western Japan, and as a result must have greatly affected a wide variety of people, impressing them with the grandeur of the Buddhist religion and increasing the faith's prestige.

It was the Soga clan, of course, that provided the impetus for the establishment of Asuka-period Buddhism and was largely responsible for this flowering of Buddhist culture. As we have seen, the Soga had long been closely associated with immigrants in Japan and were very active in promoting relations with Paekche. Their efforts to foster Buddhism were strongly influenced by their interest in Paekche, with the result that Hōkō-ji was built using techniques from Paekche and with the active assistance of priests from Paekche. As soon as the temple was completed, in 596, the priest Hyechong, who had arrived from Paekche the previous year, took up residence there. Thus Paekche's influence on Asuka Buddhism was immense; indeed, Asuka Buddhism can be regarded as a branch of Paekche Buddhism.

About one hundred years after its transmission to Paekche, Buddhism was transmitted to Silla from the northern Korean kingdom of Koguryŏ. As a result, Silla Buddhism was similar to the northern Chinese form of the religion, not the southern Chinese form that flourished in Paekche. Silla-style temples began appearing on northern Kyushu around the beginning of the seventh century. Tamura Enchō, professor emeritus of Kyushu University, has suggested that both the images of Miroku seated in a relaxed contemplative attitude, with one leg crossed over the other, and the cult of this Buddhist messianic figure reflect the influence of Silla Buddhism. Certainly the worship of Miroku is closely linked to the activities of Prince Shōtoku, as is evidenced by the fact that images of Miroku were enshrined as the principal object of worship at Kōryū-ji (in Kyoto) and at the original Shitennō-ji (in Naniwa), temples associated with Prince Shōtoku. Furthermore, since both Shōtoku's attendant Hata no Kawakatsu (founder of Kōryū-ji) and the Naniwa no Kishi family who were involved with foreign affairs, were of Silla origin, we can assume that there was a Silla Buddhist influence at court in Shōtoku's time.

Paekche and Silla were long-standing enemies, however, and in 663

Silla joined forces with a Chinese army to attack and finally destroy its rival. In the Asuka-period Buddhism sponsored by the Soga, Paekche's influence was dominant, with that of Silla playing a subordinate role, and it seems likely that there were subtle tensions and conflicts between these two streams within Asuka Buddhism.

As the number of temples increased, so did the number of priests and nuns. By the year 623, there were 816 priests and 569 nuns—a total of 1,385 religious—according to the clerical census made by supervisory officials appointed by Empress Suiko. According to the *Nihon Shoki*, these officials were appointed to oversee the priests and nuns throughout the country and to ensure they did not "offend against the [secular] law." This represents the first appearance in Japan of a national system of control of Buddhist clerics and institutions. Moreover, that the appointments were made by the empress signifies a shift in the role of the imperial family, from secondary patrons of the new religion to its foremost patrons. In appointing Soga no Umako to examine all priests and nuns, Empress Suiko was in fact attempting to hold him responsible for any problems that might arise in the course of the propagation of Buddhism. She chose Umako because his clan had played the leading role in introducing the religion. The official connection between the imperial family and Buddhism began with this effort at regulation and control.

Prince Shōtoku

The second son of Emperor Yōmei, Prince Shōtoku was born in 574. He grew up amid the turmoil of political intrigue. His father died when he was thirteen, in the same year that the Mononobe clan was destroyed. He was eighteen when his uncle, Emperor Sushun (r. 587–92), was assassinated as the result of a Soga conspiracy. According to the *Nihon Shoki*, he was made crown prince and regent (at the age of nineteen) in 593, the year his aunt ascended the throne as Empress Suiko. He directed both domestic and foreign affairs until his death in 622, at forty-eight.

The most admired of Shōtoku's achievements is the propagation of Buddhism in Japan, a labor to which he was passionately devoted. The zeal with which he applied himself to this task and the significance of his work are demonstrated by the so-called Seventeen-Article Constitution and the *Sangyō Gisho* (Commentaries on the Three Sutras) attributed to him. Doubts have been raised about the authenticity of both these works, some scholars suggesting that they are compositions of a later date falsely ascribed to Shōtoku. Yet they definitely date from Empress Suiko's reign. Moreover, as the late historian Inoue Mitsusada has pointed out, even though Korean scholars and scholar-priests at Shōtoku's court may have had a hand in producing both the constitution and the commentaries, it was unquestionably Shōtoku who provided the leadership for both projects. It is therefore quite appropriate to view them as the clearest evidence of Prince Shōtoku's relation to Buddhism.

In the second article of the Seventeen-Article Constitution, promulgated in 604, Prince Shōtoku states: "Reverently worship the Three Treasures, namely, the Buddha, the Law, and the Order. These are the final refuge of all beings, the most sublime objects of faith in all the world. How then should anyone of any time not venerate them? There are few people who are truly depraved. If they are well taught, people will generally obey the dictates of Truth. But if they do not take refuge in the Three Treasures, with what can their crookedness be made straight?" This passage reveals Shōtoku's views both on Buddhism as a religion and on the human condition. He views evildoers not as fundamentally bad but as untaught, or badly and insufficiently taught. It would seem, then, that his purpose in making Buddhism the cornerstone of his political philosophy was primarily introspective and practical, not merely to secure prayers for the protection of the state and for material benefits.

The *Sangyō Gisho* consists of commentaries on the *Hoke-kyō* (the Lotus Sutra; in Sanskrit, *Saddharma-puṇḍarīka-sūtra*), the *Yuima-gyō* (the Vimalakīrti Sutra; in Sanskrit, *Vimalakīrti-nirdeśa-sūtra*), and the *Shōman-gyō* (the Queen Śrīmālā Sutra; in Sanskrit, *Śrīmālādevī-siṃhanāda-sūtra*). Though it, too, is a work of Suiko's reign, its year of composition is unknown. The commentary on the Vimalakīrti Sutra reveals Prince Shōtoku's intention in basing his political philosophy on Buddhism. He states that there is no difference in value between the sacred and the profane, the religious and the secular. Moreover, there is no difference in the degree of merit gained by venerating the Buddha and that gained by showing compassion for a beggar. In short, there is fundamentally no distinction between the sage and the fool: all people are equally the children of the Buddha. This is their true, original nature. All the good that people do contributes to their ultimate enlightenment. Therefore the sincere practice of secular morality and ethics, too, is part of the Buddhist Way. There is no suggestion that the supreme and uniquely effective path to enlightenment consists in leaving the secular world and becoming a cleric. At the very heart of Shōtoku's thinking is the concept of lay Buddhism and the vision of realizing Buddhist ideals while remaining in the world.

The chief figure in the Vimalakīrti Sutra is Vimalakīrti, a wealthy lay follower of the historical Buddha. The Queen Śrīmālā Sutra recounts the story of the Indian queen Śrīmālā, who preached the profound truths of Buddhism at the Buddha's direction. Both sutras center not on eminent priests or direct disciples of the Buddha but on lay believers. The Lotus Sutra, too, affirms rather than denies life in the world as an avenue of Buddhist religious practice. Prince Shōtoku's own well-defined attitudes and intentions are evident in his choice, from among the vast range of Mahāyāna scriptures, of these three sutras, with their common emphasis on the importance of the life of the lay Buddhist in the world.

Prince Shōtoku truly deserves his historical reputation as spiritual teacher of the Japanese nation by reason of his lifetime of devoted service to the propagation of Buddhism. Yet he never showed any inclination to enter the Buddhist Order. He spent his entire life as a devout lay follower of Buddhism. After his death, Buddhism attained further power and prestige in Japan. Great monasteries vied with one another in size and magnificence, and many eminent priests engaged in scholarly study and religious practice. At the same time, there was a shift toward an emphasis on Buddhism as the official servant and protector of the state, an emphasis very different from Shōtoku's more spiritual, religious intention. Thus, in one sense, the true spiritual heirs of Prince Shōtoku did not appear until the Heian period, in the person of Saichō, and the Kamakura period, in the person of Shinran.

RELIGION AS PROTECTOR OF THE STATE

Aristocratic Buddhism

In 639 Emperor Jomei (r. 629–41), who succeeded Empress Suiko, began construction of a new palace and a large temple on the banks of the Kudara River, to the north of the Asuka area. The temple was called Kudara Dai-ji, and a nine-story pagoda was erected on the site during Jomei's reign. However, in 673 Emperor Temmu (r. 672–86) ordered that the temple be moved to Asuka, and he appointed an official to supervise its completion. At that time the temple became known as Takechi Dai-ji, but in 677 its name was changed to Daikan Dai-ji. It was later moved to the new capital of Nara and was again renamed, becoming Daian-ji in 729.

Since the official introduction of Buddhism all temples had been built by the Soga or one of the other great families. The emperor or empress was never directly involved. Hōryū-ji, in Nara, may seem to be an exception, but it should be remembered that its patron, Prince Shōtoku, was not in fact an emperor and that the reigning monarch, Empress Suiko, was not directly involved in its construction. Thus Kudara Dai-ji can be regarded as the first temple to be established by a reigning monarch, and Jomei as the first Japanese emperor to be an active patron of Buddhism, for although the temple complex was completed under Temmu, it had its beginnings in the temple founded by Jomei.

It was, thus, a century after Buddhism's official introduction before a reigning emperor became an active patron of the new religion. Thereafter, Emperor Tenji (r. 661–72), son of Jomei, founded Kawara-dera (also known as Gufuku-ji), Kanzeon-ji, and Sufuku-ji. He also built a Buddha hall in the precincts of Ōtsu Palace in his new capital in Ōmi Province. Tenji's younger brother Temmu founded Yakushi-ji, in addition to his role in the construction of Kudara Dai-ji—or Takechi Dai-ji, as he renamed it. In 685, Temmu ordered that Buddhist altars be built and Buddhist images and sutras installed for worship in "all the houses of the various provinces." Moreover, Empress Saimei (r. 654–61), who had been Jomei's consort, was the first monarch to have the *Ninnō Hannya-kyō* (Sutra on the Benevolent King) ceremonially read at the palace, in 660.

Tamura Enchō argues that at this point genuine state Buddhism had not yet emerged. According to him, the above acts represented simply a continuation of the practices of the clan cult of Emperor Jomei and were fundamentally the same as the practices of the earlier clan Buddhism, in which clan temples were built to pray for the repose of ancestral spirits to the seventh generation and for living clan members' welfare in this world and the next. Tamura rejects the claim that Jomei's patronage of Buddhism represented an attempt to make the religion the protector of the nation as a whole.

It is true that the construction of Kudara Dai-ji was motivated by Emperor Jomei's religious faith, and that Kawara-dera and Kanzeon-ji were planned by Emperor Tenji to pray for the repose of the spirit of his mother, Empress Saimei. Kanzeon-ji was located at Tsukushi, on Kyushu, where the empress had died while seeing off military forces being sent to the aid of Paekche, and Kawara-dera was at Kawara, in Asuka, where her palace had been located. Yakushi-ji was built as the result of a vow made by Emperor Temmu to pray for the recovery from illness of his consort, Empress Jitō (r. 686–97). In view of these facts, it must be admitted that these temples served chiefly as private temples for the imperial family.

In the ancient period, however, the emperor was regarded as virtually identical with the state. This view prevailed from at least the reign of Empress Suiko and was further strengthened during the Taika Reform of the mid-seventh century. Even though the above-mentioned temples were private temples of members of the imperial family, they were in effect national temples as well, and the various services and prayers conducted in them had a national or official significance not shared by rites conducted in the clan temples of the other aristocratic clans. Thus, the aristocratic Buddhism inaugurated by Emperor Jomei can be said to denote the beginning of a truly national or state Buddhism.

The Regulation of Clerics

As Buddhism gained adherents in Japan, the number of priests and nuns greatly increased. As mentioned above, the control and regulation of these clerics was, by decree of Empress Suiko, vested in certain monastic officials. The first to hold the office of supervisor of the clergy was Soga no Umako. Yet the establishment of this office was a step away from the exclusive control exercised earlier by the Soga clan, which had been the principal patron of the new religion from the outset. Furthermore, after the destruction of the Soga clan at the time of the Taika Reform, the court, acting through its appointed officials, was in absolute control of the monastic regulatory system.

Under the Taika system, priests and nuns were supervised by ten officials, including the priests Fukuryō and Sōmin (d. 653), while temple finances were managed by a lay official known as the *hōzu*. By 683, during Emperor Temmu's reign, Buddhist clerics were governed by high-ranking priests known as *sōgō*, of which there were three grades—*sōjō*, *sōzu*, and *risshi*. According to the Taihō and Yōrō codes of 701 and 718, respectively, these governing officials were in fact chosen by the religious communities themselves, subject to approval by the court. In other words, under the codified system the state did not directly control religious affairs but permitted the Buddhist community considerable autonomy.

Regulation of Buddhist clerics included not only supervision of those who were already members of the Order but also regulation of ordination and enforcement of the distinction between clerical and lay status. The term *sōni*—priests and nuns—is used rather loosely, but strictly speaking the term refers only to those who had joined the Buddhist Order and were dedicated to observing the full set of precepts—two hundred and fifty for priests and a much larger number for nuns. Under the regulatory system, clerics of this category were also known as official priests (*kansō*) or major priests (*daisō*). Those who vowed to keep only the ten basic precepts after ordination were known as male novices (*shami*) and female novices (*shamini*), while lay believers were known as laymen (*ubasoku*) and laywomen (*ubai*).

The policy of distinguishing sharply between lay and clerical status was reinforced at the time of the Taika Reform, and official permission was required to enter religious life. The number of ordinands per year was fixed by government decree: as of 696, ten worthy candidates were ordained on the last day of each year. The yearly ordinands were of course registered with the government and subject to its supervision. At the same time, they were granted special privileges, such as exemption from taxes and the corvée, and their social status and financial well-being were guaranteed by the government. On the other hand, privately ordained clerics, who had not obtained official permission for their change in status, were subjected to increasingly severe measures.

Through the years, the imperial court issued several sets of regulations governing priests and nuns, which are known collectively as *Sōni Ryō*. In 701, the government ordered all clerics to assemble at Daikan Dai-ji (Daian-ji), where the government official Michi no Obitona (d. 718) read them the portion of the just-completed Taihō Code dealing with monastic regulations. This and similar incidents indicate how seriously the government took the task of regulating Buddhist clerics. Provisions of the twenty-seven-article Yōrō *Sōni Ryō* (718), which is still extant, make it clear that the government sought to prohibit preaching outside temple precincts and to force priests and nuns to live and work within their religious communities. Moreover, the daily lives and personal activities of priests and nuns were carefully regulated, and penalties were stipulated for those who failed to obey the government's regulations.

The *Sōni Ryō* is part civil law and part penal code. It embodies the conviction that it was the duty of priests and nuns to serve the state through Buddhism, that the clerics occupied a fixed, well-defined position within the framework of state Buddhism, and that filling only that role was their proper function. Thus, as Inoue Mitsusada has pointed out, that many provisions of the *Sōni Ryō* duplicate the traditional monastic precepts (*kai-*

Kansō 官僧 ⎤
daisō ⎦ → shami 沙弥 ⎤
shamini 尼 ⎦ → ubasoku 優婆塞
ubai 夷

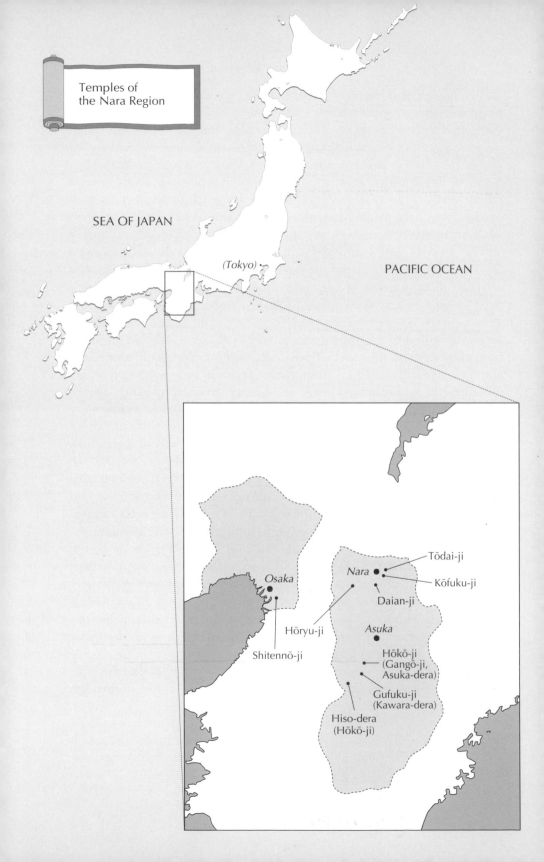

Temples of
the Nara Region

SEA OF JAPAN

PACIFIC OCEAN

(Tokyo)

Osaka

Nara • — Tōdai-ji
— Kōfuku-ji
Daian-ji

Hōryu-ji

Shitennō-ji

Asuka

Hōkō-ji
(Gangō-ji,
Asuka-dera)

Gufuku-ji
(Kawara-dera)

Hiso-dera
(Hōkō-ji)

ritsu) is due not to a concern with religious observance per se but to the recognition that illegal acts on the part of Buddhist clergy, even within the confines of their religious communities, could pose a threat to the order and security of the state and the central government.

Kokubunji *and the Tōdai-ji Great Buddha*

After about 732, relations with the Korean kingdom of Silla became strained. Year by year they worsened, and the court began to fear an invasion from the Korean peninsula. In addition, an epidemic disease, possibly smallpox, that had broken out at Tsukushi, on Kyushu, in 735 began to spread throughout western Japan. In 737 the disease reached Nara, where it claimed many victims among the aristocracy, including the minister of the left, Fujiwara no Muchimaro (680–737), and his three brothers. In March 737, with the country torn by crises at home and abroad, Emperor Shōmu (r. 724–49) decreed that each province should make images of Śākyamuni Buddha and two attendants, as well as one copy of the *Daihannya-kyō* (Great Perfection of Wisdom Sutra; in Sanskrit, *Mahā-prajñāpāramitā-sūtra*). In the light of the turmoil at the time, it is clear that the intent of Shōmu's decree was not simply to encourage Buddhism in Japan but also to enlist the aid of Buddhism in helping the state overcome the crises it faced.

In 740, Shōmu commanded that each province make ten copies of the Lotus Sutra and erect a seven-story pagoda. In March of the next year, he ordered each province to erect another seven-story pagoda and make ten copies each of the Golden Light Sutra, and the Lotus Sutra. In addition, a copy of the Golden Light Sutra transcribed in gold ink by the emperor himself was to be placed in each pagoda, with prayers to various buddhas for the protection of the nation. Finally, two provincial temples (*kokubunji*) were to be erected in each province: a monastery (*kokubunji*) to be called Konkōmyō Shitennō Gokoku no Tera (Temple to Seek the Protection of the Nation by the Four Heavenly Kings, housing a copy of the Golden Light Sutra) and a nunnery (*kokubunniji*) to be called Hokke Metsuzai no Tera (Temple for the Elimination of Sins Through the Lotus Sutra, housing a copy of that sutra). This decree of 741 established the provincial temple system.

The Golden Light Sutra promises that four heavenly kings will protect the nation and people that reverence and propagate this sutra. The heavenly kings will fend off foreign enemies and bestow prosperity and happiness

Konkyō Konkōmyō Saishōō-kyō Suvarnaprabhasa Sutra 金光明経

on the sutra's devotees. The Golden Light Sutra had long been esteemed in China as a powerful spiritual protector of the nation from calamities. Shōmu's imperial decree specifically mentions the intended recipients of the sutra's blessings. Prayers were offered for the eternal happiness of the spirits of deceased emperors and loyal officials from the Fujiwara and other major families; for the happiness and well-being of the reigning emperor and his family and of the Fujiwara, Tachibana, and other great clans; and for the defeat and destruction of wicked, rebellious subjects. Clearly, the provincial temples were not intended primarily as places for religious practice leading to enlightenment and salvation. They were institutions committed to the protection of the state and the prevention of national calamity through the quasi-magical powers of Buddhism. The provincial temple system cannot be idealized as a model achievement of Buddhist culture during Shōmu's reign.

The government in Nara devoted extraordinary efforts to the establishment and maintenance of the provincial temple system. In 741, each provincial monastery was allotted fifty households of serfs and ten *chō* (almost ten hectares) of rice fields for the maintenance of its twenty resident priests. Ten *chō* of rice fields were also allotted for each nunnery, which housed ten nuns. After the promulgation of the law on long-term private holdings of newly developed rice lands, the priests' allotments were increased to one hundred *chō* per temple and the nuns' to fifty. In addition, in each province the interest on forty thousand sheaves of seed rice lent to peasants by the government was allotted annually to defray the operating expenses of the provincial temples. In return, the priests and nuns were to perform abbreviated ritual readings of the Golden Light Sutra and the Lotus Sutra on the eighth day of each month and a ceremonial recitation of the precepts around the middle of each month. Moreover, the provincial governors were to ensure that the Buddhist prohibitions against killing animals, hunting, and fishing, as well as the other precepts, were strictly observed within their jurisdictions on the six fast days of each month.

The construction of the Great Buddha at Tōdai-ji, in Nara, marked the culmination of the development of state Buddhism. When the court official Fujiwara no Hirotsugu (d. 740) raised a rebellion in northern Kyushu in 740, Emperor Shōmu left the capital of Nara and took refuge in Kuni, Yamashiro Province. It was there that he issued the decree establishing the provincial temples. During an imperial visit to Shigaraki Palace, Ōmi Province, in 743, the emperor proclaimed that he would have a colossal image of Vairocana Buddha cast. Work on the image began at once in

Ōmi Province but was suspended in 745 when the emperor returned to Nara. It was recommenced at Konkōmyō-ji (renamed Tōdai-ji in 747), which had already been designated one of the provincial temples of Yamato Province. The Great Buddha required eight castings over a period of three years. The work was finally completed in 749, and the formal consecration, or "eye-opening," ceremony was performed in 752. It was, to quote a contemporary account, a ceremony of unprecedented splendor, attended by Shōmu (now abdicated), his consort, Kōmyō (701–60), their daughter, Empress Kōken (r. 749–58), and all the major court officials, both civil and military.

Vairocana is the principal buddha of the *Kegon-kyō* (Flower Garland Sutra; in Sanskrit, *Avataṃsaka-sūtra*), a text that describes the ideal realm of the Law in which phenomena interpenetrate without hindrance. This is a state in which noumena and phenomena—as well as individual phenomena—interact harmoniously in countless relationships. According to the Flower Garland Sutra, Vairocana Buddha can be conceived of as the great light that dwells in the Pure Land of the Lotus Womb and governs all things. It is no wonder that Shōmu was attracted to this particular text, buffeted as he was by Nara politics, in which the imperial family and the aristocratic clans, the clergy, and the local gentry vied fiercely with one another for power.

In one sense, the construction of the Great Buddha was undertaken with the same motive as the establishment of the provincial temple system—the hope of gaining peace and prosperity for the state and its subjects. However, there was a major difference between the two projects. While the temporal happiness and eternal salvation of both the imperial family and the Fujiwara and Tachibana clans are emphasized in the text of the decree establishing the provincial temples, no mention is made of the material or spiritual welfare of the great aristocratic families in the decree ordering the construction of the Great Buddha. What is emphasized instead is that the Great Buddha is to be the fruit of cooperation on the part of all devout Buddhists, a project carried out not only through imperial and aristocratic patronage but also through the labors of even the humblest peasant. Through the merits accruing from this good work, all believers will receive the same blessings as the emperor himself and will ultimately attain the same state of enlightenment.

We see here, then, the beginnings of the Buddhist universalism that was to be developed in the succeeding Heian period by Saichō and Kūkai. The provincial temples had for the most part ceased functioning by the middle of the tenth century, and their buildings quickly fell into ruin. Yet the universalist spirit expressed in Shōmu's imperial decree may have been one of the major factors in the survival of Tōdai-ji and its Great Buddha over the centuries despite the many natural and human-caused disasters to which it has been subjected.

The Six Nara Schools

The world of Nara Buddhism is usually described in terms of the six schools of Nara, the southern capital: the Hossō, Sanron, Kegon, Jōjitsu, Kusha, and Ritsu schools. Unlike the Tendai and Shingon sects of the Heian period and the Pure Land and other sects of the Kamakura period, these schools were not sects or distinct religious bodies. As in the case of the later sects, the names of the Nara schools generally derive from a particular doctrine. But it is significant that two different Sino-Japanese ideographic characters having the same pronunciation (*shū*) but different meanings can be used to identify the Nara schools. One *shū* means denomination or sect, and this ideographic character is used with the names of the Heian and Kamakura religious organizations. The other *shū* means group, and its connotation is approximately equivalent to what would be called a study group today. The latter ideographic character was the more widely used in the Nara period. Thus the Sanron school identifies the group of people who gathered to study the Sanron doctrine, and little more than that. At any rate, to interpret the Nara schools as independent religious sects is wrong.

According to the *Shoku Nihongi* (Further Chronicles of Japan; 797) and the *Shōsō-in Monjo* (Shōsō-in Documents; eighth century), students interested in a specific doctrinal system gathered at an institution where scriptures and commentaries relevant to that doctrinal system were available and devoted themselves to study under the tutelage of experts in that doctrine. This group of students and teachers constituted a school. Of the six Nara schools, only the Kegon school focused on a sutra (a sermon or discourse of the Buddha), in this case, the *Kegon-kyō*, or Flower Garland Sutra. Four of the other schools focused on particular treatises or commentaries reflecting the views of various Buddhist scholars; and the fifth, the Ritsu school, focused on the section of the canon concerned with monastic precepts: the Vinaya (*ritsu* in Japanese).

According to Inoue Mitsusada, the dates and sequence of the founding of the various schools cannot be determined—with the exception of the

Kegon school, which was founded at Tōdai-ji around 751. A decree issued by the Dajōkan (Grand Council of State) to the official priestly hierarchy (*sōgō*) in 718 urges that since the doctrines of the five schools differ, each school should designate an expert in its own doctrines. We know, then, that in 718 there were five officially recognized schools, but there is no agreement on their identity, since Nara Buddhism encompassed more than the well-known six schools.

As a matter of fact, the temples of the Nara period were not exclusively affiliated with any school. The Sanron school was found not only at Gangō-ji (usually named as its center) but also at Hōryū-ji, Daian-ji, and Tōdai-ji. The so-called six schools of Nara are the schools that had established study institutes within the precincts of Tōdai-ji by 751: the Hossō, Sanron, Kegon, Jōjitsu, Kusha, and Ritsu schools.

Strictly speaking, then, the term "six schools" refers only to the academic schools affiliated with Tōdai-ji, not to the whole of Nara Buddhism. Those not counted among the six schools probably had relatively weak ties to Tōdai-ji, a fact that helps put both the nature of the six schools and the importance of Tōdai-ji in perspective. For instance, the Shōron school, devoted to study of the *Shōdaijō-ron* (Comprehensive Treatise on Mahāyāna Buddhism; in Sanskrit, *Mahāyāna-saṃgraha*), flourished at Gangō-ji, Daian-ji, and Kōfuku-ji but was not found at Tōdai-ji. The Shutara school, which studied the Great Perfection of Wisdom Sutra, existed at Daian-ji, Gufuku-ji, and Tōdai-ji; although it remained active at Daian-ji, it died out at Tōdai-ji. All the above-mentioned temples were major, officially recognized religious centers, and all the schools found at these temples were also officially recognized.

Mountain Buddhism

Instead of joining schools at one of the official government- or clan-sponsored temples, some Nara-period priests devoted themselves to religious disciplines in remote mountain temples, such as Hiso-dera (also called Hōkō-ji), in the Yoshino district of Yamato Province. Priests who had gained extraordinary powers as a result of religious practice in such isolated spots often went on to become special ritualists at court or at the major temples. This stream of Nara Buddhism is generally called mountain Buddhism, and its influence was immense, especially in the evolution of magical and quasi-magical practices as a fundamental characteristic of ancient Buddhism in Japan. One can agree with the observation by Professor Sonoda

Kōyū of Kansai University that mountain Buddhism provided one of the great stimuli for the development of Nara Buddhism and that its magical practices rank with the academic studies pursued in the official temples as pillars of the Buddhism of that period.

The term "mountain Buddhism" usually calls to mind the Jinenchi (Natural Wisdom) school, centered at Hiso-dera, which specialized in practices based on a mystical memory-enhancing ritual called Kokūzō Gumonji Hō, or the priest Dōkyō (d. 772), who is said to have cured Empress Kōken of a serious illness through astrological and mystical practices he had mastered while in seclusion on Mount Katsuragi, in Yamato Province. However, the adepts of mountain Buddhism were found not only in the nation's heartland but also in distant provincial districts.

Taichō (682–767) was known as the Great Sage of Koshi, the region comprising Echizen, Kaga, Noto, Etchū, and Echigo provinces. Hōon Daishi (d. 795) was revered by the people of Kibi, the region consisting of Bingo, Bitchū, Bizen, and Mimasaka provinces. Both of these priests represented a popular, provincial Buddhism quite unconnected with the officially recognized temples. Fictitious biographies describing Taichō as an eminent priest within the official system began to appear around the middle of the Heian period, but these are inventions of the aristocrats and high-ranking priests of Kyoto inspired by the strength of the Hakusan mountain cult so successfully reorganized by Taichō. Hōon Daishi, on the other hand, who did not benefit from such fictionalization, was virtually unknown in the Nara region by the middle of the Heian period.

Those adepts who did not conform to the manners and standards of the capital were rejected by the secular and religious authorities as undesirables. The greater their spiritual powers and the closer they were to the common people, the more severely they were persecuted, usually on two grounds. First, they were privately ordained, in violation of the clerical regulations (*Sōni Ryō*); second, they were popular with ordinary citizens, which led to their being charged with disturbing the status quo of church and state. They were accused of going into the mountains on their own and setting up hermitages and of abiding in isolated spots and pretending to teach the Law of the Buddha.

Because of the frequency of such accusations in the *Shoku Nihongi*, it is often assumed that the quasi-magical practices of the Nara period—represented, for example, by the activities of such privately ordained figures as En no Gyōja (fl. late seventh century) of Mount Katsuragi—were entirely Buddhist in character. In fact, however, Buddhist magic constituted only one segment of the spectrum of such activities, though a very important segment, to be sure. There were also shamanist magic practices from the continent, as well as indigenous pre-Buddhist magic. Chinese Taoist magic in particular was widely popular. Many magical terms appearing in literature of the Nara and Heian periods are in fact Taoist. The prevailing tendency to look on all these terms as Buddhist is simply mistaken. The word for charm or spell, *jugon*, is a good example. Though often considered a Buddhist term, it is definitely of Taoist origin. Likewise, the view that all those who engaged in religious practice in isolated mountains and forests were Buddhists is erroneous. It is simplistic to classify all those adepts who were unconnected with officially sponsored or clan-sponsored temples as folk or popular Buddhists. This entire subject calls for careful reinvestigation and rethinking.

Chishiki *and Their Temples*

An understanding of the term *chishiki*, or ordinary believer, is important to an understanding of popular Buddhism, which had little connection with officially sanctioned Buddhism. *Chishiki* originally denoted a friend or associate in the practice of Buddhism, a fellow believer. In that sense, there is no distinction among imperial, aristocratic, and ordinary believers: all are *chishiki*. However, in the Nara period the term was customarily used not for the imperial and aristocratic classes but only for the common people, that is, Buddhist believers of the provincial gentry class and below. In particular, the term was used to describe those members of the general populace who devoted money, time, and energy to such good works as copying sutras and building temples, pagodas, and Buddhist images. The activities of these ordinary believers naturally tended to be linked to popular rather than aristocratic, official Buddhism. The best examples of such activities are probably the so-called temples of ordinary believers (*chishiki-ji*) and sutra copying sponsored by ordinary believers (*chishiki-kyō*).

Chishiki-ji were temples built and maintained through the efforts of groups of everyday citizens, in contrast to temples that were sponsored by an aristocratic clan. A representative example is Kawachi Chishiki-ji, famed because Emperor Shōmu is said to have worshiped an image of Vairocana Buddha there in 740 while on a trip to the Ōgata district of Kawachi Province. That experience is supposed to have led directly to his vow and proclamation in 741 to build the Great Buddha of Tōdai-ji. The *Nihon Ryōiki* accounts of Yakuō-ji in Kii Province and the Uda-dō hall in

Tōtōmi Province suggest that there were many temples supported by ordinary believers in outlying provinces, as well. The rapid increase in the number of temples receiving official allotments (*jōgaku-ji*) in the late Nara and early Heian periods is related to the diffusion of *chishiki-ji*. The government was attempting to bring the clan and private temples of the aristocracy and the local gentry under control of the official temple system. As the scholar Usami Masatoshi points out, most of the *chishiki-ji* appear to have been built by local gentry actually residing in the provinces; therefore, these temples cannot be ignored when considering the development of popular Buddhism.

Sutra copying was like temple building in that it required both a high level of technical competence and ample funds. Thus the central government established large-scale scriptoria at Tōdai-ji and in Empress Kōmyō's household affairs bureau and set scribes to work there. *Chishiki* could hope to participate in sutra copying only by forming large cooperative groups to support sutra-copying projects. For instance, a *chishiki*-sponsored copy of the *Yugashiji-ron* (Treatise on the Stages of Yoga Practice; in Sanskrit, *Yogācārabhūmi-śāstra*) that was dated the ninth month of 703 in the postscript on fascicle 26 involved 709 believers of both sexes. The group was led by Kusakabe no Obitomaro, a district governor in Izumi Province. This is the usual way that ordinary people participated in sutra copying, both in the Nara region and in outlying provinces. Low-level officials or middle- or low-ranking members of the local gentry frequently acted as leaders of *chishiki* groups.

Unlike the dedicatory inscriptions for sutras copied at the official scriptoria by or for high-ranking courtiers and priests, those for the *chishiki* sutras contain few references to the concerns of state Buddhism. Furthermore, Nemoto Seiji, assistant professor at the University of Tsukuba, makes the highly interesting observation that the Great Perfection of Wisdom Sutra, the (Treatise on the Great Perfection of Wisdom Sutra; in Sanskrit, *Mahā-prajñāpāramitā-upadeśa*), the Treatise on the Stages of Yoga Practice, and the Lotus Sutra were often copied as *chishiki-kyō*, while the Flower Garland Sutra—the major scripture of official Nara Buddhism, with the Great Buddha of Tōdai-ji as its supreme symbol—is rarely encountered.

At any rate, as the Nara period drew to a close and the Heian period dawned, the Japanese people began to create new forms of Buddhism and enter into a deeper personal relationship with this pan-Asian religion.

3. Heian-Period Religion: Institutional Buddhism

THE TENDAI SECT

Saichō

In the seventh lunar month of 785 a young priest climbed Mount Hiei, in the province of Ōmi, built a simple hermitage, and embarked on intense religious practice. That young priest was Saichō, known posthumously by the title Dengyō Daishi—Great Master Who Transmitted the Teachings.

Saichō was born in 767, the son of Mitsu no Obito Momoe, a descendant of Chinese immigrants who had settled in Ōmi. (It has been suggested that Saichō may actually have been born in 766, but we will follow the traditional account in the *Eizan Daishi Den* [Biography of the Great Master of Mount Hiei; 823] in calculating his age.) At the age of eleven, he entered religious life under the guidance of the priest Gyōhyō (722–97) of Ōmi Kokubun-ji. At fourteen he was ordained as a novice, and at eighteen he received the precepts of full ordination (*gusoku-kai*) in Nara, at Tōdai-ji's ordination hall, the Kaidan-in. Ordinarily, a priest who had received all the precepts was considered to be fully qualified to take up duties at a temple, but some three months after he received the precepts Saichō left Nara for the relative wilds of Mount Hiei. He had chosen isolated religious practice in the mountains and forests over the life of an official priest at Ōmi Kokubun-ji. Saichō's inner resolve, based on his profound sense of the impermanence of all things, led him to build his secluded hermitage on Mount Hiei. Saichō observed that Buddhism was in an age of decline and that people were moving further and further from the path of salvation, and he was determined to try to save them by spreading the true teachings of the Buddha.

Saichō expressed his determination in a fivefold vow that reflected the most rigorous self-examination. He began by calling himself "the greatest of fools, the maddest of madmen, a defiled priest, the base and passion-ridden, precepts-violating Saichō." His first vow stated that he would not preach to others until his six senses (sight, hearing, smell, taste, touch, and mind) had been purified by spiritual discipline and he had achieved the supranormal powers of a Buddhist adept. The second stated that he would not be involved with special arts or skills until he had attained the mental capacity to reveal the truth clearly. The third stated that he would decline all invitations to the religious observances that pious lay believers held until he was able to observe the precepts for priests strictly. The fourth vow stated that he would refrain from undertaking any task that would make excessive demands on his time and energies until he had attained true wisdom. The fifth declared that the merits he might gain through religious practice would be transferred to all sentient beings, so that all might attain the highest enlightenment.

The first four of Saichō's vows express his personal goals as a priest; the last is a manifestation of his sense of destiny as a man of religion. To achieve the fulfillment of his fivefold vow, Saichō devoted himself to the daily reading of the Lotus Sutra, the Golden Light Sutra, and the *Hannya-kyō* (Perfection of Wisdom Sutra; in Sanskrit, *Prajñāpāramita-sūtra*) in his mountain hermitage.

During this period, Saichō also studied the *Daijō-kishin-ron* (Treatise on the Awakening of Faith in the Mahāyāna), a work attributed to the second-century Indian Buddhist teacher Aśvaghoṣa but more probably composed in China (where it is called the *Ta-ch'eng ch'i-hsin-lun*), and the *Hua-yen-wu-chiao-chang* (the Chapter on the Hua-yen Classification of the Five Teachings; in Japanese, *Kegon-gokyō-shō*), an outline of the Hua-yen sect's teachings by its third patriarch, Fa-tsang (643–712). In time Saichō encountered the works of Chih-i (538–97), the founder of the Chinese T'ien-t'ai sect, among them the *Mo-ho-chih-kuan* (Great Concentration and Insight; in Japanese, *Makashikan*) and *Fa-hua-hsüan-i* (The Profound Meaning of the Lotus Sutra; in Japanese, *Hokke-gengi*).

These and other works of Chih-i were supposedly taken to Japan either by the Chinese priest Chien-chen (688–763; known in Japan as Ganjin) or by one of his disciples. This tradition was later exploited by the Nara Buddhist authorities to belittle Saichō's achievements: they claimed that it was Chien-chen of the Nara-based Ritsu school rather than Saichō who first introduced T'ien-t'ai teachings in Japan. At any rate, Saichō's encounter with Chih-i's writings had a decisive effect on his religious development. From that time on, Saichō aspired to fulfill his fivefold vow in the context of the T'ien-t'ai—in Japanese, Tendai—teachings, which are based on study of and devotion to the Lotus Sutra.

In 797 Saichō was appointed court priest, which brought him close to Emperor Kammu (r. 781–806). The appointment was probably obtained through the influence of Jukō, another court priest, who had read Saichō's fivefold vow and was on familiar terms with him. With his appointment as personal priest to the emperor, Saichō's sphere of activity spread beyond Mount Hiei.

In the eleventh month of 798 he began a series of ten lectures on the meaning of the so-called Threefold Lotus Sutra, three independent texts that had been grouped in the Chinese T'ien-t'ai tradition. The Threefold Lotus Sutra opens with the Sutra of Innumerable Meanings (*Muryōgi-kyō;* in Chinese, *Wu-liang-i-ching*), in one fascicle, which is regarded as a preface to the Lotus Sutra (*Myōhō-renge-kyō,* or *Hoke-kyō;* in Sanskrit, *Saddharma-puṇḍarīka-sūtra*). The eight fascicles of the Lotus Sutra follow; and the Sutra of Meditation on the Bodhisattva Universal Virtue (*Kan-fugen-bosatsu-gyōbō-kyō;* in Chinese, *Kuan-p'u-hsien-p'u-sa-hsing-fa-ching*), also in one fascicle, is regarded as the epilogue of the Lotus Sutra. The total of ten fascicles provided the organizational structure for Saichō's ten lectures. The twenty-fourth of this same month was the anniversary of Chih-i's death, which no doubt figured in Saichō's decision to begin his lecture series at that time.

In 801 a similar lecture series was held on Mount Hiei, with ten eminent priests from Nara as guest lecturers. The following year, Emperor Kammu's officials Wakè no Hiroyo and his younger brother Matsuna (783–846) sponsored lectures on the Lotus Sutra at Jingo-ji, in Kyoto, with Saichō as one of the guest lecturers. This initial contact with the powerful Wakè clan was instrumental in later enabling Saichō to pursue advanced studies of Buddhism in China.

In 804 Saichō was sent to China as a government-sponsored student for intensive study and observation of Chinese Buddhism. A member of the embassy led by the courtier Fujiwara no Kadonomaro (755–818), Saichō traveled on the second of four ships, while his slightly younger contemporary Kūkai traveled on the first. Saichō's disciple Gishin (781–833) accompanied him as an interpreter.

Saichō's stay in China was brief; he returned to Japan in the seventh month of 805. Nonetheless, during his time in China he received instruction in T'ien-t'ai doctrine and was administered the Mahāyāna, or bodhisattva, precepts at the hands of Tao-sui and Hsing-man on Mount T'ien-t'ai, in the province of Che-kiang. He was also initiated into the teachings of esoteric Buddhism by Shun-hsiao, who was then staying at the Lung-hsing-ssu temple in Yüeh-chou. In addition, he had some 230 works in 460 fascicles copied to take back to Japan. Most of these sutras, treatises, and commentaries dealt with T'ien-t'ai doctrine.

On his return to Japan, he was welcomed by Emperor Kammu as a teacher of the esoteric doctrines then new to Japan. That imperial interest centered on esoteric Buddhism (*mikkyō*) is evident from the fact that Emperor Kammu ordered Wakè no Hiroyo to build an ordination platform for esoteric Buddhist initiations at Takaosan-ji and had Saichō administer the rites there, as well as perform the esoteric rites of Vairocana Buddha, the prime focus of esoteric Buddhism, in the palace itself.

Government Recognition

In the first month of 806, Saichō successfully petitioned the court for two annual ordinands for the Tendai sect, which meant that the government would officially approve the ordination of two aspirants to religious life within the Tendai sect each year. The government had established the annual ordinand system to prevent undue numbers of the populace from entering religious life, which would have imperiled the state's financial stability, dependent as it was on taxation of lands and the corvée. Thus the authorization of a fixed number of annual ordinands for the Tendai sect signified its official recognition by the government.

The first ordinations did not take place until 810, however, owing to Emperor Kammu's death and to inaction on the part of his successor, Heizei (r. 806–9). One of the first two ordinands was Kōjō (779–858), who later attained high rank at Enryaku-ji, the Tendai headquarters on Mount Hiei. Ennin and Enchin, who became patriarchs of the sect, were also among the early official ordinands. The authorization of annual ordinands ensured a succession of competent leaders for the Tendai sect after Saichō's death.

It should be noted, however, that of the two annual ordinands only one was assigned the "practice of concentration and insight" (*shikan gō*), which was distinctively Tendai in character; the other was to devote himself to the rites of Vairocana (*shana gō*), an esoteric Buddhist practice. This illustrates the fervent interest of the emperor and others in esoteric Buddhism and the extent to which Saichō tried to respond to that interest. Thus even during Saichō's lifetime, circumstances demanded that esoteric teachings and practices be included within the Tendai system.

The strong demand for esoteric teachings led Saichō to approach another major Buddhist leader of the age, Kūkai, who was already regarded by the Japanese court as the principal source of information on esoteric Buddhism. Though Kūkai was his junior and they had traveled to China in the same embassy, Saichō humbled himself and, adopting the role of a disciple, requested instruction in the esoteric teachings from Kūkai and borrowed relevant texts from him. He also sent Taihan (b. 778), one of his favorite disciples, to study directly under Kūkai. But when in 813 Kūkai's refusal of Saichō's request for the loan of an esoteric text was followed by Taihan's defection to Kūkai's school, relations between these two Buddhist leaders were severed. The problem arose in part because Kūkai regarded himself as the heir and transmitter of the orthodox lineage of esoteric teachings to Japan and Saichō as a specialist in T'ien-t'ai teachings, lacking the proper training to represent esoteric Buddhism correctly. At any rate, from that time on the two men followed separate paths. To Saichō, at least, the incident was a profound shock.

In 816 Saichō traveled to eastern Honshu, preaching the distinctive Tendai doctrine of One Vehicle (ekayāna) of salvation, derived from the Lotus Sutra, to the public at Mitono-dera, in Kōzuke Province, and Ono-dera, in Shimotsuke Province. This preaching tour undoubtedly gave Saichō renewed courage and energy, saddened as he was by the rupture in his relations with Kūkai and the suspension of his esoteric studies. It was on this preaching tour that Saichō encountered a formidable opponent whose attacks on Tendai doctrines demanded rebuttal.

Saichō's Dispute with Tokuitsu

At that time the Hossō priest Tokuitsu was engaged in disseminating the teachings of his school in the area around E'nichi-ji at Aizu, in Iwashiro Province, and Tsukubasan-ji, in Hitachi Province. Tokuitsu was revered by the local people as a living bodhisattva. In his Busshō Shō (On the Buddha-nature) he criticized Tendai doctrines from the viewpoint of the Hossō school. Saichō responded with the Shō Gonjitsu Kyō (The Mirror Illuminating the Provisional and the Ultimate Teachings), refuting Tokuitsu's claims. A long controversy ensued, Tokuitsu expressing his views in several works—*E'nichi Usoku* (Winged Feet of E'nichi-ji), *Chū Hen Gi Kyō* (The Mirror of Central and Peripheral Meanings), and *Hokke Kanjin* (Essentials of the Lotus Sutra)—while Saichō wrote *Hokke Kowaku* (The Lotus Sutra Driving Away Perplexity), *Shugo Kokkai Shō* (Essay on the Protection of the Nation), *Ketsu Gonjitsu Ron* (On Deciding Between the Provisional and the True Teachings), and *Hokke Shūku* (Wonderful Passages of the Lotus Sutra).

The principal subject of dispute between Saichō and Tokuitsu was an important doctrinal point: whether all sentient beings possess the buddha-nature, the potential for attaining buddhahood. Tokuitsu, following orthodox Hossō doctrine, argued that the "five natures" are separate and distinct. These five natures, or five types of beings, are the *śrāvaka* (hearer), the *pratyekabuddha* (solitary buddha), the bodhisattva (buddha-to-be), those of indeterminate nature, and the *icchantika* (those with no potential for attaining enlightenment). Hossō teachings regard these as immutable states of being determining the individual's spiritual development. While possessors of the first four natures are thought to be able to attain either full or partial enlightenment, members of the last category are doomed to wander forever in the realm of delusion, never able to escape from suffering. Thus, according to Hossō teaching, there is a class of beings incapable of enlightenment.

In opposition to this view, Saichō taught that all sentient beings are fully capable of the highest enlightenment, or buddhahood. The debate between Saichō and Tokuitsu, Tendai and Hossō, was a contest between egalitarian and elitist views of salvation. Both men presented their views clearly, with sincerity and conviction. Saichō would not compromise on this crucial point, and vigorously pressed the claims of Tendai. At the same time, he laid the foundations for the autonomy of the Tendai clergy by insisting on the need for Tendai priests to receive precepts appropriate to their sect. This constituted a virtual declaration of independence from the control of the Nara schools.

In 818 Saichō announced his abandonment of the full precepts that he had received as a youth in Nara and devised two sets of regulations—*gakushō shiki*, or regulations for student priests—providing unique methods of training for Tendai student priests. (One regulation, for example, stipulated that all who aspired to formal status in the Tendai sect confine themselves on Mount Hiei for twelve years of rigorous study and spiritual training.) Saichō then petitioned Emperor Saga (r. 809–23) for official approval of his regulations, which were referred for review to the official priestly hierarchy (*sōgō*), consisting of Nara priests, who proceeded to ignore them, refusing any comment. The following year, Saichō submitted a new set of regulations, in which he characterized the precepts given at Nara as Hīnayāna in spirit and argued the need for Tendai ordinands to receive Mahāyāna precepts instead. The Nara clergy were outraged, and the *sōgō* requested that the government issue a summons to Saichō on grounds of violation of the official regulations for clergy. Saichō's three sets of regulations are known collectively as the *Sange Gakushō Shiki* (Regulations for Student Priests of Mount Hiei).

In response to the opposition of the Nara *sōgō*, Saichō wrote his *Kenkai Ron* (Treatise on Manifesting the Precepts) to put forward his own position. In both the *Kenkai Ron* and the earlier sets of regulations, Saichō emphasized several points. First, Tendai priests should live in an institution where the study of Mahāyāna Buddhism can be pursued, and that institution is the temple complex Hieizan-ji (later renamed Enryaku-ji), centered on Ichijō Shikan-in (the One-Vehicle Concentration-and-Insight Temple).

Second, Tendai priests living in a Mahāyāna temple should be bodhisattva-priests who realize that helping to save others is the way to save oneself. Bodhisattva-priests are to be classified as *kokuhō* (national treasures), *kokushi* (national teachers), or *kokuyū* (national resources), according to their abilities and degree of progress in religious practice. The *kokuhō* are to become leaders of the monastic order, while the *kokushi* and *kokuyū* are to serve as teachers and preachers throughout the land. Clearly, Saichō aimed at disseminating Tendai Buddhism through the activities of his priests in the most distant provinces of Japan.

Third, the Tendai bodhisattva-priests ought to receive precepts appropriate to their convictions: the *daisō kai* (precepts for ordained priests), *daijō kai* (Mahāyāna precepts), or *en kai* (perfect precepts), as they were variously called. Specifically, Saichō meant the ten major and forty-eight minor precepts set forth in the Sutra of the Perfect Net (*Fan-wang-ching*), purportedly a translation of a Sanskrit original but probably of Chinese provenance. Saichō further maintained that there was no need for Tendai priests to receive the full two hundred and fifty precepts of the Hīnayāna tradition given by the Nara schools.

Evident in these points is Saichō's affirmation that Tendai priests are in fact Mahāyāna bodhisattva-priests, separate from the priests of the Nara schools, and that they have a right to give and receive their own distinctive Mahāyāna precepts and to maintain their own Mahāyāna monastic establishment as the locus of their activities. In all this, we see the young

Saichō's strong sense of personal mission expressed in maturity as a quest for autonomy for the Tendai sect and its practitioners.

Naturally, Saichō's suit provoked ever-stronger opposition from the Nara schools. Saichō died on the fourth day of the sixth month of 822, without seeing the realization of the major project of his last years. Within seven days of his death, however, the court official Fujiwara no Fuyutsugu (775–826) and Yoshimine no Yasuyo (785–830), a son of Emperor Kammu, secured an imperial decree that fulfilled Saichō's hopes. In the second month of 823, Ichijō Shikan-in was given the official name Enryaku-ji, and in the fourth month the Mahāyāna precepts were administered for the first time in the temple's main hall, the Kompon Chū-dō. Thus Saichō's earnest desire to establish the autonomy of the Tendai sect was fulfilled after his death. In a sense, we can date the true foundation of the Tendai sect in Japan to the year 823.

Ennin's Journey to China

In his last years, Saichō devoted most of his energy to the disputes with Tokuitsu and with the Nara clergy and the *sōgō*. As a result, the development of Tendai esotericism was left to his disciples. It was primarily Ennin (794–864), Enchin (814–91), and Annen (841?–901?) who adapted esoteric teachings and practices to the Tendai doctrinal system, developing both the theory and practice of what was later called Taimitsu, or esoteric Tendai. The term Taimitsu first appeared in the *Genkō Shakusho* (Genkō-era History of Buddhism; 1322), the first history of Japanese Buddhism, by the Rinzai priest Kokan Shiren (1278–1346).

Born into the Mibu clan in the Tsuga district of Shimotsuke Province, Ennin became a disciple of Saichō on Mount Hiei in 808. That someone from Shimotsuke should come to study under Saichō eight years before his preaching tour in eastern Japan suggests that Saichō's influence extended to that region at a very early date.

In 838, after thirty years' study on Mount Hiei, Ennin went to China as part of an official embassy, remaining there about nine years. His experiences are described in his celebrated diary *Nittō Guhō Junrei Kōki* (An Account of a Pilgrimage to China in Quest of the Law). In 845 Emperor Wu-tsung (r. 840–47) initiated a major persecution of Buddhism that brought about the religion's decline throughout China and resulted in two years' internment for Ennin. Nonetheless, Ennin was able to devote his energies to an intensive study of Chinese Buddhism, and of esoteric teachings in particular.

At first he studied T'ien-t'ai on Mount Wu-t'ai, Shan-hsi Province, under Chih-yüan. There he encountered the practice known in Chinese as *nien-fo* and in Japanese as *nembutsu:* the practice of meditation on (or invocation of the sacred name of) one of the buddhas, especially Amitābha. The practice as Ennin studied it traced back to the eighth-century priest Fa-chao and drew on the earlier practice of Hui-yüan (334–416) as transmitted at the temple Chu-lin-ssu on Mount Wu-t'ai. Ennin in turn took the Mount Wu-t'ai–style *nembutsu* to Mount Hiei where, under the name "mountain *nembutsu*," it formed the nucleus of Tendai practices related to Amitābha (in Japanese, Amida) and his Pure Land.

Later Ennin went to the city of Ch'ang-an, where over a period of three years he mastered the principal rites of esoteric Buddhism: the *kongo kai* (diamond realm) ritual under Yüan-cheng of the temple Ta-hsing-shan-ssu and the *taizō kai* (womb realm) and *soshitsuji* (most ultimate, secret ritual in the *Soshitsuji-kyō* that teaches the unity of the diamond and womb realms) rituals under I-chen of the temple Ch'ing-lung-ssu. He also studied *taizō giki*, or ritual manuals for the womb realm, under Fa-ch'uan of the temple Hsüan-fa-ssu. Many years earlier, Kūkai had studied esoteric teachings under Hui-kuo (746–805) at Ch'ing-lung-ssu; now Ennin, as a representative of Tendai, was able to learn esoteric rituals from Hui-kuo's direct disciple I-chen and second-generation disciple Fa-ch'uan, and thus establish himself within the orthodox lineage of esoteric Buddhism. He went on to learn Sanskrit orthography from Hsüan-chien of Ta-an-kuo-ssu and Sanskrit pronunciation from an Indian priest known by the Chinese name Pao-yüeh, and transmitted these skills—vital to the practice of esoteric Buddhism—to Mount Hiei after his return.

In 848, the year after he returned to Japan, Ennin was appointed court priest and prayer priest for the welfare of Emperor Nimmyō (r. 833–50). In 850, inspired by the example of Ch'ing-lung-ssu in China, he built the subtemple Sōji-in on Mount Hiei to pray for the buddhas' protection of the imperial house. In the same year the number of official annual ordinands for the Tendai sect was increased to four, of whom two were to devote themselves to the study of Tendai proper and one each to the study of the two principal esoteric Buddhist texts: the *Kongōchō-kyō* (Diamond Peak Sutra; in Sanskrit, *Vajraśekhara-sūtra*) and the *Soshitsuji-kyō* (Sutra of Good Accomplishment; in Sanskrit, *Susiddhikara-sūtra*). Ennin was appointed

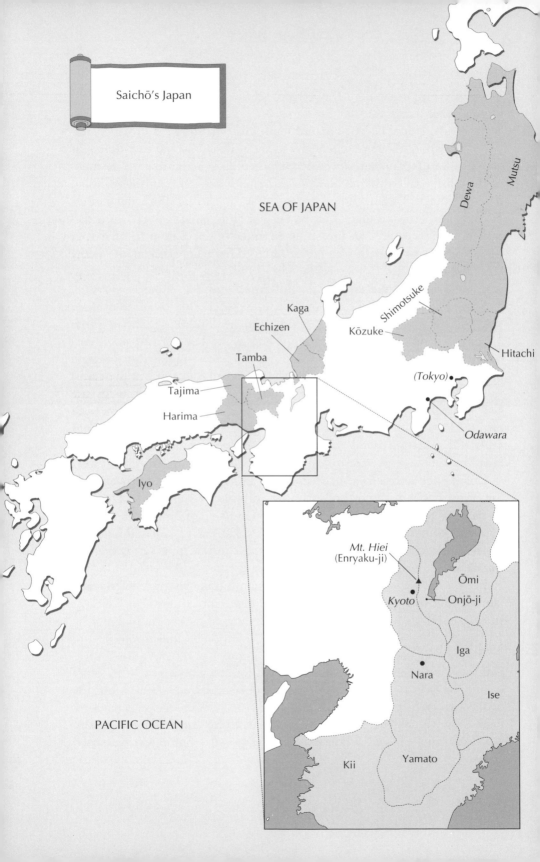

Saichō's Japan

SEA OF JAPAN

Dewa

Mutsu

Shimotsuke

Kaga

Echizen

Kōzuke

Hitachi

Tamba

(Tokyo)

Tajima

Odawara

Harima

Iyo

Mt. Hiei
(Enryaku-ji)

Ōmi

Kyoto

Onjō-ji

Iga

Nara

Ise

PACIFIC OCEAN

Kii

Yamato

grand abbot of Enryaku-ji in 854 and in following years administered esoteric Buddhist initiation to Emperor Montoku (r. 850–58), other members of the imperial family, and members of the aristocracy.

At the same time, Ennin labored to lay the theoretical foundations for esoteric Tendai. Kūkai's Shingon was based on the literature and rituals of the diamond- and womb-realm mandalas. In contrast, at the hands of Ennin, esoteric Tendai came to be based on a threefold system formed by adding the literature and ritual associated with the Sutra of Good Accomplishment to those of the diamond and womb realms. The Sutra of Good Accomplishment and the rites derived from it, which were widely studied and practiced in China at the time that Ennin studied there, represented a new element in esoteric Buddhism in Japan.

Moreover, Ennin divided the doctrines of various schools of Buddhism into exoteric and esoteric teachings, classifying the teaching of the Three Vehicles of salvation (the view that there are three modes of salvation corresponding to the varying capacities of sentient beings) as the exoteric teaching and the One Vehicle teaching (the view expounded in the Lotus Sutra that the Three Vehicles are merely temporary expedients for the One, Universal Vehicle) as the esoteric teaching. According to Ennin, both the Lotus Sutra and the esoteric teachings are the teaching of the One Vehicle. Doctrinally or theoretically they are identical; but in practice and ritual, he claimed, esoteric Buddhism is superior.

In addition to making theoretical contributions, Ennin helped develop the distinctive Tendai meditational practice of concentration and insight, or *shikan gō*, which is at the very heart of Tendai practice. He introduced the "four modes of meditation" (*shishu zammai*) at Enryaku-ji and incorporated into one of them—meditation while constantly walking, or *jōgyō zammai*—the form of *nembutsu* he had learned on Mount Wu-t'ai. This became the foundation on which Tendai Pure Land thought and practice later developed.

Enchin's Development of Esoteric Buddhism

Enchin carried Ennin's ideas further. Enchin was born into the Wakè clan in the Naka district of Sanuki Province, on Shikoku, in 814. His mother was Kūkai's niece. At the age of fourteen he began studying esoteric Tendai on Mount Hiei under Gishin, the disciple who had accompanied Saichō to China. In 853 Enchin went to China on a private Chinese merchant ship, since Japan was no longer dispatching official missions to the

T'ang court. In China he went first to Mount T'ien-t'ai and then to Ch'ang-an, where, like Ennin, he was initiated into the lineages of the esoteric diamond and womb rituals by Fa-ch'uan at Ch'ing-lung-ssu. He also received the special *samaya* precepts of esoteric Buddhism. Later, at the temple K'ai-yüan-ssu in Yüeh-chou, he studied T'ien-t'ai teaching under Liang-hsü and made copies of important T'ien-t'ai texts. In 858, after a stay of five years, Enchin returned to Japan on another Chinese merchant vessel.

Ennin, twenty years older than Enchin, remained active, administering the precepts to eminent individuals, including Emperor Seiwa (r. 858–76) and Empress Dowager Junna (809–79). Following Ennin's death in 864, Enchin grew very active: for example, in the fall of that year, at imperial command, he administered the womb initiation rite at the Ninju-den in the palace in Kyoto to more than thirty people, including Emperor Seiwa and his maternal grandfather, the immensely powerful regent Fujiwara no Yoshifusa (804–72). In 866, the year he assumed the regency, Yoshifusa built a private altar in the Reizei-in auxiliary palace in Kyoto and had Enchin offer prayers there for the well-being of the emperor. In addition, he appointed Enchin spiritual advisor to his daughter Akirakeiko (829–900), mother of the emperor.

Links between the powerful Fujiwara clan and the Tendai sect were forged under both Ennin and Enchin, links that were significant in the power struggles among the aristocratic clans allied with the imperial family by marriage. For example, two of Emperor Montoku's sons were Prince Koretaka (844–97), by Shizuko, daughter of the courtier Ki no Natora (d. 847), and Prince Korehito (850–80), by Akirakeiko, daughter of Yoshifusa. The Ki and Fujiwara clans were rivals, and each tried to advance the claims of its candidate to be named crown prince and thus heir to the throne. One weapon in these power struggles was esoteric Buddhist rites. The Tendai priest Eryō (802–60) is said to have prayed for Prince Korehito's success to great effect: Korehito was named crown prince at the tender age of eight months. This occurred while Enchin was still in China.

In 859, the year after Crown Prince Korehito ascended the throne as Emperor Seiwa, two additional annual ordinands were approved for the Tendai sect in response to an appeal from Eryō. This patronage of esoteric Buddhism and the previously mentioned esoteric initiation administered to Emperor Seiwa by Ennin unquestionably resulted from the belief that esoteric Tendai rituals were efficacious in securing worldly benefits. The relationship between Enchin and Yoshifusa after Ennin's death should be seen as a continuation of this belief. Their relationship, based on the esoteric Buddhist practitioner's willingness to respond to the circumstances and needs of the aristocracy, resulted in the aristocratization of Enryaku-ji and of the Tendai sect as a whole. The same process occurred in Kūkai's Shingon sect, which grew ever more closely linked with the aristocracy as its members became high-ranking clerics in the Shingon hierarchy and the sect responded to the great families' demands for rituals and prayers.

After Ennin's death in 864, Anne (794–868) became grand abbot of Enryaku-ji, and when he died four years later Enchin succeeded him. In 859, the year after his return from China, Enchin had been appointed administrator of Onjō-ji, in Ōtsu, Ōmi Province. Also known as Miidera, Onjō-ji was an important Tendai temple complex. After his appointment as grand abbot of Enryaku-ji, he designated Onjō-ji as the site for special esoteric initiations and left there a generous library of sutras and treatises that he had brought back from China. Later Onjō-ji became the center of the so-called Enchin group within Tendai.

Enchin went even further than Ennin had in the attempt to define the relationship between the Lotus Sutra elements and the esoteric elements in Tendai. Ennin, as we have seen, granted pride of place to esoteric Buddhism in the realm of practice but insisted that the teachings of the Lotus Sutra and esoteric doctrines were equivalent on the level of theory. Enchin, however, in his *Dainichi-kyō Sho* (Commentary on the Great Sun Sutra), states that the esoteric Buddhism preached in this sutra is "the king of the Mahāyāna, the secret of secrets"; even the Lotus Sutra is inferior to it—how much more so all other teachings. Enchin concluded that esoteric Buddhism is superior to the teaching of the Lotus Sutra not only in practice but in theory and content, as well. Thus under the leadership of Ennin and Enchin the development of esoteric Tendai—indeed, the esotericization of Tendai—proceeded apace. With the next great figure in the Tendai lineage, Annen, this process reached its climax.

Annen's Esoteric Tendai

Annen first studied under Ennin, but after Ennin's death he became a disciple of Henjō (816–90) at Gangyō-ji in Kyoto. In 876 he learned the womb ritual from Dōkai. The following year he traveled to Dazaifu, on northern Kyushu, in hope of setting sail for China, but that proved to be impossible. He studied the Siddha script for some time under Chōi, a dis-

ciple of Ennin, and was appointed master of transmitting the Dharma at
Gangyō-ji in 884. Later Annen built the subtemple Godai-in on Mount
Hiei, where he retired to devote himself to writing. He further refined and
developed the esoteric Tendai that he had learned from Ennin, Henjō,
Dōkai, and Chōi. The knowledge of Sanskrit that he gained from Chōi
was later embodied in his *Shittan Zō* (Siddhaṃ Treasury), compiled at the
behest of Emperor Seiwa. This work is one of the classics of premodern
Japanese Sanskrit studies.

In his other writings, Annen sought to place esoteric Buddhism within
the Tendai system of the classification of the Buddha's teachings. In Tendai,
all the doctrines attributed to Śākyamuni are classified by form and content. The classification by content yields the four teachings for the salvation
of all sentient beings: *zōkyō*, or the teachings of the Hīnayāna canon; *tsūgyō*,
or the teachings common to all Mahāyāna sutras; *bekkyō*, or the teachings
unique to Mahāyāna, in contrast to Hīnayāna; and *engyō*, or the perfect
teaching. In the original Tendai classification, the perfect teaching is the
Lotus Sutra. Annen, however, added the esoteric teachings to the fourfold
classification and placed them above even the perfect teaching of the Lotus
Sutra. He thus radically reordered the Tendai doctrinal system.

Annen went on to assert the superiority of esoteric Buddhism from the
four standpoints of the superiority of the buddha who preaches the fundamental sutra, the superiority of the time at which it is preached, the superiority of the place or circumstances in which it is preached, and the
superiority of the nature of the doctrine that is preached. Finally, he made
a distinction between the Tendai sect and esoteric Tendai, to the advantage of the latter, and proposed distinguishing esoteric Tendai by giving it
a new name: Shingon. Given Annen's new theory of the five, rather than
four, teachings and the renaming of esoteric Tendai as Shingon, it is difficult to avoid concluding that the basic framework of the Tendai sect was
in danger of being destroyed.

As a result of the efforts of Ennin, Enchin, and Annen in developing
both the practical and the theoretical aspects of esoteric Tendai, a rich
variety of esoteric practices and rites evolved within Tendai, differing in
techniques and the lineage of their transmission. Among the various subschools within esoteric Tendai, that descending from Ennin through
Kakuchō (960–1034) and Kōgei (977–1049) stands out. It was usually referred to as the River school or the Valley school because of the sites on
Mount Hiei where its leading practitioners lived. The Valley school had
immense influence and gave rise to many smaller subschools. The majority

of the thirteen schools of esoteric Tendai transmitted to later ages were in fact offshoots of the Valley school.

Ryōgen

It was Ryōgen (912–85) who enriched and strengthened Enryaku-ji in the mid-Heian period by further developing the links with the Fujiwara clan that had been forged in the time of Ennin and Enchin. Ryōgen was a resident priest in the Yokawa section of Mount Hiei and was appointed grand abbot of Tendai in the eighth month of 966. Toward the end of that year, a great fire destroyed most of the numerous halls, pagodas, residence halls, and other buildings on Mount Hiei. Ryōgen's first task as grand abbot was to repair that tremendous loss.

Reconstruction took about fifteen years, but by 980 most of the buildings had been restored. The support for this monumental project was supplemented by financial donations by Fujiwara no Morosuke (908–60), a high court official who had long been a devoted lay disciple of Ryōgen. When Morosuke was alive, he made donations to Ryōgen for the promotion of the Yokawa section. At that time the Fujiwara clan effectively controlled the government through a system of rule by Fujiwara regents who continued to act in the name of the emperor even after he had attained his majority. The Fujiwara had a virtual monopoly on political power and exercised dictatorial authority. Support from Morosuke was therefore immensely helpful to Ryōgen.

At the same time that Ryōgen worked at rebuilding the Enryaku-ji temple complex, he also sought to advance learning on Mount Hiei by sponsoring a system of examinations, lectures, and debates (called *kōgaku ryūgi*) held each year on the fourth day of the sixth month, the anniversary of Saichō's death. His intent was to encourage broad and deep study of Tendai doctrine by publicly honoring those who had shown exceptional ability in their studies. That proved to be an excellent stimulus for all the student priests on Mount Hiei. Thus, through his twin projects of physical reconstruction and encouragement of scholarship, Ryōgen inaugurated a brilliant period in the history of Enryaku-ji and the Tendai sect as a whole.

As the links between the Tendai sect and the aristocracy strengthened under Ryōgen, both the number of aristocrats within the Tendai clergy and their power and status grew. For example, Jinzen (943–90), a son of Fujiwara no Morosuke, became a direct disciple of Ryōgen and rose extraordinarily rapidly through the Tendai hierarchy, entirely bypassing some of the lower ranks. Eventually he was given the special rank of *isshin ajari* (one-generation master of esoteric doctrines), with the stipulation that the rank could not be passed on to a disciple. This was unprecedented. Finally, in 985, after Ryōgen's death that year, Jinzen was appointed grand abbot. None of that would have been possible without the strong support of the Fujiwara clan.

In strengthening the Tendai sect's links with the Heian aristocracy, Ryōgen fostered within Enryaku-ji an atmosphere of favoritism toward the scions of noble families, in which ancestry and family alliances counted for more than ability or character. Since Ryōgen was instrumental in that unfortunate shift, we can assume that opposition to his emphasis on family connections and status played a part in the decisions of one disciple, Zōga (917–1003), to move to Tōnomine-dera, in Sakurai, and of another disciple, Genshin (942–1017), to retire to Yokawa and live in seclusion, abandoning the office of priestly official.

Ryōgen's connection with the Pure Land traditions transmitted at Yokawa is worthy of note. As we have seen, Ennin incorporated the Mount Wu-t'ai–style *nembutsu* practice he had learned in China into Tendai as *jōgyō zammai*, or constantly walking meditation. His disciple Sōō (831–918) transformed this practice into what he called *fudan nembutsu*, the uninterrupted practice of the *nembutsu*. Yokawa had thus been associated with Tendai-style Pure Land practice ever since the site had been developed by Ennin. That background figured in Ryōgen's *Gokuraku Jōdo Kuhon Ōjō Gi* (On the Nine Types of Rebirth in the Pure Land of Perfect Bliss). Though more a scholarly study than a work concerned with religious practice, this treatise is a clear manifestation of the contemporary Tendai Pure Land teaching. It was left to Genshin to further develop that important tradition associated with the Yokawa area on Mount Hiei.

The Sammon School and the Jimon School

Two major factions arose among the priests of Enryaku-ji: one claiming allegiance to Enchin and the other to Ennin. Known as the Enchin group and the Ennin group, the factions were also called the Chishō group and the Jikaku group, after the posthumous titles of the two priests. Before his death, Enchin had warned his followers to avoid conflict with the Ennin group, no doubt sensing the danger a rift would pose to the Tendai sect as a whole. In any case, the rivalry was between the two groups of disciples, not between Ennin and Enchin themselves. There was increasing hostility and strife between the two groups over the issue of succession to the post of grand abbot. Of the thirteen grand abbots of Enryaku-ji from Enchin, the sixth, through Ryōgen, the eighteenth, seven were associated with Enchin's lineage and six with Ennin's. But for approximately fifty years, during the tenures of the fourteenth through the eighteenth abbots, the Ennin group monopolized the office, effectively shutting out the Enchin group.

Ryōgen's successor, Jinzen, resigned the abbacy in 989, after four years' tenure, and in the ninth month of that year Yokei (919–91), of the Enchin 7 group, was appointed to take his place. Though this was the first appointment for the Enchin group in many decades, the Ennin faction refused to countenance it, and Yokei was forced to resign in the twelfth month. Two abbots from the Ennin faction were then appointed in succession—Yōshō (904–90) and Senga.

The Enchin group's outrage finally erupted in violence in 993, when Kaisan (963–1053) led armed priests of this faction in an attack on Sekizan Zen-in, a temple on Mount Hiei sacred to Ennin's memory. In retaliation, priests of the Ennin group attacked and destroyed worship halls and residence halls used by their rivals and drove them from Mount Hiei. Over a thousand priests of the Enchin faction fled to Onjō-ji, which they made their base. Thereafter the Ennin group came to be known as the Sammon, or Mountain, school, while Enchin's followers were called the Jimon, or Temple, school, because of their flight to Onjō-ji. Thus at the close of the tenth century the Tendai sect found itself divided into two implacably hostile camps.

The question of the abbacy, the cause of the initial rift, continued to fuel the flames of enmity over the years. As long as the Ennin group controlled Mount Hiei, it was impossible for anyone from the Enchin group to exercise actual control of the sect's affairs. Even though, with the strong support of the Fujiwara, a member of the Enchin group might be appointed grand abbot, in the face of unrelenting opposition from the Ennin group, entrenched on Mount Hiei, he would be forced to resign. For example, the twenty-ninth abbot, Myōson (971–1063), supported by the regent Fujiwara no Yorimichi (990–1074), eldest son of the statesman Michinaga (966–1027), and the thirty-first abbot, Gensen (977–1055), both resigned after only three days in office. The case of Yorimichi's son Kakuen (1031–98) was the most extreme: that scion of one of Japan's most influential families was appointed the thirty-fourth grand abbot of Enryaku-ji in 1077 but resigned on the following day. Later, too, several candidates from the Enchin faction were appointed by the court, but the outcome was always the same. After the failure of the appointment of Kōken (1110–93) as six-tieth abbot, there were no more attempts to name candidates from the Temple school for the abbacy of Mount Hiei.

Of the greatest importance to Tendai priests was ordination at the Kaidan-in, the ordination hall on Mount Hiei established in accordance with Saichō's wishes. Strictly speaking, a novice became a full-fledged Tendai priest only after receiving the precepts at the Kaidan-in. That was true for all Tendai priests, whether from Mount Hiei or from the provinces. From all over Japan, novices gathered at Mount Hiei to receive ordination as orthodox Tendai priests. The Temple school had a problem ordaining its young novices once it had been driven from Mount Hiei. The only solution was for the Temple school to erect its own Kaidan-in, where it could administer the Mahāyāna precepts to its novices. For almost fifty years the Temple school sought to realize this goal.

In 1039 Myōson petitioned for imperial permission to build an ordination platform and hall at Onjō-ji. The granting of that permission would have amounted to official recognition of Onjō-ji's autonomy, in both name and reality, just as similar permission two centuries earlier had signaled the independence of Saichō's Buddhism from that of the Nara schools. The Mountain school of course opposed the granting of permission, and Myōson's efforts came to nothing. Several times in later years the process was repeated: the Temple school petitioned, and the Mountain school opposed the request; the Mountain school attacked Onjō-ji, and the Temple school retaliated by attacking Mount Hiei. In the end, the Temple school's hopes for establishing an independent ordination platform were crushed.

As we have seen, military force was sometimes used in the struggle between the Mountain and Temple schools of the Tendai sect. It also figured in conflicts between the main and branch temples of other sects. The actual fighting was done by armed bands of warrior-priests, called *sōhei*. Enryaku-ji, Tōdai-ji, Kōfuku-ji, and other great monasteries had bands of warrior-priests who made various demands on the court and aristocracy and enforced them. In addition, martial force was sometimes used inside a monastery, for instance, at Enryaku-ji, where conflict often arose between the elite student priests (*gakushō*), and the rank-and-file hall priests (*dōshū*). In the face of monastic strife and violence, ordinary believers were filled with foreboding that true Buddhism was dying, that the period of the Decay of the Law (*Mappō*) was upon them.

The Propagation of Tendai in the Provinces

From the very beginning, Saichō had aimed at the propagation of the Tendai sect in outlying provinces. He himself traveled only to Kyushu and to eastern Honshu, but he sought to have the priests he was training on Mount Hiei appointed as provincial lecturers throughout the land. Assigned to individual provinces for six-year terms, the government-appointed lecturers (originally styled teachers of the nation and later divided into two classes, lecturers and reciters) were responsible for administering the affairs of the local Buddhist clergy and institutions in cooperation with the provincial governors.

Even given their six-year limit, these appointments provided invaluable opportunities for the Tendai and Shingon sects to disseminate their teachings in the provinces at a time when the free proselytizing of ordinary citizens was forbidden by law. Saichō, in fact, was far more interested in using the lecturer and reciter system to establish Tendai in the provinces than in winning the appointment of Tendai priests to the official priestly hierarchy, which was monopolized by the Nara schools.

No doubt it was a specific request from Saichō that led the government to stipulate that the Tendai yearly ordinands should be appointed as provincial lecturers after ordination. It was not until 835, however, over a dozen years after Saichō's death, that the system went into effect—with the annual appointment of one lecturer and one reciter from among the Tendai clergy. Two years later the Shingon sect was accorded the same privilege. Thus the two great Heian-period Buddhist sects began to compete in the provinces, as well as in the capital.

With the appointment of Tendai provincial lecturers, outlying temples began to affiliate themselves with Enryaku-ji as branch temples. This system of a network of branch temples controlled by a head temple became very important in the history of Japanese Buddhism. The first recorded instance of a temple affiliating itself with Enrayku-ji as a branch temple is that of Tado Jingū-ji in Ise Province in 839; throughout the ninth and tenth centuries provincial temples frequently affiliated themselves with temples in the capital. The phenomenon was particularly widespread in the central provinces of Ōmi and Yamashiro, but it also extended to more remote areas, including Mutsu, Dewa, Kōzuke, Shimotsuke, Ise, Echizen, Kaga, Harima, Tamba, Tajima, Kii, and Iyo provinces. In some cases the change to Enryaku-ji branch-temple status was officially acknowledged and approved by the government.

The gradual proliferation of branch temples in the provinces seems to have come about mainly through the efforts of Tendai clergy serving as lecturers and reciters or engaged in other activities in the provinces. Enryaku-ji exercised complete control over personnel at the branch temples, sending out priests to head them as it saw fit. Consequently, the establishment of numerous branch temples was simultaneously the result of the successful advance of Tendai into the provinces and the firm foundation for further activity.

Thus a network of main and branch temple relationships, with Enryaku-ji at the center, emerged in the Heian period. In some cases, Tendai priests established new temples as Enryaku-ji branch temples in the provinces; in others, existing temples chose to put themselves under Enryaku-ji's protection. In both cases, the branch temples incurred certain burdens and responsibilities by virtue of their subordinate status. The growth of the main-and-branch-temple system parallels that of the practice of provincial proprietors' placing their landed estates under the protection of more powerful nobles, which became prevalent around the same time. Provincial temples generally became branches of one of the great monasteries in the capital area to ensure financial and political support for their religious activities. At the same time, branch temples were obliged to pay an annual assessment to the head temple and to participate in special ceremonies at its command. Inevitably, the large central monasteries vied for possession and control of the provincial branch temples.

Tendai branch temples served not only as bases for proselytizing the provincial populace but also as facilities for training local Tendai clergy. Novices from provincial temples were ultimately sent to Mount Hiei for ordination and advanced training. Having taken advantage of the extensive library of sutras, treatises, and commentaries on Mount Hiei and of other facilities for study and practice there, provincial priests would return to their branch temples to share what they had gained. Thus the main-and-branch-temple system provided both a route for the propagation of Tendai teachings throughout the country and a means by which Enryaku-ji could become a major holder of estates and fiefs, in the manner of the secular elite.

Devotion to the Lotus Sutra

The Lotus Sutra is the principal scripture of the Tendai sect. One feature that distinguishes the Tendai and Shingon sects from the earlier Nara

schools is that these two Heian-period sects based their teachings on sutras, while the Nara schools (with the sole exception of the Kegon school)
based theirs on *śāstras*—treatises that summarize or comment on ideas
and doctrines in the sutras. Sutras were regarded as containing the direct
teachings of the buddhas, whereas *śāstras* are indirect, being the words of
a learned master rather than of a buddha himself. Sects founded on a sutra tended to have a more markedly devotional character, seeking to em-
body in practice the doctrinal spirit of the sutra.

The founding of Tendai and Shingon in the early Heian period marked
the beginning of denominational, or sectarian, Buddhism in Japan. However, both Tendai and Shingon were clerical orders, full membership being restricted to ordained clergy. Ordinary lay believers were, in a sense,
outsiders. The only path open to them was to enter into a votary relationship with a particular priest or temple. It was not until the Kamakura
period that lay believers came to be regarded as full members of a sect. In
the Heian period, even lay believers who were devoted to the Lotus Sutra,
the basic scripture of Tendai, had no place within the Tendai organization
proper.

The Lotus Sutra had been introduced into Japan quite early and had
long been reverenced for two reasons. First, like the Golden Light Sutra
and the Sutra on the Benevolent King, it was considered to be a sutra
that would protect the nation. Copies of the Lotus Sutra were housed and
worshiped in the Temples for the Elimination of Sins Through the Lotus
Sutra (Hokke Metsuzai no Tera), the *kokubunniji* established as part of the
provincial-temple system discussed in chapter 2. The name given to the
kokubunniji clearly indicates the second virtue popularly ascribed to the sutra: its efficacy in cleansing individual believers of sin. The "Devadatta"
chapter of the Lotus Sutra, in particular, was revered in this connection
because it relates that anyone—even great evildoers and women, who
were thought to be incapable of religious attainment—can attain perfect
enlightenment. It was this teaching that made the Lotus Sutra popular as
a vehicle for individual salvation, quite apart from the reverence it received as a protector of the nation. In the Nara period the Lotus Sutra
was already being copied for the spiritual benefit of the dead, in the belief
that the merit gained by copying the sacred text could be transferred to
the deceased.

Saichō's view of the Lotus Sutra incorporated both of these Nara-period
elements. On the one hand, he designated the Lotus Sutra as one of the
three sutras to protect the nation (together with the Golden Light Sutra and

the Sutra on the Benevolent King). Saichō was strongly committed to the idea of Buddhism as protector of the nation. This belief was reflected in his styling Tendai Lotus Sutra priests treasures of the nation, teachers of the nation, and resources of the nation and in his establishment of the Perpetual Lectures on the Lotus Sutra (Hokke Jōgō) so that spiritual benefits might accrue to the nation into the infinite future. On the other hand, he stressed the value of the Lotus Sutra as a means of universal salvation—an especially important point in the light of his heated dispute with the Hossō priest Tokuitsu over universalism versus exclusivism.

Thus Saichō adapted to the needs of the new Tendai order the two principal focal points inherited from the Nara-period Lotus Sutra cult: protection of the nation and personal salvation. Of course, Lotus Sutra pietism was not confined to Tendai. It was manifested in various forms by the populace at large, notably in such practices as copying the sutra, burying copies of it to preserve it for future generations, and conducting formal lectures on its contents.

Lectures on the Lotus Sutra

The first recorded formal lecture on the Lotus Sutra occurred in 746, during the Nara period, when the Kegon patriarch and Tōdai-ji abbot Rōben (689–773) conducted a Lotus Sutra service in Kenjaku-in at Tōdai-ji to pray for the well-being of the emperor, the aristocracy, and high officials and for seasonable weather, an abundant harvest, and the happiness and prosperity of the general population. Then, in 796, the eminent Sanron priest Gonzō (754–827) and others instituted the Eight Lectures on the Lotus Sutra (Hokke Hakkō) in a service for the benefit of the dead. Rōben's Lotus Sutra service reflects the sutra's function as a protector of the nation, while Gonzō's Eight Lectures manifest its relation to personal salvation.

In the Heian period the Eight Lectures on the Lotus Sutra were the most popular form of devotion, though in addition there were the Ten Lectures (Hokke Jikkō), based on the eight fascicles of the Lotus Sutra plus its one-fascicle opening and closing sutras—the Sutra of Innumerable Meanings and the Sutra of Meditation on the Bodhisattva Universal Virtue; the Thirty Lectures (Hokke Sanjikkō), based on the twenty-eight chapters of the Lotus Sutra plus the Sutra of Innumerable Meanings and the Sutra of Meditation on the Bodhisattva Universal Virtue; and the Perpetual Lectures on the Lotus Sutra, mentioned above. The Eight Lectures services were conducted for such purposes as the protection of the nation, the salvation of the dead, and even the religious edification of ordinary people. The ritual was standardized. On four consecutive days, one of the eight fascicles of the Lotus Sutra was the subject of a lecture each morning and evening. The high point of the lecture series was the presentation of the "Devadatta" chapter, included in the fifth fascicle of the sutra. On the day of that lecture, lay believers made offerings and the rites were conducted with special solemnity. When the Eight Lectures were sponsored by an individual family or clan, they served a dual social function: strengthening solidarity among kindred and demonstrating the family's or clan's wealth and status to outsiders.

Within the Tendai sect, the Ten Lectures and the Perpetual Lectures had been initiated by Saichō (in 798 and 807, respectively), while the Eight Lectures seem to have become popular, especially among the aristocracy, in the late tenth century, around the time of Ryōgen. The Eight Lectures were sometimes sponsored by families or individuals for the eventual repose of the spirit of someone still living; that unusual practice was known as a prior memorial service (*yoshu* or *gyakushu*).

Lotus Sutra Waka *and Songs of the Law*

Thirty-one-syllable poems called Lotus Sutra *waka* (*Hokekyō waka*) were often composed on the occasion of Lotus Sutra lectures or memorial services. These poems were generally called *shakkyōka* (songs of Śākyamuni's teachings). *Shakkyōka* refers not only to the Lotus Sutra but also to the Vimalakīrti Sutra and other scriptures. They were the poems that expressed their authors' understanding of and feelings toward the teachings of Buddhism. The Lotus Sutra *waka* first appeared at the beginning of the eleventh century, in the time of the great statesman Fujiwara no Michinaga. A single line of the Chinese text of the sutra would be expanded in a Japanese poem. For instance, "Not one fails to become a buddha," from the "Tactfulness" chapter, becomes

> "All will attain Buddhahood," the sutra says,
> And we unenlightened mortals,
> Hearing it, are glad.

That of the twenty-eight chapters of the Lotus Sutra, "Devadatta" was the source of the greatest number of Lotus Sutra *waka* indicates the great popularity of this chapter, with its emphasis on the salvation of all.

In contrast to *shakkyōka*, written in the traditional thirty-one syllable form, *hōmonka* (songs of the Law) were written in the freer, more popular *imayō*, or contemporary, style. Conveying the doctrines of Buddhism in simple language and urging the devout to deeper faith, they were sometimes sung chorally at formal religious services. Almost all surviving examples come from the partially extant collection *Ryōjin Hishō* (Secret Selection of Rafter Dust; ca. 1169), compiled by the cloistered emperor Goshirakawa (r. 1155–58). Called *Hokekyō Hōmonka*, the Lotus Sutra supplied the text for most of them. Typically, a passage from the sutra is simplified and Japanized:

> After seeing a thousand painful springs and autumns,
> Breaking the ice to scoop up water
> And wiping away the frost to collect firewood,
> At last we have heard the Wonderful Law
> Of the One Vehicle.

Devotion to the sutra is also urged:

> Most wonderful of all the eight-fascicle
>   Lotus Sutra is the chapter on
>   Skillful Means,
> Because it tells us with assurance,
> "Of all who hear the holy Law,
> Not one will fail to find salvation."

Expressions of faith in the Lotus Sutra became staples in both the traditional world of the classical *waka* and the new realm of contemporary song.

Sutra Copying and Burial

The Lotus Sutra was often copied for the spiritual benefit of the dead (the fruit of *tsuizen*, or transferral of merit) as well as that of the living (for the prior memorial services mentioned above). The work of copying required many scribes and large sums of money. Usually a number of sutras were copied together as a set—for instance, the three texts of the Threefold Lotus Sutra, or the *Amida-kyō* (Amitābha Sutra; in Sanskrit, the Smaller *Sukhāvatī-vyūha*), together with the *Shinjikan-gyō* (the Mahāyāna Sutra of Meditation on the Origin of the Mind). Of course, sutra copies were also made for use as texts in sutra reading; but with increasing frequency, they were made for memorial and prior memorial services, as well.

In addition, sutras were sometimes copied specifically for ceremonial burial. These sutras were placed in copper or clay containers and buried in sutra mounds (*kyōzuka*). Sutra burial was practiced for a variety of reasons: to pray for temporal well-being, for a felicitous rebirth, for rebirth in one of the Pure Lands, or for the ultimate salvation of all sentient beings; or to preserve the sutra for that distant age in which the buddha of the future, Maitreya, will descend from Tuṣita Heaven and be born into this world. Sutra burial flourished from the middle to late Heian period. The earliest known example, unearthed in the Kimpu Mountains, at Yoshino, in present-day Nara Prefecture, is a copy of the Lotus Sutra dated 998, which was buried by Fujiwara no Michinaga in a cylindrical sutra case dated 1007.

Activities of Lotus Sutra Devotees

In many instances, lectures, sutra copying, and sutra burial were prompted by individual vows, but in numerous other cases these activities were carried out by groups of people under the direction of priests and holy men (*hijiri*) who traveled about preaching, teaching, and converting the general population. *Hijiri* were especially active from the mid-Heian period onward. They followed a new mode of religious life and practice that had developed among priests who had drifted away from the established schools and orders to devote themselves to preaching, teaching, and forming lay believers' associations (*kō*) among ordinary people.

Many *hijiri* were especially devoted to the Lotus Sutra, they were known as practitioners of the Lotus Sutra (*jikyōsha*). During Ryōgen's abbacy, in the late tenth century, most *jikyōsha* left Enryaku-ji to pursue religious practice in solitude in the mountains and forests, where they aimed chiefly at their own spiritual development. But hagiographies of the late Heian period indicate that many of the Lotus Sutra practitioners began to travel among the people, proselytizing. By preaching the virtues of the Lotus Sutra, they sought to benefit all sentient beings.

Also according to hagiographies, many priestly Lotus Sutra practitioners and lay Lotus Sutra devotees were able to attain rebirth in one of the Pure Lands by reciting on their deathbeds one of the important verses from the Lotus Sutra, for example, "Of those who hear the Law / Not one fails to become a buddha." Indeed, devotion to the Lotus Sutra tended to focus on smaller and smaller segments of the text: first the entire sutra, then a single chapter (for example, "Revelation of the [Eternal] Life of the Tathāgata"), and finally especially important verses. In the late Heian period we find devotees involved in sutra copying who chant the sacred name of Amitābha or the *daimoku,* the sacred title of the Lotus Sutra (in Japanese, *Namu-myōhō-renge-kyō*), and Tendai priests who preach the efficacy of reciting the title of the sutra at the hour of death. Thus, Lotus Sutra pietism increasingly took the form of recitation of the title of the sutra, a development that culminated in the teachings of Nichiren in the Kamakura period.

THE SHINGON SECT

Kūkai

Kūkai, founder of the Japanese Shingon sect, was born in Sanuki Province in 774, near the end of the Nara period. The son of Saeki no Tagimi, a member of the provincial gentry, he had the childhood name of Mao. Unlike Saichō, who entered the clergy as a child, Kūkai remained at home until the age of fourteen studying Confucianism, mastery of which was a prerequisite for becoming a government official. To pursue higher studies, he went to the capital, Kyoto, with his uncle Ato no Ōtari, a noted scholar. In 791, at the age of seventeen, he passed the entrance examination for the university that the central government had established along Chinese lines and there began serious study of the Confucian texts known as the Four Books and the Five Classics. There was only one institution of higher learning in the entire country, and successful completion of its course opened the road to rapid advancement for civil servants. Thus Kūkai had embarked on the elite path that was the dream of children of the provincial gentry. Both he and his family must have had the greatest hopes for his future wealth, power, and fame.

In his Confucian studies at the university, Kūkai quickly gained a reputation for brilliance, which augured well for his future. But suddenly he turned his back on the world, leaving the university and retiring to the mountains to devote himself to Buddhist practice. He seemed to make a complete turnabout to pursue a path that led in the opposite direction from fame and wealth. The Buddhist ascetics among whom he went to live were mostly privately ordained men, unrecognized by the government, and independent lay believers living in an entirely different world from that of the official priests of the great temples and monasteries. The government in fact was wary and suspicious of these religious, fearing they might by their words and actions subvert the social order. The Buddhist establishment was indifferent or even hostile to them, since the religion's nation-protecting, state-serving functions were of prime importance to its hierarchy.

What made Kūkai decide to take up this new way of life? The view that his origins in the provincial gentry were decisive has gained ground in recent years. According to this hypothesis, the provincial gentry had a dual character, since its members represented central-government authority on the local level and yet were closely bound to the localities where they resided. Thus they were sensitive to contradictions in the central government's policies, to the sufferings of the local peasantry, and to their own ambiguous social position. It has been suggested that having been raised in such an atmosphere, the young Kūkai could not help feeling discontented with his life as a student whose ultimate objective was government service and that finally he decided to seek salvation for himself and the suffering general population by following the Buddhist path.

Persuasive though this argument may be, it does not provide a completely satisfying explanation for Kūkai's actions. In his first work, the *Sangō Shiiki* (Guide to the Three Teachings), written in 797, when he was twenty-three, Kūkai recalled when he was ordained some years earlier: "A priest taught me the Kokūzō Gumonji Hō rite. The sutra [entitled Kokūzō Gumonji Hō (*Hsü-k'ung-tsang-ch'iu-wen-ch'ih-fa*), in which the rite is described] says, 'If people recite the mantra [true word] of Kokūzō [the bodhisattva Ākāśagarbha] one million times, in accord with the teaching [in the sutra], they will achieve the ability to memorize the words and understand the real meaning of all the scriptures [they study].'"

Surely Kūkai's encounter with that Buddhist priest—an encounter that Kūkai himself says changed his life—was significant. Kūkai was not, after all, the only scion of the provincial gentry engaged in studies in the capital at the end of the eighth century, yet no one else is recorded as having undergone the same sort of conversion. Only Kūkai abandoned his secular studies midway, turning his back on the promise of a brilliant civil service career to devote himself to the hard, lonely life of a practitioner of Buddhist ascetic disciplines in the mountains. Therefore, it seems likely that Kūkai's encounter with the Buddhist priest was at least as influential as his social and economic environment. History must acknowledge the genius of that solitary priest, who, meeting the young Kūkai for the first time, was able to recognize and draw forth his latent religious feelings. Kūkai's first contact with the esoteric Kokūzō Gumonji Hō rite may seem to have been fortuitous, yet it was decisive in the making of Kūkai the priest and man of religion. We must conclude that the effort to attribute Kūkai's conversion totally to the influence of the relations between the provincial gentry and the central government is misguided.

Shingon Esotericism

After his conversion, Kūkai retired to the wilderness of Shikoku to devote himself to religious practice. In the introduction to the *Sangō Shiiki* he writes: "Trusting in those authoritative words of the Great Holy One [Śākyamuni Buddha], I had undertaken practice earnestly and without cease, like kindling a fire by rubbing pieces of wood together; scaling Tairyō Peak in the province of Awa and earnestly practicing recitation of mantra at Cape Muroto in Toshū [Tosa Province]; finally the valleys echoed [attainment of practice], and the morning star [transformation of Kokūzō promised to earnest devotees by the sutra] made its appearance."

Kūkai's ascetic practice in the mountains must have been severe indeed. The *Go-yuigō* (Final Words of the Master; 835) states that Kūkai spent a long period alone in the depths of the mountains practicing asceticism. This practice took the form chiefly of pilgrimages to holy mountains and other sacred sites on Shikoku, undertaken with the aim of gaining religious insight and spiritual powers. This and similar practices associated with Buddhist asceticism were popular from the middle of the eighth century onward, and Kūkai's activities were not unusual. Yet, if the actual mode of life and religious practice was much the same, there was nonetheless a significant difference between Kūkai's aims and those of most other mountain ascetics.

The basic patterns of Kūkai's religious thought are already discernible in the *Sangō Shiiki*. In this work, his first, his priestly ideal is embodied in the person of Kamei Kotsuji (literally, the pseudonymous beggar boy). Kamei Kotsuji is not the powerful abbot of a government-sponsored temple or a famous priest venerated by the entire nation. In Kūkai's account, the "beggar boy" clothes himself in rags that would shame a beggar; his possessions are fewer than those of the meanest thief locked away in a prison cell. He looks so poor and miserable that should he slip into the public market to beg, passersby would be likely to shout and drive him off with a hail of pebbles or horse dung. And yet he is a model priest, zealous in pursuit of the Buddha's path, careful to avoid worldly defilements, accepting offerings from devout Buddhist believers, and claiming as his closest friend a privately ordained priest of lofty character.

The idealized figure of Kamei Kotsuji reveals that the aim of Kūkai's ascetic practice was not the life of a priest at one of the official temples but that of a privately ordained novice or a lay believer seeking only to live in accord with the Way. In fact, we can assume that prior to his journey to China as a government-sponsored student Kūkai was a lay believer. This distinguishes him from most of the Buddhist ascetics practicing in mountain hermitages, who often went on to become priests at official temples after having gained supranormal powers through their ascetic practices.

It appears that Kūkai first encountered the *Dainichi-kyō* (Great Sun Sutra; in Sanskrit, *Mahāvairocana-sūtra*), the principal sutra of the Shingon sect, during his period of solitary practice in the wilds of Shikoku. A hybrid form of esoteric Buddhism was already known in Japan in the Nara period, but orthodox Shingon esotericism, centered on Mahāvairocana Buddha and the doctrine of becoming a buddha in one's present body (*sokushin jōbutsu*, or attaining union with the vital life force of the universe itself), had not yet developed.

What is called Shingon in Japan appears to have originated in India around the middle of the seventh century of the common era. It was introduced into China around the beginning of the eighth century by the Indian priest Śubhakarasiṃha (637–735) at the invitation of Emperor Hsüan Tsung (r. 712–56). Through the energetic dissemination activities of two other Indian priests, Vajrabodhi (671–741) and Amoghavajra (705–74), it reached its zenith during the T'ang dynasty, winning the support of successive emperors. In the early ninth century, when Kūkai traveled to China to study esoteric Buddhism, the most eminent teacher was Hui-kuo, a direct disciple of Amoghavajra.

Kūkai took his first vows as a novice only in 804, when he was already thirty years old. In the fourth month of the same year, he received the full precepts at Tōdai-ji, at last becoming an officially recognized priest. Later that year he traveled to China as part of the official embassy led by Fujiwara no Kadonomaro, whose other members included Saichō and the court official Tachibana no Hayanari (d. 842). The extant records provide no clue to why someone who appears to have been just another lay ascetic until shortly before the embassy left should have been chosen for the coveted position of government-appointed scholar-priest and sent to T'ang China.

When he reached the T'ang capital, Ch'ang-an, Kūkai visited various major temples, including Ch'ing-lung-ssu, where he met Hui-kuo. From Hui-kuo he received initiation in the two most esoteric teachings of Shingon, the diamond realm and the womb realm, and he was granted the

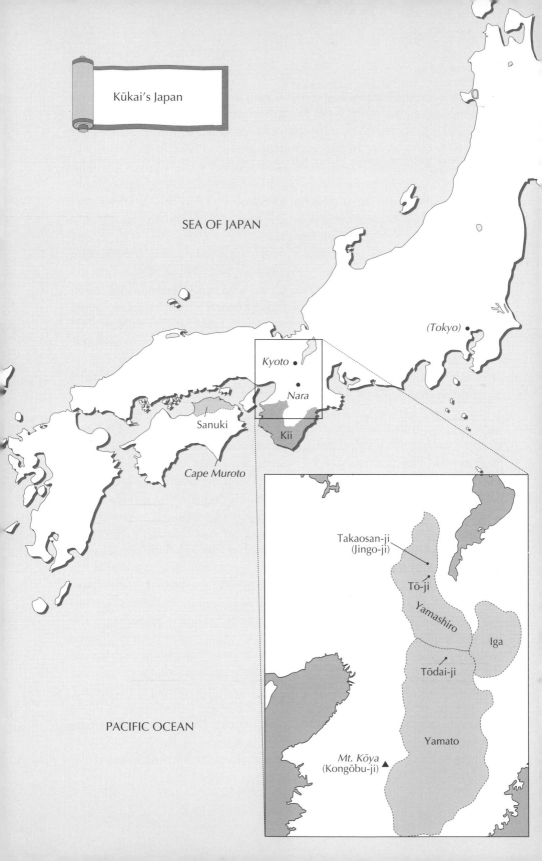

Kūkai's Japan

SEA OF JAPAN

(Tokyo)

Kyoto

Nara

Sanuki

Kii

Cape Muroto

PACIFIC OCEAN

Takaosan-ji
(Jingo-ji)

Tō-ji

Yamashiro

Iga

Tōdai-ji

Yamato

Mt. Kōya
(Kongōbu-ji)

rank *dembō ajari* (master of esoteric Buddhism empowered to initiate others). Vajrabodhi gave him some relics of the Buddha, Buddhist icons, and ritual objects. Kūkai was able to study not only esoteric scriptures but also the Sanskrit language and Hindu teachings from a Kashmiri priest named Prajñā and a northern Indian priest named Muniśrī (d. 806). In the tenth lunar month of 806 he returned to Japan, landing in northern Kyushu. He took back with him 142 esoteric works in 247 fascicles, forty-two collections of Sanskrit mantras and others in forty-four fascicles, thirty-two collections of treatises and commentaries in 170 fascicles, ten painted icons, eighteen esoteric ritual implements of nine kinds, and thirteen items given him personally by Hui-kuo. Orthodox Shingon teachings had finally arrived in Japan, where they would develop and flourish.

Shingon and the Nara Schools

Under Emperor Heizei, Kūkai was denied permission to enter the capital and live there. Not until the seventh month of 809, following Emperor Saga's accession, was he was allowed to do so and take up residence at Takaosan-ji, a temple in the northern suburbs. Emperor Heizei had driven his younger brother Prince Iyo (d. 807) to his death, suspecting him of plotting treason. Since Kūkai's uncle and Confucian tutor, Ato no Ōtari, had tutored Prince Iyo, Emperor Heizei may have assumed that the prince and Kūkai were friends and been displeased with Kūkai for that reason.

In contrast, Emperor Saga and his court treated Kūkai with great respect, while Saichō and the Tendai sect suddenly fell into eclipse. These developments were due less to the strength of Emperor Saga's interest in Shingon than to his high regard for literary skill in Chinese. As the preface to the *Keikokushū* (Passages on Governance), an early-Heian-period anthology of Chinese verse and prose written in Japan, put it: "Letters are a major element in the governance of a country." Kūkai won the emperor's esteem because of his illustrious literary and calligraphic talents, and their friendship was lifelong. Through his relationship with the emperor, Kūkai was drawn into court circles and became friendly with many members of the aristocracy. His mode of life at this period contrasted sharply with that of the unworldly, uncompromising Saichō.

In the latter half of his life, much of Kūkai's time and energy were devoted to refined literary pastimes in the company of the emperor and his courtiers. This was a clear departure from the aims and ideals held by the young Kūkai in his days of solitary ascetic practice and could be seen as the decay and ruin of a pure religious spirit. Yet without Kūkai's special relationship with the court, it would have been impossible to foster the robust establishment of the new Shingon sect, not only in the capital but throughout the entire nation, in such a short time.

The date of the establishment of the Shingon sect in Japan is open to debate. Officially the Shingon sect dates its founding to the year 807 on the basis of statements in the *Daishi Gogyōjō Shūki* (Record of Kūkai's Activities; 1089) and other late documents to the effect that Emperor Heizei issued a proclamation urging the propagation of Shingon throughout the land in that year. Another view dates the sect's founding to the year 830, the year that Kūkai's *Himitsu Mandara Jūjūshin Ron* (Treatise on the Secret Mandala of the Ten Stages of the Mind) appeared in the *Rokuhon Shūsho* (Works on the Six Principal Sects), commissioned by Emperor Junna (r. 823–33). This publication is seen as official acknowledgment of Shingon's equal ranking with Hossō, Kegon, Ritsu, Sanron, and Tendai in a new grouping of six schools, or sects, superseding the earlier six schools of Nara (the Hossō, Jōjitsu, Kegon, Kusha, Ritsu, and Sanron schools). Finally, those who argue that the appointment of annual ordinands constitutes true official recognition of a sect maintain that 835 should be taken as the date of the official founding of Shingon, since three annual ordinands for the sect were first authorized in that year.

In 810 Emperor Saga quelled an attempt to usurp his throne. The same year, Kūkai petitioned for and was granted imperial permission to perform an esoteric ritual for the protection of the nation. Conducted at Takaosan-ji, it was the first public ritual performed by Kūkai after his return from China. Two years later, he conducted the first rituals of initiation into the diamond and womb realms to be performed in Japan. The two rituals initiated a total of more than one hundred and fifty people, including twenty-two high-ranking priests from various Nara monasteries, Saichō, and three of his disciples: Enchō (772–837), Kōjō (779–858), and Taihan (b. 778).

Also in 812, Kūkai appointed Jitsue (786–847) and two other disciples to important positions in charge of temple affairs. Thus it appears that Takaosan-ji had been transformed into a mecca for esoteric studies in Japan in the space of just two or three years. In 824 the temple was given official status and financial support by the government and its name was changed to Jingo Kokuso Shingon-ji (Shingon Temple of Divine Protection for the National Weal), usually abbreviated to Jingo-ji, and in 829 the Wakè family gave the temple to Kūkai in perpetuity. It went on to become, together with Tō-ji (East Temple) and Mount Kōya, one of the three great centers of the Shingon sect in Japan.

Kūkai's relations with the Nara schools were very good, as is evident from the large number of Nara clerics who visited Takaosan-ji to receive instruction in Shingon. This clearly contrasts with the case of Saichō. The root of this contrast no doubt lay in the differences in the two men's temperaments and modes of thought. At the same time, it should be re-membered that the Nara clergy were inclined to be receptive to esoteric Buddhism because of the earlier introduction of esoteric Buddhist ele-ments—during the Nara period—and that the mystical, magical rituals of the new sect well suited the tastes and needs of the age.

Two facts are particularly important for an understanding of Kūkai's relations with the Nara schools. The first is his personal relationship with Gomyō (750–834) of Gangō-ji. Gomyō was a learned priest who had suc-ceeded in making Hossō studies at Gangō-ji the major current in Nara Buddhism, causing that temple to displace Kōfuku-ji, which had been preeminent in Hossō studies since the time of Gembō (d. 746). When Emperor Junna ordered the compilation of the *Rokuhon Shūsho*, Gomyō, as the representative of the Hossō school, compiled the *Daijō Hossō Kenjin Shō* (A Description of the Essential Teachings of the Hossō Sect; ca. 822). Further, it was Gomyō who, by virtue of his high rank and seniority, led the Nara opposition when Saichō launched his effort to establish an inde-pendent Mahāyāna ordination platform on Mount Hiei. From at least 814 on, Kūkai was on good terms with this eminent Nara cleric, and in 827 Gomyō was appointed to a high post at Tō-ji, after the temple had been put in Kūkai's charge.

The second important point is Kūkai's relationship with Tōdai-ji. A hall known as Shingon-in, devoted to esoteric Buddhist initiation rituals, was built within the precincts of Tōdai-ji in 822, the year of Saichō's death. The same Nara clerics who opposed Saichō until his death gave a warm re-ception to Shingon, welcoming it into the precincts of Tōdai-ji. That gave Kūkai an opportunity to conduct rites for the well-being and prosperity of the emperor at the grand central temple of Nara, which was a giant step forward in his long-cherished aim of winning official recognition of the efficacy of the Shingon teachings in securing benefits, both temporal and spiritual, for the nation and its rulers. Kūkai's hopes were fully realized some twelve years later with the construction of a Shingon-in within the imperial palace itself.

In 823, just prior to abdicating the throne, Emperor Saga named

Kūkai abbot of Tō-ji in Kyoto, entrusting it to him in perpetuity. Tō-ji was one of the two official temples erected by Emperor Kammu in 796 on either side of the great Rajō Gate for the spiritual protection of the newly established capital. It was a great prize, and the words attributed to Kūkai in the *Go-yuigō* concerning its administration have the ring of truth: "The emperor has graciously given me Tō-ji. I am overjoyed and will make it a center for the study of esoteric doctrines. Outsiders must under no circumstances be allowed to dwell within the Tō-ji precincts. I say this not out of pettiness or partisan spirit but in order to safeguard the truth."

Kūkai's desire to restrict residence at Kyōō Gokoku-ji, as Tō-ji was renamed, to Shingon priests was realized. An official document issued at the order of newly enthroned Emperor Junna states that fifty priests of the Shingon sect are to live at Tō-ji, and that "the path to be taught is esoteric Buddhism, and priests of other schools are not to be allowed to reside there." Kūkai soon shifted his base from Jingo-ji, in northwestern Kyoto, to the centrally located Tō-ji. The temple ultimately lent its name to esoteric Buddhism of the Shingon lineage, which came to be called Tōmitsu, or the esoteric Buddhism of Tō-ji. At Tō-ji we see a new phenomenon: a temple devoted to the study of a single sect's doctrines, as opposed to the more traditional Nara pattern of concurrent study of various sects' doctrines.

Finally, we should note that with the acquisition of Tō-ji esoteric Buddhism's influence on the great Nara temples also increased significantly, leading in turn to greater esoteric influence on the Buddhist rites for the protection of the nation that were conducted in the imperial palace, primarily by Nara clergy.

Mount Kōya and Tō-ji

In 816, before becoming active at Tō-ji, Kūkai petitioned Emperor Saga for lands encompassing Mount Kōya, in Kii Province, and the emperor granted his request. Kūkai's petition states that successive generations of emperors have shown favor to Buddhism, as a result of which the land is full of splendid temples where numerous learned priests engage in discussion of Buddhism's teachings. Apparently, then, nothing is lacking in the flourishing condition of Japanese Buddhism. But, he continues, "Alas, practitioners of the four kinds of meditation are few among the high peaks and deep mountains; and rare are the masters of *samādhi* [concentration] who dwell within the dark groves among the impenetrable cliffs." This statement suggests that Kūkai's original view that one must seek a place of solitude and withdraw from the world to devote oneself to meditation and other practices conducive to self-perfection remained basic to his religious outlook even as he found himself caught up in secular activities at the imperial court.

After receiving permission to develop Mount Kōya as a religious center, Kūkai began making arrangements to carry out that project. His subsequent involvement with the affairs of Tō-ji, in Kyoto, forced him to leave much of the administration of Mount Kōya to his disciples. It was not until 832 that he went to live there; but once settled on Mount Kōya he remained there until his death on the twenty-first day of the third month of 835, at the age of sixty-one.

Legends and traditions relating to Kūkai abound throughout Japan, and many temples claim some sort of connection with him. But the three sites that are most closely associated with him and are regarded with special reverence in the Shingon sect are the temple renamed Jingo-ji, Tō-ji, and Mount Kōya. The Shingon sect came to be centered almost equally at the two monastic complexes of Tō-ji and Mount Kōya. Tō-ji functioned as the main center for the training of Shingon priests, and Mount Kōya was revered as Kūkai's resting place. After his death, the sect's seat of power oscillated between the two rival complexes.

As mentioned earlier, three annual ordinands were authorized for the Shingon sect in 835, just prior to Kūkai's death. The examination of candidates and actual ordinations were to take place on Mount Kōya. Since the annual ordinands were to play a major role in the development of the sect, Mount Kōya's monopoly on their selection greatly increased its power and prestige within Shingon and at the same time set the stage for protracted bitter rivalry between Mount Kōya and Tō-ji.

In response to a petition from Shinzei (800–860), abbot of Tō-ji, in 853 the government increased the number of annual ordinands to six. Three were to be ordained at both Mount Kōya and Jingo-ji, but all six were to be examined at Tō-ji. Mount Kōya was able to have this procedure rescinded, but only after a long struggle. In 882, in response to a petition from Shinnen (804–91), head priest of Kongōbu-ji, the chief temple on Mount Kōya, the government returned to the mountain complex full jurisdiction over all annual ordinands. Although the government decree stipulated that any temple of the Shingon sect could nominate candidates, in fact it meant the end of Tō-ji's role as the principal training center for the Shingon sect.

Relations between Tō-ji and Mount Kōya deteriorated until the middle of the Heian period (794–1185), when a compromise was finally reached. In 907 the government issued an edict stating that since the deaths of Kūkai and Shinzei each monastery had presented numerous arguments concerning its superiority over its rival. Resolution of the conflict was difficult, since both sides had legitimate claims, but the government had settled on a compromise: the current six annual ordinands would be divided into two groups of three, with Mount Kōya and Jingo-ji having complete jurisdiction over one group each. In addition, a new group of four annual ordinands under the jurisdiction of Tō-ji would be authorized. The edict of 907 resulted from the painstaking efforts of Emperor Daigo (r. 897–930) to settle a persistent problem fairly. The new arrangement seemed to satisfy the chief demands of all three establishments. Yet the basic problem of divided authority within Shingon had not been resolved. There were still three centers of power and two major contenders for dominance, Mount Kōya and Tō-ji.

Further discord within the sect stemmed from a quarrel over possession of the text *Shingon Hōmon Sasshi Sanjū Jō* (Thirty Notebooks of Writings on the Shingon Teachings; 804), usually known by its short title, *Sanjū Jō Sasshi*. This work is a collection of notes—originally thirty-eight volumes, of which thirty survive—that Kūkai wrote or dictated summarizing the contents of major esoteric scriptures that he encountered during his sojourn in T'ang China. In terms of both its doctrinal content and its historical origins, it was the single most precious treasure of the Shingon sect. Kūkai had given this work directly to his favorite disciple, Jitsue; he in turn had passed it on to Shinzei, who gave it to Shinga (801–79), abbot of Tō-ji.

For years the *Sanjū Jō Sasshi* was preserved in Tō-ji's library, and removing it from the temple precincts was strictly forbidden. But in 876 Shinnen of Mount Kōya borrowed the text from Shinga and took it to Mount Kōya. He returned the notebooks soon after, but in 881, after Shinga had died, Shinnen once again removed the precious volumes to Mount Kōya, arguing that they were in danger of destruction by fire in the turbulent capital. Ignoring the strong opposition of the Tō-ji clergy, he attempted to have the volumes installed permanently in the Mount Kōya library.

In 915 the abbot of Tō-ji, Kangen (854–925), armed with an edict from the cloistered emperor Uda, pressed Mount Kōya for the return of the

Sanjū Jō Sasshi. The abbot of Mount Kōya, Mukū, fled with the manuscript and a party of disciples, seeking safety in Yamashiro and Iga provinces. Mukū died en route, however, and his disciples were forced to return the manuscript to Tō-ji in 918. The following year Emperor Daigo formally deposited the *Sanjū Jō Sasshi* in the Tō-ji library and commanded that it not be removed again, making the abbot of Tō-ji responsible for its safe-keeping. The question of custody was thus settled—until 1186, when the imperial prince and Shingon priest Shukaku (1150–1202) "borrowed" the manuscript and took it to Ninna-ji in Kyoto (now the head temple of an independent branch of Shingon), in whose library it remains to this day.

The strong rivalry between Mount Kōya and Tō-ji gave rise to many disputes during the ninth and tenth centuries, in which Tō-ji was almost always victorious. Mount Kōya's position was further weakened by the fact that the ablest priests of the period—such as Shinzei, Shūei (809–84), Yakushin (827–906), Shōbō (832–909), and Kangen—were almost all associated with Tō-ji.

In 919, by order of Emperor Daigo, Kangen, who had won the contest over possession of the *Sanjū Jō Sasshi* for Tō-ji, was made first abbot of Daigo-ji, in Kyoto, and superintendent of Kongōbu-ji, on Mount Kōya, while remaining head of Tō-ji. And in 921 the emperor bestowed the posthumous title Kōbō Daishi on Kūkai in response to repeated petitions from Kangen. With these achievements, the abbot of Tō-ji gradually came to dominate the Shingon sect as a whole. From 919 on, Mount Kōya was relegated to a position clearly subordinate to Tō-ji. The administration of the Shingon sect was centered at Tō-ji, though Shingon practice and study continued at other temples.

The Hirosawa and Ono Schools

Unfortunately, Tō-ji's triumph in the contest with Mount Kōya did not end division within the sect. Two highly respected Shingon priests in Kyoto, Yakushin, from Shūei's lineage, and Shōbō, from Shinga's, would become the founders of the two main schools of the Shingon sect: the Hirosawa school and the Ono school. Though Yakushin is regarded as founder of the Hirosawa school and Shōbō that of the Ono school, the schools were not named until many years after their founders had died. Each school is named after the location of its head temple.

Yakushin was highly revered by Emperor Uda (r. 887–97) and became his preceptor at the time the emperor was ordained, following his abdication of the throne. Yakushin administered the esoteric initiation of transmitting the Dharma to the cloistered emperor at Tō-ji in 901, initiating him into the rites and doctrines developed in Shingon since the time of Kūkai. Uda resided at Ninna-ji, with the result that this originally Tendai temple became a Shingon center. Ninna-ji was regarded as the most prestigious imperially connected temple in the sect. The Dharma tradition was transmitted to Kangū (884–972) and then to Kanchō (916–98), grandson of Emperor Uda. Kanchō was the first abbot of Tō-ji. Toward the end of his life, in 989, he founded Henshō-ji on the banks of Hirosawa Pond in Kyoto's Saga district and made it a center for Shingon studies. The Hirosawa school took its name from the location of Henshō-ji. The Hirosawa school produced six principal subschools, including the Ninna-ji imperial school (Ninna-ji *goryū*), which then further subdivided.

Shōbō lived and worked in Kyoto at the same time as Yakushin. He was a native of Sanuki Province, on Shikoku, and is alleged to have been a descendant of Emperor Kōnin (r. 770–81), though there is no clear evidence for this. He studied Shingon under Shinga and was named abbot of Jōkan-ji, in Kyoto, on Shinga's recommendation. In 874 he founded Daigo-ji in the Daigo district of Kyoto and worked to make it the greatest center for Shingon in the capital. His tradition was transmitted from Kangen and Shunnyū (890–953) of Tō-ji to Ningai (951–1046). Ningai had been ordained at Mount Kōya but began to distinguish himself after transferring to Daigo-ji. He was given a high priestly rank and made abbot of Tō-ji. Famed for his magical ability to cause rain to fall in dry seasons, he was nicknamed the Rain High Priest. Shortly before his death he founded Mandara-ji, or Zuishin-in, in Ono (near the Daigo district), from which his school took its name. The Ono school divided into six major subschools, which then produced several dozen smaller groups.

As of the eleventh century, the Hirosawa school, centered at Ninna-ji in western Kyoto, and the Ono school, centered at Daigo-ji in eastern Kyoto, constituted the two major currents within the Shingon sect. It is important to understand, however, that the formation and division of these schools and subschools did not always mean actual development of the tradition as a whole.

Several contrasts are easily drawn between the two schools: the Hirosawa school attracted priests of noble lineage and tended to emphasize the formal, ritual aspects of the teachings. The Ono school drew most of its members from clergy of plebeian birth and emphasized mystical experience gained through actual practice. The two schools were alike, though, in that they were not based chiefly on doctrine or theory. Both were based on direct transmission of teachings from a qualified master. That transmission consisted mainly of instruction not in religious doctrine but in ritual practice, and this was usually carried out in secret. Interest focused overwhelmingly on ritual and its magical efficacy.

Minamoto no Tsuneyori (976–1039), a middle-ranking aristocrat, wrote in his diary on the first day of the fifth month of 1032: "The priest Ningai said in the course of conversation that there have been seven priests who have employed the rain-making ritual in times of drought since the time of Kōbō Daishi: Daishi himself, Shinga, Shōbō, Kangū, Gengō [914–95], Genshin, and Ningai. Of these, Daishi's rituals were efficacious; the evidence is not clear in the cases of Shinga and Shōbō; in Kangū's case, no rain fell during the ritual itself, but when he reached the mouth of the stream in the east garden of the palace on his way to the palace with sutra scrolls, it rained heavily; Gengō's rituals were effective but Genshin's were not. Ningai's efforts met with success last year, and this year rain fell three times in twenty-seven days."

This passage represents not only Tsuneyori's own interest in the magical side of Buddhism but also the general expectation of people of the time that Shingon Buddhism would provide practical, worldly benefits—in this case, rain in time of drought. It also demonstrates that Shingon clergy, responding to believers' demands, became more and more concerned with the secondary, temporal aspects of Buddhist practice. The cause of Shingon's failure to develop fully as a religion during the Kamakura period and later can be traced to this worldly spirit. By the end of the Heian period, Shingon had lost most of the religious spirit of its founder Kūkai, and it was not prepared to meet the challenge presented by the new Buddhist sects of the Kamakura period or to contribute to their development. This emphasis on worldly benefits is the principal difference between Shingon and Tendai, its great Heian-period rival.

The Cult of Kōbō Daishi

After Kūkai's death on Mount Kōya, his body was committed to flames, in accord with usual Buddhist practice, and the remains were buried on the mountain. This fact is well established by contemporary documents. In 921, eighty-six years after his death, the court granted Kūkai the posthumous title Kōbō Daishi. The *Daishi Gogyōjō Shūki*, compiled in 1089 by

Keihan (1031–1104), relates an incident that supposedly occurred in 921: "Kangen went to Mount Kōya bearing the imperial edict granting the posthumous title and vestments bestowed by Emperor Daigo. Arriving at Okuno-in, where Kūkai is buried, he opened the door of the tomb and found the body of the Master uncorrupted and the color of the face as natural as in life. Kūkai's hair had grown very long and his robes were in tatters, so Kangen shaved the head with a razor and clothed the body in the imperial vestments. When his disciple Shunnyū accidentally touched Kūkai's legs, he found them as warm as in life."

Of course this is a legendary rather than historical account; but it confirms that by the close of the tenth century at the latest—if not as early as the time of Kangen—the belief that Kūkai had not in fact died in 835 but had entered into a profound trance had gained currency. It was believed that he would remain deep in meditation until the advent of the buddha of the future, Maitreya. This tradition is documented in the *Kongōbu-ji Konryū Shugyō Engi* (A Brief Biography of Kūkai and Description of Kongōbu-ji), composed in 968, which has Kūkai himself declare: "'I, [Kūkai,] will enter into a trance at four o'clock in the morning on the twenty-first day [of the third month]. Do not fast on my account; neither let there be grieving or weeping for me; and let no one wear mourning. . . . I will sit in the full-lotus posture and make the mudrā of Dainichi [Mahā-vairocana Buddha] with my hands, . . . closing my eyes, and without a word I will enter into a trance. My body will remain as it was in life.' . . .

"When, on the forty-ninth day after his withdrawal, the Master's disciples, following the usual custom, opened the chamber where Kūkai sat, they found his facial color unchanged and his hair grown longer. They therefore shaved him and changed his vestments. They then closed the chamber with a stone slab, precluding access to it. They summoned a stonemason and had a five-stage stupa built above the chamber, and in this they placed various Sanskrit texts and *dhāraṇī* spells. The stupa was then enclosed in a pagoda, and relics of the Buddha were enshrined there. All this was done under the direction of the high priest Shinnen."

From this and similar accounts, it is clear that pious Shingon followers began to believe in Kōbō Daishi's trance around the middle of the Heian period. This belief became the kernel around which the cult of Kōbō Daishi developed. He became the object not simply of respect and veneration as a great teacher but also of worship as a deity.

A belief in the advent of the bodhisattva Maitreya as the future buddha was widespread in the Heian period, and the cult of Kōbō Daishi gained quick acceptance among the common people in part because it accorded so well with Maitreya beliefs. In fact, Kōbō Daishi came to be regarded as an incarnation of Maitreya, and Mount Kōya as part of Tuṣita Heaven, Maitreya's realm.

It is remarkable that in contrast to Mount Hiei, where there are no graves apart from Saichō's, on Mount Kōya graves line the two-kilometer path between Ichinohashi and the tomb of Kōbō Daishi. Most of the tens of thousands of graves date from the sixteenth century or later, but the custom of burial on Mount Kōya dates back at least to the twelfth century and is directly related to the cult of Kōbō Daishi. The belief that Kōbō Daishi sits in trance in his tomb waiting for the advent of Maitreya and the notion that Mount Kōya is itself a part of Tuṣita Heaven date from the end of the tenth century at the latest. Such beliefs led to a desire to form a spiritual bond with that sacred spot by having one's bones or hair buried there. Not only priests of the Shingon sect but lay believers as well sought the benefits of burial on Mount Kōya for themselves and their deceased relatives. Mount Kōya gradually acquired the character it has today—a sacred site suited to pious Buddhist burial.

In 1107 Emperor Horikawa (r. 1086–1107) died at the age of twenty-eight. Among his effects his attendants found a lock of hair that had been cut from his head at his coming-of-age ceremony years before. After much discussion of the proper disposition of this relic, it was finally decided that it should be buried in front of Kūkai's tomb on Mount Kōya, since the late emperor had been a fervent devotee of the Maitreya cult. The practice was carried out the following year. This is the first recorded instance of the burial of a deceased person's hair on Mount Koya.

Later, in 1160, the cloistered emperor Toba's favorite consort, Bifuku-mon'in, stipulated as her last request that her bones be buried on Mount Kōya. She had been deeply devoted to Kūkai and Mount Kōya and had always regretted that she could not make a pilgrimage there. (Until 1872, the mountain was closed to women.) Prior to his death four years earlier, Toba had ordered the construction of a tomb for Bifukumon'in in the grounds of his palace. Nevertheless, in accordance with her last wishes, her remains were sent to Mount Kōya and buried in the subtemple Bodaishin-in. This is the first recorded instance of the burial of a person's bones on the mountain, and in view of Mount Kōya's long tradition of excluding women from its sacred precincts, it is both remarkable and ironic that the first bones to be interred there should have been those of a woman.

Pure Land Buddhism in Japan

Pure Land Buddhism is based on the idea of the Original Vow (*hongan*) made in the immeasurably distant past by the buddha Amitābha or Amitāyus (in Japanese, Amida) when he was a bodhisattva named Dharmākara. Prior to attaining enlightenment, Dharmākara made forty-eight vows, the most important of which declared his determination to save all sentient beings and his unwillingness to attain buddhahood if he could not accomplish this goal.

Pure Land faith and practice aim at rebirth in Amitābha's paradise, the Pure Land of Perfect Bliss, said to be located in the west. The textual sources of the Pure Land teaching, known as the Three Pure Land Sutras, are the *Muryōju-kyō* (the Larger *Sukhāvatī-vyūha*), the *Amida-kyō* (Amitābha Sutra, or the Smaller *Sukhāvatī-vyūha*), and the *Kan Muryōju-kyō* (Sutra of Meditation on Amitāyus, or *Amitāyur-dhyāna-sūtra*).

The doctrine's earliest exponent in India is supposed to have been the great Mahāyāna philosopher Nāgārjuna (ca. 150–ca. 250), who, according to Pure Land teachings, classified Buddhist practice as easy or difficult and taught that praising and worshiping Amitābha is an easy practice consistent with Amitābha's Original Vow. According to tradition, the next great Indian master of the Pure Land teachings was Vasubandhu (ca. 320–ca. 400). An exegesis of the Pure Land teaching attributed to Vasubandhu is included in the Chinese canon: the *Ching-t'u-lun* (On the Pure Land; formally, *Wu-liang-shou-ching-yu-p'o-t'i-she-yüan-sheng-chi*), which attempts to systematize the doctrine. In it Vasubandhu teaches that one can be reborn in paradise through wholehearted faith in Amitābha. It does seem that by the third and fourth centuries of the Christian era, when Nāgārjuna and Vasubandhu flourished, the principal Pure Land sutras were widely known in India.

In China, the Indian priest Saṃghavarman translated the Larger *Sukhāvatī-vyūha* in 252, and Kumārajīva (344–413) translated the Smaller *Sukhāvatī-vyūha* around 402. Under the widespread influence of Buddhism in both northern and southern China at the time, an increasing number of people engaged in Pure Land practices—reciting the sutras, erecting images of Amitābha, and praying to be reborn in his paradise. The Sutra of Meditation on Amitāyus, probably translated by Kālayaśas around the beginning of the fifth century, was the foundation for the propagation of the Pure Land doctrine by its early Chinese masters T'an-luan (476–542), Tao-ch'o (562–645), Shan-tao (613–81), and Fa-chao (fl. eighth century). Shan-tao took the teachings to the T'ang capital of Ch'ang-an. As a result of his zealous efforts among rich and poor alike, the practice of invoking the name of Amitābha (in Chinese, *nien-fo;* in Japanese, *nembutsu*) spread throughout the capital in just three years.

Chinese Pure Land Buddhism was introduced into Japan via the Korean peninsula. The exact date of the introduction of these teachings is not clear; but judging from the inscription on the mandorla of the Śākyamuni image in the Kondō (the main hall) at Hōryū-ji and from the occurrence of the term "Pure Land" in Prince Shōtoku's commentary on the Vimalakīrti Sutra in the *Sangyō Gisho,* some scholars have suggested that Amidism, as faith in Amitābha, or Amida, is known in a Japanese context, had already entered Japan by the early seventh century. Yet it would be presumptuous to infer a mature faith in Amitābha from the use of the term Pure Land. In addition to Amitābha's Pure Land of Perfect Bliss in the west, the Gṛdhrakūṭa (Vulture Peak) Pure Land of Śākyamuni Buddha and the Tuṣita Pure Land of the bodhisattva Maitreya are mentioned in scriptures.

A Land of Heavenly Longevity (Tenjukoku) is depicted in a celebrated embroidered mandala at Chūgū-ji, in Nara, but this identification is disputed. Some argue that the mandala in fact represents Amida's Pure Land. This view is based on the colophon of a copy of fascicle forty-six of the Flower Garland Sutra made in China in 513, which states: "May my deceased parents be reborn in the western land of heavenly longevity and always be able to hear the true Law there." It is suggested both that the ideographic character translated here as "heavenly" may in fact be a variant of an ideographic character meaning "limitless" and that since "limitless life" is one of the epithets of Amida, Tenjukoku is in fact Amida's Pure Land.

Firm evidence of the introduction of elements of Pure Land teachings and practices in Japan dates to the seventh century: the priest Hui-yin, a Chinese resident of Ōmi, was sent to China in 608 and returned to Japan in 639, during Emperor Jomei's reign (629–41), and lectured on the Larger *Sukhāvatī-vyūha* the following year; an Amida triad is depicted on a wall at Hōryū-ji, which was constructed between 601 and 607; and the Larger *Sukhāvatī-vyūha* is quoted in Prince Shōtoku's commentary on the Vimalakīrti Sutra. Thus we can conclude that Amidism had taken root in Japan by the mid-seventh century.

In the wake of regular missions to T'ang China during the Nara period, Chinese culture flowed into Japan. From around that time, the number of images of Amida (and portrayals of his Pure Land) increased, far exceeding those of other buddhas and bodhisattvas. According to documents preserved in the Shōsō-in, the imperial repository at Tōdai-ji, a large number of Amidist literary and religious works were imported and copied in this period. One was the *Hsiu-chu-ching li-ch'an-i* (Collection of Passages Concerning the Veneration of the Buddha and Repentance of Sins in Buddhist Sources; eighth century) by the priest Chih-sheng (fl. eighth century), which was influenced by Shan-tao's *Wang-sheng-li-tsan* (Praises of Rebirth) and is thought to have been compiled around 730.

Still, for the scholar-priests of Nara, engrossed in study of Sanron and Kegon doctrines, the Pure Land teachings must have been a secondary pursuit. Among the Nara scholars interested in Pure Land teachings were Chikō (ca. 709–ca. 780) of the Sanron school, Chikyō (fl. 741) of Kegon, and Zenju (723–97) of Hossō. Chikō's works include the extant *Muryōju-kyō Ron Shaku,* a five-fascicle commentary on the Vasubandhu's *Ching-t'u-lun,* and the Chikō Mandala, a detailed depiction of the Pure Land as seen by Chikō in a vision, which is known only through a copy. Chikyō wrote the *Muryōju-kyō Shūyō Shiji* (A Guide to the Essentials of the Larger *Sukhāvatī-vyūha*) and *Muryōju-kyō Shiji Shiki* (A Personal Guide to the Larger *Sukhāvatī-vyūha*), both based on a commentary on the Larger *Sukhāvatī-vyūha* by Won-hyo (b. 617), a Pure Land master from the Korean kingdom of Silla. Zenju's *Muryōju-kyō Sanshō* (Praises of the Larger *Sukhāvatī-vyūha*) and *Muryōju-kyō Chūji Shaku* (Notes and Comments on the Larger *Sukhāvatī-vyūha*) are derivative commentaries based on a major work by the Silla priest Ging-sing (fl. seventh century). Thus Pure Land practice and doctrine in Silla had a significant influence on the early development of the Pure Land teachings in Japan.

Zenju, who had studied Hossō doctrines and the Indian logic system *hetu-vidyā* under Gembō of Kōfuku-ji in Nara, was invited by Saichō to officiate at the consecration of the main hall on Mount Hiei in the ninth lunar month of 794. Saichō's Tendai sect, which was officially recognized in 806, taught a method of concentrating and purifying the mind by means of four types of meditative practice: seated meditation, walking meditation, mixed seated and walking meditation, and neither seated nor walking meditation. The walking meditation involved slow circumambulation of an image of Amida over a period of ninety days, all the while contemplating this buddha and his Pure Land. This practice was introduced on Mount Hiei by Saichō's disciple Ennin.

Soon after his return from China in 847, Ennin established a Hall for Walking Meditation (Jōgyō Zammai-dō) inspired by the *nien-fo* (*nembutsu*) practice he had observed at the great Buddhist center on Mount Wu-t'ai. The Wu-t'ai–style *nembutsu* was also known as the fivefold *nembutsu*, because Amida's name was chanted in five different musical modes. Ennin was drawn to this form of *nembutsu*, which couples musical intonation of the name with meditative insight. He originally built the Hall for Walking Meditation in the Kokūzōbi area of Mount Hiei, but his disciple Sōō moved it to a site north of the lecture hall in the Eastern Precincts. In 893 Zōmyō (843–927) founded a similar hall in the Western Precincts, and in 968 Ryōgen founded one in the Yokawa area.

Thus each of the major areas on Mount Hiei had its own Hall for Walking Meditation, where the *nembutsu* was practiced from the eleventh through the seventeenth of the eighth lunar month, climaxing on the fifteenth—no doubt because on that day Amida was supposed to descend from the Pure Land. With the growth of *nembutsu* practice came a need for consistent doctrinal and theoretical foundations. These were developed by such figures as Ryōgen, Senkan (918–83), and Zen'yu (912–90), each of whom composed treatises on the subject.

Ryōgen wrote the *Gokuraku Jōdo Kuhon Ōjō Gi* (On the Nine Types of Rebirth in the Pure Land of Perfect Bliss); Senkan composed the *Jūgan Hosshin Ki* (A Record of Aspiration to the Ten Vows), and Zen'yu produced the *Amida Shin Jū Gi* (Ten New Questions Concerning Amida). Ryōgen's work explains the *nembutsu* as "fixing one's mind on the Buddha" and classifies it together with fixing one's mind on the Law (*nempō*), fixing one's mind on the Order (*nensō*), fixing one's mind on charitable works (*nense*), fixing one's mind on the precepts (*nenkai*), and fixing one's mind on the celestial realms (*nenten*). Thus, Ryōgen emphasized the meditative aspect of *nembutsu* more than the oral invocation of the Buddha's name. His view that meditative *nembutsu* is superior to oral *nembutsu* became the traditional Tendai view.

Pure Land Teachings in the Nara Schools

In Nara a Pure Land tradition distinct from that cultivated on Mount Hiei developed in the Hossō and Sanron schools. The Hossō priests

Zenju (723–97), Shōkai (fl. ca. ninth century), and Seikai (d. 1017) all prayed to be reborn in Amida's Pure Land. Zenju expressed his desire for rebirth in the Pure Land in his *Yuishiki Gitō Zōmyō Ki* (A Record of the Illumination of the Lamp of Consciousness Only). Zenju's disciple Shōkai wrote two guides to Pure Land doctrines, *Amida Keka* (Repentance and Faith in Amida) and *Saihō Nembutsu Shū* (The Western Paradise *Nembutsu* Collection), expressing his deep faith in Amidism. Seikai made a painting of the Pure Land popularly known as the Seikai Mandala.

Pure Land devotees in the Sanron school included Ryūkai (815–86), Eikan (also called Yōkan; 1033–1111), Kakuju (1084–1139), Chinkai (1092–1152), and Chōyo (fl. twelfth century). Ryūkai, following in the footsteps of Chikō and Raikō (fl. ca. eighth century), studied Sanron doctrine under Gangyō (d. 864) at Gangō-ji. We know little about the immediate heirs to Ryūkai's Pure Land activities within the Sanron school. In the eleventh century, however, Eikan, author of *Ōjō Jūin* (Ten Causes for Rebirth in the Pure Land), appeared. A disciple of Jinkan (1010–57), Eikan was well known for his scholarship. He was chosen to participate in a lecture-debate at Byōdō-in, south of Kyoto, in 1057, and to serve as one who answers questions by establishing a doctrinal principle at Hōjō-ji in Kyoto in 1064.

Eikan won the support of the powerful Fujiwara family and frequently lectured at the imperial court. His reputation was at its height when he suddenly went into seclusion at Kōmyōsen-ji, in southern Yamashiro Province. Apparently he feared that he was neglecting his religious training because of his worldly involvements. He spent the next ten years at Kōmyōsen-ji, a subtemple of Tōdai-ji, devoting himself to *nembutsu* practice. Again sought out by the aristocracy, he was invited to lecture on the Vimalakīrti Sutra in 1086 and appointed superintendent of Tōdai-ji in 1100, but he resigned this position after only three years. He again turned to *nembutsu* practice, at Zenrin-ji, in Kyoto, and conducted a *mukae kō*, or *gōshō e*, a ritual imitating the welcome of Amida and his bodhisattvas at a *nembutsu* practitioner's deathbed on Yoshida Hill, in eastern Kyoto.

Eikan devoted himself to *nembutsu* practice because he believed it was the most appropriate path to deliverance for sentient beings living in the *Mappō*, the period of the Decay of the Law. In his *Ōjō Jūin*, he states: "There are several ways of freeing oneself from the bondage of delusion. But the best way for people to free themselves during the Decay of the Law is to cling to faith in Amida Buddha, who dwells in the western [Pure

Land]. Fortunately, we have been able to encounter the Original Vow of Amida Buddha in this life. This encounter can be likened to happening upon a ferry just when one needs to cross a great stream or to having an ideal ruler who is concerned for the welfare of his people. Even a heavy rock can be safely transported ten thousand leagues across the sea once it is loaded onto a ship. If aspirants realize this, they will attain rebirth in the Pure Land without fail, in accordance with [Amida's] Original Vow. But if, having heard the teaching, we postpone commitment, time passes. Therefore, let us cast aside all worldly concerns, immediately begin invoking Amida's name, as Tao-ch'o says in his final instructions, and energetically recite the *nembutsu*, as Huai-kan teaches. At some time prostrating yourself upon the ground or placing your folded hands upon your forehead, recite the holy name! Do not heed the mockery or criticism of others—just practice!"

As this passage implies, Eikan's spiritual teachers were the Chinese Pure Land masters Tao-ch'o and Huai-kan (fl. seventh century). Eikan tells his readers to say the *nembutsu* wholeheartedly, following the example of these eminent masters, to assure rebirth in the Pure Land. Eikan's views on the *nembutsu*, which place considerable emphasis on the contemplative aspect, show greater affinity with the views of Tao-ch'o and Huai-kan than with those of Shan-tao. Eikan wrote: "Steadfastly recite the *nembutsu*, fixing your mind on the tuft of white hair in the middle of the Buddha's forehead."

In addition to the *Ōjō Jūin*, Eikan wrote the *Amida-kyō Yō Ki* (Essentials of the Smaller *Sukhāvatī-vyūha*) and the *Ōjō Kōshiki* (Rituals for Pure Land Assemblies). The latter work gives rules for *nembutsu* recitation by groups of devotees who assemble on the fifteenth of each month to pray for rebirth in the Pure Land. Eikan himself joined these groups and practiced with them. Such group rituals were variously known as *ōjō kō* (rebirth assemblies), *raigō e*, or *mukae kō*. *Raigō* and *mukae* both refer to the belief that Amida welcomes believers into his Pure Land.

Kakuju, who studied under a direct disciple of Eikan, wrote only one well-known work, the *Jūni Rai Sho* (On the Twelve Adorations). His disciple Chinkai compiled the *Ketsujō Ōjō Shū* (A Collection of Passages Assuring Rebirth), which states: "The essence of the Pure Land teaching is attaining assurance of one's rebirth in the Pure Land. The proper method is found in all the Pure Land scriptures and treatises, which say that invoking the name of Amida makes no distinction between the wise and the foolish. Truly this teaching can be said to 'suit the times and the nature of people.' It pains me greatly to hear that there are some who know of this method and yet fail to practice it. Let us cast aside our reservations and earnestly invoke the holy name!"

Chinkai's chief authority was the Chinese Pure Land master Shan-tao, who wrote in the *Kuan-ching-su* (Commentary on the Sutra of Meditation on Amitābha Buddha): "To wholeheartedly recite Amitābha only, without regard to whether one is standing, walking, sitting, or lying and irrespective of whether the period of practice is long or short, and to cast aside [delusions] moment by moment—this is called 'the rightly determined practice' because it accords with Amitābha's Vow." The reference to wholeheartedly reciting Amitābha's name illustrates the shift from interpreting the *nien-fo* as a meditative practice to viewing it as the oral invocation of Amitābha's name.

Chinkai was not the first to quote from Shan-tao's *Kuan-ching-shu*. Eikan had done so in his *Ōjō Jūin*, though he had not emphasized the superiority of the recited *nembutsu* as clearly as Chinkai. At any rate, the increasingly high regard for Shan-tao's ideas marked a major development in the history of Pure Land theory in Japan.

Pure Land Teachings in the Shingon Sect

Mukū, who became abbot of Kongōbu-ji, on Mount Kōya, in 894, regularly practiced the *nembutsu* and can be regarded as the originator of the Shingon lineage of Pure Land teachings. In addition, the Heian-period popular biographies of those who supposedly had attained rebirth in the Pure Land, a literary genre known as *ōjō den*, mention such Shingon priests as Jōshō (906–83), Gengō, and Jinkaku (955–1043). All these figures were devoted to Pure Land practices as individuals, but in the eleventh century groups of devotees began to form on Mount Kōya, centering on the Hossō priest and scholar Kyōkai (1001–93), popularly known as the Holy Man of Odawara.

At Kōfuku-ji, in Nara, Kyōkai specialized in study of the doctrines of the Consciousness Only school of Buddhist philosophy. He later moved to a subtemple of Kōfuku-ji at Odawara, in Yamashiro Province, and devoted himself to Pure Land practice. Still later he moved to Mount Kōya, where he daily recited Amida's name, calling it the Great Mantra of Amida, and undertook other practices. He seems to have spent the last two decades or so of his life in Odawara, living there from about 1070 on.

Kyōkai devoted himself to both Shingon and Pure Land practices, reciting both Shingon mantras and the Great Mantra of Amida. In Kyōkai's practice the two traditions were not fully integrated. It was Kakuban (1095–1143) who actively worked to fuse Shingon and Pure Land teachings. He had studied Sanron and Consciousness Only doctrines in Nara and had gone on to immerse himself in Shingon and Pure Land practice, as well. In the twelfth month of 1113, he went to Mount Kōya to study esoteric mudrās, symbolic gestures with the hands or fingers, with the *nembutsu* practitioner Myōjaku at Saizen-in. He also practiced *nembutsu* under Shōren, known as the Holy Man of Awa, and Chōchi. Moreover, he received Shingon initiation at Ninna-ji, Tendai esoteric initiation at Onjō-ji, and a special fivefold Shingon initiation at Daigo-ji. Kakuban went on to found Negoro-ji in Kii Province in 1126 and Daidembō-in on Mount Kōya in 1132. Eventually he was named abbot of Kongōbu-ji but was driven out by the scholar-priests of Mount Kōya, who were offended by his explicit policy of combining Shingon and Pure Land Buddhism and by the fact that the training he had received, mainly from masters not affiliated with Mount Kōya, emphasized practice rather than scholarship.

In 1140, after his ouster from the abbacy of Kongōbu-ji, Kakuban retreated to Negoro-ji and tried to organize a group that would be able to combat the power of the Mount Kōya faction. In explaining his doctrinal position, he stated: "Dainichi [Mahāvairocana] and Amida are in essence the same; only the names differ. The Pure Land of Perfect Bliss and the esoteric Pure Land are one and the same." He also stated: "The esoteric Pure Land is the place where Dainichi Nyorai [the tathāgata Mahāvairocana] truly resides; the Pure Land of Perfect Bliss is the spiritual home of Amida. Amida is produced by the action of Dainichi's wisdom; Dainichi is the actual manifestation of Amida's form. The esoteric Pure Land contains and includes the Pure Land of Perfect Bliss; the Pure Land of Perfect Bliss is but another name for the esoteric Pure Land. The Pure Land of Perfect Bliss is the specific name for Amida's Pure Land. If one asks its whereabouts, I answer that it pervades the ten directions; any place where we meditate or practice is itself the Pure Land of Perfect Bliss."

Kakuban's position is characterized by belief in the Shingon teaching of the attainment of enlightenment in one's present body (*sokushin jōbutsu*): "One can at once be reborn in the Pure Land without leaving this world of dust; one's present body can enter into the mind of Amida; Amida himself is seen, without change, to be Dainichi. This is the significance of 'attaining enlightenment in one's present body'" This Pure Land version of the Shingon teaching of attaining enlightenment in one's present body is characteristic of Kakuban's thought and distinguishes his teaching from the tradition of Tendai Pure Land practice, with its emphasis on rebirth in the Pure Land after death.

Subtemples and the Development of Pure Land Teachings

Kakuban created a place for the increasingly popular *nembutsu* within Shingon. Soon groups of *nembutsu* practitioners, mostly of aristocratic origin, formed around holy men living in subtemples on Mount Kōya. This development was not limited to Mount Kōya. Tōdai-ji had a subtemple on Mount Kōmyō, and Mount Hiei had one at Kurodani, in Kyoto. Priests from the main temple could isolate themselves at these subtemples to devote more time to *nembutsu* and other specialized forms of practice, and the laity could go to the subtemples for instruction. Often they also served as centers for lay associations devoted specifically to *nembutsu* or other forms of practice, such as Hokke Hakkō (the Eight Lectures on the Lotus Sutra), the *nehan kō* (observances of Śākyamuni Buddha's death), or *mukae kō*.

It is not clear just when the building of such subtemples began. The earliest reference to a subtemple is found in the *Honchō Hokke Gengi* (Records of Miracles and Visions Connected with the Lotus Sutra; 1040–44), in the biography of the Tendai grand abbot Yōshō (904–90), which states that Yōshō had lived at a subtemple in a bamboo grove. However, it is not clear whether the subtemple already existed in Yōshō's time or he lived on the site of a later subtemple. The Minami subtemple is known to have existed at Tōnomine-dera in 1045, and it is generally conceded that the subtemple system emerged in the first half of the eleventh century. According to the late Takagi Yutaka, professor of Buddhist studies at Rissho University, by the late eleventh century there were sixty-four subtemples scattered between Ōmi Province, just east of Kyoto, and Satsuma and Ōsumi provinces, at the southern tip of Kyushu. They were especially numerous in the area around the capital, with twelve in Ōmi Province, ten in Yamashiro, eight in Yamato, and eight in Kii (three on Mount Kōya alone: the eastern, central, and southern subtemples).

Seventy-three priests named in collections of stories of rebirth lived in subtemples. Of these, forty-four (60 percent) had come from Mount Hiei or temples affiliated with Mount Hiei. Apparently they either wanted to cut their ties with that increasingly decadent religious establishment or believed that such ascetic practices as eremitism and long pilgrimages would help them attain rebirth in the Pure Land of Perfect Bliss or Tuṣita Heaven. They seem to have moved from subtemple to subtemple, which suggests that there were reciprocal relationships among the subtemples independent of their relationships with the head temple. The priests at the subtemples employed the *nembutsu* in various intercessory rituals—a practice that led to popularization of Pure Land ideas and to their spread.

Genshin and His Ōjō Yōshū

Genshin (942–1017) was born at Taima, in Yamato Province. The Taima area had a rich religious heritage, and Genshin's mother was a pious Buddhist. He went to Mount Hiei to study under the Tendai master Ryōgen. Since two of Ryōgen's disciples—Genshin and Kakuun (953–1007)— went on to become distinguished Pure Land practitioners, the master, too, must have had elements of Pure Land ideas in his teaching. Kakuun, interested primarily in traditional Tendai meditative *nembutsu,* wrote such works as the *Nembutsu Hōgō* (The Precious Name of the *Nembutsu*) and the *Kanjin Nembutsu* (Meditative *Nembutsu*). Genshin, too, was interested in meditative *nembutsu,* but he also attached considerable importance to reciting the *nembutsu.*

By the age of forty Genshin had had a brilliant career as a priest, composing a work on Buddhist logic, *Immyō Ronsho Shisōi Ryaku Chūshaku* (Commentary on the Four Kinds of Contradictory Trope Described in the [K'uei-chi's] Commentary on Buddhist Logic; 978), and serving as an imperial court priest. Gradually, however, he moved away from the world of the aristocratic clergy and eventually retired to the secluded Yokawa section of Mount Hiei. The impetus for this change seems to have been his pious mother's words that her ardent wish for him was to seek not fame and power but practice of the way of buddhahood, separated from worldly affairs. From that time on, Genshin devoted himself to Pure Land practice with unflagging zeal and showed no interest in worldly success. His practice took the form of Tendai-style meditative *nembutsu.*

Between the eleventh month of 984 and the fourth month of 985, Genshin wrote the *Ōjō Yōshū* (Essentials of Rebirth), summing up all he had gained from half a lifetime of study and practice. The *Ōjō Yōshū* states: "The doctrine that teaches us how to be reborn in the Pure Land is truly wonderful, like eyes and limbs for people of these days of the Decay of the Law. Is there anyone, priest or lay believer, noble or base, who would not wish to espouse such a doctrine? The Pure Land teaching is so excellent

that all should turn to it! True, there are many varieties of teaching, esoteric and exoteric. Though these may be accessible to some very gifted individuals, for the vast number of us who are weak and foolish, what hope
is there? For people like us, the Buddha has graciously prepared the
teaching of the *nembutsu*."

Genshin divided his work into ten sections: (1) "Separating from This
Defiled World by Being Weary of It," (2) "Longing for the Pure Land,"
(3) "Evidence for the Land of Perfect Bliss," (4) "Correctly Practicing the
Nembutsu," (5) "Methods of Auxiliary Practice of the *Nembutsu*," (6) "*Nembutsu*
Practice at Special Times," (7) "The Benefits of the *Nembutsu*," (8) "Results
of the *Nembutsu*," (9) "Various Practices Leading to Rebirth," and (10)
"Commentary on the Doctrine through Questions and Answers."

Section one includes harrowing descriptions of the sufferings of deluded
mortals, especially in the hells. Section two describes the state of the blessed
dwelling in the Pure Land with countless bodhisattvas, listening to wonderful celestial music amid beautiful flowers and ponds. Section three explains that there are many Pure Lands but that Amida's Pure Land of
Perfect Bliss is the most excellent of them all and states that the author
wishes everyone to be reborn there, through the virtue of the *nembutsu*.

Section four sets forth specific methods of praising and worshiping
Amida Buddha and names correct meditation as the most important of
these. However, since beginners find it difficult to meditate correctly, they
should first learn to concentrate separately on each of the Buddha's thirty-
two primary and eighty secondary physical marks of excellence and on
the excellences of his Pure Land. Practitioners progress from separate
meditations, for example, on the Buddha's eyes or the tuft of white hair
between his eyebrows, to comprehensive meditation on the Buddha's form
as a whole. Practitioners move from the individual parts to the whole.
Ultimately, practitioners achieve total identity with the Buddha being
meditated upon.

Obviously, not everyone is suited to this method, since it requires both
extraordinary ability and great effort. Thus Genshin offered another
method: the meditation on a specific subject. In this method, meditation
on a single one of the Buddha's marks (his eyes, for example) produces an
awareness of his radiance, which pervades the worlds in the ten directions
and saves all sentient beings who practice the *nembutsu*. Ordinarily people
do not see the Buddha's light because of the darkness of delusion within
their own minds. Yet, though they are not aware of it, they are constantly

surrounded by Amida's light. Genshin urged people to develop the ability to perceive Amida's light by means of meditation on a specific subject.

For those incapable even of this simplified meditation, Genshin suggested fervent invocation of the Buddha's name. He held that any practice, be it recitation of sutras or the *nembutsu*, is efficacious as long as it is related to Amida. In this inclusiveness we see Genshin's characteristically Tendai attitude. Nonetheless, though Genshin encouraged recitation of the *nembutsu*, he did not recommend it as either the best or the only practice. He gave pride of place to contemplative *nembutsu*. Recitation of the *nembutsu* is a secondary practice designed for those incapable of meditation.

Not long after it was completed, the aristocrat Fujiwara no Yukinari ✓ (972–1027) borrowed a copy of *Ōjō Yōshū* from the great statesman Fujiwara no Michinaga and made his own copy. In his *Chūyū Ki* (Fujiwara no Mune- *Chūyū Ki* tada's Diary), covering the years 1087–1138, another aristocrat, Fujiwara no Munetada (1062–1141), recounted that "as the dawn bell rang, in a dream I saw sentences [from the *Ōjō Yōshū*] about the ten kinds of joy [one can have in the Pure Land]. Was it because lately I've been memorizing important passages from it, so that they are engraved on my heart? At any rate, it made me very happy." It is evident that the *Ōjō Yōshū* was widely read among both the aristocratic laity and the clergy. After completing his great work, Genshin continued to practice and teach both forms of *nembutsu* until his death at age seventy-five, in the sixth month of 1017.

Pure Land Teachings and the Concept of Mappō

Relatively early in its history, Buddhism developed the concept of three periods of the Buddhist Law. Though the exact lengths of these periods differ from text to text and calculations of their beginnings and endings range widely, there is general agreement on the names and the natures of the periods. The period in which the teachings of Śākyamuni Buddha are transmitted faithfully by those who form the core of the Buddhist Order and in which practitioners are able to attain enlightenment is known as the period of the Righteous Law (*Shōbō*). The age in which, though the teachings are preserved and practiced, enlightenment is no longer possible is known as the period of the Counterfeit Law (*Zōbō*). The age in which only the written teachings remain and neither practice nor attainment is possible is known as the period of the Decay of the Law (*Mappō*). In Japan, the periods of the Righteous Law and the Counterfeit Law were thought to last one thousand years each, and it was believed that the world had entered the period of the Decay of the Law around 1052, somewhat more than a century before the Heian period ended.

The late Heian period was characterized by epidemics and natural disasters, coupled with civil and religious strife. In the sixth month of 988, the court was forced to forbid priests to wear secular clothes and bear arms. A long dispute between Enryaku-ji, controlled by Ennin's school, and Onjō-ji, under Enchin's faction, began in the ninth month of 989 as a result of the appointment of Yokei of Onjō-ji as grand abbot of the Tendai sect. Despite the imperial edict, armed conflict continued, and even escalated. In the eighth month of 993 Ennin's group attacked and destroyed Senju-in on Mount Hiei, driving a thousand followers of Enchin from the mountain; in the same year there was a severe influenza epidemic. Four years earlier a great storm had destroyed many major buildings in the capital, and the rivers had overflowed, flooding the surrounding fields and doing unprecedented damage.

Rivalry between religious institutions continued to increase. In the first month of 1037 the priests of Kōfuku-ji attacked Tōdai-ji. In the fourth month of the same year Minamoto no Norisato, governor of Tajima Province, fought a battle against the Shintō priests in charge of Iwashimizu Hachiman Shrine, south of Kyoto. In the tenth month of 1038 the priests of Enryaku-ji rioted upon learning that Myōson, abbot of Onjō-ji, had been named patriarch of the Tendai sect. When in the fifth month of 1041 the priests of Enryaku-ji learned that an ordination platform was to be established at the rival Onjō-ji, they put up violent resistance; and in the third month of 1042 they attacked Onjō-ji and burned it to the ground.

Many people believed that the reason for the natural disasters and civil strife was that the final period of the Buddhist Law, the Decay of the Law, was approaching. This view was expressed in the *Eiga Monogatari* (Tales of Splendor), the eleventh-century work that recounts Fujiwara no Michinaga's illustrious career: "The world today is full of calamities and human deaths. Yet the emperor is of a kind and peaceful disposition, and the government under Lord Michinaga is by no means a bad one. The reason for the ills that befall us is that we are entering the Decay of the Law. Year by year, the state of the world grows worse: many people die unnecessarily, and tragedies multiply."

In such times, the Pure Land faith, with its rejection of this world and its longing for the Pure Land of Amida, was most welcome. Pure Land Buddhism offered a path of salvation grounded in both theory and practice. Theoretical underpinnings were provided by scholar-priests like Genshin, while *gōshō e*, temples devoted to Amida (Amida-dō), and paintings depicting him coming to save his devotees at the time of their death (*raigō zu*) were concrete manifestations of the Pure Land faith. These expressions of Pure Land belief became particularly widespread in the late Heian period, as more and more people sought salvation through faith in Amida.

The *gōshō e* rituals are said to have been initiated by Genshin. Fujiwara no Michinaga sponsored one at Urin-in, in Kyoto, around 1019; and it is reported that others were held by Eikan at Yoshida-dera, in Yamanaka; by a figure identified as the Holy Man of Daigo-ji, near Kiyomizu-dera, in Higashiyama; and by Sensai (fl. ca. twelfth century) at Ungo-ji, in Higashiyama.

Raigo zu paintings depicted Amida, accompanied by his twenty-five attendant bodhisattvas and other heavenly beings, descending from the Pure Land on a purple cloud to welcome the devotee at the hour of death. There were many different kinds of portrayal within the genre: evidence suggests a general shift from static images of the Buddha and bodhisattvas seated preaching in the Pure Land to dynamic images of Amida standing and moving forward to greet the devotee. In time, greater movement and even depictions of speed appeared, particularly in the rendering of the characteristic purple clouds that bear Amida and his attendants, suggesting Amida's desire to save the believer without a moment's delay.

Depictions of the Buddha's descent were not limited to paintings. Occasionally groups of statues were enshrined in Amida-dō (Amida halls) to suggest Amida's descent to welcome his devotees. Examples of Amida-dō include Muryōju-in and Byōdō-in at Uji. Fujiwara no Sanesuke (957–1046), minister of the right, wrote of Byōdō-in in his diary, the *Shōyū Ki:* "I secluded myself in the hall, feeling as if I were in the Pure Land of Perfect Bliss itself!" Not all Amida-dō were as splendid as Byōdō-in, of course. But aristocrats who built Amida-dō did try to make them as beautiful as possible, as replicas of the Pure Land, an endeavor that required not only great financial resources but also a highly refined aesthetic sense.

Despite the aristocrats' protestations of faith in Amida and their desire for rebirth in his Pure Land, their art and writings convey no sense of urgency inspired by the dawning of the Decay of the Law. For a serious response to the idea of the Decay of the Law, one must turn to people more actively and directly involved in Buddhist practice.

Ryōnin and the Yūzū Nembutsu

Ryōnin (1073–1132) studied Tendai doctrines under Ryōga on Mount Hiei. He also received the Mahāyāna precepts under Zennin at Onjō-ji. He is said to have lived at the Amida-dō in the Eastern Precincts of Mount Hiei, where he engaged in the Tendai practice of reciting *nembutsu* while circumambulating the image of Amida. In time, however, he became disillusioned with the atmosphere of Enryaku-ji, where armed warrior-priests ruled by force and most clergy were bent on winning fame and fortune.

Seeking a place where he could quietly serve the Buddha and pursue his religious practice, Ryōnin retired to Shōrin-in in Ōhara, on Kyoto's northern outskirts, in 1094. Ōhara was the site of the Akuo subtemple, which was affiliated with Enryaku-ji. Shōrin-in had been founded in 1013 by Minamoto no Tokinobu (960–1024). Toward the end of the Heian period it became a center for the Valley school of esoteric Tendai, since many students of that system moved there from the Eastern Precincts of Mount Hiei. Like Ryōnin, they seem to have wished to escape the corruption and worldliness of the Tendai headquarters.

Ryōnin prayed earnestly for rebirth in the Pure Land, reciting the Lotus Sutra and repeating the *nembutsu* some sixty thousand times per day. Reciting the Lotus Sutra in the morning and repeating the *nembutsu* in the evening had long been a favorite mode of practice on Mount Hiei. But Ryōnin originated what he called the *yūzū*, or "mutually inclusive," *nembutsu*.

Ryōnin described the *yūzū nembutsu* as being based on the truth that one person is all people and all people are one person; one practice is all practices and all practices are one practice. Each person's *nembutsu* merges with that of everyone else to produce great merit that enables all to attain rebirth. At the root of this concept lies the Tendai teaching that each of the ten realms of existence—the hells and the worlds of hungry spirits, animals, *asuras* (demons), human beings, gods, *śrāvakas*, *pratyekabuddhas*, bodhisattvas, and buddhas—contains elements of all the other nine. Thus a denizen of a hell can become a buddha, and through karmic processes a buddha can become a dweller in hell. No being is perfectly evil or perfectly good. Also apparent in Ryōnin's *yūzū nembutsu* is the influence of the Kegon school and its teaching that all phenomena interpenetrate and do not obstruct one another.

The phrase "perfectly penetrating *nembutsu*" and the sentence "Because one person's practice is taken as all people's practice, the merit is immense" are found in the *Kokon Chomon Shū* (A Collection of Tales with Moral Lessons for the Young, compiled by Tachibana no Narisue in 1254). According to this work, Tamonten (in Sanskrit, Vaiśravaṇa), the deity of Kurama-dera, in Kyoto, appeared to Ryōnin in a dream and told him: "Save suffering sentient beings by propagating the *yūzū nembutsu*. It is far better to recite the *nembutsu* together than to recite it singly." Ryōnin then went to Kyoto with his *yūzū nembutsu* pledge book, in which was written: "Wishing that all may be reborn in the Pure Land, I accept pledges from all—nobles and commoners, men and women—to recite the *nembutsu* daily and inscribe herein the names of those who so pledge." The concept of a pledge and list of those making the pledge was Ryōnin's contribution to Pure Land practice.

Ryōnin traveled widely to disseminate the teaching of the *yūzū nembutsu*, as far east as Mikawa and Owari provinces and as far west as the San'yōdō area (Aki, Bingo, Bitchū, Bizen, and Harima provinces). As the *dainembutsu* (great *nembutsu*), the *yūzū nembutsu* is still practiced to an extent in a number of areas. *Yūzū nembutsu* societies survive in Iga and Ise provinces. Ryōnin devoted only the last nine years of his life to disseminating the *yūzū nembutsu*, but his influence on Japanese society was far-reaching and enduring.

4. Heian-Period Religion: Popular Religion

THE CULTS OF MIROKU, KANNON, AND JIZŌ

Miroku's Paradise

The belief in the bodhisattva Maitreya (in Japanese, Miroku) began in the Northern Wei–dynasty period (386–534) in China. Strictly speaking, Maitreya is a bodhisattva—that is, a being on the path to enlightenment—but he is also recognized as the buddha of the future, the buddha who will appear next in our world. Thus Maitreya is worshiped as both a future buddha and a bodhisattva. Maitreya is believed to live in Tuṣita Heaven, where he practices and also preaches the Law to heavenly beings. His enlightenment lies in the distant future, some 5.67 billion years after Śākyamuni's death. At that time he will be reborn in this world and attain enlightenment under the dragon-flower tree in the flower-grove garden and preach three sermons for the benefit of those beings who have formed a karmic bond with him. These are known as the three sermons of Maitreya or the three sermons under the dragon-flower tree.

One of the main goals of followers of the Maitreya cult was to encounter Maitreya when he appears as a buddha in the future and hear those sermons, which would enhance their own efforts to attain enlightenment. Because it is impossible to prolong one's life for that immense period of time, they focused on practices to earn merit in the present so that after death they might be reborn in Tuṣita Heaven with Maitreya and descend with him to earth when it is time for him to preach his three sermons under the dragon-flower tree. This form of Maitreya devotion is known as the cult of rebirth in Maitreya's Tuṣita Heaven. Adherents of a related cult, the cult of encounter with the descended Maitreya in this world, sought rebirth on this earth at the time of Maitreya's advent, without spending the intervening eons with him in his heaven.

It is not clear just when the Maitreya cult entered Japan. An entry in the *Nihon Shoki* (Chronicles of Japan; 720) dated the ninth month of 584 states that one Kōka no Omi took a stone image of Maitreya to Japan from the Korean kingdom of Paekche. This entry derives from the ancient histories in the *Gangō-ji Garan Engi Narabi ni Ruki Shizai Chō* (History of the Gangō-ji Monastery and Record of the Temple's Assets; 747). Though there are slight differences in the two accounts—the ancient history gives the year as 583 and uses different ideograms for the name, read Kōga no Omi—most scholars accept the ancient history record, since the ancient histories in the *Gangō-ji Engi* predate the *Nihon Shoki,* and conclude that a powerful family in the Kōga district of Ōmi Province first introduced a Miroku image into Japan. Moreover, the celebrated image of Miroku at Kōryū-ji, in Kyoto, is thought to date to the first half of the seventh century. It seems certain, then, that Miroku images were produced in Japan from an early date. However, the creation of images does not necessarily imply a full-blown devotional cult.

In Japan the first instance of the copying of a sutra related to Miroku was recorded in the eighth month of 730, when Ishikawa no Toshitari (688–762) copied the *Miroku Jōbutsu-kyō* (Sutra of Maitreya's Attainment of Buddhahood; *Mi-le-ch'eng-fo-ching*). Copies of the *Miroku Bosatsu Shomon Hongan-kyō* (Sutra of the Original Vow of Maitreya Bodhisattva; *Mi-le-p'u-sa-suo-wen-pen-yüan-ching*) and the *Kan Miroku Bosatsu Jōshō Tosotsuten-kyō* (Sutra of Meditation on Maitreya Bodhisattva's Ascent to Tuṣita Heaven; *Kuan-Mi-le-p'u-sa-shang-sheng-tou-shuo-t'ien-ching*) were made in 737 and 738, respectively. Buddhists of the Nara period sought rebirth in one of four Pure Lands: that of Miroku (Maitreya), Amida (Amitābha), Śākyamuni, or Birushana (Vairocana). At first Miroku's paradise was most popular, but later it was displaced by Amida's Pure Land. The decline of the Maitreya cult on the continent and the introduction of works by Pure Land masters like Tao-ch'o and Huai-kan, extolling the superior merits of Amitābha's Pure Land, seem to have been important factors in the shift from the cult of Miroku to that of Amida.

From the middle Heian period on, the Kimpu Mountains, in southern

Yamato Province, were regarded as the manifestation of Miroku's Pure Land. Thus in 1007 Fujiwara no Michinaga visited the Kimpu Mountains and buried a gilt-bronze sutra case containing copies of the Lotus Sutra, the Sutra of Innumerable Meanings, the Sutra of Meditation on the Bodhisattva Universal Virtue, the *Amida-kyō*, the *Hannya Haramitta Shin-gyō* (Heart of Wisdom Sutra; in Sanskrit, *Prajñāpāramitā-hṛdaya-sūtra*), the Sutra of Meditation on Maitreya Bodhisattva's Ascent to Tuṣita Heaven, the *Miroku Geshō-kyō* (Sutra of Maitreya's Descent; *Mi-le-hsia-sheng-ching*), and the Sutra of Maitreya's Attainment of Buddhahood. Together, the first three of these sutras are known as the Threefold Lotus Sutra, and the Maitreya sutras are known collectively as the Three Maitreya Sutras.

Michinaga's dedicatory text declared that the Lotus Sutra was being buried as an expression of gratitude to Śākyamuni Buddha, the *Amida-kyō* as an expression of Michinaga's desire to be blessed with a peaceful death and rebirth in Amida's Pure Land, and the Maitreya sutras as an expression of his hope that his sins would be expunged and that, pure in heart and mind, he would be able to encounter Miroku when he descends to this world. Michinaga vowed to leave Amida's Pure Land and go to the dragon-flower tree as soon as Miroku finished his bodhisattva practice and became a buddha. Sitting beneath the tree, Michinaga would hear Miroku Buddha's preaching and attain enlightenment, which would be acknowledged by Miroku himself. Then the sutras that Michinaga had buried in the Kimpu Mountains would spring from the earth, causing great wonderment and delight among the people—or such was the hope Michinaga recorded for posterity.

Michinaga believed in the Lotus Sutra, in Amida, and in Miroku simultaneously. Refusal to be confined to only one form of religious devotion or practice characterized the religious faith of the Heian-period aristocracy. No one found this syncretism odd or contradictory. That it was widespread is evident from such statements as "Let us go to Tuṣita [Heaven] above and also meet with Amida in the West," a wish expressed in the *Honchō Monzui* (Literary Essence of Our Land; ca. 1060), an anthology of poetry and prose in classical Chinese compiled by the scholar Fujiwara no Akihira (989–1066). The *Gō Totoku Nagon Gammon Shū* (The Collected Petitions of Ōe no Masafusa; 1061–1111) comments: "Moving across [the long distance to the west], we encounter Amida, and moving up we enter Tuṣita." People of that time had faith in both Amida and Miroku; they would have been equally happy reborn in the Western Pure Land of Perfect

Bliss or in Tuṣita Heaven. Their sole concern was to attain an auspicious rebirth.

The Cult of Rebirth Together with Miroku

Beginning around the twelfth century, as the Pure Land faith burgeoned, devotion to Miroku increasingly took the form of prayers to be reborn with him on earth rather than in Tuṣita Heaven. As Fujiwara no Michinaga's early act of piety demonstrates, the custom of burying sutras is related to this form of religious aspiration. Through the activities of the popular holy men called *hijiri*, sutra burial was gradually adopted by the general population.

Some 270 sutra mounds have been discovered, of which over two-thirds (186) date to the Heian period. Dedicatory verses written on the occasion of sutra burials clearly state the purposes of this ritual activity. To paraphrase several such verses: "In burying this sutra, we pray that it will become a scripture more valuable than the seven precious stones; that it will be enshrined in a seven-jeweled pagoda; that it will be preserved until Miroku himself descends to earth; that its teachings will be preserved even if the Law preached by Śākyamuni is lost, so that later generations may know the truth." "We reverently pray that Miroku Bodhisattva may fulfill his great vow and save us all."

All this is evidence of the vitality of the Miroku cult, which was rooted in the notion of *Mappō*, the period of the Decay of the Law, with Miroku seen as the savior for that age. Believers looked to him for their future happiness and for the purification of this degenerate world. For them, the salvation of the world during the period of the Decay of the Law was inextricably linked to Miroku's advent, as is shown by another dedicatory verse:

From calculations based on ancient texts, it is clear that some 2,052 years have passed between the time of Great Master Śākya[muni Buddha]'s entry into nirvana and the present year of Kōwa 5 [1103] of the Japanese calendar. On this, the third day of the tenth month, I, the priest Kyōson, offer an eight-fascicle set of sutras to the great deity of Ichinomiya, who dwells in Kawamura Higashigō, in Hōki Province, in the San'in region, and enshrine it on the hill southeast of the shrine. I pray that by the merits of this offering all people with whom I am linked by karma—whether they be close or distant and regardless of the Pure Land in which they are reborn as a result of their practice—may meet

him in this world when Miroku Buddha appears here. I pray also that
the sutras buried here will come to light at that time.

The figure 2,052 years signified that the two one-thousand-year periods
of the Righteous Law and the Counterfeit Law had already passed and
the world was then fifty-two years into the period of the Decay of the
Law. As we saw in the discussion of the Pure Land faith in the Heian period,
the supposed arrival of the period of the Decay of the Law was brought
home vividly to the people of the time by a series of natural calamities and
almost continuous warfare. Waiting for the advent of Miroku was an act of
hope. The period of the Decay of the Law was to last ten thousand years,
and by the end of that period Buddhism would have withered, its scriptures and doctrines lost. The practice of sutra burial was inspired by the perceived need to preserve at least part of the canon until Miroku's advent.

The so-called pledge-book priests (kanjin sō), itinerant priests who carried pledge books in which they recorded the names of those who contributed to their projects, sought to involve as many people as possible in
the work of sutra burial and preservation. In 1082, the priest Jōe wrote
this vow: "I have erected a three-shaku [about ninety-one centimeters] image of Miroku on Yasugamine, one of the seven lofty mountains of Japan,
and have copied the Lotus Sutra so that it can be buried there. My hope
is that it will be of use when Miroku comes to preach the Law beneath the
dragon-flower tree. May all those who have established karmic bonds with
me be saved by the merits of this act." By those who had "established
karmic bonds," Jōe meant those who had contributed to his cause. The
act of contributing was believed to assure salvation when Miroku arrived.

Another practice of devotees of Miroku at this time—a practice consistent with the syncretism discussed earlier—was to seek rebirth in Amida's
Pure Land and wait there for Miroku's advent. When that occurred, believers hoped, they would be reborn on earth from Amida's Pure Land
and hear Miroku's teaching directly. This hope was often expressed in a
simile: "The teachings of Śākya[muni] are like a plank floating [on a vast
ocean]. We who [have been fortunate enough to] encounter the teachings
are like a turtle [adrift in that boundless ocean, which yet manages to bump
against the plank]. Let us [wait in Amida's Pure Land], free from all doubt,
[until the time when we can encounter] Miroku in his three sermons in the
future." It was believed that this long-awaited direct encounter with a buddha would ensure salvation. In this fashion, the cult of rebirth in this world
with Miroku developed in tandem with Pure Land beliefs. Both forms of

devotion placed salvation in the hands of a buddha or bodhisattva—a current in Japanese Buddhism that, under the name of other-power (*tariki*) faith, played an important role in later Japanese religious history.

The Kannon Cult

The principal figures of devotion for the Nara-period aristocracy were Amida, Miroku, Śākyamuni, and Kannon (Avalokiteśvara). For instance, a record of treasures of Saidai-ji, in Nara, lists four images each of Yakushi Nyorai (Bhaiṣajyaguru, the buddha of healing), Shō Kannon (Ārya Avalokiteśvara), Jūichimen Kannon (the eleven-headed manifestation of Avalokiteśvara known as Ekādaśamukha), and Miroku; two of Fukūkensaku Kannon (the manifestation of Avalokiteśvara known as Amoghapāśa); and one each of Batō Kannon (Hayagrīva, the horse-headed Avalokiteśvara), Amida, and Śākyamuni. This list cites a total of eleven Kannon images in various manifestations.

Saidai-ji was a major temple established in 765 by Empress Regnant Shōtoku, and the images listed among its treasures are doubtless indicative of the Buddhist faith of the period. That more than half of the images depict Kannon demonstrates the vitality of the Kannon cult, as does the large number of tales centered on Kannon that appear in the *Nihon Ryōiki* (Miracle Stories of Japan), compiled about half a century after the founding of Saidai-ji. These tales include accounts of people spared from death and granted various worldly blessings through supplicating Kannon. The *Nihon Ryōiki* also contains many stories of miracles connected with images of Kannon.

In 881 the scholar, poet, and court official Sugawara no Michizane (845–903) sponsored a ceremonial reading of the Lotus Sutra in memory of his parents, with prayers that Kannon would allow them to be reborn in his Pure Land. Michizane especially venerated Kannon because as a child he had been cured of a serious illness in answer to his parents' prayers to the bodhisattva.

In 901 Michizane was demoted from the lofty rank of minister of the right to the post of governor of Dazaifu, on Kyushu, as a result of false accusations by his enemies. From that time on, he sought deliverance in the next world from his troubles in this through the intercession of Kannon. A poem he composed in exile (paraphrased here) reveals Michizane's belief in the bodhisattva: "My hair is as white as the snows of early spring. All feelings of grief and resentment that I had for a time have diminished.

With now peaceful heart I place green leaves and white plum blossoms before the Buddha and, folding my hands in prayer, think reverently, reverently, of Kannon." Michizane's parents had beseeched Kannon for a worldly benefit—the restoration of their son's health; in his prime Michizane had prayed to the same bodhisattva for his parents' eternal salvation; in his later years he prayed for his own salvation in Kannon's Pure Land, Potalaka, popularly supposed to lie somewhere beyond the sea. (Because of this belief sites sacred to Kannon were often located near the coast and facing the sea.)

From the tenth century on, the Kannon cult spread rapidly among the upper classes, as is evidenced by the proliferation of temples dedicated to this bodhisattva. Believers sought both worldly benefits and rebirth in Kannon's Pure Land, but the desire to be freed from the sufferings of the six realms of existence (the hells and the worlds of hungry spirits, animals, *asuras*, human beings, and gods) was central to the Kannon cult.

An important variant of Kannon worship was worship of the six manifestations of the bodhisattva: Shō Kannon, Senju Kannon (the Sahasrabhuja, or thousand-armed, manifestation of Avalokiteśvara), Batō Kannon, Jūichimen Kannon, Juntei Kannon (Cuṇḍī), and Nyoirin Kannon (Cintāmaṇi-cakra Avalokiteśvara, or Avalokiteśvara of the Wish-fulfilling Jewel). This is the case with the Tendai sect. In the Shingon sect Fukūkensaku Kannon replaces Juntei Kannon. Each of these six manifestations governs one of the six realms, seeking to save the suffering sentient beings in his own realm. Shō Kannon governs the hells; Senju Kannon, the world of hungry spirits; Batō Kannon, the world of animals; Jūichimen Kannon, the world of *asuras*; Juntei Kannon, the world of human beings; and Nyoirin Kannon, the world of deities.

Devotion to the six manifestations of Kannon seems to date to the early tenth century. In 910 the Tendai grand abbot Sōō (831–918) had images of the six manifestations of Kannon and an image of Amida made to help all sentient beings in the six realms attain rebirth in the Pure Land. This is the first recorded instance of images of the six manifestations of Kannon in Japan. In the third month of 947 the cloistered emperor Suzaku (r. 930–46) ordered the creation of six images of Kannon and six copies of the Lotus Sutra, as well as the performance of a ritual in the lecture hall of Enryaku-ji, for the repose of the spirits of those who had died in the rebellions led by the warrior Taira no Masakado (d. 940) and the former court official Fujiwara no Sumitomo (d. 941).

As devotion to the six Kannon became widespread in aristocratic circles, in about the eleventh century, reigning and cloistered emperors and the great nobles began vying in making images of the bodhisattva's six manifestations and in sponsoring rituals to ensure safe childbirth, recovery from illness, worldly success, and other practical benefits. Some people sought to win appointments to major posts, such as provincial governorships, by paying part of the costs of major rituals sponsored by the imperial household or powerful aristocratic families—which was indeed a direct route to the attainment of worldly benefits.

In addition to the cult of the six manifestations of Kannon, centers of Kannon worship connected with miracle tales also developed. The famous miscellany by the court lady Sei Shōnagon, the *Makura no Sōshi* (The Pillow Book; late tenth century), for example, lists Hase-dera, Hōrin-ji, Ishiyama-dera, Kasagi-dera, Kiyomizu-dera, Kokawa-dera, Ryōzen-ji, and Tsubosaka-dera as sites of Kannon worship; and Hase-dera, Ishiyama-dera, Kiyomizu-dera, and Kurama-dera are cited in the *Sarashina Nikki* (Sarashina Diary; ca. 1060), the memoirs of a court lady. The nobility made pilgrimages to these locations to pray for the prosperity of their families and for their own health and safety.

Most of the temples lay some distance from the capital, and the priests living in them were generally the holy men known as *hijiri*, who chose to devote themselves to austere religious practice in relatively secluded temples and avoid the worldliness of established religious centers. The custom of making pilgrimages to a series of sacred sites associated with holy men seems to have arisen in the late eleventh or early twelfth century, since Gyōson (1055–1135) of Mii-dera (Onjō-ji) is credited with having chosen the famed thirty-three pilgrimage sites of western Japan.

The Jizō Cult

According to Buddhist tradition, the role of the bodhisattva Kṣitigarbha (Jizō, in Japanese), who dwells in Trāyastriṃśa Heaven, is to save deluded sentient beings living in that degenerate age when there is no buddha in the world—that is, between the death of Śākyamuni and the advent of Maitreya. We do not know precisely when the cult of Kṣitigarbha was introduced into Japan, but it may have been relatively late, since in China devotion to this bodhisattva had first developed in the seventh century. In the tenth century he appeared in Japan as one of the bodhisattvas in Amida's retinue.

The Japanese cult of Jizō was given impetus by Genshin's *Ōjō Yōshū*, which lent great credence to the idea of hell by means of vivid, detailed descriptions of the torments awaiting mortals there. Hell was seen as the most fearful realm imaginable, yet even there, Jizō could save believers. Called the Buddha's messenger in hell, he was especially revered for his role there. Though at first the cult of Jizō was linked with that of Amida, by the end of the Heian period he was seen as capable of granting relief to those suffering in hell through his own power, which equaled that of Amida.

In the Pure Land faith of the aristocracy, Amida and the bodhisattvas Kannon, Daiseishi (Mahāsthāmaprāpta), Monju (Mañjuśrī), and Fugen (Samantabhadra) were all seen as saving the inhabitants of hell. However, in the collection *Konjaku Monogatari Shū* (Tales of Times Now Past; eleventh century) and other popular works, Jizō is portrayed as the special savior of those in hell. Here we see the beginnings of the cult of devotion to Jizō exclusively.

Like Kannon, Jizō was worshiped in Japan in six manifestations, one associated with each of the six realms of existence. It was the role of Danda Jizō to save those in hell, of Hōju Jizō to save those in the realm of hungry spirits, of Hōin Jizō to save those born as animals, of Jiji Jizō to save those born in the realm of *asuras*, of Jogaishō Jizō to save human beings, and of Nikkō Jizō to save those born in the realm of deities. In the Tendai sect, devotion to the six Kannon developed in the tenth century. In the Shingon sect, it started in the eleventh century. Devotion to the six Jizō seems to have developed in the eleventh century, at roughly the same time.

Though both Kannon and Jizō were seen as saviors of suffering sentient beings in the six realms of existence, there is a major difference between the cults of the two. The cult of the six manifestations of Kannon can be traced back to the Chinese T'ien-t'ai master Chih-i's work *Mo-ho-chih-kuan* and was long practiced in China. The cult of the six manifestations of Jizō, on the other hand, has no foundation in scripture or the writings of Buddhist patriarchs. Nor are depictions of Kṣitigarbha found in the ancient Chinese cave temples, where most figures of popular Buddhist devotion in East Asia are represented in paintings and statuary sponsored by both religious and lay organizations.

Although Jizō is described in the *Jizō Bosatsu Hosshin Innen Jūō-kyō* (Sutra of the Ten Kings and the Story of Kṣitigarbha's Aspiration for Enlightenment), this is clearly a spurious sutra of Japanese origin that probably postdates the development of the six-Jizō cult. At any rate, devotion to Jizō developed from an adjunct of Pure Land faith into an independent cult and began to gain adherents among the overall population in the middle of the eleventh century, as is evident from stories contained in popular secular literature, such as the *Konjaku Monogatari Shū* and the *Jizō Bosatsu Reigen Ki* (Records of Kṣitigarbha Bodhisattva's Miracles; eleventh century), compiled by Jitsuei, a priest of Onjō-ji. In contrast to the largely aristocratic followers of the six-Kannon cult, devotees of the six-Jizō cult were almost without exception ordinary people.

SHINTŌ-BUDDHIST SYNCRETISM

Two Types of Syncretism

Shintō-Buddhist syncretism *(shimbutsu shūgō)* is the amalgam of two religions: the indigenous Japanese "way of the *kami* (deities)" and the foreign faith of Buddhism. Though it can claim descent from both religions, it has distinct characteristics of its own and is properly seen as a separate intellectual and religious development.

Shintō-Buddhist syncretism is generally studied in terms of a single theory, that of the "original prototype and local manifestation" *(honji suijaku)*. This theory interprets Shintō deities in Buddhist terms, the "original prototype" of each indigenous deity being identified as a particular buddha or bodhisattva. The Shintō deity is regarded as the "local manifestation" of that Buddhist deity. The *honji suijaku* theory was an important idea in the history of Japanese religion; however, that Shintō-Buddhist syncretism can be summed up by this theory does not mean that it explains the entire phenomenon. In fact, Shintō-Buddhist syncretism has numerous sources and two major streams.

In view of the conditions under which Buddhism first developed in Japan, it is easy to understand why there were two major trends in the syncretic system that eventually emerged. As we saw earlier, the introduction of Buddhism into Japan was largely an official enterprise, the faith being transmitted to the Yamato court by the court of Paekche in Korea. The Buddhism of the Asuka and Nara periods was the fruit of this organized transmission of the religion from the ruling class of one country to that of another. State Buddhism—characterized by large government-sponsored temples in Nara and other important centers where government-authorized priests prayed for the welfare of the state in solemn rites—continued into the Heian period. Long before the introduction of Buddhism, of course, the indigenous religion had been the state cult, institutionalized to serve the ruling class and the government. The Shintō-Buddhist syncretism that engendered and was in turn shaped by the *honji suijaku* theory was the descendant of state Buddhism and its encounter and rapprochement with state Shintō.

In addition to the official transmission, there was private transmission of Buddhism, effected mainly by the large numbers of ordinary immigrants (many of whom lived in the provinces) rather than by authorized priests serving in the capital. Through direct contact with the indigenous population, this form of Buddhism spread in the provinces, not in the capital district; to small, unprepossessing shrines and temples, not to the great official temples; among peasants and rural shamans, not among aristocrats. To the ordinary people, the Buddha was one deity among many—and a newly arrived one, at that. Hence, it would have been natural for villagers to exclude him from the pantheon of ancestral *kami* at the heart of their worship. On the other hand, precisely because he was new, the Buddha seemed to offer novel spiritual powers. The syncretizing of Buddhism and Shintō that occurred at this level at first lacked a systematic conceptual framework.

Beginning in the late Heian period, however, Shintō-Buddhist syncretism informed by the *honji suijaku* theory was widely accepted among the populace. Indeed, it dominated popular religion during the medieval period, but not simply because it was imposed on the provinces and the general citizenry from above, by fiat of aristocrats and the priests of the great central temples. The natural syncretism developed by the general population over the centuries laid the foundation for the acceptance of the later, official syncretism.

Deities and Buddhas

The *Nihon Ryōiki* (ca. 822) is the earliest collection of Buddhist tales in Japan. It was compiled by Kyōkai, a priest at Yakushi-ji, in Nara, and many of its tales convey the Nara view of the relation between the deities and the buddhas. One story (the twenty-fourth story in volume three) set toward the end of the Nara period tells of the priest Eshō, from Daian-ji, who was staying in seclusion at Taga Shrine, in Ōmi Province, when a deity appeared to him in a dream as a monkey. The deity declared that he had been forced to take simian form because of his evil karma and piteously begged Eshō to help release him from his present sufferings by reciting the Lotus Sutra.

This well-known story depicts a deity as a deluded sentient being subject to the effects of karma, as do tales appearing in such works as the *Ruijū Kokushi* (Classified National History; 892), compiled by Sugawara no Michizane, the *Jingan-ji Engi* (History of Jingan-ji; 1546), and the *Tado Jingū-ji Garan Engi Narabi ni Shizai Chō* (History of Tado Shrine Temple and Record of Its Treasures; 788). In these stories the deities are on the same plane as human beings or on an even lower plane. They are unenlightened, suffering beings, hardly worthy of worship. It seems that this negative view of the Shintō *kami* was held by at least part of the Nara clergy.

The *Nihon Ryōiki* contains other stories that are similar. The seventh tale in volume one tells the story of a member of the provincial gentry of Bingo Province who, during the reign of Empress Saimei (r. 654–61), vowed to build a temple for the gods if he were allowed to return safely from the expedition to Korea in aid of the Paekche kingdom. He made a safe return and fulfilled his promise. The twelfth story of volume two tells of a woman who saw a snake about to devour a frog. She begged for the frog's life, promising to make offerings and worship the snake as a deity; but the snake refused the offer and made her become his wife instead. The first tale shows that erecting a Buddhist temple for a deity paid the deity greater honor than erecting a Shintō shrine. Apparently the point of the second story is that the snake refused to be satisfied with divine honors, since a deity is a relatively lowly being in comparison with the buddhas. Like the tale of the deity at Taga Shrine, these stories emphasize the superiority of the buddhas and the inferiority of the deities.

Murayama Shūichi, professor emeritus of Osaka Women's University, and others have suggested that since such tales appear in popular collections, they must have originated among the general population or perhaps were devised by Buddhist priests attempting to appeal to the emotions and beliefs of the people of provincial Japan. But in most cases these tales originated with the clergy. Though they are included in collections of popular tales, they underwent the editorial scrutiny of priestly compilers like Kyōkai. They may well have been revised to reflect a Buddhist view of the Shintō deities. Thus, not even stories that may have originated among the ordinary citizens can be assumed to faithfully reflect popular sentiment.

Anecdotal literature was directed primarily at the ordinary people in the provinces rather than at the upper classes in the capital district. In their emphasis on the *kami* as simply another class of deluded sentient beings, the tales amount to a Buddhist attack on the indigenous pantheon. As such they preach the absolute superiority of the buddhas over the deities. Thus we conclude that the Shintō-Buddhist syncretism impelled by Buddhism not only was controlled by the Buddhist clergy but also, at least through the Nara period, was aimed at the total defeat of the Shintō *kami*—the complete surrender of their divine dignity—rather than at any genuine synthesis of the two religions.

The Honji Suijaku Theory

In the Heian period, we find more and more instances of indigenous deities designated by Buddhist titles; for example, the deity Hachiman was called the Great Bodhisattva Hachiman, and the deity of Tado was known as the Great Bodhisattva Tado. Increasingly, priests were sent to read sutras at the major Shintō shrines: Munakata, Usa, and Aso. Bodhisattvas are just one step from the full enlightenment of buddhas, so that to designate Shintō deities as bodhisattvas was to accord them an elevated status entirely different from that of ordinary sentient beings. The ceremonial reading of scriptures was a Buddhist rite; thus, reading them before Shintō deities was an act of reverence. By the Heian period, clearly, the Buddhist approach to the Shintō deities had undergone a major change.

There is no evidence that Saichō and Kūkai, the founders of Tendai and Shingon, respectively, made any intellectual contributions to Shintō-Buddhist syncretism. Yet immediately after the founder's death each sect established relations with major shrines, had sutras read before the *kami*, and forged other links to Shintō. Moreover, it was claimed that Saichō had lectured on the Lotus Sutra at Usa Hachiman Shrine before his journey to T'ang China and that the deity Nifu had revealed an oracle to Kūkai when he founded his temple on Mount Kōya. Attempts to introduce Shintō elements into Saichō's and Kūkai's biographies were also made immediately after their deaths.

These developments represent a major change in attitude, due no doubt to the Buddhist establishment's awareness that earlier attempts to divest the Shintō *kami* of their dignity by fiat had not been effective. A different method was needed to ensure Buddhism's complete acceptance in Japan. Once harmonious coexistence with the indigenous deities had been chosen over conflict with and contempt for them, the Buddhists, whose understanding of philosophy was far more advanced than that of the indigenous priests, rapidly formulated a philosophy of Shintō-Buddhist syncretism.

The result was the *honji suijaku* theory, which began to reach maturity around the middle of the Heian period.

In traditional Buddhist theory, *honji* (original prototype) referred to "buddha" as an absolute and eternal ideal, while *suijaku* (local manifestation) referred to Śākyamuni as the actual historical embodiment of that ideal, manifested in this world for the salvation of sentient beings. Applied to the Shintō-Buddhist relationship, this theory was interpreted to mean that the absolute, eternal Buddha, wishing to save deluded sentient beings in Japan, had manifested himself as the Shintō deities. Thus all the Japanese *kami* originated in the buddhas and bodhisattvas. In effect, the terms deity, buddha, and bodhisattva referred to the same essence, the original truth of Buddhism.

Eryō of Enryaku-ji used the term local manifestation as early as 859, in a memorial to the Dajōkan: "The Sovereign Enlightened One [the Buddha] leads beings, sometimes to the absolutely true, and sometimes to the provisionally true. The Great Sage manifests himself locally, becoming now a king and now a deity." Nevertheless, it was only later that specific "original prototype" buddhas became associated with individual Japanese *kami*.

In the Nara period, Hachiman was the clearest example of a Shintō deity adopted by Buddhism; yet even in his case, it was not until the late eleventh century at the earliest that Amida was identified as his original prototype. Toward the end of the eleventh century the deity of Kumano Hongū Shrine, in Kii Province, was identified with Amida and the deity of Kumano Nachi Shrine with Kannon. Not until the twelfth century was the deity of Kumano Shingū Shrine identified with Yakushi Nyorai and the five deities—Nyakuōji, Zenjinomiya, Hijirinomiya, Chigonomiya, and Komorinomiya were identified with Jūichimen Kannon, Jizō, Nāgārjuna, Nyoirin Kannon, and Shō Kannon, respectively. Clearly, it took a long time for the *honji suijaku* theory to permeate the popular religious consciousness. The principal Shintō deities were finally linked to appropriate original prototype buddhas between the late Heian and early Kamakura periods.

In assigning original prototype buddhas to the principal *kami*, the Buddhists seem to have been concerned less with the character of the deities than with the status of their shrines. For example, the original prototype of the deity Katori, worshiped at Kasuga Shrine, in Nara, was Yakushi Nyorai, while the original prototypes for the deities of Katori Shrine, in Shimōsa Province, were Śākyamuni, Yakushi Nyorai, Jūichimen Kannon, and Jizō. Major shrines like these, with close ties to the imperial court and the great noble families, were generally assigned major original prototype buddhas or bodhisattvas. Thus the development of Shintō-Buddhist syncretism informed by the *honji suijaku* theory cannot be understood from a religious viewpoint alone.

TAOISM AND SHUGENDŌ ASCETICISM

Taoism in Japan

The ancient Japanese did not believe that life was confined to the world they saw before them. For instance, they spoke of Tokoyo no Kuni, the eternal land far beyond the seas. According to the Izumo myth cycle, related in volume one of the *Kojiki* (Record of Ancient Matters; 712), the diety Sukunabikona appeared from beyond the seas when the deity Ōkuninushi no Mikoto was at the Cape of Miho in Izumo, creating the land. The two deities governed the country jointly, but Sukunabikona later returned to Tokoyo no Kuni, whence he had come. The deities moved freely between Tokoyo no Kuni and this world and brought blessings and benefits to the land. Tokoyo no Kuni was regarded as the motherland, land of ancestral spirits, or land of wondrous beings. (It seems to have links with the Niraikanai realm, which figures in Okinawan myths.)

In the *Nihon Shoki*, in the account of the reign of the legendary emperor Suinin, Tajimamori, putative founder of the Miyake no Muraji clan, is said to have crossed the "great sea-plain" in search of the "timeless, fragrant fruit" and to have spent ten years on his long journey to and from Tokoyo no Kuni. On his return, he described Tokoyo no Kuni as "a sacred realm of deities and supernatural beings, not a place where ordinary mortals can easily go." In the *Nihon Shoki* account of the reign of the semi-legendary emperor Yūryaku, Urashimako of Mizunoe, who married a maiden who had been disguised as a turtle, is said to have gone into the sea with her and "traveled to Tokoyo no Kuni, where he encountered many immortals."

The term immortals refers to the ageless, deathless figures already known in Chinese Taoism by the third century before the common era. The story of Urashimako represents Tokoyo no Kuni not simply as a happy land of abundance but as a supernatural domain of longevity and even immortality. Over time, this supernatural view of Tokoyo no Kuni grew more widespread in Japan, but it was already discernible in the sixth century of the common era. Obviously, this vision of Tokoyo no Kuni was different from the one held earlier, when "wondrous beings" traveled between Tokoyo no Kuni and our realm. The later view developed under the influence of Taoist beliefs in immortals, which entered Japan from Korea and China over a long period, beginning in the fourth century. The change in the concept of Tokoyo no Kuni did not originate with the wealthy ruling class but resulted from contacts between the ordinary people and immigrants scattered throughout the country. The ideas were then gradually absorbed by the ruling classes.

According to the earlier notion, Tokoyo no Kuni was a marvelous place of blessings, a land of ancestral spirits, like the Okinawan Niraikanai; but only wondrous beings could travel there. It was a place for deities like Sukunabikona, not for ordinary mortals. Beginning in the eighth century, this older view of Tokoyo no Kuni became associated with the idea of Takamagahara, the High Heavenly Plain, from which the Sun Goddess's offspring had descended to rule Japan. Takamagahara was the very source of imperial authority, and only the aristocratic elite could hope to go there after death. The earlier view of Tokoyo no Kuni seems to have been similarly elitist and exclusive in nature.

Tokoyo no Kuni was a more accessible realm in the later, Taoist-influenced view. Of course, it was seen as the dwelling place of deities and immortals; yet Tajimamori was able to bring back the "timeless, fragrant fruit" after a journey of ten years. Tajimamori was not a divine being—he was the human ancestor of the Miyake no Muraji clan. And Urashimako was able to go to Tokoyo no Kuni, with the help of a supernatural female, and experience longevity and exquisite pleasures. Yet he was just a humble fisherman. Clearly the Taoist-influenced concept of Tokoyo no Kuni was more egalitarian and universal than the notion that originated among the aristocratic classes.

For the most part, Taoism was transmitted to Japan not by priests but by secular immigrants from Korea and China. From the seventh century on, the agents of transmission included Japanese students returning from the continent with a fund of experiences and documents. Though Taoism was, like Buddhism, a foreign faith, its mode of transmission to Japan was very different from that of Buddhism, which was introduced in an organized, systematic way through exchanges between the ruling classes of Japan and other lands. The effects of the unofficial mode by which Taoism was transmitted are apparent when we compare the notion of immortals in Japan with that on the Asian continent.

Taoist priests on the continent developed the idea of immortals not as imaginary or mythic beings but as actual people who had practiced the Way of the Immortals and thus managed to attain immortality. In Japan, however, there was neither institutional Taoism nor systematic practice of the Way of the Immortals. There was simply a body of indigenous traditions regarding supernatural beings. Popular attention tended to focus on female beings. Although in China the immortal was more often male, the female immortal became the dominant type in Japan.

Tales of swan-maidens, found all over the world, are familiar in Japan through the ancient, well-known story of the Feather-Robe (*hagoromo*) Maiden. Several variants of the story are known, but in all of them a supernatural maiden brings some sort of good fortune to mortals on earth. The *hagoromo* legend set at Lake Yogo, in Ōmi Province, was passed down in the Ikako district. In this version of the tale, a young man named Ikatomi manages to hide the feather robe of a supernatural maiden while she is bathing. Without her robe, the maiden cannot return to heaven, so she accepts the young man's proposal of marriage. She brings him happiness and good fortune and bears him four children. Later she discovers her feathery robe and returns to heaven. Her children become the ancestors of the Ikako no Muraji clan. In short, for a time the supernatural maiden became a human being, and she gave birth to ordinary human beings. From this we see that the general population, faced with the idea of immortals, sought to incorporate them into the fabric of their own lives and community.

This conception of immortal beings is quite different from the original continental idea of immortals, male or female. The difference is even more pronounced in the *hagoromo* legend connected with Manai Pond, on Mount Hiji, in Tango Province. In this version, an elderly couple hide the feather robe of a supernatural maiden they have discovered bathing. Unable to return to heaven without her robe, the maiden agrees to become their adopted child and enriches them by brewing a marvelous liquor. The old couple, now very rich, decide they have no more use for their "daughter" and drive her from their home. Grieving, she wanders from district to district until finally "she reaches the village of Nagu, in Funaki, and says to the people there: 'My heart is at ease here!' She settles in the village and becomes the goddess Toyoukanome no Mikoto, worshiped at Nagu Shrine in the Takano district." As her divine name implies, she became the goddess who governs the food the people live on and thus a vital part of the popular religion that dominated the daily lives of the ordinary citizens. In this way, the supernatural female became not an abstract figure in the Japanese pantheon but an integral part of the everyday religious life of the people.

To recapitulate, in Japan the idea of immortals was not linked to institutional Taoism. As informal Taoism found a place in the religious life of the Japanese people, emphasis shifted from male to female immortals, and a parent-child relationship between a female immortal and a local family was posited. In this way, the foreign idea of immortals merged with the indigenous cult of ancestral deities.

Though the institutional Taoism of the continent had little effect on Japanese beliefs, one tantalizing incident suggests that under different circumstances a similar religion might have evolved in Japan. The *Nihon Shoki* entry for the seventh month of the third year of the reign of Empress Kōgyoku (r. 642–45) describes the sudden appearance of a strange religious movement among the peasants of the Fuji River region in Suruga Province:

> One Ōfube no Ō, who seems to have been a member of the local gentry, began to preach the virtues of the deity of Tokoyo. The local shamans, both male and female, joined the movement, telling the peasants that the poor would become rich and the old regain their youth through worship of this deity. The populace, suffering from various hardships, eagerly accepted the new faith, offering sakè and whatever resources they had and singing and dancing wildly to cries of "New riches have come! New riches have come!" The central government, seeing that the peasants were being duped by this worthless, harmful superstition, sent Hata no Miyatsuko Kawakatsu [Hata no Kawakatsu] to punish Ōfube no Ō. The official's treatment of the offender was so severe that people were amazed, saying, "Kawakatsu is quite a man! How severely he punishes the priest of the deity of Tokoyo, who is said to be especially powerful among the *kami!*"

The Tokoyo mentioned here is not a land of ancestral spirits but a domain of the longevity and immortality represented by the Taoist immortals. The peasants were praying for youth, longevity, and wealth. No concern for those communal matters that lie at the very heart of the cult of the indigenous gods is evident. The emphasis is solely on fulfilling the material needs and desires of individual worshipers.

The new religion seems to have incorporated Taoist ideas and elements of shamanism and other folk beliefs. It spread quite widely and must have affected a significant number of the peasantry. There seems to have been a rudimentary religious organization, centered on the founder, Ōfube no Ō, and on local shamans and cult leaders. Of course, the nascent religion of the deity of Tokoyo was not identical with the organized Taoist faith of the continent, but it might have evolved into something similar.

The second and third centuries had seen the development of several Taoist organizations in China, and one can well imagine a similar development in seventh-century Japan based on the Tokoyo cult, had the government not intervened. But in fact the movement was swiftly suppressed. Terrified by the government's harsh treatment of Ōfube no Ō, his shaman associates stopped proselytizing and the faith disappeared from history. Thus, organized Taoism was stamped out by the government in the mid-seventh century.

Shugendō

Shugendō, the religion of the *yamabushi*, or "mountain-dwelling ascetics," was also known as the Shugen sect or "miscellaneous sect" (*zōshū*) during the Edo period (1603–1868). Physically, it is difficult to distinguish *yamabushi* from Buddhist priests, secular warriors of old, or Shintō priests. For example, the adherents of the Tōzan group, centered on Sambō-in, at Daigo-ji, Kyoto, shave their heads completely, like Buddhist priests, while the adherents of the Honzan group, centered on Shōgo-in, Kyoto, have a full head of hair. Nor is the elusive nature of Shugendō limited to its priests' physical appearance; its doctrines, too, are exceedingly difficult to classify.

There are three views of Shugendō: (1) It is a form of Shintō, since its followers seek to gain mystical powers through ascetic practice in mountains that, without exception, are associated with the cults of powerful indigenous mountain deities. (2) It is a form of Buddhism, because the *yamabushi* recite *dhāraṇīs*, mantras, and such sutras as the Heart of Wisdom Sutra and because since the twelfth century almost all *yamabushi* have been affiliated with either the Shingon (at Sambō-in) or the Tendai (at Shōgo-in) sect (even the five schools of Kojima *yamabushi*—Sonryū-in, Taihō-in, Kentoku-in, Dempō-in, and Hōon-in base their ascetic practice on esoteric Buddhism). (3) It is a form of yin-yang practice, since the aristocracy, the warrior class, and, from the twelfth century on, the peasantry thought of *yamabushi* as ascetics who had gained magical powers to cure illness and prevent accidents and other calamities through prayers and incantations. The prayers and incantations are varied, but most derive from Heian-period yin-yang magic, which developed from the Nara-period rituals of yin-yang experts and traditional healers.

Depending on the elements emphasized, then, views of Shugendō vary, and no single theory has gained general acceptance. Clearly, it is difficult to pigeonhole Shugendō, given its numerous disparate elements. In fact, any attempt to do so is misguided. We must not forget that Shugendō is an amalgam of traditional Japanese beliefs about indigenous deities and the beliefs of such foreign faiths as Buddhism and Taoism blended over a long period in the crucible of Japanese society, particularly that of the general population. It is thus a uniquely Japanese religious belief and practice.

In every age, Shugendō was an irritant to the religions that were firmly entrenched in the political power structure. It was regarded as heterodox by so-called Shrine Shintō, centered on the major shrines of the indigenous faith, and was attacked as an "evil teaching" by the major sects of Kamakura-period Buddhism, which warned their adherents against any involvement with it. Yet we cannot understand the religious life of the populace in the cities and in farming and fishing villages without taking into consideration the activities of the *yamabushi*.

THE RELIGIOUS LIFE OF THE VILLAGES

Popular Preachers

The theories and methods of attaining buddhahood or rebirth developed through long study and hard ascetic practice in such centers of institutional Buddhism as Mount Hiei and Mount Kōya were not transmitted directly to the ordinary people in the villages and towns. The members of the elite who were able to persevere in the long course of study and practice at these monastic centers remained there permanently. This does not mean, however, that the salvation offered by early Buddhism in Japan was entirely beyond the reach of the average man or woman. There were priests who preached various paths of salvation for the benefit of the ordinary people; these priests were known variously as *hijiri hōshi* (holy teachers), *shōnin* (holy men), and *shami* (literally, novices).

These popular preachers, who represented a disaffected element in the world of Buddhist monasticism, left the traditional centers and went to live among the general population in cities, towns, and villages. Though the names of many such preachers are known, by far the most famous are Kūya (903–72) and Kyōshin (d. 866), who was popularly known as the *Shami* of Kako.

Kūya left Mount Hiei to preach the doctrine of rebirth in the Pure Land through recitation of Amida's name. Kyōshin, who lived in Kako, in Harima Province, was an exemplar for those who aspired to rebirth in the Pure Land, including such pioneers of Kamakura-period Pure Land Buddhism as Shinran (1173–1262) and Ippen (1239–89). Kyōshin rejected the seclusion of the monastery and the search for personal salvation as a hermit isolated from the masses of ordinary people. He taught instead that believers should pursue their own practice while proselytizing. He not only spent many hours reciting the *nembutsu* but also preached to the masses, urging them to take refuge in Amida. His attitude exemplified the Mahāyāna Buddhist concern with compassionate acts for the sake of all sentient beings.

Of course, not all the popular preachers were as purely compassionate in their motives as Kūya and Kyōshin. There were also many ill-trained priests, failed students from the monasteries, and others of doubtful religious conviction. They wore priestly garb as a ruse to ease their way in life. Since they were neither learned nor diligent, they could not give the masses true guidance on matters of salvation, enlightenment, or rebirth. Collections of popular Heian-period tales contain numerous stories about sham clergy. Let us look at two examples.

The first tale, from the *Uji Shūi Monogatari* (A Collection of Tales from Uji; 1212–21), records the phenomenon of itinerant "holy" teachers of dubious accomplishments in a humorous fashion. One day an itinerant "holy teacher" appeared at the home of the courtier Minamoto no Morotoki (1077–1136), author of the diary *Chōshū Ki* (Long Autumn Record). The "holy" man began to speak piteously and eloquently of the painful, delusory nature of humans. He went on to say that since sexual desire is the very root of human delusions, he had some time before cut off his own "root" of passion as an expression of his desire to attain purity.

Morotoki, made suspicious by this announcement, asked for proof, whereupon the "holy" man rolled up the front of his robe and displayed his nakedness to the courtier. Indeed there was only hair to be seen where his genitals should have been. But the persistent Morotoki ordered some of his men to make a closer examination. It was apparent that the "holy" man had somehow tucked his penis into his scrotum and then glued hair over the whole area with rice paste in order to impress people with his asceticism and thus receive generous offerings. Morotoki and the others clapped their hands and roared with laughter at the discovery of this bold imposture; and the "holy" man himself, seeing the humor of his position, began to roll about on the ground in an uncontrollable fit of mirth.

The second story, also from the *Uji Shūi Monogatari*, tells of a "holy teacher" who announced that he would drown himself in order to be reborn at once in the Pure Land. In preparation, he performed the recitation of the Lotus Sutra for repentance of sins at Gidarin-ji, in Kyoto, for one hundred days. The news spread widely, not only in Kyoto but in the surrounding provinces as well, and soon the roads to Gidarin-ji were choked with masses of the devout, eager to see the "holy" man.

For one hundred days the "holy" man's reputation grew and grew. But when the final day came, the "holy" man kept putting off his entry into the water. He seemed to have lost his enthusiasm for the idea, but he could hardly ignore the expectations of the pious crowd gathered around him, so at last he reluctantly entered the water. Suddenly a man on the riverbank jumped in and pulled him from the water, whereupon the priest said, "I'll return this great favor in the Pure Land of Perfect Bliss!" and set off along the riverbank at a run. The angry crowd pursued him, throwing stones, but at last he reached the safety of his dwelling, badly bruised. From that day on, this fellow was said to have signed his letters "the 'holy man' who previously entered the water." Aside from making us laugh, this story tells us of the ordinary people's deep interest in rebirth in the Pure Land and of the ways unscrupulous priests preyed on them.

The popular preachers, then, were of all sorts. Since most of them were not learned, it was hard for them to preach the path of enlightenment or rebirth by quoting scriptural texts or through logical exposition. The most popular method of proselytism in the Heian period was the telling of stories of actual instances of salvation or enlightenment rather than the logical explanation of doctrines: in other words, the appeal to experience rather than to logic.

The Twenty-five *Samādhi* Association, a *nembutsu* group on Mount Hiei, was never active outside the monastery itself. Yet its leader, Yoshishige no Yasutane (ca. 931–1002), spread faith in the *nembutsu* among the general population by recording the biographies of people who had attained rebirth through *nembutsu* practice. Yasutane compiled the first collection of such biographies, the *Nihon Ōjō Gokuraku Ki* (Japanese Accounts of Rebirth in the Pure Land), sometime between 983 and 986. It contained biographies of approximately forty devotees, clerical and lay, male and female. Yasutane assembled his accounts by visiting cities and villages and collecting stories of the lives of such people. He also consulted historical sources for information in compiling his hagiographic stories, but more important than factually accurate accounts were stories that had been accepted and handed down by ordinary citizens as true accounts of salvation by Amida.

In his preface to the *Nihon Ōjō Gokuraku Ki,* Yasutane explains his motives in compiling it:

I have performed devotions to Amida Buddha daily since my early youth, and since reaching my fortieth year my faith in him has grown even stronger. Reciting his name, I visualize the excellences of his holy form. I have never failed to do this even for a moment. I am sure to always find even a few seconds for this devotion. An image or painting of Amida is enshrined in a hall or pagoda, and I always pay reverence to the image or painting. If there is anyone, male or female, clerical or lay, who aspires to [Amida's Pure Land of] Perfect Bliss and wishes for rebirth in his Pure Land, I do not fail to associate with that person. If I learn of a scripture, treatise, or commentary that treats of [Amida and] his glorious merits, I make a point of referring to it.

Shih Chia-ts'ai [fl. seventh century] of the temple Hung-fa-ssu in Great T'ang China wrote *Ching-t'u-lun* [Treatise on the Pure Land] containing accounts of twenty devotees who attained rebirth. Chia-ts'ai stated: "I have demonstrated the truth of rebirth through logic and quotations from both sutras and treatises. This is, I believe, great evidence. Yet most people, who are of limited intellect, are unable to understand the logic of [Amitābha's] salvation. Without accounts of actual instances of salvation, it is impossible to convince people and bring them to believe." How true his words are!

Another [Chinese work by the priests Wen-shen and Shao-k'ang (d. 805)], the *Shui-ying-chuan* [Hagiography of Good Omen], contains accounts of over forty devotees, some of whom slaughtered cows and others of whom sold fowl for a living—yet all of whom gained salvation. They encountered a good teacher, invoked the [Buddha's] name ten times, and attained rebirth. When I think of these people, my aspiration [to rebirth in the Pure Land] grows all the stronger!

Reading our national histories and the lives of various great men of the past, I became aware of various types of devotees who have been saved. I visited elders, and I learned of some forty people [who attained rebirth in the Pure Land of Perfect Bliss]. I was impressed. Keeping them in mind, I have compiled their biographies, and I have called this collection the *Nihon Ōjō Gokuraku Ki*. I hope that those who read this work in later times will cast aside doubt, and I pray that together with all sentient beings I may attain rebirth in the Land of Peace and Delight [Pure Land of Perfect Bliss].

We should note Yasutane's claim that arguments based on logic and on sutras and treatises are not adequate to lead ordinary people to faith because of their inferior intellectual capacity. Thus accounts of actual people who had been saved were needed to demonstrate the efficacy of the teaching. In short, empirical evidence was more important than theory in popular proselytism.

Yasutane's view dominated through the rest of the Heian period, leading to the production of many collections of pious biographies. Sometime between 1101 and 1111, the court official Ōe no Masafusa (1041–1111) compiled the *Zoku Honchō Ōjō Den* (Further Biographies of Japanese Who Attained Rebirth in the Pure Land), giving accounts of forty-two people ranging from emperors and state ministers to commoners. This work was used widely in popular proselytism. Around 1111, the man of letters Miyoshi Tameyasu (1049–1139) compiled the *Shūi Ōjō Den* (Gleanings of Accounts of Rebirth in the Pure Land); and sometime between 1123 and 1139 he compiled a sequel, *Go Shūi Ōjō Den* (Further Gleanings of Accounts of Rebirth in the Pure Land). The *shami* Renzen (fl. ca. twelfth century) compiled the *Sange Ōjō Ki* (A Record of Rebirths in the Pure Land Not Previously Recorded) shortly afterward, and the court noble Fujiwara no Munetomo (fl. twelfth century) compiled the *Honchō Shinshū Ōjō Den* (A New Edition of Biographies of Japanese Who Attained Rebirth in the Pure Land) in 1151. This hagiographic literature provides a well-defined view of the religious expectations and beliefs of the ordinary people.

Criteria for Rebirth

The accounts of rebirth in the Pure Land emphasize that rebirth is attained through the accumulated merits of a variety of buddhas, teachings, and practices. That is, the nonexclusive, polytheistic, and ascetic emphases of Nara and Heian Buddhism were reflected directly in the religious life of the general population and in the religious criteria believed necessary for rebirth or enlightenment.

The forms of practice cited in Heian-period hagiographies include recitation of the Lotus Sutra, devotion to the *nembutsu*, copying of the Lotus Sutra, recitation of the *Amida-kyō*, recitation of the *Ninnō Hannya-kyō*, memorization of the Lotus Sutra, *tendoku* reading (that is, reading just the first few lines of a sutra) of the Mahāyāna sutras, copying of the *Konkōmyō Saishōō-kyō*, *tendoku* reading of the *Konkōmyō Saishōō-kyō*, esoteric Buddhist rituals, vows to pray before statues of Kannon or Śākyamuni, fashioning of images of various buddhas, and construction of Buddhist halls and pago-das. There are also instances in which the spiritual aid of others—family, relatives, fellow believers, friends—is deemed necessary for rebirth.

In addition to religious criteria, personal criteria or qualifications—for example, certain desirable personality traits—were seen as necessary for salvation. The biographies frequently mention such traits as purity of heart; being undefiled by worldly concerns; not engaging in religious practice in an unworthy spiritual state; and meekness, sincerity, gentle-heartedness, compassion, and freedom from extremes of emotion. An interesting soci-ological note is that these qualities were deemed especially desirable for female believers.

The virtues of compassion and sincerity are most consistently noted as criteria for rebirth. Although it is important to perform meritorious reli-gious acts, of which reciting the *nembutsu* is perhaps most important, the compilers of the hagiographies assure readers that no matter how much merit is acquired through religious practice, rebirth is qualitatively differ-ent unless the twin virtues of compassion and sincerity are manifested. Moreover, sincerity is ranked above compassion in several tales. Miyoshi Tameyasu stresses the importance of sincerity as a personal qualification for rebirth in his preface to the *Shūi Ōjō Den:* "We understand that sincerity itself is the very gate to the Pure Land. Is this not why the sutra says, 'All those who are gentle and sincere will enter the Pure Land and behold the Buddha'?"

The primacy of sincerity is also evident in certain tales of the rebirth of people of indifferent, deeply flawed, or even evil character. Such people can attain rebirth if they eventually repent their misdeeds with sincerity and finally, with honest, open hearts, desire to be reborn in the Pure

Land. Some tales explain the rebirth of evil people in the Pure Land as the fruit of the karma of good deeds in past lives. It seems the compilers of the hagiographies wished to avoid discouraging anyone, whatever the person's social station or moral state, from despairing of the possibility of rebirth.

5. The Birth of Kamakura Buddhism

CHARACTERISTICS OF KAMAKURA BUDDHISM

Choice, Exclusive Practice, and Easy Practice

Hōnen (1133–1212), Shinran (1173–1262), Eisai (1141–1215), Dōgen (1200–1253), and Nichiren (1222–82), founders of major sects of Buddhism in the Kamakura period (1185–1336), all went to Mount Hiei to study at Enryaku-ji, the most influential center of traditional Buddhist learning and practice. Hōnen and Shinran discovered there a new form of Buddhist salvation suited to the new age. Nichiren, on the other hand, despaired of conditions at this stronghold of traditional Buddhism and left in quest of a new path to salvation—an intellectual pilgrimage that took him to most of the other traditional centers of Buddhist practice and study. Eisai and Dōgen found it necessary to leave Japan and seek new forms of practice in China. Ippen (1239–89), who never studied at any of the traditional centers, was greatly influenced by Hōnen's ideas in systematizing his own new form of faith.

These six religious leaders were the patriarchs of the new Buddhism that evolved in the Kamakura period. Extremely able and strong-willed individuals, they met the severe test of religious practice on Mount Hiei and at other traditional centers of Japanese Buddhism, as well as, in the cases of Eisai and Dōgen, in China. They went beyond the various forms of practice and devotion that Nara and Heian Buddhism had preserved, always seeking the true path of Buddhist salvation for those living in the new age.

From among the so-called eighty-four thousand gates to salvation, Hōnen, Shinran, and Ippen chose practice of the *nembutsu* as the sole path leading to rebirth in the Western Pure Land. They held that it was necessary only to recite the formula *Namu Amida Butsu* and to believe sincerely in Amida's power to save sentient beings. Eisai and Dōgen chose seated meditation (known as *shikan taza* or *senju zazen*) as the sole path by which mortals bound by delusion could sever those bonds and gain enlightenment, in the firm belief that this was the method directly and correctly handed down from the time of Śākyamuni himself. Nichiren became convinced that the Lotus Sutra represented the essence of the Buddha's teachings and chose the exclusive practice of the *daimoku*, recitation of the sutra's title, the formula *Namu-myōhō-renge-kyō*, as the practice leading to buddhahood.

Thus founders of the Kamakura sects taught that believers could choose a single practice—the *nembutsu*, Zen meditation, or the *daimoku*—and attain salvation through devotion to that practice alone. This was an "easy" mode of practice, in comparison with the arduous ascetic regimens of the Nara- and Heian-period Buddhist sects. Indeed, the three principles of choice, exclusive practice, and easy practice distinguish Kamakura Buddhism from earlier Japanese Buddhism. By rejecting the polytheism inherent in earlier Buddhism and focusing on a single buddha, sutra, or practice for salvation, the new sects introduced the first monotheistic beliefs in Japan's religious history.

The enlightenment pursued in the traditional monastic centers was reserved for those few who could endure the most rigorous study and religious practice. The founders of the new sects rejected the need for such rigor, which placed enlightenment beyond attainment by any but the full-time religious practitioner, isolated from the world. They claimed instead that any believer could be saved by a single recitation of the *nembutsu* with faith, by seated meditation unaccompanied by academic learning, or by recitation of the *daimoku*—very easy paths to salvation when compared with the methods of the earlier sects.

The traditional centers of Japanese Buddhism, especially Mount Hiei, had given birth to leaders who challenged the basic tenets of the older sects. It was unthinkable for the traditional centers to allow these reformers to remain in or return to the fold after their spiritual pilgrimages had led them to new beliefs and practices. Once the founders of the new faiths had rejected the teachings of the established sects and begun to preach their new insights, proselytizing among the general population, they cut themselves off from the traditional centers. In fact, no sooner had Hōnen chosen the *nembutsu* as his sole practice than he left Mount Hiei. Shinran also abandoned Mount Hiei, where he had lived for twenty years, and went to work among the populace.

In general, the founders of the new sects did not wait for opposition or for orders of expulsion. Once they had a clear understanding of their new position, they left the great monastic centers of their own accord and began their new task of proselytizing the masses.

Buddhism for the Common People

On leaving their monasteries, the founders of the sects of Kamakura Buddhism discovered a mass of potential followers, of both sexes and all social ranks. For most of them, this was a new experience. Moreover, the traditional centers were regarded as sacred precincts, to which no woman was admitted. Now the teachers found themselves surrounded by people of all sorts wanting to learn about the new paths of salvation, and there were numerous women among them—indeed, women outnumbered men in many cases. The new Buddhist leaders had to address a question never encountered at the monastic centers, namely, the possibility of salvation for women.

The old stories of miracles and wondrous rebirths were of little use in these new circumstances, because the personal and religious criteria for rebirth or enlightenment were coming to be viewed very differently. Kamakura Buddhism completely rejected the principles of nonexclusivity, polytheistic devotion, and ascetic practice that were central to the established sects and replaced them with the principles of choice, exclusive practice, and easy practice. The leaders of the new sects regarded the many buddhas, doctrines, and practices as "miscellaneous teachings" and rejected them as impediments to rebirth or enlightenment. It was also necessary to clearly reject the exemplars of the saved and enlightened who figured in earlier hagiographic literature; as a consequence, the new sects did not use these ready materials in their proselytism among ordinary people.

The new sects regarded as unnecessary the virtues of honesty, compassion, and gentleness, which the earlier Buddhism had insisted upon as essential for rebirth. In the case of Shinran, such thinking led to the doctrine known as *akunin shōki*, meaning that it is the "evil person" who has the right disposition for attaining rebirth in the Pure Land. According to

Shinran, the evil person burdened with lusts and passions is the clearest manifestation of humankind's real nature, and humankind's lusts and passions are so deeply rooted that they are unconquerable. Naturally, then, such virtues as honesty, compassion, and gentleness cannot be regarded as essential criteria for rebirth.

In the *Senchaku Hongan Nembutsu Shū* (The Choice of the *Nembutsu* of the Original Vow; 1198), Hōnen explains why he chose the *nembutsu* as the means of leading all sentient beings to rebirth:

> Because the *nembutsu* is easy, it provides universal salvation for all. Other practices are difficult and cannot be practiced by everyone. If making buddha images and erecting pagodas were a criterion for rebirth, the poor would lose all hope of salvation. . . . And far more people are poor than rich! If wisdom and intellectual abilities were criteria for rebirth, the dull and stupid or less intellectual would lose all hope of salvation. And far more people are stupid than wise! If breadth of knowledge were a criterion for rebirth, then the unknowledgeable would have no hope of salvation. And far more people are unknowledgeable than knowledgeable! If keeping the holy precepts and rules of morality were a criterion for rebirth, then those who break them or who lack them would have no hope of salvation. And far more people break the precepts than keep them! And so it is with all the other good works. You should know that none of them is essential for rebirth. For, as you can clearly see, if any of the various virtues and good works are made essential criteria for rebirth, then those who can be saved will be few, while those who cannot will be many. That is why Tathāgata Amida, when he was still the bodhisattva Dharmākara, wishing to save all sentient beings with equal compassion, chose not to make the erection of pagodas or buddha images a criterion for rebirth. The only criterion was the single practice of the *nembutsu*.

Thus did Hōnen, for the sake of the universal salvation of sentient beings, deny the necessity of the religious and personal criteria or qualifications that the general population of the Heian period had believed to be essential, and insist on practice of the *nembutsu* alone as a criterion for rebirth.

From Hagiography to Doctrine

In their preaching, the Kamakura sects could not use the Heian-period hagiographies to provide examples of holy men and devotees of the Pure Land teaching, since this literature embodied the very principles, criteria, and qualifications that the Kamakura Buddhist leaders had rejected. But neither did the founders of the Kamakura sects attempt to create their own hagiographic works extolling choice, exclusive practice, and easy practice, because there was as yet no popular tradition of Pure Land holy men and devotees consonant with the new Kamakura-period point of view.

In any case, while proselytizing among the masses, the Kamakura religious teachers did not need the traditional pious biographies and miracle stories. As elite scholar-priests from the traditional centers of Buddhist learning, they could judge the needs and abilities of their audiences and explain the profoundest doctrines in easily understood terms for the benefit of the uneducated. Through direct oral instruction, letters, and essays, they explained logically how the ordinary person could attain rebirth in paradise or buddhahood. Thus it was no longer necessary to bring people to faith by relying chiefly on the pious biographies of earlier times. The religious logic of salvation was no longer entirely beyond the people's grasp. The words quoted in the preface to the tenth-century collection *Nihon Ōjō Gokuraku Ki*—"Most people, foolish and of limited intellect, are unable to understand the logic of Amitābha's salvation. Without accounts of actual instances of salvation, it is impossible to convince people and bring them to believe"—were no longer relevant.

The founders of Kamakura Buddhism and their successors were able to explain the logic of salvation in terms that even uneducated people could understand. In contrast to the earlier reliance on pious biographies, appeals to the masses in the Kamakura period were based on reasoning. In the Heian period, biography, or empirical evidence, was stressed. In the subsequent period, the stress shifted to logic. This shift is evinced by the dearth of Kamakura-period Pure Land hagiographies.

Such hagiographies reappeared in large numbers in the Edo period (1603–1868), when they were once again used in proselytism. The preface to the *Shibyaku Ōjō Den*, a collection of stories of the rebirths of eighty-five people, both lay and clergy, compiled in 1688 by Ryōchi (d. 1751) of the Jōdo sect, notes the revival of Pure Land hagiography: "Many hagiographic collections were compiled in India, China, and Japan. In recent times, too, I observe numerous examples of devotees who have attained rebirth. Yet, since the middle of the thirteenth century, very few hagiographies have been preserved and handed down—to our loss! It is as if a great treasure were buried in the earth and not circulated. This is a matter of grave importance!" However, Pure Land hagiography disappeared during the Kamakura period not because it was hidden in the earth but because there was no need for it.

TRADITIONAL BUDDHISM IN THE KAMAKURA PERIOD

The Tendai Sect

By the twelfth century, new currents had appeared in Tendai doctrine. These developments can be regarded as an aspect of "medieval Tendai." Three are particularly important: the idea of original enlightenment (*hongaku*), emphasis on meditation, and high regard for private, oral transmission (*kuden*).

The term original enlightenment is used in contrast to gradual enlightenment (*shikaku*), which refers to the process of destroying delusions and ultimately attaining enlightenment or buddhahood. Original enlightenment identifies the idea that all sentient beings possess from the outset the essential nature of enlightenment. According to this concept, enlightenment is achieved through direct insight into one's own essentially enlightened nature, and other forms of religious practice are unnecessary.

Meditation (the means of attaining that insight into one's nature) and the state of original enlightenment are highly intuitive and experiential in nature. Thus oral transmission of the profoundest aspects of the doctrine was deemed best, and this resulted in an extremely subjective, nonsystematic means of imparting doctrine. One reason for this development was the generally positive attitude toward human nature at the time—the tendency to emphasize the innate capacity of human beings who were able to survive the violent transition from the Heian period to the Kamakura period. Though a strongly pessimistic view of life also persisted, the positive view dominated.

Yet there were other currents in the Tendai sect. The grand abbot Jien (1155–1225) sponsored lectures on Tendai theory, asking, "How can one withstand the decadence of the Decay of the Law without providing the expedient means of doctrinal theory?" In emphasizing lectures and debates on doctrine, Jien was following in the footsteps of Ryōgen (912–85). For both, mastery of Buddhist doctrine and theory was as important as meditation. Shōshin (fl. twelfth century) greatly helped Jien promote the formal study of Tendai doctrine. As is evident in his three works, collectively called the *Sandaibu Shiki* (Personal Account of the [Chih-i's] Three Major Works), Shōshin was typical of early medieval Tendai scholastic priests: he was deeply interested in textual study and was an empiricist.

The emphasis on textual and doctrinal studies favored by Jien and Shōshin contrasts sharply with the intuitive, meditative current also present in early medieval Tendai. The founders of the Kamakura sects inherited the textual and doctrinal tradition, and the intuitive, meditative tradition gave rise to two subsects within Tendai, the Eshin subsect and the Danna subsect. The Eshin subsect traces itself to Genshin (942–1017) of Eshin-in, in Ōtsu, and the Danna subsect claims Kakuun (953–1007) of Danna-in, on Mount Hiei, as its founder, though those connections are now known to be late inventions. Both subsects later split into smaller groups. The Eshin subsect spread in the Kantō region of Honshu during the Kamakura period and, under the nicknames "country Tendai" and "the country Eshin school," came to dominate Tendai thought in the early Edo period.

Under Annen (841?–901?), esoteric Tendai developed two subschools, the River school and the Valley school. Between 1242 and 1281 Shōchō (1205–82) wrote the *Asaba Shō* (Description of All Phases of Esoteric Tendai), summarizing the main points of esoteric Tendai theory and practice. Shōchō's work is as valuable as the masterwork of the Shingon scholar Kakuzen (1143–ca. 1217), the *Kakuzen Shō* (Collection of Kakuzen's Essays), composed between 1176 and 1213.

The Shingon Sect

The principal centers of Shingon were Tō-ji, in Kyoto, and Kongōbu-ji, on Mount Kōya, but Mount Kōya steadily declined in influence, partly because it lay so far from the center of power in the capital, eventually becoming little more than a branch temple under Tō-ji. In the twelfth century, however, Kakuban (1095–1143) largely restored Mount Kōya's fortunes, reviving the tradition of pilgrimage to Kūkai's tomb. But conflicts between Kakuban's supporters and the Kongōbu-ji clergy resulted in Kakuban's withdrawal to Negoro, in Kii Province, in 1139.

In the Kamakura period, too, there was friction between the priests of Daidembō-in, founded by Kakuban on Mount Kōya, and those of Kongōbu-ji. Finally, in 1288, Daidembō-in, together with its subtemple Mitsugon-in, was moved to Negoro. This move, overseen by Raiyu (1226–1304), led to the division of the sect into Old Shingon, based on Mount Kōya, and New Shingon, based at Negoro. Tō-ji, which was over-

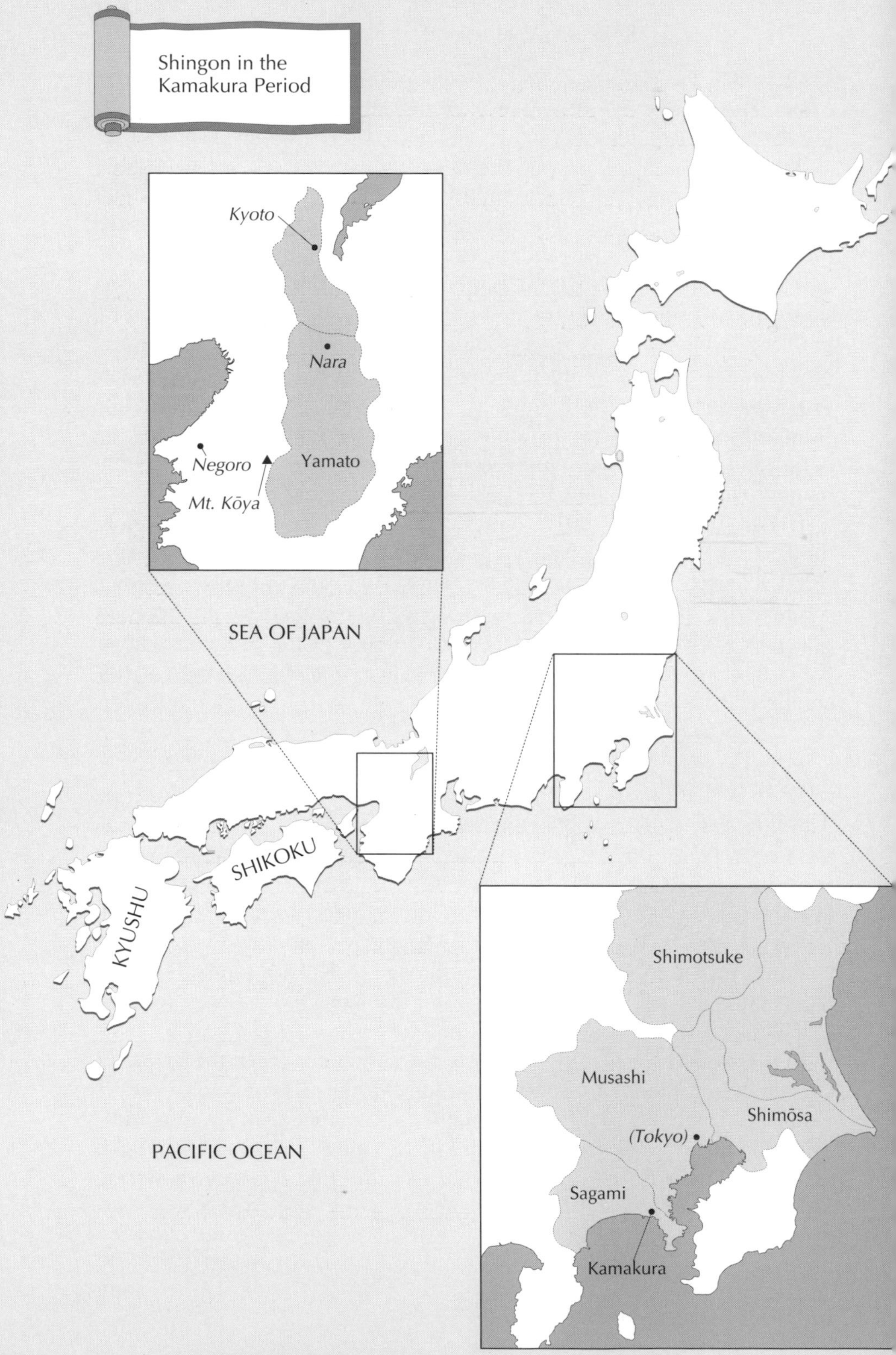

Shingon in the
Kamakura Period

Kyoto

Nara

Negoro

Mt. Kōya

Yamato

SEA OF JAPAN

KYUSHU

SHIKOKU

PACIFIC OCEAN

Shimotsuke

Musashi

Shimōsa

(Tokyo)

Sagami

Kamakura

shadowed by Ninna-ji and Daigo-ji during this period, recovered much of its earlier power in the general revival of Shingon under the patronage of the cloistered emperor Gouda (r. 1274–87).

As the center of political power shifted eastward, from Kyoto to Kamakura, so did Shingon activities. Raiken (1196–1273), of Sambō-in, a sub-temple at Daigo-ji, founded Jōraku-in in Kamakura and became the first patriarch of the Igyō subsect, which became the principal school of Shingon in the Kantō region. Of his disciples, Gangyō (d. 1295) spread Shingon in Sagami Province, and Jimyō (1212–77), of Yakushi-ji, in Shimotsuke Province, spread Shingon in Shimotsuke, Shimōsa, and Musashi provinces. Jimyō's lineage prospered through the efforts of his disciple Raison (d. 1316), the thirty-second head priest of Keisoku-ji, in Shimotsuke Province. By the Muromachi period (1336–1568), it not only dominated the Kantō region but also had spread to Hokurokudō, Shikoku, and Kyushu.

In the fourteenth and fifteenth centuries Shingon doctrine was systematized under the leadership of Raiyu and Shōken (1307–92), of Negoro; Yūkai (1345–1416) and Chōkaku (1340–1416), of Mount Kōya; and Gōhō (1306–62), of Tō-ji. In a sense, their activity was the Shingon response to the challenge of the new Kamakura sects. Also during this period, the Shingon priest Eikai (1278–1347) compiled the *Shingon Den* (The Transmission of Shingon; 1325), an account of the history of esoteric Buddhism in India, China, and Japan and of the lives of eminent priests of Shingon and of esoteric Tendai.

Pilgrimage to Mount Kōya, where, it was widely believed, Kūkai remained in a trance state, became more and more popular. *Hijiri* from Mount Kōya traveled about Japan urging faith in the cult of the living Kūkai and pious pilgrimage to his tomb. Gradually, Mount Kōya became popular as a burial site for believers. The Mount Kōya *hijiri* provided pilgrims with lodgings and guidance, and a relationship of spiritual teacher and pupil often developed between *hijiri* and pilgrim.

Finally, both medieval Tendai and medieval Shingon tended to form links with Shintō as filtered through esoteric Buddhist interpretations. These links were embodied as Sannō Shintō, in the case of Tendai, and Ryōbu Shintō, in the case of Shingon, both of which are discussed in chapter 12 (pp. 306–9).

The Nara Schools

At the end of 1180, in the early months of the Taira-Minamoto War

(1180–85), the warrior Taira no Shigehira (1157–85) attacked the old capital of Nara, burning important ancient temples, such as Tōdai-ji and Kōfuku-ji. The shocking destruction of venerable centers of Japanese Buddhism led many members of the clergy and the aristocracy to feel that they were witnessing the beginning of the end of Buddhism. A movement to restore Nara to its former glory arose, resulting in the imperial appointment of Chōgen (1121–1206) to direct the rebuilding of Tōdai-ji. However, in this early medieval period the Nara schools had to withstand another challenge, not material but religious: the exclusive practice of the *nembutsu*. Learning from the encounter, the Nara schools attempted their own response to the new age.

Hōnen had turned to exclusive practice of the *nembutsu* as early as 1175 and had spread this teaching and won many converts. Earlier, Kakuken (1131–1212), of Kōfuku-ji, grieving over the decadence of Buddhism's followers, had called for deeper faith and wisdom. His call was an acknowledgment of a spiritual crisis within Nara Buddhism. Kakuken's nephew and disciple Jōkei (1155–1213) attacked the exclusive practice of the *nembutsu* as preached by Hōnen and in 1205, in his well-known Kōfuku-ji Petition, called on the court to suppress it. Jōkei nurtured a new generation of scholars versed in the Buddhist precepts; and although devoted to the historical Buddha, Śākyamuni, he also fostered the cults of Miroku and Kannon. He also worked to develop the Hossō school into a more active and practicable branch of Buddhism.

Kōben (1173–1232) of the Kegon school also criticized the exclusive practice of the *nembutsu* in such works as the *Zaijarin* (The Error-destroying Wheel; 1212) and the *Zaijarin Shōgon Ki* (The Record of the Sublime Error-destroying Wheel; 1213). Like Jōkei, Kōben profoundly revered the historical Buddha. Twice he made plans to visit the holy sites in India associated with Śākyamuni, but they came to nothing. Kōben attempted to make the Kegon school more accessible and practicable, and three times each day he practiced veneration of the icon of the Three Treasures as the Aspiration to Enlightenment. Inscribed in the center of the icon was the formula "We take refuge in the Three Treasures—the Buddha, the Law, and the Order—Abiding in Their United, Differentiated, and Preserved Aspects." To the right was inscribed "The Wondrously Adorned Adamantine-Realm Mind in Its Myriad Aspects" and "The Great, Valorous, Wise, Compassionate Storehouse Mind." To the left was written "The Mind Firm as the Adamantine Guardians of the Law," and above and below this was written "The Mind That Is Inexhaustible as the Great Ocean of Sentient

Beings." Above and to the sides were the Sanskrit words for the Three Treasures, in Indic script.

Discernible in this Kegon icon are not only esoteric Buddhist elements but also the influence of the exclusive practice of the *nembutsu*. In fact, Kōben suggested that to attain salvation it was sufficient for lay believers to recite the formula "We take refuge in the Three Treasures! Save us after death!" He also preached the importance of a form of meditation on the Buddha's light, and he offered a simplified meditation on the mantra of radiant light (*kōmyō shingon*): "Reverently we take refuge. *Fukū Henjō Son! Daiinja!* Manifest the radiance of the jewel [*mani*] and the Lotus! *Hūṃ* [a secret word meaning 'as indestructible as a diamond']!" Kōben taught that recitation of this mantra would help avert illness and catastrophe and expiate sins in this life, while sand blessed with this invocation and sprinkled on a corpse would help the deceased attain a more fortunate rebirth. In effect, Kōben was practicing esoteric Buddhism.

Both Jippan (d. 1144), of Nakanokawa-dera, in Yamato Province, and Jōkei were active in a movement to revive observance of the monastic precepts. The Tendai priest Shunjō (1166–1227) studied the precepts in China and returned to propagate them at Sennyū-ji, in Kyoto. The priests gathered to study the precepts (*ritsu*) at Sennyū-ji came to be known as the Hokkyō (Northern Capital) Ritsu school to distinguish them from the Nankyō (Southern Capital) Ritsu school of Nara.

Such activities lent great impetus to the revival of interest in Buddhist discipline. But the custom of giving and receiving the orthodox precepts had long been dormant, and there were no qualified preceptors. In 1236 Kakujō (1194–1249), Eizon (1201–90), Yūgon (1186–1275), and Ensei (1180–1241)—who had studied the precepts at Jōki-in, a subtemple of Tōdai-ji founded by Jōkei—administered the precepts to themselves at the Great Buddha Hall of Tōdai-ji, in the absence of a qualified preceptor. The four then set about restoring the Ritsu school.

Kakujō worked at the Nara temple Tōshōdai-ji, associated with the Ritsu school since the days of the Chinese master Chien-chen (688–763). Eizon established himself at Saidai-ji, in Nara, where in addition to promoting observance of the precepts he spread devotion to the bodhisattva Monju, Prince Shōtoku (574–622), and the itinerant priest Gyōki (also known as Gyōgi; 668–749). He urged the general population to recite what he called "the Śākyamuni *nembutsu*" and the mantra of radiant light, and generally labored to make the Ritsu school a living religious movement that appealed to ordinary people. At the invitation of the former regent Hōjō

Tokiyori (1227–63) and his kinsman Hōjō Sanetoki (1224–76), Eizon traveled to eastern Japan, but it was his disciple Ninshō (1217–1303) who actually spread the knowledge and practice of the precepts in eastern Japan. Like his master, Ninshō did a good deal of religious work among the various outcast groups known as *hinin* (literally, nonhumans), through the Monju cult.

Thus the revival of the Buddhist schools of Nara and their response to the challenges of the Kamakura period relied on major borrowings from esoteric Buddhism and were strongly influenced by Pure Land teachings. Elements of the cult of Miroku, the buddha of the future, were also adopted.

At the same time, a current of historical reflection inspired by the sense of crisis in contemporary Buddhism resulted in such works as the *Sangoku Dentō Ki* (A Record of the Transmission of the Lamp in India, China, and Japan; 1173) by Kakuken and the *Nihon Kōsō Den Yōmon Shō* (Important Passages from the Biographies of Eminent Japanese Priests; 1249–51) by Sōshō (1202–78), of Tōdai-ji. Toward the end of the Kamakura period, Gyōnen (1240–1321), of Tōdai-ji, compiled the *Sangoku Buppō Denzū Engi* (An Account of the Transmission of Buddhism in India, China, and Japan; 1311). In the section on Japanese Buddhism, Gyōnen discusses the six Nara schools and the two sects of Heian-period Buddhism, Tendai and Shingon. For him, these eight sects or schools constitute orthodox Japanese Buddhism, and he does not mention either Pure Land or Zen.

Clearly, traditional Nara and Heian Buddhism not only attempted to respond to the challenge of the new Kamakura sects but succeeded in maintaining and even enhancing its strong position in medieval Japanese society.

6. The Jōdo Sect

THE JŌDO SECT IN THE KAMAKURA PERIOD

Hōnen

Hōnen (1133–1212), founder of the Jōdo, or Pure Land, sect, was the son of Uruma no Tokikuni, the head of a powerful local family and also constable of the Kume Nanjō Inaoka estate, in Mimasaka Province. One night in 1141 Tokikuni was suddenly attacked by the estate steward. As constable, Tokikuni maintained law and order on the estate, while the steward managed the estate for its absent landlord. Animosity between the two was fed by the question of the expansion of the estate. Mortally wounded, Tokikuni called Seishimaru, as Hōnen was known as a child, to his side and, as Hōnen later recalled, admonished him thus: "I do not want you to avenge my death. I have realized that this might be karmic retribution from my previous life. My wound is very painful and my suffering is great. For the first time, I realize how others suffer. If you cling to hatred and kill my enemy, then his son will surely turn his blade on you and inflict the same suffering I now endure. If we attack, they must counterattack—that is the way of the warrior. Therefore, however hard it may be for you, I want you to cast aside all hatred of our enemy, embrace religion, and pray for my salvation. This is my final request of you, my son."

The fatherless boy reached Mount Hiei in 1145 after having taken refuge with an uncle, the priest Kangaku, who soon realized that the boy's talents would be wasted in a country temple and entrusted him to an old friend on Mount Hiei, Genkō. Later young Hōnen was sent to study under

Kōen (d. 1169), a priest and scholar from the Fujiwara clan, who urged his young charge to devote his life to study and become a pillar of Tendai scholasticism. However, Mount Hiei had become a place where birth counted as much as learning, and a young priest from a ruined family of the provincial gentry could not expect to rise in its hierarchy. Nevertheless, Hōnen devoted himself to study and practice on Mount Hiei for twelve years.

In a sense, Mount Hiei's reputation as the supreme center for the academic study of Buddhism in Japan was exaggerated. Its atmosphere was hardly conducive to quiet study and earnest practice. Warrior-priests were employed by both sides in the strife between Mount Hiei and Onjō-ji, and occasional raids on the capital enforced Mount Hiei's demands on the court and its ministers. What had been the seat of Japanese Buddhist scholarship was fast becoming a constant battleground.

Hōnen's desire to devote himself to peaceful study and practice was finally realized when he retired to Kurodani, in the Western Precincts on Mount Hiei, where the well-known Eikū (d. 1179) lived. Hōnen is reputed to have read the entire Buddhist canon, consisting of thousands of scrolls, several times in the course of his religious career.

The first Pure Land text that Hōnen read was Genshin's *Ōjō Yōshū* (Essentials of Rebirth; 984–85), which he encountered at Kurodani. The *Ōjō Yōshū* stresses meditation on Amida's form and visualization of the excellences of the Pure Land. If meditation is beyond a practitioner's abilities, the practitioner should recite the Buddha's name. Meditation is regarded as superior and recitation as inferior. But Eikan's *Ōjō Jūin* (Ten Causes for Rebirth in the Pure Land; eleventh century), which Hōnen read while studying in Nara, treats invocation of the Buddha's name as primary and meditation as secondary. The source of Eikan's interpretation is said to be the *Kuan-ching-su* (Commentary on the Sutra of Meditation on Amitābha Buddha) by the seventh-century Chinese master Shan-tao.

Hōnen encountered Shan-tao's work while reading the canon in the spring of 1175. He discovered a critical passage in the section titled "San-shan-i": "The correct practice for salvation is simply to wholeheartedly recite Amitābha's name only, without regard to whether one is standing, walking, sitting, or lying and irrespective of whether the period of recitation is long or short, and to continue to do so moment by moment—this is called 'the rightly determined practice' because it accords with Amitābha's Great Vow." On reading these words, Hōnen realized that recitation of Amida's name was sufficient to ensure rebirth.

Shan-tao's *Kuan-nien-fa-men* (The Doctrine of Meditation) states that of one hundred people who recite the *nembutsu*, one hundred will be reborn in the Pure Land. To meditate on the Buddha and his Pure Land is difficult for ordinary people, but anyone can invoke the Buddha's name. For average mortals, no practice but the *nembutsu* leads to salvation. As far as salvation is concerned, there is no distinction between clergy and laity, men and women, wise and foolish, rich and poor, or old and young. The *nembutsu* constitutes a path to salvation open to all who suffer in the present world, in which it is impossible to live without sinning. The realization of this fact constitutes "conversion of the mind" (*eshin*), which is the basic tenet of Hōnen's religious teaching.

The Buddha's great compassion is directed toward all who suffer. To find salvation, human beings must discover a religion suited to their condition, the age in which they live, and their capacities. In his *Jōdo Shū Taii* (The Great Meaning of the Pure Land Sect; ca. 1190), Hōnen affirms: "If one wishes to be free of the cycle of birth and death, one must understand three things: the nature of the age, the nature of one's capacities, and the nature of the teachings." According to Hōnen, the present age is that of the Decay of the Law, and the ordinary person is sunk in a deep pit of suffering. People are not learned in Buddhist doctrine, and even if they try to keep the precepts they fail. It was precisely for such people, living in such an age, that Śākyamuni Buddha long ago prepared the Pure Land path to salvation.

Hōnen goes on to say that Tendai, Shingon, and Kegon possess profound doctrinal systems and the path to enlightenment through their teachings requires both deep knowledge and strict religious discipline. The great majority of people are unable to master those sects' doctrines, which Hōnen calls the Gate of the Holy Path. Nor can ordinary people practice the complex rituals of the Shingon sect. No matter how venerable the Gate of the Holy Path, if most people cannot pass through it, it must be classified as the Path of Difficult Practice. The great compassion of the Buddha, who seeks to save all sentient beings without exception, is directed toward the mass of ordinary people, without distinction between clergy and laity, man and woman, rich and poor, or noble and commoner. The Buddha's compassion offers solace to those who, living in an age of conflict and violent change, are stricken with guilt over their own sinfulness. Hōnen says that by assuring the "evildoers" that they can attain salvation by invoking his name, the Buddha tries to help them rise out of the depths of their despair.

Having converted to the exclusive practice of the *nembutsu*, Hōnen soon

Hōnen and
the Jōdo Sect

SEA OF JAPAN

Echigo

Echizen

Shinano

Hitachi

Musashi   KANTŌ

Kyoto

Ōmi   (Tokyo)   Shimōsa

Sagami

Settsu

Kamakura

PACIFIC OCEAN

left Mount Hiei and went to visit Enshō (1139–77). In the *Myōgi Shingyō Shū*, biographies of the eight eminent priests who attained rebirth in the Pure Land through reciting the name of Amida and their religious concepts, compiled by his second-generation disciple Shinzui (d. 1279), Hōnen says of this meeting: "Learning of the doctrine of the Pure Land and encountering Yūrenbō [Enshō] are the two greatest memories of the life I was given in the realm of human beings." His joy at discovering the Pure Land teaching was equaled only by his joy at meeting Enshō, a *nembutsu hijiri* who owned no scriptural or scholarly texts and devoted himself exclusively to the *nembutsu*. It was rumored that Enshō had been blessed with supernatural visions as proof that he would attain rebirth through this exclusive practice. Hōnen probably stayed with him in his hermitage in Hirodani, Nishiyama, in Yamashiro Province for a year or two, and he greatly influenced Hōnen's thinking.

Enshō was the son of the courtier and scholar Fujiwara no Michinori (1106–59). When Enshō died, after years of *nembutsu* practice, his hermitage was given to Hōnen, who removed it to Yoshimizu, in the Higashiyama district of Kyoto. It became known as the Yoshimizu Central Hermitage and was one of a group of buildings that multiplied with the increase of Hōnen's followers: the Eastern New Hermitage, the Western Old Hermitage, and the Buddha Hall. The Western Old Hermitage seems to have been built first. Some followers lived in the compound, but most came from their own lodgings to hear Hōnen preach in the Buddha Hall. Hōnen is said to have had 190 ordained followers, and the number of lay believers of all ages and both sexes who gathered to hear the teachings must have been far greater.

Hōnen spent a good deal of time and energy teaching by means of epistles, long, instructive letters to those who could not come to hear him preach. In his epistles he answered a wide variety of questions with common sense and a deep understanding of the principles of Buddhism. For example, he denied that breaking the rule of Buddhist discipline against eating certain foods would prevent one from attaining enlightenment. One follower asked about the practice of linking an image of Amida to a believer near death with a five-colored cord to ensure quick rebirth in the Pure Land: "It is said that a five-colored cord should be attached to the left hand of Amida's image when someone is at the point of death. When I die, which hand should I use to grasp the other end of the cord?" Hōnen lightly replied: "Both hands should be used." He denied the existence of taboos in Buddhism, labeling them secular beliefs. He challenged the common belief, stemming from filial piety, that it is wrong to die before one's parents: "In this defiled realm, such things often happen. People cannot control whether they die before or after their parents."

Thus did Hōnen teach his followers directly. Toward the beginning of 1198, Hōnen developed a high fever after catching cold, and it seemed that he might die. This experience made his disciples aware of the need to have him record his teachings systematically. Responding to the requests of his disciples and of influential supporters like the courtier Kujō Kanezane (1149–1207), Hōnen wrote the *Senchaku Hongan Nembutsu Shū* (The Choice of the *Nembutsu* of the Original Vow; 1198). Toward the end of this work he writes:

> If one wishes to be free of this suffering-filled world of birth and death, there are two excellent paths. One should for now set aside the Gate of the Holy Path leading to attainment of enlightenment in this life and choose the Gate of the Pure Land, in which one receives salvation through other-power [*tariki*]. Wishing to receive such salvation, one discovers two kinds of practice: the right, single practice and other, miscellaneous practices. One must cast aside the miscellaneous practices and throw oneself wholeheartedly into the right, single practice. . . . This single right form of practice is none other than recitation of the name of Amida. If you recite the name, you can surely be reborn in the Pure Land, because this is in accord with Amida's original vow.

Hōnen's major contributions to Japanese Buddhist thought and practice are all here: exclusive practice of the *nembutsu*, belief in Amida's vow, and reliance on Amida's power—as Hōnen puts it, other-power, in contrast to self-power (*jiriki*), or relying on one's own efforts to attain enlightenment.

Opposition to Exclusive Practice of the Nembutsu

Open opposition to Hōnen and his teachings began in the tenth month of 1204, when priests at Enryaku-ji appealed to the Tendai grand abbot Shinshō (1167–1230) to suppress the exclusive practice of the *nembutsu*. They claimed that some of Hōnen's followers were preaching that sin was of no consequence if one practiced the *nembutsu*. Allowing such ideas to spread would only encourage evildoers, they insisted, and exclusive practice of the *nembutsu* should be forbidden at once. Shinshō immediately informed Hōnen of this complaint, and Hōnen adopted a conciliatory attitude. He issued his *Shichikajō Kishō Mon* (Seven Articles; 1204), rebuking those of his followers who misrepresented his teachings and warning them to take care in their preaching not to distort or exaggerate his message.

The grand abbot, well aware that Hōnen had been trained on Mount Hiei, wished to settle the dispute quietly, as an internal matter of the Tendai sect. But the Nara clergy objected strongly to Hōnen's teachings and attacked him on nine points. These included charges that he ignored and slighted Śākyamuni Buddha, giving precedence to Amida; that he stigmatized all practices other than the *nembutsu* as "miscellaneous" and urged people to abandon practices that were universally acknowledged to be rich sources of merit; that he despised the indigenous deities; and, interestingly, that he and his followers composed pictures in which Buddhists who do not practice the *nembutsu* are excluded from Amida's radiant light.

Led by Jōkei (1155–1213), the Nara clergy appealed to the cloistered emperor Gotoba (r. 1183 98) to forbid exclusive practice of the *nembutsu* and to punish its supporters, above all, Hōnen. The court responded by ordering certain ministers to look into the matter and recommend appropriate action. Of the four ministers appointed to the task, two strongly supported the Nara clergy's position, but two urged the government to proceed with caution. The ministers supporting Hōnen feared that strife and repression within the ranks of the clergy would lead only to disillusionment with Buddhism as a whole and increase civil unrest.

The Nara clergy wished to suppress the *nembutsu*, first, out of fear that the popularity of the practice would lead to a decline of interest in and support for the more traditional sects and, second, out of fear that the spread of *nembutsu* faith would encourage all manner of evil and vice, since Hōnen taught that even sinners would be saved by Amida if they recited the *nembutsu*. Eventually Gotoba bowed to the wishes of the Nara clergy. He ordered Hōnen's disciple Junsai (d. 1207) executed and exiled Hōnen and several other disciples, including Gyōkū (fl. thirteenth century), Kōsai, and Shinran (who later founded the Jōdo Shin sect). Hōnen lived outside Kyoto for four years and nine months, from the second month of 1207 to the eleventh month of 1211. He probably stayed in his designated place of exile no longer than nine months; but unable to receive permission to reenter the capital after that, he spent a long time at Kachio-dera, in Settsu Province.

Within three months of his return to the capital in 1211 Hōnen died, perhaps because of the hardships of his journey into exile and the sorrow and strain he suffered. The reaction against the *nembutsu* movement grew stronger following his death. As was noted earlier, Kōben of the Kegon school composed anti-*nembutsu* treatises, the *Zaijarin* and the *Zaijarin Shōgon Ki*, in 1212 and 1213. Later, in the sixth month of 1227, priests from Enryaku-ji violated Hōnen's grave in an attempt to unearth his body and throw it into the Kamo River. Kōben's doctrinal criticism of Hōnen's teaching was reinforced by Jōshō (fl. thirteenth century), who wrote the *Dan Senchaku* (An Attack on Hōnen's *Senchaku Hongan Nembutsu Shū;* 1225), and Kōin (1145–1216) of Onjō-ji, who wrote the *Jōdo Ketsugi Shō* (On Definite Doubts Concerning the Pure Land; thirteenth century).

Kōben's main grievances were that Hōnen had ignored the "aspiration to enlightenment" (*bodaishin*), which Kōben considered to be fundamental to all Buddhism, and that Hōnen had outrageously compared the Gate of the Holy Path—the Tendai, Shingon, and Kegon sects—to a band of robbers. (The doctrine of the aspiration to enlightenment implies that all living things possess the potential for enlightenment and that they need to arouse and realize that potential.) Kōben also claimed that Hōnen rejected the attainment of enlightenment in this life as a Difficult Practice and insisted that the *nembutsu* alone was sufficient to ensure rebirth in the Pure Land, there being no need for the aspiration to enlightenment. Yet for Kōben, there could be no Buddhism without the aspiration to enlightenment.

Kōben described Hōnen as "the chief destroyer of the Law in the present age," "the greatest enemy of Buddhism in the three worlds of the past, present, and future," and "a great misleader of sentient beings." In their objections and the vehemence of their rhetoric, the writings of Kōin and Jōshō resembled those of Kōben; together these works fueled the controversy surrounding *nembutsu* practice and the community of *nembutsu* believers.

The Nembutsu Community in Kyoto

Followers of the exclusive practice of the *nembutsu* wore black robes, recited devotions six times daily, and lived communally in places in and near Kyoto, such as Gion, Nakayama (near Kurodani), Higashiyama Ōtani, and Kiyomizu, and at Seiryō-ji, in Saga. Higashiyama Ōtani, where Hōnen's tomb was located, was the center of their spiritual activities. In addition to Hōnen's body being enshrined there, an image of him carved from life had a special place. The work of Hōnen's lay disciple Kuwabara Saemon (fl. thirteenth century), the image was tended day and night as if it were the master himself. On the twenty-fifth day of each month a host of people gathered to honor Hōnen's memory. It was said that on these memorial days Higashiyama Ōtani was as crowded as a public fair. In this way, the tomb at Higashiyama Ōtani became the mecca of Hōnen's Jōdo sect, a focus of devotion for all believers.

After Hōnen's death Shinkū (1146–1228), his senior disciple, was in charge of the sect's affairs. In 1227, when Enryaku-ji priests attacked his tomb, Hōnen's body was saved from the hands of the raiders and transferred to Ao in Nishiyama, where it was finally cremated. Hōnen's ashes were eventually divided among his principal disciples and enshrined at various spots associated with him.

Shinkū in Higashiyama Ōtani, Genchi (1183–1238) in Shirakawa Hombō, Tankū (1176–1253) at Nison-in, in Saga, and Shōkū (1177–1247) at Ao in Nishiyama, constructed tombs for Hōnen's ashes, providing focuses for the devotion of *nembutsu* followers. As a result, Hōnen's followers separated into distinct groups: the Shirakawa group, led by Shinkū; the Murasakino group, led by Genchi; the Saga group, led by Tankū; and the Seizan group, led by Shōkū. Somewhat later, such temples as Chion-in, Hyakumanben Chion-ji, and Nison-in (all in Kyoto), and Kōmyō-ji (in Yamashiro Province) were founded. Each temple possessed a tomb containing a portion of Hōnen's ashes and functioned as a center of Jōdo sect devotion.

Some of Hōnen's disciples—such as Ryūkan (1148–1227), Kōsai (1163–1247), and Chōsai (1184–1266)—founded their own groups of like-minded followers based on differing interpretations of Hōnen's teachings. All these subgroups rapidly declined, however, because they lacked tombs containing relics of Hōnen.

Shinkū was Hōnen's favorite disciple. He had joined Hōnen at the age of eleven, when Hōnen was still on Mount Hiei. Both were students of Eikū, and when Hōnen discovered the doctrine of exclusive practice of the *nembutsu*, Shinkū was the first to be converted and become Hōnen's disciple. For the next fifty years, Shinkū studied the doctrine directly under his teacher. Since he was never banished from the capital, it seems likely that he spent his days quietly in the Ōtani center, trying to unite the disciples and preserve the new community. Genchi and Tankū cooperated with him in this task.

It was Shōkū who showed the greatest enthusiasm for the development of the Jōdo sect. The adopted son of the inner minister Koga Michichika (1149–1202), Shōkū was able to emerge unscathed from the persecution of the mid-1220s, and he was largely responsible for the acceptance that the new Jōdo teaching gained among the aristocracy. But above all he labored to introduce adherents of his Seizan group into other temples, beginning with the important temple Chion-in. Having succeeded at Chion-in, he gained great influence at a large number of lesser temples as well.

Around the end of the thirteenth century the Chinzei group, which traced its origin back to Shōkō (1162–1238), began making rapid advances in the capital. Shōkō, who had been with Hōnen for only about eight years, had been occupied mainly in spreading the Jōdo sect on northern Kyushu. The desire to acquire a tomb enshrining Hōnen's ashes provided the impetus for the Chinzei group's advance into the capital almost one hundred years after Hōnen's death. Hōnen's ashes and a statue of Hōnen carved while he was alive were essential objects of devotion for the groups of Hōnen's followers. By compromising with other groups and asserting its own orthodoxy, the Chinzei group was able to gain administrative control of Nison-in from the Seizan group and eventually control of Chion-in itself, which contained Hōnen's primary tomb.

Ryōchū

Shōkō's disciple Ryōchū (1199–1287) quickly moved into the Kantō region. He had reported the presence of more than thirty followers of exclusive practice of the *nembutsu* in Musashi Province alone before Hōnen's death. Moreover, since these thirty-odd believers were members of the warrior class, it seems likely that a number of their retainers and dependents also were *nembutsu* believers. At that time Shibuya Shichirō (fl. ca. 1200), whose religious name was Dōhen and who had received the teaching directly from Hōnen, was in Ishikawa, in Sagami Province. When he learned that Ryōchū was in the nearby province of Shimōsa, he expressed a strong desire to meet him.

Hōnen had converted the leaders of the samurai houses of Ōgo, Kumagai, and Chiba, and the younger generation inherited their parents' devotion to the *nembutsu*. Hidemura (fl. ca. thirteenth century), grandson of Ōgo no Koshirō Takayoshi (ca. early thirteenth century), was said to chant the *nembutsu* day and night, faithfully following directions given in Hōnen's letters. The dependents of the military leader Kumagai Naozane (1141–1208) apparently built a hall for recitation of the *nembutsu* within their manor, with a mandala depicting the descent and welcome of Amida and his bodhisattvas painted by Hōnen himself as the principal object of devotion. Supported by such families, Ryōchū traveled along the reaches of the Tone River in Shimōsa and succeeded in converting the entire Chiba clan to exclusive practice of the *nembutsu*. In addition to zealous missionary activity in Shimōsa, he devoted himself to writing. While he could and did expound the *nembutsu* to ordinary people in an intimate, personal way, he was basically a scholar.

Ryōchū advocated reciting the *nembutsu* as many times as possible. However, there were people in eastern Japan who advocated salvation by means of a single invocation of Amida's name; and others, under the influence of the Tendai and Shingon sects, claimed that the *nembutsu* was not the only practice chosen by Amida in his vows, but that one could gain rebirth in the Pure Land by means of various practices. Indeed, doctrines that Hōnen would have deemed heterodox were highly influential among *nembutsu* followers in eastern Japan.

Those who advocated exclusive practice of the *nembutsu* were subjected to strong pressure from the established sects, because insistence on sole practice of the *nembutsu* denied the possibility of rebirth in the Pure Land through the practices of other sects and led to the abandonment of many hallowed religious practices. Eventually Ryōchū, too, began to feel these pressures.

Around 1260, having endured considerable financial and emotional difficulty, Ryōchū left Shimōsa and went to Kamakura, the seat of the military government. But in Kamakura he was able to gain the use of a small temple only through the goodwill of a local *hijiri* known as Jōkō. His followers were forced to engage in commerce, hearing the teachings and spreading what they had learned when not occupied in buying and selling. Gradually, local estate holders and influential stewards were converted, and when the warrior Hōjō Tomonao (1206–64) and his son became believers, they contributed paddy fields for rice growing and living quarters to Ryōchū's group.

Ryōchū's preaching incorporated interpretations colored by Tendai and Shingon doctrines. As cooperative relations with the established sects developed, Ryōchū's group began to prosper and Ryōchū became known as a leading representative of the *nembutsu* movement in Kamakura. In his *Gyōbin Sojō On Etsū*, a letter of 1253 replying to Gyōbin's petition submitted to the imperial court, Nichiren, a vehement opponent of the *nembutsu* movement, spoke in the same breath of "Ryōkan, the priest best known in the land for keeping the precepts, and Hōnen's second-generation disciples Nen Amida Butsu and Dō Amida Butsu." Nen Amida Butsu was Ryōchū, and Dō Amida Butsu was Dōkyō (fl. early thirteenth century).

Nichiren ranked them with Ryōkan—that is, Ninshō (1217–1303)—of Gokuraku-ji, in Kamakura, a leading figure in the Buddhist world of the time. Nichiren's statement was made around 1271—little more than ten years after Ryōchū arrived in Kamakura.

From then on, the Jōdo sect developed around Chion-in, in Kyoto, and Kōmyō-ji, the seat of Ryōchū's group, in Kamakura. Ryōchū's followers divided into six subgroups: the Shirahata, led by Jakue (1251–1328); the Nagoe, led by Sonkan (1239–1316); the Fujita, led by Shōshin (d. 1299); the Kobata, led by Jishin (d. 1297); the Ichijō, led by Raia (d. 1297); and the Sanjō, led by Dōkō (1243–1330). Today the Jōdo sect counts Ryōchū as the third patriarch and Jakue as the fourth, based on the assumption that the Shirahata subgroup was the orthodox successor of Hōnen. Ryōchū seems to have stressed his status as third patriarch to an extraordinary degree, which suggests that many others must also have claimed to be Hōnen's sole legitimate successor. This defensiveness was transmitted to Ryōchū's disciples. Shōshin gave his disciple Ryōshin (d. 1314) a copy of Ryōchū's *Kettō Jushuin Gimon Jō* (Definite Answers to Questions About the *Nembutsu;* 1257) in 1293. He added a postscript on the copy that he himself had copied. In the postscript, Shōshin said: "The teachings of Hōnembō Genkū [Hōnen] were all transmitted to Ben A[mida Butsu] Shōkō, just like water poured from one vessel to another. Shōkō's teachings in turn were received by Nen A[mida Butsu] Ryōchū, who transmitted them to me. I myself am the fourth-generation heir in the direct line of succession from Hōnen."

The six subgroups did not differ doctrinally; they were simply seated in different areas. The sole exception was the difference of opinion between Sonkan and Jakue regarding the efficacy of a single invocation versus multiple invocations of Amida's name. Sonkan stated: "Even one invocation is sufficient, in accordance with the Buddha's plan. When devotees profoundly believe the teaching, responding to the Buddha's Original Vow to save all those who recite his name, their rebirth is from that moment assured. Therefore there is no special need to recite a great number of *nembutsu* daily, or on the point of death. People can receive the benefit of rebirth by reciting even a single *nembutsu*, since each and every *nembutsu* contains the same infinite merit." Jakue, on the other hand, claimed: "Whether one is to be reborn or not depends on the number of *nembutsu*. Many repetitions of the name are a condition for rebirth."

Sonkan's Nagoe subgroup spread from northern Kantō to northeastern Honshu, and Jakue's Shirahata subgroup from southern Kantō to southwestern Honshu. The Ichijō, Sanjō, and Kobata subgroups, on the other hand, were centered in Kyoto. The headquarters of the Ryōchū group as a whole remained Kōmyō-ji, in Kamakura. Kōmyō-ji's historical position is corroborated by a stone monument in its precincts naming it the general headquarters of the Jōdo sect in the Kantō region, as well as by the general acceptance of Kōmyō-ji as the headquarters and the temples of other groups as subordinate.

THE JŌDO SECT IN THE MUROMACHI PERIOD

Shōgei and a Doctrinal Foundation

Though successive patriarchs of the Jōdo sect stressed the orthodoxy and legitimacy of their sect vis-à-vis various groups that later branched off from Hōnen's movement, they could not claim to be independent of Shingon and Tendai. Chion-in, as the possessor of Hōnen's principal tomb, was dominant within the Jōdo sect but remained under the control of the nearby Tendai temple Shōren-in. Chion-in could not act independently of Shōren-in, nor could any other Jōdo temple. The Jōdo sect was regarded as an offshoot of the Tendai sect and was often referred to as a "temporary sect" or a "subsidiary sect." Gaining autonomy necessitated organizing both the Jōdo sect and its doctrines more fully and systematically.

It was the noted scholar and Rinzai Zen priest Kokan Shiren (1278–1346) who described the Jōdo sect as "temporary" and "subsidiary," on the grounds that it had not been transmitted to Japan from India through China and that its doctrinal theory was weak. Documentation of the transmission of the teachings from master to disciple was very important to both the older schools and sects and the newer Zen sects. In their view, a group that lacked a documented lineage of transmission from master to disciple was not a school or sect at all. When he was young, Hōnen had rejected this view, stating that the Jōdo sect did not depend on any doctrinal lineage or on direct oral transmission of doctrine from master to disciple. Of course Hōnen also said that he based his teachings faithfully on the writings of the Chinese Pure Land master Shan-tao. But there was a gap of some five hundred years between the Chinese master and Hōnen, and obviously there could have been no direct, personal transmission of the doctrine from Shan-tao to Hōnen.

The established schools and sects were not willing to ignore the matter.

Hōnen's severest critics attacked him for pride and presumption in founding a sect without a direct lineage of teachings passed from master to disciple and on those grounds rejected the orthodoxy of the Jōdo sect. In response to these attacks, Hōnen prepared a lineage of transmission of the Jōdo sect teachings from India to China and Japan. He listed five Chinese Pure Land patriarchs: T'an-luan (476–542), Tao-ch'o (562–645), Shan-tao (613–81), Huai-kan (fl. seventh century), and Shao-k'ang (d. 805). Nonetheless, his critics continued to insist that though Hōnen might claim to have grasped Shan-tao's real intent through reading his writings, he had in fact never met the Chinese master and therefore could not be said to have received a legitimate transmission of the teachings.

In an attempt to refute this argument, Shōgei (1341–1420), of the Chinzei group, composed the *Jōdo Shin Shū Fuhō Den* (The Jōdo Sect's True Transmission of the Law; 1363), which claimed that the Jōdo teachings passed from Aśvaghoṣa (fl. second century), Nāgārjuna (ca. 150–ca. 250), Vasubandhu (ca. 320–ca. 400), and Bodhiruci (fl. ca. 508–35) in India to T'an-luan, Tao-ch'o, and Shan-tao in China, and then to Japan. Shōgei thus took the lead in promoting the idea of an Indo-Sino-Japanese lineage of the transmission of the Pure Land teachings.

Doctrinally, Shōgei spoke of two vehicles, two teachings, and two sudden modes of enlightenment. The two vehicles were the Lesser Vehicle (Hīnayāna) and the Greater Vehicle (Mahāyāna). Like many Buddhist thinkers of the past, he further divided Mahāyāna teachings into gradual and sudden teachings. The gradual teachings sought to lead people to the attainment of enlightenment through study and practice, beginning with relatively simple teachings and gradually progressing to more profound ones. The sudden teachings sought to lead people to enlightenment quickly and directly. The sudden teachings could be further divided into "internal essence" (*shō*) and "external aspect" (*sō*) sudden teachings. Internal-essence teachings involved academic study, an attempt to attain buddhahood quickly by engaging in theoretical speculation. External-aspect teachings, on the other hand, centered on the doctrine of the Western Pure Land of Perfect Bliss. The Jōdo sect's teachings belonged to this category.

Shōgei claimed that the external-aspect sudden teaching is the most excellent, since it allows ordinary people living during the period of the Decay of the Law to attain salvation by means of the *nembutsu* alone. To ensure systematic teaching of the Pure Land doctrine, Shōgei established centers called *dangisho*, or academies, where young priests could be well trained in both the theory and the practice of Jōdo-sect doctrine. Shōgei was convinced that the future of the sect could be assured only through an able, well-educated clergy.

Those who had completed a certain degree of training at an academy received a special Jōdo initiation known as the fivefold transmission (*gojū sōden*), which was based on five texts, one for each of the five levels of the transmission. First to be transmitted was the *Ōjō Ki* (Record of Rebirths), attributed to Hōnen. Next was Shōkō's *Matsudai Nembutsu Jushuin* (Book of *Nembutsu* Rightly Transmitted from Hōnen; 1228). At the third level the *Ryōge Matsudai Nembutsu Jushuin Shō* (Understanding of the *Matsudai Nembutsu Jushuin;* 1237), Ryōchū's commentary on the preceding work, was transmitted. At the fourth level the student received Ryōchū's *Kettō Jushuin Gimon Jō.* Finally, at the fifth level was transmitted a practice called the Concentration on Ten *Nembutsu,* which had been handed down from the time of T'an-luan.

Each of the five transmissions was equated with a stage of *nembutsu* practice. The first stage was concerned with the capacity of the believer. The second stage was associated with the wholehearted practice of the *nembutsu* for rebirth in the Pure Land. The third stage was concerned with the realization that rebirth in the Pure Land is possible. The fourth stage dealt with the attainment of a mind free from doubts. The fifth was concerned with complete faith in Amida and the recitation of his name.

The Popularization of Doctrine

Shōgei labored to establish a foundation for the Jōdo sect and its doctrines, so that adherents of the established schools and sects would no longer be able to criticize and scorn the Jōdo sect. But even the profoundest doctrine is of little worth if it is too complex for people to comprehend. The Buddhist canon was difficult for ordinary people to read and understand fully. It could not serve them as an introduction to Buddhist teachings. Yet religion should be accessible to everyone. Shōken (1265–1345) composed for this audience three works, collectively known as the *Sambu Kana Shō* (Three *Kana* Compositions; ca. 1321), written in the simple *kana* syllabary, obviating the difficulties of orthography and literary style that Chinese ideograms presented.

The first work, the *Kimyō Hongan Shō* (On Taking Refuge in the Original Vow), tells of the time that Shōken, troubled by doubt, decided to ask the advice of a friend. Shōken went to visit his friend, only to find that the friend had died shortly before. Greatly upset, Shōken visited Shinnyo-dō, in Kyoto, where he spent the night quietly reciting the *nembutsu*. While reciting he had a vision of Amida, who appeared before him and answered all his questions. Following this story, Shōken explains and comments on each of Amida's forty-eight vows.

The second work is the *Fushi Sōkō* (Father and Son Seeking Each Other). It advocates recitation of the *nembutsu* by explaining that Amida and all sentient beings originally were born into the same household. Amida originally had been the master of the household, called the Pure Land of Perfect Bliss. After many years of wandering and earnest religious practice, Amida was able to return to his Pure Land home. Sentient beings, however, continue to wander in delusion and end by dwelling in a foreign land—this world. It seems impossible for them to return to their true homeland; and, in fact, their return is impeded by their attachment to this defiled world. At home, the father waits eagerly for the return of his children. Shōken ends his parable by advising his readers to recite the *nembutsu* so that they may be reborn in the Pure Land and thus be reunited with the loving father who awaits them there.

The third composition is the *Saiyō Shō* (Essentials Concerning the Western Pure Land), a collection of twenty questions and answers about the Pure Land teachings. Religious instruction for ordinary people must reflect their needs and desires and respond on their level, employing language they can understand. Shōken's *kana* writings are a clear example of that approach to disseminating the teachings of the Jōdo sect.

Dōzan and the Nagoe Subgroup

Shōken and Ryūgyō (1369–1449) belonged to the Ichijō subgroup, headquartered at Shōjōke-in, in Kyoto. Konkaikōmyō-ji, in Shin Kurodani, was also under the control of this subgroup. On the other hand, Hyakumanben Chion-ji, in Kyoto, was held by the Fujita subgroup, while Chion-in, in Kyoto, served as headquarters for the Shirahata subgroup. The only subgroups without headquarters in Kyoto were the Sanjō, Kobata, and Nagoe subgroups. Though the first two in fact had little power, the Nagoe subgroup had great concealed strength in the region stretching from northern Kantō to northernmost Honshu, and it sought to gain headquarters in Kyoto.

It was primarily Dōzan (d. 1593) who planned to establish the Nagoe subgroup in Kyoto. He was a disciple of Ryōga (1507–85), who preached the *nembutsu* at the Great South Gate of Zenkō-ji, in Shinano Province, for some thirty years. Dōzan at first had thought to expand his subgroup's activities along the Shinano River and into Echigo Province, but the Fujita subgroup was extremely strong there, having gained the backing of the Uesugi, a powerful local clan. Wishing to avoid conflict, he moved into Shōgaku-ji, in Fuchū, Echizen Province, where he had been born and brought up. Exactly when he moved to Echizen is unclear. He may still have been with Ryōga as late as 1566.

By 1575 Dōzan had moved from Shōgaku-ji to Saifuku-ji, in Matsubara, Echizen Province. This move was dictated by Dōzan's quest for a head-quarters temple for the Nagoe subgroup. Having established himself at Saifuku-ji, Dōzan maintained the secret rituals and traditions transmitted by the Nagoe subgroup, based on what he had learned from his master, Ryōga. He insisted that his own disciples must not study the doctrines of any other subgroup.

Saifuku-ji had belonged to the Ichijō subgroup; but with Dōzan's coming, the temple converted completely to the Nagoe subgroup and its traditions. All other teachings, including those of the formerly dominant Ichijō subgroup, were eliminated. Gradually the temples in the area from Hokurokudō to northern Ōmi Province that had belonged to the Ichijō subgroup joined the Nagoe subgroup, following the lead of their head temple, Saifuku-ji. This temple came to serve both as a training center for the Nagoe subgroup throughout Hokurokudō and as a base for the subgroup's planned expansion into Kyoto.

Dōzan entered Kyoto in the third month of 1582 after having gained imperial favor and attendant honors through the mediation of Shōjōke-in, which had ties to the Ichijo subgroup. Dōzan's arrival in Kyoto is recorded in a document of the time as follows: "The Elder [Dōzan], from a branch temple of Shōjōke-in [i.e., Saifuku-ji], has entered the capital and will be teaching doctrine to the younger priests at Shōjōke-in." After his appointment as director of studies, Dōzan's abilities gradually won increasing recognition, resulting in his appointment as head priest of both Shōjōke-in and its Kyoto branch temple, Konkaikōmyō-ji, in Shin Kurodani. He worked hard for the advancement of his own group and eventually made Shōjōke-in the headquarters of the entire Nagoe group.

Dōzan largely succeeded in his ambitions, but Shōjōke-in had no historical connection with Hōnen. Konkaikōmyō-ji, however, as a subtemple of the original Kurodani center on Mount Hiei, had long been associated with the memory of both Eikū and Hōnen. In fact, since about the time of its seventeenth head priest, Rishō (d. 1530), there had been agitation for Konkaikōmyō-ji's independence from Shōjōke-in on precisely those grounds. Dōzan was well aware of all this.

In the fourth month of 1590 Dōzan addressed the clergy of Shōjōke-in, appealing for Konkaikōmyō-ji's autonomy on the grounds of its unique character. Hoping to make Konkaikōmyō-ji the new headquarters of the Nagoe group, he argued as follows: "The lineage of transmission at Kuro-dani [Konkaikōmyō-ji] is unique to that temple and must be preserved to the end of time. It is a precious possession whose integrity must be carefully guarded. At the same time, Kurodani enjoys a special relationship with Shōjōke-in and must never act contrary to the latter's wishes." Dōzan's argument failed to win over the majority of the clergy at Shōjōke-in.

We can see how hard Dōzan struggled to win a site connected with Hōnen as headquarters for the Nagoe group, which was the ultimate purpose of his move to Kyoto and his takeover of Shōjōke-in. He was so fierce in his determination that he acquired the nickname "Mountain-Storm" Dōzan, implying that he was a ravager of other groups' temples. His tactics were also employed by other groups (the Fujita and Shirahata, for example) in their attempts to secure a Kyoto headquarters—especially one possessing Hōnen's ashes or an image of him carved while he was alive. Konkaikōmyō-ji had a tomb, an image, and the famed *Ichimai Kishōmon* (One-Page Testament; 1212), written by Hōnen as a summary of his teachings just two days before his death. All these objects testified to the orthodoxy of Konkaikōmyō-ji's lineage.

The Two Major Groups in Kantō

Ryōchū was succeeded by Jakue, and their tradition was maintained by the clergy of Kōmyō-ji, in Kamakura, Sagami Province. Kamakura became a fount from which the teachings spread throughout the entire Kantō region. Kōmyō-ji had 98 branch temples in Sagami—a number that invites comparison with the 114 branch temples of Zōjō-ji at Kaizuka, in Musashi Province. Zōjō-ji originally was a Shingon sect temple called Kōmyō-ji. It was converted in 1393 by Shōgei's disciple Shōsō (1366–1440), and its affiliation was changed to the Jōdo sect. In 1598 it was moved to its present location in Tokyo.

Jakue had three gifted disciples: Jōe (1296–1370), Renshō (1282–1362), and Chien (1290–1371). Chien went to China, where he visited the ancient sites on Mount Lu associated with Hui-yüan (334–416) and studied what survived of the traditions of Hui-yüan's White Lotus Society. Returning to Japan, he founded the Rising Sun Lotus Society in Sakai, Settsu Province, where he taught the Mount Lu *nembutsu* tradition widely to both clergy and laity. Renshō founded Hōnen-ji, at Ōta, Hitachi Province. Renshō's disciple Ryōjitsu (1303–86) trained Shōgei, whose doctrinal innovations are discussed above.

Shōgei's times did not allow much opportunity for tranquil, uninterrupted study. During one period of political upheaval, for example, he took refuge in a cave on Mount Fukei, in the Kuji district of Hitachi Province, where the water that seeped from the cave walls served him for drinking and for mixing ink. It is said that in 1393 he wrote the *Jikitetsu*, a ten-fascicle commentary on a work by Ryōchū that replies to questions concerning Hōnen's *Senchaku Hongan Nembutsu Shū*, by the dim light that penetrated his refuge. The cave was only three meters high, four meters wide, and six meters deep; within it was carved a low-relief Amida triad dating to the late Heian period.

Shōgei's disciple Shōsō described his master's situation at the time in a letter to Ryōjō (d. 1438), head of the training center at Yokosone in Shimōsa Province: "Since I must hurry to Musashi Province, I haven't time to meet you and tell you in person all that has happened at Jōfuku-ji [in Urizura, Hitachi Province]. Urizura was devastated by the fighting and the populace has fled. The clergy, too, have sought safety elsewhere—no priests remain, whether of the Zen sects or the older schools and sects. Truly, it is a tragic thing to witness. Our master, Shōgei, also had to flee and is now living in great hardship on Mount Amida. His lot is most sad and painful to consider."

Even in such circumstances, Shōgei worked on comprehensive regulations to govern the Shirahata group of the Jōdo sect. The main provisions of his regulations were: (1) anyone who had received initiation (*sōden*) into the Shirahata group was forbidden to affiliate with another group or sect for any reason whatsoever; (2) initiates were forbidden to show to outsiders not only documents received directly from their teachers at the time of initiation but also any writings dealing with sectarian matters; (3) initiates were forbidden to discuss with outsiders the manner of the transmission and the content of the doctrines and precepts of the group; (4) the preceding proscription also extended to initiates' seniors or fellow students in the group; (5) absolute obedience to orders was demanded; (6) all those who had been instructed as *nembutsu* practitioners in the Jōdo sect were enjoined to hold firmly to the teachings and earnestly desire rebirth in the Pure Land.

Ryōchū's doctrinal tradition was preserved at Kōmyō-ji, which remained the official headquarters of this tradition. Its abbots devoted themselves to the training of promising disciples. But as the center of political power shifted from Kantō and back to Kyoto toward the end of the Kamakura period, Kōmyō-ji lost much of its authority and even its function as an important training center. Kōmyō-ji also suffered a lack of gifted clergy in later years. On the other hand, the temples subordinate to Kōmyō-ji began to develop rapidly thanks to such talented and active priests as Shōgei and Shōsō.

The development of a strong religious community required not only active leaders but also secure headquarters and places to gather and study—in a word, temples. Indeed, the number of temples (as well as clergy) was looked on as a barometer of a group's progress. Certainly Shōsō held that view. He stated that he hoped to see several different priestly groups integrated into the Jōdo sect: the *zammai* (*samādhi*) priests, comprising *zammai hijiri* and *onbō hijiri*, who took charge of funerals and cremations; the *dōshin* priests, or Kōya *hijiri*, who wandered about the provinces collecting the ashes of the dead for interment at Mount Kōya's Okuno-in; and the *kanjin sō* (pledge-book priests), who traveled about collecting money for pious causes.

Virtually all these holy men were involved to one degree or another with funeral ceremonies, at which it had been customary for centuries to recite the *nembutsu* as a prayer for the deceased's rebirth in the Pure Land. No doubt this ancient connection of the *nembutsu* with funeral rites led Shōsō to see common ground between the Jōdo sect and these unaffiliated priests devoted to funeral services. But for the most part the holy men were not regularly ordained priests. Their status was somewhere between lay and priestly. Thus, when such men entered the Jōdo sect, it was necessary . to give them solid clerical training and then transmit the established Jōdo-sect doctrines to them.

The number of temples increased rapidly as the newly enrolled priests converted their religious centers into Jōdo temples and drew their followers into the sect. On the basis of regional and family connections, the new temples were organized into a main-temple and branch-temple system that centered on such key temples as Kōmyō-ji, in Sagami Province, Daigan-ji, in Shimōsa Province, and Jōfuku-ji, in Hitachi Province. The various Kyoto headquarters stood at the summit of the system, and Chion-in ranked first among them.

Unification Under the Shirahata Group

Chion-in attained its commanding position among the various headquarters at the beginning of the sixteenth century. Keijiku (1403–59) of Shōgei's group went to Hyakumanben Chion-ji in 1442 and became its nineteenth abbot. The following year Emperor Gohanazono (r. 1428–64) issued a decree stating that "since your temple is of the highest rank within the entire Jōdo sect, you are entitled to wear a robe and attend at court." In 1450 Keijiku was named the twenty-first abbot of Chion-in. It is not clear to which lineage his predecessors Hōa (d. 1403), Nyūa (d. 1448), Ryūa (1413–81), and Kūzen (d. 1450) belonged, but Ryūa seems to have been a disciple of Ryūgyō of Jōgon-in, in Azuchi, Ōmi Province, and thus he may well have belonged to the Ichijō group. At any rate, Keijiku probably was the first member of the Shirahata group to join the Chion-in clergy.

Succeeding Keijiku as the twenty-second abbot of Chion-in was Shurin (d. 1511), a disciple of Ryōgyō (d. 1483) of Kōkyō-ji, in Iinuma, Shimōsa Province. Since Keijiku and Ryōgyō were disciples of the same master, Keijiku was probably happy to bequeath his position to Shurin. During Shurin's abbacy Kyoto was devastated by the Ōnin War (1467–77). Like the other temples in the Higashiyama area, Chion-in was reduced to ashes. Shurin fled to Ikadachi, in Ōmi Province, and remained there for about ten years. In 1478 he returned to Kyoto and set to work to restore Chion-in, a labor at which he was eminently successful. Shurin expended great energy on the restoration project because Hōnen's principal tomb was located at Chion-in, and Shurin hoped to make the temple the focal point of devotion for the entire Jōdo sect.

The later restoration of Hyakumanben Chion-ji, also belonging to the Shirahata group, did not proceed as smoothly as that of Chion-in. Nonetheless, its abbot, Keishū (1476–1559), made the startling assertion that Chion-ji was the main temple and Chion-in a branch temple, on the grounds that the suffix in identifies a subtemple rather than an autonomous temple. Chion-in appealed to the imperial court and the military government, insisting on its own status as supreme headquarters of the Jōdo sect. Ultimately the court decided that Chion-in's claim was justified but at the same time stipulated that when petitions for promotion in rank were submitted to the court they could be passed through either of the two temples. Thus the court formally acknowledged the special position of both temples, although it recognized Chion-in as the headquarters, stating: "[Chion-ji] is assuredly the most eminent among all the branch temples, yet it must not ever maintain an attitude of disaffection toward Chion-in as the main temple."

The monks Donryū (1556–1623) and Banzuii (1542–1615), originally members of the Fujita group, received the fivefold transmission of the Shirahata group and formally affiliated themselves with it. Donryū had been a disciple of Kyūben (fl. sixteenth century), while Banzuii had studied under Kyūkō (fl. sixteenth century). Donryū and Banzuii were highly influential members of the Fujita group, and their defection was a sign of the group's decline. Soon only the Shirahata group survived in Kyoto, with control of the entire Jōdo sect in its hands. Chion-in, in Kyoto, with its image and tomb of Hōnen, became the center of power for the whole sect, while Kōmyō-ji, in Kamakura, also belonging to the Shirahata group, assumed general responsibility for overseeing matters of doctrine and clerical training.

7. The Jōdo Shin Sect

THE JŌDO SHIN SECT IN THE KAMAKURA PERIOD

Shinran

Shinran (1173–1262) was the son of Hino Arinori, a descendant of the
northern branch of the Fujiwara clan. In 1181, at the age of eight, he went
to the great Tendai center Enryaku-ji, on Mount Hiei. As a young novice
and priest, he seems to have been a model student. At about the age of
twenty-eight, after twenty years of study and practice at Enryaku-ji, Shinran
became certain that rebirth in the Pure Land was assured at the moment
one attained true faith in Amida and his Original Vow, without extin-
guishing the passions. Shinran came to this realization during a one-hun-
dred-day retreat at Rokkaku-dō, in Karasuma, Kyoto. On the ninety-fifth
day he had a revelation, telling him that in Hōnen, who was propagating
the *nembutsu* in Yoshimizu, Kyoto, he would find a master to teach him
the path to salvation.

Immediately after this retreat Shinran visited Hōnen's hermitage and
asked him about the path to salvation for ordinary, passion-bound humans.
Hōnen's reply was simple and direct: the true path was the *nembutsu*, by
means of which all sentient beings could attain rebirth in the Pure Land.
From his study and practice on Mount Hiei, Shinran was already familiar
with the idea that sinful mortals can be saved through reliance on Amida.
Now he sought to realize that idea in his own life, benefiting from Hōnen's
rich experience as a *nembutsu* devotee and teacher. For the next hundred
days, he questioned Hōnen about such matters as why the *nembutsu* is ab-

solutely necessary for rebirth. Finally he was able to resolve his doubts and believe in the *nembutsu* as the sole path to salvation for evildoers like himself.

After choosing the *nembutsu* as his practice, Shinran made no attempt to return to Enryaku-ji. Instead, he remained in Kyoto and, as one of Hōnen's leading disciples, worked to bring to others the joy he had come to know in salvation through the *nembutsu*. Shinran's mission continued from the time of his conversion at twenty-eight until his death at eighty-nine. Naturally, he attracted considerable attention, since in his preaching he expressed an uncompromising attitude toward faith and doctrine.

At the heart of Shinran's conception of the *nembutsu* lay two related elements: the conviction that "the evildoer is the principal object of Amida's compassion," or *akunin shōki*; and the doctrine of other-power (*tariki*) *nembutsu*. The first gave comfort and hope to ordinary men and women, with its promise that passion-bound mortals could attain enlightenment without conquering their passions. There was no need for people to pray to myriad deities and buddhas for salvation, nor were academic study and ascetic practice required, as the older Buddhist sects asserted. Indeed, such "attainments" could be impediments to rebirth if believers took pride in them.

Shinran taught ordinary people that it is the human condition to be born amid passion, to suffer, and to die there. He taught that passion cannot be uprooted by religious practice or other human effort and that the *nembutsu* of itself can raise sinful mortals to the level of buddhas—just as they are. According to Shinran, the "sinful, passion-bound buddhas" will, after death, become buddhas dwelling in the Pure Land, free at last from the bonds of delusion. Shinran therefore did not require the same kinds of personal qualifications that the older sects had established for salvation or rebirth, that is, honesty, compassion, and meekness. Since he believed humans to be naturally and inevitably bound by delusions, passions, and evil, to make such virtues requirements for salvation was inconceivable. Similarly, he did not consider the keeping of the precepts to have any bearing on salvation.

The other-power *nembutsu* is Shinran's unique contribution to the tradition of *nembutsu* practice and the culmination of the doctrinal elaboration of the *nembutsu*. By "other-power *nembutsu*" Shinran meant a *nembutsu* based on the principle of other-power—namely, the absolute power of Amida and the absolute lack of power on the plane of human endeavor. Shinran's *nembutsu* is not recited as a practice to gain rebirth in the Pure Land, for that is already assured by Amida's vow. The other-power *nembutsu* is instead an expression of relentless introspection and of the gratitude of those who, through that introspection, realize that they are already saved by Amida. Shinran's interpretation of the *nembutsu* is quite distinct from the earlier tradition of *nembutsu* thought and practice that had dominated in China and in Nara- and Heian-period Japan. It also represents further development of his teacher Hōnen's interpretation of the *nembutsu*.

Shinran's teachings were based on personal revelation and his twenty years of study and ascetic practice on Mount Hiei. As his teachings spread, they made a tremendous impression on many Japanese. Shinran boldly practiced what he preached. He first married at the age of thirty-one or thirty-two—and not secretly but openly, in defiance of the precepts regulating the life of a Buddhist priest. There are several theories regarding the identity of Shinran's wife. One, unsupported by historical fact, is that around 1204 he married Tamahi, the daughter of the powerful courtier Kujō Kanezane (1149–1207). Another theory holds that Shinran had two wives, one in Kyoto and one in Echigo Province, to which he traveled after he was exiled during the first persecution of Hōnen and his followers. Whatever the reasons for Shinran's marriage (or marriages), it served as his living testament to the possibility of salvation through the *nembutsu* even if one is enmeshed in the passions and violates the Buddhist precepts.

The propagation of the *nembutsu*, interpreted variously by Hōnen's disciples, and its acceptance by the populace led to intellectual opposition to and forceful suppression of Hōnen's group by the established sects and the imperial court. Despite fierce opposition, however, Shinran continued to preach the *nembutsu*. His soteriology as it developed in the context of his preaching activities deserves close examination.

Insight into Shinran's thought is gained from his writings, including the *Kyō Gyō Shin Shō* (Teaching, Practice, Faith, and Attainment; ca. 1224), the *Mattō Shō* (Lamp for the Latter Days, a collection of letters and lectures compiled in 1338), and other treatises and letters, as well as sayings collected and edited by his disciple Yuien (fl. thirteenth century) in the *Tanni Shō* (Lamenting the Deviations). Here is a passage from the *Tanni Shō*:

Amida's Original Vow is beyond the conception of ordinary passion-bound mortals like ourselves. The moment we believe that we can be saved and enlightened through the power of Amida's Original Vow, and conceive the desire to call upon his name, he at once deigns to save us, never casting us aside. In the Original Vow, there is no distinction between old and young, good and evil. Always remember that faith alone is needed. This is because that vow was made precisely to save us mortals who are consumed with lusts and heavily burdened with sin and evil. Therefore, if we truly believe in the Original Vow, there is no need for other good works. The *nembutsu* is absolutely effective. What good works can compare with it? Nor is there any need to be anxious about the evil we may do under the influence of karma from our past lives or the delusions of the passions. There is no evil we can do that is great enough to obstruct the grace of salvation offered us through Amida's Original Vow.

Shinran preached that Amida's Original Vow does not distinguish between old and young, good and evil, and requires only faith on the part of the devotee. The reason is that the infinite power of Amida's vow transcends all things, including the virtues and vices of ordinary mortals. Regarding the life of the saved *nembutsu* devotees, in the *Tanni Shō* Shinran wrote:

Nembutsu devotees can lead a life of joy that no one can impede or obstruct. The very deities of heaven and earth pay reverence to them, and demons and unbelievers cannot harm them. No matter how grave and numerous their sins, they will not suffer karmic retribution. And no matter what their virtues, none can surpass the merit of the *nembutsu*. Thus, *nembutsu* devotees can lead a life of unimpeded progress toward perfect enlightenment.

The following well-known passage from chapter 3 of the *Tanni Shō* expresses the idea that the passion-bound evildoer is precisely the proper object of Amida's vow:

Even the good person can attain rebirth; how much more so the evil person! Now, people usually say the opposite: even the evil person can attain rebirth; how much more so the good person! On the face of it, this seems reasonable, yet it is contrary to the spirit of the Original Vow of the other-power. The reason is that those good people who accumulate merit through self-effort are not in accord with the Original Vow as long as they lack the attitude of total dependence on the other-power. But if they turn from self-power and earnestly rely on the other-power, they will be reborn in the Land of True Recompense [Amida's Pure Land]. Since it was to save evil people, unable by any practice whatsoever to find release from the cycle of birth and death, that Amida made his vow, we can say that the evil person who comes to rely on the vow is the principal object of Amida's compassion. Thus it is properly said, "Even the good person can attain rebirth; how much more so the evil person!"

The concept of the evil person as the principal object of the Original Vow is developed even more clearly in Shinran's dialogue with Yuien in the ninth chapter of the *Tanni Shō,* which states that if one does *not* suffer from passions and delusions one cannot benefit from the salvation offered by Amida.

In the second month of 1207, after six years of preaching these and similar ideas among the people, Shinran was sentenced to banishment, together with his master, Hōnen, and the other principal disciples. The imperial court had adopted a policy of suppression of Hōnen's group because its forceful and successful proselytizing antagonized the Buddhist establishment. Shinran was exiled to Kou, in Echigo Province. There he began a new life of proselytization at the age of thirty-four.

Development of the Jōdo Shin Sect

Shinran was outraged by the sentence of banishment. He expressed his feelings years later in the conclusion to the section "The Land of the Transformation Body of the Buddha" in his monumental work the *Kyō Gyō Shin Shō:*

At the beginning of the second month of 1207 a petition was submitted to the cloistered emperor Gotoba [r. 1183–98] and Emperor Tsuchimikado [r. 1198–1210] asking that the *nembutsu* be banned. How unjust that was! The emperor and his courtiers, turning away from the Great Law of the universe and departing from the principle of justice, gave in to unreasonable anger and baseless resentment. Accepting the petition of the anti-*nembutsu* scoundrels, they arbitrarily sentenced Master Hōnen and his most prominent disciples to death or banishment. In the latter case, the victims were stripped of priestly rank and given lay names before being exiled to distant provinces. I, foolish, bald-headed Shinran, was one of those exiled. Thus I became neither true priest nor true layman. I therefore took the ideographic character meaning "bald-

Shinran, Rennyo, and the Jōdo Shin Sect

SEA OF JAPAN
Echigo
Kaga
Echizen
KANTŌ
Hita
(Tokyo)
Ishiyama Hongan-ji
Kyoto
KANSAI
PACIFIC OCEAN

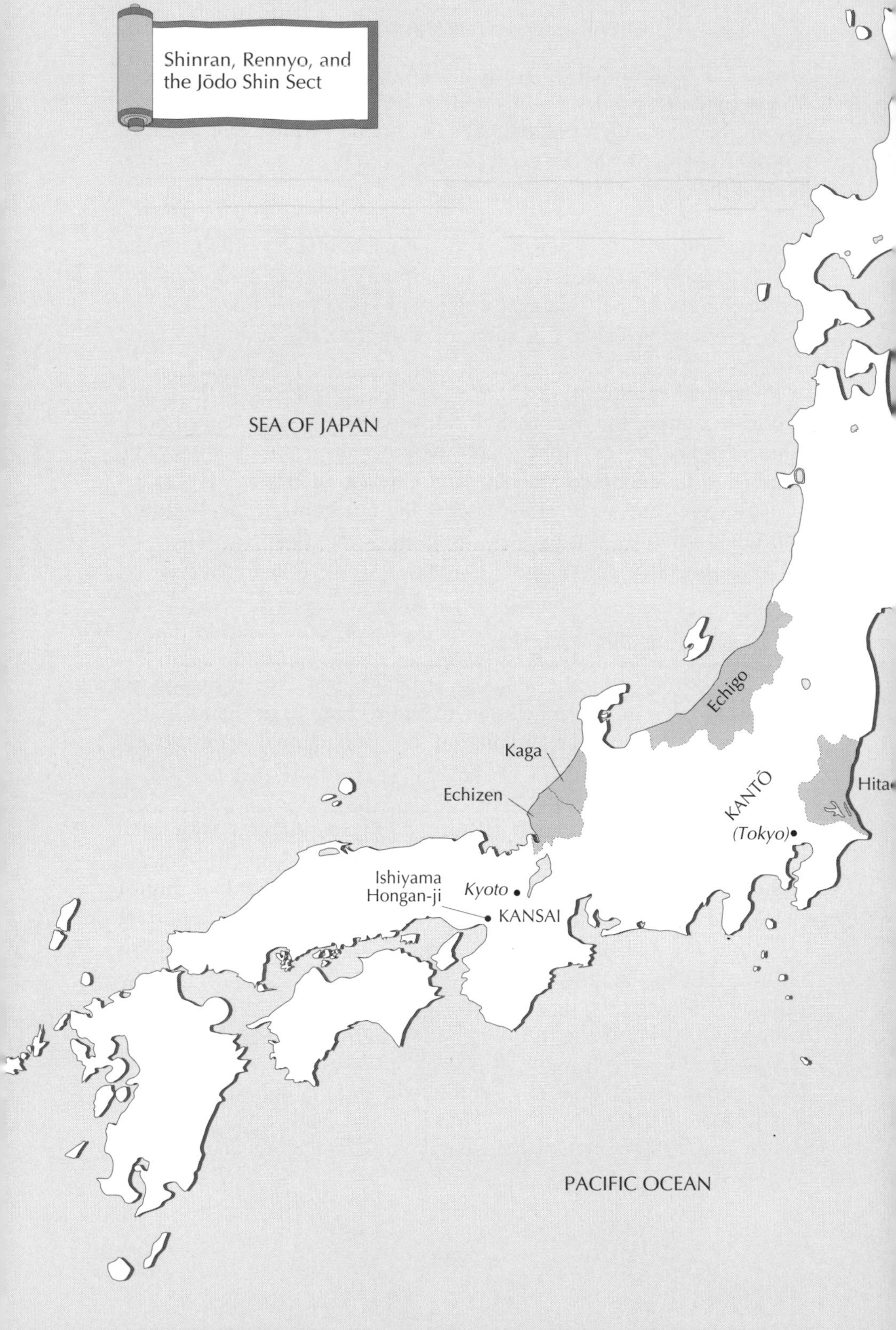

headed," a derisive term for a fallen, unworthy priest, and added it to my name.

In Echigo Shinran had to give up his mission of preaching the *nembutsu* in gratitude for Amida's grace. Until the sentence of exile was lifted, he had to live quietly, carefully watched by the clergy of the established sects, which were strongly entrenched in the villages of the area. Finally, after three and a half years, his sentence was commuted, along with those of the other *nembutsu* leaders. In the meantime Shinran had taken a second wife, Eshin, the daughter of an estate holder in Kyoto. His exile ended, he had to decide whether to return to Kyoto or remain in Echigo to preach the *nembutsu* there. The news of the death of his teacher Hōnen in Kyoto helped him decide to devote his life to the conversion of the people of the Echigo area. Free at last to preach, he showed even greater zeal than he had in Kyoto.

No extant documents tell us exactly how successful Shinran was in his efforts to convert the villagers of Echigo to the *nembutsu*. Yet we can infer that he achieved striking results. In many villages groups of fifty, a hundred, or more believers were organized under the leadership of direct disciples of Shinran just three or four years after he began to preach. The new converts were filled with a sense of solidarity: they believed that all devotees were equal in the sight of Amida and were enabled to lead a life of unimpeded progress toward the goal of ultimate enlightenment. The rapid growth of Shinran's sect, which came to be called the Jōdo Shin, or True Pure Land, sect, greatly alarmed the village authorities, since faith in the *nembutsu* gave the general population a new confidence, spirit of equality, and form of organization. Gradually the alarm felt by the local warriors and gentry led to suppression of the *nembutsu* followers.

Shinran was once again threatened by the authorities, and he knew from experience how painful and deleterious to his religious life exile could be. Therefore he decided to leave Echigo before the authorities acted. In moving, he had to consider not only his own needs but also those of his family. Would people in the new area accept a *nembutsu* preacher with a wife and children? Faced with such problems, Shinran was influenced by the fact that his wife Eshin's family had landholdings in Kantō, probably in Inada, in Hitachi Province. With the income from a small number of paddies and dry fields, Shinran could provide a livelihood for his family. Thus it is likely that he chose Kantō as the new site for his religious activities because he could depend on the land given him by his wife's family as a farewell gift to provide for his material needs. At any rate, he moved to the Kantō region in 1214, at the age of forty-one.

Shinran went to Kantō without invitation or sponsor. Since ancient times the area had been dominated by the older sects, with the *yamabushi* mountain ascetics playing a leading role in local faith and practice. Shinran's first task was a religious confrontation with the *yamabushi*. If he could not win a public debate with this powerful group, he could not hope to spread the *nembutsu* in the villages of the area. In fact, Shinran did win, and an account of his victory over the *yamabushi* Ben'en (1183–1251) is found in the *Shinran Shōnin Eden* (Illustrated Biography of Shinran; fourteenth century).

Attempting to spread the *nembutsu* unaided, and beset with various problems, Shinran needed unshakable faith in the *nembutsu* as the sole path to salvation for ordinary mortals. He spent some twenty years proselytizing in the Kantō region. There are very few materials on which to base an accurate estimate of the success of his efforts, but the *Shinran Shōnin Monryo Kyōmyō Chō* (The Genealogy of Shinran's Disciples; 1342), the *Mattō Shō*, and the *Tanni Shō* provide hints.

According to the *Kyōmyō Chō*, twenty-nine of Shinran's direct disciples lived in the Kantō region. Of these, nineteen lived in Hitachi Province, where Shinran had settled. Even if the names of disciples not listed in the *Kyōmyō Chō* but cited in other sources are included, the number of direct disciples in the whole Kantō region was no more than sixty. From this apparently small number, one might conclude that all Shinran's zealous religious activity in the Kantō area bore little fruit. But it is really a matter of how one calculates.

Sixty is not an insignificant number of disciples whose names have survived to the present day. The names of only one in several hundred, or perhaps one in several thousand, of the ordinary, humble *nembutsu* devotees would have come down to us. In the *Kyōmyō Chō* we find after the names of Shinran's direct disciples a list of second-generation disciples, and after their names the statement: "We omit the names of the third-generation disciples."

If we assume that Shinran had, for example, fifty direct disciples and that each of those had ten disciples of his own, we arrive at the figure of five hundred second-generation *nembutsu* leaders engaged full time in spreading the *nembutsu* in the villages. The real question is how many people these *nembutsu* preachers converted. If we knew that, we could make a fair assessment of Shinran's success in spreading the *nembutsu* in the Kantō region.

One name that appears in a letter is Chūtarō (d. 1261) of Ōbugō, in the Naka district of Hitachi Province. Chūtarō was a poor peasant, yet at least one hundred people were converted to the *nembutsu* and organized into a Jōdo Shin sect group by this lay believer. If each of the five hundred full-time *nembutsu* preachers had the same success as Chūtarō, then the number of believers in Kantō, including the fifty direct disciples, would have exceeded fifty thousand out of some 1.5 million, the entire population of the Kantō region at the time. From this, we can begin to assess the development of the *nembutsu* faith in the Kantō region.

As the peasants in Kantō began to lead the lives of *nembutsu* devotees, forming close-knit groups whose members were invigorated by their new-found faith, the local authorities—landowners, stewards, and constables—started to suppress the *nembutsu* and persecute believers. This persecution was prompted by the extreme language and actions of one segment of *nembutsu* believers. These zealots argued, on the basis of the teaching that evildoers were the proper object of Amida's compassion, that the ideal *nembutsu* devotee was one who flouted all rules and conventions in thought, word, and deed. They held that acting on every evil impulse and denying respect to the deities and buddhas acknowledged Amida's salvation.

Persecution soon spread from the local villages to the military government in Kamakura itself, and Shinran was forced to make another decision. It was clear that if he continued to spread the *nembutsu* faith in the Kantō region he would be driven out by the authorities. Therefore, toward the end of his sixty-first year, he returned with his family to his native Kyoto, leaving Kantō and the believers he had gained over a period of twenty years. Whenever conflict with the authorities developed, Shinran's policy was to leave the area and seek a new one, more favorable to the propagation of the *nembutsu*. He had followed this rule in both Echigo and Kantō and forced his disciples to follow it as well.

Having returned at last to Kyoto, Shinran continued to foster and encourage the faith of the *nembutsu* believers in the Kantō region through letters and other writings until his death on the twenty-eighth day of the eleventh month of 1262, at the age of eighty-nine.

The Founding of Hongan-ji

Nembutsu devotees in the Kantō region had disagreed strongly over the correct interpretation of Shinran's doctrines during his lifetime. After his death, sectarian division became more pronounced, since there was no authority to settle doctrinal disputes. In these circumstances, Shinran's ashes and image came to have special importance as a focus of devotion uniting all members of the Jōdo Shin sect.

A tomb for Shinran was built at Ōtani, in Kyoto, in 1272. On the site was a hall containing an image of Shinran said to have been carved by his own hand in 1243, when he was seventy, and given to his youngest daughter, Kakushin (1224–83). Because the tomb and the image formed a nucleus around which Jōdo Shin sect believers united, whoever controlled them also controlled the sect as a whole. Everyone was opposed to allowing any of Shinran's direct disciples (each of whom headed a suborganization in Kantō) to control the tomb site. Thus Kakushin was named custodian of the tomb with the consent of all the major disciples.

After Kakushin's death her son Kakue (d. 1307) was appointed custodian of the tomb, but the site was forcibly taken over by his half brother Yuizen (b. 1266), who denied access to members of the Jōdo Shin sect at large. The most powerful leaders of the sect joined with Kakue's eldest son, Kakunyo (1270–1351), to drive out Yuizen and regain control of the tomb for Kakue and themselves.

It was assumed that after Kakue's death custodianship of the tomb would pass to Kakunyo, who had played an important role in recovering the site. But after the bitter experience with Yuizen, there was opposition to entrusting the site unconditionally to someone simply on the basis of ancestry. It was feared that automatically granting unrestricted custodianship of the tomb to Shinran's descendants would generate a hereditary elite that might wrest control of the entire sect from the powerful local leaders who had inherited the lineage of Shinran's teachings. Thus the leading figures of the Jōdo Shin sect insisted that Shinran's tomb was the common property of all his disciples and that it was their right to decide who should be entrusted with its custodianship.

On the twenty-sixth day of the seventh month of 1309 Kakunyo presented to the sect leaders a written promise whose terms can only be described as humiliating. In his effort to win appointment as tomb custodian, Kakunyo made a promise of total obedience to the sect leaders consisting of some twelve clauses specifying that he would perform services in the image hall each day without fail; that he would raise no objections if at a later date he were deprived of the custodianship by the decision of the leaders; that he would never disobey the instructions of the leaders; that he would not involve the leaders in any problems that might arise from personal debts that he contracted; and that he would not conduct himself in a willful, egotistical manner if he were appointed custodian.

Even after Kakunyo formally promised all this, his appointment was not forthcoming. At last, deciding to act independently of the sect's leaders, he toured the Kantō region to collect funds for the establishment of a new temple. At the same time he continued to appeal to various leaders for support in his endeavor to win appointment as custodian of Shinran's tomb.

As a result of these efforts, Kakunyo was eventually made custodian, but the painful process of winning the appointment convinced him that it was essential to guarantee for Shinran's descendants a central role in the Jōdo Shin sect. To achieve this, he turned the tomb at Otani into a full-scale temple centered on the hall that housed the founder's image. This occurred early in the fourteenth century and represents the beginning of Hongan-ji. Initially, however, Hongan-ji had no support from the sect's leaders and had to vie with other Jōdo Shin groups for preeminance.

Although the Jōdo Shin subgroups competed with one another, they all opposed Hongan-ji, which had appropriated the founder's tomb and image. Meanwhile, Hongan-ji argued that it was the most orthodox interpreter of Shinran's original teaching. To combat Hongan-ji's influence, the other groups had to devise new methods of preaching and proselytizing. From the late fourteenth to the early fifteenth century, the Bukkō-ji, Gōshō-ji, Kinshoku-ji, Sammonto, and Senshū-ji groups were particularly active. The development of the Bukkō-ji group is of special interest.

Bukkō-ji was founded in Kyoto by Ryōgen (1295–1336), a disciple of Shimbutsu (1209–58) from the Kantō region. In 1320 Ryōgen left Kantō for Kyoto and received instruction from Zonkaku (1290–1373), Kakunyo's eldest son, at Hongan-ji. In time, the Bukkō-ji group far surpassed Hongan-ji in both popularity and power.

Hongan-ji maintained the orthodox doctrine that it is Amida alone who saves sinful mortals and that the *nembutsu* priests and preachers are no more than Amida's representatives, transmitting the news of salvation to others. In contrast, Bukkō-ji taught that all its priests and teachers were incarnations of Amida himself, manifested in this world in various forms to save humankind. Thus Bukkō-ji's clergy were veritable buddhas and bodhisattvas, and devotees who faithfully accepted Bukkō-ji's teachings were assured of rebirth in the Pure Land. One so assured was termed a *nyorai*, from the Sanskrit *tathāgata*, an epithet of a buddha meaning "thus come [from the absolute Truth]." The faithful Bukkō-ji devotee was also called "lord of the other-power *nembutsu*." The Bukkō-ji group insisted that because of its distinctive teachings it was especially entitled to be called "the True Jōdo sect" (Jōdo Shin sect).

Since the Bukkō-ji clergy were regarded as incarnations of Amida rather than merely his representatives, it could be said that they themselves were the saviors of humankind. By the same token, they could also revoke the salvation that they had certified. In other words, they held the power of spiritual redemption or damnation in their hands.

One factor in the Bukkō-ji group's success was its use of lists of the saved (*myōchō*) and illustrated genealogies (*e keizu*), devices reflecting the notion that the Bukkō-ji clergy were equivalent to Amida. The lists of the saved were prefaced with the promise that all whose names were included were assured of rebirth in the Pure Land. The moment a priest, or earthly Amida, inscribed a devotee's name with his own hand, the believer was guaranteed salvation. On the other hand, the name of a believer who dared oppose the clergy could be struck from the list and that person's salvation canceled. Much later Rennyo, the eighth grand abbot of Hongan-ji, criticized these Bukkō-ji practices as attempts to buy and sell salvation.

The illustrated genealogies were devised to permit the Bukkō-ji headquarters to control the many small groups of believers converted through the use of the salvation lists. If a priest was included in an illustrated genealogy, that proved he was an orthodox heir of the Bukkō-ji doctrinal lineage. If he was not included, or was removed, his orthodoxy and authority were challenged. Obviously, in the hands of the headquarters this was a potent weapon for preventing the defection of individual temples.

The use of salvation lists and illustrated genealogies and the distinctive features of Bukkō-ji preaching were patently heterodox from the standpoint of Shinran's original teaching. Kakunyo, the founder of Hongan-ji, vigorously attacked these practices at the start of his treatise the *Gaija Shō* (On Correcting Evils; 1337). Nonetheless, the Bukkō-ji group built an exceptionally strong base despite the attacks of Hongan-ji. By the early fifteenth century, the influence of Bukkō-ji exceeded that of Hongan-ji. The *Hompuku-ji Yurai Ki* (The History of Hompuku-ji; sixteenth century) and the *Hompuku-ji Atogaki* (Accounts of the Origin of Hompuku-ji; sixteenth century) describe Hongan-ji at that time as "virtually deserted, without pilgrims, and desolate in the extreme." By contrast, Bukkō-ji was said to "amaze the beholder with its crowds of worshipers, as dense as clouds or mist."

THE JŌDO SHIN SECT IN THE MUROMACHI PERIOD

Rennyo

Rennyo (1415–99) was born at Hongan-ji in a period when the temple was almost without pilgrims. He was the child of an illicit union between a serving maid and the young Zonnyo (1396–1457), who later became the seventh grand abbot. His mother abandoned him when he was only six, and he seemed destined to spend his life as a ward of the temple. Hongan-ji itself was at its lowest ebb and could provide Rennyo with only the most meager of livelihoods. As child and youth, he witnessed the mass of Jōdo Shin believers abandon Hongan-ji, while Bukkō-ji and other groups thrived.

Until his early forties, Rennyo lived in poverty and obscurity, but when Zonnyo died, Rennyo was chosen to succeed him as eighth grand abbot of Hongan-ji. With this unexpected turn of events, Rennyo was in a position to develop Hongan-ji. The method he adopted was proselytization via epistles (*ofumi*). Each letter discussed a vital point of Shinran's teachings and the deviations of the heterodox Jōdo Shin groups, based on knowledge Rennyo had gleaned through his years of study while living in obscurity at Hongan-ji. Through these letters, Rennyo attacked heretical opinions and elucidated the true teachings for the benefit of the uninformed multitudes throughout Japan. Before composing an epistle, Rennyo would assiduously study appropriate sections of Shinran's *Kyō Gyō Shin Shō* and Zonkaku's *Roku Yō Shō* (Commentary on the *Kyō Gyō Shin Shō;* 1360). He would take as his theme a few words from one of these works and elaborate on them so that the average person would be able to understand them and thus attain faith.

After becoming grand abbot, he wrote numerous epistles. The earliest of these to survive was written in the third month of 1461 and addressed to Kanagamori no Dōsai (1399–1488) of Katada, who was Rennyo's principal aide. It summarizes Shinran's ideas on salvation. The following excerpt illustrates Rennyo's epistolary style:

The faith preached by Shinran, the holy founder of the Jōdo Shin sect, does not concern itself with the degree of sinfulness of the believer or whether the believer is still bound by worldly delusions and attachments. It teaches simply that humans living in this world of delusion should cast aside all evil attachment to miscellaneous works and practices and, taking refuge in the compassionate vow of Amida, believe in it single-heartedly, without doubting. The moment they do so, Amida will illuminate them with his radiance and save them without fail. This is what is meant by the spirit of the other-power—salvation coming to us from Amida. Furthermore, even the will to believe is itself Amida's gift. Thus, once we have received the gift of faith, we must not think "Save us, Amida" when we recite the *nembutsu*. We should understand our *nembutsu* to be a spontaneous expression of thanks to Amida for having already saved us from the first moment we felt faith. This is the proper attitude for a follower of the exclusive, other-power *nembutsu*.

The proselytizing of Rennyo and the many associates who received his epistles was fruitful. The power of the rival Jōdo Shin sect groups in Kyoto and Ōmi Province was quickly undermined. Hongan-ji's rapid development aroused the wrath of the priests at Enryaku-ji and led to an armed attack on Hongan-ji by warrior-priests from Mount Hiei as early as 1465. Finally, after being persecuted by the Mount Hiei clergy on several occasions, Rennyo became convinced that continuing to proselytize in the Kansai region was too difficult and dangerous and decided to move to Hokurokudō.

In the early summer of 1471, a base for proselytizing was established at Yoshizaki, in Echizen Province, near the border with Kaga Province. This was done with the aid of a few Hongan-ji branch temples that stood like isolated fortresses in a region dominated by rival groups within the Jōdo Shin sect. Rennyo pressed his cause with great energy. He declared that in recent times the faith of many Jōdo Shin priests had become extraordinarily unorthodox. In an epistle composed toward the middle of the ninth month of 1473, for example, Rennyo wrote:

The priests call those believers who make generous contributions "good disciples" and "people of deep faith." This is a grave error. And the believers, for their part, think that if they give generous donations, they will be saved by the favor of the priests, even if their own faith is not very firm. This too is a totally false belief. So we see that there is no correct understanding of the true meaning of Jōdo Shin faith among either clergy or laity. How shameful! And there is no doubt that such priests and lay people will not attain rebirth but instead will fall into the depths of hell! What could be more lamentable, what more grievous? Therefore from now on let the priests attend people who understand what true faith is, confirm their own faith, and then transmit the true faith to the laity. Then clergy and laity alike will be able to attain the blessings of rebirth.

The heresies Rennyo attacked here were clerical reliance on donations and lay reliance on the clergy in lieu of absolute reliance on Amida's grace. The notion of the salvation list propagated by the Bukkō-ji group, with its insistence on the right of the clergy to grant or deny salvation, was such a heresy. In an epistle dated the twentieth day of the fifth month of 1474, Rennyo attacked excessive reliance on a clerical teacher as "characteristic of one who lacks true Jōdo Shin faith." From Rennyo's point of view, the only function of a teacher was to urge people to put complete faith in Amida. To cast aside Amida, who was the sole proper object of faith, and rely on the teacher, who was no more than his representative, was an absurd error.

Rennyo's epistles were copied and sent to areas where Hongan-ji missionaries were at work. His vigorous critiques of heresy and presentation of Shinran's orthodox teachings bore great fruit: within two or three years of his move to Yoshizaki, the peasants of Hokurokudō had largely been won over. A massive organization of peasant believers was being formed under the leadership of the Hongan-ji clergy. Peasants from all over the region made pilgrimages to Yoshizaki to see Rennyo. Within two or three years, there were perhaps two hundred lodging houses in Yoshizaki that catered to the hordes of pilgrims.

Naturally, the established sects and the warrior class were keenly interested in Rennyo's extraordinary success in Hokurokudō. The peasants who had found faith in Amida continued forming tightly knit groups in their villages, with Hongan-ji priests as leaders. Soon the organization had spread throughout the entire Hokurokudō region, with Rennyo, in Yoshizaki, at its head. In time, Jōdo Shin believers, strengthened by their faith and by the power of their organization, began to challenge the political, social, and religious establishments. A severe backlash resulted, giving rise to calls to attack Hongan-ji believers and Rennyo. The greater Rennyo's success in his missionary work in Hokurokudō, the greater the friction between Hongan-ji and the political and religious establishments. Later the full-scale uprisings (*ikki*) that eventually occurred will be discussed; here it is important to consider Rennyo's religious thought and mode of proselytizing. For example, in an epistle dated the eighteenth day of the twelfth month of 1471, shortly after Rennyo had established himself in Yoshizaki, he wrote:

> First, the meaning of "peace of mind" in our tradition has nothing to do with trying to reform the evil in our hearts or free ourselves from delusions and attachments through moral effort. We are simply to carry on our trades and fulfill our worldly duties. We can even hunt and fish. We will unfailingly be saved by the Buddha if only we sincerely believe in Amida's compassionate vow and realize his willingness to save base and worthless people like us, who wander day and night in the labyrinths of delusion. Once we have received this gift of faith, we should continue to recite the *nembutsu* throughout our lives as a sign of gratitude to Amida for his salvation. One who lives like this can be called in our tradition a true *nembutsu* devotee, possessed of true faith and right assurance of salvation.

The general population of the age sought not only rebirth in the Pure Land but also secular benefits in this world. Rennyo commented on this in an undated epistle: "There is no doubt that one who with firm faith prays for rebirth, knowing salvation to be the one great issue, will indeed attain the blessed state in the next life. But in addition the *nembutsu* naturally functions as a kind of prayer that ensures worldly blessings without our asking for them." Rennyo thus affirmed that the *nembutsu* also yields worldly benefits.

It was not merely the content of Rennyo's preaching that won over the ordinary people of his turbulent age. His genuine concern for his followers' well-being was evident in both his preaching and his practice. Rennyo was always ready for friendly, informal discussion with any believer. When he preached, he drew his listeners close to him. He well knew that people would be put off by an arrogant, standoffish attitude. He was the first preacher to step down from the priest's dais to the level on which the listeners sat. He repeatedly stressed that all believers were brothers and sisters. He never forgot that his financial support came from ordinary believers and took care that the cut and color of his priestly robes were modest and simple. When preaching, if he felt his audience growing bored, he introduced topics that he knew would interest or amuse them and then gradually returned to Buddhist themes.

Rennyo not only displayed a profound understanding of the psychology of the people of his day but also gave thought to the social structure of their village communities. Thus the *Eigen Ki* (Eigen's Accounts; 1689) relates: "Rennyo often said that there are three individuals in a community whom it is important to convert—the local priest, the elder, and the headman. If these three individuals come to believe, then the other members of the community will follow suit and the Dharma will flourish." This strategy shows how well Rennyo understood the social structure of rural Japan.

As a result of Rennyo's skill in preaching and organizing and of the content of his message, Hongan-ji's power grew rapidly. Meanwhile, statements and acts by Jōdo Shin believers challenging the authorities increased in number and boldness.

The Hongan-ji Jōdo Shin Sect

In 1473, two years after Rennyo had established himself in Yoshizaki, a movement criticizing other schools, sects, and religions arose among Hongan-ji believers. The many buddhas, bodhisattvas, and deities other than Amida were belittled, and the other schools and sects were criticized for differing with Jōdo Shin doctrinally. Jōdo Shin sermons generally criticized the traditional practice of observing taboos, and the more radical believers were now demanding that similar criticism be leveled at the other schools and sects and at the political and social establishment. Protests began to be made against the government's local representatives, such as the principal military governors and stewards.

The stronger Hongan-ji grew, the greater was the disruption of the peace of Hokurokudō society—a peace long maintained jointly by the political and religious powers of the region. It was no wonder, then, that cries to rise against Hongan-ji at Yoshizaki were heard from both secular and religious circles. The secular authorities suspected Hongan-ji of trying to control the Hokurokudō region politically, as well as religiously, through the tightknit organization of peasant believers that it had created. By the tenth month of 1473, there were rumors of an impending attack on Yoshizaki by the samurai of Kaga Province. In response, the priests who operated the many pilgrim lodges in Yoshizaki publicly declared their readiness to meet any attack with armed force.

By 1474 the Jōdo Shin devotees' criticism of other faiths had grown more acrimonious, and their efforts to spread the *nembutsu* more bold. At the same time, many devotees began refusing to pay tribute or taxes. In the seventh month of 1474 there was a major uprising centered on Yoshizaki. This *ikkō ikki* (uprising of those of the one-directed faith, as the rebellions of Hongan-ji–connected peasants are termed) ended in a resounding victory for Hongan-ji, with the provincial governor's representative dead in battle and his troops driven out of the province. But the Jōdo Shin believers also suffered heavy losses. According to the *Kōfuku-ji Daijō-in Jisha Zōji Ki*, a collection of the diaries of three abbots of the Kōfuku-ji subtemple Daijō-in covering the years from 1450 through 1527, "Some two thousand *ikkō* believers were killed, and the province was greatly devastated by fire."

Their victory in the uprising of 1474 propelled the Jōdo Shin believers into still more violent political struggle. Contributing to the upheaval were disaffected samurai who had joined the Jōdo Shin sect hoping to harness its religious fervor and energy to gain political power. These Hongan-ji samurai began to invade the Hokurokudō holdings of the major shrines and temples. Soon Hongan-ji–connected uprisings and land seizures spread throughout Hokurokudō, provoking an attack in 1488 by Togashi Masachika (1455–88), the military governor of Kaga Province. The major battle that ensued ended in victory for the Jōdo Shin forces and annihilation of the Togashi clan. By that time, however, Rennyo had left Hokurokudō to preach and work near the capital, Kyoto. He had opposed the violence of the Hongan-ji believers from the beginning but had been unable to restrain it.

For the next hundred years the Hongan-ji believers reigned in their Hokurokudō fiefdom. In other areas where Hongan-ji was influential, declarations and acts against the government continued right up to the decisive defeat of the Jōdo Shin forces by the warlord Oda Nobunaga (1534–82) at Ishiyama Hongan-ji, in Osaka, in 1580.

Shinran, in founding the Jōdo Shin sect, chose the *nembutsu* as the sect's sole practice and insisted that the attainment of salvation did not require devotion to any buddha other than Amida. Furthermore, he denied the need for such moral qualifications as honesty, compassion, and meekness to ensure rebirth in the Pure Land, preaching instead that the evildoer is the proper object of Amida's vow. He did not utterly reject the deities and buddhas, however. He taught that they should be respected, though not invoked to attain rebirth and ultimate salvation. Indeed, he taught that the deities and buddhas protect and aid *nembutsu* believers in this life. He also urged *nembutsu* followers to recite the *nembutsu* for the welfare of the nation, the court, and the people and for peace. He even recommended prayers for the well-being of the political authorities who tried to suppress the *nembutsu*'s spread among the peasantry.

Rennyo, as Shinran's orthodox heir, exhibited no trace of a negative attitude toward the deities and buddhas or toward the political authorities or society in general. Yet the rejection of the deities and buddhas by most Jōdo Shin believers during the fifteenth and sixteenth centuries was a natural consequence of the sect's exclusive viewpoint, with its emphasis on invocation of Amida's name alone.

Rennyo's attitude toward the more radical antiestablishment Jōdo Shin believers is discernible in his epistles. He expressed his views on the proper attitude for Hongan-ji believers in several writings, including the eleven regulations he issued in the eleventh month of 1473, his letters of the eleventh day of the first month and the seventeenth day of the second month of 1474, his letter of the seventh day of the fifth month of 1475, and his six regulations of the fifteenth day of the seventh month of 1475. In the letter dated the seventh day of the fifth month of 1475 he wrote:

Since leaving the south branch temple at Ōtsu Chikamatsu, in the Shiga district, at the beginning of the summer of 1471 I have been residing at this temple [in Yoshizaki] in order to propagate the Dharma and thus express my gratitude to Amida for his gift of salvation. I have endeavored to rouse unbelieving, indolent people—clerical and lay, male and female—to belief in the original vow of the other-power so that they may be reborn in the Pure Land of True Recompense. Yet for the past four or five years, I have been troubled by the turbulent conditions in this province and especially by the threat from the samurai of Kaga, who suspect us of preaching false and seditious doctrines. Even though this temple was founded solely as a place where the *nembutsu* could be practiced and the people could be aided on the path of salvation, for some reason the Kaga samurai have decided to attack us. And so the last three or four years have been spent helping the clergy here prepare to defend themselves against such an unreasonable, unjustifiable attack. However, all this has nothing to do with the real meaning of the Buddha's teaching, and it makes me increasingly eager to quit this place. From now on I would like to devote myself completely to the quiet practice of the *nembutsu*. Therefore, I have established the following ten regulations for all Jōdo Shin followers, who are to observe the rules strictly and exert themselves faithfully to practice the *nembutsu* alone:

(1) The deities, buddhas, and bodhisattvas are not to be spoken of with contempt; (2) the guide to physical conduct is the secular law, and the basis of one's inner life is the Dharma; (3) there must be no flouting of the authority of military governors or stewards; (4) one should seek to understand the nature of true faith according to our tradition and assure oneself of rebirth in the Pure Land; (5) after having attained assurance of salvation, one should continue to recite the *nembutsu* for the remainder of one's life out of gratitude to Amida; (6) one who wishes to gain true faith in the other-power and ensure personal salvation should seek to convert others and lead them to salvation as well; (7) priests should settle their own faith, ensure their salvation, and exert themselves to lead many believers to the same blessed state; (8) let no one presume to pervert the teachings by using my name in preaching new doctrines without permission; (9) let no one teach anything that harms the Dharma, even though it may seem true to the teacher; and (10) let no one reveal to outsiders private matters concerning our sect.

The above ten items are to be strictly observed from now on.

Rennyo commanded his followers to strictly respect the existing order, both secular and religious. He continued to oppose all radical, antiestablishment words and acts on the part of Jōdo Shin believers. Yet the popular misinterpretation of Shinran's and Rennyo's ideas gave an appearance of reasonableness to the radical actions of the Hongan-ji followers. Both men preached that all believers were brothers and sisters, equal in Amida's sight. It was the misinterpretation and exaggeration of this idea that led to disrespect for the local authorities, refusal to pay taxes, contempt for the deities and buddhas, disregard of civil laws, and denial of ordinary morality, all on the grounds that one "had attained true faith."

The peasant followers of the Jōdo Shin sect tried to extend to everyday life and ordinary society the idea of human equality that had been intended only for application within the Jōdo Shin community of believers. Thus they challenged authority in all spheres—religious, political, and social—believing they were justified in doing so because they had found true faith and become Hongan-ji devotees.

8. The Ji Sect

THE JI SECT IN THE KAMAKURA PERIOD

Ippen

Ippen (1239–89) was the son of Kōno Shichirō Michihiro (d. 1263), scion of an influential family in Iyo Province, on Shikoku. The Kōno family had been one of the principal naval powers in the Inland Sea; but owing to its alliance with the court when it rebelled against the shogunate, in the Jōkyū Disturbance (1221), the family lost all its ancestral landholdings and some members of the family were banished. Ippen's grandfather Michinobu was exiled to Esashi, in Ōshū Province, on northern Honshu, while his uncle Michimasa was executed at Hahiro, in Shinano Province. His father, Michihiro, barely escaped with his life and passed the remainder of his days in obscurity at the Tendai temple Hōgon-ji, in Iyo Province, under the religious name Nyobutsu.

When Ippen was ten years old, his mother died, which led him to enter the Buddhist order. He practiced religious austerities with *hijiri* at Dazaifu, on Kyushu, and studied formally under Kadai at the Hossō-sect temple Kiyomizu-dera, in Kyoto. Then, in 1271, while at the Jōdo temple Zenkō-ji, in Shinano Province, he saw the painting *The Two Rivers and the White Path*, which convinced him that rebirth in the Pure Land is assured for all those who rely on the *nembutsu*.

This painting was inspired by a well-known Pure Land parable described in the section "San-shan-i" of Shan-tao's *Kuan-ching-su*. A traveler has walked four thousand kilometers westward along a path. He now stands on the bank of a river some fifty meters wide, which he must cross. He sees a narrow white path some fourteen or fifteen centimeters wide divide this extraordinary river that is composed of water on the north side and fire on the south side. If he treads this narrow way, the traveler can reach the opposite bank, but the path is ceaselessly lashed by waves of water and tongues of fire. Terrified, the traveler looks back, only to see a band of brigands and a pack of wild beasts fast approaching. He can move neither forward nor backward. Suddenly he hears a voice telling him to "go forward with courage, for there is nothing to fear." Heartened by this strong, confident voice, the traveler goes on and reaches the other bank safely.

In this parable, the opposite, or western, bank is the Pure Land of Amida, while the eastern bank is this defiled world. The bandits and wild beasts following in pursuit are the advocates of the holy path of self-perfection. The seeker is not to give ear to their threats or blandishments but simply to proceed with the Pure Land as his goal.

This vivid painting did not merely impress Ippen, it transformed his life. He copied the painting and used it as the focal point of his devotions in his retreat at Kubo-dera, in Iyo Province. After three years of solitary practice, he came to the following realization:

> Ten *kalpas* [eons] ago, in the inconceivably distant past, the bodhisattva Dharmākara attained enlightenment and became the buddha Amida. When he became a buddha, he made certain vows: he stated that he would not become a buddha unless all sentient beings could be reborn in his Pure Land. Yet he *did* become a buddha after making forty-eight vows, as is shown by his being called Amida Buddha. Thus the possibility of universal salvation in the Pure Land is assured by the Buddha's promise given in the form of the vows made ten *kalpas* ago. Sentient beings can attain rebirth in the Pure Land while living in this world simply by reciting the *nembutsu* even once, sincerely asking Amida Buddha to save them. There is no need for many recitations. One is enough. Through a single repetition, both buddhas and ordinary sentient beings can attain rebirth. With respect to rebirth, buddhas and sentient beings are one and the same. Rebirth can be assured even while one lives in this world, since "Amida's Pure Land" and "this world of sentient beings" are simply different names for the same world. In Amida's realm, buddhas and sentient beings are seated together on the same throne; there is no longer a distinction between them.

This realization notwithstanding, Ippen's practice at Kubo-dera was highly ascetic. In Japanese Pure Land terms, it would be described as a self-power practice—that is to say, Ippen was relying on his own efforts to attain enlightenment. According to biographies of Ippen, through an oracle the deity of Kumano Shrine, in Kii Province, was responsible for Ippen's conversion to complete reliance on Amida: "You are wrong to think that the salvation of sentient beings depends on your preaching of the *nembutsu*. Rebirth in the Pure Land is not something new. Rebirth has been assured ever since the bodhisattva Dharmākara became the buddha Amida. It is wrong to say of those who have in fact been assured of rebirth, 'One must have faith' or 'Unbelievers are lost.' Just give everyone whom the providence of the Buddha brings to you a talisman declaring that all are reborn in the Pure Land!" Acting on these words, Ippen set out on a proselytizing tour. These tours, or journeys (*yugyō*), became a central part of Ippen's practice and integral to the sect he founded, the Ji, or Timely, sect.

In the summer of 1274, Ippen received the oracle from the deity of Kumano and set forth on his journey. His principal methods of proselytizing were to distribute *nembutsu* talismans and practice the dancing *nembutsu*, an expression of—and a method of inducing—religious ecstasy inspired by the realization that all are saved by virtue of the *nembutsu*. For fifteen years he traveled about rural Japan, from Ōshū Province, on northern Honshu, to Ōsumi Province, on southern Kyushu, omitting only the Hoku-rokudo region. Reasoning that people in the capital would always be able to encounter the *nembutsu* teachings but those in the countryside would not, Ippen concentrated on preaching in remote provinces.

One reason that Ippen chose the life of a wandering holy man, without security or station, was his conviction that he was of low spiritual capacity. He believed that *nembutsu* devotees fell into three categories. The highest were those who could recite the *nembutsu* with sincere faith and pure detachment even while living in the world with a spouse and children. On the middle level were those who had to forgo marriage but could still recite the *nembutsu* devoutly while living an ordinary, settled life. The lowest were those who could truly devote themselves to the practice of the *nembutsu* only by casting aside all worldly things.

While envious of those fortunate enough to fall into the first two categories, Ippen was convinced that he himself was of the lowest type. It has been suggested that Ippen regarded Shinran as an example of the first category and Hōnen as an example of the second, but there is no clear indication of this in any of Ippen's works. What is clear is that he placed

Ippen, Shinkyō,
and the Ji Sect

SEA OF JAPAN

Dewa

Esashi

Echigo

Ōshū

Hitachi

Echizen

Shinano

(Tokyo)

Shimōsa

Mino

Taima

Harima

Sagami

Kyoto

Owari

Fujisawa

Aki

Ōmi

Izu

Dazaifu

Iyo

SHIKOKU

Kii

KYUSHU

Ōsumi

PACIFIC OCEAN

himself in the last category and regarded family and possessions as a grave hindrance to his practice, an "evil path" to be shunned.

Ippen found true faith and peace of mind in simple recitation of Amida's name, free from concern with worldly matters and from such dualisms as wisdom and folly, good and evil, heaven and hell. Mental and emotional involvements led to mental turmoil, a state of mind incompatible with faith and inner peace. To recite the *nembutsu* truly meant to become one with the object of the invocation, Amida. To do this, it was necessary to trust completely in Amida's Original Vow and invoke his name. From that moment on, people's thoughts, words, deeds, and very lives would become Amida's own. Ippen described this state as follows: "From the moment people sincerely take refuge in the name, reciting the *nembutsu—Namu Amida Butsu—*they are no longer themselves, for their minds are Amida's mind, their acts Amida's acts, their words Amida's words, and their lives Amida's life."

In 1279, in the village of Odagiri, in Shinano Province, Ippen began his dancing *nembutsu*, to the accompaniment of a metal bowl used in lieu of the traditional Buddhist gong. The dance expressed the unutterable joy of assurance of salvation through the *nembutsu*, and it is reported that the first dancers became so carried away that they broke through the plank floor of the home of Ōi Tarō, a direct retainer of the shōgun, where Ippen lodged. Within two or three years, the wild, rustic dancing *nembutsu* of Odagiri had become a more refined and artistic dance that influenced not only Japanese religious practices but the performing arts, such as what eventually was to become Kabuki, as well.

Many people came to know the joy of the *nembutsu* through these dances. Having received Ippen's *nembutsu* talismans, people felt their salvation was assured, and in their relief and joy they danced about as they invoked Amida's name. In an age when there were few amusements for the common people, these group dances were a means of expressing joy.

Ippen's doctrines, together with his dancing *nembutsu*, spread rapidly throughout the land. On his first journey, he had been treated contemptuously, as an eccentric, in Kyoto and in Shinano and Ōshū provinces. But on his return trip, he was welcomed by huge crowds of people in Owari, Mino, and Ōmi provinces, as well as Kyoto. Placards urged the crowds to be careful lest someone be injured in the crush, and Ippen was forced to extend his planned stay from one week to two to accommodate all those who came to hear him. In the fifteen years of preaching prior to his death, Ippen distributed *nembutsu* talismans to 2,501,724 people, an average of 166,781 people a year, or 13,898 people each month.

Ippen usually preached at Shintō shrines, Buddhist temples, or market-places, wherever large crowds could gather. One distinctive feature of his religious thought was its integration of the cult of the indigenous deities. Hōnen and Shinran had preached the sole practice of the *nembutsu*, denying the need to worship the deities. Ippen, on the other hand, made pilgrimages to Mishima Shrine, in Izu Province, Kumano Shrine, in Kii Province, and shrines of Hachiman, whom he regarded as a Japanese manifestation of Amida. He believed that to spread the *nembutsu* in a region it was important to pay respect to the local tutelary deity—in part to help win the support of the local gentry and government officials.

The many years spent in constant journeys weakened Ippen. He died of illness at the Kannon-dō, in Hyōgo, Settsu Province on the twenty-third day of the eighth month of 1289. The temple Shinkō-ji was erected there, and Ippen's grave lies within its precincts. According to the *Ippen Hijiri E* (Illustrated Life of Ippen), a memorial hall was also built and an image of Ippen enshrined within it. Ippen was a popular subject of illustrated biographies. The *Ippen Hijiri E*, compiled by Shōkai (1261–1323), Ippen's younger brother and disciple, is dated the eighth month of 1299, the tenth anniversary of Ippen's death. The *Ippen Shōnin Ekotoba Den* (Illustrated Biography of Ippen; ca. 1304–5) was compiled to prove Shinkyō's right to be regarded as Ippen's true successor. Fourteen scrolls from this work survive.

Shinkyō

Before he died, Ippen stated that "the holy teachings [of Śākyamuni, which Ippen believed to be concentrated in the *nembutsu*] are finished: all have been resolved into *Namu Amida Butsu*." He had devoted his life to spreading the *nembutsu*; he wished his body to be thrown into the wilds to become food for the birds and beasts. He also told his followers that there was no need to maintain a sect based on his teachings. As a result, some followers threw themselves into the sea before the Kannon-dō, where he had died, while others simply returned to their native villages.

Shinkyō (1237–1319), accompanied by a number of grieving followers, climbed Mount Tanjō, in Harima Province, and resolved to await death quietly there while continuously reciting the *nembutsu*. But Sasuke Tokitoshi, governor of Aki Province and lord of Awakawa, went to the mountain to

receive a *nembutsu* talisman. Tokitoshi urged Shinkyō to reconsider, arguing that it was pointless, indeed irresponsible, to allow himself to die when
so many people were eager to hear the *nembutsu* teaching and receive talismans. The choice was to follow his teacher in death or to live and continue
the work his teacher had begun.

Tokitoshi's reasoning convinced a number of Shinkyō's companions,
who finally decided to preserve the precious tradition handed down by
Ippen. The Ji sect would not be allowed to die out but would begin anew
under the leadership of Ippen's chief disciple, Shinkyō. Shinkyō was persuaded that this was indeed the correct path and agreed to lead the sect,
following Ippen's example of traveling about Japan distributing *nembutsu*
talismans. Shinkyō came to be regarded as the founder of the Ji sect as an
organization, and his portrait was often enshrined in Ji temples as an object of worship.

Shinkyō went to the capital of Echizen Province in 1290. He traveled
about the Hokurokudō region for five years, then went briefly to northern
Kantō and returned to Hokurokudō. From 1294 to 1300 he was in Shinano, Shimōsa, and Sagami provinces, and his last years were spent at
Muryōkō-ji, in Taima, Sagami Province. Unlike Ippen, who had rarely
visited the same area twice, Shinkyō went again and again to certain regions. The simple distribution of talismans and encouragement of ecstatic
dancing *nembutsu* yielded only a weak, rootless faith. Realizing the dangers
of such superficial proselytizing, Shinkyō revisited some areas and also
wrote letters about matters of faith whenever the need arose.

When Shinkyō had asked his master Ippen about building and maintaining memorial halls and pagodas on sites associated with earlier holy
men, Ippen had replied that there was no need to do so, since those priests
usually had no fixed abode. The general assumption was that memorial
halls and other religious centers should be built at sites hallowed by association with eminent holy men. But Ippen felt that there was no need for
large, formal religious centers. It was enough to provide places where a
number of believers could gather to recite the *nembutsu*. Under Shinkyō,
however, increasing numbers of formal centers were established. By 1316,
there were approximately one hundred centers, to which male and female
priests were dispatched at the request of the local patron who donated
land and a building for a Ji-sect center. Thus within twenty-six years of
Shinkyō's establishment of the Ji sect there were one hundred centers and,
no doubt, several times that number of clergy.

In dispatching clergy to these local centers, Shinkyō had two goals: (1)

to strengthen the local community's faith and help the members attain salvation and (2) to foster in the Ji sect clergy a spirit of independence and of service to believers—a spirit that was less likely to develop if the clergy remained clustered around the sect leader. Shinkyō sought not only to develop the organization of the sect but also to cultivate strong, magnanimous leaders. In recognition of his accomplishments as second patriarch of the Ji sect, Shinkyō is known as Ōshōnin, the Great Holy Man, and his tomb at Muryōkō-ji, in Taima, was long regarded as the sect's headquarters. In contrast, though it is the site of Ippen's tomb, Shinkō-ji soon became little more than an ordinary local temple.

The Two Major Schools

Clerical offenses caused Shinkyō the greatest problems. He found it necessary to institute separate seating for the male and female priests. On occasion he expelled clergy from the Order and revoked the "certificates of rebirth" they had been given when they entered. Just as he had the right to certify assurance of salvation, he had the right to revoke it for major offenses against the sect's regulations, such as improper conduct between male and female priests, conduct showing a lack of responsibility as a cleric, demonstrated indifference to matters of faith and salvation, flagrant disobedience to the sect leader, and similar offenses.

Shinkyō was succeeded as sect leader by Chitoku (1261–1320), who died within a year of taking office—a year spent not traveling about the country but residing at Muryōkō-ji. The responsibility of traveling he delegated to Donkai (1265–1327), who was then working in the San'indō-San'yōdō region. Chitoku wrote Donkai a warm letter, urging him to take time and work steadily for the conversion of that region, in which the Ji sect had not been active.

Nine months later Chitoku was dead. His disciple Shinkō (1280–1333) succeeded him, taking the name Ta Amida Butsu. Shinkō wrote to Donkai under that new name to inform him of Chitoku's death and his own succession. Stunned by the news, Donkai replied that the name Ta Amida Butsu was reserved for the person who had inherited the responsibility of traveling and that that person was himself, Donkai. His indignant letter was signed "Ta Amida Butsu."

The stage was set for a major quarrel between two successors of Chitoku, each strongly asserting his own claim. Shinkō insisted he was the sect's leader on the basis of his succession to Muryōkō-ji, and Donkai made the same claim on the grounds that the responsibility of traveling and of distributing *nembutsu* talismans had been entrusted to him. Neither relinquished his claim, and in 1325 Donkai set up rival headquarters at Shōjōkō-ji, in Fujisawa, in the Kantō region.

Donkai asserted his own legitimacy and orthodoxy: "I have carried on the work of my three holy predecessors and shall continue to do so. Journeying about the provinces, I have worked to convert both nobles and commoners. The results have been extraordinary, unheard of in previous ages." He claimed to have received the tradition of Ippen, Shinkyō, and Chitoku intact: "The four generations [the previous three plus himself] of teachers differ outwardly, but over these fifty years their work has been one and the same." "Fifty years" refers to the period from the inception of Ippen's travels down to the time of Donkai's own activities. The phrase "the four generations of teachers" reflects Donkai's firm belief in the legitimacy of his claim to leadership of the Ji sect.

On the other hand, Muryōkō-ji maintained its position as the sect's headquarters in the Muromachi period (1336–1568) partly because it possessed a much-venerated image of Ippen, the tomb of Shinkyō, and the sole copy of a major biography of Ippen, the *Ippen Shōnin Ekotoba Den*, which recounts the transmission of the doctrine from Ippen to Shinkyō.

A third center of the Ji sect was Konren-ji, at Shijō, in Kyoto, where Jōa (1276–1341) was permitted to distribute *nembutsu* talismans, carrying on the tradition handed down by Shinkyō. Konren-ji had been built under the patronage of the high-ranking government official Hōjō Nobutoki (1238–1323), who as a priest was known as Izumo no Gorōzaemon. It was said that there were four holy men, or *shōnin*, in the Ji sect of that period: the Fujisawa Shōnin, at Shōjōkō-ji, in the Kantō region (Donkai and his successors); the Yugyō Shōnin, who journeyed throughout the country; the Taima Shōnin, at Muryōkō-ji, who had great influence in the southern Kantō region (Shinkō and his successors); and the Shijō Shōnin, at Konren-ji, who proselytized the Kyoto area (Jōa Shinkan and his successors).

THE JI SECT IN THE MUROMACHI PERIOD

Systematization of the Doctrine

Before Ippen died, he burned all his books and writings. The *Ippen Shōnin Goroku* (Sayings of Ippen; 1763), compiled and edited by the fifty-second

Yugyō Shōnin, Taa Ikkai (1688–1766), long after his death, is by no means a systematic presentation of his doctrine but rather a fragmentary record of statements that had been remembered and written down. The two major biographies of Ippen, the *Ippen Hijiri E* and the *Ippen Shōnin Ekotoba Den*, were not written by direct disciples. Shōkai, who compiled the *Ippen Hijiri E*, seems to have been close to Ippen before his crucial pilgrimage to Kumano and again in his last years, but there is no evidence that he accompanied Ippen on his travels to various provinces.

As long as the charismatic Ippen and his direct disciple Shinkyō were alive, the content of the preaching of Ji-sect priests presented no particular doctrinal problems; but after the founders' deaths, the clergy began to wonder what their message should be. The problem became acute for the succeeding generation of disciples, who had never known their sect's founders. The clergy's strongly felt need for an authoritative textual basis for the sect moved Chitoku to compose several works, including the *Chishin Shūyō Ki* (Essentials of the Knowledge of the Mind; ca. fourteenth century), the *Nembutsu Ōjō Kōyō* (Essentials of Salvation through the *Nembutsu;* ca. fourteenth century), and the *Sanjin Ryōken Ki* (Thoughts on the Three Minds; ca. fourteenth century). But even these works did not constitute the comprehensive presentation that the clergy believed was required to furnish the Ji sect with a firm doctrinal foundation that would help demonstrate the sect's superiority over other Buddhist sects.

In response to this need, Takuga (1285–1354) wrote the *Kiboku Ron*, a collection of Ji-sect teachings. He divided Buddhism into the holy path of self-perfection and the Pure Land teaching—the doctrine preached by Amida, and the only certain path to salvation in the period of the Decay of the Law. The Pure Land exists everywhere, Takuga declared, as does the light of Amida's radiance; in fact, this very world is the Pure Land. The Pure Land is described as being in the west simply to provide a focus of devotion for those beginning on the spiritual path. If such people were told that Amida and his paradise exist everywhere, they would find it hard to concentrate heart and mind, and without such concentration, true faith is impossible. The idea that the head of the Ji sect is a living buddha or a manifestation of Ippen is linked to the view that this very world is the Pure Land. Both concepts are related to the esoteric Buddhist doctrine of the attainment of buddhahood in one's present body, examined in chapter 3, in the discussion of Shingon.

As a living buddha, the head of the Ji sect can distribute talismans assuring rebirth in the Pure Land and can also withdraw that assurance, expelling anyone who flagrantly violates the rules of the sect. If the head of the sect is Amida, then wherever he is, is the Pure Land. Thus followers of the Ji sect came to view Taima and Fujisawa as Pure Lands and sought to be buried at these holy sites.

Development of the Ji Sect

In the time of Shinkyō there were approximately 100 Ji-sect centers. Documents from the early Edo period (1603–1868) indicate the existence of 275 temples. From this, it appears that the Ji sect grew very little in three centuries. Yet the Ikkō sect, founded by Ikkō Shunjō (1239–87) and regarded as a branch of the Ji sect, grew appreciably in the late Kamakura period. During the time of the thirteenth Yugyō Shōnin, Sommyō (1350–1417), great numbers were converted from the aristocracy, the warrior class, and the general population. Sommyō's followers were so numerous that a popular market grew up in front of the training center, or *dōjō*, at Shichijō, in Kyoto, where he lived.

Shōjōkō-ji, in Fujisawa, also underwent considerable expansion, which testifies to the growth of the sect. During the term of the sixth abbot, Itchin (1277–1355), its main hall was approximately 270 square meters in size; but when the hall was rebuilt after a fire during the term of the eleventh abbot, Jikū (1329–1412), it was enlarged to roughly 330 square meters. Under the fourteenth abbot, Taikū (1375–1439), it grew to 400 square meters. Since each reconstruction was financed by donations from believers, the increasing size of the building tells us something about their number and their wealth. The main hall was rebuilt twice in twenty years, each time on a larger scale. As suggested by the *Yugyō Engi,* an anonymous pictorial scroll depicting Sommyō, Taikū, and Son'e, along with some of their words, one reason for this was the increasing support that the feudal lords of the Kantō region gave to Shōjōkō-ji. However, another important factor was the growing number of ordinary believers, each of whom contributed a small amount to the sect's projects. Some 11,342 people made small donations of money or material for the second reconstruction.

The Ji sect developed as a cultural institution, as well. The heads of the sect were usually well versed in the traditions of *waka* and *renga* poetry. Shinkyō was the compiler of the *Taikyō Shū* (Great Mirror Anthology; early fourteenth century), an anthology of *waka,* and his poetry was included in imperially sponsored collections. The abbots of the Shijō center, in Kyoto, were well known for their poetic ability. Perhaps the most distinguished of them was Yūa (b. 1291), who devoted his life to study of the *Man'yōshū* (eighth century), Japan's oldest poetry anthology, writing many learned commentaries on it. From the period ca. fourteenth-sixteenth century, especially well known in the *renga* field are Zen'ami, Sōami (d. 1525), and Ryōami of the Shijō center, Kakua of Shōmyō-ji, at Ōhama in Mikawa Province, and Jōa (1540–1619) of Ikka-dō, at Sumpu (present-day Shizuoka City).

Others who were famous flower arrangers during this time were another Sōami, Ryūami, and Fūami. The celebrated painter Kaku Amida Butsu of An'yō-ji, in Kyōto, produced an illustrated scroll, the *Itsukushima Engi* (The History of Itsukushima Shrine; early sixteenth century). A special kind of fan, the *miei-dō ōgi*, was designed by a priest named Ami, who was connected with the Ji sect. Finally, there seem to have been close connections between the Ji sect and the Noh drama. The themes of such plays as *Sanemori*, *Yugyō Yanagi*, and *Taema* reflect the teachings of the sect.

In the Muromachi period, the Ji sect drew its members from the general population and the warrior class. Early descriptions of the travels of Ippen and his immediate successors suggest that the majority of followers at that time were ordinary people—farmers, fishers, and even beggars and other social outcasts. The *Ippen Hijiri E* lists eight warrior followers of Ippen, including Ōtomo Yoriyasu (1222–1300), the commander of armory. The *Taa Shōnin Hōgo* (Sayings of Taa) lists more than twenty warriors converted by Ippen and Shinkyō. Many Muromachi-period warriors took Ji-sect clergy with them to battle. These battlefield priests would tell stories and recite *waka* and *renga* for the warriors during the lulls in fighting and, when the time came, would recite funerary *nembutsu* for the repose of the dead. After the battle, these priests would return to their temples and tell the tale of all they had witnessed or visit relatives of the slain to deliver mementos and relay last messages.

From early in its history, then, there was a close relationship between the Ji sect and the warrior class. This may have been in part because of Ippen's own warrior-class origins. It also seems likely that many warriors were attracted by the quasi-feudal character of the master-disciple relationship in the Ji sect. The disciple was given assurance of salvation in return for absolute reliance on and obedience to the sect's leader in a relation similar to that of lord and vassal—benevolent benefaction from above and faithful service from below.

Only about twenty disciples accompanied Ippen on his travels. In the early days of the sect, during the lifetimes of Ippen and Shinkyō, it would have been difficult to arrange food and lodging for larger parties. Even small parties sometimes found it necessary to go without food or to sleep outdoors around an open fire, with a guard to watch against wild beasts. The establishment of centers in outlying provinces, however, ensured lodging for the traveling parties. The routes were never fixed: the parties traveled from one place to another in response to requests and invitations from the local communities and patrons, preaching, performing the dancing *nembutsu*, and distributing talismans.

Since these journeys were one of the principal duties of the Yugyō Shōnin, they were continued even during the frequent civil wars and other disturbances of the age. In the fifth month of 1513, Shōjōkō-ji was reduced to ashes in a battle between the forces of the powerful warrior Hōjō Sōun (1432–1519) and the warrior Miura Dōsun (1451?–1516), and the Fujisawa Shōnin was forced to give up residence there and move to a related center. In the eighth month of 1558, Sōun's grandson Hōjō Ujiyasu (1515–71) informed the Yugyō Shōnin Taikō (1501–62) that he wished to buy the Fujisawa site for a sizable sum and give it to one of his retainers. Ujiyasu felt that since reconstruction of the temple had not been undertaken, the site might as well be sold to him. Taikō's view was quite different. He argued that it had been understood that the sum of money offered by Ujiyasu was to be a donation to be used for rebuilding Shōjōkō-ji on its old site. However, Taikō refused to stay in Fujisawa and devote himself to the task of reconstruction, preferring to honor previous commitments to travel to various provincial centers.

It is not clear how many people constituted a traveling party in this later period, but the government issued official permits for the Yugyō Shōnin and his companions to travel the country freely, passing unhindered through the checkpoints set up to regulate the movements of the populace. A directive to that effect was issued on the third day of the fourth month of 1416. We do not know how long this directive remained in effect, but through the sixteenth century the Yugyō Shōnin seem to have traveled freely. We know, for example, that Taikō was able to journey from northern Kantō to Daihōji (present-day Tsuruoka), in Dewa Province, in 1558.

The thirty-first Yugyō Shōnin, Dōnen (1513–87), was from Kenshō-ji, in

Hitachi Province. When Dōnen toured Kyushu in 1583, his party numbered three or four hundred people, and local feudal lords were asked to supply eighty mounts and three hundred pack horses for it. The number of mounts indicates that there were at least eighty Ji clergy, and if we assume there was one groom for every two pack horses, there were at least one hundred and fifty attendants. In addition, there would have been at least one groom-attendant for each mount, making a total of some three hundred and ten people in the party, including both clergy and attendants. Nor was this party especially large.

The travels of the Yugyō Shōnin appear to have been burdensome undertakings. That the local feudal lords nonetheless welcomed the Ji-sect parties warmly indicates the strength of the sect's influence at that time. The large amount of baggage carried on these tours included not only the personal belongings of the Yugyō Shōnin and his companions but also religious paraphernalia, such as talismans, paintings of Amida and the Pure Land, calligraphic inscriptions of the Buddha's name, gifts received from local lords and patrons, and gifts to be presented in return by the Yugyō Shōnin.

Organization of the Ji Sect

When traveling, the Yugyō Shōnin made a point of visiting every Ji-sect center and temple along his route and inspecting the documents and treasures that they housed. The centers were regarded not as the personal property of the priests residing in them but as the communal property of the sect. The Yugyō Shōnin's tours permitted him to survey their holdings, as well as assess the effectiveness of the resident clergy's proselytizing.

Nonetheless, the extent of central control of the sect varied greatly from age to age. Ippen had preached the doctrine of "reliance on the teacher" and demanded absolute obedience from his disciples. Ippen's *Ji Shū Seikai* (Regulations for the Ji Clergy) states: "One must adhere to the doctrines of our teacher and not make willful decisions on the basis of one's personal viewpoint." When, in Shinkyō's time, centers were established in outlying provinces, a set of ordinances (or *dōjō seimon*) was devised for Ji centers. Sent out on the fifteenth day of the ninth month of 1306, the ordinances were intended to perpetuate central control of the provincial clergy. Shinkyō appears to have communicated the ordinances from a need to warn against moral problems that might arise from male and female priests living in the same centers. As he stated in a letter to Donkai, "The difference between the clergy and the laity is not fundamental but a matter of transitory appearances. Yet if one is a priest, one must resolve to cast aside all attachments and refrain from all improper conduct. It is to impress this on our clergy that I have written and sent out the ordinances."

No doubt the practice of expulsion and revocation of the formal assurance of salvation was also designed to prevent or punish the moral lapses of followers that might arise from their conviction that their salvation was assured. The revocation of the assurance of salvation fell into disuse after the time of Sonkan (1349–1400), the twelfth Yugyō Shōnin; but that did not mean there was no longer any need for sanctions against immoral conduct in the sect. Rather, it meant that the head of the sect could no longer effectively control the clergy of the growing order and that the training centers were becoming more autonomous. In the sect's early days, the head of the sect would dispatch clergy to local centers at the request of believers or patrons. Gradually, though, individual local centers came to be dominated by one powerful member family, and the clergy was selected from that family. Outsiders were no longer welcome. Increasingly, the centers became purely local, clan-centered temples and slipped from the direct control of the Yugyō Shōnin.

To counteract this trend, the Yugyō Shōnin employed two devices: central appointment to the leadership of the most important local centers and the bestowal of clerical rank and title. The centers were ranked according to their size, wealth, and prestige. Obviously it was desirable for the clergy to be promoted to larger and more prestigious centers. Promotions were based on the clergy's performance in their previous positions, which gave them an incentive to do their best. In addition to having the right to promote clergy and make appointments, the Yugyō Shōnin was empowered to bestow the title Shōnin and designate temples as imperially favored or shōgun-favored.

Finally, the Yugyō Shōnin had the right to certify the loss or destruction of important documents or precious objects at all the local centers. Thus, when essential documents were lost in a fire that destroyed Senshō-ji, in Sahashi, Echigo Province, in 1456, Nan'yō (1387–1470), the sixteenth Yugyō Shōnin, acted as the temple's guarantor and enabled it to have the documents reissued with little trouble. Since the Yugyō Shōnin could claim to have inspected the documents on his tours, Nan'yō's word was accepted by the government authorities.

9. The Zen Sects

THE RINZAI SECT

Eisai

Official relations with China were restored toward the end of the Heian period, and after a hiatus of several centuries, developments in continental Buddhism again became known in Japan. As a result, Japanese priests wished to visit China and study doctrinal systems and methods of practice new to them. When the Sung capital was moved to the southern part of the country, around 1127, the Ch'an (in Japanese, Zen) school was the dominant Buddhist movement in China. Most of the Japanese priests who went to China studied and took home the Ch'an Buddhism of the Southern Sung dynasty (1127–1279). Among those priests was Myōan Eisai (1141–1215), who played a seminal role in introducing Ch'an into Japan.

Eisai, born into a priestly family serving Kibitsu Shrine in Bitchū Province, was trained in the Onjō-ji Tendai tradition by his father and others. In 1168 Eisai went to China to seek the roots of the Tendai sect, on Mount T'ien-t'ai; but when he arrived, he found that both Mount T'ien-t'ai and Mount A-yü-wang, formerly T'ien-t'ai headquarters, had become Ch'an centers. Eisai was captivated by the fresh, radiant spirit of this new religious world. He returned to Japan but in 1187 again went to China, hoping to travel as far as India. Forced to abandon that plan, Eisai decided to study Ch'an of the Huang-lung school of the Lin-chi (in Japanese, Rinzai) sect on Mount T'ien-t'ai and Mount T'ien-t'ung.

On his return to Japan in 1191, Eisai tried to convince both clergy and laity of the importance of Zen as practiced in China, zealously propagating the new doctrine in Hakata, on northern Kyushu, as well as in Kyoto. His efforts were fiercely opposed by the Tendai clergy, and as a result the imperial court formally prohibited his proselytizing. Eisai vehemently defended his position, arguing that Zen was by no means a new current of Buddhism and pointing out that Saichō had incorporated T'ang-dynasty Zen into Tendai teachings. He maintained that condemnation of Zen undermined the foundations of Tendai and that failure to comprehend Zen hindered understanding of Tendai.

Nonetheless, compared with Saichō's T'ang-style Zen, Eisai's Southern Sung–style Zen appeared clearly heterodox to the Tendai clergy. Thus, no matter how eloquently he argued his case, Eisai made no headway against the conservatism of the Tendai priests. But Eisai did not give up; he continued to insist that Japanese Tendai could be revitalized only by adopting the new Zen teachings. In 1198 he wrote the *Kōzen Gokoku Ron* (On Promoting Zen to Protect the Nation) to present his views to his compatriots.

When it became apparent that his defense of Zen was only provoking further opposition, Eisai decided to leave Kyoto and carry on his work in the Kantō region, where he could appeal to the newly powerful warrior clans for support and protection. Eisai's Zen was received warmly by the shogunate, or warrior government, in Kamakura, which was then trying to forge a culture of its own, distinct from the court-dominated culture of the Kansai region. In 1200, having won both the protection of the shogunate and the allegiance of large numbers of warriors in eastern Japan, Eisai established Jufuku-ji, in Kamakura. In 1214 he presented to the shōgun Minamoto no Sanetomo (1192–1219) a copy of his treatise *Kissa Yōjō Ki* (On Drinking Tea and Prolonging One's Life; 1211), which extols the medicinal properties of tea. One of the first Japanese texts to mention this Chinese beverage, *Kissa Yōjō Ki* is regarded as one of the sources of the tea ceremony (*chanoyu*).

With the strong support of the shogunate, Eisai made another attempt to propagate Zen in Kyoto, founding Kennin-ji in the Rokuhara district of the capital in 1202. He also revived Tōdai-ji, in Nara, and Hosshō-ji, in Kyoto, and gradually increased his influence in court circles. Eisai remained a reformer, seeking to renew the Tendai sect by incorporating continental Zen into its teachings. Though Zen was practiced at Jufuku-ji and Kennin-ji, both were founded as Tendai temples, not temples of a distinct Zen sect.

To the end of his life, Eisai was a Tendai priest. Yet he laid the foundations for the extraordinary growth of the Zen sect by establishing in Hakata, Kamakura, and Kyoto centers for Zen practice where numerous disciples were trained for the task of introducing this new current into Japan's religious world. In this light, Eisai can justly be termed the founder of Kamakura-period (1185–1336) Zen.

Kamakura Zen

After Eisai, the central figures in the world of Zen were Gyōyū (1163–1241), who succeeded to the abbacy of Jufuku-ji and enjoyed the support of the shogunate, and Eichō (1165–1247), who founded Chōraku-ji, in Serada, Kōzuke Province. Both had learned the new form of Zen from Eisai, but they were also devoted practitioners of Tendai rituals. Gyōyū's disciple Daikatsu Ryōshin (fl. thirteenth century), however, traveled to China and took new Zen-style rituals back to Japan. By the time of Daikatsu, the Tendai sect had completed the conversion of the form to Zen. The Zen of Kennin-ji and Jufuku-ji was based on the teachings of the Huang-lung (in Japanese, Ōryō) school of Lin-chi Ch'an (Rinzai Zen).

About thirty years after Eisai's death, Enni Bennen (1202–80) introduced another form of Rinzai Zen. Like Eisai, Enni at first studied the Onjō-ji Tendai teachings. Later he practiced Zen under Eichō, Gyōyū, and Daikatsu. Going to China in 1235, he studied under Wu-chun Shih-fan (1178–1249). He returned to Japan in 1241, settling on Kyushu, where he propagated the Yang-ch'i (Yōgi) school of Lin-chi Ch'an, then dominant on the continent. In 1243, with the support of the courtier Kujō Michiie (1193–1252) and members of his family, Enni founded Tōfuku-ji, in Kyoto, as a comprehensive center for the study and practice of Shingon, Tendai, and Zen. His primary goal was the propagation of Zen; but since he emphasized harmony between Zen and other sects, learned priests of other sects went to study with him, and his school flourished.

Through Enni's activities, Zen gained increasing acceptance by the Kyoto nobility and finally even by the imperial court. The cloistered emperors Gosaga (r. 1242–46), Gofukakusa (r. 1246–59), and Kameyama (r. 1259–74) all received the Zen precepts from Enni. In recognition of his achievements in promoting Zen, Enni was given the posthumous title Shōichi Kokushi, or National Master Shōichi. His school, the Shōichi school, with headquarters at Tōfuku-ji, developed into an important branch of Zen.

Mukan Gengo (1212–91) of the Shōichi school further strengthened

Eisai and
the Rinzai Sect

SEA OF JAPAN

Kōzuke

Shimotsuke

Kazusa

(Tokyo)

Mino

Kai

Kyoto ●

Sagami

Bitchū—

Kamakur

Chikuzen

Kii

Tosa

SHIKOKU

Hakata

KYUSHU

PACIFIC OCEAN

the ties between Zen and the imperial family. The cloistered emperor Kameyama granted him an imperial villa in Kyoto, which became the Zen temple Nanzen-ji. This temple played a major role in the growth of the Zen sect and flourished as a representative of Rinzai Zen.

Among Enni's disciples were a certain number of followers of older esoteric Buddhism, so his school had tendencies in that direction. Despite this, its influence spread to the imperial court and became one of the largest schools in the Gozan system, described in detail later.

In contrast to Eisai and Enni, who both began as Tendai priests, the Zen master Muhon Kakushin (1207–98) emerged from the Shingon sect. He studied Zen under Gyōyū, Eichō, and Enni and then went to China, hoping to become a disciple of Wu-chun Shih-fan. Finding that Wu-chun had died, he studied a slightly different form of Wu-chun's Yang-ch'i school of Lin-chi Ch'an under Wu-men Hui-k'ai (1183–1260). After returning to Japan, Muhon founded Saihō-ji (later renamed Kōkoku-ji), in Kii Province. Muhon Kakushin was an extremely reclusive man, devoted to the study and practice of esoteric Buddhism. He was greatly venerated by the cloistered emperor Kameyama, who bestowed on him the posthumous title Hottō Zenji, or Zen Master Hottō. The Hottō school of Rinzai Zen that he founded preserved both his reclusive habits and his dual interest in Zen and esotericism. It kept its headquarters at Kōkoku-ji, in Kii, and directed most of its energies to the propagation of Zen in outlying provinces.

Continental Zen in Japan

Twelfth-century Japanese Buddhists sought new vigor in the Buddhism of the continent. Eisai, Enni, Muhon, and others introduced various forms of Southern Sung Ch'an, which were welcomed by the aristocratic and warrior elites when they proved to be compatible with already established Japanese Buddhist ideas and practices. Most of these new forms of Zen gradually became independent schools, but others simply blended with the established Tendai and Shingon traditions. Some Zen priests, however, chose to lead lives of seclusion in an effort to preserve the purity of the continental Zen they had learned. Unfortunately, most of these masters' schools did not survive long, and even the major facts of the masters' lives are unknown.

The schools established by Eisai, Enni, and others strengthened their contacts with Chinese Zen and began to emerge as autonomous, purely Zen schools. At the same time, the Hōjō family—regents of the shogunate and de facto rulers—and other powerful aristocratic and warrior clans grew more fervent in their support of Zen and in their efforts to encourage introduction of continental forms of Zen. As major figures in Ch'an became aware of the Japanese eagerness to learn, many went to Japan as missionaries and took the lead in developing Japanese Zen.

The first to arrive was Lan-ch'i Tao-lung (in Japanese, Rankei Dōryū; 1213–78). After succeeding his teacher, Wu-ming Hui-hsing (1162–1237) of the Yang-ch'i school, Lan-ch'i went to Japan in 1246, relying on a Japanese priest. Under the patronage of the regent Hōjō Tokiyori (1227–63), he took up residence at Jōraku-ji, in Kamakura, building a special hall for Zen meditation there and converting the temple from the Pure Land to the Zen tradition. As more people gathered to learn the new Zen practice, Jōraku-ji grew cramped. Thus Tokiyori built the huge Kenchō-ji, in Kamakura, with facilities for over two hundred trainee priests, and invited Lan-ch'i to become its first abbot. Later Lan-ch'i went to Kyoto with recommendations from the shogunate in Kamakura and took up residence at Kennin-ji. He transformed that temple from a center of mixed Zen and esoteric Buddhist practice into a training center devoted exclusively to the practice of continental-style Zen.

For more than thirty years Lan-ch'i gave himself to the task of introducing contemporary Ch'an into Japan. He firmly established the new form of Zen as the faith of the warrior elite of Kamakura, including the Hōjō clan, and trained a large number of disciples, building a solid foundation for the development of Kamakura Zen. After he died, he was given the title Daikaku Zenji (Zen Master Daikaku); he was the first priest to be given the title Zenji. The Daikaku school, centered at Kenchō-ji, became a highly influential school, second only to the Shōichi school.

In 1260, roughly fifteen years after Lan-ch'i's arrival, Wu-an P'u-ning (in Japanese, Gottan Funei; 1197–1276) went to Japan at the invitation of the shogunate. He had been a disciple of Wu-chun Shih-fan and a fellow student of Enni in China. In Kamakura, he was appointed as the second abbot of Kenchō-ji. He is said to have refused to worship the principal image enshrined at Kenchō-ji on the grounds that it depicted a mere bodhisattva, whereas he himself was an enlightened buddha. His uncompromising Zen spirit must have strongly impressed the people of Kamakura, accustomed as they were to highly ritualistic Buddhism. But Hōjō Tokiyori, who esteemed Wu-an's style of Zen, died and was succeeded in the regency by an adolescent, Tokimune (1251–84). Unable to find another patron as devoted as Tokiyori, Wu-an abandoned his missionary work and returned to China after only six years in Japan.

Three years later, in 1269, Ta-hsiu Cheng-nien (in Japanese, Daikyū Shōnen; 1215–89) went to Japan at Tokimune's invitation. Ta-hsiu was a disciple of Shih-ch'i Hsin-yüeh (d. 1254), who was of the same Dharma lineage as Lan-ch'i. It is likely that he was invited on the recommendation of a Japanese fellow student, Mushō Jōshō (1234–1306). In Japan Ta-hsiu was appointed as the third abbot of Kenchō-ji at the recommendation of Lan-ch'i and, much later, the second abbot of Engaku-ji, both in Kamakura. For twenty years he was a leader in the world of Kamakura Zen. A very learned man, Ta-hsiu not only disseminated continental Zen but also undertook the spiritual, intellectual, and cultural education of the regent Tokimune, his family, and the warrior elite.

After Lan-ch'i's death, Tokimune sought a successor among the eminent priests of China. In 1279 the Chinese Ch'an authorities sent Wu-hsüeh Tsu-yüan (in Japanese, Mugaku Sogen; 1226–86), a disciple of Wu-chun Shih-fan and hence a fellow student of Enni and Wu-an P'u-ning. At Tokimune's invitation, Wu-hsüeh served as the fifth abbot of Kenchō-ji and as the founding abbot of Engaku-ji. He was not only a learned scholar but also a superbly able teacher, as is evident from the sermons he preached to Tokimune and the warrior elite of Kamakura. As he himself said, he taught "a grandmotherly sort of Zen," using gentle and courteous modes of teaching. Wu-hsüeh exerted a great influence on the Japanese Buddhist world, and though he was in Kamakura only seven years, his school of Zen became dominant there. It was known as the Bukkō school, after Wu-hsüeh's posthumous title, Bukkō Zenji.

Wu-hsüeh's greatest disciple was Kōhō Kennichi (1241–1316), a son of Emperor Gosaga who studied first under Enni, then under Wu-an, and finally under Wu-hsüeh. Kōhō converted the Tendai temple Ungan-ji, in Nasu, Shimotsuke Province, to a Zen temple, and is regarded as its true founder. He built a special priests' meditation hall, to which zealous students came from all over Japan. Ungan-ji soon flourished as one of the most prominent Zen training centers in eastern Japan. Among Kōhō's disciples was Musō Soseki, a major figure in the world of Zen whose life is discussed later in this chapter.

In 1299, twenty years after Wu-hsüeh's arrival, I-shan I-ning (in Japanese, Issan Ichinei; 1247–1317) went to Japan as an envoy of China's Mongol court. As ambassador from the new Yüan dynasty (1279–1368),

I-shan was charged with the delicate task of persuading Japan to offer tribute to the Chinese court. Since he had traveled to Japan at the behest of the Chinese government—unlike Lan-ch'i and Wu-hsüeh, who had been invited by the shogunate—the regent Hōjō Sadatoki (1271–1311) at first suspected him of espionage and had him imprisoned at Shuzen-ji, in Izu Province.

Eventually I-shan was freed and permitted to live at Kenchō-ji. In time, he gained the esteem and patronage of Sadatoki and other Hōjō leaders and came to play a major role in Kamakura Zen circles. Later he became the spiritual teacher of the cloistered emperor Gouda (r. 1274–87), took up residence at Nanzen-ji, in Kyoto, and propagated continental-style Zen among the courtiers and nobility in the capital. I-shan, a man of refinement and culture, provided guidance not only on Zen but also on literature, the arts, and other aspects of contemporary continental culture. Moreover, his influence was decisive in setting the course of Japanese Zen. His direct disciples included such brilliant priests as Musō Soseki, who was also a disciple of Kōhō, and Kokan Shiren (1278–1346).

Unlike I-shan, most of the Ch'an masters who went to Japan did so at the invitation of the shogunate. Yet a great many also went as exiles or émigrés, fleeing the factional disputes and political upheaval in China in the wake of the Mongol conquest that ushered in the Yüan dynasty. The émigré priests went to Japan voluntarily, viewing that country as a place where they could practice and propagate their faith in safety. At the same time, there was a sudden increase in the number of Japanese priests traveling to China to study authentic forms of contemporary Ch'an, often for extended periods. Thanks to those Chinese and Japanese priests, Zen rapidly grew strong and spiritually rich. As the flourishing state of Zen became known in China, ever larger numbers of influential Ch'an teachers traveled to Japan at the invitation of Japanese priests who had gone to China. By then, however, the Hōjō clan was no longer powerful enough to be the principal support of the Chinese missionaries, and its place was taken by the Ōtomo and other prominent warrior clans.

The eminent priest Ch'ing-cho Cheng-ch'eng (in Japanese, Seisetsu Shōchō; 1274–1339) arrived in Japan in 1326. At first he resided at Kenchō-ji, at the invitation of Hōjō Takatoki. Later he became the spiritual advisor of Ōtomo Sadamune (d. 1333) and his son Ujiyasu, Ogasawara Sadamune (1292–1347), and other influential warriors. Ch'ing-cho worked diligently to introduce continental Ch'an discipline and etiquette into Japanese temples. The rules he expounded were very important in defining standards of deportment in Zen. It is said that the system of etiquette he taught to the Ogasawara clan was assimilated into traditional Japanese rules of decorum, giving rise to the Ogasawara school of etiquette for samurai families.

In 1329, Ming-chi Ch'u-chun (in Japanese, Minki Soshun; 1262–1336) and Chu-hsien Fan-hsien (Jikusen Bonsen; 1292–1348) went to Japan together. At that time all the Japanese student priests in China were eager to study under Chung-feng Ming-pen (1263–1323) of Mount T'ien-mu or Ku-lin Ch'ing-mo (1262–1329) of Mount Fang-t'ai. But with Chung-feng dead, the Ch'an of Ku-lin and his disciples became the ideal of Japanese students. Thus Ōtomo Sadamune invited to Japan Chu-hsien, the most eminent of Ku-lin's disciples, and Ming-chi, a close friend of Chu-hsien and the elder brother and fellow student of Ch'ing-cho, who had arrived in Japan a few years earlier and was already famous in the Zen world.

Chinese priests in Japan established a group called "Kongō Dōge." With its highly educated priests it was to take the leading role in the Gozan system described below. The group's emphasis on culture and literary works completed the transplantation of the Chinese essence in Japan.

Gozan Culture

In the Muromachi period (1336–1568), the various schools of Zen that had been introduced into Japan were united under the Gozan temples of Kamakura and Kyoto. The term "Gozan" (literally, five mountains) originated in China, where major temples were often located on mountains. The organization of the Ch'an temples in one group of five great temples, dating to the Southern Sung period, was inspired by an Indian grouping of five major monasteries and ten major stupas erected in honor of Śākyamuni Buddha. The Ch'an sect of Sung China, which had close ties to both the Sung imperial family and the administrative class, was no doubt influenced by the hierarchical structure of the bureaucracy when it devised a three-tiered ranking system for government-sponsored temples consisting of the Five Mountains, the Ten Major Temples, and other, minor temples.

Ranks for Ch'an priests were established around the same time. After a long period of training, a priest was given the highest trainee-priest rank and was qualified to become intendant of a government-sponsored temple. The next rank was conferred when the priest was formally appointed intendant of an official temple. The path was then open for the priest to advance from intendant of a minor temple to that of a major temple, and ultimately to one of the Gozan (top five), depending on his ability.

The Gozan system was adopted in Japan around the end of the Kama-kura period. The shogunate designated the Kamakura temples Kenchō-ji, Engaku-ji, Jufuku-ji, Jōchi-ji, and one other (changing from year to year) as Gozan, the highest rank. During the Kemmu Restoration (1333–36), following the overthrow of the Kamakura shogunate, the Kyoto temples Nanzen-ji, Kennin-ji, and Tōfuku-ji were raised to the same rank. After the Ashikaga clan established its shogunate headquarters in the Muromachi district of Kyoto, Tenryū-ji, founded by the first Ashikaga shōgun, was also included in the Gozan rank. Thus from an early date there were more than five Gozan temples in Japan, and "five" came to refer to the number of ranks rather than temples. (The Gozan system in Japan also lent its name to a literary movement influenced by the Chinese learning of Zen priests.)

In the fifth month of 1341, the relative ranks of the Gozan temples were fixed for the first time. The first rank was filled by Kenchō-ji, in Kamakura, and Nanzen-ji, in Kyoto; the second by Engaku-ji, in Kamakura, and Tenryū-ji, in Kyoto; the third by Jufuku-ji, in Kamakura; the fourth by Kennin-ji, in Kyoto; the fifth by Tōfuku-ji, in Kyoto; and the "junior fifth" by Jōchi-ji, in Kamakura. The ranking subsequently changed several times, but in the seventh month of 1386 the shogun Ashikaga Yoshimitsu (1358–1408) approved the final ranking of Gozan: senior Gozan, Nanzen-ji; first rank, Tenryū-ji and Kenchō-ji; second rank, Shōkoku-ji, in Kyoto, and Engaku-ji; third rank, Kennin-ji and Jufuku-ji; fourth rank, Tōfuku-ji and Jōchi-ji; and fifth rank, Manju-ji, in Kyoto, and Jōmyō-ji, in Kamakura.

In the late Kamakura period, ten major temples, the Jissatsu, were ranked just below the Gozan. In the eighth month of 1341, the Muro-machi shogunate registered ten temples: Jōmyō-ji, Zenkō-ji, Tōshō-ji, Manju-ji in Kamakura; Manju-ji, Shinnyo-ji, and Ankoku-ji in Kyoto; Shōfuku-ji in Chikuzen Province; Chōraku-ji in Kōzuke Province; and Manju-ji in Bungo Province. Soon, however, the term Jissatsu, like Gozan, came to identify a rank rather than a specific group of temples. In 1386 Yoshimitsu named ten temples each in Kantō and the Kyoto area to that rank. From that time on the number of Jissatsu steadily increased. After the Ōnin War (1467–77), there were forty-six throughout the country, headed by Tōchi-ji, in Kyoto. Their number later rose to more than sixty.

The Shozan (other, minor temples) rank also originated in the late Kamakura period, and from the outset there was no limit to their num-ber. In response to requests from provincial estate holders, the shogunate readily gave permission for temples to assume this rank. As a result, by the sixteenth century there were some two hundred thirty Shozan temples throughout the country.

A major factor in the rapid increase in the number of officially ranked temples was the enthusiastic support of the stewards and proprietors of provincial estates, who were devout Zen votaries eager to see government-sponsored temples established in their territories. But the shogunate's policies must also be considered.

The Muromachi shogunate established a special bureau, managed by an important vassal, to exercise direct control over the three ranks of Zen temples. The temples of the Gozan system were organized nationwide in a highly centralized official pyramidal network, with the three official ranks forming the apex and middle section and thousands of branch temples and provincial temples forming the base. The shogunate reserved the right to appoint and remove intendants of official temples and to approve the promotion of clergy from private to official and from minor to major temples. In time, it became customary for a member of the clergy to pay a fee to the shogunate on appointment to an official temple. The fee for appointment to a temple of Gozan rank was three to five times that for appointment to one of lesser rank.

Under Shun'oku Myōha (1311–88), of the powerful Musō group, secular regulation of the Gozan system became unnecessary. In 1379 Shun'oku's unquestioned leadership of the entire Gozan network was formalized by his appointment as *sōroku*, or superintendent of clergy, and the shogunate was content to leave management of the group's day-to-day affairs in the hands of the clergy. The shogunate, however, retained the right to appoint and remove the clergy of official temples.

Following Shun'oku's appointment, the office of *sōroku* was held by the most eminent priests of the Musō group. After the construction of Shōkoku-ji, the memorial subtemple for Yoshimitsu in its precincts, the Rokuon-in, became the official residence of the *sōroku*. Hence the office came to be called the Rokuon *sōroku*.

The organizational structure of the Gozan group was complete. The *sōroku* stood at the top, overseeing the three official ranks: Gozan, Jissatsu, and Shozan. Below these ranks were numerous small, private temples and subtemples throughout the country. In time, the post of *sōroku* was occupied chiefly by priests from aristocratic families. As the office became a sinecure, actual power shifted to the *inryō shoku*, who served as secretary and intermediary between the *sōroku* and the shōgun. This situation continued for well over two centuries, during which time some fifty *sōroku* were appointed. Tokugawa Ieyasu, the first shōgun of the Tokugawa clan, abolished both offices in 1615.

Musō Soseki (1275–1351) and his group, the Musō school, played the leading role in the development of the Gozan system. Musō first studied Tendai of the Onjō-ji tradition at Heienzankyō-ji, in Kai Province. Later he went to Nara to study Kegon doctrine, but, dissatisfied with the traditional schools of Buddhism, he turned to Zen, studying the newly introduced continental forms under several disciples of Lan-ch'i Tao-lung. In time he gained a reputation as the most brilliant young student of Zen in Japan. Eager to study the Zen of the recently arrived I-shan I-ning, Musō hastened to become his disciple but found something in continental Ch'an that he could not accept. Becoming deeply skeptical, he frequently made solitary journeys or lived alone in simple hermitages, trying to resolve his doubts. After much anguish, he took Kōhō Kennichi as his master and at last attained enlightenment.

The Hōjō family was eager to raise Musō to a position of leadership in Kamakura Zen, but he declined their offer and retired to live quietly on Mount Kokei, in Tajimi, Mino Province, and later in Tosa Province, on Shikoku. When the Hōjō sent a special messenger to press their invitation, Musō briefly returned to Kamakura, only to leave again for a life of seclusion, first on the Miura Peninsula, southeast of Kamakura, and then across the bay in Kazusa Province.

Abruptly, however, he moved to Kyoto, taking up residence at Nanzen-ji at the invitation of Emperor Godaigo (r. 1318–39). It is conjectured that the emperor wished to establish himself as patron of this prominent religious leader to enhance his own prestige in preparation for his planned overthrow of the Kamakura shogunate. After moving to Kyoto, Musō returned briefly to Kamakura, but it was clear that the Kamakura regime's days were numbered. After the shogunate's fall, Godaigo ordered his general Ashikaga Takauji (1305–58) to summon Musō back to Kyoto, where he was installed as the first abbot of Rinsen-ji, given quarters in Nanzen-ji, and made virtual ruler of the Zen world.

The Kemmu Restoration, which had returned direct rule to the emperor, was short-lived. But after Takauji turned against his former master and assumed power himself, founding the Muromachi shogunate, he continued Godaigo's policy of supporting Musō's Zen. Musō was appointed the first abbot of Tōchi-ji, the family temple of the Ashikaga clan, and in 1339 he founded Saihō-ji in Kyoto as a Zen training center. He urged the construction of Ankoku Zen-ji (Zen temples for national peace) and Rishō-tō (pagodas for the benefit of all sentient beings) in every province in supplication for peace and for the repose of the spirits of those who had died in the Genkō Disturbance (1331–33), in which the Ashikaga clan had taken power. Finally, he persuaded the shogunate to construct Tenryū-ji in supplication for the late Emperor Godaigo's eternal well-being.

The enduring relationship of tutelage and patronage that developed between the Musō group and the Ashikaga clan formed the political and economic foundation for this group's flowering. Musō had succeeded in winning the veneration and support of the imperial family, the Kyoto aristocracy, and the Kamakura warrior elite, and he held the highest leadership position in the Zen Gozan system, indeed in the entire Japanese religious world.

Musō's disciples included such eminent figures as Shun'oku Myōha, Gidō Shūshin (1325–88), and Zekkai Chūshin (1336–1405). He is said to have had more than ten thousand followers. The Musō group, whose headquarters were at the Rinsen-ji subtemple Sanne-in, grew into the most powerful school of the Gozan, absorbing other schools until it constituted eighty percent of the entire Gozan system. Thus Musō's activities set the course for the development of the Gozan system as a whole.

Through the influence of continental Zen, Gozan priests came to have a high regard for Chinese poetry and belles-lettres, and Zen temples attracted priests with literary interests and talents. Moreover, it was customary for Zen adepts to express their enlightenment experience in Chinese verse. This led to the investment of considerable time and effort in acquiring the necessary linguistic and literary skills, and eventually to the anomalous situation of Zen priests being more interested in the study of Chinese literature than in the practice of Zen. The emphasis on Chinese literary studies gave rise to Gozan literature.

Gozan literature flourished with the emergence of people like Kokan Shiren, a disciple of I-shan I-ning, and the arrival of Chu-hsien Fan-hsien and other learned priests from China. Their intellectual and cultural exchange stimulated the movement. By the latter half of the fourteenth century, such luminaries as Chūgan Engetsu (1300–1375), Gidō Shūshin, and Zekkai Chūshin were contributing to the golden age of Gozan literature.

After Zekkai and others transmitted from the continent the *P'u-shih Shu* (Hsiao-yin Ta-hsin's documents of statements read at Buddhist services), regarded as a model of the *ssu-liu wen* style of verse, with alternating lines of four (*ssu*) and six (*liu*) characters, *ssu-liu wen* became tremendously pop-

240 THE ZEN SECTS

ular among Gozan writers. The *ssu-liu wen* style of verse had become popular in China after the Chin dynasty (265–317). A writer who had not mastered it was not considered learned. Zen priests began to vie with one another in the use of arcane words and phrases, searching them out in encyclopedic Chinese records. Frequent lectures on difficult texts resulted in a profusion of summaries of and commentaries on the works.

In the fifteenth century, Gozan literature grew increasingly specialized and recondite. At the same time, it was cloaked in secrecy and handed down by private, secret transmission. Creativity was largely discouraged. Instead, emphasis was placed on the mastery of highly formalistic and stylized expression. Chinese learning, Japanized as Gozan literature, lost its original spirit and purpose and became dominated by the mode of secret, oral transmission characteristic of Japanese culture.

The fifteenth century also saw Giyō Hōshū (1361–1424) and Keian Genju (1427–1508) contribute to the ascendancy of the Neo-Confucianism of the twelfth-century Chinese scholar Chu Hsi in the world of Japanese Confucianism. Giyō lectured on Chu Hsi's commentary on the four Confucian classics and published a new edition of this major work, making it more accessible to Japanese readers. Giyō's work, which set the standard for the later Four Classics Method (*shisho kunten*) of rendering classical Chinese into Japanese, was of inestimable value to the development of the Japanese Neo-Confucian tradition.

Invited to Kyushu by the Kikuchi family of Higo Province and the Shimazu family of Satsuma Province, Keian lectured on Chu Hsi's philosophy, devised another system of rendering classical Chinese into Japanese (the *kahō kunten*, or Family Code Method), and founded the Satsunan school of Neo-Confucianism. This school, centered in southern Kyushu, shaped the traditions of Satsuma warriors for centuries. In time, the Chu Hsi school of Neo-Confucianism flourished as the official philosophy of the Tokugawa shogunate and various domains. The great pioneers of this school were Fujiwara Seika (1561–1619) and his disciple Hayashi Razan (1583–1657). Both men had studied Gozan literature as Zen clerics, and through them the Gozan literary tradition crossed over into the Confucianism of the Edo period (1603–1868).

Daitoku-ji

During the heyday of Gozan studies, the Daiō school in the Rinzai sect emphasized Zen practice. Its founder was Nampo Jōmin (1235–1308), a nephew of Enni Bennen who had converted from Tendai to Zen, studied under Lan-ch'i, and then gone to Southern Sung China to receive the Dharma, or Buddhist teachings, from Hsü-t'ang Chih-yü (1185–1269). After returning to Japan he served as Zen instructor to the cloistered emperors Kameyama and Gouda. His school derived its appellation from his posthumous title, Entsū Daiō Kokushi (National Master Daiō [Nampo Jōmin] Who Attained Perfect Enlightenment).

Though Nampo was at one time associated with the Gozan movement, his disciple Shūhō Myōchō (1282–1337) was not. Shūhō had begun by studying Tendai on Mount Shosha, in Harima Province, but converted to Zen. He mastered the new continental forms under Nampo and developed his own innovative and strict style of Zen. His reputation grew rapidly, and he was soon summoned to court by the cloistered emperor Hanazono (r. 1308–18).

At this time representatives of the older, established sects were deeply opposed to Zen. Thus it was decided to hold a debate among the various sects in the first month of 1325. Shūhō participated in that court-sponsored debate and roundly defeated the scholar-priests of Nara and Mount Hiei. As a result, the eminent priest Genne (d. 1350) changed allegiance and became Shūhō's disciple. Genne gave his residence in northern Kyoto to Shūhō. (That structure is the Daitoku-ji subtemple called Ummon-an.) Shūhō, however, retired to Ungo-an, in Higashiyama. Later, under the patronage of his uncle Akamatsu Norimura (1277–1350), constable of Harima Province, he moved to Ummon-an and founded Daitoku-ji. All his life Shūhō remained a low-ranking priest in the Gozan system, but Daitoku-ji quickly came to rank among the greatest temples, and he was given the posthumous title Kōzen Daitō Kokushi (National Master Who Served as a Great Lamp for Promoting Zen).

Notable among Shūhō's many eminent disciples were Tettō Gikō (1295–1369) and Kanzan Egen (1277–1360), who founded Myōshin-ji, in Kyoto. Tettō Gikō had originally studied under the Gozan system but, dissatisfied, became a disciple of Shūhō and eventually succeeded him as abbot of Daitoku-ji. Tettō, an able administrator, devoted himself to the organization of his disciples, the management of the temple, and the codification of monastic regulations. His group remained ascendant at Daitoku-ji and extended its influence throughout the region around the capital and even as far away as the Chūgoku region and Shikoku.

Later, however, Daitoku-ji insisted on the right to exclude from residence at the temple all priests who were not of Shūhō's lineage. This brought the temple into conflict with the government, and Daitoku-ji was ultimately removed from the ranks of the official Gozan. It became a private temple and in 1431 closed its doors to priests outside Shūhō's lineage. Yet because of this, Shūhō's unique style of Zen was exceptionally well preserved, and priests unhappy with the increasingly literary leanings of the Gozan temples gravitated to Daitoku-ji. Among those zealous practitioners were Kasō Sōdon (1352–1428) and his disciples Ikkyū Sōjun (1394–1481) and Yōsō Sōi (1376–1458). Daitoku-ji experienced a renaissance at the hand of these priests.

Yōsō Sōi had begun studies under the Gozan system before becoming Kasō's disciple. He was a skillful manager and worked to improve Daitoku-ji's fortunes, which declined after it was excluded from the Gozan. He cultivated good relations with the court and won recognition for Daitoku-ji as a court-affiliated temple.

Yōsō's great rival at Daitoku-ji was Ikkyū Sōjun. Ikkyū was a son of Emperor Gokomatsu (r. 1382–1412), but his mother had to leave the court before his birth because she was related to an aristocratic family allied with the rival Southern Court, which claimed to hold the legitimate throne. Ikkyū, then called Shūken, originally belonged to the Musō group but, discontented, went to study under Kasō. An idealist, Ikkyū despised the decadent tendencies in the Zen of his day and was mercilessly critical. He particularly opposed Yōsō's group, regarded as the orthodox faction at Daitoku-ji, accusing the group of hypocrisy.

Ikkyū made no secret of the fact that he kept a concubine, a blind singer who had borne him a son, and he expressed his passionate love for a number of other women in a remarkable series of poems. But Ikkyū was more than simply a rebel against convention. He labored mightily for the revival of Daitoku-ji and tried earnestly to preserve its traditions. In a time of crisis he proved willing to starve himself to death in the mountains if that would further the reformation of the temple. Unconcerned with fame or reward and unawed by those in power, he tried to preserve the purity of the Buddhist tradition he had inherited, while at the same time leading a life of perfect freedom.

Among the many artists and writers drawn to Ikkyū because of his honesty and humanity were the tea master Murata Jukō (1423–1502), the *renga* poet Sōchō (1448–1532), the Noh player On'ami (1398–1467), the Noh actor and playwright Komparu Zenchiku (b. 1405), the haiku poet Yamazaki Sōkan (d. ca. 1539), and the painter Soga Jasoku (d. 1473). Ikkyū, well loved by the general public, was a popular subject of writers of the

Edo period (1603–1868) and figured in numerous stories, such as the humorous *Ikkyū Shokoku Banashi* (Tales of Ikkyū's Wanderings in the Provinces).

Under later leaders, such as Kogaku Sōkō (1465–1548) and Shun'oku Sōen (1529–1611), the Daitoku-ji group's influence spread throughout the capital region and to such distant provinces as Chikuzen, on Kyushu, and Sagami. In one of the most turbulent periods of Japan's feudal history, the group won followers among the daimyō, or warrior lords, as well as the merchant class and artistic and literary figures.

From an early date, Daitoku-ji was associated with the tea ceremony. The priest and tea master Murata Jukō was a disciple of Ikkyū. As the disciple of one of Jukō's direct disciples, the famed tea master Takeno Jōō (1502–55) succeeded to both Jukō's tea tradition and his Zen. Over time the "way of tea" (*chadō*) developed in conjunction with an appreciation of fine art objects from the Ming dynasty (1368–1662) imported via the brisk trade conducted by merchants of the port of Sakai, southwest of Kyoto. The aesthetic of the tea ceremony, influenced by both Zen Buddhism and Chinese culture, reached its highest development under the great tea master Sen no Rikyū (1522–91), who had studied Zen at Daitoku-ji. The Daitoku-ji group's long, intimate connection with the tea ceremony is one of its distinctive characteristics.

The Myōshin-ji Group

Although it too developed from the Daiō group, Kanzan Egen's Myōshin-ji group in time surpassed the Daitoku-ji group in size and influence. Like the Daitoku-ji group, it was formed by priests who had left the Gozan system because of its lack of serious Zen practice. Kanzan, the founder of Myōshin-ji, was a disciple of Shūhō Myōchō but eventually had a major disagreement with his teacher and as a result retired to a simple hermitage in Ibuka, in Mino Province. After Shūhō died, the cloistered emperor Hanazono summoned Kanzan to Kyoto to serve as his Zen master and gave him a former imperial villa. Renamed Myōshin-ji, this structure became the headquarters of Kanzan's Zen tradition, which soon flourished, outstripping all others.

Nonetheless, after the death of its powerful imperial patron, Myōshin-ji faced difficulties, since it was officially a branch temple of Daitoku-ji. In 1399 it incurred the wrath of the shōgun Ashikaga Yoshimitsu through its complicity in the rebellion raised by the warlord Ōuchi Yoshihiro (1356–99), and Myōshin-ji and its estates were confiscated for a time. After its reestablishment was permitted by the government, Nippō Sōshun (1368–1448) became the seventh abbot of Myōshin-ji, going to Kyoto from Zuisen-ji, in Owari Province. Under the patronage of the powerful warrior Hosokawa Katsumoto (1430–73), Sōshun brought the Myōshin-ji group great influence and prosperity.

Sekkō Sōshin (1408–86), the ninth abbot of Myōshin-ji, also contributed greatly to the temple's growth. He instituted major fiscal reforms, strengthening Myōshin-ji's financial base, and with the enthusiastic support of the Hosokawa family completed the restoration of the temple's fortunes. Among his eminent disciples were Gokei Sōton (1416–1500), Keisen Sōryū (1425–1500), Tokuhō Zenketsu (1419–1506), and Tōyō Eichō (1428–1504), founders of the four major subgroups of the Myōshin-ji group.

The four Myōshin-ji subgroups established a nationwide system centering on the four hermitages (*an*) they maintained at Myōshin-ji. Each subgroup occupied its hermitage only during the term of its leadership of Myōshin-ji. (The four hermitages were Reiun-an, Ryūsen-an, Shōtaku-an, and Tōkai-an.) The four Myōshin-ji subgroups established close ties with powerful local daimyō, such as the Hosokawa and the Saitō of Mino Province. As the subgroups spread throughout the land, they incorporated elements of popular piety into their practice, adding prayers, intercessory rituals, and funeral rites to their ministry to the laity. As a result, the Myōshin-ji group won adherents not only among the powerful warrior-aristocrats, but also among doctors, merchants, artisans, and the people at large. By the end of the sixteenth century, it was far more popular and powerful than its rival, Daitoku-ji.

THE SŌTŌ SECT

Dōgen

The Sōtō sect of Zen in Japan was founded by Dōgen (1200–1253). The scion of the noble Koga Michichika, Dōgen seemed destined for a position of power and wealth, but both his parents died while he was still a child. Thus made keenly aware of the impermanence of all earthly things, he went to Enryaku-ji, on Mount Hiei, and began a rigorous program of religious exercises and studies, taking the religious name Buppōbō Dōgen.

As his studies progressed, he was troubled by the difficult question of why people must engage in religious practice to gain enlightenment if, as the Tendai sect teaches, all sentient beings are already one with the Buddha. The learned scholar-priests of Mount Hiei offered no convincing answer to this question. Dōgen then went to consult the eminent Kōin (1145–1216) of Onjō-ji, but Kōin too had no answer. He did suggest, however, that Dōgen could best begin to solve this problem by traveling to Southern Sung China and mastering the new forms of Zen being practiced there.

Dōgen went first to Kennin-ji, which had been founded by Eisai, founder of the Rinzai sect, to undergo training in the fundamentals of continental Zen. In 1223 he went to China, where he studied various forms of Ch'an, but he remained dissatisfied. Finally he went to study under the austere master Chang-weng Ju-ching (1163–1228), on Mount T'ien-t'ung, and discovered the form of Ch'an he had been seeking. He formally became Ju-ching's disciple and a priest of the Ts'ao-tung (Sōtō) sect. Having been initiated into Ch'an, Dōgen returned to Japan in 1227 and again entered Kennin-ji. From that time on he stressed the absolute correctness of the tradition he had learned from Ju-ching, arguing that *zazen* (seated meditation) was both the most correct method of seeking enlightenment and the gate to peace of mind and spiritual joy.

In his *Fukan Zazen Gi* (A Universal Recommendation of *Zazen*; 1227), Dōgen introduced the teaching and practice of *zazen*, arguing that *shikan taza* ("just sitting in meditation") is the highest and best practice. *Shikan taza* is often interpreted as literally sitting silently in *zazen*, without studying the well-known Zen dialogues called *mondō*. Dōgen, however, never denied the value of *mondō*, which are very important to the Rinzai sect, and in fact wrote many commentaries on them. Dōgen's *shikan taza* is neither simple, silent *zazen* nor simple rejection of *mondō*, but an expansive practice free of formalism.

His strong advocacy of the new continental forms of Zen soon provoked the priests of Mount Hiei, and around 1230 he was forced to leave Kennin-ji for a solitary hermitage in Fukakusa near Kyoto. There he later founded Kōshō Hōrin-ji and developed a comprehensive training program for his disciples. He also began his major work, the *Shōbō Genzō* (Treasury of the Eye of the True Dharma; 1231–53). In his writings, he continued to argue that the doctrine and practice he had learned from Ju-ching were the very essence of the Buddha's teachings, and he firmly rejected attempts to give those teachings a specific label, such as "Zen sect." He also rejected the designation Sōtō Zen. Further, Dōgen dismissed many of the doctrines and practices then current in Japanese Buddhism: the *nembutsu* doctrine, with its emphasis on salvation in the next life; prayers and incantations to invoke the protection of various deities and buddhas; and the widely popular belief in the Three Ages of the Law, the present age being *Mappō*, the period of the Decay of the Law.

Eventually, many priests were drawn to the new form of Zen that Dōgen was teaching. Among them were Koun Ejō (1198–1280) from the Tendai temple Tōnomine-dera, in Sakurai; Kakuzen Ekan (d. 1251) and his disciple Tettsū Gikai (1219–1309) from the Hakusan Tendai temple Hajaku-ji, in Echizen Province (present-day Fukui in Fukui Prefecture); and others from the Daie school of the Rinzai sect. As his training hall in Fukakusa became a center of religious activity, Dōgen again drew the hostile attention of the Tendai priests on Mount Hiei. This time, however, he did not avoid confrontation.

Dōgen wrote the *Gokoku Shōbō Gi* (The True Law as Protector of the Nation; ca. 1243), in which he argued that the Zen he was teaching was precisely the Buddhist doctrine that would preserve, protect, and bring prosperity to the nation. With some support from the court, the Mount Hiei priests bitterly criticized this view, and the suppression of Dōgen's group intensified. Also at this time, the Rinzai priest Enni Bennen adopted elements of the new continental Zen and, with the strong support of the Fujiwara clan, founded the major temple Tōfuku-ji, north of Fukakusa. This constituted another threat to Dōgen's group.

Consequently, in the seventh month of 1243 Dōgen went to Echizen Province, to the Shihi estate of his devoted lay disciple Hatano Yoshishige. There he founded Daibutsu-ji, where he lived in seclusion. Dōgen moved to Echizen at the urging of those disciples who had come from Hajaku-ji and at the invitation of Yoshishige.

The Shihi estate lay in an area dominated by the Hakusan Tendai group, whose nearby temples included Heisen-ji, in present-day Katsuyama; Toyohara-dera, in Toyohara; and Hajaku-ji. Why did Dōgen choose to move there? It is likely that in the light of his experience with priests from Hajaku-ji, he thought that his teaching might be accepted by members of the Hakusan Tendai group if only he had the opportunity to present it to them. Indeed, after Dōgen's death, his group developed into a nationwide religious movement by converting many Hakusan temples. Dōgen may have foreseen that possibility at this early date.

In 1246 Dōgen changed the name of his headquarters to Eihei-ji, after the Japanese reading of the era name Yung-p'ing (C.E. 57–75), in which Buddhism was said to have reached China from India. He no doubt intended to proclaim that the true teachings of Śākyamuni Buddha, as transmitted from India to China and preached by him in Japan, would soon prosper in Japan. He devoted himself to increasingly stringent religious practices and strongly emphasized the superiority of the religious to the lay state, denying that lay believers, both men and women, could attain complete enlightenment. With Śākyamuni Buddha's monastic and ascetic path as his ideal, he naturally emphasized monastic practice, urging the priests under his direction to emulate Śākyamuni's example.

In 1247 Dōgen went to the shogunate's capital, Kamakura, at the invitation of the powerful regent Hōjō Tokiyori, but he quickly returned to Echizen, having realized that with Gozan temple Zen firmly entrenched in Kamakura his teachings would have little effect on the ruling warriors. Thereafter he spent much of his time working on the *Shōbō Genzō*, intending to expand it to one hundred fascicles. Forced to change his plans because of illness, he revised the work, reducing it to twelve fascicles. The remaining material was later edited into a work of seventy-five fascicles by Dōgen's senior disciple Koun Ejō, and the two works together are regarded as close to Dōgen's original intention.

Gravely ill, Dōgen passed the abbacy of Eihei-ji to Ejō in the seventh month of 1253 and went to Kyoto for rest and treatment. There, on the twenty-eighth day of the eighth month, dressed in the simple black robe of an ordinary priest, Dōgen died at the age of fifty-three.

The Schism at Eihei-ji

After Dōgen's death, Ejō, the most faithful heir to his ideas, became the central figure at Eihei-ji. Originally a member of the Rinzai-sect Daie group, he became a disciple of Dōgen and aided him not only in preaching and teaching activities but also in preparing the finished manuscripts of the *Shōbō Genzō*. After the move to Echizen, Ejō devoted more and more time to the *Shōbō Genzō*, eventually completing seventy-five fascicles.

Tettsū Gikai, who also had been a member of the Daie group, succeeded Ejō in the abbacy and leadership of the Sōtō sect. He had practiced under Dōgen in Fukakusa and served as administrator of Eihei-ji. When Dōgen went to Kyoto near the end of his life, Tettsū was left in charge of the temple. But Dōgen died before Tettsū was able to receive the official transmission of the full teachings from his master. Thus he became a disciple of Ejō and devoted himself to the development of the group, concentrating especially on renovation of the temple buildings and reform of monastic rules and rituals.

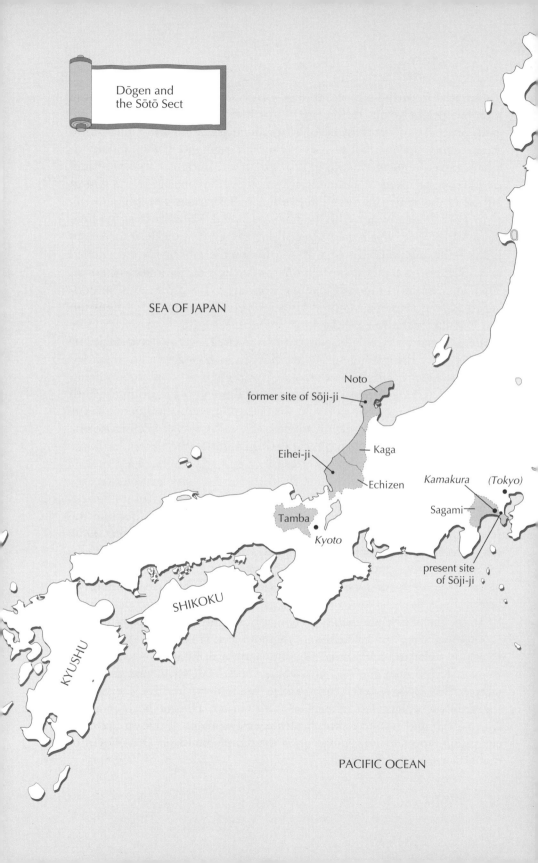

Dōgen and
the Sōtō Sect

SEA OF JAPAN

Noto

former site of Sōji-ji

Kaga

Eihei-ji

Echizen

Kamakura

(Tokyo)

Sagami

Tamba

Kyoto

present site
of Sōji-ji

SHIKOKU

KYUSHU

PACIFIC OCEAN

The Eihei-ji group was susceptible to being divided because it consisted of both disciples who had been with Dōgen from the beginning and clergy from other groups and sects who had joined later. Tettsū and others were strongly opposed by more conservative priests, such as Jakuen (1207–99) and Gien (d. 1314), who wished to preserve intact the simple, pure form of Zen practiced by Dōgen. In the second month of 1272 Tettsū finally left Eihei-ji, moving to Daijō-ji, in Kaga Province. As a result of this dispute over the third abbot, the early Sōtō sect split into a group led by Jakuen and Gien, centered at Eihei-ji, and Tettsū's group, based at Daijō-ji and spreading from Kaga Province into Noto Province. The two groups developed independently until about the sixteenth century.

Gien became the fourth abbot of Eihei-ji and was succeeded by Giun (1253–1333), who was a disciple of Jakuen. Giun worked hard to improve the material prosperity of the temple and cast a great bell that survives. He also reedited the *Shōbō Genzō*, the manuscripts of which were deteriorating, producing a new sixty-fascicle edition.

Keizan

Among Tettsū's disciples at Daijō-ji was Keizan Jōkin (1268–1325), who labored with great success for the rapid growth of the Daijō-ji branch of the Sōtō sect. Originally a disciple of Tettsū, Keizan went to Tōfuku-ji, in Kyoto, to study under Hakuun Egyō (1223–97) and then to Kii Province to learn Zen from Muhon Kakushin. From these Rinzai priests Keizan learned to combine Zen and esoteric Buddhist practices, and he concentrated on harmonizing Zen practices with those of other sects rather than preserving the Zen of Dōgen. This proved highly effective as Keizan moved from Kaga Province into Noto Province, converting Tendai temples to the Sōtō sect and absorbing the Tendai clergy and Shugendō ascetics into a burgeoning Sōtō sect.

As his activities expanded from Kaga into Noto, Keizan established his own form of Zen, strongly influenced by esoteric Buddhism. This new faith incorporated a wide variety of religious elements: the cult of the deity of Hakusan, a very ancient mountain-centered folk religion with an extremely broad following throughout Japan; the cult of Kannon, regarded by esoteric Buddhists as the original prototype of the Hakusan deity; the unique Tendai cult of the Sannō deity, worshiped at Hie Shrine, southeast of Kyoto; the cult of the deity of Kumano; and others. This development during Keizan's lifetime resulted in a new pattern for the expansion of the Sōtō sect. It spread throughout the country by exploiting the network of the Hakusan Tendai group temples and the Tendai priests and Shugendō ascetics who were closely associated with them.

Sōji-ji, in Noto Province, drew attention as a progressive new spiritual center attracting not only Sōtō priests but also the clergy of virtually all sects. Sōji-ji's fame spread far and wide, and priests from all over the country went there to study, bringing new energy and prosperity to Keizan's group. (Sōji-ji was moved to its present location in Yokohama, Kanagawa Prefecture in 1911.)

Keizan had two major disciples, Meihō Sotetsu (1277–1350) and Gasan Jōseki (1275–1365), who further advanced the fortunes of his school. Meihō succeeded Keizan as the third abbot of Daijō-ji, and his school spread through Kaga, Noto, and Echizen, and into far southern and northern Honshu. The development of the Gasan school surpassed that of the Meihō school.

Gasan succeeded Keizan as the second abbot of Sōji-ji and pursued Keizan's policies with great vigor. Believing that it was urgent to find and educate priests, he devoted most of his energies to the reeducation of clergy who entered the Sōtō sect from other sects. As a result, the Gasan group benefited from a large number of bright, highly capable members, the most eminent of whom were known as Gasan's Twenty-five Sages. Gasan remained in the remote Noto area but sent his disciples throughout the country. Through written instructions, Gasan maintained firm control of his widely scattered followers. During the forty-odd years of his leadership, both the rate of growth and the range of the school's activity were astounding.

The Sōji-ji Order

The Keizan group, spreading out from its base at Sōji-ji, continued to establish new centers of influence throughout the nation, converting and restoring the temples of older sects with the help of the provincial gentry. Especially notable for their activities were the schools headed by Taigen Sōshin (d. 1371), in the Tōkaidō region, and by Tsūgen Jakurei (1322–91), based at Yōtaku-ji, in Tamba Province. One of Tsūgen's two highest disciples, Ryōan Emyō (1337–1411), succeeded in converting the well-known Saijō-ji, in Sagami Province, from Shingon to Sōtō, and his disciples in turn spread the teaching throughout the Kantō region and into north-

THE SŌTŌ SECT 251

eastern Honshu. The other was Sekioku Shinryō (1345–1423), who carried the teachings to Kyushu, Shikoku, and the San'indō and San'yōdō regions. In time, the Tsūgen group, based at Yōtaku-ji, dominated all the subgroups of the Keizan school, its influence extending nationwide.

The reason for the extraordinary growth of the Keizan school as a whole probably lay in the popular elements in the school's teachings and practices, which appealed to ordinary believers. As mentioned earlier, the first of these elements was prayers to and invocations of the deities and buddhas, adopted as a result of the assimilation of Tendai and Shingon clergy into the Sōtō sect and the Sōtō sect's accommodation to esoteric Buddhism.

Invocations and rituals were increasingly emphasized as the sect spread through the nation. Numerous, disparate local cults were incorporated into the Sōtō sect: the Hakusan and Kumano cults, which were popular throughout Japan; that of the deity of Tateyama, in Etchū Province, whose original prototype was supposed to be Amida; that of the deity of Akiba, worshiped at Yōtaku-ji, in Tōtōmi Province, and believed to be a manifestation of Kannon who provides protection from fire; the cult of Dōryō, at Saijō-ji, in Sagami Province; the cults of the three oracles of Ise Grand Shrine, in Ise Province, Iwashimizu Hachiman Shrine, south of Kyoto, and Kasuga Shrine, in Nara; the cult of the deity Inari, especially at Toyokawa Inari Shrine, in Mikawa Province; the cult of Temman Tenjin, the deified scholar-statesman Sugawara no Michizane (845–903), centered at Kyoto; and many more. The links between the Sōtō sect and various cults are evident in any research on the historical development of Sōtō temples or the identity of their tutelary deities.

On the whole, the consolatory aspects of popular religion were emphasized, especially the rites and prayers of esoteric Buddhism. Innumerable religious practices promised worldly benefits: exorcism of demons and monsters; purification of bridges and other public works; digging of healing hot springs; development of irrigation systems; and other works that benefited the public materially or medically. Patently, Sōtō missionaries sought to convert the populace by adopting elements of popular religion and of the older, established Buddhist sects.

Furthermore, popular literature of the day records many sermons and homilies delivered at funerals and memorial services. Popular in tone, clear, and easy to understand, these sermons were evidently aimed at a broad audience, including warriors, merchants, artisans, and peasants. Clearly, the Sōtō sect had begun to reach the social classes that had been unable to participate in the formal Buddhist funerals and memorial services of the older sects—Shingon, Tendai, and the Gozan Zen schools.

At the same time, the forms of religious practice (preeminently, *zazen*) changed considerably from earlier times. For example, by the fifteenth century *missan roku*, answer books used by aspirants to prepare for interviews with their master, were widely distributed and passed privately from master to disciple as an aid to practice. In the late fifteenth century it became customary to record the transmission of the teaching from master to disciple in not only the traditional *shisho* (genealogical list) but also two other documents: the *kechimyaku* (a genealogy of the transmission of the Buddha's teaching or precepts) and the *kirigami daiji* (a piece of paper on which one subject is illustrated). The use of all three documents continues today. The *kirigami* system was originally employed by esoteric Buddhism for accurate transmission of the secret teaching from a master to his disciples. The *kirigami daiji* clearly shows the way that traditional esoteric Buddhist modes of transmission influenced the Sōtō tradition.

In addition, various ceremonies came to be widely performed by Sōtō priests: these included the *se gaki e* (feeding of the hungry spirits) rite, for the sake of the departed, and the Great Perfection of Wisdom Sutra rite, in which that voluminous work was ritually scanned (rather than read in full) in prayer for peace for the nation and the populace. Both of these originally were esoteric Buddhist rites, and their use by Sōtō priests in behalf of ordinary people appears to have been a major factor in the sect's remarkable growth in provincial Japan. Together with the adoption of these esoteric Buddhist rites, the development that characterizes the Sōtō sect of this period is the increasing popularity of the *gōko e* and the bestowing of the precepts rites.

In the *gōko e*, a traditional Buddhist practice originating in India, the participants seclude themselves for a full ninety days of religious exercises. The *gōko e* is also known as the *ango* (in Sanskrit *varṣa*, meaning rainy-season retreat) or the *kessei* practice. Dōgen himself emphasized the *gōko e*, declaring it to be the fundamental form of Zen practice handed down from the time of Śākyamuni, but it became generally popular in the Sōtō sect only after the Ōnin era (1467–69). Until then, it had been practiced in the five major Rinzai monasteries but had never been introduced to the ordinary believer. In the Sōtō sect, it became known as the *gōko* for the thousands, and under the patronage of provincial daimyō it was undertaken on a massive scale in various regions, with great numbers of ordinary believers as well as Zen clergy participating. It aroused the interest of the populace and contributed to the conversion of large numbers to Zen.

The bestowing of the precepts, too, was not restricted to a small elite, as it had been in the older, established sects. Large numbers of people of all classes—from daimyō to ordinary citizens—were able to establish direct spiritual links with eminent priests through these ceremonies, which were held in many areas and regularly attracted hundreds of participants. Moreover, the donations made at such ceremonies supported the restoration and expansion of local Sōtō temples, thus furthering the sect's growth.

As a result of all these activities, the number of Sōtō sect adherents nationwide increased greatly, and the sect's social foundation was broadened through its appeal to all classes. Futhermore, its various ceremonies, which attracted people from throughout each feudal domain, strengthened the horizontal links among the various Sōtō schools in each domain. Before, there had been little communication, except that between the main and branch temples of a school. The establishment of wider, horizontal communication networks contributed greatly to the development of the sect as a whole.

Reunification

During the fifteenth century, the various Sōtō sect schools grew and prospered throughout the country. The Keizan school became a powerful organization that overshadowed the Eihei-ji school. In the late fifteenth century, the Keizan school succeeded in taking control of Eihei-ji, with which it had had no relations since the dispute over the third abbot. The rival Jakuen school was overwhelmed, and the Keizan school promptly made Eihei-ji the center of the entire Sōtō sect, placing it over Sōji-ji, Daijō-ji, and other great temples. Thus in the last half of the fifteenth century the Sōtō sect was reunited under the direction of Eihei-ji, all of whose succeeding abbots came from the Keizan school.

Beginning in the sixteenth century, the imperial court gave the successive Keizan-school abbots the official title of Zen Master on the grounds that they were the legitimate successors of the founder, Dōgen. In the twelfth month of 1507, through the patronage of the former regent Ichijō Fuyuyoshi (1464–1514), Eihei-ji was officially termed "the preeminent Sōtō training center in Japan" in a plaque inscribed by Emperor Gokashiwabara (r. 1500–1526). With that, Eihei-ji was ranked with Nanzen-ji and a select few temples that were under imperial patronage, and imperial permission was required for official residence there. Thus Eihei-ji was in both name and fact the supreme temple in the Sōtō sect, unrivaled in power, honor, and rank. Sōji-ji, the original seat of the now dominant Keizan school, was honored as a major temple under imperial patronage in an edict of 1589.

Shortly after Tokugawa Ieyasu (1542–1616) united the nation under his rule as shōgun at the beginning of the seventeenth century, Sōnei-ji, in Shimōsa Province, Ryūon-ji, in Musashi Province, and Daichū-ji, in Shimotsuke Province, were given regulatory authority as *sōroku*, or superintendents of clergy, over other temples. In the fifth month of 1612 the Tokugawa shogunate required these three temples, as well as Daitō-in, in Suruga Province, to observe the monastic regulations of the Sōtō sect and incorporated them into the branch-temple system. In the seventh month of 1615, the shogunate recognized the imperial favor granted both Eihei-ji and Sōji-ji, including the right of their abbots to wear a purple robe, a mark of the highest distinction. This was the last step in the establishment of the branch-temple system of the Sōtō sect, with both Eihei-ji and Sōji-ji ranked as main temples. That system has survived with little change and constitutes the framework for one of Japan's largest Buddhist sects, with about 14,700 temples today.

10. The Nichiren Sect

THE NICHIREN SECT IN THE KAMAKURA PERIOD

Nichiren's Early Years

Born in Awa Province, Nichiren (1222–82) was the only one of the originators of the Buddhism of the Kamakura period (1185–1336) to come from eastern Japan. Apart from a period of study in the Kyoto area in his youth and a period of exile on Sado in middle age, he spent his whole life in eastern Japan, and his indomitable spirit mirrors the character of that region's warriors, among whom he was raised.

Nichiren was born into a family of provincial estate overseers and received his early education at a nearby Tendai temple, Seichō-ji (in present-day Amatsukominato-machi, Chiba Prefecture). In later years he said that as a child he had decided to become a priest because of his strong consciousness of the impermanence of all things. This was precisely the reason that Saichō, founder of the Tendai sect in the Heian period, and Hōnen and Dōgen, founders of the Jōdo and Sōtō sects in the Kamakura period, entered the religious life. On the basis of Nichiren's autobiographical writings, some scholars believe that he wished to determine for himself which of the ten major Buddhist sects of his day (the six Nara schools and the Tendai, Shingon, Pure Land, and Zen sects) transmitted the true teachings. However, I believe that the question of which sect was correct occupied him only later, after he had decided to become a priest.

Nichiren became a Tendai priest, adopting the name Zeshōbō. He spent many years traveling from temple to temple, studying Buddhist doctrine and practice. Seichō-ji in rustic Awa was not the best environment for finding the answers he sought. There was in fact no qualified teacher there, and so Nichiren, like most young priests at provincial Tendai temples, eventually decided to go to Mount Hiei to receive the Mahāyāna precepts and pursue more advanced study. We know little about Nichiren's early religious life, but by his own account he devoted himself to the study and practice of the Pure Land tradition, which was natural for someone who had such a strong sense of both the evanescence of worldly things and the ineluctability of death. The Tendai form of Pure Land teachings was already well known at Seichō-ji, and Hōnen's more radical version had begun to become popular in nearby Kamakura. In the Kyoto area, of course, there were many Pure Land devotees. Thus, although Nichiren later renounced the Pure Land doctrine and became one of its fiercest opponents, he was certainly at one time a follower of some form of Pure Land belief.

We do not know exactly when or how long Nichiren studied at Enryaku-ji, on Mount Hiei, but we do know that he did not discover a suitable teacher there. He never found the master that Shinran had in Hōnen, or that Dōgen had in Ju-ching. In lieu of a personal encounter, there was in Nichiren's case an encounter with scriptures—the Sutra of the Great Decease and the Lotus Sutra. Unable to find a personal master, he devoted himself to intense study of the sutras, śāstras (or treatises), and commentaries.

In Nichiren's time the Tendai sect emphasized meditational practice and doctrinal study. Though Nichiren did receive the oral transmission of meditation techniques, without question his greatest interest lay in doctrinal study. Eventually he came across the verse in the Sutra of the Great Decease that says, "Rely on the Law, not on humans." From this, Nichiren realized that he ought to seek the true Buddhist teaching rather than human teachers or masters. This principle guided and supported him for the rest of his life. Ultimately Nichiren selected the Lotus Sutra as the Law on which he would rely, and he became convinced that it was supreme among all the teachings of Buddhism.

Nichiren also seems to have studied both Shingon and Tendai esoteric teachings during his time in the Kyoto area and to have copied Kakuban's famous *Gorin Kuji Myō Himitsu Shaku* (Commentary Revealing the Secrets of the Five Spheres and the Nine Letters; ca. 1142), which attempts to subsume Pure Land doctrine under Shingon teachings and which influenced Nichiren's own thinking. However, he soon began his career as a missionary of the Lotus Sutra, preaching its superiority over all other teachings and especially opposing the increasingly popular Pure Land doctrine taught by Hōnen.

Propagating Faith in the Lotus Sutra

With the exception of Ippen, founder of the Ji sect, all the originators of Kamakura-period Buddhism first studied at Enryaku-ji and then left to establish their own groups. Their reasons for taking that step varied. In Nichiren's case, it seems likely that there was no place at the elitist, clique-ridden Enryaku-ji for a priest of relatively humble origins from the rough east country and that Nichiren himself neither expected nor wanted to be part of the Mount Hiei establishment.

By 1253 Nichiren was already back at Seichō-ji in Awa and was developing his ideas on the supremacy of the Lotus Sutra and his criticism of the Pure Land doctrine for the benefit of the clergy there. This marks the beginning of Nichiren's efforts at propagating faith in the Lotus Sutra. A large number of clergy and laity in the area were Pure Land devotees, and Nichiren's preaching, though it won over some, greatly antagonized many listeners, which led to his forced departure from Seichō-ji. Around midwinter of 1254, he left Awa for Kamakura, having had his first taste of the persecution that awaited him.

No sooner did Nichiren arrive in Kamakura than he began to disseminate his Lotus Sutra teaching. As a Tendai priest, he had acquaintances among the clergy of that sect, and some of them were his first converts. Several lay believers, too, accepted the new faith, for example, the warrior Toki Jōnin (1216–99), who became a lifelong follower of Nichiren.

At about this time a series of natural disasters occurred in the region, and Nichiren felt he could not remain silent in the face of the suffering they wreaked. Between 1256 and 1260 Kamakura experienced torrential rains, floods, and major earthquakes, and provinces throughout the country experienced heavy rains with violent wind, followed by epidemics. The bad weather led to widespread crop failure and famine. Bands of robbers increased throughout the land. In short, it was a time of much suffering, with many people falling ill, starving, and dying.

Nichiren interpreted all these tragic events in a religious light and offered a remedy on that basis. He believed that calamities occur when the guardian deities of a country abandon it and are replaced by evil spirits, and that the deities abandon a country when the people cease to revere the true Law and give themselves over to false teachings and practices. In the immediate case, these false teachings were those of Hōnen's Pure Land sect. If it were banned and correct belief in the Lotus Sutra encouraged, the well-being of the nation would be assured. Nichiren's view—that the well-being of the nation, or the cessation of the series of calamities that had struck Japan, depended on the spiritual state of the people—was essentially religious.

In 1259 Nichiren summarized his criticisms of Hōnen's Pure Land teachings in the *Shugo Kokka Ron* (On Protecting the Nation). The following year he further developed his arguments, and offered solutions to the problem, in the *Risshō Ankoku Ron* (On Establishing the Correct Teaching and Pacifying the Nation), which was presented to Hōjō Tokiyori (1227–63), the former regent and the most powerful man in Kamakura. Three times Nichiren appealed formally to the authorities for support of his views. Nichiren's act of appeal was called *kangyō*, or "remonstrance and persuasion," and the presentation of the *Risshō Ankoku Ron* in 1260 was the first occasion on which he remonstrated with and attempted to persuade the authorities.

Tokiyori, however, did not accept Nichiren's suggestions. Nichiren preached the same ideas to the ordinary people of Kamakura, arousing the opposition of the Pure Land believers in the area. Numerous acrimonious debates and even a physical attack on Nichiren followed. Since the *Risshō Ankoku Ron* suggests that natural calamities are the result of bad governance, the shogunate construed the treatise as direct criticism. In the fifth month of 1261 Nichiren was arrested and banished to Itō, on the Izu Peninsula, for about three years.

Released from exile in 1263, Nichiren returned to Awa. He promptly began to preach again and soon was surrounded by a group of believers and sympathizers, old and new. The Pure Land believers in the area, viewing Nichiren and his activities as a threat, decided to attack his group at Tōjō, under the leadership of the steward Tōjō Kagenobu (fl. thirteenth century), who had been influential in driving Nichiren from Seichō-ji years before. In the attack, which took place in the eleventh month of 1264, one disciple was killed, two were gravely injured, and Nichiren himself sustained a head wound and a broken arm. Escaping with his life, he fled Awa once again for Kamakura.

This attack and the term of exile in Izu merely deepened Nichiren's convictions as a devotee of the Lotus Sutra. He believed that since the Lotus Sutra predicts that its true devotees will suffer persecution, his experiences confirmed the truth of the scripture, as well as his own status as a true devotee. Thus, through his sufferings, both the truth of the Lotus Sutra and the validity of his own role were affirmed. With new confidence, he resumed his preaching in Kamakura.

The Mongol Court's Letter

On the basis of his reading of the Lotus Sutra, Nichiren had warned in the *Risshō Ankoku Ron* that there would be civil unrest and invasion by foreign forces if the people did not preserve faith in the Lotus. In 1268 a letter from the Mongol court of China reached Japan. It seemed the fulfillment of Nichiren's predictions. The Mongols had already conquered most of China and brought the Korean peninsula under their suzerainty and would soon establish the Yüan dynasty. Kublai Khan (1215–94), the Mongol ruler, had sent a letter to the shogunate of Japan in 1266, demanding the nation's capitulation and threatening military invasion if a positive reply was not forthcoming. The shogunate received this message in 1268 and decided to refuse the Mongol demand and prepare for the defense of the islands. The imperial court in Kyoto ordered prayers to be said for the defending forces, and the general public, including people in Kamakura, soon heard the terrifying news.

At this juncture, Nichiren—who had long predicted a foreign invasion if the people and government continued to neglect the true teachings of Buddhism—was seen increasingly as a prophet. Many of those who most feared the Mongol invasion became devout believers in the new teaching. Indeed, this was the period of the most rapid gains for Nichiren's group in his lifetime.

Gradually Nichiren turned from stressing the supremacy of the Lotus Sutra over other sutras to demanding exclusive devotion to it. At the same time, he determined to devote his life to the propagation of faith in the Lotus Sutra, regardless of threats of banishment or even death. He continued to vehemently criticize his Buddhist rivals, calling Zen the doctrine of demons, Ritsu a deceiver and misleader of the world, and *nembutsu* the cause of punishment in the lowest of the hells. The clerical and lay followers of Nichiren also became more radical in their words and actions, fiercely criticizing those who held beliefs other than the Lotus faith. It was alleged that they went so far as to burn the sacred images of other sects, or throw them into rivers. Soon the other sects were demanding that the government suppress the Nichiren group once and for all.

In the ninth month of 1271 the shogunate, no doubt spurred by fear of an impending Mongol invasion, ordered its retainers in the east to proceed to the shogunate's domains on Kyushu, which lay closest to Korea, where they were to suppress "bandits and evildoers," as well as prepare for the defense of the coast. "Evildoers" were those who in any way opposed the established order of the aristocracy and warrior class, and their suppression was to be accomplished as part of the general defense effort. This policy was also to be carried out in Kamakura, the seat of power. Nichiren and his followers, who had been engaged in radical declarations and actions against other sects in Kamakura, were regarded as another type of evildoer, and Nichiren was arrested on the twelfth day of the ninth month, one day before the order to proceed to Kyushu was given to the shogun's retainers.

The arrest was made by a group commanded by Taira no Yoritsuna (d. 1293), deputy director of the Board of Retainers. Yoritsuna was a personal retainer of Hōjō Tokimune (1251–84), director of the Board of Retainers, regent, and head of the Hōjō clan. It is reported that when he was arrested, Nichiren admonished Yoritsuna, stating that to arrest and punish him, "the support and pillar of the nation," was to work destruction upon Japan. The government should instead burn and destroy the temples of the Pure Land, Zen, and Ritsu sects and execute their clergy. Nichiren later regarded these words as his second formal remonstration with the government.

Despite his bold words, Nichiren was seized and led through the streets of Kamakura like a traitor or rebel. Finally his sentence was pronounced. According to Nichiren, it was made to appear that he would be banished, but in fact he was to be beheaded. The constable of the island of Sado, Nichiren's designated place of exile, was Hōjō Nobutoki, a member of a branch of the Hōjō family, and his deputy was Homma Rokurōzaemon Shigetsura (d. 1296). Nichiren was placed in the custody of the Homma family. At around two o'clock in the morning on the thirteenth day of the ninth month, he was led from Kamakura, bound for Homma's estate Echi in Sagami Province. It was a strange hour for departure, and Nichiren barely escaped beheading on the way, at a place called Tatsunokuchi. Nichiren finally set out for Sado in the tenth month.

The shogunate persecuted not only Nichiren but also his followers, regarding them all as evildoers. The Nichiren sect refers to Nichiren's narrow escape from death as the Tatsunokuchi Persecution, but one might better speak of a universal persecution of 1271, so extensive was the government's suppression.

Nichiren's disciples were sentenced to imprisonment, exile, confiscation of property, and dissolution of feudal ties. Nichiren wrote from the Echi estate that five disciples were imprisoned there. One of these was Nichirō (1245–1320), who later became one of Nichiren's most eminent disciples. It is likely, then, that those imprisoned were leaders of Nichiren's group. Moreover, it is safe to assume that prominent followers were exiled to Sado along with Nichiren. Though their names are unknown, Nichiren mentions such fellow exiles, as well as others who went to Sado of their own accord to visit their teacher.

While clerical followers were imprisoned and exiled, lay devotees in some cases had their lands confiscated or their relationships with their feudal lords dissolved. Since the latter punishment required that any lands held in fief be surrendered to the feoffee's lord, it was equivalent to confiscation of all property and meant the loss of the feoffee's means of livelihood. That these measures were taken by the government is known from records both of people whose lands were confiscated "because of their devotion to the Lotus Sutra" and of others who escaped such treatment thanks to the protection of their feudal masters.

During this severe persecution, many believers apostatized. Nichiren himself claimed that nine hundred ninety-nine out of a thousand fell by the wayside, but this is not a factual figure. After the arrival of the Mongol court's letter in 1268, the number of Nichiren's followers had grown rapidly, but just three years later it had been drastically reduced, and Nichiren, on his way to exile, was powerless to improve the situation.

Nichiren in Exile

The question of why devotees of the Lotus Sutra had to suffer such persecution preoccupied Nichiren throughout his period of exile on Sado. Finally, in his *Kaimoku Shō* (On Opening the Eyes; 1272), he analyzed the dialectic of suffering for the truth. He laid great emphasis on the concept of *hōbō*, or "slandering the truth." This term originally meant criticizing and obstructing the true Law, but Nichiren used it to designate the act of refusing to believe in the Lotus Sutra and thus obstructing the spread of faith in its teachings. He regarded this as the most fundamentally evil act and argued that sufferings in the present life are the result of having com-

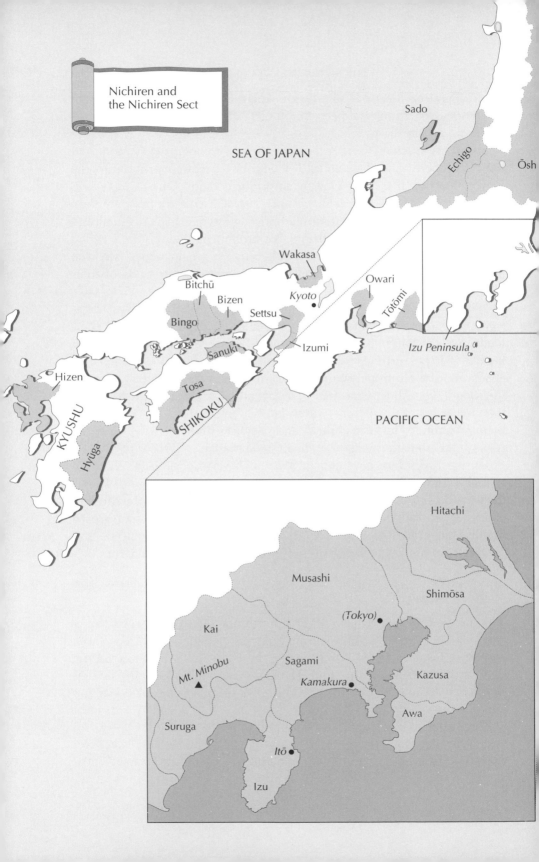

Nichiren and
the Nichiren Sect

SEA OF JAPAN

Sado

Echigo

Ōsh

Wakasa

Bitchū

Owari

Bizen

Tōtōmi

Bingo

Settsu

Kyoto

Sanuki

Izumi

Izu Peninsula

Hizen

Tosa

KYUSHU

SHIKOKU

PACIFIC OCEAN

Hyūga

Hitachi

Musashi

Shimōsa

Kai

(Tokyo)

Mt. Minobu ▲

Sagami

Kazusa

Suruga

Kamakura

Awa

Itō

Izu

mitted that sin in a previous life. To suffer in the present for the sake of the Lotus faith, however, was to expiate all past guilt; such suffering was also a sign that one would attain religious joy at some future time.

For Nichiren, suffering became an assurance of salvation. He believed that suffering was the immediate result of faith in and propagation of the Lotus Sutra, and that it was essential to maintain and increase that faith and missionary activity. Nichiren devoted himself to realizing a vow that expressed his sense of personal mission to save Japan and the Japanese people: "I will be the pillar of Japan. I will be the eyes of Japan. I will be the great ship that carries Japan to safety."

The *Kaimoku Shō* had expounded the dialectics of salvation through suffering. At the same time, Nichiren elaborated his religious philosophy that faith in the Lotus Sutra was distilled in the *daimoku*, the act of reciting the title of the sutra in the formula *Namu-myōhō-renge-kyō* (Taking refuge in the Sutra of the Lotus Flower of the Wonderful Law). He explained: "Since we are now in the period of the Decay of the Law [*Mappō*], neither the other sutras nor even the Lotus Sutra itself is of much help to us. In our dark time, there is only the invocation of its title, *Namu-myōhō-renge-kyō*."

Nichiren's reduction of faith in the Lotus Sutra to recitation of the sutra's title was influenced by both the custom of reciting the *daimoku* that had existed since the Heian period and the example of Hōnen's emphasis on the exclusive practice of the *nembutsu*. Nichiren argued that all the merits of Śākyamuni Buddha would accrue to those who recited the title of the Lotus Sutra, and their salvation would be ensured. He expressed his views on this in the *Nyorai Metsugo Go Gohyakusai Shi Kanjin Honzon Shō* (Treatise on Viewing the Mind and Realizing the Original Object of Worship for the First Time in the Fifth Five-Hundred-Year Period after the Buddha's Death), usually known by the abbreviated title *Kanjin Honzon Shō*, or simply *Honzon Shō*. Nichiren composed this work in the fourth month of 1273, the year following composition of the *Kaimoku Shō*.

In the *Kanjin Honzon Shō* Nichiren stresses the gulf that separates the Buddha from ordinary mortals and offers the recitation of the title of the Lotus Sutra as the only means to bridge that gap. In this work Nichiren abandons the idea that "the Buddha and ordinary mortals are essentially the same," so often encountered in the Tendai sect in the Kamakura, Muromachi, and Momoyama periods, with its emphasis on meditative practice.

Nichiren had composed the *Kaimoku Shō* in the second month of 1272, at Tsukahara, where he was at first exiled. In the same month, in Kamakura and Kyoto, Hōjō Tokimune's elder brother Tokisuke (1248–72) and members of his faction were murdered. Nichiren believed those deaths resulted from the Hōjō clan's suppression of the true Law. Later Nichiren was moved to Ichinotani, where he composed the *Kanjin Honzon Shō*. He also preached to the peasants he met on Sado, and the disciples who accompanied him worked to disseminate their master's doctrines there.

The Move to Mount Minobu

In the second month of 1274 Nichiren was pardoned. In the third month he left Sado for Kamakura, where he met with Taira no Yoritsuna in the fourth. The two men discussed the probable timing of the expected Mongol attack and appropriate countermeasures. They agreed that the invasion would probably come within the year. Once again, Nichiren urged that the government promote faith in the Lotus Sutra and cease supporting other sects, especially Shingon, which Nichiren said was a destructive teaching. This was, by his reckoning, his third formal remonstration with the government.

When Yoritsuna failed to take his advice, Nichiren decided to wander about Japan alone, disseminating his teachings. Leaving Kamakura in the fifth month, he traveled to Mount Minobu in Kai Province, where a lay follower named Hakii Sanenaga (1222–97) held a fief. He originally intended to stay there only a short time, but he remained on Mount Minobu for nine years, almost until his death in 1282. As his reason for remaining on Mount Minobu, Nichiren stated that with his third unheeded attempt he had finished his task of remonstrating with the government. The failure of the Mongol invasion in 1274 also may have influenced his decision. At any rate, he was no longer interested in making appeals to the government, and the official appeals made by his disciples toward the end of the Kamakura period were unrelated to Nichiren's own.

The lay followers who had heard Nichiren in Kamakura and accepted his teachings were now scattered throughout the country, as were most of the clerical disciples. Some believers proselytized in the areas where they lived. Increasingly, people went to Mount Minobu in person or exchanged letters with Nichiren, seeking his guidance. The master responded with a vigorous stream of epistles, mostly written in Japanese rather than the classical Chinese still favored by many Buddhist clerics. Like other great innovators of the period, Nichiren was a pioneer in expressing Buddhist teachings in the Japanese vernacular.

Some of Nichiren's followers caused disturbances because of their faith in exclusive devotion to the Lotus Sutra. The vertical relationships between parent and child or lord and vassal were fundamental to the society of the day, and in some cases parents or lords urged believers to abandon their faith. In such cases, Nichiren encouraged his followers, exhorting them never to give up the attempt to convert and save their parents or lords and telling them that that was the essence of true filial piety and loyalty.

If at times Nichiren counseled temporary compromise for expediency's sake, at others he himself took on the task of convincing opponents on behalf of his followers. When the peasants of Atsuhara in the Fuji district of Suruga Province were persecuted in 1279 because of their faith in the Lotus Sutra, he took up his writing brush to encourage them, seeing the persecution not merely as a local attack but as one that affected the entire community of Lotus believers. He appealed to his disciples and followers throughout Japan to develop a sense of religious community that could withstand all such persecution. Thus Nichiren continued to fight for his beliefs, even in his last years.

Nichiren's struggles took their toll on him, both physically and spiritually. The various persecutions, the years in exile, the austere life in cold, damp quarters atop Mount Minobu, and his worries over the suppression of his followers all contributed to the deterioration of his health. In the ninth month of 1282 he finally left Mount Minobu and set out for Hitachi Province to convalesce, but his illness grew worse on the way, and he was forced to stop at the house of Ikegami Munenaka, a lay follower in Ikegami (in present-day Tokyo). On the eighth day of the tenth month, knowing the end was near, Nichiren named six of his disciples as leaders of his followers. He died on the thirteenth.

Nichiren's Disciples

The six disciples named as leaders were Nisshō (1221–1323), Nichirō (1245–1320), Nikkō (1246–1333), Nikō (1253–1314), Nitchō (1252–1317), and Nichiji (b. 1250). Nichiren chose them because they were the most influential and gifted of his disciples. They worked in different geographical areas. Nisshō and Nichirō were active mainly in Kamakura, while Nikkō worked in Suruga, Kai, and Izu provinces. Nikō was based in Kazusa Province, Nitchō in Shimōsa, and Nichiji in Suruga together with Nikkō. During Nichiren's lifetime they had served as his messengers, disseminating the teachings in the provinces and acting sometimes as his official representatives.

There were also lesser disciples in Kamakura and the provinces. Some of them were still resident priests in established Tendai temples, but they accepted Nichiren's teachings and worked to disseminate them among the people. Some—such as the disciples of Nichiren and Nikkō who lived at Ryūsen-ji in the Fuji district and Kambara Shijūku-in in Ihara, both in Suruga—were driven from their temples because they taught Nichiren's doctrines. In most areas there were also disciples who offered personal guidance to and received financial support from prominent lay believers. Some of them were priests who had been driven from their own temples.

In addition, there were younger disciples studying under Nichiren on Mount Minobu. Nichiren devoted himself to their education, teaching them the essentials of the Lotus doctrine, reciting the sutra together with them, and answering their questions. This generation of disciples became very active in the mid-fourteenth century. Thus, while the second-generation disciples were out proselytizing in the provinces, the third generation was being trained by Nichiren in his last years at Minobu. During Nichiren's lifetime, the only structures on Mount Minobu were residences owned by particular disciples and priests in training. Not until after Nichiren's death was a temple for use by both clergy and laity established there.

Nichiren's Lay Followers

Like the clerical disciples, Nichiren's lay followers were scattered about the various eastern provinces (Sagami, Musashi, Kazusa, Shimōsa, Awa, Suruga, Kai, and Izu) and on Sado. They generally fell into two groups. First, there were those who encountered Nichiren directly in Kamakura and became his devotees. Since Kamakura was one of the two political and cultural centers of the day, people from outlying provinces tended to congregate there for a time and then return to their home villages. Some of these people encountered Nichiren and then carried his teachings back to their provinces. This was especially true of retainers of the shogunate on temporary duty in the military capital. Second, there were the minor officials and estate managers who met Nichiren while he was in exile on Sado. They had been appointed as his guardians and jailers, yet he was able to convert them. The bonds of faith established between Nichiren and his former jailers were so strong that in later years they journeyed all the way to Mount Minobu, on the other side of Honshu, to visit him.

In many cases, Nichiren's disciples converted the people in their own localities. These devotees came to have faith in Nichiren's teachings indirectly, through the agency of his disciples. Of the six major disciples, Nikkō was best known for his local missionary activity, but the other five also engaged in similar efforts.

Prominent among the lay followers were people of the warrior class. They were almost all low- to middle-ranking warriors (local landholders and stewards). The believers on Sado and in Suruga, however, were moderately well-to-do peasants and estate managers. Members of the warrior class were particularly attracted to Nichiren's teaching because of their strong feelings of guilt over their involvement in killing. They feared that as professional warriors they would have to endure the torments of hell after death. Hence large numbers of them were converted—not only masters and their followers but entire clans.

Nichiren certainly viewed professional warriors as evildoers, but he taught that the Lotus Sutra could save even such people. An evildoer who believed, upheld, and propagated the teaching and recited the title of the Lotus Sutra with faith would be endowed with all the merits of Śākyamuni Buddha himself. Thus, in the doctrine known as *akunin jōbutsu*, Nichiren claimed that even evildoers can attain buddhahood.

Nichiren also had many female followers. These were mostly of the same low- to middle-ranking warrior class as the male believers. They generally fell into two groups: widow-priests (*goke no ama*) and woman-priests (*ama gozen* or *ama goze*). The first group consisted of pious women whose husbands had died, and the second of those whose husbands were still living but who had, with their husbands, decided to devote themselves to the Buddhist path. These "priests" were in fact pious lay women, not orthodox female priests who had received and were bound to keep the traditional Buddhist precepts. From the beginning, Buddhist teachings held that it was particularly difficult for women to attain enlightenment; but the Lotus Sutra expounds the doctrine that women can attain buddhahood (*nyonin jōbutsu*), though that entails their being miraculously transformed into men first. Nichiren stressed the possibility of salvation for women.

Salvation through faith in the Lotus Sutra was not limited to the living. Merits gained by the living could be transferred to the dead. Thus memorial services were popular among Nichiren's followers, and the widow-priests in particular engaged in these meritorious practices for the sake of their deceased husbands. Nichiren's writings contain references to memorial services held by followers on the death day itself, as well as on the forty-ninth and hundredth days after death and on the third and thirteenth anniversaries of death.* Nichiren praised the holding of services for one's parents as filial behavior and of services for a dead husband by a widow as marital fidelity. In doing so, he gave religious support to the concepts of filial piety, loyalty, and fidelity that underlay the feudal society of his day. This was one major reason for his success in establishing his teachings in the society and age in which he lived. Other Kamakura-period Buddhist movements were similarly supportive of the feudal social structure.

THE NICHIREN SECT IN THE MUROMACHI PERIOD

Division into Schools

Immediately after Nichiren's death, his disciples built a tomb for him on Mount Minobu, as he had bid them, and agreed that the six leading disciples and other disciples would take turns guarding and maintaining it. From that time the tomb and residences on Mount Minobu came to be called Kuon-ji. Difficulties arose in fulfilling the agreement, however, and by 1284, just two years after Nichiren's death, his tomb was already showing effects of neglect. Witnessing this situation, Nikkō decided that the system of alternating custodianship did not work. Around 1285, in consultation with Hakii Sanenaga, a lay follower who was powerful in the Minobu area, he decided to live permanently at Kuon-ji.

About the same time, Nikō also went to Mount Minobu. He was warmly welcomed by Nikkō and entrusted with the education of the young priests in training. Sanenaga supported Nikkō in this, but occasionally Nikkō and Sanenaga, who regarded himself as a true first-generation disciple of Nichiren, disagreed. When Nikkō admonished Sanenaga for what he regarded as heretical views, the latter paid no attention. This led to a rupture between the two, and Nikkō left Minobu in 1288 and moved to the Fuji district of Suruga Province. Nikō, who generally supported Sanenaga in the disputes, remained at Kuon-ji, which was managed jointly by the two men and which became in effect the Hakii clan temple. From Kuon-ji the

---

* Because the day of death is counted as the first day in these figures, by Western reckoning the services are held on the forty-eighth and ninety-ninth days after death and on the second and twelfth anniversaries of death.

Nikō or Minobu school propagated Nichiren's teachings in the provinces of Kai and Kazusa.

Meanwhile, Nisshō and others in Kamakura presented the *Risshō Ankoku Ron* to the shogunate again in 1284, when Hōjō Tokimune died and was succeeded as regent by his son Sadatoki (1271–1311). This *Risshō Ankoku Ron*, completed by Nichiren before his death, seems to have been an expanded version of the treatise by the same name presented earlier to Tokiyori. It was now offered by Nichiren's disciples in commemoration of the third anniversary of their teacher's death. The earlier version had limited its attacks to Hōnen's Pure Land teaching, but the later version also criticized esoteric Buddhism. Its presentation to the government infuriated the clergy and laity of the Pure Land, Tendai, and Shingon sects and provoked a crisis that almost led to the sack and destruction of the residences of Nisshō and other priests. According to Nikkō's account, Nisshō and other priests were able to avert the calamity only by stating that they were in fact Tendai priests and approved of Tendai practices, including the esoteric Buddhist elements.

Thus, within two or three years of Nichiren's death, his followers in Kamakura were displaying a readiness to compromise with other sects. Nikkō's view of this change at the time is not clear, but in later years he severely criticized such compromises on the part of his fellow disciples, and a great rift developed between him and the other five senior disciples of Nichiren. Thus began the divisions among even the most prominent of Nichiren's followers.

After leaving Minobu, Nikkō established Taiseki-ji at Ōishigahara in the Fuji district of Suruga Province, in 1290, gaining the support of Nanjō Tokimitsu (1294–1332), a longtime follower of Nichiren and a resident of the Fuji district. Since it was established as the Nanjō family's private worship hall, Taiseki-ji inevitably had something of the character of a clan temple. In 1298, on the seventeenth anniversary of Nichiren's death, Nikkō founded Hommon-ji in Omosu, in the Fuji district, with the support of the Nanjō and Ishikawa families and local Nichiren followers. Using Hommon-ji as his base, Nikkō devoted himself to the education of young priests and encouraged the missionary activities of his disciples. The group based at both Taiseki-ji and Hommon-ji came to be known as the Nikkō or Fuji school. It spread through Kai, Suruga, Izu, and Tōtōmi provinces, and even as far as northeastern Honshu.

At about the same time, Nisshō founded Hokke-ji at Hamado, in

Kamakura, which became the base for the Nisshō or Hama school. Nichirō founded Myōhon-ji at Hikigayatsu, in Kamakura, and also headed Hommon-ji in Ikegami (which had no connection with Hommon-ji in Omosu), at the site of Nichiren's death. His school spread through Sagami and Musashi provinces and was known as the Nichirō, Hikigayatsu, or Ikegami school.

Nichiji originally proselytized in Suruga, but after Nichiren's death he moved to Musashi. He was active there around the time of the founding of Ikegami Hommon-ji and is said to have later gone overseas to disseminate Nichiren's teachings.

In Shimōsa, where Nichiren had made many influential converts, Nitchō, one of the six major disciples and the adopted son of Nichiren's lay follower Toki Jōnin, at first proselytized from Guhō-ji in Mama. When he fell out of favor with Jōnin, however, he went to Hommon-ji in Omosu, and Jōnin became the central figure in the expansion of the Nichiren group in Shimōsa. Jōnin entered religious life after Nichiren's death, taking the name Nichijō and converting his family's private worship hall in Wakamiya into an official temple, Hokke-ji (which had no connection with Hokke-ji in Kamakura), and there he carefully preserved books and letters he had received from Nichiren. Around the same time, the residence of the Ōta family in Nakayama, in Shimōsa Province, was converted into a temple called Hommyō-ji. A son of the Ōta family, Nichikō (1257–1314), became head of this temple and of Hokke-ji after Nichijō's death. In the sixteenth century, under Nichigon (1515–83), the two temples were merged and renamed Hokekyō-ji. This became the headquarters of the Nichijō or Nakayama school.

The foundations of the Nichiren sect were laid in eastern Japan after Nichiren's death by Nisshō, Nichirō, Nikkō, Nikō, and Nichijō. During the Kamakura and Muromachi periods, the schools founded by these men were never united and instead proliferated through a series of schisms. In fact, though we speak of a Nichiren sect, the Nichiren movement of this period consisted of numerous separate schools and groups.

The Hama, Hikigayatsu, and Fuji Schools

Hamado Hokke-ji, founded by Nisshō, was moved to Tamazawa, in Izu Province, and renamed Myōhokke-ji in the seventeenth century. The Hama school was heavily influenced by Tendai Buddhism. Nisshō's successor, Nichiyū (1271–1364), identified himself as a Tendai priest, writing his name even in mandalas, and in the fourteenth and fifteenth centuries other Nichiren priests criticized the clergy of the Hama school for going to Mount Hiei to receive the monastic precepts according to the Tendai tradition.

The most prominent school in Sagami and Musashi provinces was that of Nichirō, the Hikigayatsu school. Nichirin (1272–1359), the second head of the school, restored Myōhon-ji, which had burned down, and maintained it as the headquarters of the school. Nichirin was assisted by Nichiden (1277–1341), a Tendai priest who had been converted by Nichirō and became his disciple. When the Soya clan of Hiraga, in Shimōsa, converted its Jizō Hall into a Lotus Hall and asked Nichirō to visit Hiraga, he sent Nichiden in his stead. The Jizō Hall eventually became Hiraga Hondo-ji, one of the three great centers of the Hikigayatsu school. The other two, Myōhon-ji and Ikegami Hommon-ji, were regarded as a single entity. The *kanzu*, or head of the school, by custom lived at Myōhon-ji, but with Tokugawa Ieyasu's arrival in eastern Japan at the beginning of the seventeenth century, Ikegami Hommon-ji became the real center of the school.

The Hikigayatsu school's sphere of activity extended to Kazusa Province, where Hongyō-ji and Kōfuku-ji were established, in Katsuura and Ono, respectively. In addition, Nichirō's disciples Nichizō (1269–1342), Nichizen (1263–1332), and Nichigyō (1267–1330) went to the Kyoto area and proselytized in the imperial capital. Nichizen succeeded the head of Hokke-ji, in Himon'ya, Musashi Province, which Nichiren's direct disciple Nichigen (d. 1315) had converted to the Nichiren sect. Nichigyō founded Honkō-ji on Sado; Nitchō (1239–1326), who studied the Nichiren teachings under Nichirō and Nisshō, founded Nitchō-ji in Amatsu, Awa Province and Hon'en-ji in Atsuta, Owari Province; and Nichirō's disciple Rōkei (d. 1324), Hōren-ji in Ebara, Musashi. On the other hand, Nichirō's disciple Nichiin (1264–1328) left the school after his teacher's death. His successor at Honjō-ji in Echigo Province, Nichijō (1298–1369), later went to Kyoto and founded Honkoku-ji.

Taiseki-ji and Omosu Hommon-ji remained the principal centers of the Fuji school. Nikkō had bequeathed Taiseki-ji to Nichimoku (1260–1333) and Hommon-ji to Nichidai (1294–1394); but after Nichimoku's death, rifts appeared in this school too. One breach developed between Nichidō (1283–1341), who had inherited Taiseki-ji, and Nichigō (1272–1353), who later built Myōhon-ji, in Yoshihama, in Awa Province, with the aid of the Sassa clan.

When Nichimoku set out for Kyoto to admonish the imperial court, his disciples Nichigō and Nichizon (1265–1345) accompanied him. But Nichimoku died en route, and Nichigō and Nichizon had to go on to Kyoto alone to carry out their teacher's intent. After returning to Taiseki-ji, they found themselves in contention with Nichidō. Losing the struggle, they were driven from Taiseki-ji, which passed to Nichidō. Nichidō's victory owed much to the support of the Nanjō clan, who had founded Taiseki-ji, which still had a strong clan-temple character. When Nichigō left, he ordered his disciples to retain control of the Eastern Hall (Renzō-bō) and its surroundings, which had been in his possession. Nichigō's followers fought with the Taiseki-ji clergy over this issue for decades. Eventually, in 1416, they moved Renzō-bō to Koizumi, in the Fuji district of Suruga Province, where it became Koizumi Kuon-ji.

Omosu Hommon-ji was bequeathed to Nikkō's disciple Nichidai, but the influential Ishikawa clan favored Nichimyō, another disciple of Nikkō, and managed to drive Nichidai out. Nichidai then moved to nearby Nishi-yama, where he founded another Hommon-ji. Omosu Hommon-ji, which had been founded with the support of the Nanjō and Ishikawa clans and local Nichiren followers, seems to have become in effect the Ishikawa clan temple. Nichiman (1272–1360), who had supported Nichidai in his unsuccessful attempt to retain control of Omosu Hommon-ji, went to Sado and other parts of Hokurokudō to spread the school's teachings.

Hommon-ji and Hokke-ji were founded in Takase, Sanuki Province, on Shikoku, when the Akiyama clan, who were devout lay followers, moved from Kai Province to Shikoku. Moreover, Jōzen-ji was established in Hichiya, in Hyūga Province, on Kyushu, through the conversion of a local priest, who was later known as Nichiei (1309–69). Nikke (1252–1334), the priest who had accompanied the Akiyama clan, returned eventually to the Fuji district and converted the former residence of Nanjō Tokimitsu into a temple that was called Myōren-ji. The Fuji school was spread through Suruga, Ōmi, Izu, Awa, Sado, Ōshū, Sanuki, and Hyūga provinces by both priests and lay followers. Tension and conflict continued between Taiseki-ji and Myōhon-ji and between Omosu Hommon-ji and Nishiyama Hommon-ji. It is important to remember that most of this school's centers were clan temples.

The Minobu and Nakayama Schools

On Mount Minobu Nisshin (b. 1271), the third abbot, built a number of new halls and residences. He was succeeded by his disciple Nichizen (1271–1346), Nichiin (1312–73), and Nichiei (1352–1400). At this time Kuon-ji still largely retained the character of the clan temple of the Hakii clan. Nichiei succeeded briefly in uniting the Minobu and Hikigayatsu schools through the favor of the Kanō clan, influential lay followers of the Hikigayatsu school. The Hikigayatsu school as a whole opposed this development, however, and under Nichigyō (1387–1434), a disciple of Nichiei, seceded from the united school in 1400 in a clear manifestation of the partisan spirit that dominated the different Nichiren schools of the time.

Nichioku (d. 1422) and the younger brother Nichigaku (d. 1459), who were both brothers of Nichigyō, succeeded to the abbacy of Kuon-ji. Nissan (fl. fifteenth century) of Nichigaku's lineage traveled to Kyoto and founded Gakuyō-ji, which came to be regarded as the center of Nichigaku's group in the Kyoto area. In 1432 Nichiden (1393–1448) of this group boldly admonished the shōgun Ashikaga Yoshinori (1394–1441) when he went to Suruga Province to put down the rebellion of his kinsman Ashikaga Mochiuji (1398–1439).

Nisshutsu (1381–1459), a Tendai priest who had been converted to the Nichiren sect by Nichigaku, erected Hongaku-ji in Mishima, Izu Province, and then went to Kamakura, where he built a simple hermitage near Ebisu-dō bridge and began proselytizing. In a debate in 1436 he bested the Tendai priest Shinkai of Kongōhōkai-ji in Kamakura, and presented an account of his victory to Ashikaga Mochiuji, governor-general of the Kantō region.

Mochiuji responded angrily, confiscating the Nichiren temples in Kamakura and announcing the confiscation of the holdings of prominent believers, as well as sentences of banishment and beheading. He then ordered the Nichiren believers in Kamakura to assemble before him. This seems to have been an attempt to intimidate rather than to carry out his extreme sentences. In any case the believers assembled as ordered with no sign of fear or panic. At the meeting Mochiuji announced pardons for the believers, apparently out of fear that the shogunate in Kyoto would use undue severity on his part as an excuse to move against him. This brought to an end the Eikyō Persecution, so called from the name of the era during which it occurred. Nisshutsu then named his Ebisu-dō hermitage Hongaku-ji and made it a base for the Minobu school in Kamakura. It became known as the eastern Minobu.

Another great contributor to the growth of the Minobu school was Nitchō (1422–1500). As soon as he was named the eleventh abbot of

Kuon-ji, he moved its buildings to the sites they occupy today, enlarging them in the process. He devoted much time and energy to collecting copies of Nichiren's letters and other writings, developing rituals for annual ceremonies and observances, lecturing and teaching, and proselytizing in various areas. He sent his disciple Nichii (1444–1519) to found Myōden-ji in Kyoto, thus extending the school's influence into western Japan. Myōden-ji became known as the western Minobu.

The Nakayama school experienced tremendous growth under Nichiyū (1298–1374), who had succeeded Nichijō and Nichikō. Nichiyū, the adopted son of Chiba Tanesada (1287–1336), founder of the Hizen Chiba clan, not only made Nakayama Hommyō-ji the Chiba clan temple but also established other temples throughout the clan's extensive holdings. He won the support of the wealthy Mutsura clan in Mutsura, Musashi Province, across the bay from Shimōsa Province, and used Jōgyō-ji, which they built for him in Matsura, to expand his activities into neighboring Sagami Province. Tanesada had propagated the doctrines of the Nakayama school on Kyushu by establishing Kōshō-ji in Matsuo, in Hizen Province, where he had landholdings.

Nichiei (1346–1423), a disciple of Nichiyū's successor Nisson (1323–99), founded Myōsen-ji in Han'ya, Kazusa Province, with the help of the Han'ya clan. He also created lay believers' groups in various areas, establishing bases for his school in Kazusa, Shimōsa, Musashi, and Awa provinces and in Kamakura and Kyoto. At the same time, Nichiei pledged obedience to the orders of the main temple, forging direct links between it and the branch temples and local groups of Nichiren followers. Through such activities, Nakayama Hommyō-ji, which had been primarily a clan temple, gradually became a broader-based religious center. The same trend was seen at the main temples of the other schools, as well.

Propagation in Kyoto

Having remonstrated with the government three times, Nichiren had had no desire to pursue that path any further. Yet from the mid-thirteenth through the fourteenth century, the Hikigayatsu, Fuji, Minobu, and Nakayama schools all issued remonstrations addressed to the nobility and warrior classes of Kyoto. They urged the government to establish true Buddhism—to promote the Lotus Sutra—and to suppress other (false) teachings, in the spirit of Nichiren's *Risshō Ankoku Ron*. They addressed themselves to the ruling classes of Kyoto because the center of political power had shifted back to the imperial capital and the Nichiren schools, with their strongest bases in the east, felt an urgent need to be heard in the west as well. Thus they demanded official permission to proselytize in Kyoto. The Hikigayatsu and Fuji schools were the first to succeed in establishing themselves in the capital.

The Kyoto representative of the Hikigayatsu school was Nichizō, who as a youth had studied under Nichiren on Mount Minobu. He arrived in the capital in 1294 and converted a large number of merchants and artisans. Unfortunately, he also aroused the wrath of the Mount Hiei authorities and was banished from Kyoto three times. In 1321, shortly after his third period of exile ended, he established Myōken-ji.

In 1333, in the school's first contact with the Kyoto nobility, Prince Morinaga (1308–35) ordered prayers to be said at Myōken-ji for the safe return to the capital of his father, Emperor Godaigo (1288–1339), who had been exiled for plotting the overthrow of the Kamakura shogunate. When the emperor did return, Myōken-ji was designated first a private imperial worship hall and later an imperial temple. Thus the Nichiren sect gained both official status and recognition of its right to proselytize in the capital. By maintaining contacts with the nobility and warriors, as well as with the ordinary townspeople, Nichizō was able to lay a firm foundation for the growth of the Nichiren movement in Kyoto.

Nichijō, a disciple of Nichiin of the Hikigayatsu school, built Honkoku-ji, in Kyoto's Rokujō Horikawa district. The exact date of its founding is not known, but by the late fourteenth century it was important enough to be compared with Myōken-ji. Myōken-ji was the center of what came to be called the Shijō school (from its location at Shijō Kushige), while Honkoku-ji was the headquarters of the Rokujō school. Together they formed the principal bases for Nichiren activity in Kyoto, and each fostered a number of smaller branch temples.

Finally, Nichigyō and Nichizen of the Hikigayatsu school laid the foundations for what became Daimyō-ji and Hōkoku-ji.

Nikkō's disciple Nichimoku had tried to go to Kyoto to admonish the imperial court but had died en route. Nichizon who accompanied him carried it out for him and disseminated the Fuji school's teachings in the Kyoto region. Nichizon returned to Kyoto in 1338 and established Jōgyō-in in the Rokkaku Aburakōji district in 1339. In 1344 Jōgyō-in was passed to his disciple Nichiin, while another disciple, Nichidai (1309–69), established a second temple called Jōgyō-in in the Ichijō Inokuma district. Nichidai's disciple Nichigen (fl. fourteenth century) moved this Jōgyō-in to Nijō Horikawa and renamed it Jūhon-ji. These two Fuji-school temples seem to have been very much at odds with each other.

In addition, the followers of Temmoku (1245–1308), who claimed to be a direct disciple of Nichiren, built a Hommon-ji in the Nijō Nishi no Tōin Aoyagi district and engaged in proselytizing.

Nichijū and Nichijin

Nichijū (1314–92) had originally been a Tendai priest but had converted to the Nakayama school of the Nichiren sect. He went to Kyoto in 1381 and began proselytizing there, frequently traveling from Kyoto to eastern Japan, but gradually he distanced himself from the Nakayama school. Nichijū delivered formal remonstrations to the imperial regent and other high officials and attempted to deliver remonstrations to shōgun Ashikaga Yoshimitsu (1358–1408), as well, though he failed in this. With the support of the wealthy merchant Tennōjiya Tsūmyō, he established a center in the Rokujō Bōmon Muromachi district, which became Myōman-ji.

Opposed to the Nichiren groups' increasingly conciliatory attitude toward other sects, Nichijū founded a new subsect, the Myōman-ji subsect of the Kempon Hokke sect, in 1384. He argued that he was the direct heir of Nichiren, not historically but from the more correct and fundamental standpoint of fidelity to the teachings of the Lotus Sutra and to Nichiren's teachings concerning the sutra.

Nichijin (1339–1419), a contemporary of Nichijū, had been a disciple of Nichijō of the Rokujō school, at Honkoku-ji, and was entrusted with Honjō-ji in Echigo Province. In 1397 he went to Kyoto to proselytize. He adopted the doctrinal position known in Japanese as *honjaku shōretsu*, which holds that the first fourteen chapters of the Lotus Sutra represent a provisional, inferior teaching, while the last fourteen chapters represent the true, superior teaching. Nichijin attacked Nichiden (1342–1409) of Honkoku-ji for teaching the view that the two halves of the Lotus Sutra expound the same doctrine in different ways and are thus of equal value, the view known as *honjaku itchi*.

Further, Nichijin attacked the Honkoku-ji clergy for adopting the method of conversion known as *shōju*, or acceptance, instead of advancing boldly on the path of *shakubuku*, or breaking and reducing to submission. *Shōju* involves provisionally accepting the worth of other religious groups' positions while attempting to lead people to belief in the Lotus Sutra. *Shakubuku* is a more extreme method of leading people directly to the Lotus faith by emphatically denying the religious worth of other sects' teachings and practices.

Nichijin also accused the Honkoku-ji clergy of accepting offerings from nonbelievers. He held that Nichiren clergy should never accept anything from those who fail to uphold the true Law and that Nichiren lay people should never make offerings or donations to clergy of other sects. This uncompromising position is known as *fuju fuse*, or no receiving and no giving. Nichijin established Honzen-ji in the Shijō Horikawa Aburakōji district in 1406, becoming completely independent of the Rokujō school. His school was known as the Nichijin or Honjō-ji school.

Finally, Nisshū (1383–1450), a second-generation disciple of Nichijō, established Homman-ji in the Higashi no Tōin district and separated from the Rokujō school. Honkoku-ji and Homman-ji were never at odds, however, but maintained cordial relations until the late nineteenth century.

Other Temples and Nichiryū and Nisshin

The inclination to compromise and the acceptance of other doctrines for which Nichijin so strongly criticized the Honkoku-ji clergy were also characteristic of the clergy of Myōken-ji, of the Hikigayatsu school. Nichizō (1269–1342), his disciple Daikaku (1297–1364), Rōgen (1326–78), and Nissei (1349–1405) were successive abbots of this temple. A priest named Nichijitsu (1318–78) strongly opposed the appointment of Nissei and with the support of a rich merchant named Ono Myōkaku (fl. fourteenth century) left the group and founded a temple that he named Myōkaku-ji in honor of his patron. Of all the Nichiren temples in Kyoto, Myōkaku-ji was the strictest in applying the principles of noncooperation with nonbelievers and aggressive proselytization, and this tradition was maintained into the late nineteenth century.

Myōken-ji continued Nichizō's efforts to stay on good terms with the nobility and the warrior class, but this angered the priests of Enryaku-ji, who set fire to Myōken-ji in 1387. The abbot Nissei fled to Obama, in Wakasa Province. In 1393, through the patronage of Nishi no Gosho, the wife of Ashikaga Yoshimitsu, he received a large tract of land in the Sanjō Bōmon Horikawa district of Kyoto on which he rebuilt the existing temple, renaming it Myōhon-ji. The shōgun himself paid a visit to Myōhon-ji in 1398.

Nissei's successor at Myōhon-ji was Gatsumyō (1386–1440), of the noble

Sanjō family. His promotion by the court to the rank of high priest at the age of only twenty-seven outraged the priests of Enryaku-ji, who vented their wrath by burning Myōhon-ji to the ground. Gatsumyō was forced to flee to Chimi, in Tamba Province. In 1416, while Gatsumyō remained in Tamba, Myōkōbō and other disciples built a temple in Shijō Kushige, on the site of Myōhon-ji, naming it Honnō-ji rather than Myōhon-ji in deference to the feelings of the Mount Hiei clergy. Somewhat later Gatsumyō rebuilt Myōhon-ji in the Gojō Ōmiya district, but relations between the two new temples were not good, and Honnō-ji eventually became the completely independent temple Ryūhon-ji.

During Gatsumyō's lifetime Nichikei (1397–1478) founded Myōren-ji in the Ōmiya Shijō Ayakōji district with the assistance of the family of the wealthy merchant Yanagizakaya Nakaoki. The site of Myōren-ji was associated with the deceased master Nichizō. Nichiō (1433–1508), of the noble Niwata family, became the first abbot.

Nichiryū (1385–1464) also became dissatisfied with conditions at Myōhon-ji and founded an independent group. He had joined Nichizon and Nichidō (both, fl. fifteenth century) in criticizing Gatsumyō and, like them, left Myōhon-ji to proselytize on his own. Nichiryū went to Amagasaki, in Settsu Province, with an introduction from Nichidō. Gaining the support of the provincial governor, Hosokawa Mitsumoto (1378–1426), and the rice merchant Jirō Gorō, he built Honkō-ji in Amagasaki in 1423. Six years later, with the aid of the wealthy merchant Kosodeya Sōku, he built Honnō-ji in the Uchino district of Kyoto, on the site where Nichizon and Nichidō had built a hermitage after leaving Myōhon-ji. In 1433, four years after its founding, it was moved to the Rokkaku Ōmiya district and its name was changed, using different ideograms still pronounced Honnō-ji. Honnō-ji and Amagasaki Honkō-ji were regarded as a single entity and together formed the nucleus of the Hommon Hokke sect, or Nichiryū school.

Nichiryū insisted on the superiority of the second half of the Lotus Sutra, opposing the *honjaku itchi* view of Myōhon-ji that both halves are of essentially equal worth. As in the time of Nichijū and Nichijin, the impetus for reform and the establishment of new, autonomous schools stemmed from an emphasis on the superiority of the second half of the sutra. The reformers felt too that the *honjaku itchi* adherents tended to adopt moderate, conciliatory methods of propagating the faith rather than employing more aggressive techniques. *Honjaku itchi* adherents were also accused of accepting offerings from nonbelievers. The reformer Nichiryū was one of the most outstanding scholars in the Nichiren sect and a prolific writer. His works are comparable in number to those of Nitchō (1422–1500), abbot of Kuon-ji on Mount Minobu.

From the Nakayama school, Nisshin (1407–88) proselytized in Kyoto. He had studied under Nissen (1349–1422) and Nissatsu (1392–1422) and later became head of Kōshō-ji in Matsuo, Hizen Province, the Nakayama school's base on Kyushu. Kōshō-ji had been founded by Chiba Tanesada and was under the patronage of his descendant Chiba Taneshizu. Nisshin was incensed by what he felt was a lack of sincerity in Taneshizu's religious practice. During his frequent trips from Kyushu to Nakayama Hommyō-ji, in Shimōsa Province, Nisshin found it necessary to admonish Nichiyū (d. 1448), Nissatsu's successor. As a result, Nisshin was expelled from the Nakayama school in 1437.

Nisshin then went to Kyoto, where in 1439 he remonstrated with the shōgun Ashikaga Yoshinori. He wrote a work called the *Risshō Chikoku Ron* (On Establishing Righteousness and Governing the Country; 1440) in emulation of Nichiren's *Risshō Ankoku Ron*. Before Nisshin could present the *Risshō Chikoku Ron* to the shōgun, Yoshinori imprisoned him. In prison he was subjected to indignities and torture, such as having his tongue slit and having a scorching-hot metal pot placed over his head. When, in the midst of torture, Nisshin was ordered to recite the *nembutsu*, he stoutly refused and continued to chant the *daimoku*, the title of the Lotus Sutra. In commemoration of his steadfastness in the face of great cruelties, he was given the sobriquet Nisshin the Pot Wearer.

After his release from prison, Nisshin founded a center for his work in the Takakura district of Kyoto, with the aid of the Kanō clan. This center, which later became Hompō-ji, was moved first to Ichijō Horikawa and then to Sanjō Tomikōji. Around 1460 Nisshin returned to Hizen Province, on Kyushu, and won many new converts for the Nichiren faith. However, he was soon arrested, returned to Kyoto under guard, and again imprisoned. After his release he moved Hompō-ji to Sanjō Made no Kōji and began working as zealously as before to convert the populace of Kyoto. Even during the ravages of the Ōnin War (1467–77), which almost destroyed the capital, he continued proselytizing.

Another representative of the Nakayama school who was active in Kyoto during the Ōnin War was Nisshū (1437–1513). In 1495, with the support of Hosokawa Katsumasu (d. 1502), the governor of Tosa Province, on Shikoku, he moved a hermitage that he had built for himself in the Nishi no Tōin district to Made no Kōji Tomikōji, in the Nishikikōji Shijō district, and founded the temple Chōmyō-ji.

From the Minobu school Nichii (1444–1519), a disciple of the abbot Nitchō, went to Kyoto at his teacher's request and in 1475 founded Myōden-ji in the Ichijō Shirikirimachi district. Some of Nichiren's ashes were enshrined there.

Propagation in Western Japan

By the late Kamakura period, the Fuji school had built Hommon-ji in Takase, Sanuki Province, on Shikoku, and Jōzen-ji in Nichiya, Hyūga Province, on Kyushu, while the Nakayama school had founded Kōshō-ji in Matsuo, Hizen Province, on Kyushu. In the cases of Hommon-ji and Kōshō-ji, important lay believers had moved to the areas—the Akiyama clan to Takase and the Chiba clan to Matsuo. In the case of Jōzen-ji, the intendant of a temple of another sect was converted to the Nichiren sect. Moreover, temples in the Kyoto region sought to proselytize and expand in western Japan. The Nichiryū school, in particular, established temples in most of the major ports and centers of trade along the Inland Sea—in Sakai in Izumi Province, Ushimado in Bizen, Onomichi in Bingo, and Utazu in Sanuki, among others. Nichiryū's disciples Nitten (1401–63) and Nichiryō (fl. fifteenth century) also proselytized as far south as the islands Tanegashima, Yakushima, and Kuchinoerabujima, off Kyushu. Myōkaku-ji gained followers in the San'indō and San'yōdō regions, especially in Bizen Province, where the faith took strong root.

Thus the various Nichiren schools thrived not only in the eastern part of the country but on western Honshu, Shikoku, and Kyushu as well. At the same time, however, the movement was weakened by schisms and internal quarrels. To remedy this situation and in self-defense against the continuing attacks on the Nichiren movement by the clergy of Mount Hiei, attempts were made to foster solidarity among all the different Nichiren schools and groups.

When Nichijū (1403–86) of Hongaku-ji in Kyoto remonstrated with the shōgun Ashikaga Yoshimasa (1435–90) in 1465, priests from Enryaku-ji demanded the suppression of the entire Nichiren sect. This demand was not met, but in reaction in 1466 Nichijū called on all Nichiren temples throughout Japan to sign a statement of unity and amity. This agreement is known as the Kanshō Accord, from the name of the era in which it was signed. For a time it appeared that the various schools would indeed co-operate, and Nichijū worked especially hard to unite the groups in eastern Japan. In the end, however, the tendency to disagree, quarrel, and break away proved too deeply rooted. Before long Nisshin (1444–1528) broke away from Myōhon-ji over the question of the superiority of the second half of the Lotus Sutra. In 1489 he established Honryū-ji in the Shijō Ōmiya district of Kyoto, which became the headquarters of the Nisshin or Honryū-ji school.

Cults and Uprisings

As we have seen, the concepts of noncooperation with nonbelievers, intolerance of other religious ideas, and aggressive proselytization formed the core of much Nichiren doctrine in the Muromachi period. Another important element was inspired by the attempt to respond to people's desire for worldly benefits gained through religious practice (*genze riyaku*). Satisfying this desire became increasingly important as the Nichiren sect strengthened its hold on the townspeople, merchants, and artisans, and the cult of the thirty guardian deities was one of the sect's major responses.

Thirty guardian deities, one on each day of the standard lunar month, were thought to protect believers: the deity of Ise was protector on the first day, the deity of Iwashimizu on the second, the deity of Kamo on the third, and so on, ending with the deity of Kibune on the thirtieth day. The deities were of various kinds—ancestral, tutelary, agricultural, literary, and martial—but all were thought to provide protection for Nichiren believers. Moreover, each deity was thought to share in the special powers of every other deity, so the protection of all thirty deities was available to believers every day.

It was not necessary to visit numerous shrines to seek the protection of the various deities. A visit to a Nichiren temple enshrining the thirty deities was sufficient. There people implored the deities to grant them health, peace, and prosperity in the present life. The Nichiren sect strictly forbade worship at the shrines or temples of other faiths, and the sect's adoption of the thirty deities appears to be related to that prohibition.

In addition to expecting specific worldly benefits from their religious practice, the ordinary citizens of Kyoto also longed to realize the Land of Eternally Tranquil Light (Jōjakkōdo)—the ideal realm populated by sincere believers in the Lotus Sutra—in this world. Nichiren had spoken of the present world as the realm or fief of Śākyamuni Buddha. The popularity of the Nichiren sect in the Kyoto region in the Muromachi period helped fuel the hopes of the general population for the attainment of Śākya-muni's Pure Land in the present world. The organization of self-defense groups and the townspeople's growing capacity for self-government in the aftermath of the Ōnin War further strengthened the people's longing.

The larger Nichiren temples began to develop martial power that could be used for self-defense. Numerically, too, Nichiren strength was growing. With two or three new temples being established in Kyoto each month, the sect was becoming the chief religious power in the capital. The major Nichiren temples in the city were known collectively as the twenty-one head temples. In the northern districts there were Myōken-ji, Jūhon-ji, Myōden-ji, Myōkaku-ji, Chōmyō-ji, and Homman-ji; in the southern districts, Honkoku-ji, Myōman-ji, Ryūhon-ji, Honnō-ji, Myōren-ji, Jōgyō-in, Hompō-ji, Myōsen-ji, Honryū-ji, Honzen-ji, Hongaku-ji, Hōkoku-ji, and Gakuyō-ji; and in locations unknown today, Kōkyō-ji and Daimyō-ji.

Around this period Miyoshi Motonaga, the protector of the Nichiren sect in the Kyoto region, quarreled with his lord, Hosokawa Harumoto (1514–63), and was forced to commit suicide at Kempon-ji in Sakai by submitting to attacking forces of the Jōdo Shin sect. Motonaga's death was a major blow to the Nichiren sect. Afterward a rumor spread that the Jōdo Shin sect forces were about to enter Kyoto and drive the Nichiren sect out once and for all. Such a large-scale offensive was a threat not only to the Nichiren temples, which would be burned to the ground, but to a large part of the capital and its citizenry.

At this point the Nichiren sect formed an alliance of necessity with Hosokawa Harumoto, who had begun to feel threatened by the growing power of his former allies, the Jōdo Shin sect believers. A Nichiren army was raised in the seventh month of 1532, and in the following month it attacked and burned the Jōdo Shin–sect Hongan-ji in Yamashina, on the outskirts of Kyoto, in concert with the armies of Harumoto and Rokkaku Sadayori (1495–1552). From then on, the Nichiren forces cooperated completely with Harumoto, and as a result, the city of Kyoto was spared a Jōdo Shin invasion and the citizens of the town began to exercise a considerable degree of self-government.

During this period, rents owed to absentee landlords ceased to be forwarded, which prompted the landlords and estate owners to take punitive measures. Many of the estate owners were in fact large temples affiliated with the older, established sects; and the increasing autonomy of the townspeople, and their nonpayment of rents and taxes, provoked the temples to plan attacks on the city and on the much-hated Nichiren sect. Moreover, in the third month of 1536 Matsumoto Shinzaemon Hisakichi (d. ca. 1536), a lay follower of Myōkō-ji in Mobara, in Kazusa Province, debated Keōbō (fl. sixteenth century) of Kitao, in Mount Hiei's Western Precincts, in the so-called Matsumoto Debate. It was widely recognized that Keōbō had been resoundingly defeated. This so infuriated the Enryaku-ji priests that they began preparations for a major campaign against the Nichiren sect, seeking reinforcements from Tō-ji, Jingo-ji, Tōdai-ji, Kōfuku-ji, Onjō-ji, and even the Jōdo Shin–sect Hongan-ji in Ishiyama, near Osaka, and asking for the acquiescence of the government, Hosokawa Harumoto, and Rokkaku Sadayori.

In the seventh month of 1536 Enryaku-ji priests finally attacked the Nichiren temples in the capital, destroying virtually all of them. Nor were casualties limited to Nichiren priests and property. A number of townspeople also died in the fighting, and sections of the capital that had managed to rebuild after the Ōnin War were again destroyed. After the so-called Lotus War of the Temmon (or Tembun) Era, the defeated Nichiren sect was forced to move its western headquarters to Sakai, outside Osaka.

From Sakai the Nichiren sect made overtures to the imperial court, exploiting the good offices of sympathetic members of the nobility in an effort to gain permission to return to the capital and resume religious activities there. Official permission was granted in the eleventh month of 1542, although a number of temples had in fact quietly reestablished themselves earlier. But even after official permission was granted, the number of major temples in Kyoto never rose above fifteen, far short of the earlier figure of twenty-one. With the support of many townspeople, the Nichiren sect largely succeed in reviving itself in the capital. Within half a century, however, in the Tenshō (1573–92), Bunroku (1592–96), Keichō (1596–1615), and Kan'ei (1624–44) eras, the government again suppressed the Nichiren movement as a result of controversies over noncooperation with nonbelievers and other doctrinal matters.

11. Women and Buddhism

EARLY JAPANESE BUDDHISM AND WOMEN

Women and Sacred Precincts

We can do no better than turn to the reformer Hōnen (1133–1212) for an understanding of the attitude toward women held in the sacred precincts of practice and study of ancient Japanese Buddhism, such as Tōdai-ji, Enryaku-ji, Kongōbu-ji, Daigo-ji, Sūfuku-ji, and Kimbusen-ji. Hōnen, who lived well over half his life in the Heian period (794–1185), spent thirty years in ancient centers of Japanese Buddhism—Tōdai-ji in Nara and Enryaku-ji on Mount Hiei—from the age of twelve to the age of forty-two, when he left Mount Hiei to preach his doctrine of salvation through faith in Amida and recitation of the *nembutsu*. Very few men of religion were as qualified as Hōnen to comment on the situation of women in relation to the sacred precincts of centers of traditional Buddhism.

In the *Muryōju-kyō Shaku* (Commentary on the Larger *Sukhāvatī-vyūha*), Hōnen notes the practice of the temples of the Nara- and Heian-period sects of strictly excluding women from participation in their activities and even from entry into their sacred precincts: "In this land of Japan the most sacred and exalted holy places all forbid women to enter." He cites specific examples of this practice and goes on to describe the attitude toward women at ancient Buddhist centers:

> Enryaku-ji on Mount Hiei was set apart by Dengyō Daishi [Saichō] himself as a place whose mountains and valleys were not to be defiled

by the presence of women. In those sacred precincts the summit of the
One Vehicle rises loftily to the skies, and women, who are burdened with
five obstacles to enlightenment, may never trespass. The valleys are deep
and still, and women, who are subject to the five obstacles and the three
obediences, may never enter them.* A woman may hear of the blessings
of the miraculous image of Yakushi [Nyorai], the buddha of healing,
[at Enryaku-ji] on Mount Hiei, but she may not view it with her own
eyes. A woman may worship from afar the holy precincts set aside by
Dengyō Daishi, but she may never ascend the sacred mountain.

Hōnen relates that women were also denied access to Kongōbu-ji on
Mount Kōya:

Mount Kōya was set apart by Kūkai for sacred use and denied to
women. The doctrine of the supreme vehicle of Shingon flourishes there,
where the moon of the three mysteries of body, speech, and mind illuminates all things. Yet not quite all—for women, lacking the capacity
to attain buddhahood, remain unillumined. The waters of wisdom are
said to flow to all, equally. Yet they do not flow to the defiled bodies of
women. Even on Mount Hiei and Mount Kōya, the Buddha's teachings are not accessible to women. How much more right and natural is
it, then, that women should be denied entry to and be excluded from
the incomparable Pure Land of Perfect Bliss!

Mount Kōya's ostracism of women is evident in Nyojaku's *Kōyasan Ōjō
Den* (Biographies of Those on Mount Kōya Who Attained Rebirth in the
Pure Land), which numbers not a single woman among the thirty-eight
people whose lives it recounts. After noting that women were banned from
all the sacred precincts of traditional Buddhism, Hōnen states:

Sad to say, though women have legs to walk with, there are peaks of
the Law they may not climb and gardens of the Buddha they may not
enter. Again, shameful to relate, though women have eyes to see with,
there are holy places they may not look upon and miraculous images
at which they may not gaze. Thus, even the temples, like mere heaps of

* The Buddhist doctrine of the five obstacles for women holds that women cannot attain
the five highest spiritual states, supreme of which is buddhahood. The Confucian dictum
of the three obediences states that women must obey their fathers when children, their
husbands when adults, and their eldest sons in old age.

rubbish and brambles in this world of endurance, refuse entry to women, and even the crudest buddha images made of mud and sticks reject their worship. How, then, could women be allowed to be reborn in the Buddha-land and see the Buddha, possessed of every virtue and dwelling in the Pure Land of Perfect Bliss, made of countless precious gems?

In the *Shōbō Genzō* (Treasury of the Eye of the True Dharma; 1231–53), Dōgen speaks of the traditional Buddhist establishments' exclusion of women as "something ridiculous."

Chief among the reasons for excluding women from Buddhist precincts were the teachings of the five obstacles and the three obediences, to which women were deemed to be subject by virtue of their sex. At the same time, however, various sutras speak of the potence of women's passions and the grave burden of their evil karma.

Thus, in the *Nyonin Ōjō Kikigaki* (Notes on Women's Rebirth in the Pure Land; 1324), the priest Zonkaku (1290–1373) of Hongan-ji in Kyoto introduces numerous passages from sutras and treatises that testify to the sinful nature of women. From the *Nehan-gyō* (Sutra of the Great Decease), he quotes: "The passions of but a single woman and the obstacles to her attainment of buddhahood are so vast that they can be compared with all the passions and bonds of all the men in three thousand worlds." From the *Shinjikan-gyō* (Mahāyāna Sutra of Meditation on the Origin of the Mind), he cites: "Should the all-seeing eyes of the buddhas of the three worlds fall to the ground and putrefy, still no buddha whatsoever would vow to save the females of the phenomenal realms." In the *Jōyuishiki Ron* (Treatise on the Establishment of the Doctrine of Consciousness Only), he finds: "Women are messengers from hell. They have destroyed forever the seeds of the buddha-nature within them. Outwardly they are as gentle as bodhisattvas, but inwardly they are like demons."

As long as such views persisted, women would not be seen as qualified for enlightenment or rebirth, despite the assurance of universal salvation implicit in the *nembutsu* teaching that developed in the major centers of Buddhism. Yet, in the streets and alleys of Heian Japan there arose a movement that gave women an equal promise of salvation.

Women and Worldly Benefits

By the early years of the Heian period, women were already turning to

Buddhism for solace and worldly benefits, as the following tale from the *Nihon Ryōiki* (Miracle Stories of Japan; ca. 822) demonstrates.

At one time there lived on the west side of Nara, near Uetsuki-dera, a young woman who was quite alone, with no family. While her parents were alive the family had been very prosperous and had enshrined in their residence an image of the bodhisattva Kannon, whom they piously worshiped. After her parents died, all the servants fled and the livestock died of disease and neglect. Now very poor, the young woman somehow carried on, taking care of the empty house by herself.

Having heard that Kannon is ever ready to hear the prayers of mortals and to grant them help in their troubles, the young woman offered flowers, incense, and candles before the image and prayed: "I have lost my parents and am all alone in the world. I am very poor, with no assets and no way to earn a living. Please grant me the blessing of prosperity—and please, please do so as quickly as possible."

Now, in her district there lived a very wealthy man who sent a matchmaker to her with a proposal of marriage. But the young woman refused repeatedly because of her poverty. At last the man went to her in person and, almost forcing himself upon her, convinced her of his sincerity and accomplished their tryst.

Heavy rain prevented the man from leaving for three days. When he became hungry and asked for food, all the young woman could do was look in despair at the empty pots in her kitchen and shed tears of frustration and shame. Suddenly remembering the mercy of Kannon, she immediately prayed: "Send me money quickly."

That very afternoon a messenger came from her next-door neighbor bearing a tray piled high with rich delicacies, and so she was able to feed her betrothed well and avoid the shameful revelation of her poverty. Soon after her betrothed left for his residence, she went to her neighbor to thank her for the generous gift. But neither the neighbor nor her servants knew anything about the matter. They were amazed to be thanked for a gift that had not been sent.

Having returned home, the young woman was about to offer a prayer before the image of Kannon when, to her amazement, she noticed hanging from its shoulders the cheap, worn garment she had given to the "servant" who had brought the tray earlier that day. Thus she realized that all that had happened was the bodhisattva's doing. From that time on she frequently received Kannon's blessings, becoming as prosperous as when her parents were alive and living happily with her new husband.

The protagonist of this story asked for immediate, specific, material blessings from Kannon, and because of her faith and devotion, her prayer was granted. She did not despair of happiness in the present and simply seek salvation in the afterlife. But around the middle of the Heian period, the path to the other-worldly Pure Land of Perfect Bliss that had first been followed by priests on Mount Hiei was gradually opened to ordinary men and women. Let us examine this development in the lives of women as recorded in Heian-period *ōjō den,* or popular biographies of believers supposed to have attained rebirth in the Pure Land.

Women and Rebirth in the Pure Land

An early account of a woman who attained rebirth in the Pure Land is found in the *Nihon Ōjō Gokuraku Ki* (Japanese Accounts of Rebirth in the Pure Land; ca. 983–86).

> A woman said to be a granddaughter of Emperor Kōkō [830–87] married young and bore three children, all of whom soon died, as did her husband. After some years of living alone, she became a devout Pure Land believer, earnestly reciting the *nembutsu* and hoping for rebirth in the Pure Land. The woman was gentle and compassionate by nature and did not even brush away mosquitoes or flies that might alight on her. When she was about fifty years of age, she suffered a minor illness, during which she heard wonderfully beautiful music and serenely breathed her last, saying, "Amida has come to welcome me to the Pure Land. It is time for me to leave this world of edurance."

The woman in this story had a deathbed vision of Amida and attained rebirth in his Pure Land because she fulfilled the moral criteria of being gentle and compassionate and the religious criteria of having faith in and practicing the *nembutsu.* The story mentions no special criteria expressly for women.

Another hagiographic collection from the Heian period, the *Zoku Honchō Ōjō Den* (Further Biographies of Japanese Who Attained Rebirth in the Pure Land; ca. 1101–11), contains the following anecdote:

The wife of Fujiwara no Kanetsune was the daughter of Councilor Fujiwara no Takaie [979–1044]. She was virtuous and chaste, as well as beautiful. She was so even-tempered that no one in her family had ever seen her angry or overly excited. Throughout her life she reverently recited the *nembutsu,* and she finally attained such spiritual maturity that she no longer cared to live in this world of endurance. It is said that when she lay on her deathbed a wonderful perfume filled the room, signaling her imminent rebirth, and that the same perfume permeated the garments of her relatives and attendants and lingered for several months after her death.

This woman too fulfilled the moral criteria of being virtuous, chaste, and gentle and the religious criteria of being an earnest believer in and practitioner of the *nembutsu.*

A somewhat later work, the *Sange Ōjō Ki* (A Record of Rebirths in the Pure Land Not Previously Recorded; ca. 1139), contains another story in the same vein.

There lived at the foot of Mount Hira in Ōmi Province a profoundly compassionate woman who always provided food and drink for anyone who chanced upon her dwelling. If she heard that a traveler had fallen ill by the wayside, she would always prepare food and take it to the person, no matter how distant the person's resting place might be. She was as compassionate toward strangers as we are toward our own children. Furthermore, she had deep faith in Amida and had for many years longed to reach his Pure Land. When the hour of her death approached, she closed her eyes, entered into profound meditation on the Pure Land, and passed away. It is said that eight people nearby smelled a sweet fragrance like incense and that six of them saw the approach of Amida's purple clouds.

This woman, too, was able to attain rebirth because she fulfilled the moral criterion of compassion and the religious criterion of strong faith in the *nembutsu.*

A similar account is found in the *Go Shūi Ōjō Den* (Further Gleanings of Accounts of Rebirth in the Pure Land; ca. 1123–39).

The female priest Jakumyō was gentle by nature, not given to jealousy or anger. She had married and borne several children. In whatever time she could spare from household duties, she devoted herself to religious practice—reading the entire Lotus Sutra more than a thousand times and reciting the *nembutsu* some 5,300,000 times. Widowed at fifty-seven, she became a nun at seventy and, not caring for worldly things, earnestly sought the peerless Way. On the fifth day of the first month of 1116, she faced west, continuously recited the *nembutsu*, and breathed her last. Even after death, her countenance was as vibrant as it had been in life.

Here is another woman who gained salvation by fulfilling the moral criteria of gentleness and freedom from jealousy and anger and the religious criteria of repeatedly reading the Lotus Sutra and reciting the *nembutsu* a vast number of times.

A variety of sources relate numerous anecdotes of the rebirth of women in the Pure Land. Together they set down the criteria that women of the Heian period were expected to satisfy in order to qualify for rebirth. With respect to religious criteria, rebirth in the Pure Land was thought to be the fruit of the merit accumulated through a variety of practices, teachings, and devotions to various buddhas. Such thinking is of course a direct reflection of the nonexclusive, polytheistic, and ascetic nature of the Buddhism practiced in traditional Buddhist centers.

The religious practices undertaken by the women whose lives are recorded in Heian-period Pure Land hagiographies include reading the Lotus Sutra, reciting a vast number of *nembutsu*, copying the Lotus Sutra, reciting the *Amida-kyō* (Smaller *Sukhāvatī-vyūha*), reciting the *Ninnō Hannya-kyō* (Sutra on the Benevolent King), memorizing the Lotus Sutra, reading the entire Mahāyāna canon by the ritual *tendoku* method (that is, reading just the first few lines of each sutra), copying the *Konkōmyō Saishōō-kyō* (Golden Light Sutra), *tendoku* reading of the *Konkōmyō Saishōō-kyō*, practice of esoteric Buddhist rituals, praying before images of Kannon, making buddha images, and constructing Buddhist halls and pagodas. In addition, there are instances in which it was deemed necessary for the family, relatives, and friends of a female believer to perform supplemental acts of merit to ensure her rebirth in the Pure Land.

As we have noted, in addition to religious criteria, there were moral and ethical criteria as well—honesty, compassion, and gentleness among them. Such traits were emphasized equally for male and female Pure Land

believers. But in the case of women, a great change in attitudes and expectations occurred between the Heian and Kamakura periods.

KAMAKURA BUDDHISM AND REBIRTH FOR WOMEN

Hōnen and Shinran

When the founders of the new sects of the Kamakura period preached
about rebirth, salvation, and enlightenment to the ordinary women of their
day, they relied not on accounts in Heian-period hagiographies but on
theories and doctrines concerning the all-important matter of rebirth and
enlightenment. This was true also in their preaching about women's rebirth.

Hōnen's views on rebirth for women are developed in his theoretical
works and his letters. In the *Muryōju-kyō Shaku* he addresses the question of
why Amida made a special vow to save women (the thirty-fifth vow),
though he had already vowed to save evildoers and women without distinction (the eighteenth vow):

> Amida made a special promise to female believers, saying: "If, after I
> have attained buddhahood, a woman, having heard my name, should
> with joyful faith conceive the desire to be reborn in my Pure Land of
> Perfect Bliss, casting aside the hateful form of woman, and yet, when
> her present life is over, be reborn again as a woman, then I will not ac-
> cept the enlightenment I have earned." I have a question about this. In
> his earlier vow Amida promised to come to pious believers at the time
> of death and lead them to the Pure Land of Perfect Bliss, without dis-
> tinction as to sex. Moreover, his [twentieth vow] also includes both men
> and women. Why, then, did he make a special vow for women alone?

Hōnen answers his own question: "Amida did so because the obstacles
to salvation for women are formidable, and if there were no vow specifically for them, they would immediately begin to doubt the possibility of
their salvation." Another reason he gives for the specific vow is that women
are known to be disliked in the various buddha-realms and refused admit-
tance because of their many passions and failings. He then discusses in
detail the five obstacles, the three obediences, and the potency of the passions and strength of the karmic bonds of women. Hōnen cites the example
of Enryaku-ji on Mount Hiei in describing the way that the centers of tra-

ditional Buddhism discriminate against women, forbidding them entrance to the sacred precincts and denying them the possibility of rebirth or enlightenment. Since they are subject to discrimination in both doctrine and practice, women—burdened with numerous obstacles and resultant doubts—are unable to believe with simple, unquestioning faith in Amida's eighteenth vow, even though of course it includes them. Amida therefore compassionately made a special vow for them, his thirty-fifth, to give them hope.

Quoting from the *Kuan-ching-su* (Commentary on the Sutra of Meditation on Amitābha Buddha) by the seventh-century Chinese master Shantao, Hōnen explains the content of this vow:

> If they rely on the power of Amida's great vow and reverently recite his name, then when this life is over they will be able at once to exchange the form of woman for that of man. Then Amida himself will lead the woman who has been transformed into a man; the host of bodhisattvas will surround her; and she will be reborn in the Pure Land. On the other hand, if a woman does not rely on the great vow, even after countless ages she will not be able to achieve transformation into a man. Truly, Amida in his compassion works to relieve women of their sufferings and to grant them joy!

To Hōnen, Amida's thirty-fifth and eighteenth vows represented the path to salvation prepared especially for women, who—burdened with lusts and passions and subject to the five obstacles and the three obediences—had been abandoned to their fate by the other buddhas of the three worlds (past, present, and future) and the ten directions. To be sure, in female form women could not attain rebirth, but they could be transformed into men and granted salvation. Hōnen's theory of rebirth for women inevitably involved their incorporation into the ranks of males.

Shinran (1173–1262), who came to faith in the other-power *nembutsu* through his teacher Hōnen, developed the concept of the evil person as the proper object of Amida's vows. According to this view, it is specifically the person filled with passions and bound by the strongest karmic bonds—the evildoer—who is to be saved by Amida. As we have seen, the other buddhas were believed to have abandoned women precisely because of their strong passions and karmic bonds. Both traditional Buddhist thinkers and Shinran considered women the worst of a bad lot, the gravest evildoers of all. The doctrine that evildoers are the proper object of Amida's vows leads logically to the conclusion that women are the most proper object of all (*nyonin shōki*). Nonetheless, the concept of *nyonin shōki* was never part of Shinran's doctrinal system. He faithfully followed his master Hōnen's ideas regarding rebirth for women.

In his *Jōdo Wasan* (Hymns of the Pure Land; 1248), Shinran expresses his views on this topic:

> Profound is Amida's mercy!
> He shows his wondrous wisdom
> By making men of women
> And leading them to buddhahood.

Here Shinran makes it clear that women can attain rebirth and ultimately buddhahood, but like Hōnen, he insists that they must first be transformed into men. In his comments on this hymn, Shinran notes that it expresses "the intent of the thirty-fifth vow," and his interpretation of the vow faithfully conforms to the interpretations of the Chinese Pure Land patriarch Shan-tao and his successors.

The *Kōsō Wasan* (Hymns of the Patriarchs; 1248), by Shinran, also expresses his ideas about women's salvation:

> Though a billion eons pass
> The five obstacles yet remain
> And woman's form is never changed—
> Without the vow of Amida.

In other words, unless a woman relies on the vow of Amida, she will never overcome the five obstacles and never succeed in becoming a man and attaining buddhahood.

Dōgen

Dōgen (1200–1253), who harshly criticized the traditional centers of Buddhism for discriminating against women, preached the equality of the sexes with regard to practice and the attainment of enlightenment. He devoted an entire section of his *Shōbō Genzō*—the "Raihai Tokuzui" (The Essence of Worship)—to the subject. In this section he says:

> There is something ridiculous in Japan. I mean those places that, while calling themselves "sacred precincts" of "schools of Mahāyāna practice," refuse entry to female priests and lay women. This mistaken cus-

tom has continued for so long that people cannot see what is wrong with it. Even people who are learned and versed in various matters do not attempt to correct it. Even highly knowledgeable people do not regard the matter as worthy of attention. They say that it is the will of the deities and buddhas, or that it is a time-honored custom and not to be disputed. If one allowed oneself to laugh at this attitude, one would split one's sides. If one does not permit oneself to correct outmoded ways of thinking and acting, how can one possibly escape the endless cycle of birth and death?

Is there any of the three realms of existence [realms of desire, form, and formlessness] or any buddha-land in the ten directions into which a female priest may not enter? Who could prevent her from entering freely? . . . To discriminate against women and attempt to keep them from attaining buddhahood is the conduct of utter fools who seek to mislead humankind. They are like a fox that fears its den will be taken from it by other animals—no, they are far more foolish than that!

Dōgen plainly states that excluding women, discriminating against them, and refusing them opportunities for practice are unjustifiable acts of folly. He goes so far as to deny, at least indirectly, the notion of "obstacles," said to be the grounds on which the buddhas of the three worlds and the ten directions abandoned women and excluded them from enlightenment. He points out that female Buddhist priests are superior to two of the high spiritual states from which women are supposedly excluded by the five obstacles. That is, a female priest is superior to a *cakravarti-rāja* (wheel-rolling king) and a *Śakro devānām indraḥ* (a protective deity).

Dōgen's indignation over the presumption of the centers of traditional Buddhism in excluding women is clear in the "Raihai Tokuzui."

Those who live in the so-called sacred precincts in fact commit the ten evils without fear and violate each of the ten major precepts.* Their sacred precincts are places of sin, and they hate all those who do not sin like them. We rightly view the five grievous acts as the most heinous.† Do those who live within the sacred precincts not commit even these?

---

* The ten evils are killing, stealing, engaging in wrongful sexual activity, lying, using immoral language, slandering, equivocating, coveting, giving way to anger, and entertaining false views. The ten major precepts prohibit each of the ten evils.
† The five grievous acts are killing one's father, one's mother, or an enlightened person, physically injuring a buddha, and causing disunity in the community of believers.

Such demonic sacred places must be destroyed. We should learn from the Buddha in his earthly incarnation and seek to enter the true Buddha realm. To destroy the evil sacred places is the best way to requite the Buddha's benevolence. I say to the reverend patriarchs who dwell in such places: "Do you really know the meaning of 'sacred place'? From whom did you learn to raise such barriers, excluding women from practice? Who gave you the authority to do such things?"

In strong language, Dōgen condemns those who would exclude women from the holy places of Japanese Buddhism. Beginning when he was in Fukakusa in Kyoto, he preached salvation for both men and women through the practice of Zen, and developed a theory of the religious equality of men and women and of salvation for women.

Nichiren

Nichiren (1222–82) wrote many works that touch on the question of rebirth and enlightenment for women, among them the *Nyonin Jōbutsu Shō* (Notes on the Attainment of Buddhahood by Women; 1265), *Yakuōbon Tokui Shō* (Notes on Attainments in the Bodhisattva Medicine King Chapter [of the Lotus Sutra]; 1265), *Nichigennyo Shaka Butsu Kuyō Ji* (Nichigennyo's Memorial Service for Śākyamuni Buddha; 1279), *Sennichi Ama Gozen Gohenji* (Reply to the *Ama Gozen* Sennichi; 1253), and *Nyonin Ōjō Shō* (Notes on Women's Rebirth; 1253).

In his letter *Nichigennyo Shaka Butsu Kuyō Ji*, which deals with the pious act of a laywoman, Nichiren replies:

The Lotus Sutra says: "If there are people who make many images for the sake of the Buddha, they have already attained the way of buddhahood." This passage means that all women will surely attain enlightenment in the next life, as well as be freed from various troubles and trials in this, if only they perform such good works as making images of Śākyamuni Buddha. Now, in the five thousand to seven thousand fascicles of sutras that Śākyamuni preached during his lifetime, women are despised as being incapable of buddhahood. Only in the Lotus Sutra is it said that they can attain enlightenment.

In his commentary on the Lotus Sutra, Chih-i [the founder of T'ien-t'ai] says: "Nothing is said about enlightenment for women [in the other sutras]." On the other hand, the Lotus Sutra speaks of the "dragon woman attaining enlightenment." Chih-i, a great scholar who lived in China some fifteen hundred years after Śākyamuni's death, had read the entire canon fifteen times. He states that there are no instances of women attaining enlightenment and becoming buddhas except that recorded in the Lotus Sutra. Moreover, in a commentary the Great Master Miao-le [the sixth patriarch of T'ien-t'ai] says: "There is no doctrine of attainment of buddhahood by women in the entire canon."

The Lotus Sutra is like the moon as compared with the stars, or a king as compared with ordinary men, or Mount Sumeru as compared with common heights, or the ocean as compared with other waters. Since salvation for women is preached in such a splendid, surpassingly excellent sutra, what need is there to worry even if they are despised by all the other sutras in the canon? It is like being despised by a thief, robber, beggar, or leper but admired and praised by a king or emperor!

Nichiren argues that only the Lotus Sutra speaks of saving women, who are rejected by various buddhas. Yet since that most sublime of all sutras guarantees salvation to women if they are pious believers, it does not matter if they are despised in other sutras. Writing to the *ama gozen*, or lady-priest, Sennichi in the *Sennichi Ama Gozen Gohenji*, Nichiren says:

As for the vexing question of women's salvation, simply rely whole-heartedly on the fact that the Lotus Sutra, of all the Buddha's teachings, gives it greatest emphasis Always remember that among all the holy teachings expounded by Śākyamuni during his lifetime, the Lotus Sutra is the greatest, and that the greatest doctrine in the Lotus is the doctrine of salvation for women. Thus, even should all the women of Japan be despised and rejected by all the other sutras in the canon, what does it matter as long as salvation is assured by the authority of the Lotus Sutra?

In this important passage Nichiren declares that the question of women's salvation is preeminent and fundamental in the Lotus Sutra.

Finally, let us examine Nichiren's ideas as expressed in an essay on rebirth for women, the *Nyonin Ōjō Shō*.

The Buddha has told us that all the women of the entire world in the age of the Decay of the Law will be reborn in a realm of bliss where the Buddha abides if they believe even one word or one point in the Lotus Sutra. It is far better to have been born a woman in the period of the Decay of the Law than to have been born as the famous Li Fu-jen, Yang Kuei-fei, or Wang Chao-chun of China, or as Ono no Ko-machi or Izumi Shikibu of Japan. All may have been well with them while they enjoyed the favor of the powerful during this earthly life, but this life is as brief and fleeting as a dream. Now, no doubt, they find themselves in one or another of the hells. They all lived in ancient times, either before the preaching of the Law or during its early period of prosperity. Since they were born before the Decay of the Law, before the period in which the Buddha will work especially for women's salvation, their fate is uncertain at best.

How fortunate, by contrast, are the women of today, who live in an age in which women can assuredly be saved—now that the two thousand years of the periods of the Righteous Law and the Counterfeit Law have given way to that of the Decay of the Law. In nature everything has its season. In winter there is no lack of ice; in spring, of flowers; in summer there is an abundance of grass; in autumn, of fallen leaves. Just so is the present the time of salvation for women. The Buddha does not care if a woman is greedy, stupid, angry, jealous, or slothful. Why, then, should he despise a woman who is without such faults?

Here Nichiren points out the crucial factor of the times in which people live. Even such eminent and brilliant women as Li Fu-jen, Yang Kuei-fei, Wang Chao-chun, Ono no Komachi, and Izumi Shikibu probably failed to attain rebirth simply because the Buddha had not specifically promised to save women born in their historical periods. Women born in the age of the Decay of the Law, even those with many vices, will not be rejected, however, because the Buddha promised to save them in particular. In short, Nichiren does not demand that women fulfill any moral or ethical criteria in order to be saved. Even those who lack such traditional virtues as compassion, honesty, and gentleness, or are burdened with a variety of evils, can hope for rebirth. How much more so can a pious, virtuous woman.

12. Shintō and Shugendō

SHINTŌ: THE WAY OF THE *KAMI*

The Beginnings of Ise Shintō

In the ancient period of Japan's history, the indigenous religion of the Japanese had no systematized doctrine. Although the introduction of Buddhism, with its mature doctrines, spurred the crystallization of the indigenous religion, it did not begin to develop its own doctrinal system until the thirteenth century. Only with the subsequent emergence of distinct schools—such as Ise Shintō, Ryōbu Shintō, and Yoshida Shintō—is it possible to speak with validity of a Shintō religion.

In concert with these developments, the very meaning of the word *shintō* changed. For centuries *shintō* (literally, way of the *kami*, or divinities) had been virtually synonymous with *kami* and similar words meaning "deity." But in the thirteenth century the term began to be used to identify the indigenous religious system, differentiating it from Buddhism.

The earliest recorded instance of this usage is in the *Kōgi Zuiketsu Shū* (Collected Answers of Shinzui to Atsuhiro's Questions; 1256). This collection of replies by the Jōdo-sect priest Shinzui (d. 1279) to questions put by a warrior of Shinano Province, Uehara Atsuhiro (fl. thirteenth century), refers to "alms offered by adherents of Buddhism and of Shintō" and states that "Buddhism and Shintō are fundamentally one." The term is next used in this sense in the Shingon priest Tsūkai's (1234–1305) *Dai Jingū Sankei Ki* (Record of a Pilgrimage to Ise Grand Shrine; ca. 1287): "Amaterasu Ōmikami [the solar deity] is the lord of Shintō; Dainichi Nyorai

299

[Mahāvairocana] is the lord of Buddhism." Of the five occurrences of *shintō* in this work by the learned Tsūkai, however, four are in the traditional sense of *kami* rather than as the appellation of a coherent religious system.

Such phrases as "the profound meaning of Shintō," "the transformations of Shintō," and "the beautiful spirit of Buddhism and Shintō" appear in slightly later texts of the Ise and Ryōbu schools. By the time of the *Toyoashihara Jimpū Waki* (Harmonious Record of the Ways of the *Kami* of Japan; 1340), compiled by the Tendai priest Jihen (fl. 1333–40), the new usage has clearly taken root: "The imperial virtue that extends over heaven, earth, and humankind is called the Way of the Emperor. In our country this is also called the Way of the *Kami* [Shintō]."

Without question, the clergy of the major shrines played prominent roles in the relatively rapid development of Shintō doctrine. Development was especially noticeable in the thirteenth and fourteenth centuries at such major centers as Ise Grand Shrine, the shrine of Amaterasu in Ise Province; Hie Shrine, the shrine of the *kami* Sannō Gongen in Ōmi Province; and Ōmiwa Shrine, the shrine of the *kami* Miwa Myōjin in Yamato Province. In the case of Ise Shrine, changes in the shrine's economic footing and in the status of its clergy provided impetus for the elaboration of doctrine.

Ise Grand Shrine, consisting of the Inner Shrine (Naikū) and the Outer Shrine (Gekū), enjoyed great prestige after the government was centralized in the seventh and eighth centuries. The *Engi Shiki* (Procedures of the Engi Era; 905–27) states that "imperial retainers may not make unofficial offerings to the Great Deity enshrined at Ise"; that is, even ministers and other officials were forbidden to utter private prayers or make private offerings at the sacrosanct, imperially related Ise Grand Shrine. The decline of the central government's finances, however, made it impossible to maintain the Grand Shrine through imperial largess alone; it became necessary for the shrine to draw revenues from landed estates held in outlying provinces, just as the nobility, Buddhist temples, and other shrines did. The Grand Shrine's estates, known as *mikuriya*, were generally established with the cooperation of local estate holders at the urging of the shrine's *gonnegi*, or junior priests. A large number of extensive estates were established in the Kantō region, among them the Sōma and Kasai *mikuriya* in Shimōsa Province, the Yanada *mikuriya* in Shimotsuke Province, the Ōkawado *mikuriya* in Musashi Province, and the Ōba *mikuriya* in Sagami Province.

In attempting to secure these lands, the *gonnegi* of Ise Shrine stressed the shrine's sacred authority and divine virtues. Their simple emphasis on the legendary origins of the Japanese islands and people must have appealed to the warriors and landowners of eastern Honshu, a relatively undeveloped region in which the influence of the aristocratic Buddhist culture of Kyoto was weak. The persuasiveness of the *gonnegi* is evident from such records as the declaration of the donation of the Sōma *mikuriya* made by Minamoto no Yoshimune in 1161: "The entire land of Great Japan belongs to the sacred site of the deity Toyouke of the imperial Ise Grand Shrine. This is the Central Land of the Reed Plains."

Even though private prayers were ostensibly forbidden at Ise Shrine, the inner minister Fujiwara no Yorinaga (1120–56), for example, made offerings to pray for his adopted daughter Tashi's selection as imperial consort, noting in his diary that it was "a most private matter." No doubt both the rapid expansion of the shrine's estates in the Kantō region and the inclination of high officials to make private offerings resulted from the efforts of the Ise clergy, but Minamoto no Yoritomo (1147–99), founder of the Kamakura shogunate, exploited these developments. He showed great favor to the *gonnegi* of the shrine, presented estates and horses to both the Inner Shrine and the Outer Shrine, put down all opposition from local warriors living on estates owned by the shrines, and took every opportunity to demonstrate profound reverence for Ise Shrine. No doubt Yoritomo did all this to enhance the ultimate authority of Ise, whose prestige he needed to quell disputes in his own ranks while establishing a warrior government. In any case, Yoritomo's policy had a decisive, enduring effect on the religious practice of the warrior class and ushered in a new epoch in the history of Ise Shrine.

Around this time the Buddhist establishment contributed to Shintō's prestige. The Jōdo priest Chōgen (1121–1206) approached Ise Shrine in connection with the projected restoration of the ruined temple Tōdai-ji in Nara. It was widely believed that centuries earlier the court official Tachibana no Moroe (684–757), who had been sent to Ise Shrine as an emissary of Emperor Shōmu, had received an oracle saying: "The sun is identical with Dainichi Nyorai." The "sun" in this oracle was interpreted as a reference to Amaterasu. Thanks to this oracle, a tenuous connection had been established between Ise Shrine and Buddhism at an early date, and it was on the basis of this connection that Chōgen sought the blessing of Ise Shrine for his restoration project.

In 1186 he and sixty other priests from Tōdai-ji went to Ise to present the six hundred fascicles of the *Daihannya-kyō* (Great Perfection of Wisdom Sutra) to the shrine "in order that Amaterasu Ōmikami and Toyouke Ōmikami's joy in the [Buddha's] Law and their holy radiance might be increased still more." Chōgen's party was warmly received by Ōnakatomi no Yoshitaka (1146–1234), the chief priest of Ise Grand Shrine; Arakida Shigenaga (1140–93), the highest of the *negi*, or senior priests, of the Inner Shrine; and Watarai Mitsutada, the highest of the *negi* of the Outer Shrine. A formal dedication of the sutra, ritual reading of it, and lectures on its content were held at Jōmyō-ji in Yamada and Tengaku-ji in Futami, not far from Ise Shrine.

Chōgen conducted the sutra dedication ceremony primarily to further the restoration of Tōdai-ji, but the ceremony greatly benefited Ise Shrine, as well. According to contemporary sources, when the priests reached Yamada they met an emissary of Yoritomo who had been sent to convey news of grants of land to the shrine. The emissary participated in the dedication service and was so pleased to be able to do so that he gave a fine horse to Chōgen. In this fashion, Buddhist priests lent the prestige of their religion to Shintō shrines, and the shrines responded by cooperating in Buddhist religious projects. Moreover, the contact with the clergy and teachings of Buddhism stimulated the Shintō priests to begin articulating their religion in theoretical terms.

The Establishment of Ise Shintō

Largely because of Yoritomo's devoted patronage, the number of pilgrims to Ise Shrine increased greatly. Major ceremonies held at the Inner Shrine in 1266 and at the Outer Shrine in 1287 are said to have drawn millions of people of both high and low degree, from near and far. Perhaps influenced by Chōgen's example, a large number of Buddhist priests also made the pilgrimage. Among them were the Ritsu-sect priest Eizon (1201–90), who went there three times in a relatively short period, and Shinkyō (1237–1319) of the Ji sect, who made a single pilgrimage in 1301, leading a large party of *nembutsu* practitioners and lepers.

As a result of the flood of pilgrims, the priests of the shrine began to feel a need to preach the divine virtues of the *kami* enshrined there with more force and clarity. Tsūkai's *Dai Jingū Sankei Ki* served as a guidebook and basic introduction to the subject. Tsūkai, a member of the Ōnakatomi clan, had entered the Shingon sect's Daigo-ji in Kyoto and mastered the most profound doctrines of the Sambō-in school of Shingon. He eventually became abbot of Daigo-ji and later succeeded to Renge-ji, an Ōnaka-tomi clan temple on the Tanahashi *mikuriya*, near Ise Shrine, where he later built Dai Jingū Hōraku-ji (Temple of the Grand Shrine's Delight in the Law).

Tsūkai earnestly described the indigenous deities' delight in the teachings and practices of Buddhism, explaining the nature of the Inner and Outer shrines and all the lesser shrines in Buddhist or quasi-Buddhist terms. The problem of traditional prohibitions against Buddhism at Ise remained, however. Buddhist terminology had been prohibited since the early tenth century, and Buddhist priests were not allowed to proceed very far into the sacred precincts. How, then, could the pleasure of the *kami* at the offering of Buddhist sutras be explained?

One explanation was provided by the story of the Demon King of the Sixth Heaven. When the male and female *kami* Izanagi and Izanami tried to create the land of Japan, the Demon King of the Sixth Heaven, realizing that Japan would eventually become a nation in which Buddhism flourished, attempted to seize it for himself. In a ruse to deceive the Demon King, the two creator deities established a series of prohibitions against Buddhism and things Buddhist; this feigned anti-Buddhist attitude on the part of the indigenous deities was perpetuated by later generations at Ise Shrine.

Tsūkai relates this tale in the *Dai Jingū Sankei Ki*, as does Mujū (1226–1312) of the Rinzai sect in his *Shasoki Shū* (Collection of Sand and Pebbles, 1279–83). Mujū goes so far as to state that the Ise *kami* "outwardly keep themselves apart from Buddhism but inwardly guard and defend the Three Treasures [the Buddha, his teachings, and the Buddhist community]; thus, the Buddhism of our land has always depended on the august protection of the Grand Shrine." He ascribes these views to a priest of the shrine. The *Heike Monogatari* (The Tale of the Heike; thirteenth century) depicts the Demon King as trying to obstruct the spread of Buddhism by fanning the fires of such passions as conjugal love. Clearly such explanations were necessary to reconcile the traditional anti-Buddhist prohibitions at Ise with the increasing syncretism of the two religions.

Beginning in the thirteenth century, the priests of the Outer Shrine at Ise actively undertook to articulate Shintō doctrine and were more forceful, even aggressive, in their efforts to expand the influence of their institution than were the priests of the Inner Shrine. The *Engi Shiki* referred to the Inner and Outer shrines as the Grand Shrine and the Watarai Shrine, respectively; but by the late Heian period, the Inner Shrine was usually

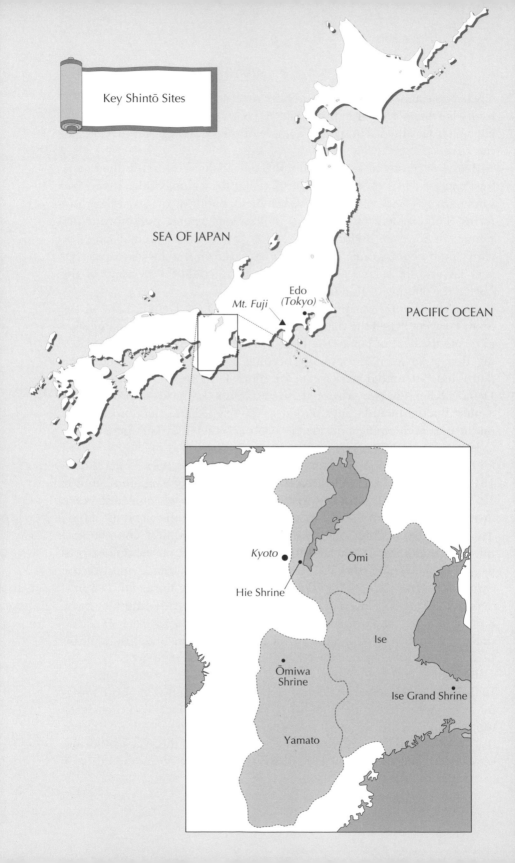

Key Shintō Sites

SEA OF JAPAN

PACIFIC OCEAN

Mt. Fuji

Edo
(Tokyo)

Kyoto

Hie Shrine

Ōmi

Ise

Ōmiwa
Shrine

Ise Grand Shrine

Yamato

called the Imperial Grand Shrine and the Outer Shrine the Toyouke Grand Shrine. References to the great imperial *kami* Amaterasu and the great imperial *kami* Toyouke—found, for example, in Chōgen's writings—indicate that the Outer Shrine was beginning to achieve status equal to that of the Inner Shrine. Moreover, in his *Dai Jingū Sankei Ki* Tsūkai states that "the *negi* of the Outer Shrine can be said to serve simultaneously at both the Outer Shrine and the Inner Shrine," since they made food offerings at two special altars that, though located in the precincts of the Outer Shrine, were dedicated to both shrines. The Outer Shrine took pride in the fact that its *kami* was the *kami* of foodstuffs, bestower of the greatest of all blessings and by extension also regarded as the *kami* of fertility and fecundity.

The assertive attitude of the priests of the Outer Shrine increasingly aroused opposition from the priests of the Inner Shrine. In 1282 the Outer Shrine *negi* Watarai Yukitada (1236–1305) was relieved of his duties as a result of a dispute between the two groups. He took that opportunity to travel to Kyoto and acquire broad learning. While there, he wrote the *Ise Nisho Daijingū Shimmei Hisho* (The Secret Work on the Divine Names of the *Kami* of the Two Grand Shrines; 1285), which was presented to the cloistered emperor Kameyama (1249–1305). Perhaps in recognition of this work, Yukitada was restored to his position in 1287. In 1296, during a disagreement with the Inner Shrine over the propriety of referring to the Outer Shrine as Toyouke Imperial Grand Shrine in a document, Yukitada infuriated the Inner Shrine clergy by demonstrating that such major thirteenth-century documents as the *Zō Ise Nisho Daijingū Hōkihon Ki* (The Jewel Record of the Fundamentals of the Two Ise Grand Shrines; ca. twelfth century) and the *Yamatohime no Mikoto Seiki* (The Life of Yamatohime no Mikoto; ca. thirteenth century) provided support for the Outer Shrine's position. These and three other documents that were already central to Shintō form what came to be known as the *Shintō Gobu Sho* (The Five Books of Shintō).

What are the tenets of the school variously termed Ise, Watarai (the clan name of the priests who served the shrine), or Outer Shrine Shintō as revealed in this canon? First, Toyouke Ōmikami, the *kami* of the Outer Shrine, also known as Miketsu no Kami, is the same *kami* who appears in the *Kojiki* (Record of Ancient Matters; 712) and the *Nihon Shoki* (Chronicles of Japan; 720) under the names Ame no Minakanushi no Kami and Kuni no Tokotachi no Mikoto, respectively. This *kami* is said to have made a divine pact with Amaterasu Ōmikami at the time of Japan's creation, agreeing to rule the land together with Amaterasu in perpetuity. Obviously this story is an attempt to establish the foundation of Amaterasu Ōmikami's power in the context of a general worldview.

Second, the *kami* of the Outer Shrine was said to rule the element of water, while the *kami* of the Inner Shrine ruled over fire. But the priests of the Outer Shrine Shintō stressed that water is especially important for nourishing all that exists, thus advancing the process of transforming Miketsu no Kami from a *kami* of foodstuffs into one of general fertility and fecundity.

In explaining the nature of the *kami*, Shintō theorists employed ideas from a variety of sources: Chinese yin-yang and five elements theory, Buddhist esotericism, and Taoist thought. Watarai Ieyuki (1256–1351), Yukitada's successor, wrote a work called *Ruijū Jingi Hongen* (Compendium of the Sources of Shintō; 1320), in which he systematized the new Shintō ideas with great erudition, even drawing on scholarly sources from Sung-dynasty China to support his arguments.

It is not clear from historical sources just how much the new Shintō theories influenced the ordinary pilgrims and devotees who went to Ise, but a nationwide network of Ise devotees did develop around this time. The increasing prestige of the Outer Shrine, thanks to its *kami*'s role as guardian of fertility and fecundity, must have contributed greatly to this development, which continued through the beginning of the seventeenth century.

The Formation of Ryōbu Shintō

It is clear that the Watarai clan assimilated many esoteric Buddhist elements into the systematization of its new Shintō theories. It seems likely that some sort of esoteric-Buddhist study group provided advice and assistance during the writing of such works as the *Ise Nisho Daijingū Shimmei Hisho* and the *Yamatohime no Mikoto Seiki*, though these works unquestionably contain traditional elements preserved from very early times at Ise, as well.

The esoteric Buddhists themselves produced many works that parallel the texts of Ise Shintō, including some that are virtually identical in content. For example, the ancient purification prayer known as *ōharae no kotoba* or Nakatomi no *harae* received a Buddhist interpretation. Buddhists referred to the ritual prayers as the *Ōnakatomi-kyō* (Ōnakatomi sutras), and their recitation was regarded as a meritorious Buddhist practice. Among the

Buddhist-style commentaries on these Shintō "sutras" that were composed, the twelfth-century *Nakatomi no Harae Kunge* (Commentary on the Nakatomi *no Harae;* twelfth century) seems to have been a relatively early work produced by an esoteric-Buddhist study group with close links to the shrine at Ise.

Around this time, Ōmiwa Shrine in Yamato Province introduced an esoteric-Buddhist interpretation of the identity of its principal *kami*, Miwa Myōjin. Eizon had frequently gone to worship Miwa Myōjin, and his disciple Shōnin (fl. thirteenth century) outlined the new theory around 1318. According to Shōnin, when the solar deity Amaterasu descended to earth, she appeared also as the *kami* of Ōmiwa on Mount Miwa in Yamato and as the great imperial *kami* of Mount Kamiji in Ise Province. Thus the three deities are actually one, and all can be regarded as manifestations of Dainichi Nyorai, or the Great Sun Buddha (Mahāvairocana), the central buddha of the esoteric Buddhist pantheon. This theory later gave rise to what is known as Miwa Shintō.

At about the same time, the esoteric-Buddhist study group at Ise developed close ties to a group of religious practitioners in the Katsuragi mountains in Yamato Province and compiled the *Yamato Katsuragi Hōzan Ki* (The Jewel Record of the Katsuragi Mountains; ca. thirteenth century). According to this text, when Ame no Minakanushi no Kami came to earth, he transformed himself into "the precious mirror without manifested aspect, of the three in one" and was enshrined in Toyouke Shrine (the Outer Shrine). "Three-in-one" refers to a threefold manifestation of the one supreme buddha Dainichi Nyorai like that posited in relation to Miwa Myōjin. In his *Korō Kujitsu Den* (Account of Truths Orally Transmitted by the Ancients; ca. 1299), Watarai Yukitada lists the *Katsuragi Hōzan Ki* as one of the most secret and sacred texts associated with Ise.

In this way various Shintō texts influenced by esoteric Buddhism were composed. Perhaps the most famous of all these is the *Tenchi Reiki Ki* (The Esoteric Teachings of the Cosmos). (*Reiki* seems to have been an ideographic pun on *shasui*, the name of an esoteric Buddhist rite, and appears to mean "secret teachings.") A series of secret texts, beginning with the *Nisho Daijingū Reiki* (The Esoteric Teachings of the Two Shrines), had developed by this time. Sometime in the late Kamakura period the *Tenchi Reiki Ki* was placed at the head of the eighteen volumes of the series and, it seems, gave its name to the entire corpus.

All these works tend to ascribe mystical, hidden meanings to the environs and precincts of the shrines, the layout and architecture of the sacred halls, and other physical features of the sites, and explain everything in terms of the two mandalas of esoteric Buddhism—the *Kongōkai*, or Diamond Realm, mandala and the *Taizōkai*, or Womb Realm, mandala. These two mandalas, known in esoteric Buddhism as the *Ryōbu* (dual) mandalas, lent the new Shintō movement the name by which it is commonly known: Ryōbu, or Dual, Shintō.

The explanations of the significance of Shintō *kami* and shrines, especially those of the Ise cult, in terms of esoteric-Buddhist concepts were widely influential. The priest Ken'a (1261–1338) of the Shingon Ritsu temple Shōmyō-ji in Musashi Province, for example, was zealous in spreading this teaching, and during the Kemmu Restoration (1333–36) people like the courtier Kitabatake Chikafusa (1293–1354) and the priest Jihen of Mount Hiei produced works on Shintō history and doctrine. Jihen's major works include the *Kuji Hongi Gengi* (The Profound Meaning of the Original Record of Ancient Events; 1332), the *Tenchi Jingi Shinchin Yōki* (Record of the Essentials of the Preservation of the Rites of the *Kami*; 1333), and the previously mentioned *Toyoashihara Jimpū Waki*. Chikafusa's best-known work in this field is the *Gengen Shū* (Collection of the Very Beginnings; 1337–38).

In 1419 the high priest Ryōhen of Mount Hiei formally transmitted to his disciples his oral interpretations of the *Tenchi Reiki Ki* and of "The Age of the *Kami*" (the first two volumes of the *Nihon Shoki*). Later, it became customary to perform a *reiki ki* initiation rite modeled on more traditional esoteric-Buddhist initiation rites. This innovation derived from Ryōhen's statement that "the initiation rite that is called *kanjō* in Shingon esotericism and *reiki* in Shintō is in fact the same. *Reiki* is simply another term for *kanjō*."

In the Muromachi period (1336–1568), a type of Shintō heavily influenced by esoteric Buddhism also came to be widely practiced on Mount Kōya. This Shingon-style Shintō, popularly known as Daishi-ryū (Kūkai's) Shintō, was later called Goryū (Honorable School) Shintō.

Esoteric versions of Shintō teachings with no connection to Ise Shrine also developed. On Mount Hiei the cult of Sannō Gongen, the tutelary deity of that mountain, was given an esoteric exegesis in the thirteenth century. This form of Shintō influenced by esoteric Buddhism, which is quite different from Ryōbu Shintō, is called Sannō Shintō or Sannō Ichijitsu Shintō. Since the seventeenth century, however, it has been customary to refer to all Buddhist-influenced Shintō by the general term Ryōbu Shintō to distinguish it from Yoshida Shintō, even though this usage blurs the significant differences between true Ryōbu Shintō and Sannō Ichijitsu Shintō.

The Origins of Yoshida Shintō

Around the time that the clergy of the Outer Shrine at Ise began to develop new Shintō theories, Urabe Kanekata compiled the *Shaku Nihongi* (Commentary on the Chronicles of Japan; 1274–75), an omnibus of all previous commentaries on the *Nihon Shoki*, or *Nihongi*. Kanekata belonged to the ancient Urabe clan, whose members had originally been in charge of divination with tortoise shells in the Jingikan, or Office of *Kami* Worship, in the Nara-period government.

The zeal and learning of the Urabe clan led to its gradual elevation, and by the end of the Heian period it monopolized several major appointments in the Jingikan. In addition, from the tenth century on, clan members served as hereditary priests at important Kyoto shrines, such as Hirano Shrine and Yoshida Shrine. Eventually the Urabe clan was widely recognized for its expertise in matters relating to the indigenous *kami* and their cult and became particularly active in preserving the knowledge of the Japanese classics, especially those that relate stories of the age of the *kami*.

The Urabe early divided into two main branches, the Hirano and the Yoshida. In the thirteenth century Urabe Kaneyori, of the Hirano branch, made copies of the *Nihon Shoki* and other classics and responded to questions about the history of Iwashimizu Hachiman Shrine, south of Kyoto. Kaneyori's son Kanefumi (fl. 1264–75) also copied classic texts and composed works on Isonokami Shrine in Yamato Province and on the *Kojiki*. Kanefumi's son Kanekata compiled the *Shaku Nihongi*. Around this time, however, the Yoshida branch became the more active of the two. In the mid- to late fourteenth century Urabe Kanetoyo (1305–76), of the Yoshida branch, wrote the *Miyaji Hiji Kuden* (An Account of Oral Transmission of Secret Matters Among the Masters of Shintō Ceremonies at the Imperial Palace). His son Kanehiro (1347–1402), who was the first to use the family name Yoshida, found an appreciative and powerful patron in the shōgun Ashikaga Yoshimitsu (1358–1408).

The Urabe clan traditionally served in three capacities: as officials in the Jingikan of the central government, as scholars of the history of Shintō, and as scholars of Japanese classics. In his daily life, the head of the clan was obliged to observe strict prohibitions relating to Shintō beliefs and practices. The prohibitions included not only abstaining from a wide variety of foods interdicted during periods of sacred observance but also extraordinarily severe restrictions on contact with death or the dead. For example, when the death of a parent approached, the parent had to be carried from the house while the head of the house knelt on the ground, refraining from looking at his dying parent. Shintō prohibitions against pollution through contact with death were rigorously observed by important priestly families.

Divine oracles were sometimes vouchsafed to members of priestly families, as is indicated by a Yoshida-clan diary entry dated the second day of the third month of 1403.

> Around two o'clock in the afternoon my wife complained of feeling unwell. While resting, she was suddenly possessed by a divine spirit and began to utter an oracle. I purified myself with cold water and then offered sakè to her. After she had taken three sips, she delivered the oracle in great detail. How fortunate we were to receive such divine favor! We must all work to further deepen our faith and serve the *kami* with even greater sincerity! To give a full account of the content of the oracle here would be sacrilegious, so I shall write nothing more.

This entry is from the time of Yoshida Kaneatsu (1368–1408), the son of Kanehiro, who was active in the late fourteenth and early fifteenth centuries. Around this time, the Yoshida clan developed its own interpretation of the *Nihon Shoki* volumes on the age of the *kami*. When Sondō (1332–1403), the imperial prince and grand abbot of the Tendai sect, expressed a desire to learn about the genesis of the Japanese islands and the origins of Shintō, the Yoshida clan agreed to formally transmit the teachings it preserved. Moreover, in addition to performing special purification rites (probably the Nakatomi *no harae*) during periods of observance of prohibitions, the Yoshida clan also practiced the formal reading of important passages from the *Nihon Shoki*, as if it were a sutra.

The Establishment of Yoshida Shintō

The emergence of Yoshida Kanetomo (1435–1511) and his remarkable attainments can be understood only in the context of his family background and the age in which he lived. The great-grandson of Kaneatsu, he experienced the horrors of the Ōnin War (1467–77) as a relatively young man. He could not have been unaffected by the sight of so much destruction—the burning of palaces and residences, of temples and shrines, and the loss of the precious and beautiful objects and ancient documents they contained. Around the age of thirty-nine he began a period of tremendous scholarly and religious activity that continued until his death, at the age of seventy-six.

His first major project was the construction of the Taigenkyū, a *saijōsho,* or hall for abstinence and ritual purification, in the precincts of Yoshida Shrine. The Taigenkyū was actually an adaptation and elaboration of the Hall of the Eight Imperial *Kami,* which the Jingikan maintained in the palace grounds. He termed it "the holiest of shrines in this land of Japan, the sacred garden where the *kami* of heaven and earth, the eight hundred myriads of *kami* from more than sixty provinces and more than three thousand shrines daily descend" and requested and received imperial sanction for its establishment. A broadly addressed appeal for donations resulted in a contribution of some forty thousand bolts of cloth from Hino Tomiko (1440–96), wife of the shōgun Ashikaga Yoshimasa (1435–90).

Kanetomo also lectured frequently on the "Age of the *Kami*" volumes of the *Nihon Shoki,* choosing appropriate lessons and principles from the ancient accounts for the benefit of his large audience. He did this confidently, relying not only on his clan's teachings concerning the *Nihon Shoki* but also on the erudite *Nihon Shoki Sanso* (Collected Notes on the Chronicles of Japan, ca. 1455–57) by the courtier and scholar Ichijō Kaneyoshi (1402–81). His lectures gave much pleasure to people, and his activities contributed greatly to the establishment of his distinctive view of the nature of Shintō.

In such works as the *Shintō Taii* (The Essence of Shintō; 1486) and the *Yuiitsu Shintō Myōbō Yōshū* (An Anthology of the Doctrines of Yuiitsu Shintō; ca. 1484), Kanetomo actually ascribed his own views to his predecessors Urabe Kanenobu (d. ca. 1004–12) and Kanenao (fl. twelfth century). In the latter work he argued that Shintō of the Original Source (Gempon Sōgen Shintō), the religion he was preaching, was quite different from the Shintō associated with regional shrines and Ryōbu Shintō: "Our Shintō is found in all things. Wind and waves, clouds and mist, movement and stillness, advances and retreats, day and night, the hidden and the manifest, warmth and chill, heat and cold, recompense for good and ill, distinction of right and wrong—there is nothing whatsoever that is not the work of the divine principle we preach."

The teachings of Buddhism and Confucianism clearly had a profound influence on the development of Shintō theory. Nonetheless, Kanetomo argued that the Shintō he taught was "of one stream, not two"—it was pure and unadulterated by foreign teachings. He quoted a purported secret memorial to the throne by Prince Shōtoku (574–622) stating that Buddhism was the flower and fruit of the myriad true doctrines, Confucianism was their branch and leaf, but Shintō was their root. Thus, according to Kanetomo, the two foreign doctrines were offshoots of Shintō, manifesting the peerless root in the form of branches and leaves, flowers and fruit. The eastward journey of Buddhism itself demonstrated that Japan was the most important of the Three Countries (India, China, and Japan, that is, the known world).

Kanetomo also set about establishing religious rituals. Since these were clearly borrowed and adapted from Shingon esotericism, we can surmise that Kanetomo hoped to establish a kind of Shintō esotericism that would supplant the traditional Buddhist esotericism.

The Development of Yoshida Shintō

After Kanetomo's death Yoshida Shintō steadily grew in power and influence under the leadership of Kanemitsu (1485–1528) and Kanemigi (1516–73), the grandson of Kanetomo. Kanetomo's third son, the influential Confucian scholar Kiyohara Nobukata (1475–1550), had been adopted by the Kiyohara clan and Nobukata's son Kanemigi was in turn adopted by the Yoshida clan. Kanemigi was assiduous in study, copying many of the classics and lecturing on the "Age of the *Kami*" volumes of the *Nihon Shoki*. He left works of his own composition, as well.

This period saw the increasing spread of Yoshida Shintō among provincial Shintō shrines throughout Japan. Yoshida Shintō was propagated not only through dissemination of its doctrines but also through a system for officially bestowing divine rank on local *kami*. It had long been customary to petition the court to bestow official rank and honors on the living. In this period petitions were submitted on behalf of local *kami*. For example, in 1498 Kanetomo, aided by Tadatomi, an official of the Jingikan, had obtained a grant of divine rank for the tutelary *kami* of Katsushika district, Shimōsa Province, as well as for two other local *kami*.

Eventually, the Yoshida clan was granted several privileges: the right to bestow divine rank and the title *daimyōjin* (great bright deity), rather than the Buddhist title *gongen* (avatar); the right to release Shintō clergy from certain clothing prohibitions; and the right to make auxiliary appointments. Divine rank and title were bestowed by means of a *Sōgen Senji* (announcement of the original source). This document title in fact alludes to the prerogatives of Yoshida Shintō in the bestowal process, since *sōgen* is an abbreviation of Gempon Sōgen Shintō, the formal name of Yoshida Shintō.

Clearly the Yoshida clan had developed a doctrinal system that enabled it to dominate and control the world of Shintō shrines. The clan already possessed expert knowledge of the rites and customs of Shintō shrines and their associated cults. In 1485, at the request of the shōgun Ashikaga Yoshimasa, Kanetomo himself had undertaken a major study of Kyoto-area shrines, their enshrined deities, the buddhas or bodhisattvas to which they correspond according to the *honji suijaku* (original prototype and local manifestation) theory, their subsidiary shrines, their associated Buddhist temples, their rites, the nature of their clergy, and their origins and subsequent development. Kanetomo thus advanced from simple investigation of past practices and precedents to research on current conditions in the world of Shintō.

Kanemigi, who was well-versed in the ancient rites and customs of shrines, is credited with having compiled the *Nijūnisha Chūshiki* (Notes on the Twenty-two Shrines). Between 1542 and 1572 he traveled widely in Iga, Ise, Echizen, Wakasa, Aki, Suō, Nagato, and other provinces, visiting village shrines, reading the documents in their possession, and inquiring into their histories. Partly as a result of Kanemigi's visits, the number of Shintō priests from the provinces who went to the Yoshida-clan center in Kyoto seeking certification from and affiliation with Yoshida Shintō greatly increased.

At first most of the priests were from western Honshu, but they were joined by priests from central Honshu. Some came from more distant areas. An examination of the identities of the one hundred and twenty-one provincial shrines and clergy who received special permits and grants of title through the good offices of the Yoshida clan between 1482 and 1569 yields the following information: twenty-eight were granted in Ōmi Province and eleven in Tamba Province, as part of a total of seventy-nine in the area around Kyoto; sixteen in the Chūbu region, including five in Echizen Province, four in Mikawa Province, and three in Wakasa Province; twelve in the Chūgoku region, of which six, the largest number, were granted in Suō Province; ten on Kyushu; and two each on Shikoku and in the Kantō region.

Significantly, many of the priests in this list were of the headman class in rural villages. For example, release from clothing prohibitions was granted to the leader in charge of performing rites at Hirano Myōjin on the Tada estate in Settsu Province. Divine rank for the local deity and an official plaque for the shrine's torii, or gateway, were granted to the local members of Koita Shrine in Tamba Province. Divine rank and title for the local deity (the eighth-century priest Dōkyō) were granted to local commoners who were members of Saeki Shrine in Tamba. Permission was granted for the shrine's *ujiko* (parishioners) to build a torii at Sasaki Shrine in the Amata district of Tamba, and for permanent caretakers to be employed at Temman Shrine on the Terada estate in the Uji district of Yamashiro Province. In the Bummei era (1469–87), it was reported that in the area around the capital the Shintō priests were largely commoners, and as the amalgamation of small villages into larger communities progressed, local warriors and headmen increasingly formed the core of the Shintō clergy.

The influence of Yoshida Shintō in outlying areas was also manifested in the services that shrines offered to believers. Yoshida Shintō shrines granted religious permission to eat animal flesh on account of old age or debility and permission for ritual ablutions to be performed with warm water rather than cold; they authorized formal dissolution of contractual obligations between clan members and between masters and retainers; they bestowed a variety of amulets, including amulets for pacifying the spirits of the vengeful dead, amulets for ensuring the safety of a household, and amulets modeled on Buddhist charms. Though Yoshida Shintō's specialized scholarly expertise in the classics and the history of major shrines remained its foundation, in response to the religious needs of local villages in the sixteenth century, it began to provide these wide-ranging religious services and in the process strengthened its position in the outlying provinces.

SHUGENDŌ: THE WAY OF MOUNTAIN ASCETICISM

The Beginnings of Shugendō

In the early Heian period both Saichō (787–822) and Kūkai (774–835) advocated secluded religious practice in mountain regions, and a great many temples were built on mountains, among which the Tendai complex on Mount Hiei and the Shingon complex on Mount Kōya are preeminent examples. As the prestige of esoteric Buddhism grew, so did the belief that the prayers of priests who had undertaken severe ascetic practice in the mountains were particularly efficacious. As a result, mountainous areas all over Japan became the haunts of both ordained priests and nonordained holy men known as *hijiri* intent on attaining spiritual powers through ascetic practice. In time the terms *shugen* (supranormal powers gained through practice) and *shugenja* (one who has acquired such powers) came into use. Since the ascetics practiced and slept deep in the mountains, they were also called *yamabushi* (those who lie down in the mountains).

Eminent practitioners of esoteric Buddhism who were also known for their ascetic practice in the mountains include Sōō (831–918) of Mount Hiei, whose practice focused on the esoteric-Buddhist deity Fudō Myōō (in Sanskrit, Acala) at Katsuragawa Falls in the western foothills of the Hira mountain range, Ōmi Province; Enchin (814–91), who founded Onjō-ji, headquarters of the Jimon school of Tendai; and Shōbō (832–909) of the Shingon sect, who practiced at Yoshino in Yamato Province. In the beginning *shugen* referred both to the Buddhist priests who had gained spiritual powers and to their mode of practice.

The general population was strongly drawn to this form of religious practice, partly because of the prestige that Buddhism accorded to ascetic practice in isolated hermitages and partly because there had always been popular religious cults centering on devotion to mountain deities. In response to the wide public appeals for spiritual aid, an increasing number of men dedicated themselves exclusively to ascetic practice in the mountains. As a result, a number of mountain sites became known as centers for this form of religious exercise, among them the Yoshino mountains and the Katsuragi mountains in Yamato Province; the three Kumano shrines in Kii Province; Mount Ishizuchi on Shikoku; Daisen in Hōki Province; the Hakusan mountains on the borders of Kaga, Hida, Echizen, and Mino provinces; Tateyama in Etchū Province; Nikkōzan in Shimotsuke Province; Hagurosan in Dewa Province; and Hikosan on Kyushu.

People had in fact secluded themselves in the mountains for religious practice as early as the Nara period. Perhaps the most famous to do so was En no Ozunu (fl. late seventh century), who is mentioned in an entry in the *Shoku Nihongi* (Further Chronicles of Japan; 797) dated the twenty-fourth day of the fifth month of 699. En no Ozunu, popularly known as En no Gyōja (the Ascetic En), was a semilegendary mountain ascetic from the Katsuragi mountains who was exiled to Ōshima, off the shore of Izu Province, because of false accusations by his disciple Karakuni no Hirotari, who is referred to in the *Shoku Nihongi* account as "the Korean noble-man." Ozunu is said to have commanded the services of daemons while he was practicing in the Katsuragi mountains, having them fetch wood and water and perform other services, and to have bound them with a spell if they disobeyed his commands.

Ozunu was a member of the Kamo clan, which had lived in the Katsuragi mountains for generations, while Hirotari, as the *Shoku Nihongi* suggests, was almost certainly from the Asian mainland. The fact that an indigenous ascetic like Ozunu was the teacher of an ascetic from the continent, where religion and culture in general were then far more mature than in Japan, is interesting. In later times, Ozunu came to be regarded as the founder of Shugendō, the Way of Mountain Asceticism. Despite the anachronism of this attribution, from the *Shoku Nihongi* account we can infer that a number of ascetics, of whom En no Ozunu was the best known, were living in the Katsuragi mountains as early as the Nara period. This was well before the advent of esoteric-Buddhist ascetic practice in the mountains.

The *Nihon Ryōiki* (Miracle Stories of Japan; ca. 822) includes a tale of Ozunu forcing a daemon to build a bridge between the Katsuragi mountains and Yoshino. This may imply that there were mountain ascetics associated with En no Ozunu not only in the Katsuragi mountains but also in the Yoshino mountains. By the Heian period many priests, beginning with Shōbō, practiced at Yoshino—or Kane no Mitake (Golden Peak), as the site was also known. Somewhat later, Fujiwara no Michinaga (966–1027) and other aristocrats began to make pilgrimages to the Yoshino mountains. The "Account of Dōken Shōnin in the Afterworld," in the *Fusō Ryakki* (Abridged Annals of Japan; late eleventh century), tells how the priest Dōken (905?–985?), while engaged in ascetic practice in the Yoshino mountains, met the fierce *kami* Kongō Zaō Gongen through the good offices of the *kami* Shū Kongō Shin. Eventually becoming the object of widespread, profound devotion, Kongō Zaō Gongen, the *kami* of the Ōmine Mountains, was made the principal deity of Shugendō. He is at present worshiped in Zaō Hall in Yoshino with distinctive Shugendō rites.

The three Kumano shrines—the Hongū, Shingū, and Nachi shrines—had been *shugen* centers since very ancient times. According to the *Kumano Gongen Gosuijaku Engi* (An Account of the Manifestations of the Deity of Kumano; 1163), a record of traditions concerning the founding of the shrines, the deity Ōjishin, originally tutelary deity of Mount T'ien-t'ai in China, descended to Kannokura (a branch shrine of Shingū Shrine) and to Asuga Shrine at Kumano, having first gone to Hikosan on Kyushu and Mount Ishizuchi on Shikoku. He then descended to Kumano Hongū Shrine "in the form of the moon." A crescent-shaped object was discovered eight years later by a hunter named Chiyosada, who had wandered into the mountains in pursuit of a wild boar. Realizing that the object was out of the ordinary, Chiyosada worshiped it. This was the beginning of the cult of the deity of Kumano. A legend in the *Shō Bodaisan Tō Engi* (Histories of Ōmine and Other Mountains; early sixteenth century) relates that several years later a Buddhist ascetic was guided deep into the mountains by Chiyosada's wife and he worshiped the object.

On the other hand, the "Kumanosan Hongū Bettō Shidai" (The Details of the Administrators of Hongū Shrine at Kumano) cited in the *Sozan Engi* (The Origins of Various Mountains; ca. twelfth century) names the ascetic Zendō (fl. 672–80) as founder of Kumano Hongū Shrine. In the *Kumano Gongen Kongō Zaō Hōden Zōkō Nikki* (Record of the Erection of the Shrines of Kumano Gongen and Kongō Zaō; ca. early thirteenth century) a tradition holds that Ragyō (fl. 708–15) revealed the figure of Jūichimen Kannon in the Nachi Falls. Finally, the *Shozan Engi* reports that En no Ozunu himself made a pilgrimage to Kumano, performing various purification rites along the way. From this it appears that during the late Heian period the ascetics at Kumano had some connections with both those in the Katsuragi mountains and those in the Yoshino mountains.

By the late Heian period several sites in the Ōmine range, which links the Yoshino and Kumano mountains, were already well known as places where *shugenja* practiced austerities—Ozasa, Shō no Iwaya, Zenkidani, and Tamakisan, among them. A mountain-ascetics' trail between the Yoshino mountains and Kumano connected the various centers, and by the late twelfth or early thirteenth century the whole area was the hub of Shugendō practice in central Honshu.

Mountain Folk and Shugenja

Semimythical accounts of the founding of centers of religious practice in the mountains indicate that the majority of mountain areas in which esoteric-Buddhist priests engaged in religious practice from the Heian period onward had earlier been developed as religious centers by non-Japanese religious leaders and their indigenous followers or by local mountain dwellers. This is true not only of such famous centers as Katsuragi, Yoshino, and Kumano but also of the many outlying provincial mountain centers.

Thus the esoteric-Buddhist *shugenja* who began entering the mountains in the Heian period no doubt had contact with mountain ascetics who were heirs of the older, pre-Buddhist traditions. Indeed, they probably sought to learn appropriate modes of practice from these older, more experienced practitioners.

Esoteric-Buddhist priests had of course established mountain centers, beginning in the Heian period. But even the most eminent of esoteric-Buddhist practitioners could not establish centers in unfamiliar mountain regions without the help of the local mountain folk. The *Kōbō Daishi Den* (The Life of Kōbō Daishi), compiled in 1315 by the cloistered emperor Gouda, tells how Kūkai founded his hermitage on Mount Kōya under the guidance of the *kami* of the mountain, who appeared in the guise of a hunter called Inukai of the Southern Mountains.

It seems safe to assume that esoteric-Buddhist founders of centers of mountain ascetic practice also sought to master the distinctive forms of prayer and asceticism that the local mountain ascetics had developed over the centuries. Largely ignorant of this, outsiders labeled the esoteric-Buddhist practitioners *shugenja* and accorded them great honor. Religious groups gradually formed around the new *shugenja*, making their bases in shrines and temples that were founded on the various mountains. The mountain asceticism that developed in these centers, however, contained elements that were not found in esoteric Buddhism but were adopted from the faith of the mountain folk and that reflected traditions that had been handed down by the mostly non-Japanese religious leaders of a much earlier age.

The Honzan Group

Around the middle of the Heian period, Kumano and Yoshino came to occupy positions of unusual importance among the centers of mountain asceticism, in part because of the frequent pilgrimages of the imperial family and the aristocracy. Ascetics from all over Japan gathered at these two centers and formed groups and orders. The three Kumano shrines became affiliated with the Tendai temple Onjō-ji around 1090, when Zōyo (1032–1116), a priest at Onjō-ji, was named superintendent of Kumano after having guided the cloistered emperor Shirakawa (1053–1129) there on pilgrimage. Appointed the abbot of Shōgo-in in Kyoto as a reward, Zōyo installed the deity of Kumano as the temple guardian and referred to the temple precincts as the Ima Kumano. In the early Kamakura period, after the priest and imperial prince Jōe (1164–1203), son of the cloistered emperor Goshirakawa (1127–92), became the abbot, Shōgo-in developed even closer ties with the Kumano shrines because of Jōe's landholdings in the Kumano area. Ultimately, the position of superintendent of the Kumano shrines became one of the hereditary offices of the abbot of Shōgo-in.

In the early Kamakura period, *shugenja* acted as *sendatsu* (or guides) to the sacred sites in Kumano, performing purification rituals at designated points for their lay followers (or *danna*, a Buddhist term of Sanskrit origin) and arranging lodging for them at pilgrim shelters (or *shukubō*), whose managers were called *oshi*. Eventually, each shelter relied on a particular *sendatsu* to supply customers from among his *danna*. Some of the shelters prospered and became influential under this system, as did some of the *sendatsu*, each of whom controlled a specific area and a large number of subordinate guides.

Shōgo-in had come to exercise general control over the more powerful *sendatsu*. In the fourteenth century Nyakuōji Shrine, in the Higashiyama district of Kyoto, which enjoyed the devout patronage of the ruling Ashikaga clan, was given administrative control of the three Kumano shrines and charged with general supervision of all *sendatsu*. Eventually a well-organized system was established, at the center of which were such major temples as Jūshin-in, Sekizen-in, and Kadai-in in Kyoto and Gaya-in in Harima Province, whose abbots were members of the imperial family or aristocrats and which had numerous *sendatsu*. Provincial *sendatsu* were supervised by these temples. The entire system remained under the general supervision of Shōgo-in, the headquarters of what came to be called the Honzan group.

The Honzan group stressed its own orthodoxy in the world of Shugendō, claiming En no Ozunu as founder and Zōyo as restorer of the sect. It also fabricated accounts of the Tendai patriarch Enchin's religious practice at Ōmine and Kumano. By emphasizing its connection with Enchin, the Honzan group hoped to win the support of Onjō-ji, which Enchin had founded. In the mid-fourteenth century, Ryōyu (1333–97), the abbot of Shōgo-in, devised new rites for the mountain centers, establishing ordination platforms for special initiations at Jinzen in the Ōmine range and Naka-tsukawa in the Katsuragi mountains. Around the same time the so-called *kasumi* system developed, under which influential *sendatsu* established their own territories (called *kasumi*) nationwide and put lower-ranking *shugenja* in charge of particular areas.

In the late fifteenth century, the abbots of Shōgo-in began to make tours of outlying provinces, trying to bring under the control of the Honzan group the various mountain centers that were focuses of *shugenja* activity. Toward the end of the fifteenth century, the abbot Dōkō (d. 1501) was particularly active. He performed austerities at Nachi Shrine and Ōmine and visited Shugendō centers throughout Japan, including the thirty-three sacred sites in the area around the capital and other shrines and temples on Honshu, Shikoku, and Kyushu. The biography of En no Ozunu that the Honzan group produced around this time suggests that that great Nara-period ascetic had traveled all over Japan, visiting each of the major mountain centers several times. But it seems likely that this claim was made simply to provide a traditional basis for the travels of the abbots of Shōgo-in.

The Tōzan Shōdai Sendatsu Group

The Yoshino mountains in Yamato Province had functioned mainly as a center for *shugenja* affiliated with shrines and temples in the Nara area. Among them the following shrines and temples were particularly well known: in Yamato, Kongōsen-ji, Abè-dera, Ōmiwa Shrine, Chōgaku-ji, Shōryaku-ji, Senkō-ji, Ryūfuku-ji, Shigisan-ji, Takama-dera, Chihara-ji, Matsunoo-dera, Yata-dera, Hōryū-ji, Nakanokawa-dera, Chōshō-ji, Tōnomine-dera, Yoshino Sakuramoto-bō, Uchiyama Eikyū-ji, and Hase-dera; in Kii Province, Kongōbu-ji, Negoro-ji Nishiza, Negoro-ji Higashiza, and Kokawa-dera; in Izumi Province, Sefuku-ji, Kamio-dera, Takakura-ji, Wada-ji, and Daiitoku-ji; in Yamashiro Province, Bodai-ji, Odawara Jōruri-ji, and Kaijūsen-ji; in Ōmi Province, the Handō-ji subtemples Iwamoto-in and Umemoto-in; in Settsu Province, Tanjō-ji and Ryōzen-ji; and in Ise Province, Segi-ji. Most of the mountain shrines and temples with which *sendatsu* were affiliated either were strongly influenced by the Shingon sect or Shingon esotericism or were branch temples of Kōfuku-ji in Nara. *Shugenja* from these temples formed the Shugendō organization known as the Tōzan Shōdai Sendatsu group, which was based at Ozasa in the Ōmine range and received the support of both the Eastern and the Western Hall of Kōfuku-ji.

The Tōzan Shōdai Sendatsu group looked on Shōbō (founder of Daigo-ji and patriarch of the Ono school of the Shingon sect) as the restorer of its tradition, on the grounds that he had performed ascetic practice in the Ōmine Mountains. According to a late-Muromachi-period legend, Shōbō had received the spiritual seal of En no Ozunu and the imperial seal of

Emperor Jomei (r. 629–41)—deposited in the Shōjō-den at Kumano Hongū Shrine by Ozunu for safekeeping—had entrusted these seals to two *sendatsu* (the *ōshuku* at Uchiyama Eikyū-ji and the *ninoshuku* at Yoshino Sakura-moto-bō), and had personally led the Shōdai Sendatsu group into the Ōmine Mountains from Yoshino.

On the basis of this legend, the Tōzan Shōdai Sendatsu group always gathered at Ozasa before the formal entry into the mountains and chose two *sendatsu* to serve as *ōshuku* and *ninoshuku* and be in charge of the entire group until the next meeting. People who wished to become *shugenja* or to rise in rank in the Tōzan Shōdai Sendatsu group had to attach themselves to one of its Shōdai Sendatsu and have their request brought before the general meeting of the guides at Ozasa by their patron. If the general meeting approved their request, the *ōshuku* and *ninoshuku* would affix both the imperial seal and the spiritual seal mentioned in the legend to a formal certificate of appointment signed by the *sendatsu* who had acted as sponsor. This system enabled the Tōzan Shōdai Sendatsu group to build up circles of disciples.

Toward the end of the Muromachi period, the Shōdai Sendatsu of the Tōzan group gradually distanced themselves from the Eastern and Western halls of Kōfuku-ji and established ties with Sambō-in at Daigo-ji, which had come to occupy a central position in the Shingon sect in the time of its abbot Mansai (1378–1435). Because Sambō-in had been founded by Shōbō, whom the Tōzan group considered its restorer, and *shugenja* were living in the Kami Daigo section of the Daigo-ji precincts, it may have been especially easy for Sambō-in to win acceptance as general headquarters for the Tōzan-affiliated ascetics. At any rate, the Tōzan Shōdai Sendatsu group's organization was established centering on Sambō-in, although it was not until the Edo period that the group became a truly powerful entity.

Provincial Shugendō Organizations

Shugendō centers and ascetics in the provinces generally affiliated themselves with either the Honzan group or the Tōzan group, but some centers preserved their independence—Hagurosan in Dewa Province, Nikkōzan in Shimotsuke Province, and Hikosan on Kyushu, for example.

The earliest mention of Hagurosan is found in the *Azuma Kagami* (Mirror of the East), a chronicle of the Kamakura shogunate during the years 1180–1266. The entry for the fifteenth day of the fifth month of 1209 re-

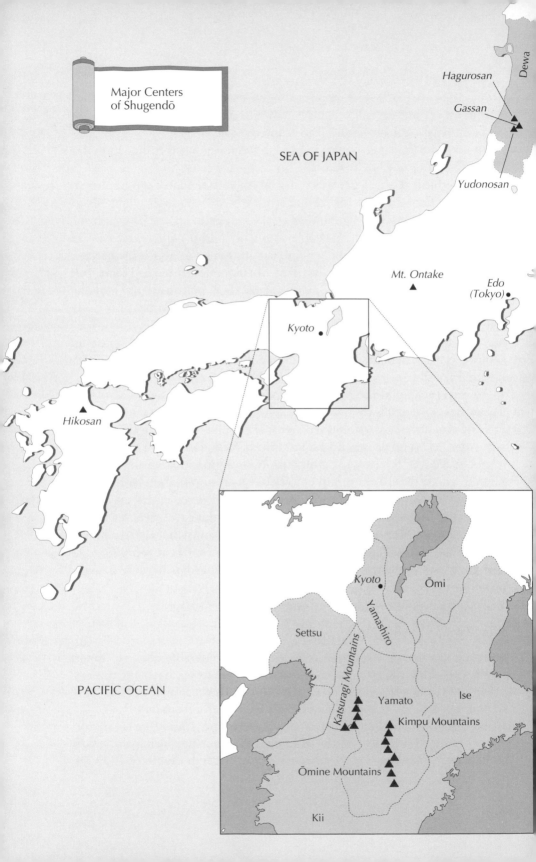

Major Centers
of Shugendō

SEA OF JAPAN

Dewa

Hagurosan

Gassan

Yudonosan

Mt. Ontake

Edo
(Tokyo)

Kyoto

Hikosan

PACIFIC OCEAN

Kyoto

Ōmi

Settsu

Yamashiro

Katsuragi Mountains

Yamato

Ise

Kimpu Mountains

Ōmine Mountains

Kii

cords the protest of the ascetics of Hagurosan against the actions of an estate steward in Dewa, who, they alleged, had seized their forest lands and was otherwise interfering in the internal affairs of their order. At the time of the Jōkyū Disturbance (1221), the cloistered emperor Gotoba (1180–1239) attempted to appoint Sonchō (fl. thirteenth century) of what was probably a Shingon temple, Hosshō-ji, in Kyoto as superintendent of Hagurosan, perhaps hoping to control the military power wielded by the ascetic order there. The government in Kamakura, however, appointed the warrior Sanada Iehisa (fl. thirteenth century) as superintendent of the mountain, with orders to prevent the entry of Gotoba's appointee, Sonchō. Thereafter, the superintendent was customarily chosen from among Iehisa's descendants at the Gyokuzō-bō and Daigo-bō subtemples on Hagurosan.

During this period Hagurosan was home to ascetic priests of both the Shingon tradition and the Tendai tradition who kept the precepts and therefore remained celibate, married ascetics affiliated with the Tendai sect, and *hijiri* who practiced the *nembutsu*. For example, Shinjōbō Shōson, who restored Kōtaku-ji (the *okuno-in* of Hagurosan) in 1310, was a *nembutsu* practitioner from Kumano Nachi Shrine. In the fourteenth century, the Tosabayashi clan, who were the lords of Fujishima Castle in Dewa Province, became administrators of Hagurosan, but in the late 1480s control passed to the family of Mutō Masauji of Daihōji Castle in Dewa.

Nikkōzan Rinnō-ji was reputedly founded by the *shugenja* Shōdō (735–817) and restored by Benkaku in 1210. Benkaku, who had undertaken ascetic practice at Kumano and was known for his spiritual powers, founded Kōmyō-in at Nikkōzan. This temple became the general headquarters for ascetics in the area and the center of Shugendō practice. By the sixteenth century, however, it had fallen into ruin, and its position was taken by Zazen-in, another subtemple in the area. After Nikkōzan lent its support to the Hōjō clan during the 1590 Odawara campaign of the warlord Toyotomi Hideyoshi (1537–98), almost all its landholdings were confiscated by the victorious Hideyoshi.

The first recorded mention of Hikosan on Kyushu is a statement in the twelfth-century *Honchō Seiki* (Chronicle of the Imperial Reigns) that in 1094 the Hikosan clergy had demanded that the governor at Dazaifu banish the vice-governor, Fujiwara no Nagafusa (1030–99). Further, it is recorded that in 1181 the cloistered emperor Goshirakawa had added Hikosan to the landholdings of Ima Kumano Shrine in Kyoto. That was the beginning of a long, close association between Hikosan and the Kumano shrines.

Hikosan comprised various holy places, centering on Minamidake, representing Śākyamuni; Kitadake, representing Amida; and Nakadake, representing the Thousand-Armed Kannon. Various halls affiliated with Reisen-ji, on Hikosan, and forty-nine caves modeled on the Pure Land of Miroku, the buddha of the future, dotted the slopes of Hikosan. More than one hundred clergy and two hundred *sendatsu* lived in the mountain's four main valleys, making Hikosan one of the major spiritual centers of Tendai esotericism.

As in the case of Hagurosan, however, Hikosan's military potential attracted the attention of the powerful. In 1333 Utsunomiya Yorifusa, the constable of Buzen Province, welcomed Prince Yasuhito, son of Emperor Gofushimi (1288–1336), to Nyohō-ji on Hikosan and made his own wife and niece titular abbots of the temple, giving them a residence at Kurokawa, near the foot of the mountain. From that time on Hikosan prospered under its abbots, becoming the most influential site of ascetic practice on Kyushu, with *shugen* exercises and other Buddhist and Shintō rites being performed there by specialists of high repute. Perhaps because of the security and peace that this system afforded those who practiced there, Hikosan was able to develop comprehensive Shugendō rituals and a systematic doctrine far earlier than did other Shugendō centers. The systematization of doctrine was accomplished chiefly under Sokuden, who went from Nikkōzan to Hikosan in the second decade of the sixteenth century.

The Ten Realms Practice

The basic goals of Shugendō are the attainment of supranormal powers through ascetic practice in secluded mountain areas and the use of those powers for magico-religious purposes. Let us explore the religious character of Shugendō in the thirteenth through the sixteenth centuries by examining the changes it underwent and their religious meaning.

It is difficult to know for certain what form ascetic practice took during the Nara period, but evidence suggests that it probably consisted of long periods of seclusion in caves close to rivers and waterfalls—where ritual ablutions were performed—and devotion to prayer and ritual invocations. It was necessary for ascetics to be able to persist in ascetic practice during long periods of isolation. The *Shoku Nihongi* mentions En no Ozunu's employing daemons to fetch water and firewood because these two items are essential to support the ascetic life. A later source lists En no Ozunu's four types of ascetic practice as picking fruit, drawing water, collecting firewood, and preparing food because these four activities are necessary to sustain life while engaging in ascetic practice and the very act of performing them could also be regarded as a form of practice. In addition, it is possible that the early ascetics set up objects of worship in their caves, before which they meditated in the hope of gaining spiritual powers.

The fourteenth-century *Yamabushi Chō* (*Yamabushi* Register; 1366), a record of procedures for the Kumano *shugenja* of that period, tells of their entering the mountains garbed in surcoats, baggy pants, and special headgear and bearing on their backs small cases for religious and personal items. Three accessories were always assembled for the rite of entering the mountains: a portable sutra case, a hat of woven reeds, and a Shintō ritual wand. An attendant carried these objects as the *shugenja* crossed the Kumano River. The ascetic then donned the hat and, with the case on his back and the wand in hand, formally entered the mountains.

It is generally believed that the ascetics of that time wandered the entire Ōmine range, from Yoshino to Kumano, or from Kumano to Yoshino. It seems more likely, though, that they secluded themselves for long periods at certain sacred sites in the Ōmine range, such as Sanjōgatake, Ozasa, Jinzen, and Fukikoshi. Formal entry into and exit from the mountains were attended with special ceremonies involving the conferral and receipt of Buddhist religious objects, but during the period of practice in the mountains the ascetics were free to choose the form that their practice would take.

Around the end of the Kamakura period, however, it became customary to enter the mountains not singly but in groups, and as a result, the form and content of practice were gradually formalized. Ascetic practices included entering the mountains, ritually "fixing" *shugenja* to their training, confessing one's sins, preparing simple foods, fasting, drawing water, abstaining from the use of water for ablutions, collecting firewood for the *goma* ritual, performing the *goma* fire ritual, receiving esoteric initiation, and leaving the mountains.

This list contains two clearly contrasting groups of practices: those that are ritualized expressions of practical acts that sustain the ascetic's life in the mountains (preparing food and drawing water) and those that are purely ascetic or magico-religious in character (fasting, abstaining from ablutions, making sacred fires, and receiving ritual initiation). Each practice in one group has a complement in the other. There were also a formalized rite for establishing the ascetic's temporary dwelling in the mountains and the distinctive Shugendō *hashiramoto goma* rite for preparing a sacred fire, which involved meditation and the setting up of bundles of wood. All these practices, centering on the confession of sins and the performance of purificatory rites, aimed at casting away attachment to the body.

Around the fifteenth century, ten practices were made obligatory for anyone engaging in ascetic practice in the mountains: choosing a dwelling, confessing, weighing one's karmic bonds (using an actual scale), abstaining from water, fetching water, ritual wrestling, ritual dancing, gathering firewood, abstaining from cereals, and performing either the esoteric initiation or the *hashiramoto goma* ceremony. Each of these practices was believed to correspond to one of the ten realms, or stages, through which sentient beings pass on their way to final enlightenment: the hells, the hungry ghosts, the beasts, *asuras,* human beings, the heavens, *śrāvakas, pratyekabuddhas,* bodhisattvas, and buddhas. It was taught that a *shugenja* who faithfully performed all the practices corresponding to the ten realms could attain buddhahood in the present body (a doctrine known as *sokushin sokubutsu*), without undergoing further transmigration or transformation. Together the practices were known as the Ten Realms Practice.

Entering the Mountains

In the fifteenth century, doctrinal explanations were devised for not only the various rites associated with mountain asceticism but also the mountains themselves, the objects of worship found there, and the distinctive garb of the *shugenja*. The Ōmine range, for example, was regarded as a mandala, a symbolic representation of the Diamond and Womb realms of esoteric Buddhism. The portion of the Ōmine range nearest Kumano was deemed the Womb Realm, while that closest to Yoshino was the Diamond Realm, and all the buddhas, bodhisattvas, and deities of the two mandalas were found in the mountain range. Thus *shugenja* who practiced in the Ōmine range could physically attain the stage identical to both mystical realms. The route from Kumano to Yoshino, identified with the Womb Realm mandala, was interpreted as "moving from cause to effect"; while the route from Yoshino to Kumano was linked to the Diamond Realm mandala and followed the reverse course, "moving from effect to cause."

In contrast to the Ōmine range, which was related to the Shingon and Tendai esoteric traditions, the Katsuragi mountains were regarded as an exoteric peaks, sacred to the Lotus Sutra and its cult. Twenty-eight sacred sites were established along the Katsuragi range, between Tomogashima at the mouth of Osaka Bay (opposite Kada in Kii Province) and Mount

Futakami in Yamato Province. A sutra mound enshrining one chapter of the twenty-eight-chapter Lotus Sutra was built at each site.

If an entire mountain is regarded as a mandala, then it is only natural to worship the rocks, caverns, and trees, indeed everything, on the mountain as part of the body of the Buddha. Between the Kamakura and Momoyama periods, precisely this view was stressed. Yet a need was felt for a specific guardian for those engaged in Shugendō practice on a mountain. This function was assigned to Kongō Zaō Gongen, the deity believed to have appeared to En no Ozunu in a vision in the seventh century. According to the *Sangoku Denki* (Biographical Accounts of India, China, and Japan; fifteenth century), when En no Ozunu, seated in his hermit's cave, invoked the protection of the *kami* and buddhas, Miroku, the Thousand-Armed Kannon, and Śākyamuni appeared before him. Unsatisfied, Ozunu continued his prayers. Finally, Kongō Zaō Gongen appeared. Ozunu at last felt he had found the right guardian for himself and for the entire Yoshino range. Kongō Zaō Gongen had been recognized as a divinity since at least Heian times, but late legends, such as this one about En no Ozunu, that began to appear in the Kamakura period indicate that he became the central deity of Shugendō.

The mythical child attendants or pages (*dōji*) of certain divinities came to be worshiped as guardian deities at the major sacred sites in the Ōmine Mountains. The eight principal *dōji* of Ōmine are Kenzō Dōji, the patron of Zenji, who offers protection through spells; Gose Dōji, the patron of Tawa, who protects the devotees of various teachings; Kokū Dōji, the patron of Shō no Iwaya, who symbolizes the unborn radiance of love that illuminates the universe; Kenkō Dōji, the patron of Ozasa, he of the radiant eyes who keeps the precepts and protects and governs; Akujo Dōji, the patron of Tamakisan, who prevents disturbance and vanquishes various demons; Kōshō Dōji, the patron of Jinzen, who symbolizes universally illuminating emptiness; Jihi Dōji, the patron of Mizunomi, who symbolizes the Mahāyāna always protecting and universally illuminating; and Joma Dōji, the patron of Fukikoshi, who symbolizes karmic obstacles disappearing of themselves.

As mentioned earlier, it was believed that the *shugenja* engaged in ascetic practice in the mountains was able to attain buddhahood in the present life by passing through the successive stages of the Ten Realms Practice. This belief was expressed in the *shugenja's* garb. The traditional costume included a surcoat (*surikake*), a collar with six colored tufts (*yuigesa*), a small stiff cap (*tokin*) with a headband, a cord (*kainoo*) around the waist, a deerskin (*hisshiki*) worn over the buttocks, leggings (*kyahan*), straw sandals (*waraji*), a sutra case (*oi*) and travel case (*katabako*) slung over the back, prayer beads (*juzu*) wound around the arm, a staff (*kongōzue*) topped with metal rings (*shakujō*), and a large conch-shell trumpet (*hora*). The surcoat and collar symbolized the Diamond Realm and the Womb Realm, respectively; the stiff cap symbolized Dainichi Nyorai; the prayer beads, conch shell, staff, deerskin, and leggings symbolized the *shugenja*'s path to buddhahood; and the sutra case, travel case, headband, and cord symbolized the *shugenja*'s ultimate rebirth as a buddha. Thus the *shugenja* was viewed as a kind of mandala of the Diamond and the Womb realms and as identical in essence with Dainichi Nyorai. The *shugenja*'s costume symbolically depicted the nonduality of the profane and sacred states and concretely expressed the possibility of the *shugenja*'s attainment of buddhahood in the present body.

In short, Kamakura- and Muromachi-period ascetics diligently devoted themselves to their mountain practice in the belief that they could attain buddhahood in this life. They clothed themselves in garments symbolizing the idea that they could become Dainichi Nyorai—the embodiment of the *Ryōbu* mandalas—because essentially the ascetics themselves were mandalas of the Diamond and Womb realms. They engaged in the Ten Realms Practice, modeled on the various stages of the path to buddhahood, and dwelled in mountains that were themselves regarded as mandalas of the Diamond and Womb realms.

The Kumano Guides

The *shugenja*'s activities were not limited to the practice of asceticism. They also acted as guides to the shrines and temples in the mountains, performed intercessory rites for believers (employing the supranormal powers they had gained through their practice), and engaged in various other religious activities. In particular, ascetics attached to Kumano acted as guides for the nobility toward the end of the Heian period and for warriors and peasants from the Kamakura period on. The Kumano guides, affiliated with specific Kumano pilgrim shelters, guided groups of believers to the shelters they were connected with. In addition to acting as guides to sacred sites, the Kumano guides performed special rites that were deemed necessary for the satisfactory completion of a pilgrimage. The believers fasted and purified themselves under the guide's direction and then recited sutras, offered food and ceremonial wands before the altars of the deities, and sometimes copied out sutra passages. If the pilgrims wished, the guides also performed intercessory rituals and answered questions concerning religious matters.

The Kumano guides traveled about Japan, propagating faith in the Kumano cult. They told tales of the history of the shrines and explained the content of the faith, illustrating their talks with picture scrolls depicting the deities and precincts of Kumano. They also distributed their own distinctive amulets, known as Kumano *goō*. Many of the Kumano shrines scattered throughout Japan owe their origins to this proselytizing by the guides. A guide who founded a shrine usually became its superintendent and the local representative of one of the pilgrim shelters. By acting as guides to the main shrines, distributing amulets, performing intercessory rituals, and giving sermons, the guides established strong religious ties to the believers living in their areas.

The guides also played an extremely important role in collecting funds for the erection of temples and shrines. The excavation of a sutra mound at Kumano Nachi Shrine yielded evidence of the activities of the *shugenja* Gyōyo, who in 1130 toured the nation and enrolled some sixty-nine thousand people as patrons. The items found at the mound include a catalogue, which describes the items buried and the votive activities of Gyōyo, and many Buddhist images and copies of the Buddhist scriptures, such as the Lotus Sutra and the Sutra on the Benevolent King. This is one recently recovered piece of evidence for the wide-ranging activities of the Kumano guides.

Kumano was not the only source of guides. They came from all the major Shugendō centers—Yoshino, Hakusan, Tateyama, Hagurosan, and Hikosan—and played a similar role everywhere. The pilgrimage to the thirty-three sacred sites of western Honshu, for example, which began at Seiganto-ji at Nachi and ended at Kegon-ji in Mino Province, included several temples that were connected with Kumano and were as a rule closely linked to the *shugenja*. Perhaps for this reason such Shugendō priests as Gyōson (1055–1135) and Kakuchū (1117–77), who were affiliated with Onjō-ji, made the western pilgrimage. So did Dōkō, the abbot of Shōgo-in, though he made his pilgrimage much later, in the Muromachi period.

In the Muromachi period, as the Kumano cult declined and pilgrimages to Ise or the temples of western Honshu became popular, the Kumano guides of eastern Honshu diversified their activities, conducting parties to Ise and the west, as well as to Kumano. It seems likely that as the *shugenja* began to travel ever more widely about Japan—guiding pilgrims, engaging in ascetic practice, or collecting donations—they conducted intercessory rites for believers. The evidence suggests that many of the rites were exorcisms employing the esoteric Buddhist formulas called *dhāraṇī*. The *shugenja* also distributed amulets from their home temples or shrines and potions and medicines made from mountain herbs. In this connection, it is interesting to note that such established centers of Shugendō as Yoshino, Mount Ontake (Shinano Province), and Tateyama later became important in the manufacture and sale of medicines. Finally, it is possible that the *shugenja* filled some of the functions of traders, selling such necessities as tea and salt on their travels.

The Martial Activities of the Yamabushi

Especially remarkable activities of the *shugenja*, or *yamabushi*, in the Kamakura and Muromachi periods were those in time of war—performing magico-religious rites, acting as messengers or spies, and practicing the martial arts. The *shugenja*, who knew the mountain trails and through their travels were familiar with conditions all over the land, were well qualified to undertake these activities. Before battle, they blessed horses, arms, and armor and prayed for the defeat of the enemy. Their intercessory rites were called for when camp was set up or broken. It is impossible to enumerate the tales of their skills as spies or messengers, such as the story of the news that the warrior Nitta Yoshisada (d. 1338) was raising troops having been transmitted throughout Echigo Province in the course of a single night. Then, too, there were significant links between the *shugenja* and the *ninja* masters of martial arts in Kōga (Ōmi Province), Iga (Iga Province), and Negoro (Kii Province). So skilled were the *shugenja* at stealthy appearances and disappearances that they were compared to the legendary mountain creatures called *tengu*, who were said to inhabit the very mountains where the ascetics had their centers.

Warlords called on the *shugenja* groups at Yoshino, Kongō Katsuragi, Kumano, Hakusan, Haguro, and Hikosan for help during such major conflicts as the Taira-Minamoto War (1180–85), the war between the Northern and the Southern Courts (1336–92), and the factional wars of the Age of the Warring Provinces (1467–1568).

The many examples of warriors relying on the aid of the *shugenja* include Minamoto no Yoshitsune (1159–89) taking refuge in Yoshino from the attacks of his brother Yoritomo (1147–99), the Southern Court's reliance on the ascetics of Yoshino and Kongō Katsuragi, and the relations

between Minamoto no Yoshinaka (1154–84) and the Hakusan order, between the Mutō clan and Hagurosan, and between the Utsunomiya clan
and Hikosan. There are also a number of tales of defeated warlords escaping by masquerading as *shugenja* on pilgrimage. For example, Yoshitsune
escaped from Yoritomo disguised as a *yamabushi*'s serving man, and Prince
Morinaga (1308–35) used the same ruse to remain hidden in the foothills
of Totsugawa, in Yamato Province, after his defeat on Mount Kasagi.

Thus the *shugenja*, or *yamabushi*, of the Kamakura and Muromachi periods
roamed the mountains of Honshu freely and exercised an influence far
greater than is usually imagined, not only on religion but on political and
military affairs as well.

13. The Tokugawa Shogunate and Religion

Up to the Edo period (1603–1868) Buddhism supported the Japanese spiritually through its concern with the questions of life and death. Buddhist priests lived among the people, often led them, and wept and rejoiced with them. With the establishment of the Tokugawa shogunate in Edo (present-day Tokyo) in 1603, however, the priests' attitudes toward their way of life changed greatly. During the Edo period, secular society was strictly stratified, divided broadly into the four classes of warriors, farmers, artisans, and merchants. Under this system, priests—like farmers, artisans, and merchants—were subject to control by the warriors.

As their way of life increasingly diverged from that of the ordinary people, the priests began to lend full support to the shogunate's policy of surveillance of the populace. Even the priests of the Hongan-ji organization, which had provided leadership for the peasant uprisings against local authorities in the preceding century, yielded to the will of the shogunate and became its minions. To the extent that Buddhist priests aided in controlling the people, the shogunate was unstinting with political and economic protection for their temples. The price of this protection, however, was tight control over all religions, Buddhism first and foremost.

As a result, Buddhism was strictly regulated down to the smallest detail by temple regulations (*jiin hatto*). Priests acceded to the wishes of the shogunate and the authorities and were encouraged by the shogunate to perform various tasks, in particular that of fostering the type of subject that the rulers considered ideal. In return, temples and priests were given ranks bearing stipends deriving from landholdings, in effect making Edo-period priests public servants of the military government. The temple regulations were civil service codes that regulated priests' lives and ranked priests under their head temples in a rigid organizational hierarchy that resembled that of society at large.

In the Edo period, each person was required to register as a parishioner (*danka*) of a temple, and the priests of those temples had to provide proof that their parishioners did not espouse beliefs that were considered dangerous, such as Christianity. The establishment of the parish system was the shogunate's greatest gift to Buddhist priests. For better or worse, even today, long after the collapse of the shogunate, Japanese temples survive by clinging to the parish system.

Of the many roles that priests played as public servants, three were particularly notable. First, priests assumed the responsibilities of village officials, acting as record keepers and providing the required official certification of important private events, such as marriages and deaths. Second, they helped mold public thought, cooperating with the government to create a compliant populace by instilling a positive attitude toward the authorities through sermons to their parishioners and the people at large. Third, they undertook public surveillance, acting as government agents to expose and stamp out underground faiths, such as those of the underground Christians, the Fuju Fuse faction of the Nichiren sect, and the underground *nembutsu* followers, all of which are discussed in chapter 15. To unmask members of these groups and other nonconformists, the Buddhist establishment, in concert with the shogunate, used a religious-affiliation census (*shūshi nimbetsu aratame*) to conduct a kind of inquisition. Of all the powers held by priests, their control of the religious census was the most burdensome to the people. Many documents criticizing priests for misuse of the census survive.

Their position as officials of the Tokugawa shogunate appeared to ensure the priests' security as long as that system survived. The actual situation was not so clear-cut, however. From around the middle of the Edo period, even the warriors found it increasingly difficult to maintain the dignity of their positions on their stipends alone. The Buddhist establishment, at best considered peripheral by the shogunate and unable to rely on it for continuous support, was also increasingly hard pressed economically, and temples were forced to look for additional sources of income.

Bolstered by the parish system and occupied by their role as supervisors of the thought of the nation, priests neglected the task of offering the people religious solutions to the questions of life and death. But no offerings come to those who cannot teach what life is about. Therefore, in order to eat, the priests began to tend the graves of their parishioners. Until the late sixteenth century, temple priests had little to do with the graves and funerals of the general population. Those responsibilities lay with itinerant priests called *kanjin hijiri* or *kanjin bōzu*, who traveled from village to village. In the Edo period, temple priests appropriated the duties of conducting funerals and tending graves from the itinerant priests, and these services became a valuable source of income for temple priests. By the middle of the period, such services were expanded by the introduction of a system of memorial rites to be conducted at prescribed intervals for parishioners' deceased family members and ancestors. This system led to the compilation of death registers. In turning to meeting the needs of the dead before those of the living, Japanese Buddhism was transformed into the funerary religion that it largely remains today.

Buddhism's complete alliance with the shogunate led to its becoming the state religion. Although subordinated to both secular and clerical authorities by the temple regulations, priests wielded considerable power over the populace, particularly through the religious-affiliation census. Thus it is not surprising that people sought living faiths outside the oppressive bounds of established, institutionalized Buddhism. Some joined underground movements, but fierce persecution by both the Buddhist establishment and the government prevented those movements from becoming major religious outlets. Hence many among the general population became devotees of local cults, the most popular of which were associated with a particular *kami* (*hayari-gami*) or buddha (*hayari-butsu*), or of cults that developed around certain charismatic religious leaders (*kyōso shinkō*) of the late Edo period.

BUDDHISM UNDER THE SHOGUNATE

Temple Regulations

Most of the regulations for Buddhist temples were issued between 1601 and 1615, in the last years of Tokugawa Ieyasu (1542–1616), founder of the Tokugawa shogunate. The first of the regulations, the *Kōyasan Jichū Hatto Jōjō* (Codified Regulations for the Temples of Mount Kōya), appeared in 1601, and others were issued at intervals until 1615, by which time the great majority of Buddhist sects were subject to official regulations. Altogether, forty-six sets of codes date from this period, governing the Hossō, Tendai, Shingon, Jōdo, Rinzai, and Sōtō sects. Of these, thirty-four applied to the Tendai and Shingon sects alone.

Ieyasu's purpose in issuing regulations at that time was fourfold. He wanted to control the temples throughout the country both politically and financially, deprive them of the special privileges they had accumulated, force the priests to concentrate on doctrinal study, and bring the activities of the temples under government control.

Interestingly, he did not issue regulations to the sects that had most vigorously opposed his power, notably the *ikkō ikki* faction of the Jōdo Shin sect, which had caused him trouble ever since the uprising in Okazaki in Mikawa Province in 1563, and the Nichiren sect, which had refused to participate in the dedication of the Great Buddha at Hōkō-ji in Kyoto in 1595. Nor did he issue regulations for the Ji sect, whose priests traveled around the country in small groups, providing religious services for the populace. Ieyasu's policy was to control first those sects that would offer the least resistance. The power of the head temples of the Tendai sect, on Mount Hiei, and the Shingon sect, on Mount Kōya, had been sharply reduced by the warlord Oda Nobunaga (1534–82) and his successors Toyotomi Hideyoshi (1537–98) and Ieyasu, and those sects could offer little resistance. Since the fifteenth century the Rinzai sect had been under government control through the Gozan system, and the Sōtō sect never offered any opposition to Ieyasu. The Jōdo sect was Ieyasu's own faith.

The central figure in the drafting of the temple regulations was Ishin Sūden (1569–1633), head of the Nanzen-ji subtemple Konchi-in in Kyoto. His regulations reflected the aspirations of each sect's head temple, and branch temples were forced to accept a subordinate role. As a representative of the Buddhist establishment, Sūden did not always bow to the will of the shogunate with regard to control over the Buddhist organization.

Clauses common to every sect included those establishing the head- and branch-temple system (*hommatsu seido*), promoting doctrinal study, regulating the lives of priests, and specifying clerical qualifications. The head- and branch-temple system was intended to increase the head temples' authority, giving them complete control over the branch temples. At the same time, to expand its own power at the head temples' expense, the shogunate concentrated on diluting the power of the sects by having them establish head temples in both the eastern and the western regions of the country. The shogunate also introduced different methods of control in different regions. Doctrinal study was strongly emphasized, both to limit the number of priests by disqualifying those who were not learned and to occupy the priests with concerns other than politics or society. However, some sects were not directly controlled by these regulations, and the details of the codes differed from district to district and sect to sect. From the government's point of view, the regulations remained inadequate for these reasons.

Temple regulations that largely incorporated the shogunate's intentions and that were uniform for all sects were finally issued in 1665 as two codes: the nine-clause *Shoshū Jiin Hatto* (Regulations for the Temples of All Buddhist Sects), or *Sadame*, formulated by the shōgun Tokugawa Ietsuna (1641–80), and the five-clause *Gechi Jō* (Proclamations of the Shōgun), or *Jōjō*, conveyed by the shogunate's senior councilors.

The *Sadame* stipulated that (1) formal religious observances of the sects should not be neglected; (2) priests ignorant of the formal religious observances of their sect could not serve as head priests of temples; (3) the head- and branch-temple system should be strictly preserved, but oppression of the branch temples would not be tolerated; (4) relationships between temples and parishioners should be defined by the wishes of the parishioners; (5) factions should not be formed and altercations would not be tolerated; (6) temples must not protect those who violate civil laws; (7) temple structures should be repaired frugally; (8) temple land must not be bought, sold, or mortgaged; and (9) permission for ordination must be obtained from the shōgun's local administrator.

Although the substance of clauses 1, 2, 5, and 6 had been included in Ieyasu's regulations, clauses 3, 4, 7, and 8 were new regulations. Clause 3 pertained to the intense disputes between the head and branch temples and attempted to address the concerns of the branch temples. Clause 4 was the shogunate's criticism of the temples' practice of forcing unilateral demands on their parishioners. Clauses 7 and 8 regulated the temples' economic activities.

The *Jōjō* stated that (1) funerals, memorial services for ancestors, and other rituals must be conducted frugally; (2) the heads of temples established by parishioners were to be appointed and dismissed at the discretion of the parishioners; (3) the office of head priest was not to be bought or sold; (4) proselytizing outside temple precincts by holding services and installing Buddhist altars in lay people's houses was forbidden; and (5) laywomen were forbidden to reside in temple precincts. These provisions, which are not found in the regulations of Ieyasu's time, appear to be aimed at rooting out abuses in the head- and branch-temple and parish systems. In the first half of the seventeenth century the shogunate had been concerned primarily with establishing the temple hierarchy and the role of the parish, but by the time of the *Jōjō* it had changed its stance and was pointing out defects in those systems and ordering their rectification.

The next set of regulations governing all sects was the twelve-clause *Shojiin Jōmoku* (General Temple Regulations), issued in 1687. It required thorough investigation of religious affiliation (*shūmon aratame*) to stamp out four proscribed sects: Christianity and three closely related Nichiren-sect groups (the Fuju Fuse, Sanchō, and Hiden factions). It also recommended alleviation of the economic burden of the parishioners; ordered that parishioners be present when decisions on temple succession were made, thereby expanding their influence; and stressed that in matters in which the interests of the Buddhist establishment and those of the state conflicted, the state's interests took priority.

The *Shoshū Sōryo Hatto* (Regulations for the Clergy of All Buddhist Sects) of 1722, consisting of eight clauses, emphasized the encouragement of learning by priests and a frugal lifestyle for them. It also encouraged simplicity in the conduct of memorial services for ancestors and other rituals and restraint in the partaking of food and drink provided by the laity on occasions of memorial services, and stressed that relations between priests and parishioners were not to be influenced by parishioners' wealth or temple attendance.

While the early codes emphasized adherence to the feudal social order, the later codes focused on the protection of parishioners from exploitation by the temples. They also offered protection for the landowners, who could not demand as much tribute from tenants who had to donate heavily to the temples.

Patronage

Tokugawa Ieyasu's first donation of temple land, to Daisen-ji in Mikawa Province, was recorded in 1556. As his influence and power grew, he awarded land to temples in other areas, as well. It should be noted, however, that in most cases these grants were made in areas already under Ieyasu's control. Later, when registers of head and branch temples were compiled, temples were ordered to report the value of their holdings. The *Kan'ei Shoshū Matsuji Chō* (Kan'ei Era Branch-Temple Registers of Various Sects; 1632–33) lists 2,838 temples, less than a quarter of all the temples in Japan. Income from temple lands was modest: 14.9 percent of the temples reporting had incomes of less than one *koku* (180 liters) of rice, and 67 percent reported incomes of between one and five *koku*. Since more than 80 percent of the temples earned less than five *koku* from their lands, it is clear that income deriving from their lands alone could not meet their economic needs.

When temple landholdings were to be confirmed by the shogunate, the land was surveyed. Often a large portion of the land had been confiscated by the time official notice of a grant was issued, and only a small part of the original holding was reallotted to the temple. The official notice of the grant was accompanied by a document of prohibition. Surviving documents indicate that the reallotment system was intended not only to reduce temples' landholdings but also to divest temples of the special rights they had acquired during the Kamakura, Muromachi, and Momoyama periods and to deprive them of the means of protesting against the government actions. The temples were weakened both politically and economically.

After 1642 the shogunate issued official certificates of authorization to temples throughout Japan, and in 1649 and 1665 "temple-land assurance certificates" were issued. The latter were reconfirmed at the accession of each new shōgun, but the amount of land generally did not change. The temples that had received these land-assurance certificates were accorded the status of officially approved temples (*shuin jiin*). These were usually temples with a long history, most of them having been founded before the seventeenth century. A few temples founded later by the shōgun, daimyō, or other influential figures were also accorded this status. As a rule, however, the *shuin jiin* were well-known old temples.

The temples whose landholdings were confirmed by the shogunate were of the highest status and had the largest revenues. Ordinary temples were also granted tax-exempt landholdings. This privilege, conferred by the lord of a domain, was held by many temples. Temples benefited from expansion of their tax-exempt lands, and as their holdings increased, temples became landlords. Large temples seemed destined to become financial powers in their own right as they profited by diverting funds received as donations for repairing their buildings, using them to make high-interest loans, and by seizing lands forfeited by borrowers who defaulted on loans. Though the lands confirmed under the shōgun's seal and tax-exempt lands were at first quite modest holdings, they soon became the springboard for increased ownership and management of land by temples.

The Hommatsu System

Not only the head temples of the various sects but also the shogunate and the daimyō were concerned with organizing branch temples into an orderly system. The problem was addressed gradually and the *hommatsu* system strengthened through the temple regulations issued in the Keichō and Genna eras (1596–1624). To make the system effective, it was necessary to compile registers, or *hommatsu chō,* of the results of investigations into head- and branch-temple relations.

The preparation of the registers offered the head temples an opportunity to investigate conditions at the branch temples, with the shogunate's authorization. The shogunate considered it imperative to bring all the scattered temples under the authority of their respective head temples and to organize them in a hierarchal system governed by feudal ties. Temples were ranked as direct branches (*jikimatsu jiin*), branches once removed (*matamatsu jiin*), branches twice removed (*magomatsu jiin*), branches thrice removed (*himagomatsu jiin*), and sectarian temples (*monto jiin*).

The first registers that the shogunate drew up were the *Kan'ei Shoshū Matsuji Chō* of 1632–33. The head temples of some sects had already compiled similar documents. For example, records compiled between roughly 1615 and 1680 by the Higashi Hongan-ji branch of the Jōdo Shin sect indicate that before 1631 Higashi Hongan-ji had already recognized some 304 temples as affiliated institutions. Among the documents of the Nichiren-sect temple Hokekyō-ji in Nakayama, Shimōsa Province, are one dated 1594 in which 91 branch temples are recorded; another, dated 1606, mentions 126 branch temples and 29 subtemples. The temples of most branches of the Rinzai sect had already been organized throughout the country under the Gozan system. Eleven Gozan temples in Kyoto and Kamakura, headed by Nanzen-ji in Kyoto, and many lower-ranking Jissatsu and Shozan temples were recognized. Clearly, to regulate their internal organization, the head temples of three sects had already compiled the equivalent of branch-temple registers, incomplete though they were. No doubt other sects also did so.

The shogunate first exerted its influence in this area in the Kan'ei era (1624–44). In the ninth month of 1631, it ordered all head temples to submit registers of their branch temples. The submissions were completed in 1633, and the forty-five extant volumes of registers are held by the National Archives of Japan, in Tokyo.

Allowing for the overlap inevitable in historical documents, nine sects are represented in these registers: Tendai, Kogi (Mount Kōya) Shingon, Shingi (Negoro) Shingon, Ritsu, Jōdo, Ji, Rinzai, Sōtō, and Nichiren. A total of 12,080 temples are recorded. The only major sect not to submit a register of its branches was the Jōdo Shin sect. Considering this sect's rapid expansion in the Hokurokudō, Kinai, and Tōkaidō regions, that omission must represent a considerable number of temples of which there is no record. The earlier Higashi Hongan-ji register alone listed 304 temples. In addition, the Tendai return is limited to a single temple, Hōkai-ji in Kamakura, with three subtemples. It is unfortunate that the registers for the powerful Enryaku-ji (the Tendai headquarters, on Mount Hiei), the Tendai subtemple Kita-in in Kawagoe, and the Jōdo-sect Chion-in in Kyoto are no longer extant.

Obviously, the surviving registers represent only part of the registers submitted in 1632–33. Two records of 1681, compiled fifty years after the first submission, list the names and numbers of temples in the registers then in the possession of the shogunate. Their information is identical to that in the documents now in the National Archives. Despite the loss of a large body of information, the existence of well over twelve thousand temples at the time of the first surveys can be inferred.

This inference is supported by other documents of the period, for example, the diary of Sūden, who was instrumental in formulating the shogunate's temple regulations. According to Sūden, the junior councilor Matsudaira Nobutsuna (1596–1662) ordered that registers of branch temples be submitted by temples throughout the country. Shūun Gentan (d. 1661) of the Rinzai-sect subtemple Kantō-in in Musashi Province submitted his report to Nobutsuna on the third day of the eleventh month of 1632, but this report is not included in the extant registers of the shogunate. Moreover, although Kantō-in had to report to Engaku-ji in Kamakura, and its register was to be transmitted to the shogunate by Engaku-ji, there are no registers from Engaku-ji among the shogunate's archives. In another entry Sūden states that on the eleventh day of the twelfth month of 1632 Ichijō-in, a subtemple of Kōfuku-ji in Nara, submitted information on the branch temples and their income at the order of Tenkai (d. 1643) of Kita-in. No register for Kōfuku-ji survives among shogunate documents, however. Support is also provided by extant documents in the archives of head temples, such as a head- and branch-temple register at Engaku-ji dated the fifteenth day of the sixth month of 1633 and a register of branch temples at Engaku-ji, titled *Matsuji Mokuroku*, dated the third month of 1633.

The documented existence of reports that have not survived among shogunate records must not be overlooked. Many of the lost records were probably in the possession of the shogunate at one time, since the government clearly required head temples throughout the country to submit registers. We can assume that a large part of the documents submitted have been lost, inferring their existence only on the basis of references to them found in other documents. It is likely that even if there were no reports on some of the temples of each sect, their number was small enough not to affect the shogunate's overall policy.

The shogunate ordered comprehensive submissions of branch-temple registers by all sects three times in later years, in 1692, 1745, and 1786–95. Most of these registers have been lost. Those that survive from 1786–95, which are deposited in the Shōkōkan archives in Mito (in present-day Ibaraki Prefecture), list some 48,500 temples, quadruple the 12,080 listed in the 1632–33 registers in the National Archives. An encyclopedic collection of Edo-period documents, the *Suijin Roku* (Blowing-Dust Record; 1890), reports the total number of temples in the Kansei era (1789–1801) as 469,934; and a Meiji-period survey dated 1870, the *Shaji Torishirabe Ruisan* (Compilation of Surveys of Shrines and Temples), lists around 465,000. The Shōkōkan archives figure is just 10.3 percent of the total number of temples in the *Suijin Roku*, and the National Archives figure is only about 2.6 percent of the total number of temples in the *Suijin Roku* and the Meiji-period survey. This indicates that the surveys were more extensive than is suggested by the evidence of extant documents.

The Terauke *System*

In 1638 the shogunate decreed that Christians be sought out, and it promised rewards to those who revealed Christians to the government. Bounties for Christians were set by category: priests (*bateren*), two hundred pieces of silver; lay brothers (*iruman*), one hundred pieces of silver; and ordinary Christians, thirty or fifty pieces of silver, depending on the accusation. One of the shogunate's most effective tools for eliminating Christianity in Japan was the temple-certification, or *terauke*, system.

Under the *terauke* system, Buddhist temples (*tera*) guaranteed (*uke*) that their parishioners were not Christians. This system was established around 1635. Several facts suggest that the *terauke* system went into effect between that date and 1638.

First, there are no extant temple-guarantee certificates dated earlier than 1635.

Second, the death registers maintained by temples show a sudden increase in the names of ordinary citizens (who did not have surnames at that time) around 1635, suggesting that temples rushed to record all members of their parishes to comply with new regulations requiring temples to guarantee the religious affiliation of their parishioners.

Third, in 1635 the shogunate established the office of secular temple and shrine commissioner (*jisha bugyō*) and appointed as the first commissioners the daimyō Andō Shigenaga (1600–1657), Matsudaira Katsutaka (1589–1666), and Hori Toshishige (1581–1638). The shogunate's employment of these men to administer the affairs of temples and shrines reflected its decision to take a more direct hand in religious affairs. Unlike the people employed earlier to devise means of controlling the temples—such insiders as Tenkai, Sūden, Gien (1558–1626), and Bonshun (1553–1632)—the daimyō were not part of the Buddhist establishment. With these appointments, the shogunate forged ahead with its new religious policy.

Fourth, the Shimabara Uprising on Kyushu, ostensibly fomented by Christians, which lasted from the tenth month of 1637 to the third month of 1638, sent a chill through the government. Within six months of its suppression, the policy of soliciting denunciations of Christians was put into effect. This policy was doubtless a major reason for the acceleration of anti-Christian activities and must have contributed to the importance of the *terauke* system.

On the basis of this evidence, it seems probable that the temple-guarantee system was put into effect sometime between 1635 and 1638. The introduction of the system was momentous from the viewpoint of the temples, since without exception every person in a settlement or village in which a temple was located was firmly bound to the temple by the *terauke* system. Because of this system, every Japanese became a parishioner of a temple, and vestiges of the system survive today.

Kitō *Buddhism*

Kitō Buddhism refers to the practice of praying to buddhas or deities for specific benefits. The shogunate had from the first opposed *kitō* Buddhism, which stressed benefits in the present life and their attainment through magico-religious rituals. However, as the *terauke* system made funerary Buddhism dominant, the ordinary people lost faith in Buddhism, and their spiritual reliance on family temples weakened. The systematization of relations between temple and parishioner meant the formalization of faith itself. Moreover, as priests increasingly devoted themselves to administration, they assumed the roles of civil registrars and funeral directors rather than religious leaders. They paid lessening attention to teaching and doctrinal study and took advantage of both their positions as shogunate functionaries and their relations with parishioners through funeral services to expand their precincts and buildings. Temples in farming villages became local landlords, and many urban temples served as moneylenders.

Yet the general population wanted from their family temples salvation in the present life, not esoteric ritual or lofty doctrine. The life of farming people in the Edo period was one of constant exploitation by the daimyō, even in times of good harvests. When a harvest was bad, suffering was unremitting. Poor nutrition led to sickness. Life was gloomy and insecure, and that caused family discord. The people were seeking relief, and they looked for it in religion.

Those who provided this help were the priests known as *kanjin bōzu,* or pledge-book priests, who lived near them in simple huts and hermitages. The *kanjin bōzu* were regarded as socially inferior and most of them could not even read the sutras, yet they were valued for their ability to cure disease. Other figures were sacerdotal diviners—who might diagnose the source of family discord as the inauspicious layout of the house and order the house rebuilt—and *yamabushi,* who traveled periodically to certain villages to distribute talismans and amulets to ward off evil, protect against lightning and fire, ensure safe childbirth, protect children, and cure disease. These figures, whom temple priests held in contempt, were the religious support of the ordinary people. The living faith of the Edo period was in fact *kitō* Buddhism.

Kitō Buddhism was from time to time banned by the shogunate and denounced by the literati, particularly the Confucianists, as superstition and heresy. Nevertheless, bound to the people by strong ties, it was, however irrational, the focus of popular faith throughout the Edo period.

SHINTŌ UNDER THE SHOGUNATE

Yuiitsu Shintō

In the Edo period, Yoshida Shintō became better known as Yuiitsu Shintō (Unique, or One-and-Only, Shintō). This designation, devised by Yoshida Kanetomo (1435–1511), the systematizer of Yoshida Shintō, was based on the statement that "this Shintō has drawn on only one stream" in his *Yuiitsu Shintō Myōbō Yōshū* (An Anthology of the Doctrines of Yuiitsu Shintō; late fifteenth century). The designation was used extensively by the shogunate.

The Yoshida clan's fortunes fluctuated in the late sixteenth century. The clan head, Yoshida Kanemi (1535–1610), a high-ranking Shintō official at court and a son of Yoshida Kanemigi (1516–73), corresponded with Oda Nobunaga regarding the restoration of shrine landholdings, but that was the extent of their contact. Kanemi enjoyed greater favor under Nobunaga's successor, Toyotomi Hideyoshi, however. Hideyoshi consistently promoted the concept of Japan as the land of the *kami*, and the influence of Yoshida Shintō is apparent in statements of principle in the opening paragraph of his order of 1587 to expel Christian missionaries and in a letter to the Spanish viceroy of the Indies in 1591, in which he wrote, "Ours is the land of the gods, and God is Mind. Everything in existence is part of Mind. . . . This God appeared in India as Buddhism, in China as Confucianism, and in Japan as Shintō."

There is no evidence that Hideyoshi gave any particular patronage to Yoshida Shintō during his lifetime, but it appears that he hoped to be enshrined as a Shintō deity after his death. It was no doubt on that account that after Hideyoshi's death his heir, Hideyori (1593–1615), summoned Kanemi and presented him a land grant with a yield of 10,000 *koku* (1.8 million liters) of rice, requesting that he enshrine Hideyoshi as a *kami*. Miyagawa-dono, the sister of Kanemi's son's father-in-law, criticized this arrangement, saying, "The Taikō [Hideyoshi] has become a deity, and the priest of the Yoshida has become a man," no doubt referring to Kanemi's achievement of daimyō status.

This is the origin of the shrine of Toyokuni Daimyōjin (Great Bright Deity Toyokuni). It is said that when the shrine was completed in 1599, perpetually lit lanterns densely lining both sides of the four-block-long road leading from the entry gate to the main shrine made a splendid sight. After the Toyotomi family's destruction following the fall of Osaka Castle in 1615, however, Tokugawa Ieyasu ordered the razing of the shrine and confiscated the land that Hideyori had granted to the Yoshida clan four its priests.

Despite this setback, Yuiitsu Shintō survived. Kanemi's brother Bonshun, a Shintō scholar and Buddhist priest, had long been Ieyasu's trusted adviser on matters related to Shintō and shrines, and in 1613 Ieyasu had attained such mastery of his studies that he was on the point of receiving Shintō initiation from Bonshun. Ieyasu fell ill early in 1616. When his illness became grave, on the fifteenth day of the fourth month, Bonshun told the lords in attendance that the interment should follow both Shintō and Buddhist rites, which suggests that there had been some controversy about the nature of Ieyasu's enshrinement. The following day it was decided that Ieyasu should be interred on Kunōzan in Suruga Province with Shintō rites. Ieyasu died the next day, the seventeenth of the month. His will directed that he be buried on Kunōzan, that his funeral be held at Zōjō-ji in Edo with Buddhist rites, that his memorial tablet be placed in Daiju-ji in Mikawa Province, and that following the first anniversary of his death a small shrine be erected on Nikkōzan in Shimotsuke Province, where the deified Ieyasu would dwell as tutelary deity of the eight provinces surrounding the country's new capital, Edo. Thus Ieyasu was interred temporarily on Kunōzan, with Shintō rites conducted by Sakakibara Teruhisa under the supervision of Bonshun.

Afterward there was a dispute about the kind of Shintō *kami* that Ieyasu should become. The Tendai priest Tenkai, who had been Ieyasu's closest religious and political adviser and would continue to serve the shogunate, favored a Shintō-Buddhist deity (in this case, one belonging to the Sannō Shintō embraced by the Tendai sect on Mount Hiei), while Bonshun wanted Yuiitsu Shintō deification. Tenkai took his campaign to the court nobles in Kyoto, and argued that the title *daimyōjin* that Yuiitsu Shintō proposed for Ieyasu had been rendered inauspicious by the fate of Hideyoshi. Two months later, the emperor decreed deification under the title *tōshō daigongen* (buddha incarnate as the sun deity of the east), proposed by Tenkai. The Yoshida faction was bested.

Though this defeat meant the Yoshida clan did not gain the influence it sought as administrators of Ieyasu's shrine, the clan did eventually assume far-reaching control of Shintō throughout the country through its system of certification of Shintō priests. In the course of gaining this control, it could not avoid conflict with Shugendō; but Shugendō, under pressure from the shogunate because of its participation in funerals, was in a vulnerable position, and no serious disputes arose. Just as the shogunate used the head- and branch-temple system and the *danka*, or parish, system to tightly control the Buddhist sects, Yuiitsu Shintō became the shogunate's umbrella organization for control of Shintō affairs throughout Japan.

In 1665, the year that the *Shoshū Jiin Hatto*, or *Sadame*, code for Buddhist sects was promulgated, the shogunate issued the *Shosha Negi Kannushi Hatto* (Regulations for the Priests and Chief Priests of All Shrines), which required that all shrine priests, of whatever rank, devote themselves exclusively to the Way of the *kami*, have knowledge of the nature of the tutelary deity (or deities) of their own shrines, and perform rituals and ceremonies according to custom. Unranked priests were ordered to wear plain white cotton robes over loose pants; no other costume could be worn without the express permission of the Yoshida clan. In addition, all trade in shrine lands was forbidden.

The *Shosha Negi Kannushi Hatto* reflects the shogunate's recognition of the Yoshida clan as the arbiter of matters concerning Shintō priests. Shrines that could be considered to belong to the Shintō-Buddhist (Ryobu Shintō) school, administered totally by *bettō* (Buddhist temple superintendents) and *gusō* (Buddhist priests serving in shrines), were scattered all over Japan. But many other shrines belonged to the Yuiitsu Shintō school. In these, the Shintō priests had full or partial responsibility for ritual and differentiated themselves from the *bettō* and *gusō*. Most of them looked to the Yoshida clan in Kyoto for leadership and were formally affiliated with it.

In many cases, precedent dating to the fourteenth through sixteenth centuries made it impossible to distinguish the limits of the authority of the shrine itself and of the *bettō-ji* (the temple of the Buddhist administrator in the shrine precincts). There were many instances in which shrine personnel wanting to be freed from the bonds of the *bettō-ji* caused disputes between the shrine and the *bettō-ji* and resorted to litigation. That the shrines "frequently lost the appeal or withdrew it" suggests that as a rule the *bettō-ji* were able to maintain their dominant position by means of the religious-affiliation census system. Shrines had been gradually break-ing free of the jurisdiction of the temples since the Age of the Warring Provinces (1467–1568), when villages began to merge and become au-tonomous. In the Edo period, however, when the stability of the feudal system became all-important, shrines were generally put under the con-trol of temples. In the latter part of the period, shrines began once again to move toward independence when shrine priests demanded the dissolu-tion of all ties with Buddhist temples, in what is called the *ridan* move-ment.

Suika Shintō

With the rapid gain in the popularity of Confucian studies in the Edo pe-riod, Shintō began to receive a Confucian interpretation. This trend is evident in the works of the Neo-Confucian scholars Hayashi Razan (1583–1657) and Kumazawa Banzan (1619–91).

It was the Neo-Confucian scholar Yamazaki Ansai (1618–82) who or-ganized Suika Shintō, a doctrine with a Neo-Confucian cast. Ansai was at first a Rinzai Zen priest. Reverting to lay status, he studied Chu Hsi Confucianism and lectured on it in Kyoto and Edo, where he had opened schools. His highly esteemed lectures gained him many followers. He de-veloped an interest in the study of Japanese history and wanted to edit historical works. Feeling that he had little chance of success, however, he concentrated on Shintō, visiting Ise to study Ise Shintō under Watarai Nobuyoshi (1615–90) and Ōnakatomi no Kiyonaga (1601–88). Returning to Kyoto, he studied Yoshikawa Shintō under Yoshikawa Koretari, its founder. Yoshikawa Shintō was an offshoot of Yoshida Shintō with strong ethical elements.

Ansai's Shintō took the name Suika from a central passage in one of the five classics of Ise Shintō, *Yamatohime no Mikoto Seiki* (The Life of Yamato-hime no Mikoto): "The revelation [*sui*] of the *kami* is invoked through earnest prayer, and marvelous blessings [*ka*] are secured through hon-esty." Ansai formulated unique Shintō theories, in particular that of *tokon no den*, which involves the concept of *tsutsushimi* (the Japanese reading of the Chinese ideogram *ching*, used in ancient Confucianism to mean "rev-erence" and by the Neo-Confucianists to denote "seriousness"). Ansai in-terpreted *tsutsushimi* in the light of the ancient Chinese theory of the five elements (wood, fire, earth, metal, and water) and concluded that the mere cultivation of a deep feeling of *tsutsushimi* brought wealth and happiness. Ansai's interpretation appears very strained, but it is typical of his bold efforts to relate Shintō to Chu Hsi's philosophy.

In the *Zatsuwa Hikki* (Miscellaneous Talks Recorded), Ansai's second-generation disciple Wakabayashi Kyōsai (1679–1732) quotes Ansai as saying: "If I talk about divine things with all my ability, the people will all accept me with admiration. However, it is not satisfactory to talk about Shintō in that way. Speaking with an almost childlike innocence while respecting the old theories is the way to interpret Shintō works." He meant that understanding the volumes on the age of the *kami* in the *Nihon Shoki*, for example, requires a childlike simplicity of mind.

As a teacher of Chu Hsi's philosophy, Ansai had many outstanding followers. Three of the most famous were Satō Naokata (1650–1719), Miyake Shōsai (1662–1741), and Asami Keisai (1652–1711). Naokata and Shōsai embraced Chu Hsi's philosophy but never supported Ansai's Shintō theories. Keisai appears to have had a little more sympathy for Shintō, although he did not address it specifically and as a strict Neo-Confucianist did not transmit Ansai's Shintō thought.

Many disciples did transmit Ansai's Shintō theories, however, in particular Ōyama Tameoki (1651–1713), a scion of the priestly family of Fushimi Inari Shrine in Kyoto, who linked Shintō and the Way of the Emperor; Tamaki Masahide (1670–1736), who compiled Ansai's secret transmissions on practice; Tanigawa Kotosuga (1709–76), Tamaki's disciple, who composed the *Nihon Shoki Tsūshō* (1762), a fine commentary on the *Nihon Shoki*; and Tani Shigetō (1663–1718), who noted the course of controversies in Ansai's school in the *Jinzan Shū* (Collection of Tani Shigetō's Works), published by his son in 1728. Others were the noble Ōgimachi Kimmichi (1653–1733), who gave *waka* poetry a Shintō interpretation. There was also one of Asami Keisai's disciples, Wakabayashi Kyōsai, whose school in Kyoto, the Bōnanken, attracted many students; its atmosphere is described in the *Zatsuwa Hikki*.

Suika Shintō became a fountain of thought on the Way of the Emperor. Among its proponents were two of the central figures in antishogunate incidents in the Hōreki (1751–64) and Meiwa (1764–72) eras. As a youth, Takenouchi Shikibu (1712–67), the son of a physician in Echigo Province, went to Kyoto, where he was influenced by the Suika Shintō of Tamaki Masahide and others. Through the agency of the noble Tokudaiji family, he lectured to court nobles on the Way of the Emperor, using the *Nihon Shoki* as his text. His influence was very great. Eventually the reaction of the conservative faction brought the situation to the attention of the au-

350 THE TOKUGAWA SHOGUNATE AND RELIGION

thorities, who in 1758 ordered several nobles confined to their homes and in 1759 banished Shikibu from Kyoto. This censure by the shogunate is known as the Hōreki Incident.

Yamagata Daini (1725–67) was the son of a lower-ranking warrior in Kai Province. He studied under Kagami Ōu (1711–82), a proponent of Suika Shintō, and under Gomi Fusen (1718–54), a disciple of the Confucianist Dazai Shundai (1680–1747). On the basis of his own theories of the structure of power, Daini emphasized a variety of restoration thought, advocating reverence for the emperor and the overthrow of the military leadership. Deemed a threat to the shogunate, he was arrested in 1766 and executed in 1767, in what is called the Meiwa Incident.

Yoshikawa Shintō and Popular Shintō

Learning and the arts flourished during the peaceful Genroku era (1688–1704). During that time, Shintō, which had been the preserve of a select few, began to spread more widely among the people.

Yoshikawa Koretari (1616–94), the founder of Yoshikawa Shintō, was the son of a fishmonger in the Nihombashi district of Edo. In 1653 he went to Kyoto, where he entered the service of Hagiwara Kaneyori (1588–1660), the head of the Yoshida clan and a grandson of Yoshida Kanemi, and was eventually initiated into the teachings of Yoshida Shintō. After returning to Edo, he gained the confidence of various daimyō, and in 1682 he was appointed *Shintō-kata*, or administrator of Shintō matters, by the shogunate. His teachings were similar to those of Yoshida Shintō but placed more emphasis on morals. Most revered of the *kami* in Koretari's pantheon was the great creator spirit, Kuni no Tokotachi no Mikoto. Koretari taught that the ideal of true love, justice, and harmony had been realized in Japan and that the act of praying for the eternal prosperity of the sacred, nonpareil nation expressed the spirit of Japan (*Yamato damashii*).

A number of independent thinkers who appeared after Koretari taught his ideas comparatively freely to the people at large. Eventually these figures came to be called Shintō *kōdan* (storytellers), or popular exponents of Shintō. Typical of them was Masuho Nokoguchi (1655–1742). Born in Bungo Province, he went to Kyoto and entered the service of the Konoe family. Eventually he began expounding Shintō teachings as a popular storyteller in a booth set up in a busy area. He used theatrical techniques to make Shintō accessible to the general population. "The atmosphere was rather vulgar," wrote the Confucianist Miwa Shissai (1669–1744) in

his *Shintō Okusetsu* (Shintō Hypotheses), "but his intention was to disseminate Shintō by whatever means he could."

According to Nokoguchi's *Kamiji no Tebikigusa* (An Introduction to the
Path of the *Kami*), if Śākyamuni and Confucius had been born in Japan,
without doubt they would have taught the Way of Yamato, in Japanese
fashion. Teachings were adapted to country and locale, and in Japan the
laws of the *kami* were to be preserved. Indians followed the teachings of
Buddhism; Chinese, the teachings of Confucius; and Japanese, the teachings of the *kami*. (For "teachings," Nokoguchi used the expression "mountain path," borrowed from a well-known *waka* that tells of numerous
paths and a single moon.) He felt that for Japanese to follow the path of
Indians or Chinese was to take the long way around; from the mountain
summit one saw the same moon.

Nokoguchi also explained that in Japan sexual intercourse between a
man and a woman was considered sacred, a belief based on the harmony
of the teachings of the *kami* and of yin and yang, which meant that male
and female were as two wings of the bird and that there was neither high
nor low, honored nor despised. The idea that women were men's slaves,
that they should be subservient in everything, arose from the mistake of
aping Chinese ways and neglecting those of Japan. Although since ancient times China had produced many wise men of surpassing virtue,
none seemed to have appeared in Japan. This was because in China such
men were rare in a large population of little virtue, and their existence
was always well recorded. In Japan, virtuous, remarkable men were too
common to stand out. Proof of this, said Nokoguchi, lay in the fact that
even in his day there was no compulsion to note men of great learning or
wisdom.

In the same work, Nokoguchi also dealt with matters concerning graves,
funerals, and memorial services. He was a captivating source of popular
Shintō and taught the importance of flexibility and avoidance of precon-
ceived notions in human relationships.

In the Bunka era (1804–18) Hirata Atsutane was widely praised for his
lectures, particularly those on the Ancient Way (*Kodō*). His work, which is
discussed later in this chapter, provides the best example of effective
teaching.

In the Tempō era (1830–44) Kamo no Norikiyo (1798–1861), born into
the priestly family of the Kamo Shrine in Kyoto, taught Shintō widely in
Edo. He said that the *Nihon Shoki* and other works cherished by scholars
taught the principles of heaven and earth allegorically and had no factual

basis. He also stressed that carving features in wood and praying to these images of the *kami* and buddhas or printing charms on pieces of paper merely duped gullible ordinary people. He warned of the growing love of luxury: the demand for silk led to the cutting down of entire forests, resulting in soil erosion and floods, all to feed the silkworm. Thus the silkworm was leading the country to ruin. Norikiyo's topics, diverse and attention getting, won him great popularity but drew the disapproval of the shogunate, leading to his banishment. It is significant that popular Shintō, propagated in a spirit of freedom outside the established system, called down on itself the rancor of the authorities.

Kokugaku

The quest for more modern scholarship, which began in the Kyōhō era (1716–36), fostered the rise of both Kokugaku (National Learning) and Western learning. At this time the world of Shintō was troubled by two problems, both of which were related to the burgeoning of Kokugaku and Western learning and were reactions to restraints imposed by the shogunate. A rival school of Shintō—that of the Shirakawa clan—had begun to challenge the monopoly of the Yoshida school. The Shirakawas, high-ranking nobles, were hereditary heads of the Jingikan. In this period they worked actively among shrine priests in outlying districts to create support for their school. Although challenges to the authority of the Yoshida school resulted in disputes, in many cases such challenges simply reflected changes in the structure of villages and farming communities. The second problem was the *ridan* movement and the repeated attempts of shrines to break free of the grip of the parish temples. *Ridan* refers to the shrine priests' efforts to free themselves of the constraints of the temples under the religious orthodoxy laws.

Through his lifelong study of the eighth-century *Man'yōshū* poetry anthology, the Shingon priest Keichū (1640–1701) had established an advanced, scientific research methodology. Kada no Azumamaro (1669–1736) inherited this tradition of classical scholarship, which was further developed by his student Kamo no Mabuchi (1697–1769) and finally systematized as Kokugaku by Motoori Norinaga (1730–1801).

Norinaga recognized the essence of Shintō in accounts of the *kami* of the Age of the *Kami*. In the *Naobi no Mitama* (The Divine Spirit of Rectification; 1771), an interpretation of ancient mythology, he wrote:

In ages long past no mention was made of the concept of "the Way" [*michi*]. "The Way" meant only the road that people walk along. The concept of "the Way" as a principle or teaching is foreign. However, as time passed, writings were brought to Japan, and as people began to read and study them, they learned Chinese ways. As foreign and Japanese ideas mingled, traditional Japanese ways came to be called the Way of the *Kami* [Shintō]. . . . The so-called teachings of Shintō, which should have been transmitted to each individual, were all contrived recently out of envy of the teachings of foreign lands.

"The Way," Norinaga taught, lay in the nonexistence of the contrived way. To know the Way, it was necessary to abandon narrow knowledge and return to childlike purity. It was good to rely on the will of the *kami* in everything, realizing the weakness of human nature.

In the *Tama Kushige* (The Precious Comb Box; 1787) and the *Hihon Tama Kushige* (The Sacred Book of the Precious Comb Box; 1787), Norinaga dwelled on contemporary social problems. The Way was founded on reverence for Amaterasu Ōmikami and reverent acceptance of the emperor as her descendant. Thus the shōgun administered political affairs because they had been entrusted to him by the emperor, and the daimyō governed as the shōgun's delegates. The land and the people were not the private possessions of the daimyō but belonged to Amaterasu. Those who wielded power were to do so with discretion and care, never forgetting that ultimately both the government and the governed had been placed in their trust by Amaterasu.

Good and evil exist in society as a result of the actions of Naobi no Kami and Magatsubi no Kami. It is impossible for people to strive against them. Norinaga, completely indifferent to the idea of a judgment in the next world, said that without exception both the good and the bad must go to the realm of darkness, "a dirty and evil land," which is the destination of all the dead. This certainly makes death the most sorrowful of all events, according to Norinaga. Kokugaku based its objectives on accounts of the Age of the *Kami* and strongly retained its aestheticism.

Restoration Shintō

Hirata Atsutane (1776–1843) drew a sharp distinction between his ideas about the next world and those of Norinaga. Hirata's system of thought, called Restoration (*Fukko*) Shintō, can be differentiated from Norinaga's mature Kokugaku. Hirata considered it a vital duty of Kokugaku scholars to consolidate the Yamato spirit, and to do that it was important to impart peace of mind about what happened after death. Consequently, it was necessary to clarify the destination of people's spirits and, by extension, to know the nature of heaven, earth, the realm of darkness, and the source of all the universe.

Atsutane recognized Takamimusubi no Kami and Kamimusubi no Kami as the deities of procreation whose creative power gave birth to all things and Ame no Minakanushi no Kami, the deity who existed before these two, as the creator and master of all the universe. Atsutane was precise about where people could expect to go after death: the realm of darkness governed by Ōkuninushi no Mikoto, a place invisible to this world but from which this world can be observed distinctly. People could achieve true peace of mind by entrusting themselves to the judgment of Ōkuninushi in the realm of darkness, according to the good or evil they had committed in life.

Atsutane held that the foundation of Ōkuninushi's judgment is the Way of the Emperor and the *Kami* (*sumegami no michi*). He stated that that Way is the principle by which the emperor governs the land and that the emperors are the link between the present and the Age of the *Kami* and between the present and the future. Atsutane strongly emphasized Norinaga's theory of the delegation of governance, but his belief that the people should never forget (and should faithfully follow) the laws issued by the eternal emperor went beyond Norinaga's position and advocated virtually unconditional obedience.

In his late years, Atsutane's writings earned the displeasure of the shogunate, and in 1841 he was banished to his birthplace in the Akita domain, in Dewa Province. He died two years later, but his influence was inspiring and lasting.

After the Tempō era (1830–44), social conditions were rife with contradictions, and apprehension was widespread. Restoration Shintō—which had introduced the concept of delegation of governance, both as an expression of reverence for the emperor and as a theory of behavior based on an ethical view of the next world—continually sought means of effecting decisive change in all parts of the country. From the viewpoint of Restoration Shintō, this theory of delegation, formally called *miyosashi*, meant that all governance was delegated by the emperor and that, in obedience to the will of the emperor, it was the duty of the village officials who came into daily contact with the people to raise people's productivity, improve the quality of their lives, and lighten their burdens, as well as help the poor.

Among Atsutane's followers were the agronomist Satō Nobuhiro (1769–1850), the agronomist and Kokugaku scholar Miyaoi Yasuo (1797–1858), and the Kokugaku scholars Kitahara Inao (1825–81) and Katsura Takashige (1817–71), all of whom acted on the teachings of Kokugaku and Restoration Shintō and actually went among the villagers to teach and guide them. Atsutane's followers also included people like Ikuta Yorozu (1801–37), who attacked the residence of a daimyō's deputy in Kashiwazaki in Echigo Province with his followers when the authorities were unwilling to provide famine relief to the farmers. In this, Yorozu was inspired by the example of the Confucian teacher Ōshio Heihachirō (1793–1837), who had staged an uprising in Osaka in protest against the lack of famine relief. There were also followers like Ōkuni Takamasa (1792–1871), who promoted Restoration Shintō throughout the country while taking part in reforms in the Tsuwano domain, in Iwami Province, toward the end of the Edo period.

In the turmoil of the late Edo period, Restoration Shintō encouraged organized criticism of the existing system and gave substance to a vision of government in which Shintō ritual and national politics were united. Its influence cannot be dismissed, considering that the inauguration of the new government of the Meiji period (1868–1912) was in essence an imperial restoration.

14. Established Religion Under the Shogunate: The Jōdo, Ji, and Zen Sects

THE JŌDO SECT

Clerical Education

The most distinctive feature of Jōdo-sect organization in the Edo period (1603–1868) was its facilities for the training of priests, widely known as the eighteen academies, or *danrin*, of the Kantō region. Early in the seventeenth century, in response to the shogunate policy of encouraging the study of doctrine as a means of educating the clergy and controlling the Buddhist establishment, all Buddhist sects began establishing their own facilities for doctrinal study and the education of priests: training academies called *danrin*, *dangisho*, *gakurin*, or *gakuryō*, depending on the sect. The Jōdo academies—organized through the efforts of Zonnō (1544–1620) of Zōjō-ji in Edo and other priests and backed by the authority of the shogunate—came to play a significant role in overseeing the activities of the sect as a whole.

In the seventh month of 1615, the shogunate issued to Jōdo temples throughout the country the thirty-five clause *Jōdo Shū Hatto* (Jōdo-Sect Regulations). These regulations became the basic rules for the sect and the foundation for later codes that governed it. The regulations provided that existing academies were to act as organs of training for all Jōdo priests. Furthermore, the establishment of new institutions was forbidden, with the result that the power to transmit the sect's teachings was restricted to the existing academies.

A seventeen-article code issued in the first month of 1671 incorporated the decisions of a committee of the heads of the Jōdo academies. This code provided the framework for the training system, setting the age for admission to *danrin* and establishing rules governing the registration of trainee priests, the subjects of study, and the formal transmission of doctrine. This committee's power grew until it became the highest decision-making body of the Jōdo sect, dominating all levels of the sect's governing apparatus. The academies were also instrumental in setting up the *hommatsu*, or head- and branch-temple, hierarchy demanded by the shogunate.

The academy system, therefore, must be considered in terms of its role in the education and training of priests, in the promotion of doctrinal study, and in the sect's internal organization. By the end of the seventeenth century, the Kantō academies had brought more than half the Jōdo temples of the Kantō region under their jurisdiction; and with the development of the *hommatsu* network in outlying areas, they came to govern the lives of the priests in branch temples in various ways. As time passed, however, the quality of education in the academies declined, leaving graduate priests ill-qualified to propagate the sect's teachings.

Jōdo-Sect Views on Propagation

The *Jōdo Shū Hatto* of 1615 was the first of the regulations handed down by the Tokugawa shogunate with the aim of institutionalizing the sect's propagation activities. The code forbade priests with inadequate knowledge of Jōdo doctrine to preach and ordered even those with permission to preach never to deviate from the sutras or the patriarchs' interpretations. Priests were forbidden to use rhetoric to draw attention to themselves or to praise themselves and criticize others. Later a large number of edicts were issued forbidding doctrinally suspect sermons, criticism of others, and self-praise.

Nevertheless, Jōdo as a sect was deeply concerned with encouraging propagation. For example, in the sixth month of 1722 administrators at Zōjō-ji issued regulations dealing with clerical reform. Such abuses as paying other priests to preach in one's stead were forbidden, and ordinary temple priests were encouraged to be more active in preaching, though that task was primarily the responsibility of a temple's chief priest.

A letter from the academy at Jōfuku-ji in Hitachi Province to a branch temple dated the third month of 1737 states:

The branch temple is the training ground for the faith of lay parishioners. Therefore, it is the duty of the chief priest to preach to all comers, however large or small their number, on the occasions of the spring and autumn equinoxes, Bon [observances in the eighth month to honor the spirits of ancestors], the memorial observances for the sect's founder, and the ten-night *nembutsu* [held from the fifth to the fifteenth day of the tenth month]. In this way parishioners' faith will be deepened and the trainee priests' studies encouraged.

The apathy of temple priests toward teaching their parishioners Buddhist doctrine can be inferred from the popularity of the itinerant preachers who used secular stories to explain their creed. At the same time, however, there were priests like Butsujō (1734–1800), who stressed in his *Zoku Remmon Jūji Kun* (Supplementary Lessons for Temple Priests of the Lotus Gate; 1799) that even if they were not eloquent speakers temple priests should deliver their own sermons on the occasions of the two equinoxes and the ten-night *nembutsu* and at the monthly gatherings for *nembutsu* invocation.

The Zōjō-ji regulations of 1722 comment: "Recently the attitude of student priests has worsened. We have heard that they neglect the study of fundamental doctrine and commentaries to immerse themselves in training to expound the teachings publicly for propagation purposes. This is very wrong. In the future, please endeavor earnestly to correct this situation." It is ironic that academy students were disregarding doctrinal study for propagation. Propagation by academy students, as well as by religious recluses or hermits and privately ordained priests, was banned repeatedly.

In an undated directive in the Jōfuku-ji archives, the teaching duties of priests are laid out:

Above all, the head priest of a temple is the teacher of the people; therefore, you should at all times teach your parishioners the principle of good and bad causes and effects and, leading them to reject evil and do good, correct their morals and have them uphold the laws of the shogunate. Compassionately teach them to fear retribution in the next life and to do good so that they may be reborn in the Pure Land. Hold *nembutsu* meetings monthly, and exhort your parishioners to strive to practice the way of faith both for themselves and for others.

The sect's authorities expected each priest to be responsible for creating the ideal subject who follows the government's orders and acts ethically. For example, in his *Kimyō Hongan Shō Genchū Karigo*, an eighteenth-century anthology of vernacular proverbs, the *nembutsu* practitioner and teacher Kantsū (1696–1770) wrote that "loyalty and filial piety alone are the main principles on which the country is governed and the people are given peace."

It is doubtful that the priests were effective in creating the ideal subject that the government wanted. Rather than the regular priests, it was the itinerant *nembutsu* practitioners who gained the faith and trust of the people and were the best teachers of the time. Nevertheless, it is not fair to say that all temples were indifferent about teaching the people. There were temple priests who strove to kindle the faith of their parishioners, priests who could respond to the diverse religious needs of the people in villages and remote regions. We can catch glimpses of these priests in temple diaries and in the biographies of believers who were thought to have attained rebirth in the Pure Land.

Propagation Methods

In the Edo period two kinds of writings were important in the propagation of Jōdo-sect teachings: doctrinal works discussing rebirth in the Pure Land (*ōjō ron*) and collections of biographies of those who had attained such rebirth (*ōjō den*). The former genre dates back at least to the Heian period (794–1185), when it was popular, and the latter was favored later, in the Kamakura period (1185–1336). The Edo period saw the use of both genres. Doctrinal discussions of rebirth appeared in *dangibon*, storybooks used to explain Jōdo teachings to the general public. Propagation by means of biographies, a method that had been completely disregarded in recent centuries, came back into vogue, and new works were consciously modeled on those of the earlier traditions.

For example, the *Genshō Ōjō Den* (Biographies of Manifest Evidence of Pure Land Rebirth), a three-volume work compiled by the priest Keihō of Hōgyō-ji in Sakai, Izumi Province, was published in the ninth month of 1740. Its introduction offers the reasons for its compilation:

The venerable priest Keihō of Hōgyō-ji in Izumi is a man sincere, merciful, and forbearing. He has deep faith in Buddhism and has from his earliest years prayed for rebirth in the Pure Land. Thus he fervently practices the invocation of Amida's name. When he is not practicing the *nembutsu*, he records instances that he has observed of people who have attained rebirth in the Pure Land. Their number totals seventy-three, and he has recorded them in this three-volume work called *Genshō Ōjō Den*.

The title is taken from the words of our sect's founder, the venerable Hōnen, "manifest evidence of rebirth in the Pure Land [*ōjō genshō keien*]." Many years ago Yoshishige no Yasutane was deeply influenced by the words of [Shih] Chia-ts'ai in the *Ching-t'u-lun* [Discourse on the Pure Land]: "I have demonstrated the truth of rebirth through logic and quotations from both sutras and treatises. This is, I believe, of great value. Yet most people, foolish and of limited intellect, are unable to understand the logic of Amitābha's salvation. Without accounts of actual instances of salvation, it is impossible to convince people and bring them to believe. To this end I have compiled records of rebirth and included them in this work." Moved by these words, Yoshishige no Yasutane was inspired to compile his own *Nihon Ōjō Gokuraku Ki* [Japanese Accounts of Rebirth in the Pure Land]. Now the venerable Keihō has followed this example in his compilation of the *Genshō Ōjō Den*. The times are different but the need to bring people of limited intellect to faith by means of biographies of Pure Land rebirth is still exactly the same.

Keihō's collection, then, is clearly linked to those of the past, citing as it does the works of Shih Chia-ts'ai (fl. seventh century) and Yoshishige no Yasutane (ca. 931–1002). Similarly, Ryōchi (d. 1751), the author of the *Shibyaku Ōjō Den* (Biographies of Ordained and Lay People Who Attained Rebirth in the Pure Land; 1688), stated that he had collected accounts of Pure Land rebirth from men and women in both town and country because no such biographies had been compiled since the middle of the thirteenth century.

Propagation methods unique to the Jōdo sect were the fivefold transmission (*gojū sōden*, or *gojū*) and the administering of the precepts (*kechien jukai*, or *jukai*). The *gojū sōden*, originally intended to stimulate the religious practice of those whose faith was already strong, was a ceremony for the laity in which a priest transmitted the essential teachings of the Jōdo sect—the five important principles first propounded by Shōgei (1341–1420). The *Jōdo Shū Hatto* had insisted that this transmission be administered only with the greatest discretion and never to the laity. Despite the ban, however, local priests had long performed it among the laity. By the middle of the Edo period, the *gojū* had been formally recognized as a lay-training device. In 1733 temple priests of a certain rank were given official approval to administer it, and thereafter it was their duty to administer it when proselytizing. However, as the Jōdo-sect priest Teigoku (1677–1756) states in the *Gojū Hairyū Shō* (The Growth and Decline of the Fivefold Transmission; 1744), the administering of the *gojū* had already become irregular. In later times the broad popularization of this rite led to its being comparatively freely administered to all. This is evidenced in mass conferment of the *gojū* and in conferment in return for donations for the repair of monastery buildings.

The popularization of the *gojū* through its unrestricted conferment stripped it of all meaning, and it became a conventional rite. Eventually the *gojū* was advocated for the efficacy of its mystical powers, derived from Amida's Original Vow to save all sentient beings, and *nembutsu* practice was abandoned. In his *Jōgō Shimpō Ketsu* (Essential Teachings on Pure Karma and Belief in the Law; 1823), a tract on the *gojū sōden* directed to the laity, Ryūen (d. 1834) wrote: "Those who have not received the *gojū* have continued to be diligent in daily *nembutsu* practice. But recently, many of those who have received the *gojū* have thought recitation of ten *nembutsu* enough and have neglected daily *nembutsu* practice. Thus the *gojū* has drawn people away from *nembutsu* practice." The *gojū* had originally been conferred to encourage belief in Amida's Original Vow and diligence in daily *nembutsu* practice; it is ironic that this rite became an impediment to *nembutsu* practice.

The second propagation method was *kechien jukai* (conferring the precepts to forge a connection with the Buddha). The majority of contemporary descriptions suggest that this practice was not as widespread as the fivefold transmission, probably because few priests were qualified to administer the precepts. Late in the Edo period the priest Kenryō (d. 1831) wrote in his *Jōdo Shū Endonkai Gendan* (Profound Words on the Jōdo Sect's Precepts for Swift Achievement of Perfect Character) that the precepts enhance knowledge of the law of cause and effect and aid in the elimination of evil, while the fivefold transmission enables faith in Amida's Original Vow to grow and daily *nembutsu* practice to be undertaken. He also said that a combination of the two is without doubt beneficial in the present world and in the next. Thus these practices were highly important propagation methods for the Jōdo sect.

Various opportunities for preaching were also used to introduce people to the *nembutsu* teaching of the Jōdo sect. Other methods of conversion and of encouraging the faithful included persuading a lay person to pledge before a master to recite a certain number of *nembutsu* daily and receiving ten *nembutsu* (*jūnen*) from a master. According to the *Muryōju-kyō* [Larger *Sukhāvatī-vyūha*], the eighteenth of the forty-eight vows of Amida guarantees rebirth in Amida's Pure Land to all who recite ten *nembutsu*.)

Popular Buddhist Preachers

In contrast to most temple priests, who generally were not interested in teaching the general public, popular preachers working in villages were very active during the Edo period.

Jōdo-sect temples in this period can be classified in three broad categories: *kyō-in*, or official temples; *ritsu-in*, or temples in which the Vinaya (the set of precepts governing Buddhist religious communities) was studied; and *shaseiji*, or centers of the Shasei (Abandoning the World) group, a protest movement within the sect. Followers of the Shasei group severely criticized the mainstream Jōdo sect for abandoning the exclusive practice of the *nembutsu*. Leading hermitic lives and devoting themselves to the practice of invoking Amida's name, they traveled the country sowing the seeds of the Jōdo faith and encouraging villagers to practice the *nembutsu*. Shōnen (1513–54) is said to have founded the movement, and priests associated with it include Ihachi (1532–1614), Danzei (1552–1613), Ninchō (1645–1711), Chōzen (1652–1721), Munō (1683–1719), Engu (1634–1715), Kantsū (1696–1770), Unsetsu (1668–1735), Gakushin (1722–89), Hōgan (1744–1815), Hōjū (1765–1839), and Tokuhon (1758–1818).

Accounts of these itinerant preachers in biographies of famous priests and in various *ōjō den* relate how people attained rebirth in the Pure Land through these preachers' efforts. Notable among these priests is Kantsū, also known as Kōyo Shōnin. The many works describing his activities record that through him congregations in various areas forged connections (*kechien*) with the Buddha and that through his influence many people entered the Buddhist priesthood. The following passage from the *Kōyo Shōnin Gyōjō Kikigaki* (An Account of the Activities of Kōyo Shōnin) is of particular interest.

When the master was staying at Entsū-ji in Kawaramachi [in Kyoto], many gained rebirth in the Pure Land through his intensive propagation. As if carried on the wind, congregations from every direction gave him their faith, seeing the proof rather than reading about it in the scriptures. There were a great many laymen who changed their calling to that of the ordained, as well as children and women who were ordained. People who did not believe in the teachings of the Pure Land marveled, and officials, encountering people reciting the *nembutsu* in the streets, were amazed. It was surprising how many young boys and girls gained salvation and how many people left their homes and turned their minds toward the Pure Land. There have been none since ancient times who have been able thus to lead so many disciples. It is a thing of wonder among those of little faith.

Not only was it a cause of surprise that so many of the laity were ordained but their number was also probably a social problem that threatened the means of production at the village level. Priests of the Shasei group who engaged in popular propagation, such as Kantsū, were occasionally persecuted, which indicates their great influence among the people.

Kantsū not only conferred the daily *nembutsu* on people himself but also encouraged his many disciples to confer it on both ordained and lay people. As a result, his followers vied with one another in teaching practice of the *nembutsu* to all. In short, all of Kantsū's followers were propagators of the *nembutsu*. Yet the scholar-priest Teigoku, Kantsū's contemporary proselytizer, had nothing but scathing criticism for the results of this avid propagation that was often aimed more at tallying large numbers of converts than producing deeply committed *nembutsu* practitioners. In his *Kintsui Shō* (The Wooden Hammer and the Cloth-beating Table), Teigoku wrote: "His followers were so irresponsible that they would confer the daily *nembutsu* on people who pledged to recite ten *nembutsu* a day as easily as a boatman ferries people across the Sumida River. The priests conferred the *nembutsu* even on casual passersby in the streets, accepting pledges for a mere ten *nembutsu* a day. In this way they were able to report that ten thousand people who had pledged yesterday had increased to twenty or thirty thousand today."

Another type of proselytizer was the *dōshinsha,* or "one dedicated to the Way." The term originally referred to those who had aspired to enlightenment. By the Muromachi period (1336–1568) it had come to refer to a privately ordained, rather than officially licensed, priest. These priests were the lowest ranking of all Buddhist practitioners. The *dōshinsha* generally lived as caretakers of small worship halls, in hermitages, or in temples with no official priests in residence. Though they were on the lowest rung of the head- and branch-temple hierarchy, they came under the protection and control of priests of the head temples.

The number of regulations pertaining to the *dōshinsha* in the Jōdo sect attests to the vigor of their propagation in the villages. They had already drawn the attention of the authorities in the *Jōdo Shū Hatto* of 1615. They were condemned for undermining the sect's discipline by going out among the populace and encouraging people to receive the ten *nembutsu* and the transmission of the Jōdo-sect teachings. Condemnation of their religious activities continued over the years, and they were castigated for offering the fivefold transmission to the laity and for renting property from the laity for their hermitages. They were further criticized for preaching and holding special *nembutsu* services in their dormitories, accepting disciples, and being disrespectful to their elders and fellow priests.

Such criticism clearly indicates that whatever their qualifications or individual backgrounds the *dōshinsha* were very active in their particular kind of propagation and in their relations with the people as a whole. One clause in the regulations issued by Zōjō-ji in 1709 voices concern over their activities. It asks that the academies play a stronger role in controlling the propagation activities of *dōshinsha*. A document at Jōfuku-ji states:

> False *dōshinsha* are respected by men and women alike simply for their advanced age. They have free access to the homes of the laity, giving sermons without permission and granting the ten *nembutsu*. They take advantage of the support of believers who know no better, assuming the enlightened expression of sages, when their only concern is to cultivate sources of alms. Moreover, they place the mortuary tablets of parishioners in their hermitages and perform rituals for the deceased on memorial days. They decorate the interiors of worship halls to excess and hold gatherings to recite the *nembutsu*. Their behavior hardly differs from that of temple priests, in that they assemble congregations, receive benefits, and support themselves. In recent years such fellows are to be seen in many villages; it is the duty of the nearest academy to put a stop to their activities.

These documents reflect the suspicion and fear of the Jōdo-sect establishment, aroused both by the popular preachers' creation of a base of support among the general public far surpassing that of the established temple priests and by the fact that their hermitages had assumed the functions of temples. The *dōshinsha* lived very close to the people and became a nucleus of popular resistance against the repressive bonds of the parish system. They were able to respond to the needs of the people in a way that the temple priests could not.

As long as the *dōshinsha* operated outside the established system of temple-parishioner relationships, their activities were not perceived as a threat to the system. When the threat of their eroding the system became apparent, the Jōdo sect and the government united to suppress them. Nevertheless, the *dōshinsha* were not forced underground because they actually shored up the foundations of the Buddhist institutional framework, which was in fact a manifestation of the authority of the shogunate itself.

The Ideal Jōdo Follower

In general, the emphasis on public morals in Buddhist sermons of the Edo period is a responsive adaptation to secular concerns and reflects the policy of the Tokugawa shogunate and the shogunate's power to implement its policy. The sermons of the Jōdo sect are no exception, and they exhibit a bias toward the moral ideal favored by the shogunate. That ideal, as fostered by the Jōdo sect, is seen clearly in its *ōjō den* and *ōjō ron*. Through these works we can gauge the extent to which the religious ideal was influenced by secular power and ethics.

The biographies distinguished between the personal and the religious criteria for rebirth in the Pure Land. The personal qualities demanded of both men and women were sincerity and compassion. Women were additionally required to demonstrate meekness and integrity. The importance of filial piety was also emphasized. It is hardly surprising that recitation of the *nembutsu* was primary among the religious criteria believed necessary for rebirth. The *ōjō den* also indicated the striking importance of receiving the fivefold transmission and of *nembutsu* recitation combined with observance of the eight precepts for lay believers (*saikai*). The granting of the fivefold transmission became popular in the seventeenth century, but the latter practice was mentioned only in biographies of the followers of Ninchō, who combined observance of the Buddhist precepts with recitation of the *nembutsu*. When *nembutsu* practices verged on asceticism—for example, when tens of thousands of invocations were performed daily—the traditional *nembutsu* practice had merged with other religious practices.

Instructional works and collections of sermons also reveal the connection between *nembutsu* faith and the lay life. Butsujō, a scholar-priest and proselytizer in Kyoto, made it evident that both ethics and religion were important for the lay believer. He was typical of Jōdo-sect teachers of the eighteenth century, and in his *Nikka Nembutsu Tōshuku Hen* (An Encouragement to Daily *Nembutsu* Practice; 1800) he wrote:

> Lay people should be modest; fear providence always; believe deeply in the doctrine of cause and effect; be satisfied with their station in life, whether they be warrior, farmer, artisan, or merchant; not be concerned with what they lack; serve their parents and masters as if they were living buddhas; be selfless in their filial piety and loyalty; give thanks for the benefits they have received from their ancestors; and pray for the continuation of their family lines. In their relations with their families, they should strive to be gentle and modest, so that all family members are as courteous to one another as to honored guests. They should be sincere and fair in their dealings with fellow villagers and companions, never losing their trust. They rise early and go to bed late, exerting all their efforts toward their calling. Although they are frugal, they should not be thought stingy.

At the same time that Butsujō urges belief in the law of cause and effect, he appeals to lay people to adhere to the feudal ethics of contentment with one's lot and of loyalty. Behind the new Jōdo-sect emphasis on secular ethics lay the shogunate's strong pressure on religious institutions to inculcate those values in their followers. In addition, Jōdo priests were concerned with answering the charges of Confucianists and other opponents of Buddhism that Buddhism was not interested in ethics. They stressed that their religion was in fact deeply involved in the actual world of the present despite its teaching of salvation in the next world through the power of Amida.

Taiga (1709–82) had spoken of the oneness of Confucianism, Buddhism, and Shintō in his *Sankyō Teisoku Ron* (Treatise on the Three Teachings as the Three Legs of a Pot; 1751) and *San'i Kun* (Three Lessons to Be Observed; 1758), saying that all three praised good, condemned evil, and emphasized social tranquillity. Kantsū, too, in his popular propagation, proposed that the Confucian virtues of humanity, morality, and propriety were the equivalent of the three spiritual attributes important for *nembutsu* practice stressed by Amida in the *Kan Muryōju-kyō* (Sutra of Meditation on Amitāyus): loyalty and sincerity, deep faith, and a desire for rebirth through the transfer of merit. Kantsū spoke of compassion between parent and child—filial piety—and of the relations between lord and retainer in terms of these three spiritual attributes, which he frequently described as the qualities of righteousness, stressing that moral virtues and the teachings of the Jōdo sect formed a unity.

According to Teigoku, Confucianism is merely the small and narrow way to salvation only in the present, while Buddhism is far superior, since it encompasses the three worlds of past, present, and future. To stress the importance of ethics, he exploited the popularity of such works as the *Zenshō-kyō* (Sutra of Good Rebirth, a text that teaches the proper discipline for lay Buddhists). In his *Zuiki Tazen Gi* (The Meaning of Rejoicing over Other Kinds of Goodness), he discussed worldly good (defined as filial piety, loyalty, chastity, respect, and a love of harmony) and transcendent good (exemplified by the basic Buddhist doctrines of the Four Noble Truths, the Twelve-linked Chain of Dependent Origination, and the Six Perfections). He taught the need of merit transfer as well, with the understanding that worldly ethics are "auxiliary practices for rebirth in the Pure Land."

Starting from the same premise, Butsujō wrote in the *Nikka Nembutsu Tōshuku Hen:* "Though a person's physical body is covered with worldly dust, on receiving a religious name that person shall be known as a lay bodhisattva." In terms of the role of religion in supporting the ethical system, Butsujō considered two elements crucial: belief in the law of causation (good leads to good, and evil to evil) and awareness of the impermanence of all things. The secular authorities themselves urged belief in the former, but concerning the latter he made detachment from the present world and fervent prayer for rebirth essential. At the same time he emphasized daily practice. Butsujō spoke of living in the present with an awareness of impermanence:

> If the principle that human life is unpredictable and uncertain is fully realized, then one instantly, without the least effort, becomes a good person. There is no way superior to this for quickly entering the way of Buddhism. To know that one's own body is impermanent is each day to call freshly to mind, as if it were newly experienced, the nature of filial piety and loyalty. Since the present is considered important and there is no hankering after the past, the mind of itself becomes gentle and obedient. Inappropriate desires do not arise, and the mind is braced and refreshed.

In Butsujō's writings, the way that life is lived in the present is identified as the true practice of the *nembutsu* and the means to rebirth in the Pure Land.

THE JI SECT

The Travels of the Yugyō Shōnin

In 1591, when the Tokugawa clan assumed power in the Kantō region, Shōjōkō-ji, the headquarters of the Yugyō school of the Ji sect in Fujisawa, Sagami Province, was officially granted temple lands with an income of one hundred *koku* (eighteen thousand liters) of rice. Later, in 1613, the abbot of Shōjōkō-ji, under his official title Yugyō Shōnin, was awarded the right to requisition fifty post horses per day, giving him the freedom to travel throughout the country. This mark of special favor by the authorities was granted to no other religious leader. The right to requisition horses extended to their grooms as well, so that fifty horses included fifty men to lead them. The magnitude of the privilege, which may have been accorded following an example from earlier times, is indicated by the fact that even daimyō were restricted to fifty horses when traveling along the Tōkaidō, the highway between Edo and Kyoto.

When the Yugyō Shōnin visited the Naitō domain in Iwakitaira, Mutsu Province, in 1744, his retinue consisted of sixty-three priests, one hundred and thirty-six grooms, and seventy horses. This means that the Yugyō Shōnin actually provided twenty horses and eighty-six grooms. It is worth noting that an entourage of this size was deemed necessary despite official notice that the sect should keep its trappings as unostentatious as possible. The train also transported baggage containing treasures of the Ji sect— such objects of faith as a small shrine of the deity Kumano Gongen, scrolls of calligraphic representations of *nembutsu,* and illustrated biographies of the sect's founder, Ippen—as well as utensils for eating and drinking, palanquins, and much other equipment.

Lodging and meals for the Yugyō Shōnin and his train were supposed to be the responsibility of the local domain. The Yugyō Shōnin was served a relatively sumptuous meal consisting of three soups and seven vegetables, though its nature probably varied from place to place. In contrast, priests received two soups and five vegetables, and others in the retinue, one soup and five vegetables. Menials had one soup and three vegetables. Cooking on the day of arrival and the next morning was undertaken by the hosts. When stays were longer, food was prepared by cooks in the Yugyō Shōnin's train. It seems that the domain supplied the food, ranging from grain to vegetables and bean paste.

During the Yugyō Shōnin's ten-day stay in the Naitō domain, twenty bags of white rice, sixty bundles of firewood, thirty-six bags of charcoal, one hundred large carrots, sixty large burdock roots, thirty bunches of taro, and fifty-three bundles of seaweed were provided. In addition, some daimyō personally sent noodles, sugar, and sweet cakes. However, almost half the burden of food supply was shouldered by the Yugyō Shōnin—a burden that fell on the temple where he and his entourage stayed. The supplies received were turned over to the cooks who accompanied him, and they were responsible for preparing the daily meals. Others accompanying the Yugyō Shōnin had charge of the vestments, and still others made prayer beads and crafted scrolls to which were affixed the sacred names (*nembutsu*) written by the Yugyō Shōnin.

The Yugyō Shōnin's itinerary was normally announced to the domains and the branch temples months in advance. On receiving an announcement, the domain would appoint an official to take charge of all the arrangements. That official would consult with the priests who were traveling ahead, settling the itinerary and deciding on lodgings. He would assign various tasks and order the construction and repair of facilities, such as baths and toilets, for the Yugyō Shōnin's party and would even see to the rethatching of roofs when required. Tatami floor mats would have to be changed and sliding doors repapered, and even roads, bridges, and stone walls would be repaired. A daimyō's visit would not have entailed more preparation. Bodyguards were assigned around the clock for the Yugyō Shōnin's protection.

The daimyō usually traveled by the great highways, such as the Tōkaidō and the Nakasendō. The Yugyō Shōnin, however, concerned mainly with propagation, tended to use comparatively minor roads. As a result, he also often had to stay in towns and villages that had no post houses. The so-called Five Highways, frequented by both ordinary travelers and daimyō, were regularly maintained and repaired, but the lesser roads were often neglected. Thus when it was announced that an important party was to travel along a minor route, road repairs, riverbank maintenance, and bridge construction had to be undertaken.

In the fourth month of 1678 the forty-second Yugyō Shōnin, Sonnin

(1625–91), sent word to the lord of Hikone that he intended to travel in Ōmi Province from the post town of Tsuchiyama through the Sasao Pass to the post town of Aichigawa, via Kamagake, Ishihara, Okamoto, and Yōkaichi. Neither daimyō nor Yugyō Shōnin had used that particular route before; consequently, there was no provision for post horses along that route. However, since the Yugyō Shōnin had the shōgun's authorization to use post horses, they had to be provided, and the Hikone daimyō promptly sent horses and grooms to three villages along the route. The peregrinations of the Yugyō Shōnin must have put great strain on the resources of daimyō and local people alike, yet the Yugyō Shōnin played an important role in stimulating communications and the upkeep of local roads.

The Role of the Yugyō Shōnin

In his chronicle of the annual tribute mission to Edo, which he accompanied in 1691 and 1692, Engelbert Kaempfer (1651–1716), a German physician at the Dutch trading post on Dejima in Nagasaki Harbor, wrote:

> At one end of Fujisawa, on the verge of a village, there was a temple, Yugyō-ji, where lived an old gray priest, fourscore years of age, who was a native of Nagasaki. He had spent the greatest part of his life in holy pilgrimages, running up and down the country, and visiting almost all the temples of the Japanese empire. The superstitious vulgar had got such a high notion of his holiness that even in his lifetime they canonized and reverenced him as a great saint and would worship his statue, which he caused to be carved of stone, exceeding in this even Alexander the Great, who was granted no such honors befitting a divinity during his lifetime. Those of his countrymen who were of our retinue did not fail to run thither while we were at dinner, to see and pay their respects to that holy man.

Because he traveled the country widely, the Yugyō Shōnin was known by name to a great many Japanese. He was the focus of a cult that believed he could provide various worldly benefits in this life and guarantee rebirth in the Pure Land after death. Because he traveled so much, however, those who wanted to meet him were often unable to do so. For the people in Kaempfer's party, being able to go to Fujisawa was the chance of a lifetime, because the former Yugyō Shōnin, who had received the title Fujisawa Shōnin, was living there in retirement. Thus the Japanese members of Kaempfer's party used the little time they had to visit Shōjōkō-ji (also called Yugyō-ji) in Fujisawa.

The *Yugyō Engi*, a collection of biographies of the thirteenth, fourteenth, and fifteenth Yugyō Shōnin compiled around 1417, records examples of the supposed immediate efficacy of the *nembutsu* tablets the Yugyō Shōnin distributed. One anecdote concerns the travels of the fifteenth Yugyō Shōnin, Son'e (1364–1429), in the area of the Iruma River in Musashi Province. A mute man known to all the local residents went up to the Yugyō Shōnin, who was distributing *nembutsu* tablets, and silently held out his hand. Not knowing of the man's condition, the Yugyō Shōnin admonished him. "You must recite 'Namu Amida Butsu' before I can give you a tablet." The onlookers waited with trepidation; miraculously, the mute man suddenly began to recite the *nembutsu* loudly. The event was recorded as a joyful instance of immediate benefit gained through the merits of the *nembutsu* tablet. Countless other incidents attest to the wondrous powers of the Yugyō Shōnin and the tablets he distributed.

In the second month of 1744 the Yugyō Shōnin was staying at Jōsai-ji in Iwakitaira, Mutsu Province. People flocked to the temple daily to receive the tablets he was distributing. Surviving records give the following figures: on the first day 925 were distributed; on the second day, 2,950; on the third day, 5,379; on the fourth day, 5,996; on the fifth day, 3,933; on the sixth day, 4,858; on the seventh day, 4,890; on the eighth day, 3,780; on the ninth day, 3,250; and on the tenth day, 339. The first and last figures represent the days of arrival and departure and are therefore small. Over a ten-day period some 36,300 tablets were distributed, an average of 3,630 a day. Such was the extent to which the tablets were valued. The Iwakitaira total is not exceptional; similar quantities of tablets were distributed wherever the Yugyō Shōnin went.

While it is not clear exactly what people expected from the tablets, there were obvious differences according to age, sex, station, and circumstances. The elderly probably looked on the tablets as passports to the Pure Land; pregnant women wanted safe childbirth; and the sick saw the tablets as talismans to relieve illness. The Yugyō Shōnin himself determined which tablet was most suitable for each recipient. According to an entry dated the twenty-fourth day of the second month of 1727 in the *Yugyō Nikkan* (Diaries of the Yugyō Shōnin), travel diaries covering the early eighteenth century to the nineteenth century, he distributed "for the wife, a tablet for the deflection of lightning and a tablet of Aizen [Myōō]; for the lord of the domain, a tablet to protect from arrows; for the six government officers of the highest position, tablets to protect from arrows and tablets of Benten; for their wives, tablets to avert illness; and for the shrine and temple officials, tablets to protect from arrows and tablets of Benten." An entry six months later reads: "For the master, tablets to protect from arrows and tablets of Benten and Daikoku[ten]; for his wife, tablets for protection against lightning and for safe childbirth; for Kyūtarō, tablets to avert harm by arrows and sickness; for Kansuke, a tablet for protection from illness; for the daughter, a tablet of Aizen; and for the son, a tablet for protection against illness." The general public clearly sought the tablets as charms, amulets to protect from harm, and talismans of various deities.

In the instances cited above, the tablet bestowed corresponded with the desires of its recipient. Benten is a deity of wealth; Aizen is a deity of love; and Daikoku is worshiped for the granting of requests. Because Aizen is supposed to be able to bestow good looks, his charm was especially valued by women. Charms for protection against weapons were not inappropriate, even in the peace of the Edo period, for members of the warrior class continued to carry two swords. Amulets for protection against lightning were given mostly to women, perhaps because they tended to fear it more than men. Merchants received amulets of Daikoku. Because he conferred these benefits, the Yugyō Shōnin was worshiped as a living buddha, able to bestow both benefits in this world and salvation in the next.

The Training Facilities of the Ji Sect

For the daimyō, the travels of the Yugyō Shōnin must have been above all a financial burden. Though the Ji-sect temples had to bear a certain portion of the costs, they were able to claim reimbursement from public funds for repairs and improvements. The Yugyō Shōnin's visit was most important to the local priests, for it offered a chance of promotion in rank.

The Ji sect had five ranks: *chashitsuji, jisshitsu, goken, nian,* and *shiin*. The *chashitsuji* (literally, tea steward) were priests who served the Yugyō Shōnin or the Fujisawa Shōnin (the retired Yugyō Shōnin) as personal attendants for a period of four years after ordination. Ji-sect priests next advanced to the rank of *jisshitsu* (literally, ten rooms), followed three years later by *goken* (five houses), when they received the qualification *kashō* (qualified priest who is able to teach) and could wear a purple robe. After a further four years of training, they attained the rank of *nian* (two hermitages), at which point they could visit the imperial palace if invited. Eleven years of training took priests to that point. In the seventeenth or eighteenth year after ordination, they had to write commentaries on the sect's doctrinal works and preach to the common people and answer their questions. Priests advanced to the rank of *shiin* (four temples) when authorized lecturers recognized them as masters of Ji doctrine. Thus those who had achieved the rank of *shiin* were confirmed as authorities on both doctrine and practice.

Since the necessary training was available only at Shōjōkō-ji, at the training center at Shichijō in Kyoto, or under the Yugyō Shōnin as he traveled the country, it was not easy to advance smoothly along this course. Still less could priests in country temples hope for an opportunity to advance. For many, the Yugyō Shōnin's visit to the temple in which they resided was their sole chance. By serving him diligently they might be promoted in the hierarchy of their sect.

Training academies (*gakuryō*) were established at Shōjōkō-ji and at the Shichijō training center in the fifth month of 1748. Before that time the Ji sect had no educational facilities of its own; the only training available to priests was the scanty amount to be had by attaching themselves to the Yugyō Shōnin or some other learned priest as a personal attendant. Because of the lack of an organized, long-term training program, priests who wanted to pursue more advanced doctrinal studies could receive permission to study in one of the academies of the Jōdo sect. Since those academies were the official organs for the training of the Jōdo-sect clergy, however, Ji priests were not allowed to pursue courses of study outside the established syllabus. It was perhaps inevitable that Ji priests who studied at Jōdo academies leaned toward a Jōdo-influenced interpretation of the doctrines of their own sect. As a result of the increasing erosion of an independent understanding of the Ji sect's teachings, many priests advocated the establishment of training facilities within the sect.

Students in the Ji-sect training facilities studied both texts relating specifically to the Ji sect and texts with a broader Buddhist foundation. Among the Ji-sect works were the *Banshū Mondō Shū*, an anthology of Ippen's teachings compiled in 1688, and the *Kiboku Ron*, a collection of Ji teachings by the seventh patriarch, Takuga (1285–1354). The writings of Buddhist masters outside the Ji sect included Hōnen's *Senchaku Hongan Nembutsu Shū* (The Choice of the *Nembutsu* of the Original Vow; 1198); the *Chiao-chieh-lü-i* (Teachings on the Rules and Precepts), by Tao-hsüan (596–667), founder of the Vinaya sect in China; and the *Tendai Shikyō Gi* (An Outline of the Fourfold Teachings of Tendai), compiled by the late-tenth-century Korean scholar Chegwan.

In addition to the Shōjōkō-ji and Shichijō academies, there was a Ji-sect training center known as the Asakusa academy at Nichirin-ji in the Asakusa district of Edo, but the date of its establishment is not known. The third edition of the *Ippen Shōnin Goroku* (Sayings of Ippen Shōnin) was published under its auspices in 1811.

Because these schools were intended to train priests to the sect's specifications, religious practice was stressed as much as academic study. Priests had to spend a period (termed *zaikan*) in service at the head temples, where their performance of the daily round of ceremonies was strictly enforced. Seven years of service—a period that included both study and religious training—enabled a priest to become head priest of a temple. The subjects offered at the training centers appear to have varied from year to year, but the main elements of the doctrines of Ji and of other sects of Japanese Buddhism were to be mastered during the period of residence. If a priest had to take up duties in a temple before the seven years had been completed, ninety days of annual service at a head temple was accepted as an alternative training system.

The Schools of the Ji Sect

Historically the Ji sect recognized twelve schools: the Yugyō school (based at Shōjōkō-ji in Fujisawa), Taima school (based at Muryōkō-ji in Sagami Province), Ikkō school (based at Renge-ji in Ōmi Province), Tendō school (based at Bukkō-ji in Dewa Province), Shijō school (based at Konren-ji in Kyoto), Kokua school (based at Sōrin-ji in Kyoto), Ryōzen school (based at Shōbō-ji in Kyoto), Okutani school (based at Hōgon-ji in Iyo Province), Rokujō school (based at Kankikō-ji in Kyoto), Ichiya school (based at Konkō-ji in Kyoto), Mieidō school (based at Shinzenkō-ji in Kyoto), and Gei school (based at Shinzenkō-ji in Hitachi Province). By the time registers of branch temples were submitted to the shogunate in the middle of the Edo period, the Okutani and Rokujō schools had already disappeared. The Okutani school became extinct during the lifetime of the seventh Yugyō Shōnin, Takuga. It is recorded that when Takuga was traveling in Iyo Province in 1344 the master of the Okutani school applied to join the Yugyō school. The Rokujō school was absorbed into the Yugyō school sometime before the tenth month of 1396. Though the ten remaining schools survived, the *Hommatsu Kakiage Oboe* (Notes on Head and Branch Temples) of 1788 indicates that the Mieidō school possessed only twenty-two temples, the Kokua school eight, the Gei school seven, and the Ichiya school two.

Of the thriving schools, the Ikkō school (together with the Tendō school) had ninety-eight branch temples, the Ryōzen school fifty-five, the Shijō school fifty-two, and the Taima school forty-two. These were not great numbers in comparison with the 564 (plus 217 subtemples) of the Yugyō school, but these schools succeeded in preserving the lineage of teaching on which they had been founded and in maintaining their individuality. In the Edo period the Ikkō-school Renge-ji, Taima-school Muryōkō-ji, Shijō-school Konren-ji, and Ryōzen-school Shōbō-ji were recognized as special temples (*tokubetsu jiin*) and allowed to use the title "grand head temple" (*daihonzan*). Muryōkō-ji in particular claimed to be the chief of all the head temples by virtue of housing the tombs of the sect's patriarchs, maintaining the teachings of Ippen and his successor Shinkyō, and preserving the title Ta Amida Butsu, the title of the active successors of Ippen.

As the Tokugawa shogunate became more securely established, the Ikkō school, founded by Ippen's contemporary Ikkō Shunjō, intensified its declarations that it was not originally of the lineage of Ippen and that it had been forced to merge with the Ji sect because of the similarity of the practices of the two masters. The school brought several suits against Shōjōkō-ji, sometimes claiming independence, sometimes seeking permission to join the Jōdo sect. But the suits were always dismissed on the strength of the branch-temple registers of the Kan'ei era (1624–44). The Yugyō school appears to have attempted to bring the Ikkō school under the jurisdiction of Shōjōkō-ji at one time. The ability of Shōjōkō-ji to block attempts to attain independence or secede accounted for much of the Yugyō school's strength and the number of its branch temples.

The heads of the various schools, Taa Shōnin of the Taima school, Jōa Shōnin of the Shijō school, and Kokua Shōnin of the Kokua school, also engaged in ritual travel and the dispensing of *nembutsu* tablets.

Neither the founder of the Shijō school, Jōa (1276–1341), nor the founder of the Kokua school, Kokua Zuishin (1314–1405), was initially trained in the Ji sect. Jōa first studied Zen under Kakushin (1207–98) at Yura in Kii Province and later, while visiting the grand shrine of Kumano, encountered the *nembutsu* teaching. That encounter was the impetus for his travels around the country to propagate the *nembutsu* teaching. It was by chance that he met Shinkyō in Kazusa Province in 1300 and became his disciple.

Kokua's background was similar. According to the *Kokua Shōnin Den* (A Biography of Kokua Shōnin; early fifteenth century), after studying Tendai doctrine at Enkyō-ji in Harima Province, Kokua made a vow to save all sentient beings by becoming a practitioner of the *nembutsu* and traveling throughout the country. It was at this time that he encountered Takuga and became his disciple. Thus the Ji sect took shape as small groups with similar practices joined forces to form a larger community.

During the Kamakura, Muromachi, and Momoyama periods, the Taima school received much of its support from warriors and landholding farmers. In contrast, the Shijō school established three of its four main temples in port cities and attracted members of the merchant class. The Jōa Shōnin was permitted to distribute tablets only within Kyoto. Finding itself unable to match the training provided by the Yugyō Shōnin, the Shijō training center abandoned doctrinal instruction and developed into a kind of cultural salon, sponsoring poetry meetings, *nembutsu* dances, and even a bathhouse. Because the Yugyō school was dominant south of the Kantō region, the Taima school concentrated on extending its influence in the northeast, in the provinces of Musashi, Shimōsa, and Sagami. It was so effective that by the end of the Edo period small *nembutsu* towers commemorating the direct link between Ippen and the current Taa Shōnin had been erected all over the region by the school's lay groups.

THE ZEN SECTS

The Ōbaku Sect

During the early Edo period, many Chinese fled the upheavals that occurred in their country with the fall of the Ming dynasty in 1644 and settled in Nagasaki and other Japanese port cities, where they were allowed to engage in business by the Tokugawa shogunate. These émigrés built temples in the areas where they lived and invited priests from the continent to teach at their temples.

One famous priest, Tao-che Ch'ao-yüan (d. 1660), arrived in Nagasaki in 1651. He had serious differences with Yin-yüan, a priest who arrived from China shortly after him, however, and returned to China eight years later; consequently, Tao-che is not as well known as Yin-yüan. Yet in the brief time he resided in Japan, many Zen priests congregated under him, including such influential figures in Zen circles of the time as the Sōtō priest Gesshū Sōko (1618–96), who worked to restore the Sōtō sect to the purity of Dōgen's teachings, and the Rinzai priest Bankei Yōtaku (1622–93), who became the abbot of Myōshin-ji.

Three years after Tao-che, Yin-yüan Lung-chi (in Japanese, Ingen Ryūki; 1592–1673) arrived in Japan accompanied by twenty priests and ten artisans. It is popularly believed that the Zen sect that Yin-yüan introduced in Japan, the Ōbaku sect, was an independent Chinese school of Zen; no such sect existed in China, however. The Japanese Ōbaku sect derived from Rinzai Zen. Ōbaku is the Japanese pronunciation of the Chinese Huang-po, the mountain on which the temple Wan-fu-ssu (in Japanese, Mampuku-ji) was located. When Yin-yüan, who had been the abbot of Wan-fu-ssu, established a temple in the Uji district of Yamashiro Province, it was named Ōbakusan Mampuku-ji (Mount Huang-po Wan-fu-ssu), in commemoration of the Chinese site.

Yin-yüan, a famed authority in continental Zen circles, traveled to Japan in 1654 both to fulfill the wishes of a beloved disciple who had drowned on the way there some time before and because of the entreaties of Chinese residents in Nagasaki. He first went to live at the temple Sūfuku-ji in Nagasaki; later, through the mediation of Ryūkei Shōsen (1602–70), who had relinquished the abbacy of Myōshin-ji in Kyoto to become a disciple, he took up residence at Fumon-ji in Tonda, Settsu Province. It was also through Ryūkei that he was cleared of suspicions of being a spy for China. Yin-yüan went on to gain the respect and veneration of the cloistered emperor Gomizunoo (1596–1680), as well as of the court and the military.

As Yin-yüan's fame grew, he came to the attention of the shōgun Tokugawa Ietsuna (1641–80). He traveled to Edo, where he was received in audience. In 1661 he gained the shogunate's permission to construct a temple in the Uji district and was given a land grant for the purpose. That temple, Mampuku-ji, became the center of a surge of continental culture in Japan. The Ming style of Zen that developed there closely followed Chinese models in all aspects, from architecture down to the daily regimen of the priests. From the gates of Mampuku-ji emerged not only eminent Chinese priests, such as Mu-an (in Japanese, Mokuan; 1611–84) and Chi-fei (in Japanese, Sokuhi; 1616–71), but also Japanese Sōtō and Rinzai priests who flocked to study the new continental Zen. These figures exerted a great influence both on their own sects and on the thought of the Edo period in general. They contributed a great deal to the reinvigoration of the religious life of their times.

Besides providing Edo-period Japan with cultural and religious leadership, Yin-yüan and the other Chinese priests who went to Japan took with them artisans and men of letters. Together with continental Zen, new trends in poetry, architecture, crafts, painting, and cooking were transmitted from China to Japan. Because of their superlative calligraphy, Yin-yüan, Mu-an, and Chi-fei were known as the "Three Brushes" of Ōbaku, and their Ōbaku-style calligraphy, with its strong curves and thick strokes, stimulated the stagnant circles of Japanese calligraphy. New types of food and styles of cooking also had a great impact. Yin-yüan is credited with taking string beans to Japan and introducing a Chinese style of vegetarian temple cooking that is called *fusa ryōri* in Japanese.

Mu-an, who had helped establish Mampuku-ji, eventually succeeded Yin-yüan as its abbot. He had earlier founded Zuishō-ji in the Shirogane district of Edo, a temple that prospered and in time rivaled the head temple in influence. Other famous names associated with the Ōbaku sect include Tu-li Hsing-i (in Japanese, Dokuryū Shōeki; 1596–1672), who had taken Chinese medical techniques to Japan, particularly for the treatment of smallpox; Tetsugyū Dōki (1628–1700), who carried out land reclamation projects in Shimōsa Province and made vast amounts of new farmland available; Tetsugen Dōkō (1630–82), who initiated an Ōbaku edition of the Buddhist canon; Ch'ien-ai Hsing-an (in Japanese, Sengai Shōan; 1636–1705), who distributed relief to thousands during the great famine of 1682; and Gekkai Genshō (1675–1763), nicknamed "the Old Tea-seller" (Maisaō), who built a hermitage in the Higashiyama district of Kyoto and helped popularize the drinking of tea for its spiritual and medicinal benefits.

The Sōtō Sect

By the beginning of the Edo period, the Sōtō sect as a religious organization had grown rather large. There was considerable disorder, however, in the formalities of transmission and in the sect's regulations in general, and abuse was rampant in such areas as the direct transmission from master to disciple (*menju*) and the tradition of succession from a single Dharma master (*isshi injō*). For example, to become head of a temple, a priest might arbitrarily change Dharma masters and join the Dharma lineage of that temple. As a result, one person could be heir to two Dharma lines, and teaching and temple lineages became muddled. Inevitably a movement arose to correct these abuses in the sect's traditions and restore the Sōtō sect to the spiritual plane of Dōgen's time. In the vanguard of that restoration movement was Bannan Eishu.

Bannan (1591–1654), who deplored the decadence of Sōtō Zen, lived a hermit's existence. He built huts in various mountainous areas and led the simple life of the Zen ideal. Wishing to bring about a renaissance in the sect, he restored Kōshō-ji, the temple that Dōgen had built in Fuka-kusa, in Kyoto, and moved it to its present site in Uji. Many prominent exponents of the Sōtō restoration movement studied under him.

Suzuki Shōsan (1579–1655), also known as Sekihei Dōnin, was a close associate of Bannan. One of the famous band of warriors known as the Mikawa Bushi, he had fought for the Tokugawa clan at both Sekigahara and Osaka. In his early forties he became a priest and studied Zen, first under Gudō Tōshoku (1577–1661) of the Rinzai sect and then under Bannan. Suzuki taught that in an age of upheaval there was no use in re-treating to a quiet place to practice; warriors in particular had to immerse themselves vigorously in practice, a battle cry constantly on their lips.

Gesshū Sōko (1618–96) of Daijō-ji in Kanazawa, Kaga Province, was one of the central figures in restoring vigor to the religious life of the Sōtō sect. He had inherited Bannan's commitment to religious restoration and had gone to Nagasaki, where he learned of continental Zen from Tao-che Ch'ao-yüan. The spirit of Tao-che's Zen inspired him to redouble his ef-forts to bring about a restoration of the Sōtō sect. To that end, he pro-moted the study of Dōgen's *Shōbō Genzō* (Treasury of the Eye of the True Dharma; 1231–53) and strove to correct errors in the daily rules of the sect. Many of the priests he trained became leaders of the movement. Among them was Manzan Dōhaku.

Manzan (1636–1715), who called himself Fukko Dōnin (Wayfaring Restorer), became Gesshū's successor. Disturbed by the abuses in trans-mission and succession, he set out for Edo with Baihō Jikushin (1633–1707) and others from Kōshō-ji in Uji to appeal to the shogunate to regulate matters so that the transmission would be maintained strictly between a single master and disciple. As a result, regulations favoring the principles of direct and single transmission were issued in the eighth month of 1703. An aspirant who succeeded to a temple received from his or her master a lineage chart (*kechimyaku*) and a diagram outlining Buddhism's fundamen-tal teachings (*kirigami daiji*). (The master had earlier conferred a certificate of transmission of the Dharma, *shisho.*) As a result, long-standing abuses in the system of transmission were eliminated. As the number of Manzan's disciples increased, he came to be regarded as the greatest Sōtō Zen mas-ter of the time.

Gesshū belonged to the Meihō school, centered at Daijō-ji. Another school, the Gasan, also produced a number of prominent priests, notably

Tenkei Denson (1648–1735). Like Gesshū, Tenkei desired a return to the Sōtō sect of Dōgen, and he devoted his life to studying the *Shōbō Genzō* and enhancing the stature of Dōgen's Zen. Because his Zen was unconventional and very strict, some regarded it as heretical. Somewhat later appeared Menzan Zuihō (1683–1769), who also yearned for Dōgen's Zen and devoted his life to its restoration. He traveled far and wide propagating his beliefs, and he also collated Sōtō manuscripts, including that for *Shōbō Genzō*. His painstaking preaching earned him the nickname "Old Woman" Menzan.

The reconsideration of and attention to the study of the *Shōbō Genzō* and other Sōtō works was the result of the movement to restore the Sōtō sect. By the Genroku era (1688–1704) there were about a thousand priests studying at the two Sōtō academies in Edo: Sendanrin at Kichijō-ji, in the Komagome district, and Shishikutsu at Seishō-ji, in the Shiba district. In quality, the Sōtō schools were in no way inferior to the official academy of the shogunate, the Shōheizaka Gakumonjo, which was devoted to Confucian teachings, not Buddhist. As the value of learning became more highly regarded, the number of Sōtō-sect scholars increased, lending further impetus to the sect's renaissance.

Outside the Sōtō-sect mainstream, a number of Sōtō-affiliated priests had adopted a mendicant lifestyle or built hermitages and isolated themselves from society. Rejecting fame and power and keeping themselves far away from the mainstream of the sect, they led a life of wandering and had almost nothing to do with the secular world. They often succeeded in preserving the lofty spirit of the clergy that Dōgen had advocated. In many cases, because of their personalities or deep learning, they caught the attention of people around them and came to exert a considerable influence on society.

One such person was Fūgai Ekun (1568–ca. 1650), nicknamed Ana (Cave) Fūgai. Using a skull for his bowl, he dwelled alone in caves in the mountains or at the seaside of Sagami Province, earning his living by drawing idiosyncratic pictures of the legendary Chinese priest Pu-tai (in Japanese, Hotei) and of Bodhidharma, the first Zen patriarch in China, as the mood struck him. He spent his life as a wandering priest. Tōsui Unkei (1612–83), whose nickname was Kojiki (Beggar) Tōsui, also craved anonymity and roamed the countryside, although he practiced genuine Zen. Wearing rags and letting his beard grow wild, he joined a band of beggars. In their mendicant aspects, at least, the lives of these priests approached the ideals of early Buddhism.

Perhaps the most typical of these wandering sages was Ryōkan (1758–1831), the eldest son of Yamamoto Iori (d. 1795), the village headman of Izumozaki, Echigo Province. From his writings, we learn that Ryōkan did not feel fit to take on his father's work of supervising the affairs of the poverty-stricken local fishermen. He soon concluded that there was no path open to him but Buddhism. Choosing to be ordained, he entered a nearby Sōtō temple, where he received the name Ryōkan.

He then traveled to Entsū-ji in Tamashima, Bitchū Province, where he became a disciple of its abbot, Dainin Kokusen (1723–91), who was of the lineage of Gesshū. Ryōkan stayed with Dainin almost ten years, studying the teachings of Dōgen, whom he deeply admired, and absorbing the essence of Dōgen's Zen. Later he built a small hermitage on Mount Kugami in Echigo, which he called Gogō-an. There he led an austere mendicant life, doubtless influenced by the ideals that Dōgen advocated.

In gentle poetry, Ryōkan expressed his boundless love and his indifference to fame and fortune. He did not preach to people, nor did he lecture on the sutras or teach Zen. Rather, it was his gentle manner that taught people the Buddhist spirit of selflessness. Dearly loved by many, he possessed in his compassion the true strength of Zen.

Though Ryōkan distanced himself from the mainstream of the Sōtō sect, he came closer than most to realizing the basic religious attitude that Dōgen himself had reached. It is significant that Hara Tanzan (1819–92), a luminary in Buddhist studies in the Meiji period (1868–1912), regarded Ryōkan as the greatest figure in Sōtō Zen since Dōgen.

The Rinzai Sect

In the Edo period the Rinzai mainstream consisted of the non-Gozan schools of the Daiō-school lineage. They centered on the Kyoto temples Daitoku-ji and Myōshin-ji. By the end of the sixteenth century, the strict style of Zen that had formerly characterized both temples had degenerated. Myōshin-ji even had no *zazen* hall, which is the heart of any center of Zen practice. It was with the emergence of Takuan of Daitoku-ji and Gudō of Myōshin-ji that signs of a renaissance began to appear.

After studying Zen under a number of masters, Takuan Sōhō (1573–1645) went to practice under Ittō Shoteki (1539–1612) of Yōshun-ji in Sakai, near Osaka, known as the foremost proponent of the strict Daiō-school Zen, and became his disciple. He became the one hundred forty-fourth chief abbot of Daitoku-ji, but after he retired from the position and left the temple, he became concerned about the direction in which Daitoku-ji Zen was heading.

In 1626 the shogunate ordered both Daitoku-ji and Myoshin-ji to obey certain rules that it had laid down regarding, among other things, the appointment of abbots. There was consternation among temple elders because the new regulations required the chief abbot to have had thirty years of Zen practice. Traditionally, the abbots of Daitoku-ji and Myōshin-ji had been appointed by imperial decree.

When the shogunate decided to oppose the installation of Shōin, proposed by Takuan to Emperor Gomizunoo, who approved the appointment, the repercussions were great. Takuan wrote a protest and submitted it to the shogunate, but to no avail. The affair ended with the emperor's abdication and the exile of Takuan and other high-ranking priests to Dewa Province, on the northern tip of Honshu. Takuan later was pardoned and received special favor from the shōgun, Tokugawa Iemitsu (1604–51), and from the renowned master swordsman Yagyū Munenori (1571–1646), becoming their guide in Zen matters. Takuan's treatise on swordsmanship, *Fudōchi Shimmyō Roku* (A Record of the Wonders of Wisdom and Determination; ca. 1635), in which he expounded for Munenori the oneness of the sword and Zen, is well known.

Gudō Tōshoku of the Myōshin-ji school served as the chief abbot of Myōshin-ji three times and was spiritual adviser to both Emperor Gomizunoo and Tokugawa Iemitsu. In the vanguard of a reform movement in his school, he worked hard to revive Myōshin-ji. One of the many fine disciples that he trained was Shidō Bunan (1603–76), who was spiritual adviser to many daimyō and established the temple Tōhoku-in in the Azabu district of Edo. Later Shidō went into retirement at his hermitage, Shidō-an, in Edo's Koishikawa district. Throughout his life, he shunned wealth and honor, never rising above the rank of *shuso*, or senior trainee in a Zen temple. He was a forerunner of Hakuin Ekaku in that he composed easily accessible poetry and prose in the colloquial style and taught Zen to ordinary citizens in a popular way.

Still later, Bankei Yōtaku (1622–93) emerged as a leading figure of the Myōshin-ji school. After studying Zen under Gudō, he went to Nagasaki, where he gained great illumination under Tao-che. Later he joined bands of beggars in Kyoto and Edo. The spiritual adviser of powerful daimyō— such as the Matsura clan of the Hirado domain, just off Kyushu, and Katō Yasuoki, lord of the Ōsu domain, on Shikoku—Bankei established many temples in western Japan. Because he taught that all are endowed with the buddha-nature, which neither is born nor dies (*fushō fumetsu*), his Zen was popularly called Fushō Zen.

He tried to teach Zen in the simplest way possible, doing without the traditional *kōan* teaching device. It was an error, he held, simply to assume the formal sitting position and use a *kōan* in order to gain enlightenment. Rather, everyday life itself in every aspect should be regarded as Zen. Further, Buddhism should be taught to the Japanese people in their own language, since employing abstruse Chinese terminology did not convey the message of Buddhism adequately. In more than forty years as a teacher, he attracted multitudes of followers through his propagating of an easily accessible Zen.

Two men were especially important in the reinvigoration of Rinzai Zen: Kogetsu Zenzai (1667–1751) in the west of Japan and Hakuin Ekaku (1685–1768) in the east. Kogetsu valued learning and practice equally. He taught mainly on Kyushu, where he was based at the temples Daikō-ji in Hyūga Province and Bairin-ji in Chikugo Province. He was invited to serve as the abbot of Myōshin-ji but declined. Many priests received the transmission of the teachings from him, and his influence was felt throughout the nation.

Hakuin entered Shōin-ji in Hara, Suruga Province, as a boy. He later took up the life of a wandering priest and traveled the country visiting various masters. Eventually he settled in Iiyama, Shinano Province, at Shōju-an under the master Dōkyō Etan (1642–1721). Etan, known as Shōju Rōjin, was a master in the Myōshin-ji lineage of Gudō and Shidō, and under him Hakuin absorbed the Myōshin-ji Zen tradition, learning Shidō's simple and popular preaching style, his aloofness from secular power, and his strict Zen.

Hakuin resumed his life of wandering and undertook austerities in mountain hermitages. He returned to Shōin-ji in 1716 as its master, and subsequently his style of Zen gained great acclaim. Soon Shōin-ji became one of the most popular Zen retreats in eastern Japan, open to all. Hakuin expounded on the teachings to many people—men and women, rich and poor, from court nobles and members of the warrior class to peasants and townspeople in neighboring districts—traveling from one end of the country to the other with hardly a pause to rest. He lectured on the sutras of the Zen sect and on the records of the masters. He trained a large number of remarkable disciples, such as Tōrei Enji (1721–92); his biographer, Suiō Genro (1717–89); and Gasan Jitō (1727–97).

Despite his continual ill health from tuberculosis, Hakuin was a vigorous teacher and a prolific writer. Many of his works were written in an easily accessible style using the native Japanese syllabary instead of difficult Chinese ideographic characters, and his tales about the nature of causality were laced with humor. He strove to interpret Zen for his contemporaries. In his *Orategama* (The Embossed Tea-Ceremony Kettle; 1749 and 1751), he spoke of Zen for the daimyō, whose responsibility it was to govern; in the *Komoriuta* (Lullaby) he spoke simply about bringing up a child. The euphony and simplicity of his *Zazen Wasan* (Verses on *Zazen;* 1760) made them easy to recite.

In works like the *Yaemugura* (Trailing Creepers; 1759) he drew on sermons on miraculous virtue, striving for ways to make his teaching comprehensible to ordinary people. In explaining karmic retribution and the nature of causality, he skillfully employed stories of virtuous lay people. Thus in the verse accompanying his drawing of a prawn, he wrote: "If you want to live so long that your back is bent and your beard long, eat in moderation and sleep alone." At first glance many of the verses resemble popular songs, but they convey an incisive Zen message with charm and clarity.

Hakuin stressed both the efficacy of *zazen* and its worldly benefits. He taught that anyone could achieve long life and eternal youth by concentrating the body's energy at the points known as the *tanden* and the *kikai*, situated in the abdomen, below the navel. Even the uneducated and illiterate could warm to his teaching, offered directly without reliance on elaborate reasoning. Few Zen teachers in Japan have been as loved by the everyday citizen as Hakuin.

The popular aspect of Hakuin's Zen was paralleled by an almost inexpressibly difficult side. He was relentless in his own practice and encouraged his disciples in a strict form of Zen. Hakuin's greatness lay in his achievement of harmony between the popular and ascetic elements of Zen practice. Through his efforts to bring about a renaissance in such practice, Rinzai Zen revived dramatically, and today all Rinzai masters trace their lineages to Hakuin.

The Fuke Sect

A minor stream in Edo-period Zen was the Fuke, the sect of the shakuhachi-playing priests known as *komusō*. Fuke Zen considers the T'ang-dynasty Chinese master P'u-hua (ninth century) as its founder and takes its name from the Japanese pronunciation of his name, Fuke. P'u-hua is said to have been an eccentric Zen master who always rang a large bell near people's ears before reciting a Buddhist verse and going on his way. The Fuke sect is believed to have had its beginnings in Japan when the Rinzai master Muhon Kakushin (1207–98) took a P'u-hua priest with him on his return from China in 1254.

Members of the sect did not shave their heads, and they led a life of wandering. Because they wore a straw mat (*komo*) tied to their hips, they were also known as *komosō*. During the fifteenth and sixteenth centuries, they formed into bands and called themselves the Fuke sect, though they were popularly designated *komusō* (priests of nothingness). They adopted no particular sutra as their doctrinal foundation, and wandered about the country begging for donations by playing the shakuhachi, or bamboo flute.

The sect flourished in the Edo period. It divided into several schools, including the Kaka and the Kinzen, and was centered at such temples as Myōan-ji in Kyoto; Reihō-ji in Ōme, Musashi Province; and Ichige-dera in Kogane, Shimōsa Province.

In the Fuke sect there were also ordinary priests with shaven heads, who were called resident priests (*jūjishoku*). The unshaven priests—who wore a straw, basket-shaped hat that covered the face and, instead of priestly garb, a *rakusu* (abbreviated priest's robe) over dark blue or black robes— were called *kansu*. They always carried a shakuhachi and a seal verifying their status. Associated with the *komusō*, though not actually members of the Fuke sect, were wandering ascetics who also played the shakuhachi. They were called *sōen*, or "attached to the sect." At their request, the Fuke sect would sponsor them for specific periods of time, during which they were called *josui*, or "assistant players."

Eventually the sect became a refuge for members of the warrior class who had committed crimes or otherwise run afoul of the authorities, as well as for commoners with a variety of backgrounds and motivations. Many Fuke-sect followers wantonly committed a variety of abuses, and the shogunate repeatedly banned the sect. In the tenth month of 1871, it was finally suppressed, but it survives to the present as *kyōkai* (religious associations), such as Myōan and Fuke.

15. Underground Buddhist Movements in the Edo Period

THE NICHIREN SECT AND THE FUJU FUSE MOVEMENT

The Nichiren Sect Under Japan's Unifiers

After the destruction it sustained in 1536 during the Lotus War of the Temmon (or Tembun) Era, the Nichiren sect reestablished itself in Kyoto. Eventually its power and influence were greater than they had been before the Lotus War. Nevertheless, it was soon assimilated into the system of government that the warlords Oda Nobunaga (1534–82), Toyotomi Hideyoshi (1537–98), and Tokugawa Ieyasu (1542–1616) were fashioning and that culminated in the Tokugawa shogunate.

Nobunaga brought political and military pressure to bear on all sects of Buddhism, the older Nara- and Heian-period sects and the newer Kamakura-period sects alike. He used military force against uprisings by adherents of the Jōdo Shin sect and against Enryaku-ji, the Tendai complex on Mount Hiei; and in 1579, as a means of subduing Nichiren followers, he proclaimed a ban on religious debate (*shūron*).

That ban was a consequence of the Azuchi *shūron*, a government-sponsored religious debate between priests of the Jōdo and Nichiren sects held in the castle town of Azuchi, Ōmi Province, in 1579. The debate was precipitated by challenges by Nichiren followers to local priests of the Jōdo sect. In response to acrimonious claims by both sides, Nobunaga's government ordered a public debate between representatives of the two sects. Shōyo Teian (1539–1615) of Saikō-ji in Azuchi and Reiyo Gyokunen (d. 1586) led the Jōdo speakers, and Nikkō (1532–98) of Chōmyō-ji in Kyoto,

Nittai (d. 1585), and Nichien (1529–1609) spoke for the Nichiren sect. Nobunaga was represented by his nephew Oda Nobuzumi (1555–83), and the commissioners (*bugyō*) Hasegawa Hidekazu (d. 1594), Sugenoya Nagayori (d. 1582), and Hori Kyūtarō (1553–90) were also present. For his own purposes, Nobunaga arranged that the Nichiren sect should be judged the loser.

After the debate, Nikkō, his fellow speakers, and representatives of the Kyoto Nichiren temples were ordered to subscribe to a three-article pledge to be submitted to the commissioners. In it they acknowledged that they had been defeated in debate, agreed that they would never again attack the religious teachings of another sect, and affirmed that they were grateful that the Nichiren sect had been spared destruction. Nikkō, Nittai, and Nichien had to pledge further that they would not object to punishment of the entire sect if they themselves should break the oath. In addition, Nobunaga imposed stiff fines on those temples whose priests had participated in the debate.

Doctrinal debate was an important means of propagation for the Nichiren sect. It was an integral element of *shakubuku*, or conversion by aggressive refutation of other beliefs, a practice of major importance to the sect. With debate banned, *shakubuku* could no longer be employed and priests were forced to use an alternative method, *shōju*, or measured guidance leading to conversion without vigorous refutation. The Nichiren sect was in retreat, and political pressure led it to appease the government.

Toyotomi Hideyoshi continued Nobunaga's violence toward religious organizations. In 1585 his army destroyed Negoro-ji, Kii Province, and subjugated its warrior-priests. Later he suppressed the Jōdo Shin *ikkō ikki* congregations in the Saiga district of Kii and disarmed Tōnomine-dera in Sakurai. His "sword hunt" (*katana-gari*) of 1588 stripped both farmers and temples of their weapons, effectively separating the peasant and warrior classes for the first time. The metal from the swords was used to make nails and cramp irons for the construction of the Great Buddha Hall of the Tendai-sect Hōkō-ji in Kyoto. The question of attendance at the dedication ceremonies for this building in 1595 caused controversy within the Nichiren sect.

Nevertheless, Hideyoshi's policy toward Buddhism was conciliatory to a degree. He contributed to the rebuilding of a number of temples and in 1594 required that temple regulations be formulated and strictly observed. In 1585 he had revoked the three-article pledge imposed on the Nichiren sect by Nobunaga. Even so, when Kyoto was partially restored to the plan of the ancient capital under Hideyoshi's sponsorship, Nichiren temples found themselves moved from the heart of the city to its outskirts, where they remain to this day.

Tokugawa Ieyasu brought the temples under his control both by issuing temple regulations to all sects and by encouraging the clergy to turn away from secular concerns and concentrate on doctrinal study. While all-embracing codes were issued to other sects, at first only one set of regulations was issued to the Nichiren sect, and they applied to but a single temple, Kuon-ji on Mount Minobu, Kai Province, far to the east of Kyoto. Yet Ieyasu involved himself in internecine controversies of the Nichiren sect and in 1600 exiled Nichiō (1565–1630), the leader of the sect's most uncompromising group, to the island of Tsushima, north of Kyushu, as a disruptive force. Later, when Nichikyō (1560–1620) of the Myōman-ji subsect criticized the Jōdo sect and belittled the efficacy of the *nembutsu*, Ieyasu punished him and his fellow priests in 1609 by having their ears and noses cut off. At the same time a pledge was extracted from the Nichiren-sect Minobu school, Ikegami school (based in Kamakura), and temples in Kyoto that they would not make the *nembutsu* the subject of religious debate. Nichion (1572–1642) of the Minobu school opposed the order, but the other representatives complied.

Such government actions typify the coercion of the Nichiren sect at the beginning of the seventeenth century in attempts to force the sect to temper its fundamental practices of *shakubuku* and religious debate and, an issue of growing importance, the refusal of certain Nichiren-sect followers to receive anything from members of others sects. Under Nichiō's leadership this group of followers evolved into the Fuju Fuse (No Receiving and No Giving) faction; the sect's more conciliatory group was known as the Ju (Receiving) faction.

At this time, the Nichiren-sect schools from the Kyoto area made conspicuous advances into the Kantō region, where the most influential Nichiren-sect temples were Hokekyō-ji in Nakayama, Shimōsa Province, and Kuon-ji on Mount Minobu. In 1594 Nikkō of Chōmyō-ji in Kyoto brought a suit against Nichiden (1528–92), the abbot of Hokekyō-ji, claiming that he was not qualified to act as a *kanzu*, or abbot of a main temple. As a result, three Nakayama-school temples in the Kinai region—Hompō-ji and Chōmyō-ji in Kyoto and Myōkoku-ji in Sakai—were instructed to appoint the Hokekyō-ji abbot in rotation, and Nikkō was the first abbot so appointed. Subsequently the order of rotation was maintained, despite occasional dissension between the abbot and the temple officials and branch temples.

In 1603 Kuon-ji, the center of the Minobu school, invited Nichiken (1560–1635) of Homman-ji in Kyoto to be abbot and transferred to him the absolute right to select successive abbots. Through this act, the concept of the integrity of lineage was abandoned. Nichiō's Fuju Fuse–faction followers denounced Minobu as a betrayer of the Buddhist Law for appointing as abbot a follower of the rival Ju faction. Nichiken answered the challenge by bringing a suit against Nichiju (1574–1631) and others of Ikegami Hommon-ji in Edo and, with the support of the shogunate, succeeded in exerting pressure on them. Thereafter Nichiken worked to have Kuon-ji acknowledged as head of all temples associated with the Ju faction.

By the mid-sixteenth century the Nichiren sect, like other sects, tended to emphasize doctrinal study. In 1568 at Myōkoku-ji in Sakai, Nikkō established an academy, where he lectured on the three most important texts of T'ien-t'ai Buddhism, the *Fa-hua-hsüan-i* (The Profound Meaning of the Lotus Sutra; in Japanese, *Hokke-gengi*), *Fa-hua-wen-chü* (Textual Commentary on the Lotus Sutra; in Japanese, *Hokke-mongu*), and *Mo-ho-chih-kuan* (Great Concentration and Insight; in Japanese, *Makashikan*). The Iidaka Academy in Shimōsa Province was set up by Nittō (d. 1579) and Nisshō (1553–95), and the Matsugazaki Academy in Kyoto was founded by Nisshō. By the 1660s, a large number of Nichiren-sect academies for the training of priests had been established in both the Kantō region and the Kyoto area. Tendai doctrine was predominant in studies at these academies.

To meet the needs of students, publishing, employing the new technology of movable type, burgeoned in the first half of the seventeenth century. Honkoku-ji and Yōbō-ji in Kyoto published various texts, among which editions of Nichiren's surviving works stood out. Numerous editions of Nichiren's works appeared: the Keichō-era (1596–1615) edition issued by Nichiken and Nichion of Kuon-ji, the Genna-era (1615–24) edition of Honkoku-ji, and two Kan'ei-era (1624–44) editions. Both of the Kan'ei-era editions were published by booksellers and were printed from wood blocks rather than movable type. The Kan'ei-era editions marked the withdrawal of the temples from active publishing. In addition, illustrated biographies of Nichiren, including the *Nichiren Shōnin Chūgasan* (A Biography of Nichiren in Words and Pictures) and *Renkōsatta Ryakuden* (A Biographical Sketch of the Bodhisattva Nichiren; 1566) compiled by Nisshū (1532–92), were published. The former was originally published by Nitchō (1441–1510) in Chinese ideographic characters, but later editions were published in the more accessible mixture of Chinese characters and the Japanese syllabary. As published works proliferated, Nichiren's followers, both priests and the laity, were provided with material with which to take a fresh look at his traditional image.

The Fuju Fuse Movement

The Fuju Fuse movement arose out of Nichiō's refusal to attend the dedication service for the Great Buddha of Hōkō-ji in the Higashiyama district of Kyoto, held in 1595 under Toyotomi Hideyoshi's sponsorship. The ostensible purpose of the service, to be conducted by an assembly of one thousand priests, was to offer prayers for the repose of Hideyoshi's ancestors. In building the lavish Great Buddha Hall, however, Hideyoshi seems also to have fulfilled a long-standing plan to publicly display his power in order to awe both the imperial court in Kyoto and the temples and shrines of the region.

With his sword hunt in 1588, Hideyoshi hoped to simultaneously disarm the peasantry, focus attention on his rule through a national project on a grand scale, and gain religious merit. No trace of his Great Buddha remains today. The site of the precincts of what had been a spectacular complex lies in the vicinity of the present Toyokuni Shrine. Only the great bell survives. In 1588 a wooden buddha was built to a height of 19.8 meters, and large stones were brought from all over the country to build a stone wall around it. By 1591 a hall to house the Great Buddha had risen to a height of 66 meters, and ancillary structures, such as surrounding corridors and a gate housing images of two guardian deities, were completed. When finished in 1595, the Great Buddha was about two meters taller than the Great Buddha at Tōdai-ji in Nara, and the hall that housed the image was about twenty-four meters taller than the Great Buddha Hall at Tōdai-ji.

Summonses were issued requiring the attendance of one hundred priests from each of ten Buddhist sects at the dedication ceremony on the tenth day of the ninth month of 1595—and at the monthly memorial services for Hideyoshi's ancestors at the Great Buddha Hall of Hōkō-ji—to be followed by the offering of a meal to the priests. There had long been a tradition of holding *sensō kuyō*, or memorial services, attended by one thousand priests. At these services the priests would perform an abbreviated (*tendoku*) reading of the *Daihannya-kyō* (Great Perfection of Wisdom Sutra) and then be offered a meal. Such services were conducted from time to time as national endeavors sponsored by the imperial family or powerful landholders, and the merit accrued by the sponsor was believed to be very great.

Priests from the sixteen Nichiren head temples in Kyoto gathered at Honkoku-ji to discuss whether to attend as commanded. They decided that the sect would participate once, since that seemed unavoidable and disobedience might lead to its temples' destruction, but that the sect would thereafter refuse, having explained to Hideyoshi the principle of *fuju fuse*—neither receiving from nor giving to those who were not believers in the Lotus Sutra. Nichiō alone strongly objected to the compromise as being contrary to the basic tenets of the sect handed down from the time of Nichiren, and he flatly refused to have any part in the proceedings. He maintained that the principle, once violated, would not survive.

The priests of all Nichiren factions except Nichiō's attended the service under the conditions they had devised for themselves. As Nichiō had prophesied, however, they had to continue to take part in the monthly memorial services and accept what Nichiō said were tainted donations. The Fuju Fuse movement arose out of Nichiō's refusal to compromise on that principle. He continued to stress the orthodoxy of his action, saying that he was upholding a doctrine central to the teachings of the Nichiren sect.

Information about other sects' attendance at the dedication ceremony is found in the diary of Gien (1558–1626), the abbot of the Shingon temple Tō-ji in Kyoto. "First was Shingon, second Tendai, third Ritsu, fourth Zen, fifth Jōdo, sixth Nichiren, seventh Ji, and eighth Ikkō [Jōdo Shin]." The order of precedence caused controversy, especially since the Nichiren sect's position was inferior to that of its traditional enemy, the Jōdo sect. To Nichiō in particular that was unforgivable.

Nichiō was not the only priest to refuse Hideyoshi's summons. Of the Nara schools Gien says: "Hossō, Sanron, and Kegon received summons to attend but sent their regrets because of the distance involved." Further, on the twenty-ninth day of the fifth month of 1596, he writes: "Because of today's heavy rain, attendance was unpardonably small. Only sixty or seventy [Shingon] priests went. The numbers will have to be strictly enforced next month." Similar entries concerning Shingon participation are scattered through the diary. The number of Shingon priests the diary notes as attending the monthly service reveals that Shingon had great difficulty in assembling the requisite number. No doubt the same could be said of the other sects, as well. In reality the thousand-priest services were attended by perhaps five or six hundred. There was even one service, in the eighth month of 1598, that had a scant two hundred priests.

The records suggest that the sponsors put no particular pressure on the sects to participate, and it seems safe to say that at that time refusal to participate did not automatically lead to suppression and punishment. The pressure applied later to the Fuju Fuse faction was not apparent at this stage. No penalty was imposed on the three Nara sects for not attending, nor on the sects that could not send sufficient numbers. The Fuju Fuse faction's refusal to attend was an internal problem for the Nichiren sect rather than a matter of concern to the government of Hideyoshi. The question of participation was used as the rationale for isolating the conservatives, Nichiō's faction. However much Nichiō maintained the contrary in his writings, Hideyoshi was not particularly concerned about the existence of Nichiō's movement.

Nichiō and the Myōkaku-ji Community

The existence of Nichiō's Fuju Fuse faction was a great problem for the Nichiren sect. From a doctrinal viewpoint, if Nichiō's assertion went unchallenged, the sect's other factions would be branded as heretical. In maintaining his stance and attacking those who advocated compromise with nonbelievers, Nichiō always returned to the issue of attendance at the Hōkō-ji services and emphasized his own orthodoxy in contrast to the stance of those who attended. In an attempt to settle the question, a debate between the opposing factions of the Nichiren sect was held at Osaka Castle.

The debate, held at the insistence of the Ju faction, took place on the twentieth day of the eleventh month of 1599 in the presence of Tokugawa Ieyasu. Nichiō, who had left the abbacy of Myōkaku-ji and was forced to participate against his wishes, represented the Fuju Fuse faction against Nisshō (1542–1622) of Myōken-ji in Kyoto and Nittō (1549–1603) of Myōkoku-ji in Sakai. The central issue was attendance at Hōkō-ji services.

Nichiō maintained that he had consistently upheld the principle of neither receiving from nor giving to those who did not believe in the Lotus Sutra. Nichiren himself, he said, had defied the authorities on pain of exile. If it was necessary to defy authority and be persecuted in order to establish Buddhism, as Nichiren had taught, then Nichiō was doing no more than following the teachings of his school's founder. Nisshō and Nittō responded by asserting that propagating the Buddha's Law did not necessitate defiance of the authorities; rather, Buddhism and the law of the country were like the two wheels of a cart. The Buddha taught that his Law was to exist in alliance with secular rule and that Buddhism was to be propounded according to the wishes of the ruler of the country. Since representatives of the majority of Nichiren-sect priests had been attending monthly memorial services at Hōkō-ji during the four years since 1595, the view of Nisshō and Nittō clearly represented the new orthodoxy of the sect. As was expected, the Ju faction was judged the victor in the debate. In the following year, 1600, Nichiō was exiled to the island of Tsushima, where he remained until 1612, when he was pardoned.

After the debate, the Ju faction's influence within the Nichiren sect grew, and, with what amounted to Ieyasu's sanction, it gained stability and strength. Nevertheless, those who interpreted the teachings of Nichiren strictly were deeply troubled, and Nichiō's exile caused much agitation.

After his release, Nichiō worked actively for reform in the Nichiren sect and set about strengthening the Fuju Fuse faction, based at Myōkaku-ji. In 1616 he wrote what can be considered the vade mecum of the Fuju Fuse faction, the *Shūgi Seihō Ron* (On the Regulation of Our Sect's Doctrine). In the eleventh month of 1623 he issued the *Myōkaku-ji Hatto Jōjō* and *Myōkaku-ji Hosshiki*, regulations based on Nichiren's teachings, to govern the Fuju Fuse faction. The first clause of the *Myōkaku-ji Hatto Jōjō* reads:

> Since it is important to uphold the law of the school [that is, the principle of *fuju fuse*, neither receiving nor giving] the nine-clause code [of Myōkaku-ji] has been set forth in detail; of greatest importance are the first three clauses. It is forbidden [for believers in the Lotus Sutra] to visit the temples and shrines of those who slander the Law [that is, criticize the Lotus Sutra]. It is forbidden [for Lotus believers] to give to those who slander the Law. It is forbidden [for Lotus believers] to accept offerings from those who slander the Law. These three clauses are the essence of regulations concerning the doctrine [of the Fuju Fuse faction].

Plainly, these regulations severely restricted contact with anyone not a Lotus believer of the Fuju Fuse faction. The first three clauses were the principal rules that the Myōkaku-ji faction required its branch temples and followers to observe. Myōkaku-ji priests were told that they must always be ready to give up their lives for their Lotus faith. Lay people were told: "If the husband is a believer but not the wife, the wife will be subject to *shakubuku* [forceful attempts at conversion] for three years. If she does not convert, both husband and wife will be expelled [from the community of believers]."

The nature of the Myōkaku-ji group is clearly revealed in its insistence on strict observance of these three clauses by its branch temples and lay believers as well as in its teachings to priests and laity alike. That efforts were made to avoid dispute and dissension within the Nichiren sect can be inferred from the injunction in the Myōkaku-ji code that "there should be no loose talk to outsiders regarding the errors of priests." The inviolability of the principle of *fuju fuse* was firmly stressed. Persecution by secular authorities and the destruction of temple properties were not reasons to abandon one's convictions. "Even if there is religious persecution and the temples are demolished, no injury should be done to the Law. Buildings destroyed can be built again with the support of lay followers, but injuries done to the Law will fester for all eternity."

As a result of Nichiō's exile, the Fuju Fuse faction strove to present its teachings more clearly, and it worked to establish both control over its priests and solidarity among its supporters. The Fuju Fuse movement's activities thereafter were governed by the three chief principles of the Myōkaku-ji regulations.

Conflict Between the Ju and Fuju Fuse Factions

With Nichiō's reorganization of the Fuju Fuse faction at Myōkaku-ji, Kuon-ji on Mount Minobu bore the brunt of his criticism. A passage in his *Shūgi Seihō Ron* reads: "Now on Mount Minobu, although monastery buildings range roof to roof and Buddha images stand side by side, in the time of Nichiken [1560–1635] the intention of our founder in establishing the sect has been frustrated, and heresy has been persistently encouraged. Is this not the extinction of the Law of the Buddha, the destruction of the sect [of Nichiren]? A pitiful thing. A pitiful thing." The *Shūgi Seihō Ron* is devoted almost entirely to condemning the Ju faction. But Minobu did not remain silent. Its side of the dispute was presented in such works as the *Haō Ki* (Against Nichiō; 1616), by Nissen (1586–1648) of Kuon-ji.

Eventually, on the sixteenth day of the second month of 1629, Nissen appealed to the shogunate to suppress Nichiō, Nichiju (the abbot of Ikegami Hommon-ji), and the entire Fuju Fuse faction. Nissen submitted three reasons for his appeal. First, he held that it was absurd for Nichiō to persist with his unfounded accusations against the Ju faction for attending the ceremonies at Hōkō-ji; second, it was outrageous that Nichiō encouraged believers not to hold memorial services at Minobu, saying that it was a place where the Law was defiled and threatening them with rebirth in the lowest hell if they visited there; and third, though Nichiō and Nichiju had made a point of refusing donations from the secular authorities, Nichiō had in fact accepted a donation of land from a daimyō.

In reply, on the twenty-first day of the second month of 1630 Nichiju submitted a report to the office of the *jisha bugyō*, or temple and shrine commissioners, heatedly denying the accusations. He explained that it was essential for Nichiren followers to observe the principle of *fuju fuse* because it had been a rule of the sect since the time of Nichiren. Further, he insisted that in the light of the sect's doctrine Minobu was clearly violating the Law and thus it was natural for the followers of the Fuju Fuse faction to criticize Minobu. He also denied the contention that the temple lands in question were a donation.

The Minobu group was not swayed and on the day the report was submitted confronted the Fuju Fuse faction and designated a place to settle the argument. The chief debaters, Nissen of Mount Minobu and Nichiju of Ikegami Hommon-ji, argued heatedly for some two hours. That meeting became popularly known as the Minobu-Ikegami Debate. There were six debaters on each side, all leading priests of the Nichiren sect. Sakai Tadayo (1572–1636), Doi Toshikatsu (1573–1644), Shimada Toshimasa (1576–1642), Hayashi Razan (1583–1657), and Eiki Shinchō represented the shogunate. The judges were the Rinzai priest Ishin Sūden (1569–1633) and Tenkai (d. 1643) and four other Tendai priests. Debate centered on two questions: Why did Nichiō revive the outlawed Fuju Fuse faction? Was temple land to be regarded as a donation? In answer to the first question, Nichiju held that the restoration of the Fuju Fuse faction was a natural consequence because Ieyasu probably repented his folly and pardoned Nichiō. To the second, he said: "[The granting of] temple land is [an expression of] the gratitude and benevolence of the civil government. The making of a donation is an act of faith in Buddhism; it is creating merit. In principle the two are quite different." Thus the distinction between granting land and making an offering lay in whether the act was prompted by faith. Mount Minobu took an entirely different view.

Nichiju's argument did not win the shogunate's approval, and he was exiled to the village of Iida in Shinano Province, where he died the following year, 1631, at the age of fifty-seven. Twenty days before the judgment

was announced, Nichiō had died in Kyoto at the age of sixty-five. Nevertheless, he was again sentenced to exile on Tsushima, this time posthumously.

In 1631 the shogunate ordered the main temples of all sects to submit
lists of their branch temples. With the shogunate's sanction, Kuon-ji ordered all Nichiren-sect temples to submit branch-temple registers. Those
that agreed to do so were accepting de facto governance by Kuon-ji, and
they thus significantly strengthened Kuon-ji's control of branch temples.
Many of the branch temples of the two leading temples of the Fuju Fuse
faction—Hommon-ji in Ikegami and Myōkaku-ji in Kyoto—refused to
change their allegiance, however. Remaining firmly loyal were 134 of the
165 branch temples of Hommon-ji and eighty-four of the one hundred
affiliated with Myōkaku-ji. Their allegiance demonstrated the vitality of
the Fuju Fuse faction, while their continued existence was striking evidence of the leniency of the shogunate's regulation of Buddhism. Despite
Kuon-ji's insistence, the shogunate seems not yet to have been particularly
worried by the Fuju Fuse faction.

The Minobu group had secured a foothold in gaining control of the
sect as a whole by complying with the shogunate's orders to compile
branch-temple registers and thus establishing the head- and branch-temple
system in the Nichiren sect. As Minobu continued to appeal to the shogunate on the subject of the Fuju Fuse faction, its position as the head of the
entire sect gradually became confirmed.

The Kambun Suppression

During the Kambun era (1661–73), Mount Minobu attacked the Fuju
Fuse faction more vigorously, and the shogunate was finally prevailed on
to act. On the eighteenth day of the third month of 1661, Mount Minobu
petitioned the commissioner of temples and shrines to prosecute the Fuju
Fuse faction. When the shogunate took no action, a second petition followed on the ninth day of the second month of 1663. The second petition, which stresses that requests to restrict the Fuju Fuse faction had
been made in the past, reads in part:

Since that time the Fuju Fuse faction continued its activities as before
and did not send even one person to participate in the funeral ceremonies of the late shōgun Tokugawa Iemitsu in the fourth month of
1651. For this reason, Minobu has continually asked in the twelve years
since the shōgun Iemitsu's death that strong pressure be brought to

bear on the faction that did not attend the funeral ceremonies. The matter has not been taken up, however. Because this year marks the thirteenth annual memorial service for Iemitsu, it would be truly appreciated if that faction could be punished, as it has been by past shōguns.

Three months later, on the ninth day of the fifth month, Mount Minobu wrote to the commissioner of temples and shrines, Inoue Masatoshi, saying that Mount Minobu was ready at any time to confront the Fuju Fuse faction. Two months later, on the ninth day of the seventh month, a nine-clause statement was sent to various high officials, including the senior councilor Sakai Tadakiyo (1624–81) and Inaba Masatoshi. It was pointed out that three temples—Hondo-ji in Hiraga, Tanjō-ji in Kominato, and Hokke-ji in Himon'ya—would not obey the orders of Minobu, that the Fuju Fuse faction had gained in strength, and that the shōgun Ietsuna was much more lenient with the faction than his three predecessors had been. Suppression was urged. On the last day of the ninth month, a ten-clause statement was submitted to Inoue. In view of Minobu's persistence, the shogunate was at last compelled to act.

In the seventh month of 1665, the shogunate informed all Buddhist sects of its regulations governing sects and temples (the *Shoshū Jiin Hatto*). The first clause of these regulations, a warning against internal disputes, stated: "There shall be no breaking of the laws of the sects; those who do so must be brought to trial." The rules appended to the second clause forbade the establishment of new sects: "No new doctrine, no heterodox teachings, will be permitted." Both provisions were probably directed at the Fuju Fuse faction.

In the eleventh month of the same year, the shogunate banned the Nichiren lay associations that had burgeoned in the towns and ordered Nichiren-sect temples to acknowledge that they accepted temple lands as donations to Buddhism in the customary sense. Many temples of the Fuju Fuse faction, however, refused to obey this order. As a consequence, those temples considered leaders of the faction were punished. On the third day of the twelfth month, Nichijutsu (1611–81) of Hondo-ji in Hiraga, Shimōsa Province, and Nichikan (d. 1673) of Hōren-ji in Ōno, Shimōsa Province, were placed in the custody of Datè Munezumi of the Yoshida domain in Iyo Province, on Shikoku; while Nichigyō (1620–84) of Myōkaku-ji in Okitsu, Kazusa Province, and Nichiryō (1634–88) of Hōmyō-ji in Zōshigaya, Musashi Province, were placed in the custody of Kyōgoku

Takatoyo of the Marugame domain in Sanuki Province, on Shikoku. On the eighth day of the same month, the two Kyoto temples Myōman-ji and Jōgyō-ji were put under the supervision of Itō Sukezane of the Obi domain in Hyūga Province, on Kyushu.

On the tenth day of the twelfth month of 1665, temple lands were granted to several temples on condition that they abandon allegiance to the Fuju Fuse faction. These temples included Kannō-ji and Hokke-ji in Musashi Province, Tanjō-ji and Kyōnin-ji in Awa Province, Myōnō-ji in Sagami Province, and Jusen-ji in Kazusa Province. It is probable that this stratagem was originally conceived by Mount Minobu and suggested to the shogunate as a means of ensuring changes of allegiance.

On the twenty-second day of the second month of 1667, Mount Minobu put further pressure on the Fuju Fuse faction by submitting to the shogunate a list of temples affiliated with the faction and urging their punishment. A copy of this register survives at Kuon-ji, on Mount Minobu. Its three volumes—the *Fuju Fuse Jiin Chō* (The Register of Fuju Fuse Temples), *Fuju Fuse no Chō: Ji An Oboe* (The Fuju Fuse Register: Memorandum Concerning Temples and Hermitages), and *Ikegami Matsuji Fuju Fuse Chō* (The Fuju Fuse Register of Branch Temples of Ikegami)—mention a total of 439 temples adhering to the *fuju fuse* doctrine. The vast majority of these temples were in the Kantō region, in the provinces of Musashi, Sagami, and Shimōsa. Of their number, 243, or 55.4 percent, were in Edo, Musashi Province. Notes in the register give fragmentary accounts of the punishments meted out to temples of the Fuju Fuse faction. Temples that transferred their allegiance are also noted. An afterword contains expressions of gratitude to the shogunate for acceding to Mount Minobu's urging and inflicting punishment on temples affiliated with the Fuju Fuse faction.

In the fourth month of 1669, temples associated with the Fuju Fuse faction were forbidden to certify the religious affiliation of parishioners under the *terauke* system. Deprived first of their land and then of their parishioners, the temples found themselves with no financial base. Clearly the shogunate used economic pressure to persuade them to abandon their position.

The influence of the shogunate's policy toward the Fuju Fuse faction extended to the outlying feudal domains. When temples in the Okayama domain, Bizen Province, were reorganized in 1666, the Fuju Fuse faction was subjected to severe pressure. According to a letter submitted by the Okayama domain to the shogunate's senior councilor, Sakai Tadakiyo, in the fourth month of 1667, of the 1,044 temples in the domain, 563 (54 percent) were demolished. Of these, 313 (56 percent), inhabited by 585 priests, were affiliated with the Fuju Fuse faction. The germ of the reorganization seems to have been an attempt by the daimyō of Okayama, Ikeda Mitsumasa (1609–82), to subjugate the Fuju Fuse faction, which was firmly rooted in the region. About one-third of all temples affiliated with the Fuju Fuse faction were concentrated there, and the teachings of the group had continued to diffuse despite the shogunate's bans.

Another domain that took the lead in exerting pressure on temples was Mito, Hitachi Province. Its daimyō, Tokugawa Mitsukuni (1628–1700), abolished 1,098 (46 percent) of the domain's 2,377 temples, although he focused on the esoteric groups related to Tendai, Shingon, and Shugendō rather than the Fuju Fuse temples. In all probability, this reflects the paucity of Fuju Fuse–affiliated temples in the domain. There were a few, however, and they were forced to transfer allegiance to a different main temple or be razed.

The shogunate initially effected its policy governing religious orthodoxy at the urging of Mount Minobu. This policy, extended to the domains, resulted in the regulation of the beliefs of the people across the land. Although the policy originally addressed an internal, intrasectarian controversy of the Nichiren sect, it ultimately weakened the entire sect.

Persecution

The policy of suppression of the Fuju Fuse faction pursued by the shogunate and the domains made it increasingly difficult for the faction to publicly propagate its teachings. Harsh pressure was brought to bear on unauthorized religious activity in 1718 and 1794 through the persecution of Fuju Fuse congregations in Namekawa, Kazusa Province, and in Shimōsa Province.

The Namekawa Persecution occurred in the sixth month of 1718. The authorities arrested eleven priests and thirty-two lay people—adherents and supporters of the Fuju Fuse faction. Of the forty-three arrested, fourteen were imprisoned (of whom twelve died while incarcerated), five were exiled, six banished, three deprived of their stipends, fourteen pardoned, and one exonerated.

The Shimōsa Persecution took place in the ninth month of 1794, after a priest had provided the authorities with information about the local Fuju Fuse faction. Seventy-two people were punished. Eighteen died in prison, five were exiled to the countryside, one was placed under house arrest, two were forbidden to come within ten *ri* (about forty kilometers) of Edo, ten were fined, fifteen were deprived of office, nine received severe rebukes, and twelve received mild rebukes. A report made at the time reads: "All the priests submitted letters of protest, and as a result eleven were martyred . . . as were seven lay people who had given them lodging. As the saying goes, 'Our bodies are light but the Law is heavy.' They sacrificed their bodies to uphold the Law." The report stressed that to the end, neither the priests nor the lay followers renounced their belief in the forceful method of conversion known as *shakubuku*. The local daimyō probably intended the persecution as a lesson to discourage people from adopting ideas associated with the Fuju Fuse faction, and the severe punishments inflicted on both clergy and laity were designed to eradicate the faction and its adherents. Those who were lightly punished were mainly village officials who were responsible for the community as a whole and had to shoulder the blame officially. It may be supposed that the heavier punishments fell on members of the Fuju Fuse faction, and the lighter on those outside it but somehow involved or officially responsible.

Suppression, however, not only drove the faction underground but also made it more resolute. As the Fuju Fuse faction lost its centers for doctrinal education, it placed increasing emphasis on ritual.

The Secret Daimoku Confraternities

In 1609 Nichikyō (1560–1620), of the Kyoto Myōman-ji subsect and the lineage of Nichijū (1314–92), criticized the Jōdo sect fiercely. He was arrested and his nose and ears were cut off. Exiled to various sites around the country afterward, he used the opportunity to teach people the doctrines of Nichiren in the hope that they would be preserved. Much earlier Nittai (1432–1506), also of Nichijū's lineage, had gained the support of the Sakai clan, lords of Toke, Kazusa Province. As a result, the whole area had been converted to the Lotus faith through the local lord's influence. Going to Toke, Nichikyō established Hōfun-ji at Higashi Yokokawa as a center for such religious practices as chanting the Lotus Sutra and reciting the *daimoku*, or sacred title of the sutra. This was the origin of what became the secret *daimoku* confraternities.

After Nichikyō's death in 1620, Nichiyō (d. 1628), a disciple based at Hōfun-ji, engaged in proselytizing. His uncompromising orthodoxy drew a reaction from the priests of the various temples of the Nichijū lineage in Kazusa; and in response to their complaint, Nichiyō, Raichō, and three lay followers were arrested in 1627. Hōfun-ji was razed by order of the shogunate's representative in Ōami.

In 1634 Nichikyō's disciple Nichijō (d. 1635) built Hongaku-ji in Noda, Shimōsa Province, and introduced the people of Noda to Nichikyō's practice of reciting the *daimoku* five million times. He incurred the enmity of the other local temples, and a complaint was lodged against him. Nichijō and eight others, both clergy and laity (among them the wives of male lay followers), were taken to Edo under guard, where they were sentenced to crucifixion, which took place later at Toke. Hongaku-ji was burned to the ground by order of the shōgun's representative.

Somewhat earlier Nisshō (d. 1674), a disciple in the lineage of Nichikyō, moved from Myōhō-ji in Aizu, Iwashiro Province, to Kazusa Province and built a temple called Hōfun-ji in Minami Yokokawa. A complaint was lodged against him in 1660, and he was exiled to the island of Miyakejima in the Pacific Ocean, about eighty kilometers from the Izu Peninsula. At the same time, his companions Nittei and Nissei were banished to the island of Ōshima, about twenty kilometers off the Izu Peninsula. Seven others were also sent to various places of exile, where they died. According to the *Tokugawa Jikki* (The Chronicle of the Tokugawas), an account of the achievements of the first ten shōguns compiled between 1809 and 1849, Nisshō was punished for his advocacy of the Jōraku-in school and his forcible acquisition of branch temples; Genna- and Kan'ei-era (1615–44) precedents for the sentence are cited. Additional grounds were found in the reaction of other temples in Kazusa to Nisshō's criticism that they had violated Nichijū's rule against receiving donations from nonbelievers.

Nisshō's followers sent messengers to him in exile, bearing money, valuables, and reports on the numbers of *daimoku* they chanted. Others went to serve him and receive instruction. He sent in return a large number of the Nichiren-sect mandalas known as *honzon,* which are the focus of devotion for the faithful when chanting the *daimoku.*

Some lay followers of the secret *daimoku* confraternities abandoned the places of their birth. Their names were removed from the local temples' registers of parishioners, and they were recorded as *rōnin* (literally, prisoners) in the annual census. *Rōnin* received money from the exiled priests and acted as religious leaders of the congregation in their absence. In documents related to the *daimoku* societies, the *rōnin* are called "outcasts for the sake of the Law" and "outcasts for the sake of the True Teaching."

They maintained and led the cult of the *daimoku,* which sprang up around them and the exiled priests. It was an underground movement, and its various names reflect its clandestine nature: the secret *daimoku,* the store-room *daimoku,* the inner believers, the secret believers, and the new followers. Formally, its believers are called the Nichijū Koshō Gi (Followers of the Ancient and Correct Principle of Nichijū) or Hommon Shōgi Shū (Group Upholding the Correct Teaching of the Essence of the Lotus Sutra).

There is still much that is not known about the secret *daimoku* confraternities of the Edo period, which existed independent of the Fuju Fuse faction. Scholars have not established their distribution, but these societies appear to have been centered on the provinces of Kazusa and Shimōsa and were also found in Edo.

The Ju Faction and the Populace

With the Fuju Fuse faction forced underground, the Nichiren sect centered on the Ju faction, dominated by Mount Minobu, which was also the focus of a nationwide popular cult, since it had been Nichiren's final abode. In 1712 Kuon-ji on Mount Minobu boasted more than 130 subtemples, which provided lodgings for pilgrims.

Kuon-ji and the other head temples of the sect were supported by the daimyō and other families of the warrior class, and they constructed impressive temple complexes. Their branch temples were also supported by the parish system. The branch temples were obliged to participate in ceremonies and memorial services of the head temples and to collect donations known as branch-temple funds (*matsuji kin*).

Priests were assigned to the various branches but needed the permission of the chief of the head temple to preach sermons. The heads of the branch temples were required to have completed studies at one of the sect's academies. Clerical rank was indicated by colors and patterns of robes: ordinary priests wore a *kesa* (outer robe) of five or seven strips of cloth pieced together and a black cotton inner robe; high-ranking priests with the title of *shōnin* (holy man) could wear a purple *kesa* and colored robes; while the abbot of a head temple might don a *kesa* of gold silk brocade and elaborate robes, such as a wide-sleeved silk robe with a pleat at the hem or the scarlet *jikitotsu,* with matching outer and inner robes. The title *shōnin* was bestowed on those heads of branch temples whose contributions to the main temple had been remarkable; first bestowed on individuals, *shōnin* evolved into the temple rank *shōseki*, which was often conferred in perpetuity as *eishōseki*.

During the Edo period, the Nichiren sect was frequently subjected to anti-Buddhist attacks, mainly by followers of Shintō, Confucianism, and Kokugaku (National Learning). At first criticism had come from Shintō and Confucian quarters; later it came from Kokugaku and Shintō scholars. The harshest critic was Hirata Atsutane (1776–1843), who regarded the Nichiren and Jōdo Shin sects as the enemies of Shintō. His *Shutsujō Shōgo* (Laughter After Meditation; 1811), a six-volume work attacking Buddhism, includes a section titled "The Two Enemies of Shintō." Hirata's antipathy toward the Nichiren sect was inspired by the prevalence of Nichiren temples and parishioners in the area where Hirata's adherents lived and by the activities of lay Nichiren believers in the early decades of the nineteenth century. Nichiren scholars sought to avert criticism by advocating the view that Shintō, Buddhism, and Confucianism were fundamentally one.

Though oral religious debate was forbidden, written criticism was tolerated. Extant tracts set forth the arguments exchanged by priests of the Jōdo, Jōdo Shin, and Kegon sects. Early in the Edo period, doctrinal argument predominated; later, however, criticism of attitudes toward religious faith and institutions was dominant. From the middle of the period onward, lay leaders increasingly figured in the exchanges, in particular those popular leaders who became heads of the "founder cults."

Popular cults prospered in the Nichiren sect, unhindered by class distinctions. The cults centered either on Nichiren as the sect's founder or on numerous protective deities, such as the thirty guardian deities (*sanjū banjin*); the ten female *rākṣasas* (*jū rasetsunyo*), guardians of Buddhism; Kishimojin (in Sanskrit, Hārītī); Shichimen Tennyo (the Seven-Headed Goddess); the Bodhisattva of the Polar Star (in Sanskrit, Sudṛṣṭi), the deification of the Great Bear constellation; Inari, the indigenous harvest deity; Taishakuten (Indra); and Bishamonten (Vaiśravaṇa). The Nichiren cults went beyond merely venerating the founder and flourished by teaching that worldly benefits could be obtained by worshiping images of Nichiren. The images, known by the generic title Yakuyoke Soshi (Founder Who Prevents Misfortune), were believed to bring luck, prevent fires, ensure safe childbirth, and grant wishes within a certain period of time.

A practice that gained great popularity was the display by certain temples affiliated with Nichiren of *kaichō*, sacred relics and images of Nichiren normally kept hidden. Worshipers were allowed a glimpse of these objects at the climax of a religious service. The objects were displayed not only at the temple that owned them (the display referred to as *igaichō*) but also when priests of that temple took them to another Nichiren-sect temple for display under similar conditions (the display then being called *degaichō*). The objects were carried from one temple to another in procession by priests from the proprietary temple. The first such procession to Edo was made in 1705 by priests of Honkoku-ji in Kyoto. Further processions were organized by Mount Minobu and many other temples affiliated with the Nichiren sect that had made themselves centers of pilgrimage. The public displays of relics and images of Nichiren reached a peak between 1818 and 1844, and chronicles relating the objects' miraculous powers were sold.

Devotional associations, or *kōjū*, supported the display of images and relics. For example, the day the image of Nichiren arrived in Edo from Mount Minobu, the associations were in a state of high excitement. A contemporary source states that they celebrated the event by parading with banners

> recording in gold and silver embroidery the highlights of Nichiren's life. . . . Some of them were made of gold brocade and velvet costing a hundred pieces of gold. Each banner, suspended between two poles, was carried by several people, some of whom held guy ropes to support it in the wind. It was truly a magnificent sight. There were seventy associations in Edo. When they all paraded, bringing out their banners, the parade extended the four or five blocks of the district, and the effect was spectacular. However, because of the procession's size, the Edo commissioners halted it.

The associations were also actively involved in the *oeshiki*, celebrations of the anniversary of Nichiren's death, and paraded with *mandō*, staffs crowned with elaborately decorated lanterns. Thanks to the cults surrounding Nichiren, popular understanding of his teachings grew, and by the middle of the nineteenth century lay teachers and writers, dissatisfied with clerical failings, were editing his works and publishing criticism of other sects.

Mid-Nineteenth-Century Lay Movements

The arrival of Commodore Matthew C. Perry (1794–1858) in Uraga, at the mouth of Edo Bay, in 1853, the consequent signing of a treaty with the United States in 1854, and the Ansei Purge of 1858 shocked the Buddhist establishment out of its slumber and enveloped it in an air of crisis. It was in this climate that the Nichiren-sect priests Nitchi (1819–54) and Nikki (1800–1859) worked to lay the foundation of modern study of the sect's doctrine. Especially noteworthy was Nikki's Jūgō-en, a training center set up at Ryūzō-ji in Kanazawa, Kaga Province. Many of those who shouldered positions of responsibility in the Nichiren sect during the Meiji period (1868–1912) were trained at Jūgō-en.

Conspicuous during the last decades of the Edo period and the first decades of the Meiji period is the increasing importance of the religious activity of lay people in contrast to the waning influence of the clergy on the masses. In this period many popular religious groups—the new religions—emerged in response to people's feelings of uncertainty in the midst of political turmoil. A significant number of these groups became associated with Shintō out of dissatisfaction with Edo-period Buddhism. In the Nichiren sect, two men developed lay confraternities into popular Buddhist-based religious groups. They were Matsudaira Yorikane (1809–68) of the Takamatsu Happon Society and Nagamatsu Seifū (Nissen; 1817–90) of the Butsuryū Society.

At the beginning of the nineteenth century, the Happon Society, organized in Edo by Nissō (1776–1837) of the Nichiryū school (which became the Hommon Hokke sect), flourished and spread to areas as distant as the Tōkai region (along the southern coast of Honshu between the Kantō region and Shikoku), Kyoto-Osaka, and Shikoku. The Nichiryū school was also called the Happon school (the school of the eight chapters) because its founder, Nichiryū (1385–1464), held that the essence of the Lotus Sutra was contained in chapters 15 through 22 of the sutra. In the town of Takamatsu in Sanuki Province, on Shikoku, Matsudaira Yorikane injected new life into the Nichiryū school and established the Takamatsu Happon Society.

Yorikane, an illegitimate son of Matsudaira Yorinori (1775–1829), the lord of the Takamatsu domain, had come to the Lotus faith after studying both the Jōdo and Zen traditions. He became the student of Nichigi of Hongaku-ji in Takamatsu. Afterward, he introduced the Happon Society to Takamatsu and won converts by using *shakubuku*, the Nichiren-sect method of forceful conversion. He preached and distributed the *honzon*, or mandala of the Nichiren sect. To preach, the permission of the abbot of a head temple was necessary; further, the distribution of the *honzon* was a prerogative of the abbot and could not in any case be undertaken by a lay person. Yorikane's position as the son of a daimyō exempted him from these restrictions. Eventually the Takamatsu Happon Society had branches in forty-one provinces, from Hizen on Kyushu to the northernmost area of Honshu. The society's total membership reached 4,459. With Yorikane's death in 1868, however, its vitality ebbed rapidly.

Nagamatsu Seifū was influenced by Yorikane and received his patronage. Whereas the Takamatsu Happon Society withered after the death of its founder, Seifū's Butsuryū Society grew into the present-day Hommon Butsuryū sect. Seifū was born into a family of townspeople in Kyoto and as a young man studied painting, calligraphy, Japanese poetry, and Kokugaku. His interest in Buddhism deepened, and after studying in the Jōdo and Zen traditions, he embraced the faith of the Lotus under the instruction of Nichiō of Honnō-ji in Kyoto, the head temple of the Nichiryū school. He was ordained in 1848 and intended to study at the Nichiryū-school academy at Honkō-ji in Amagasaki, Settsu Province; but he was ostracized by his fellow students, who were jealous of his scholastic attainments and contemptuous of his becoming a priest at the late age of thirty-two.

Disappointed by and distrustful of the clergy, Seifū returned to Kyoto and to the secular life. In 1857 he established the Butsuryū Society in Kyoto. Earlier, he had written a work refuting the doctrine that the denizens of the three lowest realms of existence (the hells and the worlds of hungry spirits and animals) could attain buddhahood and had sent it to Yorikane in Takamatsu. Yorikane invited Seifū to Takamatsu. Meeting Yorikane and observing for himself how the Takamatsu Happon Society functioned inspired him to establish his own society the following year. Even the name Butsuryū Society was chosen with the approval of Yorikane, who was publicly thought to be its author. The commissioner of Kyoto presented Seifū with a hanging scroll inscribed with the society's name and that of its supposed author, Yorikane. That a public official should make such a gift signified the de facto official recognition of the Butsuryū Society.

Seifū, however, faced more problems in his propagation than had the aristocratic Yorikane. Concerned with propagating its teachings widely and converting as many new believers as possible, the Butsuryū Society criticized other teachings and bitterly condemned the lapses of the priests. Seifū's criticism naturally brought clerical retaliation, and in 1865 sixty-four temples of all sects (including the Nichiren sect) in Ōtsu, Ōmi Province, accused Seifū of harboring Christian beliefs and of preaching without having been ordained. Since lay people were forbidden to preach and even the clergy needed the permission of the abbot of their head temple to do so, Seifū's activities were a brazen challenge to the feudal religious organization. Furthermore, because Seifū's sermons were based on the writings of Nichiren, on which he also wrote commentaries, the Butsuryū Society seemed to be calling for a return to Nichiren's original ideals.

In 1868 Seifū was imprisoned under the anti-Christian law for willfully misleading the general public. He was eventually pardoned by the governor of Kyoto, who arranged for him to be reordained, and an established Nichiren temple authorized him to preach. He continued to be censured by the priests of other sects and was twice again imprisoned. Despite the pressure brought to bear on him, his confraternity survived, and in 1878, when it became an officially recognized religious body, it had over ten thousand members.

THE JŌDO SHIN SECT
AND THE UNDERGROUND *NEMBUTSU* MOVEMENT

The Religious Ideal

Religious organizations of the Edo period were under the jurisdiction and protection of the secular authorities, and priests were compelled to teach the populace a Buddhism imbued with the values of the rulers. How this was accomplished by the three principal groups of the Jōdo Shin sect and the approach the sect developed toward propagation will be examined below.

Documents that provide keys to the nature of Edo-period Jōdo Shin–sect teachings are the pastoral letters called *shōsoku* or *gosho* sent by the abbots of the three principal schools—the Hongan-ji establishment, the Bukkō-ji school, and the Takada Senju-ji school—to their followers and propagation materials, such as *ōjō den*, the popular collections of accounts of *nembutsu* followers' rebirth in the Pure Land compiled mainly by priests in branch temples. The pastoral letters represent the public posture of the sect, showing how it interpreted the will of the secular authorities, while the *ōjō den* record how the *nembutsu* practice was taught to Jōdo Shin–sect followers by branch-temple priests. The religious ideal promoted in these works is the *myōkōnin,* or wondrously good person, the *nembutsu* practitioner who is also a model subject of the shogunate.

The Hongan-ji Establishment

A portrait of the Hongan-ji establishment can be drawn from the pastoral letters of its leaders, which reveal the establishment's interpretation of the ideal Buddhist. In a letter dated the nineteenth day of the fourth month of 1787, Hōnyo (1707–89), the seventeenth abbot (*hossu*) of Nishi Hongan-ji in Kyoto, wrote: "It is important that you obey the laws of the world and practice loyalty and filial piety in order to inherit the faith of the Jōdo Shin sect."

In the sixth month of 1792 Hōnyo's son, Bunnyo (d. 1799), the eighteenth abbot, wrote:

Make the law of the country your prime concern, giving priority to charity and justice above all. Never forget the gratitude owed those in political authority. Do not neglect to pay either your annual tax or the miscellaneous taxes required. Practice the five virtues of benevolence, justice, propriety, wisdom, and honesty and the five relationships—between master and follower, father and child, spouses, elder and younger siblings, and friends. These are the foundation of the faith of the Jōdo Shin sect.

Bunnyo invokes the pillars of the Confucian ethical system, the official philosophy of the Edo period.

In the eleventh month of 1799 Honnyo (1778–1826), the nineteenth abbot and son of Bunnyo, wrote: "Having attained faith, do not neglect the *nembutsu* of thanks for having been saved. Observe the regulations and obey the secular authorities, and your faith will deepen. This is important."

Shortly before the collapse of the shogunate, in a letter dated the twenty-fifth day of the second month of 1867, Gonnyo (1817–94), the twenty-first abbot of Higashi Hongan-ji in Kyoto, wrote:

When we consider the state of the world in recent times, we can imagine the extent to which the authorities are troubled. In such circumstances, the followers of the Jōdo Shin sect should keep in mind the following. As I have told you before, it is only through the benevolence of the authorities that the teachings of the Jōdo Shin sect flourish and do not stagnate. Followers of the Jōdo Shin sect obey the orders of the shōgun and practice benevolence and justice in society.

Pay honestly to the government the crop taxes that have been levied, and be not halfhearted about paying other miscellaneous taxes. Be content with your station and what you have and practice moderation. Fervently contemplate the gratitude you owe the state, and in your hearts achieve the steadfast faith that leads to rebirth in the Pure Land of Perfect Bliss. Having attained that state, constantly recite the *nembutsu*, giving thanks to Amida. Succeed in your belief in a wonderful and correct manner. . . . Priests of the Jōdo Shin sect and followers, strive well in unity to walk both the Buddhist Way and the secular way.

Gonnyo, more than previous abbots, inculcated in Jōdo Shin–sect followers a strong feeling of gratitude to the authorities, promoting loyalty to and cooperation with the shogunate. The restoration of imperial rule lay but ten months away. These were the final days before the collapse of the Tokugawa shogunate, which had ruled for two hundred and sixty-five years. This was also the time of the birth of the powerful new political forces that coalesced to form the Meiji government. In the face of change, the Hongan-ji establishment urged its followers to cooperate with the shogunate. Aware that the survival of the shogunate ensured the survival of the Buddhist establishment, the Edo-period abbots of Hongan-ji made observance of the values advocated by the shogunate a requisite spiritual practice of Jōdo Shin followers.

Between 1808 and 1858 Gyōsei, Sōjun, and Zōō, three priests of a branch temple of Hongan-ji, compiled the *Myōkōnin Den* (Biographies of Wondrously Good People), a twelve-volume collection of 157 biographies of ideal *nembutsu* practitioners. Let us look at two of the biographies.

Seikurō was born into a poor farming family in Yamato Province, near Kyoto. He had lost his father in infancy and from the time he could remember had worked to help his mother support them. She worked at cotton ginning, while he was the servant of a farmer in a nearby village. Seikurō was dull-witted and had been so since birth. He was illiterate, unable even to read or write his own name. Nevertheless, he worked hard and was an obedient, faithful, model servant. He also faithfully obeyed the laws and orders of the shōgun. Not only was he never derelict in the payment of his annual taxes but he also cultivated fields abandoned by runaway farmers and paid the taxes owed by others. As a result he was commended by the shōgun as a model peasant.

Seikurō also showed deep filial devotion to his mother. After his day's work was finished, he would immediately return to her house to ask how she was and cut firewood and draw water for her. When he had finished these tasks, he would go back to his master's house, where, alone in the kitchen, he would eat cold leftovers. Throughout his life he diligently recited the *nembutsu* and was a fervent practitioner of a type rarely seen. He led his life so that he would attain rebirth in the Pure Land of Amida and there find eternal happiness.

Shōsuke, a poor peasant of Chikuzen Province, on Kyushu, was likewise known for his filial piety. Once as he set out on an errand his father said to him, "The roads will be muddy after the rain, so wear your clogs." His mother, however, said, "It stopped raining some time ago, so the roads are dry. Wear your straw sandals." A dutiful child, Shōsuke was bewildered and finally went out wearing a straw sandal on one foot and a wooden clog on the other. Moreover, whenever the daimyō's procession passed by on the occasion of the regular formal visit to Edo, Shōsuke would prostrate himself, reverently thanking his lord for all that he had done in Shōsuke's behalf.

The *myōkōnin* in this collection all demonstrated loyalty to the government, filial devotion to their parents, and deep faith in the *nembutsu*. The first two attributes represented fundamental secular values of the age, while the third of course embodied the central teaching of the Jōdo Shin sect. The *myōkōnin* are portrayed as people who know no discontent and have no desires in this life. Their stories reveal that the ideal *nembutsu* practitioner, as conceived by the Hongan-ji establishment, possessed the qualities of loyalty and filial devotion required by the shogunate, crowned by religious faith. Of all the groups in the Jōdo Shin sect, the Hongan-ji establishment most vigorously encouraged this passive and malleable religious ideal as a means of convincing the authorities that its followers were free of any taint of the rebelliousness and independence that had characterized the Hongan-ji establishment during the uprisings of *nembutsu* followers in earlier ages.

The Bukkō-ji School

Like the Hongan-ji school, the Bukkō-ji school incorporated official values in its beliefs during the Edo period. This is clear in *gosho,* or letters, from the abbot to his followers. One *gosho* reads:

> The four classes of people—warriors, farmers, artisans, and merchants—should contemplate the four debts of gratitude. These are gratitude to heaven and earth, gratitude to the ruler of the country, gratitude to parents, and gratitude to society. Farmers in particular should take their public service very seriously and strictly observe the laws. If there are *nembutsu* practitioners who defy the government, it is your duty to remonstrate with them with all your might. If there is one who disobeys the laws of the shogunate, even if that person is a member of your family, you must write down the malefactor's name, immediately reveal the facts, and take the complaint to the local authorities or to the temple. This is as was pledged long ago. Farmers should pay their taxes as levied by the authorities. There should be no selfish reluctance because of the size of the harvest. Those who treat the authorities with contempt act contrary to the true faith of the Jōdo Shin sect. Since those without true faith disdain the authorities, it is impossible for them to escape punishment.

Nembutsu practitioners were required to show gratitude, particularly to their rulers. They had to obey the law and not evade their duties—in particular, their taxes. The pastoral letters further reason that those who disobey the authorities cannot have true faith, or put another way, those who do not have true faith will unfailingly disobey the authorities. The ideal subject of the Tokugawa shogunate and the ideal *nembutsu* practitioner, as viewed by the Bukkō-ji school, were identical. This belief was taught to Bukkō-ji followers by priests of the branch temples, and the kind of person they sought is depicted in the *Kinsei Ōjō Den* (Recent Records of Rebirth), a famous collection of accounts of Pure Land rebirth.

The *Kinsei Ōjō Den* was compiled by the Bukkō-ji-school priest Nyogen Myōshun (d. 1694). It was published posthumously in 1695 by his friend Kōken, also a Jōdo Shin–sect priest. Myōshun first embraced the Jōdo-sect faith before becoming a priest of the Takada Senju-ji school of the Jōdo Shin sect. Only later did he join the Bukkō-ji school. He explained that he collected biographies of members of the Jōdo Shin sect who attained rebirth because he ardently wished to save the people of the world. He divided the accounts into four sections and brought them together in a single volume to be used as a text for *nembutsu* propagation. The book contains the stories of forty-eight followers who attained rebirth in the Pure Land. Two of the accounts are summarized here.

Hanajo lived in the town of Renjaku in the Hamamatsu district of Tōtōmi Province. In the summer of 1669 she became ill, and her condition suddenly worsened at the beginning of the ninth month. She seemed to be near death. When she was thought to be drawing her last breath, she began breathing easily again and spoke as if she were quite comfortable. "My pain has suddenly gone, and I feel happiness welling up in my heart. I think I will attain rebirth in the Pure Land today. If you want to see me, look at the person standing to the left of Amida Buddha," she said. Her mother and father asked what proof she had that she would attain rebirth. She answered that she had faith. She then asked everyone to chant the *nembutsu*, in which she joined in a loud voice before attaining rebirth in the Pure Land, just as if she had fallen asleep. A purple cloud—the indication that rebirth in the Pure Land had been attained—then surrounded the house up to the eaves and did not disappear until the next morning. Hanajo attained rebirth because of her compassion and faith in the *nembutsu*.

Another account tells of Chōsuke of Ise Province, a poor man who lived in the village of Ikuratsu in the Ichishi district. He was honest and gentle, with a deep respect for Buddhism. Though poor, he never forgot the gratitude he owed his ancestors, nor did he neglect to pray for the repose of their spirits and have memorial services held on the anniversaries of their deaths. In the middle of the eleventh month of 1677, he fell ill and took to his bed. His family called a physician, who prescribed treatment, but Chōsuke took the medicines only once and thereafter refused them. He reasoned that taking medicines would only make him worse. He believed that the present life is determined by the karma of past lives and that it is impossible to break those karmic bonds by taking medicines. There was nothing to do but resign his fate to the heavens and chant the *nembutsu*.

He predicted that he would die at the end of the month. He sent his wife to a priest to ask him to confer on Chōsuke the Buddhist name by which he would be known after death. He was given the name Saijun. On the night of the twenty-fifth day of the eleventh month, he turned to his wife and said, "You must not regret that some day you will leave this world of endurance. I think I will be departing tonight. I feel no pain now, either in my body or in my mind. Help me recite the *nembutsu*. You and the others chant with me." Then he said, "When the cock crows, I will set off for the Pure Land of Perfect Bliss." Bringing the palms of his hands together, he recited the *nembutsu* six or seven times in a loud voice, and when the cock crowed he suddenly departed from this world, as he had foretold. He shouted his last *nembutsu* so loudly that it woke the people next door. He was thirty-seven.

Hanajo was said to have been reborn in the Pure Land because of her compassion and faith. Chōsuke's attainment of rebirth in the Pure Land was due to the combination of his honesty, gentleness, and devotion to *nembutsu* belief. The *nembutsu* practitioners whose stories are told in the *Kinsei Ōjō Den* manifest long years of faith, exclusive *nembutsu* practice, and an unswerving determination to achieve rebirth in the Pure Land. More-over, they have the personal qualities of goodness, gentleness, obedience, malleability, compassion, honesty, and selflessness. These were in fact the qualities valued and encouraged by the shogunate in its subjects.

Myōshun compiled the *Kinsei Ōjō Den* not only out of a desire to save the people of the world but also, as he states in his preface, to encourage people to respect and obey the secular authorities. Myōshun believed that if his collection were distributed to every family and if all subjects became believers in the *nembutsu* and accumulated merit leading to Pure Land re-birth, their debt of gratitude to both the government and the Buddha would be repaid. The *Kinsei Ōjō Den* shows clearly that the Bukkō-ji school tried to instill in its followers the ideal of behavior set forth by the authori-ties, identifying the goals of Buddhism with those of the government.

The Takada Senju-ji School

The Takada Senju-ji school, like the Hongan-ji and Bukkō-ji schools, in-terpreted the wishes of the shogunate through *gosho* to its followers from the abbot (known in the Edo period as the *monzeki*). Of interest here are two letters from the collection of the *gosho* of the fourteenth abbot of the school, Gyōshū (1582–1666), that were published in four volumes in 1657 as the *Takada Gosho* (Pastoral Letters of the Takada Senju-ji School).

The following letter appears at the beginning of volume one. Gyōshū writes:

The essence of the teachings of our revered founder and holy teacher is twofold. In public you must revere the laws of the rulers, respect the shōgun, obey the regulations of the domain lords and local officials, fully comply with duties for taxes and labor service, and give your master loyalty and your parents filial devotion. In terms of the Dharma, you must never slight the buddhas, bodhisattvas, or deities, nor criticize other sects or groups. Now, it is the faith of this sect to call on Amida with single-minded purpose and rely on his Original Vow to attain rebirth in the Pure Land. Never doubt Amida, but as long as you live, whether asleep or awake, be alert and recite "Namu Amida Butsu."

In a letter from the beginning of the second volume, Gyōshū says:

Generally speaking, this sect teaches that we must call on Amida with single-minded purpose, relying on the Original Vow of the Tathāgata [Buddha] for rebirth and never doubting. Just invoke the holy name of Amida at all times and repay the debt of gratitude for his great compassionate Original Vow. Next, as a member of society, you must deeply revere the rulers, obey the regulations of the lords and the local officials, fully render your taxes and labor service, and in general do nothing to violate the five virtues. Do not neglect the deities or the buddhas. Ignorant as you are, avoid doctrinal dispute with the learned. Be charitable with one another, since you are all *nembutsu* followers, and pay reverence with body and mind by decorating the altar according to your means, placing incense, flowers, and candles on it, and keeping it clean.

Let us examine the order of the contents of these two letters. The first is organized as follows: (1) the attitude toward the authorities, (2) the attitude toward other sects and groups, and (3) the religious life of *nembutsu* practitioners. The second speaks of (1) the faith of *nembutsu* practitioners, (2) the attitude toward the authorities, (3) the attitude toward other sects and schools, and (4) daily religious practice. While the former speaks first of a cooperative attitude toward the government, the latter speaks first of the faith of the *nembutsu* practitioner. The first letter reflects the attitude of the Takada Senju-ji school toward the government and society. The second reveals the school's attitude toward its followers. Gyōshū calls for cooperation with the government in both these letters and reinforces his words by appending to his *gosho* copies of letters by Shinran, the Jōdo Shin–sect founder, expressing the same views.

The *Shinsen Ōjō Kenki* (Newly Selected Records of Pure-Land Rebirth Experiences) was compiled in 1830 by Shinkyō (1791–1867), a priest of the Takada Senju-ji school. Shinkyō states that he edited the collection in the hope that more people would practice the *nembutsu* and attain rebirth in the Pure Land. The *Shinsen Ōjō Kenki* presents mainly stories of *nembutsu* practitioners of Ise Province (the location of Senju-ji). Let us examine summaries of a few of the fifty-two biographies in the collection.

Enkō Shunjō Koji, a lay believer whose secular name was Ōsumi Ryōzō, lived in the town of Tsuyumi in Ise Province. He had a dream of good omen in which he saw the Pure Land. On the sixth day of the eighth month of 1812, he attained rebirth there because he was "malleable and filial" and "a believer in Buddhism, who, not shirking his public duties, never neglected, day or night, to chant the sutra and recite the *nembutsu*."

Edō Hōni was the mother of the priest Hōzan of Sempuku-ji in the village of Oyamato in the Ichishi district of Ise. When she was forty-seven, she took the tonsure and became a cleric, receiving the name Edō. She attained rebirth in the Pure Land on the eighth day of the second month of 1814. Shortly before, a bodhisattva had appeared to her in a dream and told her that her death was near. Her attainment of rebirth in the Pure Land was due to her chastity and mildness and to her belief in the *nembutsu*.

Because of his personal attributes of filial devotion, compassion, kindness, calm, and nobility and his faith in the *nembutsu*, Jōkan'in-dono attained rebirth in the Pure Land on the twenty-seventh day of the eleventh month of 1822 as peacefully as if falling asleep. Likewise, Tokunin Seikō Shōnin had attained rebirth in the Pure Land on the second day of the third month of 1801 because of his "honesty and kindness" and the "sincerity of his *nembutsu* practice."

In these biographies, both certain personal qualities (compassion, honesty, malleability, and filial devotion) and *nembutsu* practice were criteria for rebirth in the Pure Land. In these criteria there was very little difference between the teachings of the Takada Senju-ji and Bukkō-ji schools.

The Kakure Nembutsu *Movement*

Bolstered by the *hommatsu* (head and branch temple) and parish systems and the government power that sanctioned them, the established sects, including the Jōdo Shin sect, eventually grew complacent about their position in Edo-period society. In many ways, the religious establishment exploited its followers, sometimes in concert with the government and sometimes on its own. Followers were exploited through the parish system, the religious-affiliation census, the temples' acting as landlords and moneylenders, and the government-inspired indoctrination that equated the pursuit of religious ideals with obedience to the secular authorities.

One means of resisting this combined secular and religious exploitation was to resort to violence, as peasants did periodically in agrarian uprisings (*hyakushō ikki*). Another was to turn to new religions for salvation. As if in answer to the people's needs, popular cults known as *hayari-gami* and *hayari-butsu* sprang up one after another, attracting followers by curing people of sickness and providing various worldly benefits. Yet another alternative was to reject the official Buddhism approved by the shogunate and to seek to restore a sect's teachings in accordance with the intentions of its founder, as in the case of the Fuju Fuse faction of the Nichiren sect. These cults were forced underground. A similar group of *nembutsu* followers, the *kakure* (underground) *nembutsu* movement, emerged from the Hongan-ji group in the middle years of the Edo period.

The *kakure nembutsu* cults were known by a number of names, most connoting secrecy. Typical names were Okura Hōmon or Dozō Hōmon (Storehouse Teachings) and Kuri Hōmon (Kitchen Teachings). The *kakure nembutsu* movement was characterized by a strong rejection of the faith taught by the Hongan-ji establishment. Because the cults denied the authority of the Hongan-ji establishment, they were forced underground. The members of the *kakure nembutsu* cults bitterly criticized the formalism, hollowness, and ossification at Hongan-ji and that establishment's obsequious attitude toward the authorities. Their members' attitude caused the *kakure nembutsu* cults to be branded heretical.

The philosophy of the *kakure nembutsu* cults is conveyed clearly in the *Hōyō Shō* (Essay on the Essentials of the Law; ca. mid-eighteenth century), the central theoretical work of the movement, which considerably influenced the activities and outlook of cult followers. Of interest is its criticism of the concept of faith as taught by the Hongan-ji establishment.

The followers of Hongan-ji neither come into contact with the good teacher (*zen chishiki*), who resembles a buddha living in the world to lead people to the Buddhist Way, nor have any clear awareness of the experience of conversion. They remain ignorant of the precise moment they attained faith. At some point they become conscious of the impermanence of all things and go to a temple or other place of practice and gratefully listen to a sermon. It is for miserable people like us that Amida sat in meditation for five eons and continues to practice for all eternity. Thus we should never forget our debt of gratitude to him. One who doubts nothing and simply recites the *nembutsu* is considered a *nembutsu* practitioner, one who has attained faith. Such cannot possibly be attainment of true faith.

The *Hōyō Shō* idealistically criticizes the empty formalistic faith of Hongan-ji followers. It also rejects the authority of the abbots of Hongan-ji.

Regarding a good teacher, some say that this can be only Shinran or one of the successive abbots of Hongan-ji. Were that so, even if we were told we should find a good teacher to learn the true, orthodox *nembutsu*, it would be impossible to do so today, since Shinran died five centuries ago. And no one visits the abbot seeking knowledge of faith. Even if we were to go, the abbot would not readily bequeath faith to us. If he could do so, the settlement before the gates of Hongan-ji would be teeming like a marketplace, but no such thing can be seen. So we say that no one visits the abbot asking for the true faith. It therefore follows that it is impossible to find a good teacher. But if we cannot find one, it is impossible to attain rebirth.

The *kakure nembutsu* followers raised questions about the nature of Shinran's true teachings and the true faith, which, they claimed, was not the formalistic faith taught by the establishment. According to the *kakure nembutsu* movement, "Shinran's orthodox faith consisted of single-minded devotion [*kimyō no ichinen*] and nothing else. As Rennyo [1415–99; the eighth abbot of Hongan-ji] says in his pastoral letters, faith consists of concentrating on Amida's name with no distraction whatsoever. We must call on Amida with single-minded devotion so that, miserable and wretched as we are, we can be assured of that great goal, our afterlife." However, "we cannot, just as we are, achieve that single-minded devotion." The writer's point is that "since Shinran's most important orthodox teachings are very difficult to explain, they can be understood only through prolonged discussion with someone who has true faith. If only we ask and seek as is taught by the sacred works of our *kakure nembutsu* movement, we will achieve single-minded devotion."

The *Hōyō Shō* then goes on to discuss the best way to attain that faith.

Bow your head in adoration, strain your ears toward release, listen to the sacred teachings, kneel before the image of the Buddha, discard all miscellaneous practices and thoughts of your own power, know that you are a sinner and a rogue, rid yourself of your grave sins and errors, and then at once call on Amida with all your heart so that at that very instant he may help you attain the great goal, your afterlife. Be not of two minds; just firmly concentrate on the thought that you are clinging tightly to the sleeve of the Buddha, and with an unwavering mind directed entirely toward the Buddha beg for salvation with no thought other than the *nembutsu* in mind.

Kakure nembutsu followers observed strict secrecy. The substance of the transmission received at the time of the attainment of faith could never be mentioned to anyone—parent or child, husband or wife—who had not yet attained faith. Silence in the presence of outsiders was the strictest of the movement's rules. Followers, in seeking true faith, were taught that they could not find a good teacher, or *zen chishiki*, among the clergy of the Hongan-ji establishment, since the true transmission of faith existed only within the *kakure nembutsu* movement.

The movement's writings show it to be convinced of its own orthodoxy. Its followers made a point of continually stressing the heretical nature of Hongan-ji doctrine and the behavior of its priests and followers. They declared that they themselves embraced living teachings that correctly transmitted the doctrines of Shinran and Rennyo. Their insistence on reliance on a good teacher, however, was controversial, since both Shinran and Rennyo insisted that only Amida could be relied on. Though the reaction of the *kakure nembutsu* movement against the Hongan-ji establishment is understandable in the context of the times, the movement's insistence and dependence on a good teacher as a religious leader led it into doctrinal conflict with Jōdo Shin–sect teachings.

The most explicit, though certainly biased, account of the movement is in the *Kuri Hōmon Ki* (A Record of the Kitchen Teachings), published around 1765. The author, Tatematsu Kaishi, a faithful parishioner of Hongan-ji, lived in the Naitō Shinjuku district of Edo. He came into contact with the *kakure nembutsu* movement by chance and out of loyalty to the secular authorities decided to become an informer. Because of the information he divulged, in 1767 the movement was subjected to severe oppression and punishment, the circumstances of which are recorded in his book. The *Kuri Hōmon Ki* contains a colorful account of the initiation—a protracted ceremony that concluded with the declaration that the believer had been saved and was a living buddha—and of the great secrecy that surrounded it.

In the 1750s Teigin, a female cleric at Nishi Hongan-ji, had joined the movement as a spy and reported its activities to the Nishi Hongan-ji authorities. Having made contact with the movement cautiously but with eagerness, she was able to take part in the secret initiation ceremony. Her information about *kakure nembutsu* beliefs and activities is very similar to that given in the *Kuri Hōmon Ki*. As a result of Teigin's report, the authorities of Nishi Hongan-ji put pressure on the movement in 1755, which led to criminal proceedings and punishment by the government.

Around 1790, under orders from Nishi Hongan-ji, the priest in charge of a temple called Shinjō-ji investigated the situation of the *kakure nembutsu* movement and its organization in Kyoto. After long efforts to make contact, he gained the group's trust and, in the fourth month after making contact, was admitted to its ranks. From the start he kept a daily record of his observations, which he turned over to the authorities.

One interesting feature of the *kakure nembutsu* movement is that its followers were urged to pretend to cooperate with religious and secular authorities and to reveal no signs of resistance or rebellion—to conform, outwardly, in every way. Yet both religious and secular authorities were relentless in their efforts to eradicate the movement. As a result, it was driven even further underground, and secrecy became its main goal. During the Meiji period, when there was no longer any need to hide, the followers of the *kakure nembutsu* continued to maintain their traditional secrecy. After centuries of hiding, they were unable to come out in the open, and thus the movement failed to survive into the modern period.

16. Christianity in the Edo Period

THE INTRODUCTION OF CHRISTIANITY

Francis Xavier

Together with two companions, Francis Xavier (1506–52) of the Society of Jesus (who wrote in a letter to King João III of Portugal dated June 20, 1549, that his going to Japan was service to God) landed in Kagoshima, Satsuma Province, on Kyushu, on August 15, 1549. For the next twenty-seven months, until he left Japan in November 1551, he traveled in the Kyushu area—visiting the Hizen Province island of Hirado; Hakata, Chikuzen Province; Funai, Bungo Province; and Yamaguchi, Suō Province, on Honshu opposite Kyushu—and as far east as Sakai and Kyoto, preaching and striving to lay the foundations for the propagation of Christianity in Japan.

The daimyō of Satsuma, Shimazu Takahisa (1514–71), regarded the religion introduced by Xavier as a new "Indian teaching." In a letter dated November 5, 1549, Xavier wrote to the Jesuit mission in Goa: "The lord was so delighted at seeing a picture of Our Lord Jesus Christ and the Blessed Virgin Mary that he knelt before it, worshiping them with a show of deep reverence and ordering all his attendants to do the same." Xavier's experience in Kagoshima strengthened his hopes for the success of the mission in Japan. In the same letter he wrote: "According to all that I know of the Japanese from my experience of associating with them, they are the most admirable people we have yet discovered. We cannot hope to find a better people among the heathens. They are in general agreeable, good-natured, and without malice."

In Kagoshima Xavier preached the Christian gospel in his very limited Japanese and criticized the corruption of the Buddhist clergy. His denunciation provoked the wrath of the Buddhists, and the daimyō was forced to issue an edict against the Christians. As a result, Xavier left Kagoshima in August 1550 and set off for Kyoto, by way of Hirado and Yamaguchi, to secure from the highest authorities permission to evangelize throughout the land. The daimyō of Hirado, Matsura Takanobu (1529–99), and the daimyō of Yamaguchi, Ōuchi Yoshitaka (1507–51), received Xavier and his companions warmly. Cosme de Torres (1510?–70), a Spanish Jesuit, remained behind at Hirado to preach. Xavier and the Spanish Jesuit Juan Fernández (1526–67) went on to Yamaguchi, where they preached twice a day at crossroads the entire two months they were there.

In Kyoto, where his hopes had lain, however, Xavier was able neither to see the emperor and receive permission to preach nor to conduct a desired religious debate with the priests of Enryaku-ji, "one of the universities." Realizing that the political unrest in Kyoto was a serious obstacle to evangelizing and judging Ōuchi Yoshitaka to be a suitable patron, Xavier returned to Yamaguchi. There he requested Yoshitaka's cooperation in his missionary activities and presented the daimyō with letters of friendship from the Portuguese governor of the Indies, Garcia de Sá, and from the bishop of Goa, João de Albuquerque, and with such novelties as a clock, mirrors, spectacles, and small arms.

The mission in Yamaguchi, housed in an abandoned temple donated by Yoshitaka, expanded vigorously under the shield of the daimyō's permission. In a letter to the Jesuits in Europe dated January 29, 1552, Xavier wrote that the missionaries preached twice a day and a great number of people came to hear their sermons on Jesus Christ's teachings, and the missionaries had to spend much time afterward answering people's questions. Although Xavier's fierce criticism of Buddhism aroused resistance in different quarters, he was well satisfied with the situation. He wrote: "I have passed two months here in the town of Yamaguchi. About five hundred people have been baptized after receiving instruction, and by the grace of God many more are baptized each day."

In September 1551, still full of optimism about the future of the Christian mission in Japan, Xavier went to Funai at the invitation of the daimyō of Bungo, Ōtomo Sōrin (also called Yoshishige; 1530–87). Two months later he boarded a Portuguese vessel there, knowing that his presence as apostolic delegate was needed in Goa, and bid a sad farewell to Japan and the Japanese faithful.

Xavier's stay in Japan had been beset with difficulties, not least of which was his failure to gain permission to evangelize throughout the country. Despite the interest his teachings had aroused, he had baptized only a thousand or fewer converts (between one hundred and 150 in Kagoshima, between fifteen and twenty in Ichiki, 180 in Hirado, three on the way to Yamaguchi, between five hundred and six hundred in Yamaguchi, and between thirty and fifty in Funai), compared with the ten thousand he is said to have baptized in a single month in the Travancore region of India. His lack of success, however, did not dim his hopes for the future of the mission and for gaining Japanese converts.

Xavier proposed new missionary methods for Japan. Based on his observations during his stay he recommended that missionaries should be ready to endure privation and hardship, and that they be humble and modest. They should be people of great philosophical and dialectical knowledge with a rich spiritual life to enable them to withstand the opposition of the Buddhist priests. He added that a knowledge of astronomy would be very useful. Moreover, missionaries had to be excellent judges of character. It was of particular importance that they obtain permission to teach from the daimyōs and earn their goodwill, and that they be able to refute the claims of the Buddhists in those temples that he called "Japanese universities." His successors inherited this strategy as the basis for proselytizing in Japan.

Cosme de Torres

After Xavier's return to India, Cosme de Torres in Hirado became head of the mission in Japan. As mission superior, Torres made his base in Yamaguchi. With the help of Juan Fernández, the newcomer Balthazar Gago (1515–83), a Portuguese Jesuit who served in Japan from 1552 to 1561, and Brother Lourenço (1526–92), one of the most important of the mission's Japanese converts, Torres won two thousand converts in the region in five years. Among them were members of the warrior class. To a great extent, the mission's success was the fruit of its systematic program of charitable works that was carried out at Daidō-ji, the first Christian church in Japan, built in Yamaguchi in 1552 by Ōuchi Yoshinaga (d. 1557).

In 1553 the Christians of Yamaguchi placed an alms box in front of

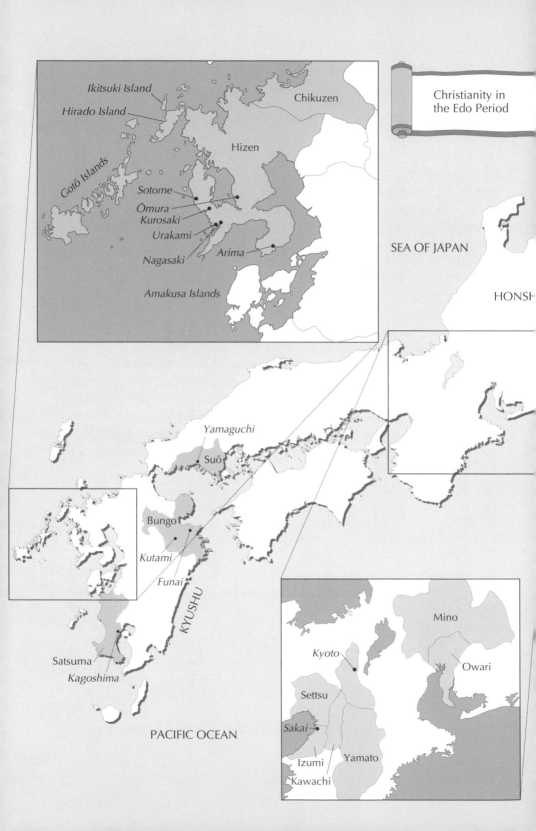

Christianity in the Edo Period

Ikitsuki Island
Hirado Island
Chikuzen
Hizen
Gotō Islands
Sotome
Ōmura
Kurosaki
Urakami
Nagasaki
Arima
Amakusa Islands

SEA OF JAPAN

HONSH

Yamaguchi
Suō

Bungo
Kutami
Funai

KYUSHU

Satsuma
Kagoshima

PACIFIC OCEAN

Mino
Kyoto
Owari
Settsu
Sakai
Yamato
Izumi
Kawachi

the church, and the contents were distributed to the needy regardless of whether they were Christian. It was also decided that rice would be distributed to the poor once a month, and a special tub was prepared to collect the donated rice. During the great Christian feasts, such as Christmas and Easter, there were special rice distributions.

Gago, recognizing the importance the Japanese attached to funerals, gave special attention to memorial services. He designated a "day for the departed" once a month for these services, which included a mass for the dead. Christian cemeteries were created and burials conducted with pomp and ceremony regardless of whether the deceased had been rich or poor. The missionaries used a variety of means to create a broad social base for Christianity, from building poorhouses to attending to the ritual needs of the Japanese.

Despite this hopeful start, the activities of the Christians in Yamaguchi were brought to a standstill in 1554, when Yamaguchi became a battleground, and their church was dissolved completely when the Mōri family came to power there in 1557.

Torres, meanwhile, had moved to Funai, where he was joined by two newly arrived priests and five friars. Together these men consolidated the church on Kyushu, which prospered under the goodwill of the Ōtomo lords of Bungo. Further help came when Luis de Almeida (1525–83), who had at one time been a physician on a Portuguese merchant ship, joined the mission. Charitable institutions established in Funai under his supervision—such as an orphanage for abandoned children and a maternity hospital—won the regard of the people. One result of his work, however, was that Christianity came to be regarded as the religion of the poor, and this perception interfered with the missionaries' efforts to convert members of the warrior class.

Beginning in 1559 the prospects for the church in Japan were complicated by increasing pressure brought to bear on Christians in the Hirado and Hakata regions by the anti-Christian Matsura daimyō. The mission was also in financial difficulties. Torres decided that this crisis could be overcome only by investing in the Portuguese silk trade. It was also imperative to adopt Xavier's suggestion to convert the ruling class and thereby gain influence throughout Japan. To this end, Torres decided to establish a mission in Kyoto.

Gaspar Vilela (1525–72), a Portuguese Jesuit, was entrusted with the Kyoto mission. Accompanied by Lourenço, he arrived in Kyoto in the autumn of 1559. The following year he succeeded in extracting from the shōgun, Ashikaga Yoshiteru (1536–65), permission to evangelize. Missionary activity in the capital, however, was hindered by the persistent obstructionism of Enryaku-ji. Nevertheless, Vilela and Lourenço overcame the interference of Matsunaga Hisahide (1510–77), a powerful figure in the shogunate who supported the complaints of Enryaku-ji, and were able to expand the mission into the neighboring provinces of Izumi, Yamato, Kawachi, and Settsu. Among the converts at this time were the court noble Kiyohara no Shigekata (1520–90) and the powerful daimyō Takayama Zusho (d. 1596) and his son Ukon (1552–1615) and their retainers. As a result of their conversion, the church rapidly gained a foothold in the Kyoto area.

Within ten years of Xavier's arrival, the church in Japan, under the leadership of Torres, had gained the desired missionary base in the central provinces and succeeded in converting powerful members of the ruling class. By around 1561, when missionary activity around the capital gained momentum, there were a total of six Jesuits in Japan—the priests Torres and Vilela and the friars Fernández, Duarte da Silva, Almeida, and Guilherme Pereira (ca. 1540–1603)—and missions in eight towns: Funai, Kutami, Hirado, Hakata, Kagoshima, Yamaguchi, Kyoto, and Sakai. There were churches or chapels in each town, including six in Hirado. In a semiofficial letter sent from Goa dated September 20, 1571, Vilela mentions that in 1569 there were a total of 26,500 Christians in Japan: 20,000 in the area of Shimo (northern Kyushu), 5,000 in the Bungo area, and 1,500 in the Kyoto area. As a result of the work of Torres (the mission's first superior), Vilela, and others, the church in Japan was entering its first period of ascendancy.

Francisco Cabral and Organtino Gnecchi-Soldo

Francisco Cabral (1533–1609) went to Japan in 1570 as the second mission superior, a position that he held until 1581. A member of an old Portuguese noble family, Cabral was a man of deep learning; yet he was often led astray by pride in himself as a scion of the nobility and by a desire for fame. He was also inclined to factionalism. In direct contrast was the self-proclaimed serf, Organtino Gnecchi-Soldo (1533–1609). The two men had arrived in Japan on the same ship, landing at Shiki in the Amakusa Islands, west of Kyushu, but thereafter often found themselves in conflict in the course of their mission work.

Having been confirmed in his post at a conference of missionaries in

Shiki, Cabral traveled as mission superior to Bungo by way of Kabashima, Nagasaki, Fukuda, and Ōmura, and thence to the Kyoto region. His opinion of Japan, gained through two visits of inspection of churches and training facilities in the Kyoto region and other areas where the church was active, was diametrically opposed to that of Xavier and Torres. He had a completely negative view of the Japanese, considering them hypocritical and their government barbaric. He felt that the daimyōs' only interest in Christianity and the Jesuits lay in the profits they might gain from the Portuguese trade. He complained bitterly about the Japanese, faulting their meekness as the demeanor assumed when no other course was open to them. As soon as their situation improved, he said, they at once started to act like lords.

This interpretation emphasized the dark side of Xavier's view of the Japanese as "people of honor." Cabral took for granted the ties with the ruling classes that had been established only through the hard work of Xavier and Torres. Unlike his predecessors, Cabral had no empathy with those of a different culture. Proselytizing through the ruling class, he soon concluded that feudal lords made the best missionaries. Although he adopted this aspect of Xavier's strategy, he lacked the earlier missionaries' sympathy for the populace.

Cabral thought that the daimyōs could be induced to convert through the lure of the Portuguese trade and through military benefits. They would then compel their subjects to convert. The political situation was far from stable, however. Ōmura Sumitada (1533–87), a Christian daimyō in Hizen Province whom Cabral trusted, was subjected to the attacks of such anti-Christian daimyōs as Matsura and Ryūzōji and to a rebellion of his retainers. Despite the pessimism that these conditions generated, Cabral would not allow any alternative missionary method to be tried. There were serious problems on Kyushu, not only between the Jesuits and the Japanese at large but also within the order itself. The professional lay assistants (*dōjuku*) seemed prepared to rebel because of the low esteem in which Cabral held them and the arrogance with which he insisted on exercising his authority over them.

Organtino Gnecchi-Soldo, the mission superior in Kyoto, complied closely with the wishes of Xavier, respecting the customs of the country and the feelings, culture, and preferences of the people. He worked hard to avoid any suggestion of incompatibility. Believing that appearances prompted many Japanese to convert, he had a fine church built in 1576, the three-story Church of the Assumption of Our Lady. Popularly called

Namban-ji, or the Temple of the Southern Barbarians, this church was one of the landmarks of Kyoto. Organtino's goodwill toward the Japanese made him well loved, and he became known in Kyoto as Urugan-sama.

Organtino's efforts were rewarded with rapid growth in the number of Christians, as typified by the host of conversions in Kawachi and Settsu provinces in 1577. Believers in various districts competed among themselves to demonstrate the strength of their faith through the number of converts they won. Each year the number of Christians in the Kyoto region increased by more than ten thousand, far exceeding the number of converts on Kyushu. Such success was due not only to the judicious adaptation of missionary methods to the needs of the Japanese by Organtino and his assistants but also to the conversion of great lords like Takayama Ukon and his father. The missionaries' situation also benefited from the strong protection they received from Oda Nobunaga (1534–82), the de facto leader of the nation.

The differences between the reception of Christianity on Kyushu and in Kyoto can only be attributed to the differences in outlook of the two mission superiors. It was recognized that a new, unified missionary approach based on Xavier's ideas was urgently needed to remedy the internal discord that Cabral had provoked.

Alessandro Valignano

Alessandro Valignano (1539–1606), making his first inspection of the mission in Japan, landed at Kuchinotsu, on the Shimabara Peninsula, in July 1579. He was to review the mission's results in the thirty years since Xavier's arrival and consider its prospects. The church had made rapid progress and had more than one hundred thousand believers in the area extending from Satsuma Province, on southern Kyushu, to Mino and Owari provinces, northeast of Kyoto. Nagasaki, Shimabara, the Amakusa Islands, the Gotō Islands, the island of Hirado, Hakata, Bungo Province, Yamaguchi, Kyoto, Takatsuki, Sakai, Kawachi Province, and Azuchi all had active Christian groups. Despite the need for people to minister to these groups, Valignano found that the twenty-odd missionaries he had sent to Japan could not speak Japanese. Faced with a situation that Cabral had precipitated, the grieved and anxious Valignano set about seeking a policy to resolve the problem.

He turned first to promoting the missionaries' study of Japanese. He ordered the compilation of a Japanese grammar and a Japanese-Portuguese dictionary. Besides concentrating on developing the missionaries' proficiency in the vernacular, he worked to dispel the distrust between the missionaries and the Japanese.

Cabral, mistrustful of the Japanese, did not seem to comprehend the problem and would not listen to Valignano's recommendations on the necessity of learning their language in order to undertake their conversion, conforming to the country's manners and customs, and training Japanese priests. Valignano was puzzled by Cabral's obstinacy and, after a year's study of the customs and attitudes of the Japanese, concluded that the Society of Jesus was in a state of crisis in Japan because of the mission superior's view that the Japanese were an inferior race. Valignano charged Cabral with seven errors, which can be reduced to three basic points: Cabral was contemptuous of the Japanese, he refused to treat them as equals, and he rejected language study, be it of Portuguese and Latin by Japanese or of Japanese by Europeans.

Faced with the need to reform and strengthen the mission, Valignano convoked a consultation of its members. Through this consultation—consisting of three meetings held in Usuki (Bungo Province), Azuchi, and Nagasaki between October 1580 and the end of 1581—Valignano hoped to achieve agreement among all the missionaries concerning the mission in Japan and the growth of the church there. The agendas of the meetings centered on questions arising out of two drafts he had prepared in June 1580, "Private Regulations for the Mission Superior in Japan" and "Guiding Regulations for Seminaries."

In the "Private Regulations" Valignano proposed four courses of action: (1) Japan should be divided into three missionary districts—Shimo (northern Kyushu), Bungo (eastern Kyushu), and Miyako (the Kyoto region). (2) Because of the unstable political situation, educational facilities should be dispersed. A central novitiate, accepting novices from all three districts, should be established at Funai. Shimo was the appropriate site for a seminary for language study. (3) Once every three years, the mission superior should inspect the seminaries and other institutions under his supervision. The district superiors should make an inspection tour of their own districts once a year. And (4) Japanese should be permitted to join the Society of Jesus, and the Society should make good use of its Japanese members.

The "Guiding Regulations" covered all aspects of seminary life, from specifics concerning food, clothing, and living quarters to subjects for study, such as the transliteration of Japanese in the Latin alphabet, the

Japanese writing system, and Japanese music. Above all, missionaries were required to act according to Japanese custom. Valignano's policy promoted the strategy of adaptation advocated by Xavier and Torres and confirmed Organtino's approach rather than Cabral's. At that point Cabral resigned as mission superior, leaving the way open for the mission to develop as Valignano wished.

The three sessions of the consultation resulted in an accord among the missionaries regarding missionary work and the establishment of the church in Japan. They agreed on nine main points: (1) Japan should become a vice-province, distinct from the province of India (Goa). (2) The donation of the Mogi district of Nagasaki would be accepted. (When Ōmura Sumitada had offered to cede Mogi to the church, Valignano had been concerned that the church's motives might be misconstrued as territorial ambition. After much vacillation he decided to accept, taking into account the church's need for an economic and political base). (3) The vice-province of Japan would be divided into three districts, Shimo, Bungo, and the Kyoto region. (4) Seminaries would be established in each district. (5) Japanese clergy would be trained. (6) Japanese would be admitted into the Society of Jesus. (7) It was stipulated that clergy in Japan should be permitted to wear silk robes whenever necessary, so that they would be accepted in Japanese society. This was based on the fact that Buddhist priests wore silk robes according to their rank. (8) The training necessary for *dōjuku* to become clergy and the roles they should play in dissemination should be specified. It would also be necessary to strive to develop a mutual understanding of the differences in ways of life and customs between the Europeans and the Japanese, a mutual awareness of their overall equality, and a unity of purpose and general consensus on the necessity to overcome the barriers separating them. And (9) annual mission reports would be submitted by the Society in Japan. These should include the status of the Jesuits in Japan, details about the Japanese political and social situations, and other subjects. A communications system would be established so that each missionary district would specifically report to the general of the Society of Jesus on their dissemination activities and the condition of their followers.

The Growth of the Church

Following the reform of the Christian mission in Japan under Alessandro Valignano's guidance, a wave of conversions like those in the Kyoto region in the mid-1570s swept through all the mission districts. In 1569 converts in the Kyoto region accounted for only 5.7 percent of all converts, but by 1582 their number had grown to 16.7 percent, surpassing Bungo, then under Cabral's supervision. Bungo had accounted for 18.9 percent of the converts in 1567, but that had fallen to 6.7 percent by 1582. Valignano's *Sumario de las Cosas de Japón* (Summary of the Situation in Japan) of 1583 reported that there were some two hundred churches and 150,000 Christians in the three missionary districts, with 115,000 converts in Shimo, 10,000 in Bungo, and 25,000 in the Kyoto region. Valignano's resolute implementation of reform and his decision on the best missionary approach allowed the church to develop on a firm footing in Japan. As missionary work became more systematic, the church entered a period of rapid growth.

After 1574 the numbers of converts increased, particularly in the wake of mass conversions that owed much to the leadership of Christian daimyōs, such as Takayama Ukon. The church continued to grow year by year, like a "fire from heaven." Even Bungo, which had stagnated under Cabral, made gains, with 2,779 baptisms in 1584. This was due to the diligent work of the thirty-five Jesuits stationed there, staffing the college in Funai, the novitiate in Usuki, and two other residences. Of the thirty-five, eight were priests and twenty-seven friars (fourteen of whom were Japanese and thirteen European). By 1590 Bungo had 30,000 Christians—triple the number eight years earlier and far surpassing the number in the Kyoto region—and accounted for 12.5 percent of Japan's Christian population.

In the Kyoto region, mission activity expanded to the extent that missionaries could not meet the needs of believers. The Jesuits' annual report of 1585 testified to the severe shortage of missionary personnel. It stated that while progress could be expected, the number of priests available to visit Christians and work for conversions was inadequate. Only one-twentieth of the number needed were actually available. In truth, the church's prospects seemed limitless as it looked forward to a bountiful harvest of the numerous seeds it had sown.

For Christians, Nagasaki was a true paradise, thriving as a result of the Portuguese trade and served by four priests and two friars in permanent residence. Only Christians were permitted to live in the settlement. Inhabitants followed an ordered and devout religious life, going to church three times a day—for mass in the morning, hymns and doctrinal study (using the *Doctrina Christam*) at midday, and recitation of the rosary in the evening.

The church grew rapidly in Bungo and the Kyoto region, but it grew even more rapidly in Shimo. In 1569 Shimo accounted for 75.4 percent of the total Christian population of Japan, and although the figure had fallen to 66.7 percent by 1590, that was still two-thirds of the total. This large Christian population was to an extent the fruit of the charity work that had been conducted throughout the Shimo district from the mission's early days.

Christian Charity

Charity, as demonstrated by acts of the church in Yamaguchi and of Almeida, was a direct expression of Christian belief. The doctrinal manual *Doctrina Christam* states that the hallmark of a Christian is not only faith in Jesus Christ's teachings but also obedience to them in word and deed. The *Doctrina Christam* based its teaching on Matthew 22:37–40, where the commandments given to Moses are reduced to just two: "Thou shalt love the Lord thy God with thy whole heart, and with thy whole soul, and with thy whole mind. This is the greatest and the first commandment. And the second is like to this: Thou shalt love thy neighbor as thyself. On these two commandments dependeth the whole law and the prophets." The *Doctrina Christam* identifies fourteen acts of charity as expressions of neighborly love.

Christians were, among other things, obligated to feed the hungry, give drink to the thirsty, clothe the naked, succor the sick and those in prison, give lodging to travelers, support newly released prisoners, and inter the bones of the dead. The missionaries engaged in these activities among those left destitute by war. In a letter dated October 8, 1561, Fernández reported to the society that by arranging funerals and caring for the sick in hospitals (supplying them with medicines), the missionaries ministered to both the spiritual and the physical needs of Christians and led nonbelievers to the faith. Such work established trust in Christianity and earned the missionaries the support and praise of the populace.

These charitable works roused Japanese society. Lay Christians assisted missionaries in their labors of love and themselves worked as good neighbors. They usually undertook works of mercy in the company of others, as members of confraternities, rather than as individuals. The Misericordia confraternity, established in Nagasaki in 1583, was followed by devout associations formed voluntarily in other places. The confraternities had strict rules. They not only evangelized and supported the faith in various ways but also devoted themselves to works of charity as an expression of their faith.

The Jesuits' annual report of 1585 commends the Nagasaki Misericordia confraternity for observing the feast day to commemorate the Holy Mother's visit to Saint Elizabeth and honoring it with splendid ceremony. The report mentions that the confraternity held funerals and joined in funeral processions and notes the many works of mercy that the confraternity undertook, such as collecting alms in the streets for the poor. Moreover, the report says that the confraternity did these things as efficiently as the Jesuit missionaries.

The Christians in Nagasaki established a variety of charitable facilities (including an old people's home, an orphanage, and an aid station for the homeless) and hospitals (including a leprosarium). They supervised cemeteries, provided various services for Nagasaki residents, acted as pallbearers for the poor, dug graves, aided prostitutes and slaves, helped the bereaved families of the persecuted, and so on. Such concern exerted a great influence both in Nagasaki and outside the community.

Methods of Catechesis

The missionaries' greatest task was to teach the fundamentals of faith to a society completely ignorant of Christianity. With that in mind, Xavier preached that God is the creator of all things, refuted the claims of the Japanese Buddhists, explained Jesus Christ's sufferings on the cross, taught the fundamentals of Christian belief, and spoke of the Ten Commandments. Luis Frois (1532–97), the dynamic leader of the mission in the Kyoto region, surveyed the methods of instruction from the time of Christianity's entry into Japan. In his two-part *História de Japam*, covering the years 1549–82, he notes:

> First of all we prove that there is a creator of the universe, that the universe had a beginning and is not eternal as some people believe, and that the sun and moon are not gods and are not even endowed with life. We then prove that the soul lives on forever after its separation from the body and show the difference between the rational and sensible soul, a distinction that is unknown to the people here. After that we discuss all kinds of objections and difficulties as they are brought forward and answer questions that are asked about various phenomena of nature. The next step is to discuss those Japanese sects to which

each individual belongs in order that they can compare their old be-liefs with what we have told them and can see the difference. Each of the errors must then be refuted with clear-cut proofs so that the people can understand that those beliefs are mistaken.

Once all these things have been understood, we seek according to the intellectual caliber of each to explain the mystery of the Trinity, the creation of the world, the fall of Lucifer, and the sin of Adam, and from this point we lead up to the Incarnation, the holiness of Christ's life, His death, resurrection, and ascension, the power and mystery of the Cross, the Last Judgment, the pains of Hell, and the happiness of Heaven.

When all these truths have been made clear to the people by means of fixed and standardized sermons that have been prepared in Japa-nese, additional pre-baptismal instructions are given concerning the Ten Commandments, the necessity of avoiding their traditional superstitions, their obligation of persevering in the observance of God's Law, and the meaning and the need for contrition, etc. Baptism is then administered, but not before its meaning and necessity have been explained.*

Catechesis progressed in three stages: (1) instruction in doctrines con-cerning God the creator, the immortality of the soul, and salvation, to-gether with an adapted refutation of the teachings of the Buddhist sects; (2) a chronological exposition of Christian doctrine; and (3) preparation for baptism, with an explanation of the Ten Commandments and Jesus Christ's teachings. Catechumens went through this strict training at a church before being able to receive baptism.

The Japanese catechism that Valignano compiled according to these principles, the *Catechismus Christianae fidei in quo veritas nostrae religionis ostenditur et fectae Iaponenses confutantur* (1586), became the basic instructional work. Christianity was also taught through plays and songs based on Bible sto-ries. These devices helped the general population gain familiarity with Christianity and begin to understand its message. Dramatic interpreta-tions included *The Story of Adam and Eve* (performed in Yamaguchi in 1553; in Funai in 1560, 1563, 1565, and 1566; and in Ikitsuki in 1563); *The Story of Moses* (Yamaguchi, 1553); nativity plays, such as *The Nativity of Our Lord;* and passion plays, such as *The Burial of Our Lord.* In the main, their themes came from stories in the Old Testament and from the life of Jesus

* Luis Frois, *História de Japam*, trans. Hubert Cieslik in Hubert Cieslik, "Father Luis Frois, Historian of the Mission," *Missionary Bulletin* (Tokyo) 8 (1954): 156–57.

and they emphasized such teachings as the meaning of redemption. Tales from the Bible set to music were said to have been sung in Japanese musical styles.

The training of missionaries was undertaken in the seminaries and colleges. The purpose of the seminaries was to train large numbers of evangelists and Japanese clergy to compensate for the shortage of European preachers. The seminaries provided basic training for novices who aspired to become priests or friars. They also trained organists, choristers, painters, copperplate engravers, and printers. The colleges were of two levels. The elementary level, intended as centers of missionary activity, taught children the reading and writing of Japanese and Latin, vocal music, and religion. The higher level, for religious workers, focused on advanced and specialized studies; these colleges taught theology, philosophy, music, and art and undertook research on and taught Japanese religion, literature, language, and customs.

This organized educational structure established by Valignano was intended not only to train missionaries but also to create Christian leaders in many walks of life.

THE SUPPRESSION OF CHRISTIANITY

Christianity Proscribed

In the sixth month of 1587 Toyotomi Hideyoshi (1537–98), who had just conquered Kyushu and established virtual hegemony over all Japan, issued a five-article edict expelling the foreign Jesuits. This action reflected Hideyoshi's increasing doubts about Christianity, in particular its concept of the "kingdom of God" as symbolized by Nagasaki, which he had heard about in detail while on Kyushu. To Hideyoshi, Christians were like the Jōdo Shin *ikkō* groups, harmful to the nation. This edict ended the friendly relations that had existed between Hideyoshi and the missionaries.

Hideyoshi's expulsion edict is best understood as a declaration of his political, economic, and ideological authority. Hideyoshi's anti-Christian edict, issued on the nineteenth day of the sixth month of 1587, which proscribed Christianity entirely, shocked the missionaries and caused Christians great anxiety. In the Christian settlement of Nagasaki, people were panic-stricken, fearing a major persecution. The Jesuits' annual report for 1587 says that all the townspeople fled for a short time, thinking that Hideyoshi's retainers were going to destroy and plunder the town. A large number of people shouldered their belongings and hid in the hills. The Jesuit clergy, fearing that the churches would come to harm, removed holy pictures and statues and barred church doors. The prosperous settlement became a ghost town.

The proscription edict remained largely unenforced, however. Valignano returned to Japan as visitor a second time in July 1590 in the company of the embassy of Japanese youths that had gone to Europe in 1582. His visit paved the way for a renaissance of the Japanese church. The church pressed forward with the charitable works emphasized by Valignano, and the plan of the vice-provincial, Gaspar Coelho (ca. 1531–90), to establish a fort at Nagasaki was abandoned. Amicable relations with the government were restored when Hideyoshi received Valignano in audience in the third month of 1591. As long as the anti-Christian edict was not enforced, the prospects for development of the church seemed to be good.

With the arrival of the Dominican friar Juan Cobo (d. 1592) in 1592 and of the Franciscan friar Pedro Baptista Blásquez y Blásquez (1549–97) the following year, however, the Jesuit monopoly of the Japan mission that Valignano had envisioned ended, leading to animosity among the religious orders and disorder in missionary activities. The secular authorities intervened, and Blásquez and twenty-five others—Franciscan and Jesuit clerics and lay Christians—were executed in Nagasaki in 1597. The deaths of these twenty-six were both an augury of the long period of martyrdom that followed and the first demand that Japanese Christians give proof of their faith.

Hideyoshi's successor, Tokugawa Ieyasu (1542–1616), continued to enact anti-Christian measures as he strove to establish his rule and the Tokugawa shogunate. Repression became increasingly systematic under the second and third Tokugawa shōguns, Hidetada (1579–1632) and Iemitsu (1604–51). The successive proscription decrees issued in 1612, 1613, and 1616 were integrated with the seclusion edicts of 1633, 1634, 1635, 1636, and 1639 that closed Japan to the outside world. These decrees were enforced all the more harshly because many of those who took part in the Shimabara Uprising, from the tenth month of 1637 to the third month of 1638, were Christians. Beginning in 1632, when Iemitsu assumed power on the death of his father, Hidetada, records of the execution of Christians throughout Japan testify to the long-delayed enforcement of the Christian proscriptions.

Proscription was enforced through the *shūmon aratame* (national reli-

THE SUPPRESSION OF CHRISTIANITY   437

gious-affiliation census) and the *terauke* (temple-certification) system. It was strengthened by the practice, particularly around Nagasaki, of "picture treading" (*efumi*), whereby suspected Christians were required to trample on Christian images; by the five-family system of joint responsibility instituted in 1634, which linked unrelated households as a means of social control; and by the offer of rewards to informers. Finally, in 1687 an investigation of Christian families to the fifth generation (*ruizoku aratame*) was begun. The goal of these various measures was to eradicate Christianity from the country.

Punishments for violation of the proscription were Draconian and included crucifixion, burning at the stake, water torture, suspending the prisoner head down over a pit of excrement, and mutilation. Despite the cruelty of their punishment, many Christians remained steadfast in their faith to the end. Their bravery in the face of martyrdom stemmed from their religious life, which was nurtured by confraternities. The more that Christians found themselves assailed by the forces of persecution, the more they looked to the confraternities as sources of practical and spiritual aid and encouragement in their shared faith.

The Kakure Christians

Confraternities were established throughout Japan after Valignano returned in 1590 for his second visit. He intended to organize lay believers in preparation for the persecution that was sure to come. Even if the churches were lost and suppression prevented public worship or missionary activities, if devout associations of lay believers survived, they could play a major role in evangelization and pastoral work and in maintaining and encouraging the faith. As a result of the concerted efforts of each of the orders, by around 1600 Christian lay associations could be found in all parts of the nation.

Jesuit confraternities on Kyushu—the Sacramento, the Santa Maria, and the Annunciation, in Nagasaki, Arima, and Ōmura, respectively— developed active programs similar to the charity work conducted by the Misericordia confraternity in Nagasaki. Confraternities established by other orders included the Franciscan Cordón de Francisco in Edo and the Dominican Rosario in Ōmura. Thus various confraternities were established where Christian communities existed and became the source of support of the faith and protection of the lives of Christians when the religion was proscribed.

A concise statement of the role of the confraternities is found in the regulations of the Santa Maria confraternity: "The confraternity is established to work for the salvation of souls and to aid the teaching of the Christian faith, not solely out of thought for the benefit of its members. Through its various groups and subgroups, Christians can better and more easily receive guidance and help in regard to all things. In times of persecution it is truly the one unequaled beneficial body."

The confraternities were organized into both small groups of about fifty people (consisting of male believers and their wives and children) and large groups of five hundred to six hundred people (consisting of an assemblage of several small groups). In addition, there was a parent organization in each district. The small groups were headed by two leaders, the principal leader (*ōoya*) and the assistant leader (*kooya*), who were also among the leaders of the large groups and the parent organization. The regulations specified that the leaders were to be men of standing, able to encourage and protect the organization's holy work through both their personal authority and acts of philanthropy. They were chosen from among the village elders or the headman class.

The group leaders were assisted by those assigned to foster charity and pastoral work, to collect and distribute donations, and to promote communications. An older woman oversaw the charitable work of the women. Appointments to office were decided by consultation between priests and leaders, as were such matters as admission to or expulsion from the confraternity.

The members of the confraternities led devout lives, helping with evangelization and performing charitable works like visiting the poor and the ill. They met for mass, private worship, the reading of devotional works, and religious instruction. With all the churches destroyed, these meetings took place in private homes. The activities of the confraternities not only strengthened group solidarity among Christians but also deepened their individual faith. The confraternities attempted to prepare believers to face martyrdom.

The Christians who practiced their faith in secrecy in the villages and hamlets maintained a firm religious structure under the guidance of the *sōgashira*, the elder who interpreted the Christian liturgical calendar to direct his fellows concerning which activities were permitted and which were not. Below him in the organization were the *furegashira*, who transmitted the faith to smaller groups, and the *kikiyaku*, who stood between the *furegashira* and individual Christians and worked with a very small group of several families.

Isolated and outlawed as they were, Christian organizations were united by a strong fellow feeling that eventually excluded non-Christians. According to Toshiyuki Toya's *Kirishitan Nōmin no Keizai Seikatsu* (Economic Life of the Christian Farmers; 1943), "Last year, when Christians suffered distress from sickness and misfortune, fellow Christians distributed rice and money among them. Those who were unbelievers, slanderers of the faith, be they even master, parent, child, brother, or sister, were ignored, regardless of their distress." The idea of helping one's neighbor, the cornerstone of the confraternities' activities, vanished when Christians found themselves under close surveillance. In its stead ties of sympathy between members and vigilance against outsiders were emphasized.

Christians were found at all levels of village society, from the official class to laborers. In times of persecution, however—for example, that in Urakami, near Nagasaki, in the Kansei era (1789–1801)—many among the wealthier classes cooled toward the faith and apostatized. Eventually, the surviving Christian communities were largely isolated, rural, and poor.

The Isolated Christian Communities

The Christians who remained underground while the proscription edict was in force perpetuated the faith of their ancestors as tradition. Following the reopening of the country after 1854, the surviving Christians split into two groups, those who were "resurrected" when the Catholic church resumed missionary activity and those who remained segregated, preserving their traditional practices. The latter are known as "old" Christians, and because they did not rejoin the Catholic church they are also called *hanare* (isolated) Christians.

The *hanare* Christian communities clung to their distinctive faith, which had evolved during two and a half centuries of isolation. These communities survived in Hizen Province in the remote regions of Ikitsuki Island, Kurosaki, and the Gotō Islands. The believers revered various relics of their faith, including articles connected with their martyred ancestors; "closet gods" (*nando-gami*), crude reproductions of sacred pictures affixed to scrolls and hung in the back of storage closets; and the forty-six-cord whips used by flagellants.

In the Sotome region, northwest of Nagasaki, the Christian groups were led by a number of people, such as the elder and keeper of records (*chōkata* or *ochōyaku*), the baptizer (*mizukata* or *osazukeyaku*), and the catechist (*kikiyaku* or *minaraiyaku*). In the Gotō Islands the hierarchy consisted of the elder and keeper of records, the baptizer (*kambōyaku*), and the assistant (*fureyaku* or *toritsugiyaku*). Recognized group members were called "those within the group" (*kumiuchi*) or "those in the register" (*chōuchi*).

The elder's duties were those of the principal leader described in the Santa Maria confraternity regulations. He was responsible for preserving observance of the liturgical calendar and for transmitting the traditions of worship (*orasho*) and doctrine. The baptizer of course administered baptism, and the catechist was virtually the assistant of the baptizer, since it was his duty to make preparations for various ceremonies, including baptism.

The old Christians preserved their beliefs through their own religious works, such as the *Konchirisan no Riyaku* (The Merit of Contrition; first printed in 1603) and the *Tenchi Hajimari no Koto* (The Beginning of Heaven and Earth; nineteenth century). The latter document is a biblical narrative in which Christian beliefs are merged with the local traditions of the Sotome region. It depicts the realm of faith as defined by the old Christians during centuries of isolation, a blend of Christian teachings, indigenous folk beliefs, Shintō, and Buddhism.

17. Folk Religion and Shugendō

FOLK RELIGION

Urban Folk Religion

Folk religions of all periods and places are alike in having no specific founder and no codified doctrine. Japanese folk religion encompasses veneration of traditional local tutelary *kami* (deities) and of the buddhas associated with them under the theory of *honji suijaku*, which regarded the local *kami* as manifestations of those buddhas. It is, above all, a religious expression rooted in the everyday lives of people dwelling in villages and hamlets.

As a rule, farming villages in the Edo period (1603–1868) had one local tutelary deity, or *ujigami*, and a number of Buddhist temples. Within the grounds of the shrine of the *ujigami* was an associated shrine (*sessha*) or a subordinate shrine (*massha*). Along roadsides there were miniature shrines (*hokora*) dedicated to *kanjōshin*, or invoked deities, to whom appeals for particular types of assistance and succor were addressed. The roles of the various *kami* were complementary, and the *kami* and buddhas coexisted. Both the *kami* and the buddhas, as understood and worshiped by the villagers, derived from and were regarded as local protector spirits. The diversity of the *kami* and buddhas in the villages can be traced to the diversity of human desires and hopes. Perhaps it is in this sense that we can say that humans create their deities.

In the middle of the eighteenth century, popular belief in folk *kami* and buddhas increased enormously, as is evidenced by the flourishing of *ennichi* (festival days associated with particular *kami* or Buddhist deities) and *kaichō* (the exposure of normally concealed images) in the grounds of small and medium-sized local temples of the Tendai, Shingon, and Zen sects. For example, in 1690 Benzaiten (in Sanskrit, Sarasvatī) had been enshrined in thirteen places in Edo, but sixty years later, in 1749, some 134 places were associated with that deity—a tenfold increase. Similarly, temples dedicated to Kannon (in Sanskrit, Avalokiteśvara) increased from fifteen to fifty-two, temples of Yakushi Nyorai (Bhaiṣajyaguru) from fourteen to thirty-four, temples of Fudō Myōō (Acala) from seven to nineteen, temples of Jizō (Kṣitigarbha) from none at all to forty-seven, and shrines of Inari (the deity of the harvest) from twenty-four to 124. Pilgrimage circuits—such as the thirty-three Kannon temples of Edo, the forty-eight temples associated with Jizō, the eighty-eight images of Kūkai, the one hundred Emma-ō (Yama-rāja) temples, the one hundred Benzaiten shrines, and the circuit of the Shichifukujin, or Seven Deities of Good Fortune—developed at about the same time.

Kaichō drew throngs of worshipers. There were two forms of *kaichō*: *igaichō* and *degaichō*. *Igaichō* was the display of the images of a temple or shrine in its own quarters. *Degaichō* was the display of the images of a temple or shrine in quarters borrowed from another temple or shrine for that purpose. As a rule, *degaichō* lasted sixty days.

Research by the scholar Hiruma Hisashi indicates that numerous temples and shrines outside Edo held *degaichō* in Edo, in Iwakiyama Shrine (in Mutsu Province, far to the north), and in Zendō-ji (in Chikugo Province, on Kyushu, far to the west). Moreover, of 1,565 recorded instances of *kaichō* in Edo between 1654 and 1868, nearly half (47.3 percent) were *degaichō*. The percentage of *degaichō* among *kaichō* was significantly higher in Edo than in Kyoto, making a high percentage of *degaichō* a feature of *kaichō* in Edo.

Temples and shrines did not necessarily hold *kaichō* every year. Most of the *degaichō* initiated in Edo by temples and shrines outside the city were held at the Jōdo-sect Ekō-in in the Honjo district, Eitai-ji in the precincts of Tomioka Hachiman Shrine in Fukagawa, the Shingon-sect Gokoku-ji in Koishikawa, and Tenjin Shrine in Yushima. The areas around *degaichō* facilities developed into thriving markets to serve the crowds of visitors.

It was essential for the famous provincial temples to attract crowds when they held a *degaichō* in Edo. At the time of the *degaichō* of an image known as the Satte Fudō in 1807, a huge party of *yamabushi* (mountain-dwelling ascetics) in their distinctive garb paraded through Edo, welcoming the sacred image. Leading a five- or six-block-long procession of several thousand people, they carried small bells and staffs crowned with small metal rings and blew on conch-shell trumpets. The highlight of the spectacle, which attracted great attention, was an exhibition of fire-walking by the *yamabushi* inside a specially erected palisade of bamboo.

Not all *degaichō* pilgrims were drawn by pageantry, however. Many people with sincere religious vows or petitions avoided the crowds and made early morning pilgrimages (*asamairi*), a popular theme of Edo-period woodblock prints. Such prints offer glimpses of mothers carrying children on their backs and young women risen early, their makeup hurriedly applied, making for the shrine or temple of their favorite deity between five and six in the morning. They sought to avoid the crowds and deliver their petitions directly to a *kami* or buddha.

Ennichi, the Buddhist equivalent of shrine festivals, provided an opportunity for worshipers to visit temples and pray to the buddhas or bodhisattvas in whom they had placed their faith. The custom of holding *ennichi* on certain days can be traced back to the late Heian period (794–1185). It was widely believed that the eighth of the month was sacred to Yakushi Nyorai, the nineteenth to Kannon, the twenty-fourth to Jizō, and the twenty-eighth to Fudō Myōō.

Seasonal Festivals

Ennichi and *kaichō* were largely Buddhist events. Traditional Shintō festivals also continued, and coexistence of the two traditions characterized Japanese folk religion. Reflecting the rhythms of an agrarian society, the traditional festivals were most frequent in spring and autumn. Festivals in the spring welcomed the *kami* of the paddies at the time of rice planting, and those in autumn celebrated the harvest. At midwinter festivals the people prayed for the return of the sun, and at summer festivals they prayed for protection against misfortune.

One function of festivals was to secure bountiful harvests by inviting the *kami* to descend to the paddies and then entertaining them. Then, too, malevolent *kami* had to be propitiated and banished. Kyoto's principal summer festival is an excellent example of the latter belief. The *kami* of the Gion Festival is Gozu Tennō (in Sanskrit, Gośīrṣa-devarāja), an Indian deity equated with the legendary Susanoo no Mikoto, the younger brother of Amaterasu Ōmikami, who was expelled from the High Heavenly Plain for his offensive behavior. He was enshrined as the main deity of Yasaka Shrine, in the Higashiyama district, in accordance with

the belief that once the malevolent *kami* Susanoo was appeascd his powers would be used to protect supplicants against sickness and misfortune.
After the twelfth century, the task of vanquishing *goryō* (vengeful spirits)
came to be assigned to Susanoo no Mikoto in his manifestation as Gozu
Tennō. One of the practices believed to propitiate spirits was colorful, ele-
gant dancing, and this seems to have been the origin of the Gion Festival,
with its lavish floats (*dashi*) and portable shrines (*mikoshi*) paraded through
the streets.

During the Edo period, Gion festivals came to be held in provincial
cities, where they eventually took root as local urban festivals. In some
ways townspeople enjoyed even less security than peasants, for they were
at the mercy of the frequent epidemics that swept the crowded cities.
Epidemics were thought to be the work of evil spirits, the curse of the
kami of illness. This belief had been held by townspeople as early as the
Heian period.

Like Yasaka Shrine in Kyoto, Kanda Shrine in Edo, popularly known
as Kanda Myōjin, was associated with a wrathful spirit that had been
propitiated and transformed into a protector deity. One of the *kami* enshrined at Kanda Shrine is the vengeful spirit of the warrior Taira no
Masakado, who was slain in 940 during the rebellion he led in the Kantō
region. His severed head was believed to have flown through the air and
landed in Edo at the site known as Kubizuka (Head Mound), where he
was worshiped to appease his malevolent spirit. The *Bunsei Jisha Kakiage*
(The Bunsei-Era [1818–30] Report on Temples and Shrines) indicates
that Masakado's spirit had been enshrined with the *kami* worshiped at
Kanda Shrine, made the *ubusunagami* (tutelary deity) of the Kanda district, and honored with a festival. (Even today the festival *mikoshi* of
Kanda Shrine never fail to visit Kubizuka, in modern Tokyo's Ōtemachi
district.)

Through these honors and attentions, Masakado's spirit was gradually
appeased and transformed into a local protector deity. The *mikoshi* of his
shrine even had permission to enter Edo Castle itself when the famed
towering floats of the shrine festival were paraded through the streets in
homage to Masakado, the former author of violent curses. The Kanda
Festival is another example of the practice of propitiating a malevolent
spirit, transforming it into a benevolent spirit, and calling on the now-
benevolent spirit's power to drive away the *kami* of illness.

In general, autumn festivals honored the protector *kami* of rural villages. They were large-scale rites, in which foods special to the harvest

season, especially those made with the new grain, were prepared and the deity invited to feast. The new grain was offered to the *kami*, and the celebrants ate together with the invited deity. A large banquet followed. Autumn festivals were the most typical of the festivals of agricultural communities.

One of the most important autumn rites discovered by folklorists is Ae no Koto, a folk religious practice still performed by farmers on the Noto Peninsula, on the west coast of central Honshu. The observances, which are concentrated around the fifth of December—roughly the beginning of the eleventh month of the lunar calendar—are conducted in the houses of old families whose ties to the district date back to the Edo period.

Bales of the seed rice to be used for planting the following year are placed in each house. These are revered as *shintai*, a *kami*'s temporary residence. On the evening of December 5 the head of the household, clad in formal attire, goes out to the paddies to welcome the *kami* of the paddies, under whose protection the rice has been produced, and invites the *kami* into the house. There, the *kami* is led to the bath and invited to bathe. At this point, the family head mimes the actions of the *kami* bathing. Next the *kami* is taken to the formal sitting room, where the bales of rice have been placed. In front of the bales is a large double-rooted white radish. Trays of food are placed before the bales, and the household head, naming each food as it is offered, feeds the *kami*. According to the oral tradition, this is done because the *kami*, begrimed by long labors in the paddies, can no longer see. With hunger sated, the *kami* returns to the mountains or to the sky, to descend again at planting time in the spring.

In the cycle of agricultural festivals, the paddy *kami* were bidden farewell in the autumn and welcomed back in spring. Folklore studies have shown that the autumn and winter festivals originally celebrated the rebirth of the spirit of the rice. Summer festivals, on the other hand, were the magical means of propitiating evil spirits and banishing misfortune. They were characterized by colorful processions and parades of floats and by boisterous energy. Although superficially akin to the outbursts of frenzied dancing that recurred during times of social unrest, these festivals did not escalate into a popular movement but were assimilated into custom and limited to the ritual banishment of and burning of effigies of the *kami* of bad luck.

From the beginning, shrine festivals had encompassed two dimensions of life: the extraordinary (*hare*) and the routine (*ke*). Festivals took participants from everyday life into the realm of the supranatural and back again, the religious implication being that the act of welcoming the *kami* and entertaining them courteously enables humankind to flourish. In social terms, however, festivals were opportunities for large numbers of people to participate in group activities. The individual participants knew exactly why they were involved. The summer festival provided protection against misfortune, while the autumn festival ensured that the *kami* of the rice would return the following season. The repetition of the round of festivals maintained the order of everyday life.

Dōsojin *and Phallic Deities*

Belief in the harmony of complementary opposites was a powerful force in the lives of farmers. The realization that the growth of families and villages was sustained by the generative power of men and women gave rise to the belief that agricultural bounty was sustained by the generative power of the fields. Phallicism, worship of the generative principle, is the organized expression of this belief. A representative example of phallicism in Japanese folk religion is found in worship of *dōsojin*.

Dōsojin, or guardian deities, are also known as *sai no kami*, the deities of roads or boundaries. *Dōsojin* are commonly represented as a male-female couple. Most such *dōsojin* carved of stone date from the Edo period and later. The couple *dōsojin* have been identified variously as the male and female creator *kami* Izanagi and Izanami and as the equally ancient male and female deities Sarutahiko no Kami and Ame no Uzume no Mikoto, but whatever their derivation, their powers as protectors of village boundaries are enhanced by the male-female pairing. In addition to sculptures of the couple standing side by side, there are many sculptures that are frankly sexual, depicting the couple embracing in varying degrees of intimacy.

Surveys of *dōsojin* sculptures in Niigata Prefecture, on the northwestern coast of Honshu, made by Yokoyama Kyokusaburō raise a number of interesting points. For instance, the *dōsojin* at Akatani in the town of Kawanishi was revered as a child-bestowing deity. People who wanted children prayed to this *dōsojin*, and it was believed particularly efficacious for the couple to make love before this image in the dead of night. The *dōsojin* revered at Takinomata in the village of Hirokami was called the "kissing statue." The success of prayers offered to this *kami* was believed to be assured if two small stones were thrown and two small twigs twisted together with the left hand. On May 8, the women of the village collected and cooked wild vegetables from the hills and waited for the men to come with sakè and other food. They then sat down together in front of the *dōsojin* and feasted. This custom appears to suggest sexual intercourse before the *dōsojin*.

In Itoigawa men and women petitioned *dōsojin* for restoration of the equilibrium of their generative powers, as is evidenced by the inscription on a local *dōsojin:* "Disorders of the male and female organs are cured. If an impotent man offers prayers with deep belief, vigor will be achieved in a marked fashion. Kōshin Day, 1852."

Dōsojin festivals were central to agricultural rites performed on the fourteenth and fifteenth days of the New Year season. A common feature of these festivals was the clear perception of the individual roles of the male and female deities. The *dōsojin* were venerated as two separate gods.

During the *dōsojin* festival at Yoshio in the city of Kashiwazaki, two pairs of dolls, representing a young couple (*ani fūfu*) and an old couple (*oji fūfu*), were made. The males were dressed in silver paper and the females in gold paper. On January 15 straw shelters were erected on opposite banks of the local river and the couples placed in them. Later the dolls were set afire, first the young couple, then the old.

An interesting account of a *dōsojin* festival in the Nagaoka region of Echigo Province (present-day Niigata Prefecture) is found in the *Shokoku Fūzoku Toijō Kotae* (Answers to a Questionnaire about Provincial Customs), replies to the survey on customs in the provinces, conducted around 1816 by the shogunate-appointed Confucian scholar Yashiro Hirokata (1758–1841). Yashiro describes a celebration on the fourteenth day of the New Year season as follows:

> Images of the male and female gods in the style of the dolls popular in Kyoto for the Doll Festival were made of sumac and dressed in white paper painted with patterns in red. Children led by men carried them around in *hasamibako* [boxes with shoulder poles] to the houses of relatives. When they called out the name of the family whose *dōsojin* they were carrying, they were given gifts wrapped in paper—fans, paper handkerchiefs, chestnuts, persimmons, rice cakes, or money to buy food. The men were given cups of sakè. The gifts were called the *kanjin* [pledge] for the *kami* of the boundaries.

Though this was predominantly a children's event, the *kami* were clearly adult male and female deities. The children sang a verse that seems to have been popular at the time: "It is the *kanjin* for the *kami* of the boundaries. Give us money or give us rice so that when spring comes there will be a bride or a groom from the northwest, straight and easy. *Oshare, oshare.*"

The expression "there will be a bride or a groom" appears to have a special significance. In his *Hokuetsu Seppu* (Snow-Country Tales; 1836, 1842), the essayist Suzuki Bokushi (1770–1842) wrote about the ceremony on the day of the *kanjin* for the *kami* of the boundaries.

> Beginning at dawn, large numbers of children gathered at the gates of households that had received a bride or a groom in the past year. They beat on the panels of the gate with the measuring sticks they carried, crying out in unison: "Send out your bride, send out your groom."

This ritual can be regarded as a generative rite of the lunar New Year inspired by the belief that the fervid sexual activity of newlyweds would work as sympathetic magic to promote agricultural bounty. Suzuki also describes the *dōsojin* fully:

> They make two wooden heads about five or six *sun* [fifteen to eighteen centimeters] tall. On each they paint eyes and a nose, creating a male and a female *kami*. Cotton is draped around the head of the female, and red plum blossoms and other flowers are painted on a paper robe. An *eboshi* [court cap] is placed on the head of the male, and he is given a beard of wood shavings. Designs of young pine are painted on his paper robe.

The accounts of both Yashiro and Suzuki demonstrate the centrality of the male and female deities. But even when there were no specific *shintai*, or physical manifestations of the *kami*—for instance, in the form of phallic or ktenic stones—the sacredness and centrality of special representations of the male and female genitals were apparent in a number of rites in Niigata Prefecture.

At Mugurasawa in the village of Yunotani, on the morning of January 15 a phallic tower was built of snow and crowned with a triangular kteis adorned with "hairs" of cypress leaves. In the afternoon, pine branches were placed on the platform that represented the testicles and ignited. At Ushiroyama in the town of Yamato men of an age believed to be unlucky made white fans, and women of an unlucky age made sacred wands with paper of five colors. The fans, wands, and a monetary offering were bound together with reeds. Four pairs of fans and wands were placed before the stone image of the *kami* of boundaries and later burned. At Takanosu in Kashiwazaki effigies of the *kami* of boundaries in the form of an old man and an old woman about one meter tall were made of straw, old charms, or hair. Both male and female wore a topknot, and the crotch area of their naked bodies was emphasized with the powdered flesh of red peppers. The effigies were hoisted into the air face-to-face by the villagers. All these examples imply reverence for the paired male and female deities in their role as symbols of sexual activity.

During the festival held in the hamlet of Momogawa in Nishi Kubiki District, the hamlet was divided into east and west. On the evening of January 14, the rite of going from door to door singing a song to drive harmful birds from the village was performed. Afterward a table was set up in the sitting room of each house, and on it were placed the pair of deities called Odekusan. The figures, about five centimeters in diameter and ten centimeters tall, were carved from sumac. The male was dressed in red, and the female in yellow. Specific families in the eastern and western sections of the hamlet made the images.

On the morning of January 15, the children of the village collected the *kadomatsu* (New Year's gate decorations) from each household, pulled the pine branches from the decorations and bound them to bamboo, and burned the bundles as representations of the *kami* of boundaries. This rite, called *sai no kamiyaki*, took place in the eastern and the western sections at sunset. The making of prophecies for the coming year was a part of this rite. If the burning pine branches fell toward the hills, that betokened abundant mountain produce for the year. If they fell toward the sea, fishing would be good.

When the *dōsojin* was portrayed as a male-female pair, there was a tendency to focus attention on the exposed genitals. However, this type of *dōsojin* was intended to ensure a rich harvest for an agricultural society. In fact the primary purpose of all the rites of the Little New Year (January 15), not just those connected with the *dōsojin*, was to ensure agricultural bounty. Thus the rites displayed many sexual elements, representing generative power, and were often concerned with envisioning the bounty of the next harvest.

Students of religion point out that such rites were performed as sympathetic magic. Unsophisticated peasants saw a correspondence between human fecundity and plentiful crops. Models of flowers and grains shaved from soft wood were meant to suggest ripened grain. The slight sexual allusion here was probably not accidental. As a religious phenomenon these rites represented veneration of generative power, which sustains the underlying order of an agricultural society.

Fuji Kō

One of the popular religions that developed rapidly in the Edo period was Fuji Kō, the cult of Mount Fuji. The syncretic Fuji Kō beliefs incorporated elements from many sources. This cult was especially significant because, lying outside either Buddhist or Shintō control, it suggested possibilities for the new religions of the period preceding the fall of the shogunate, in the mid-1850s. Fuji Kō's influence stemmed from the fact that it was largely a product of the mountain cult centered on Mount Fuji since earliest times and from its simple exposition of a doctrine that ordinary people could easily understand and accept.

With its beautiful mountains and valleys, the area around Mount Fuji can easily be thought of as another world. The earliest description of Mount Fuji, the *Fujisan Ki* (Mount Fuji Diary), by the courtier and poet Miyako no Yoshika (834–79), mentions that the people living at the foot of the mountain performed rites and ceremonies every year. Yoshika claims to have seen two white-robed maidens dancing on the summit, which does not seem so fanciful if we recall that white smoke from Mount Fuji's intermittent volcanic activity was visible on clear days. Hence, Konohana Sakuyahime (supposed to be the most beautiful of all mythical women) and Kaguyahime (the heroine of unsurpassed beauty in the tale *Taketori Monogatari*) were integrated into the female-*kami* cult associated with Mount Fuji. This probably explains why many *miko* (female shamanic mediums) apparently gathered on peaks in the Mount Fuji region to engage in ascetic practices. However, the earliest documented cults are those of the mountain ascetics of the Shugendō tradition.

The oldest of the routes up the mountain began at the village of Murayama, which came to be dominated by Shugendō practitioners in the Shingon lineage. Tradition holds that in the early twelfth century the legendary ascetic Matsudai climbed the mountain from Murayama and built a temple dedicated to Dainichi Nyorai on the summit. Raison, a later leader of Shugendō on Mount Fuji, was active at the beginning of the fourteenth century. The legend associating the late-seventh-century ascetic En no Ozunu with Fuji Kō appears to have originated around the fourteenth century. Shugendō, most influential at Murayama, was scarcely represented at the departure points of the other four routes up the mountain.

Although there are no old records of women climbing Mount Fuji, that they certainly must have done so from time to time is suggested by the cave cult that existed at the foot of the mountain. Legends associated with Mount Fuji often refer to women confining themselves in its caves. Kaguyahime is said to have entered a cave in the mountain, although which cave is unclear. There are many that became centers of various beliefs. The presence of *miko* is suggested by the prefix *uba* (old woman) in such place names as Uba-ana and Ubasute-ana.

Another cave designation worthy of note is *tainai* (uterine cavity). Since it is womb-shaped and is believed to have been where Konohana Sakuyahime gave birth to a child, Funatsu Tainai in Kawaguchi, in Mount Fuji's northern foothills, enshrines the deity of safe childbirth. Another cave of much the same shape is the Inno Tainai in Gotemba, southeast of Mount Fuji, which contains the image of a deity who watches over the rearing of children, as well as stones sacred to conception and safe childbirth. A phallic stone was worshiped as the manifestation of the deity. The term *tainai* may have been used as a conscious reference to such sexual elements.

The most celebrated of the caverns was Hitoana near the city of Fujinomiya, in Mount Fuji's southwestern foothills. A large cave some ninety meters deep, Hitoana was from early times a site sacred to Fuji Kō. An entry dated the third day of the sixth month of 1203 in the *Azuma Kagami* (Mirror of the East), a chronicle of the Kamakura shogunate, relates how Nitta Shirō Tadatsune (d. 1203) entered Hitoana with five companions on the shōgun's orders. But something frightful seems to have occurred in the cave, and the next day only Nitta returned. Nothing further is recorded; however, the account indicates that at the beginning of the thirteenth century the cave was a place of mystery that few people approached.

This incident inspired numerous tales. For example, the *Hōjō Godai Ki* (Chronicle of Five Generations of the Hōjō Clan; ca. 1615–24), compiled from material written by Miura Shigemasa (1565–1644), relates that the six men met the deity of Mount Fuji, the Great Bodhisattva Sengen, a frightening white-haired presence clad in white robes. Many copies of the Muromachi-period (1336–1568) *Hitoana Zōshi* (A Tale of Hitoana) were in circulation, spreading the reputation of the cave even further. The *Hitoana Zōshi* recounts that the first to enter the cave was a man called Wada Heita, who is said to have met a woman dressed in ceremonial court robes and a scarlet divided skirt. She was seated at a loom, weaving. This woman, the mistress of the cave, possessed the sacred ability to tell the fortune of the shōgun, Minamoto no Yoriie (1182–1204). Perhaps the story reflects the existence of a group of *miko* undergoing ascetic training in the cave. The woman called up an awesome wind, which swept Heita away and deposited him outside the cave. He did not try to enter a second time.

When Nitta was commanded to enter, he resigned himself to death. He saw before him a panorama of hell and paradise. The cave was another world, so to speak, governed by the Great Bodhisattva Sengen. At this point the chronicle becomes a tale of exotic travel. Nitta promised not to utter a word about what he had experienced in the cave, and he returned to the outside world. At the shōgun's urging, however, he eventually spoke of what he had seen and died under a curse.

In the Edo period this legend was made the subject of popular illustrated fiction and further popularized. Typical of such works was the *Fuji no Hitoana Kembutsu* (Sightseeing in Mount Fuji's Hitoana), by Santō Kyōden (1761–1816). In this work the rustic Nitta enters Hitoana and has a variety of sexual experiences. These make him a man of the world, able to hold his own in the most sophisticated circles. Though Kyōden's purpose was clearly to titillate and amuse, it is worth noting that he retained the basic theme of Nitta's transformation in the cave.

The legendary founder of Fuji Kō is Kakugyō (1541–1646). He secluded himself in Hitoana, where he practiced austerities and was granted a revelation. He is said to have gotten his name, written with the Chinese ideographic characters for "square" (*kaku*) and "practice" (*gyō*), from his practice of standing immobile on a square piece of wood inside Hitoana. It was at this time that he produced strange ideograms, unique symbols valued by later cult followers. One story in the Kakugyō legend tells that the shōgun Tokugawa Ieyasu (1542–1616), accompanied by the Tendai priest Tenkai (d. 1643), went to visit Kakugyō during his practice and spoke with him. By the late years of the Tokugawa shogunate, however, Fuji Kō had become so influential that it was subjected to severe regulation and even proscribed by the shogunate.

The sixth patriarch of Fuji Kō was an ascetic named Jikigyō Miroku (1671–1733). Under him the cult gradually freed itself of the magical elements that had persisted since the time of Kakugyō, and its doctrine came to be based on popular ethical teachings.

The ideographic characters of the name Miroku can be interpreted to mean "achieving happiness [*roku*] by accepting one's station in life [*mi*] and working diligently." Miroku is also the Japanese name of the future buddha Maitreya, which suggests a connection with the cult of this bodhisattva—who was also associated with mountain worship from an early period. The Japanese had cherished a belief in the utopia of Miroku's realm since ancient times.

A famine in 1731 had sent rice prices soaring, and Edo was in the throes of a depression. Hoping to make the utopia of Miroku a reality, Jikigyō Miroku starved himself to death at the summit of Mount Fuji in 1733, vowing thereby to save all sentient beings. Pietistic suicide, particularly by starvation, was practiced by some mountain ascetics, who sought to achieve buddhahood in the present body by that means. The words that Jikigyō Miroku addressed to his disciple Tanabe Jūrōemon just before his death are recorded in the *Sanjūichinichi no Maki* (An Account of the Thirty-one Days; 1733), which is still in circulation today. According to this work, Jikigyō Miroku taught four virtues—uprightness, compassion, kindness, and frugality—and said that whoever practiced them would be much better off when reborn in the next life, whatever the misfortunes of the present one.

Fuji Kō spread and flourished. At one time it was said to have 808 branches in Edo alone. Its popularity caused the authorities, always uneasy about the organizations of the ordinary people, to fear its power. The degree of regulation imposed on the cult can be judged from the number of official notices concerning Fuji Kō that the shogunate issued to the townspeople. The notices indicate that a growing number of ascetics calling themselves members of Fuji Kō were wandering through urban areas distributing amulets. Since this was a violation of the law, such people were to be arrested and closely questioned. The extent to which Fuji Kō and related beliefs had permeated the lives of the populace can be attributed to the practical appeal—promises of wealth and prosperity—of the cult's teachings, as well as its emphasis on social and natural harmony, principles that reinforced the social ideals of the age.

Fujidō

During the early part of the nineteenth century Fujidō—written with ideographic characters meaning the Way of Nonduality but obviously in part homonymic with Mount Fuji—developed as an offshoot of Fuji Kō in the post-house town of Hatogaya outside Edo on the Nikkō Highway. Fujidō was led by Kotani Sanshi (1765–1841), an heir of the lineage of Jikigyō Miroku. Fujidō fervidly stressed the idea of world reformation (*yonaori*). Itō Sangyō (1746–1809), Sanshi's spiritual master, wrote in his

Sangyō Rokuōkū Otsutae (Divine Message through Sangyō) that the world changed at the seventh hour of the morning of the fifteenth day of the sixth month of 1688. The reformation had come about because male and female ropes had been let down from Tuṣita Heaven, the abode of the Great Bodhisattva Sengen. The release and intertwining of the male and female ropes signified the realization of the logic of harmony. The mention of Tuṣita Heaven, which in Buddhist cosmology is the Pure Land of Maitreya, further connects the beliefs of the Miroku cult and the logic of harmony.

Originally the teachings of Fuji Kō were explained in terms of the principle of pairs, such as father and mother or husband and wife. The sixth patriarch, Jikigyō Miroku, embodied this male and female harmony, and his daughter Hana (1724–89), a female ascetic and the seventh patriarch, transmitted it. The union of yin and yang realized through Jikigyō Miroku and Hana was manifested in rice. The connection here between male and female harmony and the ripening of crops is clear.

Fujidō shared the Fuji Kō belief that "the birth of a person and the birth of rice are the same thing." Among the *wasan*, or hymns, sung by Fujidō members was one titled *Koumi Wasan* (A Hymn on the Birth of a Child), a portion of which reads:

> The teachings of the time of [the bodhisattva] Miroku:
> The woman opens her heart to what is above,
> The man gives his affection to what is below,
> Their union at first is mere pleasure
> But is soon made a thing of importance.
> Before you are aware of it
> The time of conception may arise.
> There is nothing unwise about this.
> Look at the seedlings to be planted in the fields.
> When the work is done halfheartedly,
> The crop will not be bountiful.
> It is the same with human beings.
> The important thing is the planting.
> When there is the blessing of menstruation,
> The time is selected and the body purified,
> The mind cleansed of wrong,
> The laws strictly followed,
> Loyalty and filial piety held firm,

Regrets and greedy desires discarded,
Friendship sought with everyone.

This song of practical morality shows deep awareness of the connection between agricultural bounty and human sexuality and childbirth. The pivotal connection is clearly harmony between man and woman.

A typical folk religion of the Edo period, Fuji Kō declined after the great persecution of 1850. Nevertheless, key components of its value system survived in religions that came into being in the nineteenth century, and in this sense it clearly influenced modern popular religion.

SHUGENDŌ

Regulation by the Shogunate

With the *Shugendō Hatto* (Shugendō Regulations) issued in 1613, the shogunate ordered all practitioners of Shugendō to affiliate themselves with either the Honzan group or the Tōzan group, depending on their original lineage, and to follow the practices of that group. It also ordered *yamabushi* of the Honzan group not to collect from *yamabushi* of the Tōzan group "performance fees" for certain rites.

Thus the *yamabushi* groups, many of which had depended on particular mountain temples and shrines and had performed martial roles, found themselves attached to either the Honzan group, whose head temple was Shōgo-in in Kyoto, or the Tōzan group, whose head temple was Sambō-in in Kyoto; but with the twelve *shōdai sendatsu* (the foremost of the ranking *yamabushi*) still at the helm. Though the community of Hikosan on Kyushu was attached to the Honzan group, the Hagurosan group in Dewa Province, which was under the direct control of the chief priest of the Tendai temple Rinnō-ji on Nikkōzan in Shimotsuke Province, retained its separate identity. While the three Shugendō streams were ostensibly independent, legally they were branches of established Buddhist sects (the Honzan group belonged to the Jimon school of the Tendai sect, the Tōzan group to Shingon, and the Hagurosan group to the Sammon school of Tendai), so strong Buddhist influence on Shugendō was inevitable.

Around the beginning of the seventeenth century, *shugenja* (Shugendō practitioners) began settling permanently in remote communities, perhaps because they had been driven from their mountain temples and shrines by warriors and then prevented from returning by the shogunate's regulations. According to the *Fudoki Goyō Kakidashi,* an official report on conditions in the Sendai domain, in Rikuzen Province, compiled between 1855 and 1862, the affiliations of Shugendō temples founded up to the end of the fifteenth century were as follows: sixteen belonged to the Honzan group, two to the Tōzan group, and thirty-two to the Hagurosan group. In the sixteenth century the respective affiliations were twenty-two, six, and twenty-four; in the seventeenth century, forty-seven, eleven, and sixty-six; and in the eighteenth century, seven, one, and twenty-two.

The rapid growth of temples associated with Shugendō in the seventeenth century is also seen in the *Yamabushi Kaiki Chō* (Report on the Founding of Shugendō Groups; 1663), compiled by the Mito domain, in Hitachi Province. The Honzan group grew gradually from the latter half of the fifteenth century, reaching its peak in the first half of the seventeenth century. The Tōzan group by contrast grew rapidly from the first half of the seventeenth century. Records for Sagami Province reflect the same trend, with a peak in the seventeenth century. At the end of the fifteenth century the Honzan group had only four temples and the Tōzan group one in Sagami, but in the sixteenth century the Honzan group had six, which increased to seventeen in the seventeenth century. Tōzan-group figures for the same periods were three and thirteen. In the eighteenth century, however, the number of Honzan-group temples fell to five, though Tōzan-group numbers remained unchanged.

These figures represent only a small number of provinces, but they indicate three trends: Honzan-group Shugendō gradually became more institutionalized after the end of the fifteenth century; the numbers of *shugenja* who settled permanently in villages increased sharply after the shogunate's regulations took effect; and the Tōzan group in particular extended its power from the seventeenth century on.

Religious Organization

Both the Honzan and the Tōzan groups set about establishing an organized system to regulate the administrative apparatus needed to control rapidly growing numbers of branch temples and to settle questions of ritual and doctrine. The various small differences in the groups' organizations reflect differences in their origins.

At the beginning of the Edo period the abbot of Shōgo-in, who superintended the three Kumano shrines, was made head of the Honzan group. Nyakuōji Shrine in the Higashiyama district of Kyoto, which was charged with administrative control of the three Kumano shrines, managed the sectarian affairs of the Honzan group. After the middle of the period, however, the managing agency moved to Shōgo-in, where various Shugendō officials participated in the conduct of the group's affairs.

At this time the Honzan group created a system for denoting clerical status. The most powerful members of the group were the *inge*, who were the *sendatsu*, or senior guides, living in such subtemples as Sekizen-in and Jūshin-in in the precincts of Shōgo-in. They had religious jurisdiction over certain areas (the territories known as *kasumi*) and controlled the *shugenja* in each *kasumi* through intermediaries, such as the *sendatsu*, *nengyōji*, and *junnengyōji*.

Sendatsu were powerful *shugenja* who might control entire provinces. They had connections with the *inge* and either administered *kasumi* on behalf of *inge* or held *kasumi* of their own. Some *sendatsu* held temporal powers through their connections with the lords of domains. The *nengyōji* (leader in charge of annual rituals) and the *junnengyōji* (assistant leader in charge of annual rituals) were responsible for day-to-day management of the *kasumi* at the district level, under the direction of the *sendatsu*.

Shōgo-in also recognized and formed ties with well-known Shugendō communities while respecting their autonomy. For example, it recognized the abbots (*zasu*) of the communities on Hikosan, Kubotesan, and Hōman-zan on Kyushu, and the *shukurō* (leaders) of the Goryū (five schools— Sonryū-in, Kentoku-in, Dempō-in, Hōon-in, and Daihō-in) Nagatoko band in Kojima, Bizen Province, on Honshu, and the *kugyō* (subleaders) under them. Other independent Shugendō centers with their own organizations, such as Hasuge in Sagami Province and Murayama at the foot of Mount Fuji, were under the personal control of the abbot of Shōgo-in as direct branch temples.

The Shōgo-in organization bestowed ranks on *yamabushi* reflecting the number of periods of practice they had undertaken in the mountains. Those with fewer than three periods of practice were called *misendatsu;* those with four or more, *sendatsu;* those with more than ten, *sanshi shūgakusha;* those with more than twenty, *jikisan;* and those with more than thirty-three, *buchū shusse.* During the Edo period rank determined all matters of precedence, including seating at rites and the color and style of priestly robes, and thus preserved a strict organizational discipline.

At the beginning of the Edo period, when Sambō-in was made head temple of the Tōzan group, the group was led by the twelve *shōdai sendatsu*, the successors to the thirty-six *shōdai sendatsu* of earlier centuries. The twelve *shōdai sendatsu* were the heads of Yoshino Sakuramoto-bō and Uchiyama Eikyū-ji in Yamato Province; Byōdō-ji on Mount Miwa, Ryōzen-ji, Takama-dera, Hōzō-in, Matsunoo-ji, and Shōryaku-ji in Yamato Province; the Handō-ji subtemples Iwamoto-in and Umemoto-in in Ōmi Province; Kongōbu-ji on Mount Kōya in Kii Province; and Segi-ji in Ise Province. The *shōdai sendatsu* commanded disciples all over the country who had personal ties to them. At their own temples, these powerful masters delegated their duties to assistant *sendatsu* who acted as stewards and to lower-ranking *sendatsu* who were subordinate officials. The *shōdai sendatsu* devoted themselves primarily to ministering to their personal followings through local leaders and their subordinates.

The three principal administrative offices of the Tōzan group were the *ōshuku, ninoshuku,* and *sannoshuku,* to which *shōdai sendatsu* were appointed on the basis of seniority. At the annual meeting at Ozasa, in the Ōmine Mountains, before formal entry into the mountains, the twelve decided, as *shōdai sendatsu* had for centuries, on the promotion of their followers and the bestowal of rankings. After Sambō-in was designated the head temple of the Tōzan group, however, the formal certificates of appointment issued at the meeting were required to have the seal of the abbot of Sambō-in, in addition to Emperor Jomei's seal and the spiritual seal of En no Ozunu. As had been the custom since the end of the Muromachi period (1336–1568), the *sendatsu* who sponsored the applicant was also required to endorse the certificate of appointment.

Around the middle of the Edo period, the abbot of Sambō-in, who had until then acted simply as guarantor for the actions of the *shōdai sendatsu,* began to bring all Tōzan-group *shugenja* throughout the nation under his direct control by issuing his own certificates of appointment. Sambō-in's control was further strengthened in 1700, when Kōken (d. 1707), the incumbent abbot of Sambō-in, merged the headships of Kaijō-in in Edo and Hōkaku-ji in Yoshino, Yamato Province, site of the grave of Shōbō (832–909), revered as the Tōzan group's restorer. Kaijō-in was renamed Edo Hōkaku-ji, and its head was appointed supervisor of all the Tōzan group's local leaders. Edo Hōkaku-ji was put in charge of all Tōzan-group *shugenja* because of the prestige of its association with Shōbō, and thereafter it made all decisions concerning appointments and ritual. Naturally the *shōdai sendatsu* strongly opposed that change, though they were powerless to stop it. The dual system of control that had emerged in the Tōzan group continued until the end of the Edo period.

In 1641 the community on Hagurosan, in Dewa Province, came under the direct control of Tōeizan (the Tendai-sect Kan'ei-ji complex in Edo) through the efforts of its superintendent, Ten'yū (1606–74). The Hagurosan community included three ranks of practitioners: the *seisō* (pure priests), also called *hombō* (main priests), who administered the whole community; the *gyōnin* (ascetics), who performed the esoteric rites of Shugendō; and low-ranking *shugenja*, who lived in the village of Tōge at the foot of the mountain. Branches at the village level throughout the nation were affiliated with one or another of the Hagurosan *shugenja* and were directed by local leaders appointed by the community on Hagurosan. Shugendō on Hagurosan differed from that of the Honzan group in that even the low-ranking practitioners who lived in Tōge had their own *kasumi*.

In the early part of the Edo period, the community on Hikosan, on Kyushu, was affiliated with the Honzan group; but like the community on Hagurosan, it strongly wished for independence. It succeeded in being recognized as a special headquarters of Tendai Shugendō through a shogunate ruling in 1696. The hereditary abbot of Reisen-ji on Hikosan retained headship, and from among his community recruited officials— *shittō* (administrator), *sō bugyō* (general superintendent), *saji bugyō* (construction superintendent), *yama bugyō* (superintendent of the mountain), and *machi bugyō* (town commissioner)—who oversaw the *shugenja*, the Tendai priests, and the Shintō priests who made up the Hikosan community. During its most prosperous period, in the years up to the middle of the Edo period, the community on Hikosan had seventy branch temples and a large number of lay supporters throughout Kyushu.

Shugendō, as we have seen, established itself as a religious organization in the Edo period, and through the work of ordinary *shugenja* became widely popular. When the government of the Meiji period (1868–1912) came to power, however, the Buddhist-Shintō syncretism of Shugendō was deemed contrary to the new rulers' policy of separating Buddhism and Shintō, and Shugendō was officially proscribed in 1872. The Honzan group was merged with the Jimon school of Tendai and the Tōzan group with the Daigo group of Shingon, and Shintō shrines replaced the communities on Hagurosan and Hikosan. While many local *shugenja* became farmers, others became either Buddhist or Shintō priests.

Shugendō reestablished itself after World War II, and a number of sects that emerged then are still active. Four of these arose from the old Honzan group: the Honzan Shugen sect, the Honshugen sect, the Shugen sect, and the Shugendō sect. Three arose from the old Tōzan group: the Shingon Daigo group; the Kimpusen Shugenhon sect, in Yoshino; and the Hagurosan Shugenhon sect, on Hagurosan.

Shugendō Literature

After Shugendō became an organized religion in the Edo period, its doctrines and rituals changed greatly. Shogunate policy encouraged doctrinal study, and as a consequence a large number of basic doctrinal works, instructional texts, and ritual manuals were written and published in swift succession. The so-called Five Books of Shugendō (*Shugen Gosho*), which had in fact been in circulation for a considerable time, appear to have been read by a large number of people.

The Five Books of Shugendō are the *Shugen Shūyō Hiketsu Shū* (A Collection of the Secrets of Practice and Doctrine of Shugendō; compiled ca. 1521–28), which was compiled from the *kirigami* notes of early-sixteenth-century residents on Hikosan that Sokuden obtained; the *Shugen Sanjūsan Tsūki* (An Account of Shugendō in Thirty-three Sections), a collection of notes assembled by Renkaku (fl. fifteenth century), priest of Reisen-ji on Hikosan and Chikō (fl. ca. latter half of the fifteenth century), *sendatsu* of Hikosan, and thought to be the source of the preceding work; the *Shugen Tonkaku Sokushō Shū* (A Collection of Actual Evidence for Shugendō Sudden Enlightenment; early sixteenth century), an account of Sokuden's Buddhist philosophy; the *Shugen Shinan Shō* (A Summary of Shugendō Instruction; ca. mid-fifteenth century), a doctrinal work based on the tales of Kumano Gongen; and the *Enkun Keisei Ki* (An Account of En no Ozunu; 1684), the biography of En no Ozunu transmitted by Kumano Shugendō, compiled by Shūkō (fl. seventeenth century).

The *Shugen Shūyō Hiketsu Shū* was considered the most basic of the Five Books of Shugendō, and it was studied carefully throughout the Edo period. Among the ten or so commentaries on it are the *Shugen Ki* (An Account of Shugendō; ca. sixteenth century) and the *Shugen Shūyō Hiketsu Denkō Hikki* (Notes on Lectures on the *Shugen Shūyō Hiketsu Shū*; mid-nineteenth century).

From the first the Five Books of Shugendō were read by Tōzan-group *shugenja*, as well. After about the last decade of the seventeenth century, however, works reflecting the distinct doctrinal standpoints of the Honzan group and the Tōzan group began to appear. Chief among them were the *Yamabushi Niji Gi* (The Meaning of the Characters for "*Yama*" and "*Bushi*"; 1645), by Yūban (fl. seventeenth century) of the Honzan group. As its title indicates, this work explains Shugendō thought by interpreting the two ideographic characters used to write "*yamabushi.*" Jōen (fl. seventeenth century) of the Tōzan group wrote two commentaries, the *Shugen Shinkan Shō* (A Summary of the Mirror of the Heart of Shugendō; 1672) and the *Shugenshū Hōgu Hiketsu Seichū* (Detailed Notes on the Secrets of the Doctrine and Ritual Implements of Shugendō; seventeenth century). The first is a commentary on the *Shugen Shinkan Sho* (The Book of the Mirror of the Heart), a work attributed to Shōbō (832–909), and the second explains Shugendō doctrine through its ritual implements. Kanken composed a commentary explaining the Ten Realms Practice titled *Shugen Hiyō Gi* (The Meaning of the Mystery of Shugendō; 1720). Another important commentary was the *Endan Jū Gi* (The Ten Meanings of En no Ozunu's Discourses; 1699), explaining Shugendō doctrines.

These works were commentaries on the personal notes that the *yamabushi* used as guides for their rituals. Moreover, their explanations of doctrine stress ideology more than practice and are strongly influenced by esoteric-Buddhist teachings and the Tendai theory of original enlightenment. The incorporation of the Honzan group and the Tōzan group into mainstream Buddhist sects may explain this.

Both groups also produced a large number of biographies of their patriarchs, particularly of En no Ozunu and Shōbō. They also made *kechimyaku*, genealogical charts tracing the transmission of the patriarchs' teachings. The two groups maintained an intense rivalry and published basic instructional texts in which they criticized each other from a variety of standpoints. Typical of such works are the *Shugen Gakusoku* (Rules for the Practical Study of Shugendō; 1799) and *Honzan Shugen Ryakuyō* (Summarized Essentials of Honzan Shugendō; 1834) of the Honzan group and the *Shugen Hiki Ryakuge* (A Brief Explanation of the Secret Writings of Shugendō), a text of the Tōzan group compiled by Bōen (1667–1736), and the priest Shunken's *Tōzanmon Genki* (The Origins of the Tōzan Group; 1742) of the Tōzan group. Outstanding scholarly works based on doctrinal research also appeared, such as Gyōzon's *Shugendō Kembun Shō* (Knowledge about Shugendō; 1687) of the Honzan group and, from the Tōzan group, the *Konohagoromo* (The Cloak of Leaves; 1832) and *Tōun Rokuji* (A Record of Stepping Among the Clouds; 1836), both by Gyōchi (1778–1841).

A number of books recorded rituals, such as entering the mountains. Typical of this genre are the *Buchū Jisshu Shugyō Sahō* (The Way of the Ten Kinds of Practice in the Mountains; early sixteenth century) and *Buchū Hiden* (The Secret Transmission of Mountain Practice; late seventeenth century). The latter work is particularly interesting, for it contains a number of secret verses.

Other works describe religious services, for example, the Honzan group's *Honzan Shugen Gongyō Yōshū* (A Collection of the Essentials of Honzan Religious Services; 1834), scriptural texts for recitation services in the morning and in the evening, compiled by Keichō, and the Tōzan group's *Shugen Jōyō Shū* (A Collection of Shugendō Scriptures for Daily Use; 1825). The procedures for vigils, such as waiting for the rising of the sun or the moon (*himachi* and *tsukimachi*), are detailed in the *Shugen Yōhō Shū* (A Collection of Shugendō Essential Methods; 1713), and those for Shugendō funeral ceremonies are described in the *Shugen Mujōyō Shū* (A Collection of Shugendō Occasional Methods; 1745). Esoteric practices are recorded in the *Shugen Jōyō Hihō Shū* (A Collection of Secret Methods of Shugendō for Daily Use; early nineteenth century). Another work of interest is the *Shugen Koji Benran* (A Compendium of Shugendō Traditions; 1730), which explains folk beliefs in Shugendō terms.

These works were not exclusive to one group or the other but were widely used by all *shugenja*. The works mentioned here represent only a fraction of the Edo-period writings relating to Shugendō, most of which are included in the five volumes of *Shugendō Shōso* (Commentary on the Chapters on Shugendō) in the *Nihon Daizōkyō* (Japan Canon; 1919–21).

Doctrinal Developments

There were several important doctrinal developments in Shugendō during the Edo period. The Ōmine Mountains were still regarded as esoteric peaks, symbolizing the mandalas of the Womb Realm (*Taizōkai*) and Diamond Realm (*Kongōkai*), and the Mount Katsuragi region as the exoteric peak, representing the twenty-eight chapters of the Lotus Sutra. Kongō Zaō Gongen and the eight principal *dōji* (mythical child attendants of divinities) of Ōmine were venerated in the Ōmine Mountains; and the bodhisattva Hokki and the eight principal *dōji* of Katsuragi were venerated in the Katsuragi mountains. During the Edo period, however, the principal deity worshiped in the majority of Shugendō-affiliated temples was in fact Fudō Myōō, who was venerated by *shugenja* as the central deity of their magico-religious rites and prayers.

The Shugendō patriarchs En no Ozunu and Shōbō were revered not only as sect founders but as sacred beings in their own right. An active cult of En no Ozunu among *shugenja* in the Ōmine Mountains dates to the end of the Muromachi period, and many images of him were made and enshrined in temples both in these mountains and elsewhere. Rituals and hymns of praise were devised with which to venerate his images. According to a legend, he died in 700. Following this legend and by the Japanese reckoning, in 1700 and 1800, on the one thousandth and the eleven hundredth anniversaries of his death, Shōgo-in sponsored large-scale memorial services. In the year before the second observance, the posthumous title Great Bodhisattva Jimben was bestowed on En no Ozunu. Likewise, for Shōbō, whom it regarded as its restorer, the Tōzan group built a tomb at Hōkaku-ji in Yoshino; devised services and hymns of praise; and celebrated his memorial days. In 1707, Shōbō was granted the posthumous title Rigen Daishi.

The proofs of religious orthodoxy—the *kechimyaku*, or genealogies of the transmission of secret teachings and initiations—drawn up by Shōgo-in and Sambō-in reflect the realities of their organizations. The genealogy of the Honzan group, the *Jinzen Kanjō Keifu* (A Record of the Lineage of the Dharma Transmission at Jinzen), names En no Ozunu as the founder. He is followed by five generations of disciples; Enchin (814–91) and other Onjō-ji priests; and Zōyo (1032–1116), a priest of Onjō-ji who was named superintendent of the three Kumano shrines and later appointed abbot of Shōgo-in in Kyoto.

The Tōzan group, on the other hand, in its *Gokujimpi Hōkechimyaku* (The Significant, Secret Genealogy of the Transmission of the Law) traces its lineage from Dainichi Nyorai (Mahāvairocana), Vajrasattva, and Nāgārjuna (ca. 150–ca. 250) to En no Ozunu, Shōbō, and the thirty-six *shōdai sendatsu*. Another Tōzan-group genealogy, the *Tōzan Shugen Dentō Kechimyaku* (The Traditional Lineage of Tōzan Shugendō), traces its lineage from Mahāvairocana, Vajrasattva, and Nāgārjuna (fl. seventh century) to En no Ozunu, Shōbō, and the hereditary abbots of Sambō-in after Shōbō. The existence of two Tōzan-group genealogies reflects the dual system of control of the organization.

Shugendō ideas on human nature can be inferred from the meanings attached to the ritual clothing and implements of the *shugenja* and from explanations of the connotations of the two characters used to write *yamabushi*. Garments and tools that symbolized the Womb Realm and Diamond Realm mandalas and the attainment of buddhahood remained unchanged from earlier times. In the Edo period, however, as works such as the *Endan Jū Gi* reveal, there was a much broader interpretation of the significance of the *shugenja*'s wearing of traditional garb to represent Fudō Myōō, one of the chief deities of Shugendō.

Another development is seen in the ideological interpretation of the characters for *yamabushi* found in the *Yamabushi Niji Gi*. The character for *yama*, or mountain, is interpreted as representing "the oneness of the three bodies of the Buddha," that is, the Law-body (*dharma-kāya*), the reward-body (*saṃbhoga-kāya*), and the manifest-body (*nirmāṇa-kāya*); as "the unity of the three parts," that is, the Lotus Sutra, the Buddha, and Kongō Zaō Gongen; and as "the triple truth [emptiness, the provisional, and the middle] in one thought." The character for *bushi*, or recumbent, is seen as representing "the nonduality of ignorance and Dharma nature," or the ultimate truth.

The aim of Shugendō, to attain buddhahood through the Ten Realms Practice, did not change from earlier times. During the Edo period, however, the practice lost much of its rigor. Previously it had been thought that buddhahood could be attained in the present life only by practice of an extremely severe form of asceticism. But the practice of entering the mountains became formalistic, and it was said that attainment of buddhahood was assured if the Ten Realms Practice were performed as prescribed. On the Yoshino side of the Ōmine range four gates were erected along the route from the foot to the summit of Sanjōgatake. These were the Hosshin-mon, or Gate of Aspiration; the Shugyō-mon, or Gate of Practice; the Tōkaku-mon, or Gate of Approximate Enlightenment; and the Myōkaku-mon, or Gate of Supreme Enlightenment. It was believed that buddhahood was assured for anyone who passed through these four gates and attained the summit.

By interpreting the phrase *sokushin jōbutsu* (buddhahood in the present body) in terms of the mind, Jōen's *Shugen Shinkan Shō* clearly demonstrates that emphasis had come to be placed on meditation techniques rather than ascetic practice. Such techniques include meditation on the character for *kaku*, or guest, recommended in the *Endan Jū Gi* and meditation on the Sanskrit syllable *A* (considered to be the root of all sounds), which is a Dharma transmission of the *ein* (hand gestures representing the precepts, concentration, and wisdom) belonging to the Tōzan group. By the time of the composition of the *Buchū Shōkanjō Geba Sahō* (Methods of Practice in Other Places for Correct Initiation in the Mountains), even the Ten Realms Practice had become a meditative practice. Perhaps these changes came about because of the need for a means of attaining buddhahood within a training hall, since the numbers of *shugenja* who were true ascetics wandering in the mountains decreased dramatically when the majority took up sedentary lives.

In earlier centuries Shugendō practitioners had been forbidden to devote themselves to any particular sutra, since nature and its sounds were believed to be buddhas in themselves and therefore worthy of being the main focus of contemplation. In the Edo period, however, both Shugendō groups reported to the shogunate that their beliefs were based on Mahāyāna Buddhist texts. The Honzan group specified the *Shugen Sempō*, or *Hokke Sempō* (Rites of Repentance through the Lotus Sutra), the *Kujaku Myōō-kyō* (Peacock Sutra; in Sanskrit, Mahāmāyūrī), the *Fudō-kyō* (Acalanātha Sutra, a sutra made by a *shugenja* on the basis of the *Sheng Wu-tung-tsuen Ta-wei-nu-wang Pi-mi-t'uo-lo-ni-ching* [Esoteric *Dhāraṇī* Sutra of Acalanātha]), the *Jimben Daibosatsu Kōshiki* (Services for the Great Bodhisattva Jimben [En no Ozunu]), the *Amida-kyō* (Amitābha Sutra), the Lotus Sutra, and various *dhāraṇī*, or mystical formulas. The Tōzan group employed a text called the *Shingon Darani* (Mantra and *Dhāraṇī*) and relied on the *Dainichi-kyō* (Great Sun Sutra; in Sanskrit, Mahāvairocana-sūtra), the *Kongōchō-kyō* (Diamond Peak Sutra), the *Soshitsuji-kyō* (Sutra of Good Accomplishment), the *Konkōmyō Saishōō-kyo* (Golden Light Sutra; in Sanskrit, *Suvarṇaprabhāsottama-sūtra*), the Lotus Sutra, the *Ninnō Hannya-kyō* (Sutra on the Benevolent King), the *Kujaku Myōō-kyō*, and the *Hannya-kyō* (Perfection of Wisdom Sutra). Shugendō's sacred works are a further indication of its integration into mainstream Buddhism.

Entering the Mountains

One of the most distinctive rituals of Edo-period Shugendō was the collective *mine-iri* (entering the mountains) for group ascetic practice in the mountains. Every year the Honzan group organized two major rituals: practice in Katsuragi mountains in spring and practice in the Ōmine range in autumn. The chief events of the ritual year for the Tōzan group were the *toake*, the year's first trip into the mountains, beginning on the eighth day of the fourth month; the *hanaku no mine*, going into the mountains in early spring to offer flowers to divinities; the *mieku no mine*, entering the mountains between the end of the fifth month and the middle of the sixth month to honor En no Ozunu; and *gyakubu*, entering the mountains from the opposite side of the range, practiced from the early part of the seventh month to the middle of the eighth month.

The greatest of the mountain-entering rituals of the Edo period were observed when the abbot made his ritual ascent to the peak. The successive abbots of Shōgo-in, who undertook the ritual at the age of nineteen, headed a large contingent of *sendatsu*, chief of whom were the *inge*. The ritual included a ceremony confirming them as abbots. The Sambō-in abbot Kōken ascended the peak in 1668, and his three successors followed his example. The ritual was conducted on the grandest scale, and *yamabushi* from throughout the nation participated.

During the Edo period the practice of entering the mountains as a group became formalistic as participants became interested more in the clerical advancement it afforded than in religious training, and the harsh severity of the practice of earlier centuries all but disappeared. The *shugenja* who had settled in remote communities tended to practice in nearby mountains. The religious authorities officially recognized such *mine-iri* and ranked them second to practice in the Ōmine range and in the Katsuragi mountains.

Shugenja *in Village Life*

The local *shugenja* who settled in villages in large numbers responded to the needs of the villagers by becoming the priests of the village Buddhist temple or of the shrine of the local tutelary *kami*. According to the *Fudoki Goyō Kakidashi*, 68 percent of the village shrines in the Sendai domain had *shugenja* as caretakers. This pattern was not unique to Sendai but was widespread in other domains, as well. The *shugenja* in charge of the tutelary *kami* became deeply involved in the lives of the people. They organized the village festival and the festivals associated with the small shrines to local protector deities. They acted as leaders of religious associations, such as those connected with ritual vigils or the veneration of Kūkai (774–835), founder of the Shingon sect.

The *shugenja* also performed certain religious services of central importance to village life. They conducted the spring divination at New Year's, rituals for the prosperity of the family, exorcisms to rid fields of harmful insects, the festival for the protection of crops against wind, and prayers for rain and for good weather. They prayed for easy childbirth and conducted the *torigo* ceremony after the child was born, entrusting the infant to the protection of a particular buddha. Later they performed the coming-of-age ceremony for the child. They performed exorcisms for those going through years of bad fortune, and they conducted funerals.

The *shugenja* employed a wide variety of practices: Taoist-type divination, esoteric prayer rituals, spells, incantations, and rites for exorcism and delivery from curses. They conducted rituals to meet a wide range of needs: relief from illness (stomach disorders, eye diseases, nervous complaints, and menstrual pain), prosperity and success, the blessing of new clothing and houses, protection against fire, prevention of public and personal discord, and protection against theft. Even today descendants of these *shugenja* preserve their personal notes outlining the principal details of the many rituals they performed for fellow villagers.

Analysis of collections of such notes—for example, the *Shugen Jimpi Gyōhō Fuju Shū* (A Collection of Incantations for Shugendō Secret Methods), *Shugen Jimpi Gyōhō Fuju Zoku Shū* (A Further Collection of Incantations for Shugendō Secret Methods), *Shugen Jōyō Hihō Shū*, and *Shugenshū Shintō Jinja Injin* (The Secret Transmission of Shugendō at Shintō Shrines; late eighteenth century)—shows that most of them deal with rites to cure illness, acquire material necessities, or reduce personal animosities. The majority of rites were concerned with health and the bearing and raising of children. These were the practical concerns that took the people to the homes of the *shugenja*, seeking ritual assistance.

Shugenja taught that illness and calamity were the curses of evil *kami* and spirits. When angered, such spirits caused bad fortune. The malevolent spirits of people who had died violent deaths were responsible for the worst curses. Even the spirits of the living could curse people they hated deeply. But if such *kami* and spirits, including animal spirits, were appealed to in a prescribed manner, people would be protected and their lives would run a normal course, free from calamity.

Shugendō held that all these spirits, whether they wrought curses or not, were embraced and governed by Dainichi Nyorai, the embodiment of the Diamond and Womb realms, which symbolized all the phenomena of the universe. Thus, through the power of Dainichi Nyorai, it was possible to enlist these spirits to protect people's lives and prevent calamities. Further, Dainichi Nyorai had charged the esoteric-Buddhist deity Fudō Myōō with the task of banishing evil spirits. Accordingly, the *shugenja* believed and taught the villagers that it was possible to dispel misfortune and gain protection by praying directly to Fudō Myōō and invoking his power.

By praying to Fudō Myōō and becoming one with him, *shugenja* could invoke his powers to protect the village and ward off misfortune. The interpretations of the garments and implements of the *shugenja* as symbols of various aspects of Fudō Myōō seem to have arisen from this belief. By undergoing austerities in the mountains—which were believed to be actual mandalas of the Diamond and Womb realms—and by receiving esoteric ordination in the course of their training, *shugenja* were endowed with the secret seal of Dainichi Nyorai and Fudō Myōō and became incarnations of Fudō Myōō. As a result, they believed that they had gained the power to perform spiritual feats. This power was displayed before the villagers during festivals. Some *shugenja* were able to walk barefoot across hot coals, which were said to symbolize the nimbus of flames that surrounded Fudō Myōō; and others, like ascetics during the Hayama Festival in Fukushima Prefecture, in the Tōhoku region of northern Honshu, consulted oracles. Still others, like the practitioners of the *gohōtobi* rite* in western Okayama Prefecture, in the San'yō region of western Honshu, displayed to the villagers their control over spirits.

Even where the old rites have become primarily theatrical performances, they still retain an element of their former mystic power. The *shugenja* is transformed, becoming an object of veneration who prays and dances for the good fortune of the villagers during performances of *kagura* (sacred song and dance), such as the *yamabushi kagura* of Iwate Prefecture, in the Tōhoku region; the Noh-related *kagura* known as *bangaku*, in Akita Prefecture, in Tōhoku; the purificatory *yudate* (boiling-water) *kagura* of various regions; the oracular *takumai* dance of Izumo, Shimane Prefecture, in the San'in district of western Honshu; and the *ennen* dance drama of Nikkō, Tochigi Prefecture, in the Kantō region. The evidence of many village performing arts in fact suggests that the *shugenja* actually becomes an avatar of the deity. Through sermons and sacred verses (*saimon*), the *shugenja* recounted tales of their practice and spiritual powers. Such tales were popular in rural areas, where entertainments were few, and were

---

* The *gohōtobi* rite (*gohō* is from *gohōzane* and Gohōzen, and *tobi* means jumping) is performed at Ryōsen-ji in the Kume district of Okayama Prefecture on August 14. A village man is chosen and kept secluded in a section of the temple complex for a week to purify himself. He is called the *gohōzane*. During that period, he goes to nearby Gohōzen Shrine every day to worship the deity Gohōzen, the protector deity of *shugenja*. After a week of purification, he is welcomed at the main hall of the temple. The *gohōzane* holds a bundle of string-bound bamboo stalks with leaves and waves it; children move around him, chanting the Sanskrit syllable, "*Gate, gate* [gone to the other shore of enlightenment]." The *gohōzane* is possessed by the deity, through the prayer of the *shugenja*, and jumps around in the precincts of the temple. The purpose of this rite is to obtain abundant crops. The rite is also performed at several other temples and shrines in the Shugendō lineage in the Kume district.

doubtless instrumental in creating a state of mind receptive to the display of the *shugenja's* powers.

Shugenja helped individual villagers by first divining the source of their personal misfortune. The numerous means of divination used included casting yarrow stalks, interpreting the sound of rice bubbling in a caldron, stringing together prayer beads of rough stones or berries, scattering grains of washed rice on a tray, and consulting astrological charts on the basis of the four pillars—year, month, day, hour—of a person's birth. Individual *shugenja* generally chose a single divination method and used it almost exclusively. For other questions or problems, *shugenja* referred to an almanac of auspicious times and directions. They used this chiefly to decide on the dates for important ceremonies and to determine the good and bad directions for the placement of new buildings.

Shugenja often practiced divination while in a state of divine possession, most often during the chanting of prayers; though in rare cases they practiced divination while possessed by a tutelary *kami*. Far more frequently, the *shugenja* summoned a spirit into the body of a *miko* and used his own spiritual powers to cause the spirit to utter oracles. In some cases a *shugenja's* wife acted as the *miko*. The Shugendō ritual *yorigitō*, a ritual to invoke a deity who would enter a medium, had its origins in the *abisha hō*, an esoteric-Buddhist rite for summoning a deity into the body of a child. By the Edo period such esoteric rituals had become associated more closely with Shugendō than with mainstream Buddhism. In many festivals, such as the Hayama Festival, the deity that entered a medium was generally a local *kami*.

Exorcism rituals varied according to the type of spirit working the curse or taking possession of someone. The spirit might be a neglected deity or spirit, an animal spirit, an evil spirit, or an *ikiryō* (the jealous spirit of a living person who bears a grudge against someone). The reason for the spirit's anger was also important in choosing the proper ritual to appease it.

When the tormenter was a high-ranking *kami*, it was believed that the cursed person had a serious fault, and the favored method of exorcism was to have the cursed person repent and enshrine that *kami*. Evil deities and spirits were exorcised by reading sutras to them to enlighten them, and then returning them to their original shrines. Animal spirits and vindictive *ikiryō* were more difficult to exorcise, however. Incantations were used to compel such spirits to leave their victims. The *shugenja* assumed the powers of Fudō Myōō and forced the spirit to leave by threatening it with fire and Fudō Myōō's sword. The specific methods included recitation of the "nine letters" charm, performance of the *hikime* rite (twanging a bowstring and shooting a hollow-headed arrow into the air), and trapping the spirit in a bamboo pipe and burying it at a crossroads. Simpler exorcisms were conducted with charms and incantations.

Though all *shugenja* were formally affiliated with one of the official Shugendō groups, they chose a shrine, temple, or area near their homes for religious austerities. When *shugenja* visited such sacred sites as the Ōmine Mountains or other shrines and temples, they received *ofuda* (charms) to distribute among the villagers on their return. They also often acted as agents for the Shugendō leaders from the mountain shrines and temples, who came at set times to distribute their talismans and deliver such goods as medicines and tea. The village *shugenja* also often guided villagers to the mountain with which they were affiliated. They not only played a role in the religious life of the community but also acted as leaders on a broader scale. Many *shugenja* participated in village politics and ran the village schools. In Iwate Prefecture, for example, most of the village schools were established by *shugenja*.

Lay Believers' Associations

By the beginning of the Edo period lay people had been inspired by the *shugenja* to undertake austerities in the mountains and visit mountain shrines and temples for religious purposes themselves. Their religious practice was centered in the activities of the lay believers' associations known as *kō*. The first documented Shugendō-affiliated *kō* dates from 1424 and was a Kumano *kō* organized in the village of San'un in the Kōga district of Ōmi Province by a member of a local warrior family called Nomura. As is clear from the membership list that the *sendatsu* Keishin submitted to his supervisor, the *oshi*, this association consisted of local warriors, small farmers, women, and Buddhist priests. At the head of the *kō*'s hierarchy was the *oshi*, under whom was the *sendatsu*, who was in turn the superior of the local leader of the *kō*. By the seventeenth century a large number of Kumano *kō* were active in the Kyoto-Osaka region, though they declined in the Edo period with the waning of the influence of Kumano Shugendō.

As the Kumano *kō* declined, Sanjō *kō*, associations for entering the Ōmine Mountains from the Yoshino side, gradually developed. The first mention of a Sanjō *kō* appears in an entry made in the third month of

1535 in the *Genjo Ōnen Ki*, a chronicle of the priest Genjo, covering the years 1494–1563. The chronicle recounts that Genjo visited Ise Grand Shrine, Murou-ji, and Hase-dera in Yamato Province with fifty-seven members of a Sanjō *kō*. Sanjō *kō* established later in Osaka and Sakai include the Iwa Bannin Kō organized in Osaka by Yoshikawa Gembei, a descendant of a warrior family associated with Kōfuku-ji in Nara, and the Torigegumi, organized chiefly by shipping agents in Sakai. Similar associations also developed in the farming villages of the region.

The special object of devotion of the Sanjō *kō* was an image of En no Ozunu dated 1426, which was kept hidden in Zaō Hall on Sanjōgatake in the Ōmine range. The *kō* made pilgrimages to Sanjōgatake mainly in early summer, starting their ascent from either Yoshino or the village of Dorogawa. The *kō*, the Iwa Bannin Kō in particular, gave rise to a number of subgroups and thereby gained great power. When Zaō Hall was rebuilt in 1691, the Iwa Bannin Kō took the lead in collecting donations for the construction in Osaka and Sakai. Eight Sanjō *kō* groups in that region—the Iwa Bannin Kō, Kōmyōgumi, Sangōgumi, and Kyōbashigumi in Osaka and the Torigegumi, Ryōgōgumi, Izutsugumi, and Goryūgumi in Sakai—were known collectively as the En Kō. Throughout the Edo period (and even today), the En Kō was the driving force behind the large-scale rites that accompany the mountain-opening and -closing ceremonies in the Ōmine range.

Other Sanjō *kō* in the Kyoto-Osaka region did not affiliate with the En Kō. These *kō* still make pilgrimages to the Ōmine Mountains during the Bon season and conduct the *mine-iri* as a rite of passage to adulthood. (In the areas where these *kō* exist, it is believed that good health is assured if one steps over the recumbent body of a person who has undergone his or her first *mine-iri*.) The pillar of the Sanjō *kō* organization was the lay leader, who was accorded the honorary rank of *sendatsu* by Shōgo-in, Sambō-in, or one of the Shugendō temples of the Yoshino area.

Early in the Edo period, *kō* affiliated with Dewa Sanzan (the three mountains of Gassan, Yudonosan, and Hagurosan in Dewa Province) spread from the northern areas of Honshu into Echigo and Shinano provinces, and by the end of the seventeenth century they could be found in the eight Kantō provinces and Tōtōmi Province. This growth can be attributed to the work of the guides based at Tōge at the foot of Hagurosan, who made the rounds of their territories every winter. *Kō* members usually visited Hagurosan in the summer and also went to Gassan and Yudonosan before returning home. A cult connected with Yudonosan burgeoned in the eighteenth century, and by the early decades of the nineteenth century it had seventeen thousand followers throughout Japan. Pilgrimage to Yudonosan was especially popular during years of the ox in the Chinese zodiac, because according to legend Yudonosan was believed to have been founded in the year of the ox.

By 1700 the Hikosan community had six hundred thousand supporters, most on Kyushu (chiefly the western part of the island) but also on the islands of Iki and Tsushima, in the Chūgoku region of Honshu, and on Shikoku. Two hundred and fifty fully ordained priests lived on the mountain and made circuits of the supporters and distributed charms, such as *goō hōin* amulets. The most important event in the community's ritual calendar, the Matsu-e in the middle of the second month, drew large crowds of pilgrims, the majority of whom were representatives of Hikosan Gongen Kō, which had been formed by adherents in each area.

During the Edo period the establishment of lay believers' associations connected with sacred mountains was stimulated by those Shugendō guides who had settled in remote communities and practiced austerities in nearby mountains, mountains that lay people often already considered places of spiritual power. Besides the associations already mentioned, there were active groups associated with sacred mountains in every area of the country—groups such as the Iwakisan Kō and Kinkazan Kō of northern Honshu; the Fuji Kō, Haruna Kō, Mitake Kō, Mitsumine Kō, Ōyama Kō, and Kominegahara Kō in the Kantō region; the Akiba Kō, Ontake Kō, and Togakushi Kō of central Honshu; the Ushiroyama Kō, Daisen Kō, Ishizuchi Kō, and Kenzan Kō in the Inland Sea area; and the Miyajidake Kō, Aso Kō, and Kirishima Kō on Kyushu. Of these, the most singular and widespread were the Fuji Kō, discussed earlier, and Ontake Kō.

Mount Ontake in the Kiso domain, Shinano Province, was associated with Zaō Gongen. Well known as a center for Shugendō practice before the Edo period, it was noted especially for the rigor of the hundred days of isolation and purification required before its ascent could be undertaken. In 1785, however, a priest from Owari Province, Kakumyō (1719–87), eliminated that requirement by establishing a new route up the mountain from Kurosawa. Another priest, Fukan (1731–1801), from Musashi Province, opened a route from Ōtaki in 1792. Thanks to these priests, lay people were able to climb the mountain freely. The Kakumyō groups formed *kō* throughout the Kiso region, while the Fukan groups had their base in the

Kantō and Tōkai regions. The Ontake *kō* inherited a number of rituals influenced by Kiso Shugendō, such as the seances (*oza*) in which a practitioner called the *maeza* (front seat) put a medium (called the *nakaza*, or middle seat) into a trance, summoned a deity into the medium's body, and questioned the deity. Other Ontake *kō* rituals were divination by the caldron method, the *goma* fire rite, and *ha watari* (walking barefoot across a bed of upright naked sword blades).

Early in the Meiji period (1868–1912), the Ontake *kō* were amalgamated by Shimoyama Ōsuke (fl. twentieth century) of Gumma Prefecture to form Ontakekyō, one of the thirteen groups formally recognized as a Shintō sect around that time.

Pilgrimages along certain circuits and visits to shrines and temples were also popular during the Edo period. In many cases *shugenja* acted as leaders and guides for groups of pilgrims. Of particular note among the places visited was the temple of Fudō Myōō in Narita, Shimōsa Province. From the early nineteenth century, it attracted believers from a wide area extending from Edo and the Kantō region to Mutsu, Shinano, and Echigo provinces. Around the beginning of the sixteenth century, the cult of a deity on Shikoku, Kompira (in Sanskrit, Kumbhīra), who protects fishermen and sailors, became known throughout Japan through the efforts of people like the superintendent of his shrine, Yūsei (also called Kongōbō), who had a strong interest in Shugendō practice. By the beginning of the seventeenth century, Ise had displaced Kumano as Japan's premier shrine, and it was a mecca for numerous cults. Compared with other shrines and temples, Ise attracted surprisingly large numbers of pilgrims in the Edo period. There were also many who visited Mount Kōya, Kii Province, inspired by a cult dedicated to interring the ashes of the dead there, and Zenkō-ji in Shinano Province.

Especially popular with pilgrims were three circuits: two of thirty-three sacred places in the western provinces of Honshu and in the eastern Tōkai region, and a third of thirty-four sacred places in the Chichibu Mountains, Musashi Province. Especially popular with residents of the Kantō region was a combination of those three circuits for a pilgrimage to one hundred places sacred to Kannon. A circuit on Shikoku attracted large numbers of pilgrims from the Kyoto-Osaka region and the areas along the Inland Sea. It started at Ryōzen-ji in Awa Province and finished at Ōkubo-ji in Sanuki Province and comprised a total of eighty-eight places associated with Kūkai. This circuit is still popular today, and pilgrims undertaking the Shikoku pilgrimage are warmly welcomed by people who live along the route. As a mark of its popularity, miniature versions of the Shikoku circuit were constructed all over Japan.

The *kō*, devoted to visiting sacred mountains, shrines, and temples, clearly had an impact on the communication network of the time. Road conditions gradually improved, making travel safer. With the expansion of a money economy, ordinary people were able to travel with comparative freedom. Nevertheless, the very popularity of pilgrimages contributed to the dilution of their religious nature, and in time they came to be merely recreational journeys.

18. Sectarian Shintō:
Tenrikyō and Konkōkyō

OVERVIEW

The disturbances that brought about the fall of the shogunate and a return to imperial rule under Emperor Meiji (1851–1912) in 1868 marked the end of seven centuries of feudalism and more than two hundred and sixty years of Tokugawa family control. The end of the domination of society by the warrior class gave rise to the modern period of Japanese history.

The traditional class system underwent great changes at this time. The system of four classes—warriors, farmers, artisans, and merchants—that had been maintained by strong military force crumbled, and the whole structure of social relations began to totter. The slogan "Equality for the Four Classes" speaks vividly of the disintegration. Moreover, during the Meiji period (1868–1912) European and American methods of industrial production were adopted and industrialization was fostered by the government for the benefit of the populace.

When the proscriptions that had isolated Japan were abolished, the country was opened not only to trade but also to other ways of thinking, ushering in a new era of religious, intellectual, and cultural ferment. For two thousand years Shintō, Buddhism, and Confucianism had dominated the Japanese religious consciousness. At an early date Buddhism and Shintō had merged to such a degree that most Buddhists considered Shintō subordinate. Confucianism, the official philosophy of the Tokugawa shogu-

475

nate, was also absorbed by Japanese of all social classes. This triad came to govern the people's spiritual life.

It is no exaggeration to say that religion had been forced on the people during the Edo period (1603–1868). They were given no choice but to assume its outward form like livery. But when Japan opened its doors, ideas and religions from all over the world flooded into the country. Buddhism, which had reigned supreme over the nation's spiritual life since its transmission from the Asian continent, found itself facing a mighty test in a new age.

In the Edo period Buddhism, aided by Shintō, had served its master, the shogunate, as a faithful lapdog. In return it received cordial protection, although its activities were strictly supervised. As long as its great patron thrived, Buddhism's future was assured. In trying to be faithful to its master, Edo-period Buddhism ignored and sacrificed its true supporters, the people. When the seemingly invincible shogunate fell, Buddhism was forced to stand on its own as an institution and to survive without special privileges among the many religions and philosophies then sweeping into Japan.

Deprived of its previous patron, Buddhism tried to win the favor of the new master. The Meiji government, however, did not accord Buddhism any special legal status. Instead, Shintō became the new state religion. The positions of the two religions were completely reversed, and Buddhism was not merely relegated to a subordinate position but was eclipsed under the decree of complete legal and institutional separation of Shintō and Buddhism that the new government issued in 1868. People who for long years had been unwillingly on the membership rolls of Buddhist temples interpreted the Meiji government's policy as anti-Buddhist and ransacked and destroyed the temples that had been the spiritual guardians of their ancestors. Two centuries of hatred had risen to the surface. Released from domination by Buddhism, Shintō was given the preeminent position as State Shintō. Its network of shrines spread to every corner of the country, as well as overseas, in conjunction with the growth of Japanese political power and prestige.

Shintō was not alone in being liberated by the new social order. Religions and cults that had been forced underground for the duration of the Edo period—such as Christianity, the underground factions of the Nichiren sect, and the underground cult of the *nembutsu*—were permitted to surface. However, these groups had been underground for so long they were too timid to reassume their place in the world. They proved unable to shake off their underground mentality, and most remained secret at their own insistence.

When the *kakure*, or underground, Christians emerged from hiding, they completely lost their bearings. Because they had preserved their faith in isolation for so many years, it had diverged greatly from Christianity in other lands. The Christianity that reached Japan in the Meiji period was not the old faith that the *kakure* Christians had kept alive but Roman Catholicism and Protestantism newly transmitted from Europe and the United States. Although the Meiji period was an age of modernization sponsored by the government through the importation of European and American political, social, and ideological models, Christian activities and growth in Japan were beset with difficulties. The situation was entirely different from that in which Christianity found itself after World War II. Nevertheless, since the beginning of the Meiji period, Christianity has tried to establish itself in Japanese religious life by performing various roles never undertaken by Japanese religion.

The enormous changes in society, not least of them the changes in traditional values, resulted in a surge in the number and types of folk religions. The previous age of great change, the Kamakura period (1185–1336), had given rise to six sects of Buddhism that inspired people suffering in the gloom of an age of upheaval, enabling them to face the challenges of a new society. The modern period of upheaval beginning with the end of the Edo period was little different. The religious reaction—the appearance of many new forms of religious belief and practice—must be understood as a historical phenomenon signaling changes in social structures. Collectively, the thirteen folk religions that came into existence at the end of the Edo period and the beginning of the Meiji period and attracted the faith of large numbers of people are usually designated Sectarian Shintō.

The course of Sectarian Shintō was not smooth. Its proselytization met great political and social obstacles. The Meiji government limited religious freedom, and the new religions were forced to cooperate with official policy in order to conduct their activities. They frequently found themselves suppressed or persecuted. The government's authority for such acts was Article 28 of the Meiji Constitution (1889), which guaranteed freedom of religion to Japanese subjects only "within limits not prejudicial to peace and order, and not antagonistic to their duties as subjects." Article 28 permitted the government to mobilize the police against a religious organization if it was judged that peace and order were being disturbed or that believers were ignoring their duties as subjects of the Meiji government. To grow, Sectarian Shintō, like Buddhism in the Edo period, had no choice but to bow to the will of the government.

The thirteen Sectarian Shintō sects around the beginning of the Meiji period were Kurozumikyō, Misogikyō, Fusōkyō, Ontakekyō, Izumo Ōyashirokyō, Shintō Shūseiha, Shintō Taikyō, Jikkōkyō, Shintō Taiseikyō, Shinrikyō, Shinshūkyō, and the two most representative, Tenrikyō and Konkōkyō. The oldest sect, Kurozumikyō, was founded in 1814 by Kurozumi Munetada (1780–1850), and the newest, Shinshūkyō, in 1881 by Yoshimura Masamochi (1839–1915). Tenrikyō and Konkōkyō, which outstripped the others, both emerged as the shogunate collapsed. Of the thirteen sects, four arose before 1867 and nine after. It is clear that these sects arose in tandem with social changes. Only one of the sects had a female founder: Tenrikyō, founded by Nakayama Miki. The largest of the sects, Tenrikyō has attracted a large following from the Meiji period to the present and today has over two million followers and some seventeen thousand places of worship (*kyōkai*). It is followed in size by Konkōkyō, founded by Kawate Bunjirō (1814–83), which claims more than half a million followers.

TENRIKYŌ

Nakayama Miki

The founder of Tenrikyō, Nakayama Miki (1798–1887), was born into a wealthy farming family in Yamato Province. At the age of twelve she was married to the eldest son of the Nakayama family in the nearby village of Shōyashiki (present site of the headquarters). The Nakayamas were hereditary village heads and one of the most affluent and best regarded families in the village. After marrying into such a family, Miki was expected to cultivate the traditional female virtues, which included the three obediences—to father, husband, and eldest son—as well as marital fidelity, attention to household duties, and concern for servants' welfare.

Observing Miki's model behavior as a wife, her mother-in-law turned over to her the keys of the household in the third year of her marriage, giving her complete responsibility for managing everything. Miki's youth was devoted to meeting the expectations of her husband's family. In contrast, her husband, Zembei (1788–1853), showed no inclination to work and led an idle and dissipated life. Nevertheless, Miki remained faithful to him, without approving of his self-indulgence. Emotionally remote from

Zembei, she went about her daily responsibilities and eventually gave birth to seven children, three of whom died.

Miki could not help looking on her husband's laziness and dissipation as her misfortune. He was free to indulge himself because of his prestige as a member of the landed class with inherited wealth. Miki began to question the nature of happiness. The wives of poor farmers who envied her worked every day beside their husbands simply to survive. Yet they seemed happy. Miki thought that however poor a couple might be, working side by side as husband and wife made them happy. She discovered a new set of principles: being poverty-stricken meant that happiness was possible, and poverty was in fact the starting point for happiness.

Miki had been sustained by her strong *nembutsu* faith since childhood. In the Edo period, however, the *nembutsu* teaching of temple priests was accompanied by moral and ethical lessons on the duties of women. But was that enough for Miki? She was exhausted physically and mentally after long years in the Nakayama family, striving to practice the three obediences, attending diligently to household affairs, suffering her husband's dissipation, and losing three children in succession. In 1837 her eldest son, Shūji (1821–81), complained of pain in his left leg, and when all the doctors from the surrounding area had failed to cure him, a *shugenja* was summoned to perform an exorcism. Despite all this treatment, Shūji's pain was not relieved. In the meantime Miki had given birth to a daughter, Kokan, her last child. This birth left her physically weak and emotionally unstable. Her fatigue had reached a peak.

When Miki was forty, Shūji again complained of leg pains; her husband, Zembei, had trouble with his eyes; and she herself suffered from back pains. Thus on the twenty-third day of the tenth month of 1838, the family once again summoned a *shugenja* to perform an exorcism. The *miko* (female shaman) could not attend, however, and Miki took her place. As the incantations continued and spiritual ecstasy mounted, Miki suddenly spoke the following words:

> I am the general of heaven. I am the true and original God. I have been predestined to reside here with the Nakayama family. I have descended from heaven to save all human beings, and I want Miki to be the shrine of God. Do as I say. If you comply, I will save people throughout the world. If you refuse, the Nakayama family will be destroyed.

This was Miki's first pronouncement as a *kami*. She subsequently re-

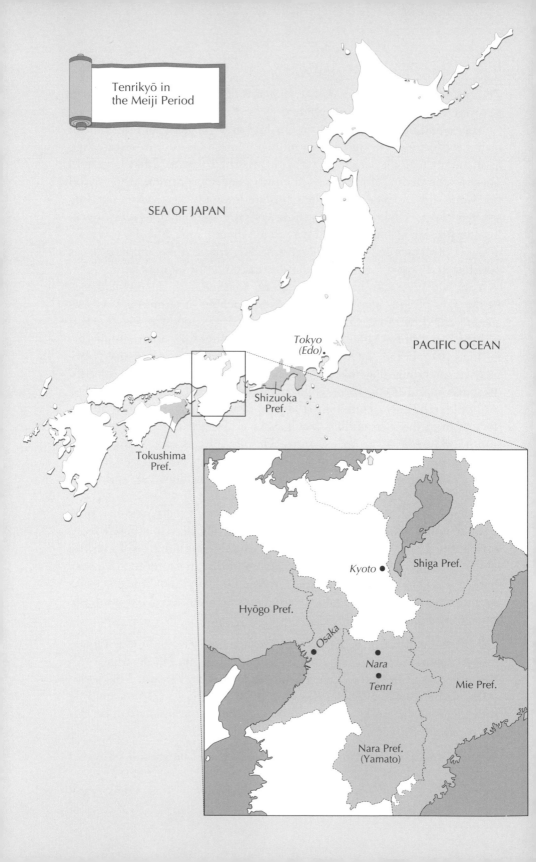

Tenrikyō in
the Meiji Period

SEA OF JAPAN

PACIFIC OCEAN

Tokyo
(Edo)

Shizuoka
Pref.

Tokushima
Pref.

Kyoto

Shiga Pref.

Hyōgo Pref.

Osaka

Nara

Tenri

Mie Pref.

Nara Pref.
(Yamato)

nounced the Nakayama wealth and lived a life of poverty. She considered her poverty the will of almighty God, the general of heaven. Revitalized by her new life, Miki eventually began to see her mission as one of relieving people's suffering. The first people she helped were women. She freed them from anxiety about bearing children by guaranteeing a safe birth. At first Miki was looked on as a *kami* who ensured trouble-free childbirth; later she was viewed as someone who could ensure conception. Finally, as her skills matured and faith in her deepened, she was able to cure a wide variety of ailments. Around the beginning of the Meiji period, she was known throughout the Kyoto-Osaka region and beyond as a *kami* who cured illness. Many people went to visit her in the village of Shōyashiki, seeking to be healed. In cases too numerous to cite, sufferers who found themselves cured became her followers.

Miki's Philosophy

Miki's healing gradually became more widely recognized, and her followers looked on her as a devoted and self-sacrificing mother. She would suck the pus from their sores and cure eye diseases by licking their eyes. Her actions were those of a highly compassionate mother figure and deeply affected her followers, winning their hearts. As their numbers increased, Tenrikyō began to develop as a religion. Its rapid growth cannot be attributed solely to the worldly benefits it promised. Miki's own religious reasoning asserted that the "manifest evidence"—the curing of disease— was not accidental but inevitable. She created for Tenrikyō a philosophy of salvation that came to have great meaning for its followers.

The foundation of Tenrikyō doctrine is contained in two of its scriptures, the *Mikagura Uta* (Songs for the *Tsutome* [Service]) and the *Ofudesaki* (Tip of the Divine Writing Brush), written by Miki between 1866 and 1882. She said that to achieve salvation it is first necessary to have sunk into poverty, for that is the point from which the search for happiness can begin. The effort to produce this happiness she called *hi no kishin*, or consecrated labor, that is, labor with no thought of reward. Thus the basic human state and starting point for Tenrikyō salvation is poverty, a universal state that many in the Edo period experienced—together with illness, social unrest, and natural calamities. Hence there is a need for the salvation of the Tenrikyō God.

Miki explained that unhappiness was caused by karma from past existences that resulted in dust (*hokori*) being lodged in a person's heart. People were unhappy because their hearts were covered with this dust. The Tenrikyō God, the *oyagami* (God the parent), swept the dust from their hearts, enabling happiness to arise. True faith was all that was necessary for salvation by the *oyagami*. The way to salvation was to be found in Tenrikyō's Kagura-zutome (Kagura [Salvation-dance] Service) and Teodori (the hand movements of the Kagura Service). Through this act of faith the Tenrikyō believer achieved a joyous life (*yōki-gurashi*) full of laughter, song, and dance. Miki constantly stressed that the entire world would be made happy if this method of salvation were disseminated to all people everywhere.

The salvation that Miki taught contributed greatly to the growth of Tenrikyō, but it was not the group's only attraction. Something more basic that drew a large number of followers lay hidden in Miki's new philosophy and personal example. Those who looked to her for salvation had been poor for generations, could not escape poverty, and believed poverty was the cause of their unhappiness. Miki, the envied wife of a rich man, had herself fallen into poverty and had joined the mass of the poor. But she taught a new attitude toward happiness, rooted in her own confidence and experience. Poverty was the starting point for happiness, and by practicing *hi no kishin* to build a new life, people would achieve true joy. According to Miki, people were unaware that poverty was the springboard for happiness and felt unhappy because they depended on outmoded values. She taught that such attitudes should be abandoned and her new ideas adopted.

Miki's views on poverty were the most important ideological basis for Tenrikyō's continuing development.

The Growth of Tenrikyō

Those to whom Miki spoke were of the lowest social stratum. In her *Ofudesaki* she denounced those she called the "high mountains" (those in power) and made many pronouncements on the priority of relief for the ordinary people (the "valley bottoms"). Angry at those with political power who were persecuting Tenrikyō, she criticized them boldly. She also wrote that salvation for scholars and the rich could wait, and that the positions of daimyō, "spear carriers," and palanquin bearers should be abolished. When Miki died at eighty-eight, in 1887, she had been arrested eighteen times. A woman of religion to the end, she continued to insist that her god and her convictions were more important than politics.

Tenrikyō grew remarkably in the 1880s, and its followers formed believers' associations, or *kō*, in many districts. Miki encouraged the establishment of these associations, which in turn stimulated the growth of Tenrikyō. In 1888, the year after Miki's death, the *kō* were renamed *kyōkai* (places of worship) under a new administrative system. In that year there were two directly affiliated *kyōkai:* one in Kōriyama, Nara Prefecture (the former Yamato Province), and one in Yamana, Shizuoka Prefecture. By 1889 ten more existed in Ashitsu, Semba, and Takayasu in Osaka; Hyōjin, Hyōgo Prefecture; Kawaramachi in Kyoto; Kōga, Shiga Prefecture; Muya, Tokushima Prefecture; Higashi and Nihombashi in Tokyo (the former Edo); and Shimagahara, Mie Prefecture. The number of *kyōkai* continued to grow in the next three years, increasing by ten in 1890, fifteen in 1891, and forty-three in 1892.

The number of *kyōkai* increased sharply in 1896, 1909, and 1925, years of social unrest generated by war or natural disaster. Between 1912 and 1922 the number of believers mushroomed from about 75,000 to 133,000, a 77.3 percent increase. Between 1928 and 1936 the number increased from 174,000 to 288,000, a 65.5 percent growth rate. A similar spurt was apparent after World War II. A survey conducted by Tenrikyō in March 1945, recorded a total of 196,000 accredited *kyōnin* (leaders qualified as heads of *kyōkai*) and *yōboku* (leaders given divine direction), which suggests that there must have been around 400,000 followers in all. A survey conducted in December 1999 records over two million members (*kyōnin, yōboku,* and ordinary members) and some seventeen thousand *kyōkai*. Propagation had extended throughout Japan and overseas to the United States, Brazil, and Congo.

Criticism and Persecution

Tenrikyō's development was by no means smooth. In fact, it faced increasing hardship as it gained followers among the lowest strata of Meiji society. As Tenrikyō grew, it was attacked bitterly from various quarters—by politicians, the established religions, journalists, and local communities.

Miki's eighteen arrests attest to the degree of official suppression of Tenrikyō. After her death in 1887, the suppression intensified and was carried out nationwide. On April 6, 1896, a secret directive was issued to all prefectural and city offices in the name of Home Minister Yoshikawa Akimasa. The order appeared to ban new religions that the government considered heretical. In reality, however, it was a ban on Tenrikyō.

Reasons for suppression cited in the directive included the indiscriminate socializing of men and women, the disregarding of medical science, and compulsory donations. The directive recommended increased police surveillance, particularly of Tenrikyō activities that the government regarded as exploitative.

Criticism of the religion in print increased significantly around the early 1890s. Between the late 1880s and the late 1890s more than thirty books attacking Tenrikyō were published. In addition, major newspapers of the time, including the *Asahi Shimbun*, *Miyako Shimbun*, *Tōkyō Nichinichi Shimbun*, *Hōchi Shimbun*, and *Chūō Shimbun*, carried articles sharply critical of Tenrikyō. The *Chūō Shimbun*, in fact, undertook a six-month campaign against the organization.

Official Recognition

Seeking to avoid being attacked from all sides, Tenrikyō initially made every effort to cooperate with the government. During the Sino-Japanese War (1894–95), it contributed 10,000 yen to the government's war fund in a show of good faith. During the Russo-Japanese War (1904–5), it helped to sell government bonds and itself bought more than 2.5 million yen worth. It also donated 14,000 yen for assistance to soldiers going to war and 2,500 yen to the war fund. It worked to improve its image by undertaking civic activities, such as street cleaning, to benefit local communities.

At the same time, Tenrikyō worked to gain official recognition as a religious sect. It made its first application to the Home Ministry's Bureau of Religious Institutions in August 1899. That bureau turned down the appeal, however, saying that recognition of Tenrikyō as a religious sect was unthinkable and that it might order the group to disband if any irregularities were discovered. The bureau also said that it would be best for it to find a way to reform itself.

The first head of the Takayasu Kyōkai, in Osaka, Matsumura Kichitarō (1867–1952), a relative of the Nakayama family, had the task of obtaining official recognition for Tenrikyō. He was one of the very few intellectuals in Tenrikyō at the time and was a talented administrator. A second application was made in June 1901, but the result was the same. Tenrikyō was not discouraged by the repeated failures, however, and set about reforming its doctrine and organization. Matsumura invited people from outside the sect—Shintō scholars, as well as journalists—to help create its "Meiji Scriptures," incorporating all the government's demands. They completed their work in January 1903. The Meiji Scriptures consisted of ten parts: "Honoring the Gods," "Revering the Emperor," "Patriotism," "Ethical Principles," "Practicing Virtue," "Purification," "Establishing the Teachings," "Gratitude to God," "Worshiping God through Dance," and "Peace of Mind." Although the Meiji Scriptures generally followed Miki's teachings, they also departed greatly from those teachings.

Tenrikyō filed a new application in August 1904. The Bureau of Religious Institutions again rejected the request and intimated that its position would not change in the future. The bureau stated that Tenrikyō's application was acceptable in form and its religious training procedures were adequate but there were still doubts about its actual practice. The Bureau of Religious Institutions recommended that the sect put its new beliefs into effect and submit a new application. In his fruitless efforts to gain official recognition for Tenrikyō, Matsumura had traveled repeatedly between the Tenrikyō headquarters in Nara Prefecture and the Bureau of Religious Institutions in Tokyo and had spent more than six months in the capital.

A fourth application was made in the same year, and it appeared that success was at last within reach, but once again the request was turned down. Tenrikyō continued to work to meet the bureau's requirements. Then, eight months after its fifth application was submitted, Tenrikyō received the following notification: "Home Ministry Confidential Document, Class B, No. 54. Your application has been approved. November 27, 1908. Baron Hirata Tōsuke, LL.D., Home Minister."

Tenrikyō's long-held dream was fulfilled, although the spiritual price of official recognition was enormous. To avert government suppression, Tenrikyō had deliberately added elements to Miki's doctrine that were not necessarily in the same spirit as her teachings, had altered the interpretation of her words, and had even changed the name of its deity at the request of the government. The multiple compromises that Tenrikyō had accepted were indicative of the extent of government control of religion at that time.

The Jiba

Throughout her life Miki had reiterated that anyone who did God's will could expect to live one hundred and fifteen years. People were unable to live out this allotted span only because they went against God's will and accumulated evil in their hearts. Miki had constantly emphasized the hundred-and-fifteen-year life span, both in her speeches and in her writings, yet she herself failed to attain it, dying a few months before her eighty-ninth birthday. The disturbance this caused among her followers was almost indescribable. To quiet the unrest, the sect's leaders issued a statement officially announcing her death and interpreting its meaning. They said that Miki had shortened her term of physical existence by twenty-five years (according to Japanese reckoning she had died at the age of ninety) to hasten the growth of those who were the children of God and to enable people to do God's will. Although she was mortal, her spirit was believed to be immortal, dwelling in the *jiba*, the sacred area at the heart of the main Tenrikyō worship hall.

By sealing Miki's spirit in the *jiba*, on the original Nakayama land, Tenrikyō was able to avert heresy and schism. That did not end the problem, however. A mediator, an interpreter of the Tenrikyō god's will, was needed. To fill that role, the office of *honseki* was established, to be held by a person who would transmit the will of the *kami* Miki. The master carpenter Iburi Izō (1833–1907), one of Miki's closest disciples, was selected as the first *honseki*.

After Miki's death the *jiba* became the center of Tenrikyō faith. In the *jiba* stands the *kanrodai*, an octagonal table, on which a wooden vessel receives divine grace. Between 1887 and 1907 in the main worship hall, with the *kanrodai* at its heart, Iburi Izō delivered what were considered Miki's directions, which were collected in the sect's third scripture, the *Osashizu* (Divine Directions). Broadly speaking, the *jiba*—which includes the main worship hall, the founder's hall, and the ancestors' hall—is equivalent to the space known in Tenrikyō as the *yashiki* (dwelling). An extension of the *yashiki* is the space in the center of the city of Tenri, Nara Prefecture, that is called Oyasato (Parent Village). The *jiba* is the space that lies at the very heart of the sacred land of Tenrikyō.

Tenrikyō faith was sustained through Iburi's *Osashizu*, which emanated from the *jiba*. When Iburi died in 1907, Ueda Naraito (1863–1937) was named to succeed him as the second *honseki*. The Nakayama family, led by Miki's grandson Shinnosuke (1866–1914), opposed the *honseki* system, however. If the sect obeyed the *honseki*, power would be transferred to the families of the mediators, the Iburis and Uedas. The Nakayamas felt that they, the blood relatives of the founder, were being ignored, and they were offended that power within the organization should be held by the *honseki* and those bound to them by faith. The Nakayamas therefore declared Naraito mad and abolished the position of *honseki*. Eventually the *jiba* passed from the hands of the Tenrikyō organization into the private possession of the Nakayamas. After World War II the Nakayamas were named hereditary patriarchs (*shimbashira*) of Tenrikyō, and rivalry between the founder's blood relations and the religious elite ended in the victory of her descendants.

KONKŌKYŌ

Kawate Bunjirō

The founder of Konkōkyō, Kawate Bunjirō (1814–83), was born the second son of a poor farmer, Kandori Jūhei, in the village of Urami in Bitchū Province. When he was eleven, he was adopted into the Kawate family in the nearby village of Ōtani. Bunjirō's circumstances did not improve noticeably after his adoption. At that time the Kawate family had only about 3.6 ares of land and lived in a small one-room shed. Bunjirō worked hard to improve his adoptive family's fortunes, laboring from morning to night beside his new father. As a result of his efforts, the family's situation gradually improved.

Yamabushi who taught of a vengeful deity, Konjin, were influential in the Ōtani area. Religious from childhood, Bunjirō deeply believed in the *yamabushi* teachings, especially regarding the power of Konjin's curses. He remained faithful to the Konjin cult and its teachings about lucky and unlucky days and directions.

Yet Bunjirō's family was afflicted with a number of misfortunes. In 1831 his adoptive mother gave birth to a son, Tsurutarō. The child died at the age of five, and twenty days later his father died. The family suffered further misfortunes between 1836 and 1851, including seven deaths (of both family members and livestock). Popular belief held that seven deaths would occur in a family cursed by the deity Konjin, and Bunjirō could not help thinking of that. In April 1855 he contracted a throat infection so severe that the doctors considered his case hopeless. His brother-in-law, however, who had been praying for his recovery, became possessed by Konjin, and as a result of an appeal to the deity, Bunjirō's health improved. His devotion to Konjin grew stronger than ever.

Bunjirō himself first became possessed and heard the deity's voice in 1858. Thereafter he repeatedly had the same mystical experience, through which he came to realize that Konjin was not a *kami* who caused suffering

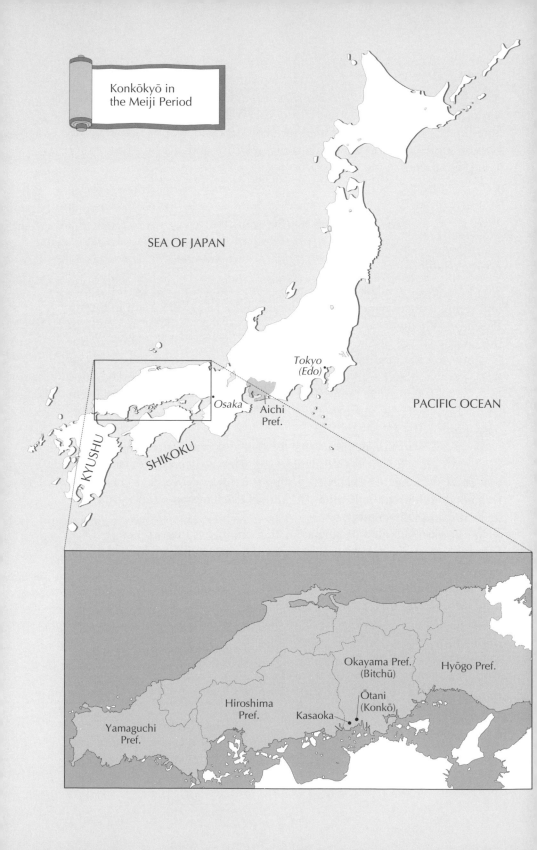

Konkōkyō in
the Meiji Period

SEA OF JAPAN

PACIFIC OCEAN

Tokyo
(Edo)

Osaka

Aichi
Pref.

KYUSHU

SHIKOKU

Okayama Pref.
(Bitchū)

Hyōgo Pref.

Ōtani
(Konkō)

Kasaoka

Hiroshima
Pref.

Yamaguchi
Pref.

but one who brought happiness. People began visiting Bunjirō to learn about the new form of salvation that Konjin promised. Finally, in 1859, Bunjirō turned his farm over to his son Asakichi (1845–1907) and devoted himself exclusively to religious activities. On the twenty-first day of the tenth month of that year, the *kami* told him:

> Many people in this world face trouble. Since you have sincere faith in the *kami*, you will help both people and the *kami* by mediating between them. You will help the *kami* and save people. People have being because of the *kami*: the *kami* has being because of people. Through your mediation, both will benefit far into the future, depending on one another like parents and children and fulfilling themselves through helping one another.

That was the beginning of Bunjirō's life as a religious figure.

Bunjirō's new religion did not stress his role as an *ikigami* (living *kami*) or its founder. He likened the relationships between Tenchi Kane no Kami (the parent *kami* of heaven and earth, another name for Konjin) and himself, between himself and other believers, and between the *kami* and other believers to the relationship between parents and children. All human beings are the children of the parent *kami*. Bunjirō, too, was a child of the *kami*, like other believers. But as the first person to hear the voice of Tenchi Kane no Kami, he stood as a mediator (*toritsugi-sha*) between other people and the *kami*, transmitting the will of the *kami* to his children. In this role Bunjirō proclaimed himself an *ikigami* called Konkō Daijin.

Bunjirō left the running of the farm to his family and sat continually before the *kami* in a small sanctuary called the *hiromae*, where he mediated for petitioners of the *kami*. The numbers of people who visited him continued to increase, so that by 1861 he had to rebuild the Kawate home to accommodate them.

Bunjirō's Teachings

Bunjirō's only formal education was a year of reading and writing. Though they were very simple and unsophisticated, his teachings were sufficient to help suffering farmers, since they were born of his own long experience as a farmer. He taught:

> It is not true to say that a person without learning cannot help others. Even learned people cannot help others if they do not know *makoto*

[the truth]. It is said that people of learning are sometimes ruined—however great their learning, it may not save them from hardship. Though I am without learning, those who listen to me will receive *okage* [worldly benefits].

These statements are characteristic of a man who entered religion not through study but through personal experience.

Bunjirō promised easy childbirth to women and urged them to abandon the restrictions and taboos traditionally associated with menstruation and childbearing. In a striking innovation for his times, when men were honored and women disdained, Bunjirō made several pronouncements that women should be esteemed. "Konjin teaches that although until now only men have built families, women may do likewise. Look at the example of Empress Jingū." "Women are near the *kami*. Women are the source of faith."

Bunjirō encouraged the poor farmer to work hard and lead a simple life. "Konjin despises fallow ground," he remonstrated. In regard to the sect's collection of donations, he said: "Konjin does not rejoice when his children are hurt by drives for donations." Warm and humane, Bunjirō continued to minister to poor farmers and women until his death at the age of sixty-nine in 1883.

The Hiromae

People's reasons for joining Konkōkyō reveal what they were searching for when they went to Bunjirō seeking salvation, as well as what Bunjirō could offer them. Illness was the most common motivation. Bunjirō and the sect's leaders practiced *toritsugi*, mediating for their followers, offering prayers to the *kami*, and obtaining the *kami*'s salvation for followers.

Adherents' prayers and petitions have been recorded by the founder and other *toritsugi-sha* in religious diaries called the *Gokinen Chō*. These records reveal that most people were seeking release from illness and other misfortunes and that temporal benefits were central to their prayers. A *Gokinen Chō* of May 1870 includes the following notes: "Three-year-old girl, [born in the] year of the dragon, an abscess on the head, quickly cured"; "Man, year of the hare, twenty-eight, fever, completely cured"; "Woman, year of the goat, sought safety in the home and success in business"; "Woman, year of the tiger, asked for cure of chest pains, thanks for rapid cure." In a *Gokinen Chō* of November 1914, the pattern was much the same as it had been almost half a century earlier: "Woman, year of the rat, thanks for complete cure of illness"; "Man, year of the cock, burn completely healed"; "Woman, year of the ox, thanks for daily work"; "Woman, year of the tiger, sixty-one, plea for cure of swelling of right shin." A *Gokinen Chō* of February 1960 records: "Suzuki Hanako, prayer in last month of pregnancy for safe childbirth"; "Yamada Taichirō, injury to face"; "Takahashi Hiroshi, prayer that he might enter Hosei University"; "Nakamura Yoshiko, prayer for a successful marriage after many difficulties"; "Saitō Yoshiko, prayer for prosperity of drinking establishment." Although there are small differences in detail from period to period, these records clearly reveal that most pleas were for temporal benefits, particularly cures for illness.

The *Gokinen Chō* have been recorded daily for nearly one hundred and forty years at the main and regional worship centers since the inception of Konkōkyō's activities. They faithfully testify to some of the main attractions that Konkōkyō has for believers.

Toritsugi is practiced and the *Gokinen Chō* are recorded in the sanctuary of Konkōkyō, the *hiromae*, which is the sect's most sacred site. The *hiromae* is not unique to the main worship center of Konkōkyō but is found in any meeting place of the sect. Thus mediation between Tenchi Kane no Kami and Konkōkyō followers can take place wherever there is a Konkōkyō meeting place. In contrast to the centralization of authority that marks Tenrikyō, authority in Konkōkyō is dispersed.

The Growth of Konkōkyō

Konkōkyō first took form in 1861 as a *kō*, or believers' association, organized by Saitō Jūemon (1823–95). Its branch organizations were first called *deyashiro*, or branch shrines. The most active of these at the beginning of the Meiji period was the Kasaoka branch in Okayama Prefecture. Over nineteen thousand members—an average of nearly sixteen hundred a month—visited it in 1868. Believers who visited Kasaoka had taken the faith to Shikoku and western Honshu by 1873. By 1881 there were twenty thousand believers in a single district of Yamaguchi Prefecture.

Thereafter Konkōkyō spread throughout every region of Japan. Propagation activities began in Osaka in 1875, on Kyushu in 1887, in Tokyo in 1888, and on Hokkaido in 1891. As a result, Konkōkyō regional meeting places were established all over Japan. In July 1885 the *deyashiro* were re-designated *bun-kyōkaisho* and *shi-kyōkaisho*, and three years later these designations were abbreviated to *bunsho* and *shisho*. The largest number of meeting places at that time was eight in Okayama Prefecture, followed by six in Osaka, three in Kyoto, two in Hiroshima Prefecture, two in Hyōgo Prefecture, and one in Aichi Prefecture. Konkōkyō's growth was modest, but the organization expanded greatly in the years around 1912 (the end of the Meiji period and the beginning of the Taishō period [1912–26]) and 1926 (the end of the Taishō period and the beginning of the Shōwa period [1926–89]). The years of greatest growth, measured in terms of new meeting places, were 1931, 1933, 1937, and 1940. When the five atypical years of extremely small growth between 1885 and 1945 are excluded, two slumps in overall growth occurred in the period 1885–90 and during World War II.

In 1942 Konkōkyō had 1,518 meeting places, but after the war it lost most of its overseas branches. As of December 31, 1953, the number had fallen to 1,332. Despite the effect of the war on Konkōkyō, the organization rebounded, and by December 31, 1999, it had 1,606 meeting places and claimed 434,000 members.

Konkōkyō and the Government

In the first month of 1863, Saitō Jūemon of Kasaoka was imprisoned for one hundred and seven days at the order of the local administrator for the shogunate. In response, Bunjirō did not defy the government but advised his followers to submit and bide their time: "This present age of the Tokugawa clan is like a stone wall, which cannot easily be toppled. But in thirty years the world will change and a way will open up." While predicting a bright future, he counseled avoiding conflict with the authorities. He told his followers to strictly obey the laws of the shogunate. "Those in charge are your superiors, just as are the *kami* above you. If you disobey the regulations of the government, there will be no *okage* [blessings] from the deity." "You might think that your annual tax is a payment to the district office, but that is not so. What you pay is your debt to the emperor."

Though Bunjirō advocated obedience to the authorities, he was not obsequious. He knew that it was meaningless to oppose those in power. To escape persecution, it was important to obey the laws and avoid provoking the authorities. Bunjirō held to this course all his life, and after his death his successors maintained it.

Konkōkyō cooperated fully with the government during the Sino-Japanese and Russo-Japanese wars, and the organization actively encouraged its members to observe the Imperial Rescript on Education (1890); the Imperial Rescript of 1908, intended to curb hedonism and abuses of free speech; and imperial edicts concerning national morals and ethics. It taught that the ideal subject envisioned by the Meiji government and the ideal Konkōkyō follower were the same. Konkōkyō published many tracts encouraging cooperation with the government. The *Kokuun no Hatten to Kokumin no Taido* (The Development of the Nation and the Attitude of Citizens; 1910) was a collection of lectures by Satō Norio (1856–1942), who played an important role in the development of Konkōkyō doctrine and organization. The collection consisted of seven chapters: "The Great Work of the Restoration," "The Imperial Rescript on Education and the Imperial Rescript of 1908," "Civilization and Diplomatic Relations," "National Power and Integrity," "Resolution of the People," "The Dignity of Establishing the Nation," and "Youth and the State."

In the chapter on imperial rescripts, Satō wrote:

It is my humble opinion that from now on the Japanese people—officials, educators, people of religion, business people, or whatever their calling—will not be able to perform their assigned tasks unless they act according to the Imperial Rescript on Education and the Imperial Rescript of 1908. I believe that the criteria for the people's integrity and the broad policy for social action must be completely based upon the two rescripts and that future development of the nation must be accomplished by observing them.

Satō had inherited Bunjirō's attitude toward the government and firmly supported the Meiji government and its policies.

At the beginning of a tract of January 1913, "The Opinion of Members Concerning the Political Situation," Satō included the Charter Oath of 1868, the five-clause statement of the philosophy of the Meiji government at its inception. Paralleling the oath, Satō quoted the "Divine Instructions of the Founder of Konkōkyō" as the five articles that Konkōkyō believers were obliged to uphold: "As one born in the country of the *kami*, never forget your deep debt of gratitude to the *kami* and to the emperor"; "Do not forget that your body does not belong to you but is part of the great body of the *kami* and the emperor"; "For the emperor and your country, carry out your daily duties with faith"; "Receive divine virtues and cultivate human ones"; and "Those with faith face everything with sincerity." Here obedience to the authorities had been elevated to active cooperation.

Unlike such sects as Tenrikyō and Ōmoto, Konkōkyō suffered scarcely any pressure from the government. On July 22, 1899, it applied to the Bureau of Religious Institutions for official recognition as a separate sect. The central figure in the movement to attain recognition was Satō Norio, who had spent almost a year in Tokyo negotiating with the Home Ministry in preparation.

As a result, Konkōkyō's application was approved on June 16, 1900, by the home minister, Marquis Saigō Tsugumichi. The process had been relatively smooth, with approval being granted after the first application. By contrast, Tenrikyō labored nine years and submitted five applications before its independence was approved in November 1908.

19. Christianity
After the Edo Period

The pressure brought to bear in 1853 by the East India Squadron of the United States Navy, commanded by Commodore Matthew C. Perry (1794–1858), persuaded the Tokugawa shogunate to open Japan the following year under the 1854 Kanagawa Treaty of Peace and Amity, which gave American ships restricted access to two unimportant ports. Similar treaties with other Western nations quickly followed. Under commercial treaties concluded with the United States, Russia, the Netherlands, Great Britain, and France in 1858, first the ports of Hakodate, Nagasaki, and Yokohama and then the ports of Kobe, Niigata, Osaka, and Tokyo were opened to foreign commerce. Christian missionary societies in various countries were eager to work in the rich field that Japan presented for propagation, and in preparation a number of missionaries visited Japan to study the language and observe conditions there firsthand.

When Christianity did return, it was active in a number of areas in which Shintō and Buddhism were not, and it greatly influenced the attitudes of the Japanese who were promoting modernization. Its vigor increased as the years passed, reflecting the efforts of growing numbers of missionaries and evangelists. In 1899 there were 1,333 missionaries in the country; by 1931 that figure had almost doubled, to 2,374.

A survey published in 1929 showed that 39 percent of Japanese Christians belonged to the Roman Catholic and Orthodox churches and 61 percent were members of Protestant denominations. Studies of the modern history of Christianity in Japan have tended to focus on the Protestant denominations and ignore the Roman Catholic and Orthodox churches. This chapter attempts to remedy that bias by examining all three streams.

Renewed Missionary Efforts

The Société des Missions Étrangères de Paris (M.E.P.) continued the work of the Jesuit, Franciscan, and Dominican religious orders, which had maintained active missions in Japan in the sixteenth and seventeenth centuries. In 1831 the Vatican created the Apostolic Vicariate of Korea to further mission work there and placed the Ryukyu Islands under its jurisdiction, apparently intending to use the Ryukyus as the gateway for reintroducing the gospel into Japan.

Continuing persecution and martyrdoms in Korea, however, made any thought of resuming mission work in Japan seem hopeless. Napoléon-François Libois, M.E.P. (1805–72), procurator-general of Macao, took the opportunity of naval maneuvers to send a missionary to the Ryukyus. In 1844 Théodore-Augustin Forcade, M.E.P. (1816–85), was taken to Naha, on Okinawa, by Admiral Jean-Baptiste Cécille, the commander of the French naval forces in the Far East; but Forcade was immediately arrested and interned in the temple Shōgen-ji, in Tomari, on the outskirts of Naha. Denied contact with the islanders, he waited for the chance to do missionary work.

In 1846 Pope Gregory XVI made Japan a vicariate, to support the early resumption of missionary work there, and Forcade was appointed first vicar apostolic. He was consecrated bishop in Hong Kong in 1847, but was forced to resign in 1851 because of ill health. Charles E. Collin, M.E.P. (1811–54), a missionary in Manchuria, was appointed to succeed Forcade, but died en route to his new post in Naha. Libois then became vicar apostolic and dispatched three priests to the Ryukyus—Prudence S. B. Girard, M.E.P. (1821–67), Louis Auguste-Théodore Furet, M.E.P. (1816–1900), and Eugène-Emmanuel Mermet de Cachon, M.E.P. (1828–71?)—to learn Japanese while waiting for the opportunity to enter Japan.

After the signing of a Franco-Japanese treaty of friendship and trade in October 1858, Girard was appointed superior of the mission in Japan. In September 1859 he arrived in Edo to act as chaplain and interpreter for the French consulate. This was the first step toward the resumption of missionary activity following the long hiatus introduced by the prohibition edicts of the seventeenth century.

Four priests were appointed to work in Japan: Girard, Furet, Mermet, and Pierre Mounicou, M.E.P. (1825–71). The four had been together in the Ryukyus. Girard, as mission superior, administered Kanagawa from nearby Edo, with Mounicou in residence there after 1861; Mermet was responsible for Hakodate, on Hokkaido, and Furet for Nagasaki, on Kyushu. Their immediate concern was to discover the descendants of the *kakure*, or underground, Christians.

To this end, Girard had churches built in Yokohama (consecrated in 1862) and Nagasaki (consecrated in 1865), ostensibly to serve the foreign community, but he also intended that they should be centers for open propagation when that was permitted. Girard had the word *tenshudō* (Roman Catholic church) inscribed on the façade of the Yokohama church in large characters, and he answered the questions of visitors, delivered sermons, and distributed prayer books whenever the opportunity arose. His activities were nothing less than a public demonstration that the Catholic Church had revived in Japan.

In Hakodate, Mermet opened a school to teach French and began to care for the sick. His efforts in education and in charitable work, together with his own sincerity and devotion, brought many from the lower strata of society to the Catholic faith.

The Integration of the Kakure Christians

Under Furet's aegis, a Catholic church was built on a steep hillside in the Ōura district of Nagasaki in 1864. The Ōura Catholic Church, an imposing building with three steeples topped by crosses, announced to Nagasaki and its environs that the Catholic priests had returned. In August 1864, Bernard T. Petitjean, M.E.P. (1829–84)—who succeeded Girard as vicar apostolic in 1866—arrived in Nagasaki from Okinawa to replace Furet, who was suffering from fatigue. Petitjean brought the Ōura church to completion.

As he guided visitors around the so-called French Temple, Petitjean secretly hoped that the "old" Christians might declare themselves. His prayers were answered on March 17, 1865, when a group of farmers from the village of Urakami visited the church and one of them, a woman named Sugimoto Isabellina Yuri (1813–93), confided to him: "Our hearts are the same as yours." This was the declaration for which the missionaries had waited so hopefully, evidence of the resuscitation of the church in Japan after long persecution.

Overjoyed, Petitjean lost no time in writing to Girard in Yokohama announcing the discovery.

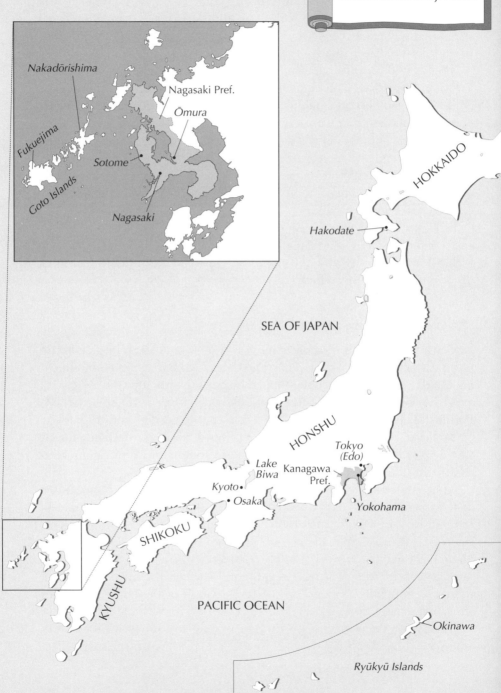

The Roman Catholic
Church in the Meiji Period

Nakadōrishima

Nagasaki Pref.

Ōmura

Fukuejima

Sotome

Goto Islands

Nagasaki

HOKKAIDO

Hakodate

SEA OF JAPAN

HONSHU

Tokyo
(Edo)

Lake
Biwa

Kanagawa
Pref.

Kyoto

Osaka

Yokohama

SHIKOKU

KYUSHU

PACIFIC OCEAN

Okinawa

Ryūkyū Islands

Today, just after midday, I saw some fifteen people—men and women, young and old—standing in a group at the church door. Something marked them as different from the usual sightseers. I immediately went and opened the door and led them down the aisle to the altar. Though I have prayed there every day since the church was consecrated, today I made a special plea to the Lord for His blessing. Just then, a woman of about forty knelt beside me and, putting her hands over her heart, said: "Our hearts are the same as yours." I was surprised and asked her where she came from. "We are from the village of Urakami, outside Nagasaki," she replied. "In our village there are many of the same heart as you. We pray to Saint Mary. Where is the statue of Saint Mary?" Once again I felt amazement, together with great joy. Were these, then, the descendants of the Old Christians? I praised God for His blessings and led them to the place where the statue of the Madonna and Child is enshrined.

Though delighted, Girard, as vicar apostolic, advised caution in view of the fact that Christianity was still proscribed. Petitjean followed Girard's instructions carefully and visited the Christian villages only late at night, in secret, working to rekindle a vigorous flame of faith. He was active not only in Urakami but also in the villages and hamlets where Christians were living in hiding, such as Shitsu in the Saga domain in Hizen Province (a village of 260 families, of whom all but that of the local doctor were Christian). Under Petitjean's guidance, these Japanese Christians studied doctrine and prayed, waiting for the day when they could at last declare their faith openly.

By 1867, however, the Urakami Christians had become increasingly reluctant to continue their lives of deception, following Buddhism publicly and hiding their Christian faith. Ignoring the Buddhist priests and conducting their own funerals, they cut formal ties with the Buddhist temple of their registration. This was a challenge to the entire *terauke* and parish system. Throughout that year and the next, similar incidents led to the persecution and exile of Christians in Ōmura and the Gotō Islands, a harbinger of the long journey into exile that the Christians were soon to face.

The newly installed Meiji government enforced the policy of proscription even more strictly than had the Tokugawa authorities. In 1868 a Nagasaki court recommendation to an imperial council stated that "since death is too pitiable a punishment for three thousand people, we submit that the leaders be severely punished and those under them banished, prevented from associating with others, and made to do hard labor." Acting on this recommendation, the government ordered the banishment of everyone in the village of Urakami for practicing Christianity. In May 114 prominent members of the community of about 3,000 were gathered up and sent to the domains of Hagi, Tsuwano, and Fukuyama, on western Honshu. Though most Christian families were broken up, they accepted persecution as a test of faith. Eventually, in February 1870, all the Urakami Christians were exiled: a total of 3,384 people were sent to fiefs throughout Japan.

The Return of the Exiles

The Christians' exile ended in 1873, when the proscription against Christianity was rescinded and Christians in Nagasaki were permitted to return to their homes. The exile had resulted in 613 deaths and 1,011 apostasies, but 1,092 people had kept their faith to the end and returned elated to their homes. Many of those who had apostatized repented their sin and returned to the Christian faith.

While the exiles of Urakami were joyful over being able to proclaim their faith openly, they returned to find almost half their homes sold, burned, or razed. Their difficulties were compounded by a strong typhoon that struck the area in 1874 and a dysentery epidemic that followed soon after. Marc de Rotz, M.E.P. (1840–1914), a priest under Petitjean, took charge of relief measures for the former exiles with the help of four volunteer nurses from among their number—Iwanaga Maki (1849–1920), Kataoka Wai, Moriyama Matsu, and Fukabori Wasa. The four women lived a communal life in a shed donated by Takayama Sen'emon, the farmers' spiritual leader, and worked under de Rotz's direction.

With regard to the hours for rising, prayer, work, and retiring, de Rotz laid down conventlike regulations for the life of the four volunteer nurses. When the epidemic ended, Iwanaga Maki embarked on a mission to provide for the children orphaned by the illness. The Takayama shed became an orphanage known as the Children's Room, and it was supported by income from the harvest of fields bought and donated by de Rotz.

In 1877 the community of women centering on Maki became a quasi order called the Congregation of the Sisters, Lovers of the Cross (Urakami Jūjikai). The women were active both in Nagasaki Prefecture and elsewhere, establishing children's homes and care centers. The self-sufficient women supported themselves by farming, raising silkworms, and spinning and weaving, and their life of work and prayer was a model for the villagers. In the Gotō Islands, west of Nagasaki, their establishments included an orphanage in Arikawa, on Nakadōrishima; an almshouse in Okuura and Saint Joseph's Institute in Kishuku, both on Fukuejima; and Saint Cecilia's Institute in Kita-uonome. Such charitable work gained Catholicism a foothold among the populace.

Besides helping Iwanaga Maki, in his parish of Sotome (which also included the villages of Kurosaki, Mie, and Kōnoura) de Rotz concentrated on bettering the life of the farmers through improved agricultural techniques. Self-support was all the more desirable because the Christians of Sotome were discriminated against as paupers of the lowest social class.

In 1883 de Rotz built a vocational institute where milling, weaving, sewing, netmaking, dyeing, edible-oil processing, and such exotic arts as bread baking and macaroni making were taught, together with such skills as record keeping and arithmetic. A similar school for young people had been opened in 1881 in Shitsu in the Saga domain to teach new agricultural techniques and provide a multifaceted education in farm management. Such practical schools were labors of love to benefit poor Catholic peasants. De Rotz's activities also included the provision of a dispensary, charitable works in the community, improvement of agricultural implements, and instruction in the planting of better crop varieties and methods of increasing sardine catches.

Thus, through its firm connection with the everyday lives of the people, propagation of the gospel bettered poor Christians socially while transmitting the Catholic faith. The strength of Catholicism lay in its concrete social measures, which made it a friend to the poor and the sick. The light of faith kindled in the villages by the period of exile was strengthened by the labors of the missionaries.

Ecclesiastical Organization and Growth

The vitality of the church in the Nagasaki area, and in Urakami in particular, bolstered missionary work in other areas. Missionaries had been dispatched to the open ports and the large cities—Tokyo, Yokohama, Nagasaki, Hakodate, Niigata, Kobe, and Osaka. The first order of religious women to go to Japan from Paris, the sisters of L'Institut des Sœurs de l'Enfant Jésus, arrived in 1872. Despite the great effort devoted to missionary work, however, results were disappointing, except in Nagasaki.

Petitjean succeeded Girard as vicar apostolic in 1866, taking charge of all missionary work in Japan. In 1875 he went to Rome and proposed the division of the vicariate into north and south to make mission work more systematic. The proposal was approved in June 1876. The Vicariate of Northern Japan, centered at Tokyo, consisted of Hokkaido and Honshu east and north of Lake Biwa. Pierre-Marie Osouf, M.E.P. (1829–1906), was appointed its vicar apostolic. The Vicariate of Southern Japan incorporated Honshu west of Lake Biwa, Shikoku, and Kyushu and had its see in Nagasaki. Petitjean remained its vicar apostolic and resided in Osaka.

At that time the northern vicariate had 14 priests and 34 catechists serving 1,235 Catholics in the five northern missions of Tokyo, Yokohama, Yokosuka, Hakodate, and Niigata. In the four missions of the southern vicariate—Nagasaki, Urakami, Kobe, and Osaka—there were 13 priests and 175 catechists serving 17,200 Catholics, more than 90 percent of the country's Catholic population. Although the religious orders were based in the Tokyo-Yokohama area, the vast majority of the entire Catholic population was in the Nagasaki-Urakami area of Kyushu, where missionary work focused primarily on the reintegrated *kakure* Christians. The Catholic population in the northern vicariate consisted of Catholics in the foreign concessions and an extremely small number of local converts.

The division of the vicariate made it possible for the missionaries to overcome areas of weakness and extend mission work throughout the country. There were two types of priests: the itinerants, who traveled from place to place preaching, and the residents, who served in chapels and churches. Thanks to the work of the itinerant priests, Catholicism spread throughout Japan.

In the northern vicariate the itinerants François-Paulin Vigroux, M.E.P. (1842–1909), and Hippolyte Louis Cadillac, M.E.P. (1859–1930), traveled through the prefectures north and east of Tokyo—Chiba, Saitama, Ibaraki, Fukushima, Tochigi, and Gumma—while Germain Testevuide, M.E.P. (1849–91), concentrated on those to the south and west—Kanagawa, Shizuoka, Aichi, and Gifu—and Felix Evrard, M.E.P. (1844–1919), and Augustin Ernest Tulpin, M.E.P. (1853–1933), worked in Aichi, Gifu, and Kanazawa prefectures. The priests were particularly active among people at the lower levels of society, such as the inhabitants of villages of outcastes. Fifteen years after the division of the vicariate, believers had increased tenfold.

The church exhibited great vitality in the southern vicariate, as efforts to locate and bring back to the fold the old Christians still living in hiding on remote islands continued and women's groups were organized in various places through the Urakami Jūjikai of de Rotz and Iwanaga Maki. In 1891 there were 27,909 Catholics in the Nagasaki area, served by fifty-four churches and oratories.

Missionary work was conducted throughout Kyushu and was particularly vigorous on western Honshu, in the area centering on Osaka. Itinerant priests worked in the prefectures of Mie, Fukui, Okayama, and Hiroshima and in the administrative district of Kyoto. They announced meetings by beating a drum. After giving a general talk on the teachings, illustrated by magic-lantern slides, they would discuss doctrine in detail with those who showed interest. As a result, by 1889 there were 2,946 Catholics registered outside Kyushu—on western Honshu and Shikoku. In the previous year the Vicariate of Central Japan, consisting of western Honshu and Shikoku, had been created out of the southern vicariate, which then came to consist of Kyushu alone. The vicar apostolic of the new vicariate was Felix Midon, M.E.P. (1840–93).

In view of the growth of Catholicism in Japan, in April 1891 Pope Leo XIII ordered the establishment of an episcopal hierarchy. On June 15, Tokyo became an archdiocese, with Osouf as archbishop. Three dioceses with suffragan bishops were formed at the same time: Nagasaki, with Jules Alphonse Cousin, M.E.P. (1842–1911), as bishop; Osaka, under Bishop Midon; and Hakodate, with Alexandre Berlioz, M.E.P. (1852–1929), as bishop. The archdiocese of Tokyo administered the area from Niigata, Fukushima, and Miyagi prefectures in the north to Fukui, Gifu, and Aichi prefectures, as far as Lake Biwa, in central Honshu. The see of Nagasaki controlled all of Kyushu, and Osaka administered Shikoku and the area of Honshu west of Lake Biwa. The diocese of Hakodate consisted of Hokkaido and northern Honshu. Thus at about the time that Japan adopted its first modern constitution, Japanese Catholics were organized into dioceses and encouraged to look forward to a new era of growth.

The Work of the Orders

As the number of Catholics increased, religious orders went to Japan and greatly aided the missionary effort. The following information regarding the orders and their dates of arrival is based on the 1972 edition of the *Catholic Yearbook*. The orders' missionary work encompassed a variety of welfare projects. Only a few orders went to Japan in the Meiji period (1868–1912), but because they found an untilled field, they worked enthusiastically. The greatest influx of missionary orders occurred after World War II.

The sisters of L'Institut des Sœurs de l'Enfant Jésus, who arrived in 1872, were devoted principally to teaching, caring for orphans, and providing medical care, pioneering work for which they were well prepared. They founded a girls' school, Shin'ei Joshi Gakuin in Tokyo, in 1875, and the Futaba Girls' High School in Tokyo in 1909. The Sisters of Chauffaillies, who arrived from France in 1877, were also devoted to education and the care of the poor and sick. Soon after their arrival they established an orphanage and a charity hospital in Kobe, and in 1879 they established an orphanage in Osaka. They administered Saint Bernard's Hospital in Nagasaki from 1895 to 1912 and operated a free elementary school for Catholics there from 1889 to 1905.

The Marist Brothers went to Japan from Bordeaux, France, at the request of Bishop Osouf. To carry out their plans for the education of boys and young men, in 1887 they established the Gyōsei School in Tokyo. They were a strong force in the spreading of French culture in Japan's capital. In 1896 the Trappists, who came from Peking at the invitation of Berlioz, established a monastery near Hakodate, where they followed their strict regimen of prayer, contemplation, and work. They supported themselves by farming and raising livestock, skills that contributed to the development of Hokkaido's dairy industry.

In whatever role the orders functioned, their aim was to serve those at the lowest rung of society. As can be inferred from the work of de Rotz in Sotome, the basic purpose of their involvement in agriculture was to protect the livelihood of Catholics and at the same time raise the standard of living in poor villages.

Catholics also played an active role in the increase of female higher education that occurred during the 1890s. Unlike the Protestants, who had been quick to establish institutions of higher education for young women, the Catholics had been primarily concerned with elementary and middle school educations. The Society of the Sacred Heart of Jesus arrived from France in Japan in 1908, with female higher education as its mission. In April 1910, it opened Seishin Joshi Gakuin in Tokyo, providing girls with kindergarten, elementary, and high school educations. Throughout the nation, people of the upper class welcomed the establishment of Catholic institutions of higher education for women, since many of them were dissatisfied with the Confucian "good wife, wise mother" focus of most other schools. Through its schools, the Catholic Church reached the upper class.

By the end of the Meiji period, the Catholic Church in Japan had gained a foothold among the very poor and the upper class through its multifaceted missionary work. Unlike the Protestants, who swayed with middle-class trends, the Catholics had indomitable confidence in their beliefs. The Japanese church endured fifteen years of suppression, between 1930 and 1945, while the country was at war. During that period, Japanese priests carried on the church's work and gained Catholicism a firm following among the upper class. After World War II a large number of Catholic clerics who had been forced to flee China in the wake of the civil war there flooded Japan and contributed to the work of the orders. At the same time, Catholics in the United States and elsewhere sent generous financial aid. As a result, the church developed greatly in Japan. Catholic education in particular prospered, giving the church a broad influence on society as a whole.

THE ORTHODOX CHURCH

Nikolai and the Church on Hokkaido

A Russian consulate was established in Hakodate, on Hokkaido, in 1859, and its chaplain, Ivan Vasilevich Mahov, became the first representative of the Orthodox Church in Japan. Poor health forced him to leave the post less than a year later. He was replaced in 1861 by Ivan Dmitrievich Kasatkin (1836–1912), better known as Père Nikolai, who became the driving force of the Orthodox mission in Japan.

Nikolai, who had developed an interest in the country after reading *Memoirs of a Captivity in Japan, during the Years 1811, 1812, and 1813,* by the naval officer and explorer Vasilii Mikhailovich Golovnin (1776–1831), applied for the position vacated by Mahov. Following his arrival in Hakodate in June 1861, Nikolai undertook the study of Japanese etiquette and customs, history, religion, and literature and attempted to translate sermons and liturgical works into Japanese while waiting for the day when it would be possible to work openly as a missionary. His initial policy and plans for the mission can be inferred from the set of fourteen rules for a proposed mission that he prepared in 1868. The rules concern mission policy, doctrine, the training of missionaries, church organization, the

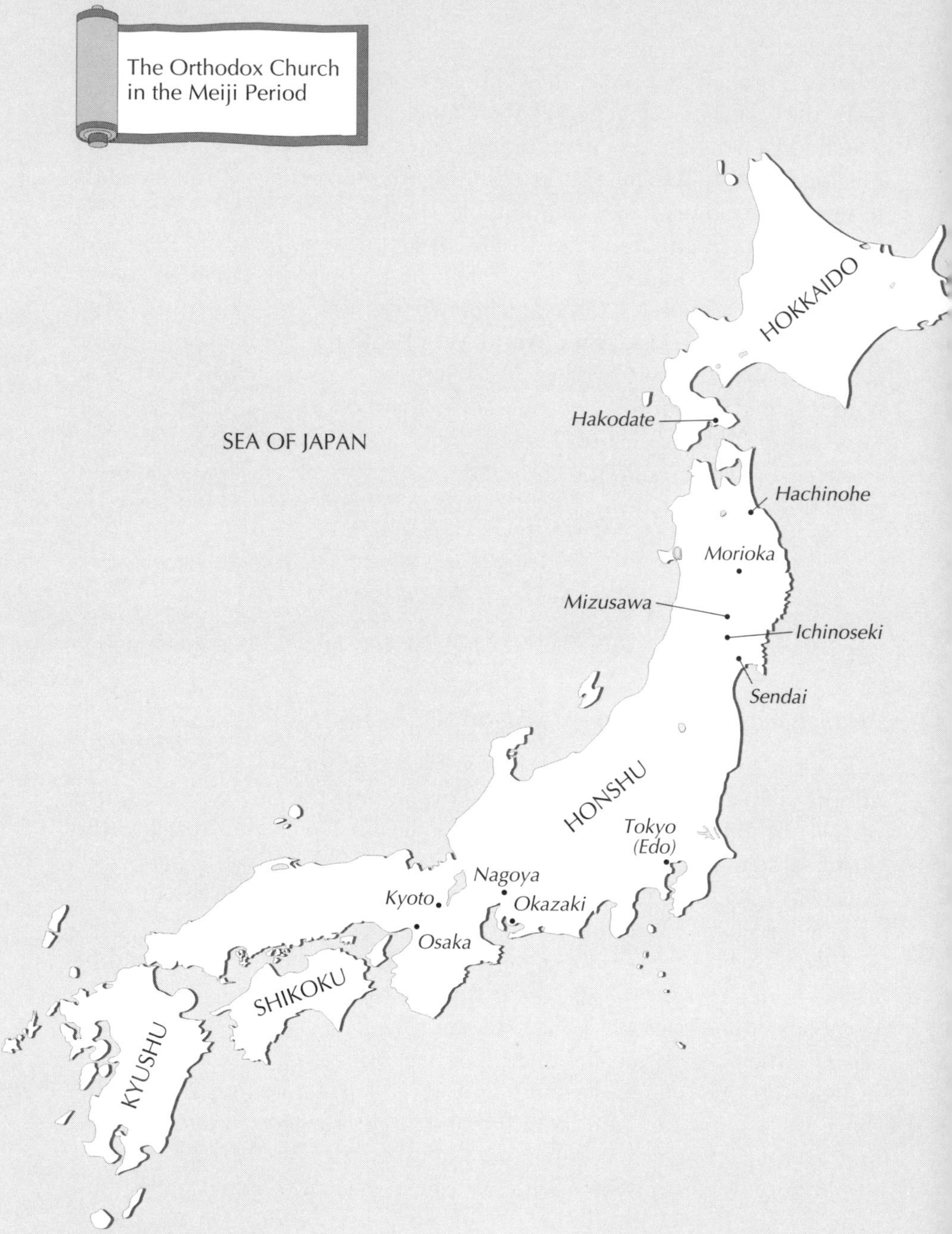

The Orthodox Church
in the Meiji Period

HOKKAIDO

SEA OF JAPAN

Hakodate

Hachinohe

Morioka

Mizusawa

Ichinoseki

Sendai

HONSHU

Tokyo
(Edo)

Nagoya

Kyoto

Okazaki

Osaka

SHIKOKU

KYUSHU

PACIFIC OCEAN

teaching of Russian, the training of medical doctors, the dispatch of Japanese youths to theological schools and medical schools in Russia, and the establishment of hospitals.

The rules stipulated two levels of instruction: general study of doctrine by beginners and more advanced study by catechists. The beginning classes were to be open to all—men, women, and children—with their curriculum the Nicene Creed, the Lord's Prayer, and the Ten Commandments. Catechists taught, and if a student was absent, the catechist was to ensure that the student received the missed explanations. Catechists studied the New Testament in the advanced classes and had to attend every session. In both classes, discussion was not to be permitted until explanations had been completed. Both classes were to meet twice a week.

In addition, catechists were to go through the town seeking converts and visiting new converts, teaching them the Nicene Creed, the Lord's Prayer, and the Ten Commandments. They were also to visit and instruct anyone who found it difficult to attend church services.

In 1868 Nikolai baptized his first converts: Sawabe Takuma (1835–1913), a priest at Shimmei Shrine in Hakodate; Sakai Tokurei (ca. 1836–81); and Urano Taizō. Through the Sendai retainer Arai Jōnoshin (1846–1922), Sawabe invited a number of men from the Sendai domain on Honshu to Hakodate in order to interest them in Christianity. Among the Sendai warriors who became priests and catechists of the Orthodox Church in Japan were Ono Shōgorō, Sasagawa Sadakichi, Tsuda Tokunoshin, Takaya Naka, and Ōtachime Kengo. Their conversions were the first step in the spreading of the faith through the Tōhoku region of northern Honshu, centering on the old Datè fief.

A great many of the early converts from the Sendai domain—which had been defeated in the struggles that resulted in the overthrow of the Tokugawa shogunate—looked to the Orthodox faith for hope for the future. Sawabe wrote to the Sendai retainers:

National reform must spring from new ways of thinking. These must spring from religious innovation, which springs from the Orthodox faith. . . .

If you are aiming at national restoration, you must hope for the unity of the people. The unity of the people depends on a true religion. If the people are brought to believe in a true religion, their unity will be achieved. If the people are united, is there anything that cannot be attained? If you truly grieve for your country, come at once to Hakodate.

Sawabe's message was political: for displaced retainers, Orthodox faith was the key to national restoration.

The Growth of the Church

In 1869 Nikolai returned to Russia for a short time. While he was there, the Holy Synod approved the establishment of the Russian Orthodox Japan Mission, appointed Nikolai as its head, and raised him to the rank of archimandrite. Nikolai returned to Japan in 1871. In December of that year he sent Ono, Sasagawa, and Takaya to Sendai for mission work and had Sawabe and Tsuda undertake propagation in Hakodate with the newly arrived hieromonk Anatolii (1838–93). In January 1872, Nikolai moved to Tokyo to direct all mission work in the nation. In September he chose a site in the Surugadai district for his headquarters and established sites for preaching in the Yotsuya, Shitaya, Asakusa, and Honjo districts.

After the restriction and persecution that it had experienced in Sendai and Hakodate, the Orthodox Church proceeded vigorously with local missionary activity. The first expansion—from Hakodate and Sendai to Mizusawa and Morioka, on northern Honshu—was followed by activity in the Nagoya and Okazaki area of central Honshu, in the nearby Osaka and Kyoto area, and in the western part of Honshu and on Kyushu. Success was particularly striking in the northern part of Honshu, centering on Sendai.

In October 1872, the Hokkaido Colonization Office ordered Sakai Tokurei to leave Hakodate and escorted him back to his registered domicile, Mizusawa. There he was placed under close surveillance. Nevertheless, he attempted to teach Christianity in nearby villages, such as Kannari, Karishiki, Izuno, and Wakayanagi. In Izuno a young man named Chiba Takusaburō (1852–83) was converted through his efforts. Chiba became a tireless fellow worker, and at the end of the year he visited Tokyo, where he was baptized by Nikolai.

Both Chiba and Sakai suffered for their beliefs and spent time in prison. This only strengthened their faith. After Sakai moved to Hachinohe to do missionary work there, Chiba actively assisted Tsuda Tokunoshin with propagation in the Tome region and was the driving force behind the establishment of the Orthodox Church in Izuno and Wakayanagi. Chiba later moved to Tokyo, where he was known by his baptismal name, Peter. He eventually became the head of an agricultural elementary school in the village of Itsukaichi in the Nishi Tama district. The focus of his activity was a study group called the Gakugei Kōdan-kai (Society for Lectures on Culture). He styled himself a doctor of law and drafted a private "Japanese imperial constitution" known as the Itsukaichi Draft Constitution.

Handa Unai, of Sanuma, in the Tome region, was another of Sakai's converts. In 1875 he devoted all his energy to the establishment of the Sanuma Ken'ei-kai, as the church was known. It grew rapidly, recording fifty-three baptisms in 1875, ninety-eight in 1876, and ninety-five in 1877. The Sanuma Ken'ei-kai became the headquarters for all propagation in the Tome district and provided leadership for the churches that were established in such neighboring villages and towns as Furukawa, Takashimizu, Tome, Tsukidate, Iwagasaki, Wakayanagi, Kanazawa, Jūmonji, Izuno, Kannari, Wakuya, Yamanome, and Ichinoseki.

Church members, as exemplified by Handa, came mainly from the local bourgeoisie. Motivated by a strong spirit of independence, in 1879 these people formed a popular organization called the Kōtsū-sha. The organization worked hard to achieve large-scale regional development. It opened an office in Ishinomaki and started a steamboat service on the Hasama River to take rice bought from local farmers to Ishinomaki for shipment to Tokyo. It also established a silk-reeling mill in Yokoyama. These undertakings failed within a year, however, and two-thirds of all the prosperous families in the Sanuma area became bankrupt. As a result, Handa left the church, and its reputation was severely damaged.

The Orthodox Church at that time encouraged progressive ideas among the middle class in agricultural areas. Thus, according to his daughter Kō, Fukasawa Yūshō, a silk manufacturer in Maebashi, Gumma Prefecture, taught female workers and students visiting from other areas "silk manufacture during the day and Christian doctrine in the evening. As a result, silk products spread throughout the neighboring regions along with the seeds of the new religion." The seeds of the faith were also sown in the silk mills of Hoshino Chōtarō and Iizuka Buichirō in the same prefecture.

On the strength of this growth, in 1874 Nikolai established the first synod of six catechists, which made twenty rules for propagation. These rules stipulated the duties of catechists, their assignment to local churches, their monthly stipends, the authority of the church in Tokyo, and the training of aspiring male catechists, young members, and female catechists. The establishment of the synod heralded the organization of the

510 CHRISTIANITY AFTER THE EDO PERIOD

Orthodox Church and the systematization of missionary efforts. In the same year, a seminary was established in Tokyo to train catechists, an act that substantially strengthened the church. Building on a solid foundation, regional churches were formed, missionaries worked actively on northern Honshu, and the Orthodox Church grew throughout Japan.

The Russo-Japanese War

In 1880 Nikolai was consecrated titular bishop of Revel (present-day Tallinn, Estonia). That year Japanese Orthodox converts numbered 6,099, and there were 96 churches and 263 meeting places. During the 1890s, however, the rapid growth of the early period slowed both because of the ruin of the rural bourgeoisie as a result of economic retrenchment under Minister of Finance Matsukata Masayoshi and because of the growing atmosphere of conservatism in the country. Conversions increased by around 3 percent each year, but the numbers baptized often fell below one thousand annually. In 1903 there were 720 baptisms. In 1904, the year the Russo-Japanese War began, there were 653—slightly more than half the number baptized in 1892. Before it ended in 1905, the Russo-Japanese War brought the church close to stagnation.

Concerned about the fate of believers all over Japan who had been branded Russian spies, Nikolai issued a statement urging cooperation with the war effort. In particular, he stressed that grand funerals should be held for the war dead. After the war, donations from Russia, on which the church had depended, dried up before the church had recovered. The resulting financial difficulties brought missionary work to a halt as the numbers of catechists grew smaller and smaller. When Nikolai died in February 1912, at the age of seventy-five, he was anxious about the future of the Orthodox Church in Japan.

The Russian Revolution and Beyond

Bishop Sergie Tihomieroff (1871–1945) succeeded Nikolai as leader of the Japanese Orthodox Church. Bishop Tihomieroff concentrated on missionary work in an attempt to reverse the decline of his church. At the beginning of the Taishō period (1912–26), membership stood at forty-five thousand. Just as the church was beginning to recover, however, it suffered another severe blow—the Russian Revolution of 1917. Church membership fell to 26,769 in 1918. Having lost the financial support of the Russian church, the Orthodox Church in Japan was forced to become independent. The revolution had threatened the very existence of the Russian church and all relations with it were severed. In 1919 the Japanese church adopted its own constitution and renamed itself the Nippon Harisutosu Sei Kyōkai (Japan Orthodox Church).

Bishop Tihomieroff went on to revive the church, and after the destruction of the Orthodox cathedral in the Tokyo Earthquake of 1923, he traveled throughout Japan, Korea, and China, soliciting donations to rebuild it. The new cathedral was completed in 1929, when the dark cloud of global war was already looming. In that year church membership was about thirteen thousand, less than half what it had been even during the Russo-Japanese War.

Revolution and war caused the Japanese church severe internal disruption, and after World War II it placed itself under the Sobor (synod) of North American Bishops. The politics of the Allied Occupation of Japan made American influence dominant in the Japanese church, but in 1970 a joint agreement between the Orthodox Church of the United States and the Moscow patriarchate made the church in Japan autocephalous, and three dioceses were established: Tokyo (the archdiocese), Sendai, and Kyoto. It was a new starting point for a church that through revolution and war had lost all the social influence it had enjoyed under Nikolai. Today it is still groping, seeking the course to rebirth.

PROTESTANTISM

Early Missionaries and the First Converts

In July 1858, the Harris Treaty (United States–Japan Treaty of Amity and Commerce) was signed by American Consul General Townsend Harris (1804–78) and the shogunate. Clause 8 contained provisions for the practice of Christianity: "Americans in Japan shall be allowed the free exercise of their religion, and for this purpose shall have the right to erect suitable places of worship." As a result, Christian activities were made legal in the foreign concessions. Moreover, the treaty's sixth clause provided for the trying of Americans accused of crimes against Japanese in American consular courts under American law. Such rights of extraterritoriality guar-

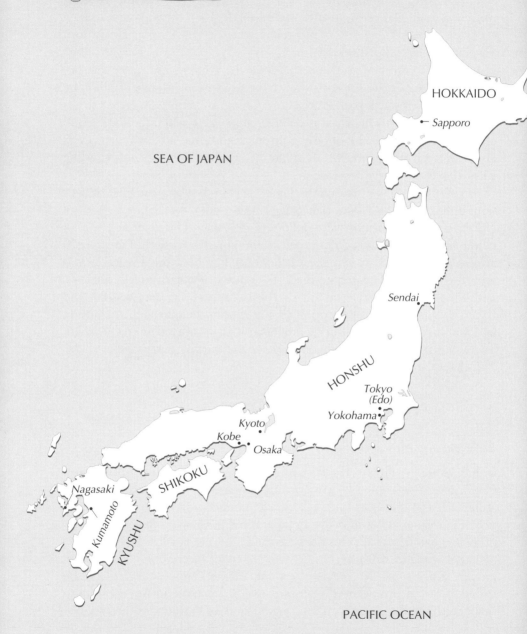

Protestant Church
in the Meiji Period

SEA OF JAPAN

HOKKAIDO

• Sapporo

Sendai

HONSHU

Tokyo
(Edo)

Yokohama•

Kyoto
•

Kobe
•

Osaka

SHIKOKU

Nagasaki
•

Kumamoto

KYUSHU

PACIFIC OCEAN

anteed the safety of missionaries. Thus legal preparations for the arrival of American Protestant missionaries were complete.

The treaty was to take effect in July the following year. Before that, however, John Liggins (1829–1912) of the American Episcopal Church, a missionary in China, received orders to proceed to Japan. He landed in Nagasaki in May 1859. In June Liggins was followed by a fellow missionary from China, Channing M. Williams (1829–1910). Going directly from the United States were James C. Hepburn (1815–1911) of the American Presbyterian Church, who reached Japan in October, and Samuel R. Brown (1810–80), Duane B. Simmons (1834–89), and Guido Herman F. Verbeck (1830–98) of the American Dutch Reformed Church, who arrived in November. The influx suggests the expectations that American churches had for Japan once it was open to foreign intercourse. More missionaries followed across the Pacific, and by the time the edict outlawing Christianity was rescinded in February 1873, there were sixty missionaries and their wives in Japan, most of them sent by American churches.

The missionaries lived in the foreign concessions, such as Yokohama and Nagasaki. They employed Japanese as house servants and language teachers. To broaden their contacts with Japanese citizens and create opportunities for mission work, the missionaries taught English and other subjects. Those who were medical doctors, such as Hepburn and Simmons, used their knowledge to make contact with the people.

At Townsend Harris's wish, the following observation was appended to Clause 8 of the Harris Treaty: "The Government of Japan has already abolished the practice of trampling on religious emblems [in Nagasaki]." This did not mean that the government had legalized Christianity, however. The ban remained, and revealing that one was a Christian still invited arrest, imprisonment, and execution. Under these circumstances, it was to be expected that Japanese who sought out missionaries were interested more in acquiring their specialized knowledge and skills than converting to their faith. Nevertheless, a few did express interest in the religion, and as their faith deepened they received baptism.

The first Protestant convert was Yano Mototaka, an acupuncturist who was baptized by James H. Ballagh (1832–1920) of the Dutch Reformed Church in November 1865. Yano, bedridden with tuberculosis, died soon afterward. On Harris's recommendation, Yano had been employed as Samuel Brown's Japanese-language teacher, and he later became Ballagh's teacher as well. Under Ballagh's direction, Yano participated in the translation of the Gospels of Mark and John. This deepened his knowledge of Christianity until finally he expressed the wish to declare his faith and be baptized. Since Yano risked his life in this, Ballagh was taken aback, and only after consulting with James Hepburn did he agree to perform the baptism. It had been six years since Hepburn and Brown had arrived in Kanagawa. Yano's conversion gave the missionaries great hope and encouragement.

The second, third, and fourth converts appeared in Nagasaki. The second was Shōmura Sukeemon, a middle-ranking warrior from the Kumamoto domain. He had been sent to Nagasaki as supervisor of the domain's personnel there and, coming into contact with Guido Verbeck and Channing Williams, he studied things Western. He was baptized by Williams in February 1866. Three months later Murata Wakasa, a senior retainer of the Saga domain, and his youngest brother Ayabe were baptized by Verbeck. While in charge of a patrol monitoring foreign ships in Nagasaki, Wakasa had obtained Dutch books from which he had learned much about European affairs. His interest in Christianity deepened after one of his men retrieved an English Bible from the sea. After about three years' study of the Bible, Wakasa visited Verbeck and asked the surprised missionary to baptize him and his brother.

Converts continued to appear in small numbers, and by 1871 there were six in the Yokohama area and fourteen in Nagasaki. Considering the number of missionaries in Japan, progress in winning converts was slow, but baptism remained a perilous undertaking while Christianity was outlawed. Though the missionaries delivered sermons and lectured on the Bible, they could not urge baptism on their hearers.

Bands of Protestant Converts

The new converts in Yokohama and Nagasaki had ties to the missionaries who baptized them, but not to each other. There was no organization of Japanese Protestants, and it was difficult to sustain faith under trying circumstances without group support. The earliest example of a Japanese Protestant group is the so-called Yokohama Band, which was established in 1872. Similar groups formed later in Kumamoto, on Kyushu, and in Sapporo, on Hokkaido.

The Kumamoto Band was formed following the conversion of thirty-five students of Capt. Leroy L. Janes (1838–1909) at the Kumamoto Yōgakkō (Kumamoto School of Western Studies). They declared their faith in a meeting on Mount Hanaoka, on the outskirts of Kumamoto, in January 1876, signing a pledge to follow the Protestant religion and support each other in their common faith. The Kumamoto region was extremely conservative, and there was strong local criticism of Christianity. The mutual protection that the young men pledged was vital in the face of the parental and social opposition they were bound to meet when they professed their faith.

On Hokkaido the social climate was much less anti-Western. Western technology was instrumental in opening the virgin territory to settlement. In March 1877, thirty-one students of William S. Clark (1826–86) at the Sapporo Agricultural College, an institution bursting with the pioneer spirit, signed a covenant in which they declared their faith in Christ and formed an association for mutual encouragement in the faith. Members of the Sapporo Band experienced none of the persecution that the members of the Kumamoto Band did, but they still needed an organization to support prayer, Bible study, and the reading of religious books.

In both Kumamoto and Sapporo the groups of young Protestants organized to maintain their faith. The Sapporo Band, with little outside pressure, was stable, but the Kumamoto Band, faced with severe opposition, was forced to break up. The majority of its members went to Kyoto to enroll at Dōshisha, the school founded in 1875 by Niijima Jō (also called Joseph Hardy Neesima; 1843–90), the first ordained Japanese Protestant. These youths became some of the main figures in the history of Protestantism in Japan.

To ensure the survival of the religious groups, it was necessary to develop beyond isolated groups and create an institutional structure. The individual converts and groups owed their existence to the missionaries, but in March 1872, the Yokohama Band reconstituted itself as the Nihon Kirisuto Kōkai (Protestant Church of Christ in Japan). The Nihon Kirisuto Kōkai, which had been organized by converts who had become Christians following a prayer week observed by James Ballagh's students of English, was presbyterian in form. In an election held under Ballagh's guidance, Ogawa Yoshiyasu (1831–1912) was elected elder and Ballagh acting pastor. A constitution set out church regulations and rules for administration. The members of the Yokohama Band had chosen the presbyterian system over the episcopal or congregational and gave their church institutional form by establishing rules and regulations for it. Their method of organization was remarkable because it differed so radically from the conventional Japanese practice of communal religious organization. With its democratic structure and individual pledges of faith, it represented a completely new pattern of Japanese religious organization.

The Revolutionary Nature of Protestantism

The faith and ethics inherent in the new organization were not merely new; they were revolutionary. Andō Ryūtarō (d. 1880), a spy for the Dajōkan (Grand Council of State) who posed as a believer and infiltrated the Yokohama congregation of the Nihon Kirisuto Kōkai, noted that three church regulations had been eliminated for fear of outside censure and attack. Missionaries had constantly impressed on new converts the importance of promising to strictly obey these three regulations, which were a basis for judging the depth of a convert's faith.

The first regulation stated that members were not to kneel in reverence before the shrines of emperors, ancestors, or local deities. The second said that they were not to submit to any order, even an imperial order, at the expense of their faith. The third forbade excessive attachment to parents or relatives. All three regulations were based directly on biblical teachings and were a clear declaration of the fundamentals of Christianity adapted to Japan. At the same time, they directly contradicted the traditional values of obedience to the *kami*, one's lord, one's parents, and others in authority and thus posed a bold challenge to the system.

The regulations conflicted sharply not only with traditional values but also with the national education policy. In June 1872, the Ministry of Religion announced that popular education should teach the following three precepts: always venerate the *kami* and love the nation; follow the law of heaven and the way of humanity; and submit to the imperial will. Clearly, these precepts advocated a system completely opposed to that proposed by the regulations of the Yokohama congregation of the Nihon Kirisuto Kōkai, which appear truly revolutionary in this context.

When the Meiji government came to power in 1868, it issued orders for the restoration of "the unity of religious ritual and governance" (*saisei itchi*), making clear its intent to establish Shintō as the national religion. Thus persecution of Christianity continued unabated, leading to the exile of the three thousand Christians from Urakami. In Nagasaki two converts—former Jōdo Shin–sect priests Shimizu Kunai, who had been baptized by Guido Verbeck, and Futagawa Ittō, who had been baptized by George Ensor (d. 1910)—were arrested and imprisoned. In Kyoto, Ichikawa Einosuke (1831?–72), the Japanese-language teacher of the missionaries

Daniel C. Greene (1843–1913) and Orramel H. Gulick (1830–1923), was arrested and died in prison. Spies for the Dajōkan operated in Tokyo, Yokohama, Osaka, Nagasaki, and Hakodate to investigate Christian activities and gather information. In the view of the new government, Christianity was a dangerous and revolutionary creed that merited surveillance and persecution. Hence, in the early years of the Meiji period, to become a Christian was to invite brutal oppression by the authorities.

Other Converts

Since conversion to Christianity entailed great personal danger and required a basic change in outlook, it must be asked why people became Christians.

Some converts found Christian teachings strongly persuasive. When the third convert, Murata Wakasa, met Verbeck, he declared: "When I first read about the personality and work of Jesus, I was moved beyond words. I had never seen, heard of, or imagined such a person. My heart was captured by his wonderful life and character." Murata had been won over by the persuasive power of the gospel. Uemura Masahisa (1858–1925), a member of the Yokohama Band, had been drawn to Protestantism as a result of a prayer meeting at Ballagh's English school. Though he found the missionary's awkward Japanese difficult to understand, he was attracted by the Christian concept of one true, merciful God who is omnipresent. A new world opened up for the fifteen-year-old youth, and he asked to be baptized. At sixteen, Uchimura Kanzō (1861–1930), later of the Sapporo Band, who had experimented with various kinds of worship in order to propitiate the anger of the gods, came to understand through Christianity that there was only one God. Both his rationalism and his conscience welcomed the concept of a single deity.

Other converts found Christianity persuasive because it seemed to endorse traditional Japanese values. For example, Matsuyama Takayoshi (1847–1935) joined Daniel Greene's Bible-study class to learn about Christianity in order to refute it but was deeply moved by the commandment "Honor thy father and thy mother" and by the action of Jesus on the cross in commending his mother to the care of a disciple. These teachings, having much in common with traditional Japanese virtues, won Matsuyama over to Christianity.

In most cases, the charisma of the Protestant missionaries was an important factor in winning converts and encouraging devotion to the Bible.

The personality of the missionary and the persuasive power of the Bible fused in converts' minds. Most of the missionaries at that time, who had risked their lives to go to Japan, were outstanding men of deep learning and high moral character.

Social Factors in Conversions

The persuasiveness of Christian doctrine and the character of the missionaries accounted for many conversions, but these were not the only contributing factors. The social and personal situations of individual converts must also be considered. Comments by the Meiji-period journalist and writer Yamaji Aizan (1864–1917), who was also a Christian, illuminate an important social factor that led many young people of the former warrior class to convert to Christianity in that era. Aizan pointed out that the young converts were frequently children of warriors who found themselves in distress under the new Meiji government. The warriors who had opposed and overthrown the shogunate held the most important positions in Meiji society. Warriors and their scions who had supported the Tokugawas were shut out of the new government, their feudal privileges abolished, and as a class they were frustrated. Christianity offered them hope.

This argument, however, cannot explain the motivation of such people as Sawayama Pōro (Paul; 1852–87), a retainer of the Chōshū domain, which had been instrumental in the overthrow of the shogunate, and Matsuyama Takayoshi, the son of a headman from Itoigawa in Echigo Province, nor can it account for the large numbers of young converts. These converts adopted the Christian faith in response to the sudden changes in their lives and in society. Conversion to a new religion is one response to sudden personal or social change. When a way of life disappears, there is a need to establish a strong self-identity as the basis for rebuilding one's life, and religious commitment often provides this inner strength.

Yet many young converts did not always completely reject their earlier beliefs. Rather, they emphasized the common ground between the two traditions. The Christian educator Kozaki Hiromichi (1856–1938), who had been a member of the Kumamoto Band, wrote in his autobiography: "When we advanced from Confucianism to Christianity, we did not throw away the one in accepting the other, but rather believed that Christianity was the fulfillment of the truth of the teachings of Confucius and the spirit of Confucianism." In his diary, Uchimura Kanzō wrote: "With the spirit of the Japanese warrior we can establish the Christian attitude," and "Our lord is Christ, we are His retainers." Following the tradition of Hirata Atsutane's school of Kokugaku (National Learning), Matsuyama Takayoshi understood Ame no Minakanushi no Kami to be the one true God, the creator of the universe, identical with the Christian Heavenly Father. All these men found in Christianity confirmation and reinforcement of traditional ideas that had been called into question by the sudden changes in society, and they sought to reestablish their personal identity through belief in this new religion.

Civilization and Enlightenment

One product of the search for a new system of values to suit a new age at the beginning of the Meiji period was the belief that Christianity was a vehicle of "civilization and enlightenment." The linking of civilization and enlightenment with religion was a feature of Japanese Protestantism in the last years of the Edo period (1603–1868) and the early years of the Meiji period. Christianity was seen clearly and simply as the foundation of Western civilization.

This view of the religion severely limited the religious experience of Japanese believers. John L. Atkinson (1842–1908), the third acting pastor of the First Church of Christ in Settsu, near Osaka, noted in a letter in September 1876 that most of the congregation believed Christianity was the true religion but they had yet to experience a spiritual renewal through the Holy Spirit. Moreover, they were not particularly interested in such an experience. They were interested more in knowledge than in salvation, and they seemed to regard the two as nearly equivalent. They were apathetic about spiritual matters.

On adopting a faith so foreign to their country's religious traditions, few Japanese converts felt that they had been filled with the Holy Spirit; most were converted through reason. Yet it cannot be denied that belief inspired by the hope of gaining civilization and enlightenment kept converts from progressing beyond an intellectual understanding of their faith. A period of religious revivalism in the 1880s in some ways righted the balance between heart and mind in early Japanese Protestantism.

Gradually, individual Japanese Protestants began to experience spiritual renewal through the Holy Spirit. In particular the revivals of the first half of the 1880s gave many believers and inquirers direct spiritual experience. The early 1880s were a conservative period, one of reaction against the earlier preoccupation with civilization and enlightenment. Christianity was also being assaulted by Western philosophy and science, especially agnosticism and the theory of evolution. It was in this climate that the great revivals blossomed.

The first revival in Japan was held in Yokohama in 1883 during a week of joint prayer. Its influence swept through the churches and Christian schools in Tokyo and Yokohama; and after the third National Convention for Christian Fellowship in May that year, it spread to Gumma Prefecture, Kobe, Osaka, and Sendai. In March 1884, Dōshisha was the scene of a great revival during another week of joint prayer, and excited students carried the revival to Kyoto, Osaka, and Kobe, to the Chūgoku region, and to the island of Shikoku. The influence of these revivals was also felt in Tokyo, Gumma Prefecture, and Sendai, and the previous year's wave of spiritual awakening was repeated in spiritual inspiration in the churches in those areas.

Though some Japanese Protestants later criticized the revivals as mass hysteria, the events gave them an experience that was necessary for the growth of the church. In Japan an intellectual, abstract understanding of Christianity preceded a more emotional, direct Christian experience. The revivals deepened the Japanese Christian experience and stimulated a spiritual renewal.

Protestantism and Society

Despite the effects of the revivals, Meiji-period Japanese continued to approach Protestantism intellectually, and in general that approach remained the dominant feature of their Christian experience. Although the numbers of converts increased as missionary work expanded, middle-class intellectuals were still the backbone of the Protestant churches. At the World's Parliament of Religions in Chicago in 1893, Kozaki Hiromichi represented the Christian churches of Japan and reported on the state of the religion there. He pointed out that believers tended to be male, young, and of the *shizoku*, or former warrior, class.

In the 1880s increasing numbers of *shizoku* families lost their source of income and were forced by economic conditions to leave their ancestral lands for the cities. As the social disintegration of the *shizoku* continued in rural areas, small capitalists and rich farmers replaced the *shizoku* as sources of Christian converts. These people were also the middle-class intellectuals.

After the 1890s public higher education advanced rapidly to provide the technicians and clerical personnel required by the growing capitalist economy. These salaried workers (the new middle-class intellectuals) and the students who would join their ranks in the future accepted Christianity in order to study English and other subjects. They thus became the main source of converts. In 1901 the United Twentieth-Century Mission, sponsored by various denominations, was organized to welcome the new century, and most of the converts it won were from this group. Mission work among the less privileged was not attempted until such rare individuals as Yamamuro Gumpei (1872–1940) of the Salvation Army and the social reformer Kagawa Toyohiko (1888–1960) came forward.

Protestantism in Japan, which was supported by intellectuals, became a powerful conduit for Western culture. Members of the *shizoku* class, with their solid background in Confucianism, were attracted to the strong ethical content of American Protestantism. As a result, their religion was not contemplative or emotional but active and ethical. They fostered moral reform movements and the abolition of prostitution, defining their ethical position in terms of Japanese society. Though as a religion Christianity attracted few Japanese, as a cultural and ethical vehicle it widely influenced the country's culture as a whole. Through its promotion of Westernization in Japan, Christianity contributed to the country's modernization.

Sects and Denominations

In June 1941, some thirty Protestant denominations, excluding the Nonchurch Christian Movement, were consolidated into the Nihon Kirisuto Kyōdan (United Church of Christ in Japan) because of pressure resulting from the Religious Organizations Law, which had gone into effect the previous year. The nucleus of the new organization consisted of such large denominations as the Nihon Kirisuto Kyōkai (Church of Christ in Japan), Nihon Mesojisuto Kyōkai (Methodist Church in Japan), and Nihon Kumiai Kirisuto Kyōkai (Congregational Church of Christ in Japan); but the organization also included such strange bedfellows as the Nihon Seikōkai (Anglican Episcopal Church of Japan), Kyūseigun (Salvation Army), YMCA, and YWCA. At its first general meeting, the organization declared: "We are Christians, but at the same time we are Japanese subjects,

and our first loyalty is to our nation." To protect themselves from government accusations of being unpatriotic and to survive, the Christian
churches had chosen the road of compromise.

Despite the churches' cooperation with the government during World
War II, there was sporadic resistance by individual Christians, which led
to their imprisonment, and often their death. The Occupation authorities
ordered the repeal of the Religious Organizations Law because it restricted
religious freedom; and at the end of December 1945, the government
promulgated the Religious Juridical Persons Ordinance, which guaranteed freedom of worship. The next year denominations left the Nihon
Kirisuto Kyōdan one after another. The denominations that broke away
in 1946 were the Kirisutokyō Kyōdai Dan (Japan Brethren in Christ),
Kassui Kirisuto Kyōdan (Christian Church of the Living Water), Nihon
Kirisuto Kaikakuha Kyōkai (Reformed Church in Japan), Nihon Seikōkai
(Anglican Episcopal Church of Japan), Kyūseigun (Salvation Army), and
Tōyō Senkyōkai Kiyome Kyōkai (Kiyome Church of the Oriental Mis-
sionary Society). They were followed in 1947 by the Nihon Fukuin Kirisuto
Kyōdan (Japan Evangelical Christian Church), Nihon Hōrinesu Kyōdan
(Japan Holiness Church), Fukuin Dendō Kyōdan (Evangelical Mission
Church), Nihon Baputesuto Remmei (Japan Baptist Convention), Kirisuto
Yūkai (Religious Society of Friends), and Nihon Fukuin Rūteru Kyōkai
(Japan Evangelical Lutheran Church), and the trend continued in 1948
and 1949. The Nihon Kirisuto Kyōdan virtually crumbled with the seces-
sion of the Nihon Kirisuto Kyōkai (Church of Christ in Japan) in 1951
and the Nihon Fukuin Kyōdan (Japan Gospel Church) in 1952.

Between 1946 and 1952, when the Nihon Kirisuto Kyōdan was disin-
tegrating, Protestant membership swelled. Christianity seemed especially
attractive until about 1950. Under General Douglas MacArthur, supreme
commander for the Allied Powers, occupation policy favored Christianity,
and a vast amount of aid, both material and spiritual, flowed from the
United States and Canadian churches to Japanese Protestant churches that
had suffered in the war. Certainly many secessions from the Nihon Kirisuto
Kyōdan were inspired by the promise of aid from foreign churches.
Churches and chapels—quickly rebuilt on their burned-out sites—attracted
the young with English classes, hymns, and an American-style democratic
organization. According to the yearbook of the Nihon Kirisuto Kyōdan,
despite the continued splintering of the Protestant sects, the number of
baptisms increased from some eleven thousand in 1947 to a peak of more
than fifteen thousand in 1950. Church attendance rose by 54 percent be-

tween 1947 and 1951. The number of believers grew from 106,000 in 1947 to 129,000 in 1951.

Japan entered a new phase after 1951. In April of that year MacArthur was dismissed from his post and left Japan; in September the peace treaty between the United States and Japan was signed; and the occupation ended when the treaty went into effect in April 1952. Japan took its place in the international community and began rescinding some of the occupation reforms. In that climate, Christian fervor waned and large numbers of the young who had thronged the churches lost interest. This reality is reflected in the statistics.

According to a recent survey by the Agency for Cultural Affairs, at the end of 1998 Japan's Protestant followers numbered 460,000, and there were some 5,700 churches and meeting halls. The denominations with the largest number of followers and churches were the Nihon Kirisuto Kyōdan, Nihon Seikōkai, Nihon Baputesuto Remmei, Nihon Fukuin Rūteru Kyōkai, Iesu no Mitama Kyōkai Kyōdan (Spirit of Jesus Church), and Matsujitsu Seito Iesu Kirisuto Kyōkai (Church of Jesus Christ of Latter-day Saints).

After more than a century of missionary activity, only four of every thousand Japanese are Protestants, a low number compared with the Christian population of Korea, for example. Nevertheless, what is not revealed by statistics is the deep and far-reaching influence of Protestantism on the religion, ethics, education, and culture of Japan.

20. State Shintō

THE EVOLUTION OF STATE SHINTŌ

The Nationalization of Shintō

The Restoration (Fukko) Shintō that Hirata Atsutane (1776–1843) advocated toward the end of the Edo period (1603–1868) attracted many adherents among lower-ranking warriors, Shintō priests, landowners, and rural merchants. It provided the ideological underpinnings for the movement to restore imperial rule and became the guiding concept behind the Meiji period (1868–1912) government's drive to make Shintō the national religion.

Shortly after its establishment, in the third month of 1868, the new government issued a directive proclaiming its intention to restore the ancient ideal of the unity of religious ritual and governance (*saisei itchi*) and revive the Jingikan (Office of *Kami* Worship), placing all shrines in the country under the Jingikan's jurisdiction. A later directive that month announced the separation of Shintō and Buddhism in a move to restore Shintō to its pure form. A little over a year later, in the seventh month of 1869, the Jingikan was separated from and ranked above the Dajōkan (Grand Council of State), making it the highest-ranking of all government offices. This was done to establish the religious authority of the modern emperor system. Powerful Restoration Shintō leaders—including Hirata Atsutane's adopted son Kanetane (1799–1880), Ōkuni Takamasa (1792–1871), and Fukuba Bisei (1831–1907)—who had been appointed to important posts in the new government were instrumental in initiating the policy of nationalizing Shintō.

Shintō priests across the nation viewed the promulgation of the directive separating Buddhism from Shintō as an opportunity to free themselves from the control of the *bettō* (temple superintendents) and the Buddhist priests serving at shrines. Aided by followers of Restoration Shintō and abetted by the animosity of the general population toward a corrupt Buddhist establishment, they set in motion a nationwide persecution of Buddhism that, despite government edicts urging moderation in carrying out the separation order, continued unabated until the abolition of the fiefs and provinces and the establishment of prefectures in 1871.

In the first month of 1870, when persecution of Buddhism was at its height, two imperial rescripts were issued. The first—introducing a new ritual for the emperor for enshrining the eight imperial *kami* (protectors of emperors), the *kami* of heaven and earth, and the spirits of dead emperors in the sanctuary of the Jingikan—made it clear that the emperor presided over worship of all the *kami* enshrined throughout the country. The second rescript announced the appointment of religious propagandists to serve in the newly established Senkyōshi (Office of Propaganda) to disseminate the Great Teaching (Taikyō) in order to exalt orthodox Shintō, that is, the way of the *kami* (*kannagara no michi*).

By the middle of 1871 the policy of nationalizing Shintō had reached its peak. In the fifth month of that year the Dajōkan issued a directive declaring that all shrines were government institutions. Since shrines could not be owned privately, the system of hereditary priesthood was abolished and all Shintō priests—from those of Ise Grand Shrine down to those of the most insignificant local shrines—were dismissed. Subsequent appointments were based on careful selection. At the same time, official shrines (*kansha*) were chosen from among the nation's shrines, excluding Ise Grand Shrine, and placed under the jurisdiction of the Jingikan.

The official shrines were divided into two classes: thirty-five imperial shrines (*kampeisha*), which performed rituals at the direction of the Jingikan, and sixty-two national shrines (*kokuheisha*), which performed rituals at the direction of prefectural governors. Shrines under local jurisdiction were also of two classes. The first consisted of metropolitan shrines (*fusha*), domainal shrines (*hansha*), and prefectural shrines (*kensha*), the second of district shrines (*gōsha*) of local tutelary deities. Shrines were ranked according to their supervisory agency, the rituals they were to perform, and their local importance. In addition, a system of ranks for priests of each rank of shrine was introduced, and the positions of the appointed priests were guaranteed by the central and regional authorities who held the power of appointment.

This reorganization was completed two months later, when Ise Grand Shrine was made the head of all the nation's shrines. At the same time, one district shrine in each administrative unit was designated the family-registration center. For administrative purposes, all other shrines in each area were designated as village shrines (*sonsha*) affiliated with the district shrine or as unranked shrines (*mukakusha*). With the most minor of shrines brought under government control, the Meiji system of shrine ranking was complete.

In conjunction with the organization and ranking of shrines in administrative areas, local residents were required to register at a local shrine in a system that replaced the Edo-period *terauke* (temple certification) system. The new registration system was more effective on paper than in practice, however, and was abolished by the Dajōkan within two years. The new system reflected the lack of a realistic understanding of the differences between Shintō shrines and Buddhist temples, and there was no prospect of success for it unless it was coupled with other moves to replace Buddhism with Shintō in daily life—for example, by substituting Shintō funeral rites for Buddhist rites. The failure of administrative measures that disregarded entrenched custom demonstrates the popular limits to the policy of nationalizing Shintō in a period of change.

In the eighth month of 1871 the Jingikan was abolished and its functions assumed by the new, lower-ranked Jingishō (Ministry of Shintō Religion). In the third month of 1872 the Jingishō, too, was abolished and the Kyōbushō, or Ministry of Religion, established. These changes suggest that contradictions between the policies of modernization and of nationalization of Shintō forced the government to revise its Shintō policy.

The Separation of Ritual and Religion

One month after the Ministry of Religion was established, the religious propagandists of the defunct Senkyōshi were replaced by religious instructors under the ministry's jurisdiction. The ministry directed them to teach three precepts: veneration of the *kami* and love of country; observance of the law of heaven (philosophy and religion) and of the way of humanity (morality and ethics); and obedience to the emperor.

Popular education was to be accomplished through two national institutions: the Daikyō-in (Great Teaching Academy), at the Jōdo-sect temple Zōjō-ji in Tokyo's Shiba district, and the Jingūkyō-in (Grand Shrine Academy), at Ise Grand Shrine in Mie Prefecture. Associated with these two national centers were numerous *chūkyō-in* (middle-ranking academies) in prefectural capitals and *shōkyō-in* (elementary academies) at large and small temples and shrines throughout the country. Shintō priests were employed as religious instructors, of course, but Buddhist clergy were also recruited, as were volunteers, among them propagators of popular religious cults, village headmen and local leaders, and entertainers, such as actors, storytellers, and comedians. In fact anyone skilled in the art of communication was mobilized as a laborer in the systematic popular education program based on Shintō nationalism.

Though Shintō priests ostensibly headed the Daikyō-in hierarchy, they were not the equals of the Buddhist clergy in doctrine, propagation, or organization and were forced to defer to their Buddhist colleagues. As a result, dissension between the two groups increased.

The hybrid Shintō-Buddhist propagation at the Daikyō-in hardly furthered the official policy of separating the two religions; yet the religious instructors were in fact forcing on the populace new religious values based on the government's three precepts. Viscount Mori Arinori (1847–89), Japan's first envoy to Washington, where he served from 1871 to 1873, was harshly critical of the government's religious policy. In an English-language booklet titled *Religious Freedom in Japan* (1872), he attacked it for mixing religion and politics and being devoid of any real concern for freedom of religion. While in Europe in 1872, Shimaji Mokurai (1838–1911), a priest at the Jōdo Shin–sect temple Nishi Hongan-ji in Kyoto, sent a petition to the government criticizing the three precepts and asking for separation of the state and religion and for the right of religious groups to dissociate themselves from the Daikyō-in. Mori and Shimaji pointed out the contradictions between the Western concept of separation of church and state and the government's program for popular education, which relied on the clergy as teachers.

On his return to Japan in 1873, Shimaji launched a movement among four of the branches of the Jōdo Shin sect to withdraw from the Daikyō-in, and in January 1875, he was told unofficially that permission to secede would be granted. In April the government formally abolished the propagation of its Shintō-Buddhist amalgamation and ordered religious instructors to establish their own educational institutions. With this step, the Daikyō-in lost its raison d'être.

In November 1875, the Ministry of Religion orally notified Shintō and Buddhist leaders that separation of religion and state would be guaranteed and stressed that it was the duty of all religious leaders to support public order and lead the people well. After this, the government's religious policy gradually moved toward toleration of religious freedom, but the thorny question of the function of shrines remained.

The Shintō faction had little hope that the Daikyō-in would survive, since it had been shaken by internal disputes and by the separation movement. Even before the government announced the dissolution of the Daikyō-in in May 1875, the Shintō faction had gained permission to set up a central Shintō agency, the Shintō Jimukyoku (Shintō Office), established in March 1875. The Shintō Jimukyoku incorporated all streams of Shintō under the supervision of the Shintō religious instructors. Nevertheless, internal conflicts continued to deepen, and in 1881 the Ise and Izumo streams quarreled over the *kami* worshiped at Ise Grand Shrine's *yōhaijo* (remote worship site) in the Shintō Jimukyoku quarters. The dispute was finally mediated by Emperor Meiji. As a result of this incident, Shintō circles reached the consensus that Shrine Shintō, as the national ritual, should be separated from religion in general and that its privileged position as the national ideology should be secured.

The government abolished the Ministry of Religion in January 1877, and its responsibilities were assumed by the Bureau of Shrines and Temples (Shajikyoku) in the Home Ministry. At the urging of the Shintō faction, the government adopted a policy of separation of ritual and religion and advocacy of Shrine Shintō as the national ideology, that is, State Shintō. Consequently, in January 1882, Shintō priests were prohibited from holding clerical and teaching posts concurrently and from officiating at funerals. In May of the same year, various religious groups in the Shintō tradition that were attached to the Shintō Jimukyoku were granted independence. Stripped of their religious elements, shrines—the official shrines in particular—were limited to the function of performing rituals and their priests restricted to conducting the rituals. The Shintō-based religions known collectively as Sectarian Shintō maintained the traditional religious functions of ministry and ritual, and the government viewed them as belonging to a category entirely different from Shrine Shintō.

State Shintō at Official Shrines

Since the policy of stripping shrines of religious elements and making them places for ritual alone was initially implemented at official shrines, the process of the establishment of State Shintō should first be examined as it affected these shrines.

The Shintō faction pressed the government to establish a shrine system befitting a national institution. They deplored priests' loss of official rank in 1887 and 1894, when the government changed its policy and turned to pursuit of modernization and treaty revision. The immediate goal of the National Association of Shintō Priests (Zenkoku Shinshoku Kai), founded in 1878, was either the restoration of the Jingikan or the creation of a special government office for Shintō affairs. The association's goal was achieved in April 1900, when the Bureau of Shrines and Temples in the Home Ministry was abolished and replaced by two new bureaus, the Bureau of Shrines (Jinjakyoku) and the Bureau of Religion (Shūkyōkyoku). The Bureau of Shrines was the administrative center for completing the establishment of State Shintō and controlled all affairs concerning shrines and shrine priests nationwide.

The institutional reform that made Ise Grand Shrine the headquarters of all shrines in the nation had begun in 1871, when the Inner Shrine (Naikū) was ranked above the Outer Shrine (Gekū), the duties of Ise Shrine priests and the method by which they were appointed were changed, and *onshi* (itinerant priests associated with Ise Grand Shrine) were deprived of their right to distribute the Ise Grand Shrine amulet (*taima*). These reforms were strictly enforced.

Further consolidation followed in January 1890, when the highest office, that of *saishu* (supreme ritualist), was conferred on a member of the imperial family, and in November 1896, when a system of Ise Grand Shrine offices was established. The supreme ritualist was appointed personally by the emperor, the *daigūji* (supreme chief priest) by imperial order, and the *shōgūji* (junior chief priest) either by imperial order or with imperial approval. Each of these offices was held by one person. In addition there were eleven *negi* (senior priests) appointed with imperial approval, as well as twenty *gonnegi* (junior priests) and forty *kujō* (attendant priests) appointed as junior officials. Ise Grand Shrine was under the direct supervision of the emperor through the *saishu*, a member of the imperial family. The *daigūji*, who assisted the *saishu* in ceremonial matters and headed administration, was under the supervision of the Home Ministry. In September 1897, a Religious Affairs Department (Jingū Kambesho) headed by the *daigūji* was established near Ise Shrine to deal with the production and distribution of almanacs and *taima* amulets. This, the final step in the organization of Ise Shrine, was the first act of the newly established Bureau of Shrines.

Responding to the demands of the Shintō faction, the Bureau of Shrines next undertook the consolidation of the imperial shrines and the national shrines. The reform of 1887 had abolished the post of *shinkan* (divine official) at these shrines and replaced it with a hierarchy of *gūji* (chief priest), *negi* (senior priest), and *shuten* (attendant priest). This revision, consolidated and expanded legally, was promulgated in February 1902.

The stipends of priests at official shrines were paid by the government, as were the costs of ceremonies and shrine upkeep. A Dajōkan decree of 1874 set the government's yearly contributions at 2,493 yen for major imperial and national shrines, 1,600 yen for middle-ranking shrines, and 1,165 yen for minor shrines. This funding was terminated in 1886, however; and in 1887 a subsidy system was introduced, with generally lower rates, a different amount for each shrine, and a fifteen-year limit (later extended to thirty years). During this time, shrines were expected to accumulate reserves for eventual self-support. Some shrines received no subsidy at all, but even those that did were assured of government assistance only until 1916. The Shintō faction opposed the restrictions on funding, and priests of imperial and national shrines were in the vanguard of the opposition movement.

In April 1906, when Japan's victory in its war with Russia had generated intensified veneration of shrines among the populace as a whole, the long-cherished hopes of the Shintō faction were realized. The government restored funding for official shrines (imperial and national shrines) from the national treasury and allowed the shrines to manage the interest from that income and from capital assets, as well as the income from offerings made in the shrine precincts. Since shrines derived only 10 percent to 20 percent of their income from government funding, however, government assistance was largely symbolic support of the national ideology rather than a guarantee of the stability of shrine administration.

State Shintō at Nonofficial Shrines

The consolidation of the organization of nonofficial shrines (*minsha*, or people's shrines) followed the pattern of that for official shrines (*kansha*). In February 1894, prefectural and metropolitan shrines (*kensha* and *fusha*) and district shrines (*gōsha*) were each permitted one *shashi* (chief priest) and a small number of *shashō* (assistant priests). Village shrines (*sonsha*) and below were allotted a small number of *shashō*. Both the numbers of *shashō* and the appointments of *shashi* and *shashō* were decided by the prefectural governors. Although both *shashi* and *shashō* were ranked as junior government functionaries, after 1873 their stipends were paid not by the government but by believers.

After 1902, priests of the imperial and national shrines (*kampeisha* and *kokuheisha*) had to pass a primary or secondary level priests' examination, but those of ordinary shrines, of the prefectural and metropolitan level and below, had to pass the examination for *shashi* and *shashō*. This requirement reflected the attempt to raise the quality of the Shintō priesthood. In 1903, once appointments were based on examination, Jingū Kōgakukan (the present-day Kōgakukan Daigaku), which had been established at Ise Shrine in 1882, became a state school for training Shintō priests under the direction of the Home Ministry.

Soon after subsidies for the official shrines were restored in 1906, ceremonial offerings to shrines of prefectural and metropolitan rank and below were established. While subsidies for official shrines came from the national treasury, ceremonial offerings to the *minsha*, or nonofficial shrines, were to be made only once a year, at the time of the shrine's annual festival, by prefectures (to prefectural shrines), cities or administrative districts (to district shrines), or towns or villages (to village shrines). Whereas all official shrines received support, only some of the *minsha*—those designated by regional officials—were granted offerings.

After the Meiji Restoration of 1868, the government established a relatively large number of official shrines, which fell into four groups. The first consisted of shrines for veneration of the spirits of those who died in the imperial cause in the struggle against the shogunate that culminated in the Restoration. Yasukuni Shrine in Tokyo, which was known as Shōkonsha (Shrine for Inviting the Spirits) until 1879, belonged to this category. The second type of shrine—exemplified by Minatogawa Shrine in Kobe, where the great warrior Kusunoki Masashige (d. 1336) is enshrined—was devoted to veneration of the loyal retainers of the Southern Court during the period of the Northern and Southern Courts (1336–92). The third type included shrines like Kashihara Shrine in Nara (where Japan's legendary first sovereign, Emperor Jimmu, is enshrined), dedicated to veneration of the imperial house and emperors of past ages. The fourth consisted of shrines established in the colonies, such as Taiwan Jinja (later called Taiwan Jingū) in Taipei, founded in 1900.

All these government-established shrines directly symbolized the ideology of State Shintō, which revolved around veneration of the emperor. Though they were newly founded, their architecture imitated the classical style and they were given high rank within the shrine system.

On the other hand, with the exception of shrines for the war dead or modern war heroes and shrines in newly settled regions like Hokkaido, there were virtually no new *minsha,* or local, nonofficial shrines. In fact, small shrines, which had no place in State Shintō, became targets for consolidation with other shrines. The merging of *minsha* was directly related to the system of designating the shrines that would receive ceremonial offerings at the time of festivals. Bureaucrats in the Home Ministry decided that there were too many small local shrines, often without a full-time priest, and that small shrines in every town or village should be merged into a single shrine with adequate capital assets. This shrine would be designated to receive ceremonial offerings.

In 1905 shrine mergers were effected on an experimental basis in Mie Prefecture, which had a particularly high density of shrines. Full-scale enforcement of the policy, so strict that it was remembered in Mie long afterward, began the following year when the decision was made to launch a nationwide merger program. The home minister, Hara Takashi, issued a directive to that effect at a conference of prefectural governors in 1906. An imperial edict issued on April 28, the day before the final session of the conference, established ceremonial offerings for *minsha.* This edict was followed on August 9 by one that allowed the transfer of an abolished shrine's land to the shrine it had merged with. With the legal and administrative underpinnings to facilitate merger thus strengthened, the national movement was launched.

Mergers on a national scale were ordered in 1906 by ministerial directives, although there was no legislation explicitly authorizing mergers. The Home Ministry merely confirmed that its policy was being carried out, and left supervision of the actual implementation to the discretion of the prefectural governors. Consequently, there was considerable difference among prefectures in the extent to which mergers were carried out. Some prefectures reported a large decrease in shrine numbers between the end of 1905 and the end of June 1910 (Mie 91 percent, Wakayama 77 percent, Ehime 58 percent, Osaka 56 percent, Gumma 56 percent, and Saitama 51 percent), but others showed little decrease at all (Fukushima 2 percent, Tottori 3 percent, Kumamoto 4 percent, and Yamanashi 5 percent).

As government-sponsored institutions, the official shrines tended to have little connection with the daily lives of the local people. This was particularly so in the case of shrines founded after the Meiji Restoration. In contrast, *minsha*, popular shrines supported by popular devotion, were intimately involved in community life. There was considerable resistance to their merger. In the areas where mergers were most rigidly enforced, the regulations were often circumvented. Popular opposition found expression in the Diet, and in April 1910 the home minister publicly stated that mergers were not compulsory. With the softening of the ministry's stance, active enforcement of the policy waned.

Most of the shrine mergers occurred between the end of 1905 and the end of June 1910. During that period, the number of shrines nationwide decreased by nearly 28 percent, from 195,000 to 141,000. More than one shrine in four was abolished. The target of the policy had been the low-ranking shrines, as is indicated by the decrease of 1 percent in district shrines, 10 percent in village shrines, and 35 percent in unranked shrines nationwide. Prefectural and metropolitan shrines largely escaped merger; their numbers actually grew by 2 percent because mergers elevated some district shrines to the rank of prefectural or metropolitan shrine.

The Establishment of State Shintō

State Shintō was established by many laws and ordinances, of which the seventy-five most important were brought together in a composite Home Ministry order in April 1913. This order completed the systematization of State Shintō. By government order, shrines of every rank throughout the nation conducted ceremonies corresponding to rites in the imperial palace. Standardized procedures were required at all shrines, and this endangered local religious customs and practices.

The construction of Meiji Shrine, in Tokyo, to enshrine the spirits of Emperor Meiji and his consort, Empress Shōken, was a great undertaking intended as a concrete expression of the establishment of State Shintō. Immediately after Emperor Meiji's death in July 1912, there was a surge of public support for the building of such a shrine, and the following year both houses of the Diet approved construction. When the empress dowager died in 1914, it was unofficially decided to enshrine both spirits there.

The Home Ministry designated Meiji Shrine an imperial shrine of the upper rank. Construction, which began in Tokyo's Yoyogi district in 1915, was supervised by the Meiji Shrine Construction Bureau (Meiji Jingū Zōeikyoku), whose president was the imperial prince Fushimi no Miya

Sadanaru (1858–1923) and whose administrator was the head of the Bureau of Shrines (Jinjakyoku). Construction on the large site of almost seventy-three hectares started with the Inner Garden, which was completed in five years and cost the government 5.22 million yen. The enshrinement took place in November 1920. Some ninety-five thousand trees from all over the nation were planted in the Inner Garden, and eleven thousand young people donated their labor for the planting. The 51.3-hectare Outer Garden, next to be constructed, was financed by some 6 million yen in public donations.

The government deftly manipulated public sentiment, intensifying popular regard for Emperor Meiji and harnessing the people's energy to complete a religious monument that symbolized all the shrines established under the restored emperor system. Four organizations—Tokyo Metropolis, the City of Tokyo, the Tokyo Chamber of Commerce and Industry, and the Meiji Shrine Supporters' Association—were appointed to administer the shrine, emphasizing its role as the city's great protector shrine.

THE DEVELOPMENT OF STATE SHINTŌ

From Religion to Ritual

The process by which Shrine Shintō was shorn of its religious functions and made a state ritual began around the end of the 1870s and was legitimized by the Meiji Constitution of 1889. Though Article 28 of the Constitution guaranteed limited religious freedom, in that "Japanese subjects shall, within limits not prejudicial to peace and order, and not antagonistic to their duties as subjects, enjoy freedom of religious belief," it was made clear that State Shintō was a suprareligious national rite. Still, insofar as a rite is not empty ritual but presupposes a divinity, the claim that State Shintō was above religion was an attempt to circumvent separation of religion and the state. Yet it was impossible to deny the religious nature of State Shintō. Since State Shintō was the religious foundation for the nation's political structure, the duties of subjects were closely related to State Shintō. Thus the freedom of religious belief that the Constitution was supposed to guarantee was compromised from the outset.

On the other hand, it is difficult to dispute that religiosity was in decline in State Shintō and that ethics eclipsed religiosity. This can be seen in the organization of shrines on the lowest tier in the pyramidal structure of State Shintō, the *minsha,* or nonofficial shrines.

To examine the effect of shrine mergers on people's ideas about *kami* and to understand the conception of Shintō held by advocates of the mergers, let us turn to the essay "Shintō Fushin no Gen'in" (The Causes of Shintō's Stagnation), by the Shintō scholar Kōno Seizō (1882–1963), who wrote it after completing graduate studies at Kokugakuin University, in Tokyo, while the mergers were underway.

> Why have shrines come to their present stagnation? First, we must account for the changes that have occurred in ideas about *kami.* Simply put, the *kami* have hitherto had a religious visage but have recently acquired an ethical one. *Kami* of great power now demonstrate merit. *Kami* believed to be eternal are now no more than [the spirits of] ancestors. In the worst interpretation, *kami* who have always been the object of gratitude have become *kami* of the past. Thus conceptions of *kami* have changed, and no doubt certain people are encouraging the tendency. Without doubt, this is why there has been a very real loss of vigor in the world of Shintō.

The change from a religious to an ethical conception of *kami,* replacing personal belief with public worship, was the prime cause of Shintō's stagnation. This conscious change of attitude is related to the division of the Bureau of Shrines and Temples into the Bureau of Shrines and the Bureau of Religion, to the later shrine mergers, and, in general, to the formation of State Shintō. Such programs as enforced shrine mergers did not arise from any religious concept. The government saw the shrines as rational and ethical, that is, as nonreligious institutions.

On another level, changes in ideas about the *kami* represented a transformation of popular Shintō into bureaucratic Shintō. Needless to say, the transformation was most obvious at official shrines.

Shrines in Village Life

Shrines—*minsha,* or nonofficial shrines, in particular—developed in the context of village life. They were venerated as the homes of the local tutelary deities, who watched over the villagers and their livelihood. Ceremonial worship at the shrines took the form of festivals rooted in the rhythms of local life. Both small and large shrines represented community solidarity.

Shrines are sacred sites for venerating the spirits that protect a locality. When they fell under government scrutiny as the smallest units in the shrine system organized after the Meiji Restoration, they were modified by a bureaucracy that ignored the attitudes and feelings of the local people.

Shrine mergers were typical of the modification. It is not surprising that the mergers met local opposition. The degree of opposition depended on whether the goal of reorganization was one shrine per administrative unit (village or town), or one shrine per hamlet (ōaza, or "natural" village). It also depended on the degree of coercion. If the goal was one shrine per hamlet, which meant merging an area's various unranked shrines (mukaku-sha) with the local village shrine (sonsha), little harm was done to either popular custom or local solidarity. And as long as there was no added inconvenience in visiting the shrine and no particular force used in achieving the merger, there was little trouble or resistance. When the authorities enforced a policy of one shrine per administrative unit and began merging shrines at the larger village (mura) and ward or town (machi) administrative levels, however, they quickly encountered strong resistance.

Though that resistance took many forms, there were very few instances of outright rejection of official demands for merger. Opposition was passive rather than active. For example, members simply continued worshiping at shrines they had been ordered to dismantle; they did not obey the merger directives regulating shrine facilities and priests' stipends; and they transferred sham sacred objects during a merger and continued to venerate the genuine objects in private. Usually, however, there was no opportunity to express opposition, and most people submitted. Yet when the old site and assets held in common were retained, a shrine dismantled at the time of merger was often rebuilt and its ceremonies revived as time passed. Of course these shrines had no official standing and remained unranked. Shrines that had not been listed in the official register of shrines could be used only clandestinely.

These acts of resistance reflect the popularity of shrines, particularly local shrines. Though the minsha might be suppressed, they were so important to the local communities that many survived.

Shrines in Newly Settled Areas

On Hokkaido, opened for settlement in the Meiji period, and in Japanese communities overseas, shrines were founded as communities matured. For example, on Hokkaido, two villages grew out of the colonist-militia settlement of former warriors at Ebetsu, east of Sapporo. In Ebetsu, a statue of Katō Kiyomasa (1562–1611), the daimyō of Kumamoto, on Kyushu, that the ex-warrior colonists had carried with them from Kumamoto as the symbol of the deity of Nishikiyama Shrine in Kumamoto at once became the guardian *kami* of the entire settlement. When a railway station was built at Ebetsu and a business district developed in response to the increase in settlers, the merchants proposed that the itinerant chief priest at Izumo Shrine, Shimane Prefecture, be asked to enshrine the spirit of Ōkuninushi no Mikoto with Kiyomasa as a joint protector deity of both the original settlement and the business district. This was done at Ebetsu Shrine, and in 1891 the shrine was moved to the top of a small hill west of the station.

In the village of Shinotsu, near Ebetsu, many people depressed by the hardships of colonial life committed suicide by drowning themselves in the Shinotsu River. The father of a settler from Tottori Prefecture took with him from his home village an amulet as the embodiment of a protective deity. Desiring that an annual festival be held to ward off misfortune, he enshrined that deity and Suitengū (the deity of water) near the bank of the Shinotsu River around 1890. That shrine eventually became Shinotsu Shrine, the unofficial guardian of the whole area.

The membership areas of both Ebetsu Shrine and Shinotsu Shrine grew with changes in the administrative districts, further unifying the community. The shrines fulfilled their function as homes for the guardian deities of the area, as providers of almanacs, and as the religious symbol of local solidarity.

There were shrines wherever Japanese lived abroad. Hilo Daijingū, founded on the island of Hawaii in 1898 and enshrining Amaterasu Ōmikami, is a typical example. Tokyo Daijingū in the Tokyo Colony in Brazil also venerated Amaterasu Ōmikami. Ryūtōzan Shrine in Pusan, Korea, was administered by the local office of the Japanese government and by groups of worshipers, while Shanhai Shrine in Shanghai, China, was supported by a local group of Japanese residents. The shrines in Pusan and Shanghai both venerated Kotohira (also called Kompira), among other deities.

Japanese expatriate communities were organized very much like the prefectural associations in Japan's big cities that maintain local identity, with the shrine as the focus of social cohesion. Overseas shrines provided a spiritual bond with the home country. An overseas shrine would send a representative to Japan to the main shrine of a particular deity to request the deity's enshrinement overseas. Thus overseas shrines helped expatriates maintain their Japanese culture.

Official Shrines Overseas

Official shrines were established alongside the nonofficial shrines on Hokkaido and overseas. The official shrine of Hokkaido was Sapporo Shrine, in Sapporo, dedicated to the three protector *kami* of the newly developed areas: Ōkunitama, Ōnamuchi, and Sukunahikona. The Hokkaido Colonization Office set aside land in Sapporo for a shrine, and the shrine was ranked as a minor national shrine in 1871, when its name was decided on. The following year it became a minor imperial shrine, when it was designated the protector of all Hokkaido, a function usurped from Hakodate Hachimangū, in Hakodate, the shrine related to the local daimyō, the Matsumae clan. In 1899 it was raised to the rank of a major imperial shrine.

The shrine system could be instituted on Hokkaido, Japan's northernmost island, with the expansion of settlement. But overseas, where Japanese were a tiny minority, nonofficial shrines could hardly claim to enshrine a local protective deity. Even less could official shrines overseas, which were no more than symbols of the Japanese state. With the extension of Japanese rule, such shrines were built on Taiwan and Sakhalin, in Korea and Manchuria, and on various Pacific islands.

Taiwan Jinja, erected in Taipei in 1900, was designated a major imperial shrine. It enshrined three protector *kami* of newly settled areas and the spirit of Prince Kitashirakawa (1847–95), who had died during the conquest of the island. Karafuto Jinja, established in Toyohara (Yuzhno Sakhalinsk) on Sakhalin in 1910, was also ranked a major imperial shrine and enshrined the same three deities. It was regarded as the shrine pacifying the northern limits of Japan's empire. Chōsen Jingū, built in Seoul in 1919, was dedicated to Amaterasu Ōmikami and Emperor Meiji. A major imperial shrine, it was intended as the ideological support for the colonial rule and pacification of Korea, which Japan had annexed in 1910. In Port Arthur, in the leased territory of Kwantung on China's Liaotung Peninsula, Kantō Jingū (also a major imperial shrine) was erected in 1938 to enshrine the same deities as in Chōsen Jingū. In the puppet state of Manchukuo,

Kenkoku Shimbyō was established in 1940 in the imperial palace in the capital, Changchun. This shrine was dedicated to Amaterasu Ōmikami as the country's founding deity, and the rites performed there followed Manchurian traditions.

Thus in its conquered colonial and semicolonial territories Japan established major imperial shrines as ideological props for colonial expansion. During the Meiji period (1868–1912) these shrines were dedicated to three protector deities; during the Taishō and Shōwa periods (1912–89) they were dedicated to Amaterasu Ōmikami and often Emperor Meiji. The same pattern was seen in the Pacific, for example, in the Palau islands, where Nan'yō Jinja—a major imperial shrine—was built in 1940 and dedicated to Amaterasu Ōmikami. Between the end of the Sino-Japanese War (1894–95) and the end of World War II, shrines were built one after another in the territories occupied by Japan as State Shintō gave full support to Japanese political and military power.

Many large and small shrines below the rank of imperial shrine were built overseas, primarily to serve Japanese worshipers. These shrines did not have the support of the indigenous peoples. The imperial shrines in particular were widely resented, since land for them had been expropriated and the indigenous people had been forced to worship at them. As the most hated symbols of Japanese militarism, they were destroyed after Japan's defeat in 1945.

State Shintō and Other Religions

Though the ritual element of State Shintō was stressed, its religious aspects were not entirely neglected, a violation of the Meiji Constitution's limited guarantee of religious freedom. The violation is especially obvious from the perspective of religions that reject the mythology and concepts of State Shintō. Christianity is a good example.

The Home Ministry attempted to promote a policy of giving shrines, especially shrines that were designated recipients of ceremonial offerings, a more important role in elementary school education. To this end, school and shrine functions were linked. During annual festivals, for example, children visited a shrine instead of attending school. In Hiroshima Prefecture in May 1907, and in Ehime Prefecture in July of the same year, schools were directed to include annual shrine festivals in their calendars. At its regular meeting in 1909 the National Association of Shintō Priests discussed requesting the Home Ministry to issue a directive requiring all schoolchildren throughout the country to visit a shrine on annual festival days. The directive was not issued, but orders at the prefectural level increased to the extent that such visits were widely enforced. For those who could not accept shrine worship as mere ritual devoid of religious meaning, the situation was intolerable.

Many Christians refused to contribute to the upkeep of the shrines of tutelary *kami* and opposed ceremonial offerings by local public bodies to shrines, saying that these supported idolatry. Naturally, Christians also opposed compulsory worship by their children at shrines on annual festival days. (Japan's Christians were not alone in opposing State Shintō; in Ehime Prefecture, for example, one government official wanted to cancel the local ceremonial offerings to the district shrine and a district school inspector arranged for elementary school pupils to be released from the obligation to visit the shrines of tutelary *kami* during the annual festival.) In Hiratsukachō, Kanagawa Prefecture, a Christian minister refused to allow his parishioners' children to worship at the local shrine on annual festival days and started a movement to prevent the school authorities from marking these children absent. For Christians with school-age children, the burden of shrine upkeep was infinitesimal compared with the anguish caused by compulsory shrine attendance.

With regard to the construction of Meiji Shrine, a Christian fellowship group said that enshrinement of the spirit of the dead emperor was not necessarily bad but seemed to violate the principle of separation of religion and the state. The group said that memory of the emperor's virtue would be better perpetuated for future generations through more positive, active works. Thus the Christian group did not directly oppose the construction of Meiji Shrine. Although opposition might have been expected from Japanese Christians, who had been taught that the worship of any deity other than Jehovah was idolatrous, apparently there was none. Some Christians viewed Meiji Shrine as a focus of national rather than religious veneration and, therefore, as not inconsistent with Christianity or freedom of belief.

The concept of shrines as centers for promoting ethical values rather than religion was fostered as State Shintō developed, and it was a view that Christians who supported nationalism found easy to accept. To them, neither financial support of nor compulsory visits to shrines was problematic. However, the concept of the nonreligiosity of shrines was unrealistic, and even the Shintō faction was not satisfied with it. Christians who saw Shintō religiosity for what it was were keenly aware of the danger that

State Shintō, as symbolized by the construction of Meiji Shrine, presented for religious freedom.

THE END OF STATE SHINTŌ

The Shintō Directive

With its organization completed early in the twentieth century, State Shintō reached its zenith in tandem with the growth of the fascism of the emperor system in the 1930s. One indicator of its status was the transformation of the Bureau of Shrines into an extraministerial body in 1940, the Agency of Shintō Worship (Jingiin). At the peak of its influence, however, the nation was defeated in World War II and the fortunes of State Shintō plummeted.

Clause ten of the Potsdam Declaration, setting out the terms for Japan's surrender, demanded the establishment of freedom of speech, religion, and thought. The Allied occupation authorities enforced this demand from the beginning of the occupation, in September 1945. In December they issued a directive titled "Abolition of Governmental Sponsorship, Support, Perpetuation, Control, and Dissemination of State Shintō." The so-called Shintō Directive forced the Japanese government to undertake complete separation of the state and religion, beginning with the abolition of State Shintō.

Specific steps toward abolition included the cessation of official sponsorship and control of Shrine Shintō and of public financial support for shrines; the abolition of the Agency of Shintō Worship and any public or private schools with Shintō characteristics; the abolition of Shintō-style education in all schools; the elimination of Shintō elements from school textbooks; the removal of Shintō symbols, such as *kamidana* (Shintō altars), from schools and local government offices; and the freeing of civil servants and the populace from the obligation to participate in Shintō events. Any hope that Shintō would retain its authority was dashed.

On New Year's Day 1946, the emperor declared in an imperial edict that he was not a *kami* incarnate (*akitsu-mikami*). This denial of his divinity came as a severe blow to many Japanese. In February, all laws and ordinances relating to shrines, including authorization for the Agency of Shintō Worship, were repealed. The legal authority of State Shintō collapsed, and the whole system was completely dismembered. Shrine Shintō, denied the protection of the state, elected to continue as a genuine religion, and, as one religion among many, to propagate on its own. The reforms were felt at the level of nonofficial shrines in November of that year, when the government forbade the sponsorship and support of Shintō by neighborhood associations and neighborhood groups.

As the new social order took shape, confusion arose. The new Constitution, which took effect in May 1947, guaranteed religious freedom as a basic right and specified the separation of the state and religion. With it, the age of State Shintō—and its eighty-year dictatorship in religious matters, its coercion of the people, and its frustration of the growth and development of religious freedom—was finally at an end.

Preventing a Revival of State Shintō

Toward the end of the occupation, as the nation began to rearm in the wake of the beginning of the Korean War in 1950, reaction set in against the democratic, pacifist Constitution. In that period, the Jinja Honchō (Association of Shintō Shrines), which embraced the majority of shrines in Japan, increasingly supported those who opposed the Constitution. The leadership of the association hoped for a revival of State Shintō.

At the center of the movement to revive State Shintō were those who wanted the government to maintain Yasukuni Shrine, in Tokyo, which had built up a strong and influential following among members of the Association of Bereaved Families and of the organization of war veterans, the Gōyū Remmei. The movement escalated after 1955 and grew in strength and numbers as the years passed. In 1969 the ruling Liberal Democratic Party, with the support of most of its members in both houses of the Diet, introduced the Yasukuni Shrine Bill. A majority of those in religious circles opposed the bill, and though it was introduced every year, it failed to pass. The Liberal Democratic Party then devised its Memorial Respect Proposal, as the reactionary forces in favor of state maintenance of Yasukuni Shrine gained modest support.

The rationale for state support of Yasukuni Shrine has been that this shrine symbolizes the nation's respect for the war dead. The common local custom of visiting shrines for special observances, like weddings or the birth of a child, is also based on Shintō rites. To oppose state support of Yasukuni Shrine and prevent the revival of State Shintō required changing people's attitudes toward those traditional observances. Such a change could not be accomplished overnight by measures like the Shintō Directive of December 1945, or the government order of November 1946.

In 1965 officials in Tsu, Mie Prefecture, not far from Ise Grand Shrine, used public funds to hold a Shrine Shintō groundbreaking ceremony, or *jichinsai* (which invokes the protection of the *kami* during construction). Suit was brought against the city on the grounds that the action violated Article 20 of the Constitution, guaranteeing freedom of religion, and Article 89, prohibiting the use of public funds for the maintenance of a religious institution. The suit was dismissed by the Tsu District Court, but in 1971 the Nagoya High Court overturned the lower court ruling and found that the *jichinsai* was not common custom but a religious act that violated Article 20 of the Constitution, and therefore spending public funds on it was illegal.

This ruling was a severe blow to the public organizations that had been having Shintō ceremonies, such as the *jichinsai*, performed. Not only could public bodies not participate directly in such ceremonies but also the general public had to question the relationships between shrines and public bodies. This was a matter of separation of state and religion at the local level. Grassroots concern was needed to prevent the revival of State Shintō and to make people aware of their constitutional right of freedom of religion. In July 1977, the Supreme Court decided that the performance of *jichinsai* at the request of public bodies was constitutional, stating that such ceremonies did not meet the test of religious activity forbidden by the Constitution. Though the specific problem raised by the actions of the Tsu officials had been resolved, doubtful points remained concerning the meaning of freedom of religion.

State Shintō was developed as the ritual and religious prop for the modern emperor system. Its fortunes linked to that system, it suffered with the system at the end of World War II. It awaits an opportunity to restore its authority once the postwar emperor system stabilizes. The Japanese people must decide whether a revival will be allowed so that State Shintō can again act as a support for the emperor system and a brake on religious freedom or whether religious freedom will be upheld and Shintō will be restricted to religious services commemorating the events of everyday life.

21. Buddhism and Modern Society

BUDDHISM AT A TURNING POINT

Anti-Buddhist Currents in the Meiji Period

Strong resistance to the Japanese Buddhist establishment developed in many quarters during the Meiji period (1868–1912). Almost from the beginning of the period, Buddhism was attacked by those who favored the separation of Shintō and Buddhism and the establishment of Shintō as the state ideology, and the attacks resulted in often violent demonstrations against Buddhist institutions across Japan. This anti-Buddhist movement inspired the government's policy of promoting its three precepts of veneration of the *kami* and love of country, observance of the way of humanity (morality and ethics) and the law of heaven (philosophy and religion), and obedience to the emperor. At the same time, Buddhism was criticized by progressive thinkers and Christian converts, who saw it as old-fashioned, feudalistic, and inappropriate for a nation emerging in the modern world.

Shintō attacked Buddhism on many fronts, starting with the separation edict and the depredation of temples across the land. A different approach to undermining Buddhism was evident in the establishment of the Daikyō-in (Great Teaching Academy) in 1872. As we have seen, the purpose of the Daikyō-in was to inculcate upon the public the three precepts advocated by the government. In 1872 the Ministry of Education directed that these precepts be taught to schoolchildren.

The Daikyō-in was clearly a hybrid Shintō-Buddhist institution, and 3,047 of its 7,247 instructors were Buddhist priests. Though this hybridism represented a drift from the tide of extreme anti-Buddhism, the general policy of assigning primacy to Shintō remained unchanged. While the Buddhists who cooperated in the Daikyō-in program justified their participation as offering the best opportunity to recover from the severe blow that anti-Buddhist persecution had dealt them, priests like Shimaji Mokurai (1838–1911) deplored such thinking and advocated Western-style separation of religion and the state, as well as freedom of religion.

The concepts of "civilization and enlightenment" were popularized by such educators and scholars of Western learning as Fukuzawa Yukichi (1835–1901) and Katō Hiroyuki (1836–1916), by the conservative followers of the educator and moralist Nishimura Shigeki (1828–1902), and by Christians. Influenced particularly by Herbert Spencer's and Charles Darwin's views on evolution, these people valued logical, critical thought and held high hopes for the development of human civilization in accordance with the theory of evolution. In the light of that theory, they concluded that people of knowledge and reason had no need for religious salvation and that religion was the solace of the irrational.

Japanese Christians also rejected Buddhism, not only on religious grounds but also because they, too, judged it unsuited to an age of reason and progress. Writing in the influential political, social, economic, and literary review *Kokumin no Tomo* (The Nation's Friend), the Christian political scientist and educator Ukita Kazutami (1859–1946) said: "I attack Buddhism simply because it regards the body as the cause of evil and pessimism as the best attitude. In its teachings I can discover no truth for civilizing and enlightening the people of this country."

The Precepts and a Return to Ancient Traditions

Anti-Buddhist harassment gave rise to a variety of movements to safeguard Buddhism. Buddhists who cherished tradition submitted a petition to the government detailing ways that Buddhism benefited the state. But thoughtful, farsighted leaders tried to set a course for Buddhism through the restoration of personal faith and religious commitment and through a Buddhist renaissance based on rediscovery of its ancient roots.

One practice that they thought would help achieve their goal was strict observance of the ten major precepts. Since this restoration movement was especially concerned about the role of Buddhism among the laity, Buddhist thinkers stressed the need to discover how ordinary people could keep the ten precepts in daily life. The doctrine of the ten precepts was one of the most influential teachings in the new Buddhist movement of the Meiji period. The ten major precepts, governing all behavior, are not to kill living beings, not to steal, not to engage in wrongful sexual activity, not to lie, not to use immoral language, not to slander, not to equivocate, not to covet, not to give way to anger, and not to hold false views.

Shaku Unshō (1827–1909), of the Shingon sect, and Fukuda Gyōkai (1809–88), of the Jōdo sect, were priests who attempted to revive observance of the precepts and to reinterpret the concept of the Decay of the Law (*Mappō*) without losing sight of prevailing ideological trends. Unshō sought to disseminate strict observance of the precepts among lay Buddhists by organizing the Jūzen-kai (Association for the Ten Precepts). Some of its members, however, finding it difficult to keep the precepts strictly in secular life, described their difficulties in letters to Unshō. He replied with a quotation from the *Bommō-kyō* (Sutra of the Perfect Net): "One precept is the radiant diamond treasure." He explained that if one kept even a single precept perfectly, one's personality would take on the radiance of a diamond. He also explained the role of repentance in awakening the mind of someone who feels distressed after violating the precepts.

Clergy and laity alike regarded Gyōkai as the standard-bearer of contemporary Buddhism. He insisted on the need for a unified Buddhist view to eliminate sectarian abuses. He also attempted to reevaluate the Theravāda tradition of the southern stream of Buddhism, which in Japan had been held in low esteem or ignored. He was convinced that this was the only way to correct "mistakes" that had entered Buddhism, and he sought to restore Buddhism to its original purity by rejecting whatever was erroneous, a policy summed up by the phrase *haja kenshō* (rejecting false teachings, manifesting truth), which became a catchword among contemporary Buddhists.

He amplified his views in the *Dōtoku Ron* (Discussion of the Same Virtue; 1870), in which he opposed making Buddhism a state religion: "Buddhism was not originally expounded for the governance of a state." Gyōkai's ideas on fostering Buddhism appear in his *Hiroshima Mondō* (Questions and Answers in Hiroshima; 1870), *Kyōbō Shihi* (The Buddhist Teachings and My Personal Criticism; 1871), and *Buppō to Sehō* (Buddhist Law and Secular Law; date uncertain); but they are dealt with most systematically in the *Dōtoku Ron*.

Like those of Unshō, Gyōkai's views on Buddhism's role in society were influenced by his belief in the importance of the precepts and the reality of the Decay of the Law. He wrote of the ten precepts in the *Isshin Chō* (Notes on Single-mindedness; ca. 1881):

> Once you sincerely accept the precepts, you will find—even when asleep, forgetful, thinking of other things, or working—that their merit continually sustains you. It does not matter whether you rest; the precepts still grow and swell. If they could take form, they would exceed both heaven and earth. This is what the Buddha taught.

Another notable figure of Meiji-period Buddhism was Hara Tanzan (1819–92), of the Sōtō sect, who reinterpreted Buddhist doctrine in a manner relevant to this turning point in the history of Japanese Buddhism. He was not swayed by the form of the precepts but set out to comprehend the source of the three poisons—the greed, anger, and foolishness that blight acts of merit that yield good fruit. He criticized the traditional interpretations and suggested applying the scientific method, which was then becoming accepted in Japan. He comments on these matters in the *Shinshō Jikken Roku* (An Experimental Record of the Mind; 1873) aroused great interest among both Buddhists and non-Buddhists.

BUDDHISM IN SECULAR SOCIETY

Lay Buddhists

Buddhism, which had been firmly established by the parish system under the temple regulations of feudal times, retained great vitality even amid the social modernization of the Meiji period. The Buddhist movements of the time attempted to find new meaning for the religion, interpreting its message in modern terms, and were on the whole fostered by former priests and lay devotees critical of sectarian Buddhism. Ōuchi Seiran (1845–1918), a former priest of the Sōtō Zen sect, for example, organized a lay movement for discussion of Buddhism and how to make it play a role in daily life.

Seiran, a "progressive" thinker of the early Meiji period, wrote for *Meikyō Shinshi* (The New Magazine of Bright Teachings; no. 598) an editorial on pressing questions for Buddhism, including reform of the clergy. For instance, should the clergy be allowed to marry and to eat meat? Seiran used these issues to urge reconsideration of the nature of the clergy and revitalization of lay Buddhism.

Beginning around 1875, Seiran published the short sermons of the deceased Shingon priest Jiun (1718–1804; also known as Onkō) and frequently discussed them in *Meikyo Shinshi*, popularizing Jiun's teaching of the importance of the ten lay precepts. Admiration of Jiun's twelve-volume *Jūzen Hōgo* (Sermons on the Ten Good Precepts; 1775) and his *Hito to Naru Michi* (On Becoming More Human; 1781) burgeoned, and Buddhist associations devoted to the ten good precepts sprang up in several places.

Seiran formulated a creed for a movement to "prevent evil, encourage good, and bring all to enlightenment." The creed consisted of the threefold faith (*sanshin*) and the three practices (*sangyō*), and its purpose was to organize the principles of enlightenment and practice—which are identical, according to Sōtō-sect teaching—and to articulate accessibly the ideas in the *Dōjō Zaike Shūshō Gi* (The Meaning of Practice and Enlightenment for Lay Members of the Sōtō Sect), which Seiran compiled in 1887. In the philosophy of Dōgen, founder of the sect, Seiran discovered four essential principles: repentance that purifies the heart and extinguishes bad karma (*sange metsuzai*); attainment of enlightenment through receiving the precepts (*jukai nyūi*); vows to be of benefit to all beings (*hotsugan rishō*); and gratitude to the Buddha for helping practitioners persevere in practice (*gyōji hōon*). His distillation of these four principles into basic teachings truly marked the start of a new epoch.

Seiran had thought at one time that the most impressive of all methods of religious practice was that taught by Shinran, founder of the Jōdo Shin sect, in his doctrine of the assurance of rebirth through a single moment of complete faith in Amida Buddha. While editing the *Dōjō Zaike Shūshō Gi*, however, Seiran was deeply influenced by Dōgen's *Shōbō Genzō* (Treasury of the Eye of the True Dharma), and he abandoned faith in rebirth through "other power" in favor of belief in salvation through complete faith in one or more buddhas.

Many criticized Seiran severely for his doctrinal about-face. In answer to these criticisms, in the second issue of *Sōtō Fushūkai Zasshi* (Magazine of the Society to Help the Sōtō Sect) Seiran wrote a moving apologia for his conversion. His ideas on religious teaching, drawn from the Sōtō Zen doctrine of the unity of practice and enlightenment, attracted much attention for their resistance to the cultural changes and "modernization" occurring in Japan and to the new ethical system that was arising with modern capitalism. Seiran was also attempting to correct the view of "progressive" thinkers that Buddhism was a religion of the foolish and superstitious.

The Meiji period offered perhaps the best opportunity for Buddhism to develop its ideas on propagation, as it ceased to be the official cult of the Tokugawa shogunate and was forced to rely on propagation to survive. Seiran, along with Shimaji Mokurai and his movement based on associations of believers, played a very important role in devising ways to popularize Buddhism.

The Popularization of Doctrine

Two popularizers of Buddhism were former Buddhist priests: Daidō Chōan (1843–1908), who founded Guzekyō, and Tanaka Chigaku (1861–1939), who devoted his life to a movement based on Nichiren's teachings.

In 1886 the Sōtō sect stripped Chōan of his priestly status after condemning as heresy his interpretation of the sect's main tenet for attaining peace of mind. He had received special promotion in priestly rank in 1883 at the age of forty and been appointed a leader of sect administration in Niigata Prefecture. Chōan had been a fervent devotee of Kannon since boyhood. He was preoccupied with the true and provisional practices leading to salvation. The true practice was emancipation from worldly attachment through meditation on holy things. The provisional practice was teaching and benefiting others by opening "the universal gate." He adhered to his belief in these practices throughout his years as a Sōtō priest, as well as after founding Guzekyō.

While still a Sōtō priest, Chōan devoted himself to propagation. He chronicled the results of his efforts in his *Benkyō Roku* (Study Records; 1875–82), in which, for example, he recorded 860 yen collected for compassionate works and 343 yen for relief, 29 precepts ceremonies conducted, 3,175 lectures given, and the precepts conferred on 11,386 people. When he criticized the Jōdo Shin sect in 1885 in an endeavor to emphasize the differences between it and the Sōtō sect, he was attacked by Jōdo Shin adherents in what is known as the Kumogaike Persecution. This prompted Chōan's petition the following year to be allowed to leave the Sōtō sect. The sect authorities, however, exacted a larger penalty by expelling him.

As the founder of Guzekyō, "the religion of salvation," Chōan devoted all his energy to finding a way for people to attain peace of mind in everyday life. To this end he saw the need "to ignore deluded people and establish groups of true believers." He began by rejecting the strictures of sectarianism. He held that meditation through *zazen* was the "difficult practice" and that rebirth through chanting the *nembutsu* was the "easy practice." In the *Guzekyō* (1891) he wrote of faith in Kannon:

> Truly you should understand that people of old, people of today, and holy people of all times have appeared in the world to bring about the salvation of all beings. . . . When you realize that the very purpose of human life is to save others, then you will also understand clearly why I look up to Bodhisattva Kannon as my model and my focus of devotion.

In the twenty-two years before his death at the age of sixty-five, Chōan propagated his teachings in an area stretching from Osaka in the south to Hokkaido in the north.

Movements propagating Nichiren's teachings were of two types: nationalistic and supranationalistic. Tanaka Chigaku exemplifies advocates of the former, and the influential writer Takayama Chogyū (1871–1902) exemplifies advocates of the latter. Despite their differences in outlook, both learned from Nichiren the primary importance of creating humane social conditions as the foundation for universal salvation rather than seeking subjective peace of mind for isolated individuals through the *nembutsu* or other religious practices.

In both thought and deed, Chigaku rejected the academic climate of the Nichiren sect in the nineteenth century. During that time the sect abandoned aggressive conversion techniques for more moderate ones taught by Nikki (1800–1859). Chigaku devoted himself to restoring what he regarded as the sect's pure doctrine. As a student, Chigaku had been taught the established interpretation of Nichiren's doctrine on conversion—rejection of aggressiveness in favor of gentle persuasion. Chigaku came to believe that forceful conversion was "not the exclusion and rejection of other sects, but a conversion through compassion, having broken down all conceit and attachment to one's own views. . . . This forceful conversion is like preventing illness, whatever the nature of the times."

Chigaku synthesized his ideas on lay Buddhism in his *Bukkyō Fūfu Ron* (The Buddhist View of Husband and Wife; 1887), in which he reexamines marriage and the enlightenment of women. The spirit of his interpretation of Nichiren's teachings is best revealed in his *Shūmon no Ishin* (The Sect's Restoration; 1898) and *Honke Shōshaku Ron* (Discussion of the

Aggressive and Moderate Methods of Conversion Used by the True Bodhisattva Nichiren; 1899).

Buddhism and Nationalism

In the middle of the Meiji period, Buddhism responded to the new nationalism that had developed in reaction to intense efforts to westernize
Japanese culture in the first decade of the period. By the middle of the
Meiji period, Buddhists had regained their confidence and were declaring
that Buddhist truths are consistent with logic and science. Buddhist scholars, newly proud of their religion's important role in forming Japan's distinctive culture and spiritual climate, supported the growing nationalistic
movement.

One such scholar was Inoue Enryō (1858–1919). His *Sangaku Ron* (The
Three Teachings; 1885) was the starting point for his ideological activities. Inoue advocated the systemization of Eastern philosophy, together
with study of the origins of Western philosophy and the adoption of its
academic tradition. He focused on three philosophical traditions and their
greatest exponents: Chinese philosophy and Confucius, Indian philosophy and Śākyamuni, and Western philosophy and Socrates and Kant. He
asserted that these philosophers taught all that there was to learn.

It is interesting that he omitted Jesus from the list. This omission emphasizes Inoue's belief that a religion should be judged by its philosophical and scientific consistency. His treatment of Christianity also reveals an
effort to use logic to overcome the psychological defensiveness of early
Meiji Buddhists faced with an "evil" religion, Christianity. In 1891 in the
third volume of the *Shinri Kinshin* (The Guiding Principle of Truth), Inoue
wrote: "Christianity is a religion, just as Buddhism is. Within limits, they
are allies and brothers against those who have no religion. The purposes
of Christianity are those of Buddhism." Despite this statement, he found
theoretical grounds for rejecting Christianity because of its philosophical
and scientific inconsistencies. Similarly, he held that piety is no more than
"stale custom arising from the delusion and superstition of fools."

Inoue combined a love of truth and strong patriotism. In his *Bukkyō
Katsu Ron* (Enlivening Buddhism; 1887) he said: "I understand the need to
study Japanese and Chinese learning but not Buddhist learning. I also realize the urgency of maintaining literary and historical studies, but do not
feel the same urgency about preserving religion." And "the love of truth
arises from a love of humanity, whereas the desire to defend the state

comes from a love of the self. The former may be termed universalism, the latter nationalism." Inoue's two great goals were attained through a flourishing system of education and religion.

MODERNIZING BUDDHISM

Buddhism and Modern Thought

Japanese Buddhism of the middle of the Meiji period was stimulated by the previously mentioned concept of *haja kenshō*—that is, rejecting false teachings and manifesting the truth. This phrase appears in the *San-lun-hsüan-i* (The Profound Meaning of the Three Treatises) by the Chinese priest Chi-tsang (549–623). *Haja kenshō* was not simply the arbitrary rejection of other doctrines but a fourfold strategy for resolving questions: refuting without accepting, accepting without refuting, refuting or accepting, and neither refuting nor accepting.

The Jōdo Shin–sect priest and eminent scholar Murakami Senshō (1851–1929) urged a reconsideration of the use of the term *haja kenshō* by Buddhists who criticized Christianity but also lacked an understanding of the careful Buddhist scholarship and Buddhist renewal that Inoue and others were calling for. In Washio Junkyō's *Bukkyō Taika Ron Shū* (Collection of the Writings by Eminent Buddhist Priests; 1903), volume three, he wrote:

> Today's priests are very inclined to assert that Buddhism is theoretically superior to Western religions and to parrot certain ideas—that Buddhism is a philosophy, a science, and that Western religions are neither true nor rational and are no match for Buddhism. They attempt to apply *haja kenshō* arbitrarily and incompletely. How absolutely misguided of them!

When the Christian Uchimura Kanzō's refusal to pay homage to the emperor's signature on the 1890 Imperial Rescript on Education precipitated a confrontation between education and religion, various questions concerning the nationalistic view of education and Christian doctrine were brought into the open. The ensuing literary debate advanced the view that any religion, be it Christianity or Buddhism, should adapt to the national polity and not obstruct the intention of the Rescript on Education. The majority of Buddhists followed the current of the times and produced a bigoted rationale for the ostracism of Christianity.

The Rise of Critical Thought

Critical thought gained popularity in Japanese intellectual circles around 1894, when the first Sino-Japanese War broke out. The important effect that critical thought had on Buddhism can be seen in the writings of several Buddhists active at the time.

Kiyozawa Manshi (1863–1903), a Jōdo Shin priest and noted philosopher, pointed out the limits of philosophy in his essay "Shisō Kaihatsu Kan" (The Development of Thought) in the journal *Bukkyō* (Buddhism): "Though Hegel comprehended that the whole of thought should be embraced, all philosophers admit the possibility that he may have misinterpreted other philosophers." Kiyozawa wrote that religion is beyond philosophy, and that one who embraces all thought transcends thought and attains a state of religious bliss.

Furukawa Rōsen (1871–99), another Jōdo Shin priest, described three stages of thought—dogmatism, skepticism, and criticism—in his essay "Kaigi Jidai ni Ireri" (Entering an Age of Skepticism), which also appeared in *Bukkyō*. He wrote:

> Those who read the history of philosophy must admit that it developed in three stages: dogmatism, skepticism, and criticism. Philosophy in a time of dogmatism is an intellectual effort to understand the universe and the immortality of the soul. In a time of skepticism it is concerned with the opposite, doubting that these things can be understood by intellectual effort. Arriving at philosophy in a time of criticism, we find, as it were, a compromise between the two positions, an evaluation of whether it is possible for the intellect to delve into its own nature. A philosophy of dogmatism gives way to a philosophy of skepticism; a philosophy of skepticism moves on to a philosophy of criticism; and a philosophy of criticism in turn shifts to a new phase: a philosophy of dogmatism. This new dogmatism, as the product of critical philosophy, accepts what must be accepted and rejects what must be rejected, and in so doing advances one stage further from the previous dogmatism.

A good example of the fruit of critical research into Buddhist doctrine is a work published in 1903, the *Daijō Bussetsu Ron Hihan* (A Critique of the Theory that Mahāyāna Is the Direct Teaching of the Buddha), by Murakami Senshō. Murakami saw the scholar Tominaga Nakamoto

(1715–46) as the pioneer of nonsectarian Buddhist studies and esteemed him for his critical research into the historical development of doctrine. As a result of historical research, Murakami had already concluded in the *Bukkyō Tōitsu Ron* (The Unity of Buddhism; 1898) that "there is no historical buddha other than Śākyamuni, who was not superhuman. Some people fear that this fact will weaken the faith of ordinary people. . . . I think it will instead give rise to the establishment of sound faith."

As a result of the controversy over the authenticity of Mahāyāna, Japanese Buddhism at the turn of the century had begun to acknowledge its own historical development. It had emerged from its periods of dogmatism and skepticism into a time of criticism. Among the pioneers in such research were four Jōdo Shin–sect priests and scholars: Murakami Senshō; Sakaino Kōyō (1871–1933); Washio Junkyō (1868–1941), who collaborated on the journal *Bukkyō Shirin* (A Historical Forest of Buddhism) in 1894; and Fujii Senshō (1859–1902), who wrote a two-volume history of Buddhism, the *Bukkyō Shōshi* (A Brief History of Buddhism; 1894). Their research on the history of Buddhism was like fresh air for those searching for true Buddhism and a living faith. One of Sakaino's essays, "Rekishiteki Bukkyō" (Historical Buddhism), published in *Bukkyō Shirin*, had a great impact both in and beyond Buddhist circles. Historical scholarship led the reformers to study primary sources for information on the lives and teachings of the Buddha and the patriarchs.

The "New Buddhists"

The New Buddhist Friends' Association (Shin Bukkyōto Dōshikai) was founded in October 1899, by Sakaino Kōyō and the lay Buddhist philosopher Takashima Beihō (1875–1949). Their faith and practice were based on a six-article creed: "(1) We make sound Buddhist faith our fundamental principle; (2) We will encourage the prosperity and diffusion of sound faith, knowledge, and moral principles and work to better society from its foundation; (3) We advocate unrestricted research into Buddhism and other religions; (4) We are resolved to eradicate superstition; (5) We see no need to maintain the present system of religious organization and ritual; (6) We reject all political patronage and interference with religion."

The creed's content is closely linked to the currents of thought that made the early twentieth century a turning point for Japanese Buddhism, and it is characteristic of one of the directions in which Buddhism turned. In the journal *Shin Bukkyō* (New Buddhism), Sakaino wrote more specifically about the nature of the "sound faith" that was the objective of the New Buddhists:

> If "faith" is defined as a still-unrefined emotion, then we must distinguish credulity, or blind faith, from true faith. . . . We must base our faith on mutual tolerance so that it does not contradict modern ideas. . . . Thus, faith in Buddhism is not blind adherence to the letter of the Buddhist scriptures but is the ability to investigate them freely; not altering basic principles, but asking what they are. New Buddhism does not teach these but respects freedom of thought, disliking whatever restricts that faith.

The New Buddhists did not attempt to establish a unified doctrine but relied on "the propagation of the idea of the new in respect to the possession of faith." Stressing the importance of secular life, they held that secular life in itself was none other than the religious life. This idea gave rise to a religious outlook based on secularism, common sense, and religious tolerance.

Kiyozawa Manshi and Spirituality

Central to the Buddhist movement at the beginning of the twentieth century, and apparent in the thought of the New Buddhists, was the question of how true faith should be understood in terms of Buddhist scholarship. Kiyozawa Manshi, attempting to answer that question, found a new direction for Japanese Buddhism and shaped the religion in modern terms through his concept of "spirituality" as the core of life.

His philosophical activities can be broadly divided into four phases: the first, from 1888 to 1898, when practice based on his own efforts, as opposed to faith in the Buddha, dominated; the second, from 1894 to 1898, when he underwent conversion; the third, from 1900 to 1901, when his activity centered on the Kōkōdō, the community he established in Tokyo's Hongō; and the final phase, from 1902 until his death in 1903.

Kiyozawa's *Shūkyō Tetsugaku Gaikotsu* (A Skeletal Outline of a Philosophy of Religion; 1892) is typical of the first period. Its central theme is the concept of the finite (*yūgen*) and the infinite (*mugen*). Philosophical infinity is, he said, "the inquiry of the rational mind doubting the verity or falsity of infinity." A person examining the question from a religious viewpoint, however, accepts the infinite.

During the second period, of conversion, Kiyozawa became convinced of the importance of faith in liberating him from his perplexity about the ability of the unaided self to attain religious enlightenment through religious practice. In this eventful period he was wracked physically and mentally—by a reversal in the sectarian reform movement that he supported, family problems, a financial crisis, and a recurrence of his tuberculosis. His conviction of the primacy of faith arose from his growing understanding of the "real" Śākyamuni—the man—and his religion as revealed in the four collections of early canonical texts known as the Āgamas, which he read in 1898, between January 22 and February 25.

Kiyozawa was also influenced at this time by the *Discourses* of the Greek Stoic philosopher Epictetus (ca. 55–ca. 135), a freed slave who was lame and suffered ill health throughout his life, and by the thirteenth-century *Tanni Shō* (Lamenting the Deviations), a collection of Shinran's teachings compiled by his disciple Yuien. From Epictetus Kiyozawa absorbed the Stoicism needed to overcome sorrow and misfortune, and from the *Tanni Shō* he learned that even the wicked can be saved and gained an understanding of salvation through merit transferred by the Buddha.

Kiyozawa's state of mind at the time is reflected in a passage from his diary of religious practice, *Rōsen Nichijō* (Useless Kiyozawa Manshi):

> Our great delusion is in not knowing the Buddha. When we know the Buddha we can for the first time understand our own limits. That is, we must become a slave of the Buddha, not a slave of anything else, if we want to know what we can and cannot attain and what is within our limitations and what is not.

This passage is characteristic of Kiyozawa's spirituality. Passive in the face of the changes that modernization had brought to his society, he looked to the "other power" of the Buddha as the inspiration for his thought and practice.

Kiyozawa was also influenced by Jiun's voluminous *Jūzen Hōgo* and understood it as an expression of a religious mind that accepts the infinite. In his interpretation of Jiun's concept of the precepts, he went so far as to say: "If one believes in the other power, one can only do more and more good." Kiyozawa's ideas on spirituality were systematized by his disciples at the Kōkōdō and published in the journal *Seishinkai* (Spiritual World). This record reveals the nature of his speculation, his deep faith, and his religious practice, all of which reflected his anxieties and personal sufferings in the face of a rapidly modernizing society.

Modernization of the Sōtō sect was begun by two priests, Kohō Chisan (1879–1967) and Nukariya Kaiten (1867–1934). Kohō criticized the rationalism in the writings of the New Buddhists, Kiyozawa's spirituality, and Takayama Chogyū's Nietzschean philosophy and propounded his own Zen-based philosophy of life. He argued that Takayama ignored reason and did not recognize the danger of either the senses or the passions. While agreeing that Kiyozawa's spirituality might be appropriate to the times, he said that it had a strong element of resignation and was therefore not a sound doctrine for that period, when the struggle for survival was hard. In particular, he felt that members of Kiyozawa's Kōkōdō were inclined to stress the emotions and as a result preach antimoralism. According to Kohō, the New Buddhists overemphasized reason and, in stressing modernism, acted contrary to basic Buddhist principles.

In *Wayūshi* (Journal for Harmony and Nondiscrimination) he explained his reasons for advocating the Zen way of life:

> Moral corruption has already allowed the karma to permeate society to its foundations, and the great tide of materialism has now surged and engulfed all levels of society. . . . Confusion and turmoil in intellectual circles have reached an extreme. This is why I expound my philosophy of the Zen way of life.

Kohō does little more than describe the Zen life in relation to the academic ideas of the five stages to correct understanding propounded by Tung-shan Liang-chieh (807–69), founder of the Ts'ao-tung (Sōtō) sect, and the four types of outlook propounded by Lin-chi I-hsüan (d. 867), founder of the Lin-chi (Rinzai) sect.

In his essay "Naisei Naikan Shugi" (Internal Reflection and Inner Insight), published in the January 1904, issue of *Wayūshi*, Nukariya wrote that the awakening to the inner self that is attained through religious training and practice is not limited to the Buddha. "Even the physical, temporary self tied to the senses is also the Buddha." With regard to the universe, in his "Zenshū Hyōron" (Critique of the Zen Sect) published in the November 1904 issue of *Wayūshi*, he wrote:

> The struggle for existence is the mother of morality, the fountainhead of progress and improvement. That being so, the cosmic will is not the

perpetrator of the wretched carnage that is caused by the struggle for survival, but is that which supplies us the fountainhead of progress and improvement.

From one perspective Nukariya's Zen ethics appear autonomous, but from another they seem heteronomous. Human beings are ethically autonomous because they have been endowed with goodness from the first; and they are heteronomous from the point of view of their original nature. That human beings seek out the Way is in itself the realization of the great Buddha spirit. At this point, autonomy and heteronomy merge. Nukariya's concluding statements in "Zenshū Hyōron" concern the oneness of progressive ethics and perfection.

I cannot completely approve of an ethics that gives supremacy to reason and slights the emotions. . . . The blind impulse of humanity's animal passions is not something that can be eradicated.

Because of this belief, he placed great emphasis on the principle of self-denial through *zazen*, Zen meditation.

22. The Growth of
New Religious Movements

DEFINING THE NEW RELIGIONS

The Rush Hour of the Gods

After World War II, new religions sprouted one after another, like bamboo shoots after rain. In part a product of the unrest that accompanied postwar social changes, they prospered with the new freedom of religion guaranteed by the postwar Constitution. The Religious Corporations Ordinance (Shūkyō Hōjin Rei, Imperial Ordinance No. 719) of December 28, 1945, reflects the spirit of the Constitution. Articles 4 and 7 of the ordinance are especially striking. Article 4 states: "A sect or denomination comes into existence by registering the establishment of its principal office; and a shrine, temple, or church by registering its seat. The particulars necessary for registration . . . shall be stipulated in an ordinance." Article 7 adds: "When a religious corporation is established, its regulations and the full names and addresses of its directors shall be reported within two weeks: to the minister of education if it is a sect or denomination, or to the prefectural governor if it is a temple, shrine, or church."

The ordinance thus abolished the government control of religion exercised under the Religious Organizations Law of 1939 and made clear that it was up to each religious organization to manage its own affairs. The government had no right to grant or withhold permission to act; religious bodies had complete autonomy, and the government's role was limited to registering them.

The ease of registering religious organizations quickly led to the restoration of the sects that had existed before enforcement of the Religious Organizations Law, which had restricted Shintō to thirteen sects, Buddhism to twenty-eight sects, and Christianity to two organizations (the Roman Catholic church and the Nihon Kirisuto Kyōdan, the federation of Protestant denominations). These mandatory coalitions quickly dissolved, and sects that had been compelled to shelter under the protection of one of the legally recognized sects during the war also became independent, breaking away from their long-standing religious superintendents. Completely new organizations were also established in rapid order.

By the end of October 1947, five times the previous number of religious organizations had been registered with the Ministry of Education. The number of registrations soon became a flood so great that it was said a new religion came into being every week, and the phenomenon was dubbed "the rush hour of the gods." By the end of 1951, shortly after the signing of the San Francisco Peace Treaty, which restored sovereignty to Japan, 720 religious organizations had been registered.

The Jiukyō Incident

Many of the religious organizations that came into being in the period of postwar confusion had only a fleeting existence. Yet an equally large number gained in strength and went on to become large, influential organizations.

In January 1947—when social unease was at its height and high unemployment and severe food shortages were compounding the shock of defeat—newspapers focused public attention on a religious group called Jiukyō after a disturbance at the sect's headquarters in Kanazawa, Kanagawa Prefecture, led to its leaders' arrest. Founded by Nagaoka Nagako (1903–84), also known as Jikōson, Jiukyō numbered among its members the famed champion *sumō* wrestler Futabayama and the celebrated *go* player Go Seigen. Nagaoka declared that since the emperor had renounced his divinity, the spirit of Amaterasu Ōmikami had entered her, and she attracted a fanatical following when she predicted a series of natural calamities. The Shintō Directive, which had been issued on December 15, 1945, had forbidden the teaching or dissemination of militaristic or ultranationalistic ideas. The police regarded Jikōson's teachings as ultranationalistic and raided her headquarters on suspicion of violations of the weapons- and food-control laws. During the raid, Futabayama was involved in a scuffle.

Though the police were unable to prove any violation, Jiukyō was attacked by the media; and as Jikōson's prophesies turned out to be false, members gradually fell away. It was the media that called the sect a *shinkō shūkyō* ("newly arisen religion")—a label that soon became pejorative—and branded it as deceitful. After the so-called Jiukyō Incident, the new religions came under increased public scrutiny in newspapers, magazines, and radio broadcasts.

Popular Cults

A number of the new religious organizations became controversial. One was led by a man known as Otasuke Jiisan (Helpful Old Man), an elderly practitioner of magicoreligious rites in the city of Ichikawa, Chiba Prefecture. Though it never developed into a large organization, it had short-lived success as a result of newspaper and railway advertisements asserting that any physical complaint could be cured quickly if the sufferer sat quietly awhile. Otasuke Jiisan had a great reputation for solving all manner of problems by brandishing a sword and shouting violently as the client sat before an altar. After the cult was severely criticized on the NHK (national public broadcasting system) radio program "Social Report," however, it went into rapid decline.

Yet other groups prospered despite adverse publicity and ridicule in the media. Journalists dubbed one the Odoru Shūkyō (Dancing Religion). Officially called Tenshō Kōtai Jingūkyō, it is a unique organization that was founded just after the war by Kitamura Sayo (1900–1967), the wife of a farmer in the remote area of Tabuse, Yamaguchi Prefecture, at the western extremity of Honshu. In July 1948 "Social Report" focused on the group.

On September 22, 1948, Kitamura visited Tokyo for the third time, and in front of Tokyo Station gave one of her "singing sermons" in thundering tones. "Wake up, you maggoty beggars," she roared. "Wake up, you common beggars. The grotto of heaven has opened; return to your true humanity. The realm of the *kami* has come into being." She then led her followers through the streets in a "dance of selflessness." With their eyes closed, they claimed to experience the joy of salvation. This group ecstasy was reported widely in newspapers and magazines and shown in newsreels, and all over the country the cult became known as the "dancing god" or the "dancing religion." Kitamura, like Nagaoka Nagako with her preaching of world renewal through natural calamities, was typical of the postwar cult leaders in that she emerged as a popular savior soon after the emperor renounced his divinity.

Sekai Kyūsei Kyō

One sect that prospered, eventually becoming Sekai Kyūsei Kyō (Church of World Messianity), was that of Okada Mokichi (1882–1955), also known as Meishu-sama (Enlightened Spiritual Leader). He had been a leader of Ōmoto, the Shintō-related sect founded by Deguchi Nao in 1892, which is discussed later, but came to feel that he was imbued with a spiritual power of his own. In 1935 Okada founded Dai Nihon Kannon Kai (Japan Kannon Society) and began practicing his own healing method, called Okada-Style Spiritual Finger-Pressure Therapy, which employed *jōrei* (purification of the spirit). The next year, following complaints that he was violating the Medical Practitioners Law, Dai Nihon Kannon Kai was superseded by the newly founded Dai Nihon Kenkō Kyōkai (Japan Health Association), which Okada had established with the idea of separating healing from religion. In 1940 he was again accused of violating the Medical Practitioners Law and was forced to sign a pledge not to practice *jōrei* therapy. Unable to practice it himself, he set about training others who could.

Okada gave *jōrei* practitioners talismans inscribed with the Sino-Japanese ideographic character for light. They believed that a sphere of light some six centimeters in diameter in Okada's abdomen emitted a steady stream of light. Practitioners, who placed their talisman in a small bag that was worn around the neck, believed that when the palm of the hand was held over an ill person this divine light was channeled through the practitioner's hand and cleansed away the ill person's spiritual clouds.

After the beginning of World War II, the talismans were revered as having miraculous power, and despite the government's restrictions on the movement, the number of believers increased steadily. Members included politicians, military men, and celebrities. In 1944, foreseeing the coming devastation of air raids on Tokyo, Okada bought two summer villas—Shinsen-sō, in Hakone, Kanagawa Prefecture, purchased from the politician Fujiyama Aiichirō, and Tōzan-sō, in Atami, Shizuoka Prefecture, purchased from Yamashita Kamesaburō, founder of Yamashita Steamship Co.—and left Tokyo. After the war these properties became the twin sacred grounds (headquarters) of the sect and the base for further expansion.

In 1947 Okada reorganized Dai Nihon Kenkō Kyōkai as Nihon Kannon

Kyōdan (Japan Kannon Church). In 1948 he established a separate group called Nihon Miroku Kyō (Japan Miroku Church), which attracted attention as a religion that could "cure any illness, with spiritual energy from the palm of the hand" at a time of shortages of medicines. It had over one hundred thousand followers eighteen months after its establishment, and by the end of 1949 the number had grown to three hundred thousand.

Okada rejected modern medicine and its reliance on drugs. A collection of his essays, the *Goshin Sho* (Divine Writings), was published in two volumes, one on religion (1953) and the other on art and society (1955). Medical and other matters are treated in the *Igaku Kankei Rombun Shū* (Writings on Medicine), and the *Jōreihō Kōza*, a ten-volume collection of lectures on *jōrei* therapy has also been published.

Okada taught that every person is constituted of a physical being and a spiritual being. The mind is at the center of the spiritual being, and the soul is at the center of the mind. The workings of the spirit, the mind, and the soul give rise to will and thought, and these govern the physical being. Since the spiritual being is primary and the physical being is secondary, clouds on the spirit cause illness. Spiritual clouds are essentially poison. Poisons, or spiritual clouds, can be inherited from ancestors (natal toxins) or absorbed after birth (acquired toxins). If a medicine, which is itself a toxin, is taken in an attempt to cure an illness, it may give temporary relief, but eventually it will accumulate in the body and make the illness worse. Okada's method of healing was to remove those poisons from the body and dispel spiritual clouds through *jōrei* therapy. He applied the same principle to agriculture, in what he called Nature Farming, rejecting the use of chemical fertilizers as poisons and promoting the use of *jōrei* to enhance crop growth.

In the postwar period, many people afflicted with illness were attracted to Okada's medical and agricultural ideas. At the same time, his methods raised serious ethical questions when a follower died after refusing conventional medical treatment. As a result, he was subjected to growing criticism from journalists. In August 1949 his premises were searched on suspicion that he was concealing gold and diamonds.

In February 1950 Nihon Kannon Kyōdan and Nihon Miroku Kyō were merged to establish Sekai Kyūsei Kyō as a religious corporation. In May that year, Sekai Kyūsei Kyō was accused of bribery and renovating a building without a construction permit, and Okada was imprisoned while being investigated. The incident caused an enormous public outcry. The religion did its best to avert criticism by reorganizing, relieving Okada of his position as head, and instituting a system of ministers. Since the founder's death, Sekai Kyūsei Kyō has continued its efforts to create a "paradise on earth," where no disease, poverty, or strife can arise.

Questionable Activities

A number of sects with strange names and teachings came into being in the early postwar period. For example, Denshinkyō (Electricity God Religion) revered Tenchi Denki no Ōkami (the God of Electricity) and Thomas Edison in gratitude for the blessings of electricity. Kanzebokyō (Compassionate Mother Religion) was founded by a former prostitute. Media criticism of fraudulent sects reached a peak with the emergence of Kōdō Chikyō (Imperial Way of Peace Religion), an association of businesses whose only aim was profit.

Registered as a religious corporation, Kōdō Chikyō had a grandiloquently named headquarters administered by its founder, Kibune Haruyoshi, and an impressive hierarchy—archbishop, bishop, superintendent of Shintō affairs, doctor of divinity, head missionary, and chief priest. At the time of its registration in 1946, it declared that it had three facilities, three instructors, and sixty-three hundred followers. When it began activities in earnest the following year, a number of questionable incidents that occurred in a short time in various parts of the nation made it widely known.

Kōdō Chikyō taught that life itself is religion. Accordingly, a restaurant, for example, could be called a church; commerce would be missionary activity; customers would be followers; the filling of empty stomachs in a time of food shortages would be salvation; and money received in payment of bills would be offerings. Because a religious corporation's income earned through its specified religious activity was tax-exempt, small businesses in areas like Shizuoka Prefecture, Aichi Prefecture, Kanagawa Prefecture, Tokyo, and Chiba Prefecture were soon vying for affiliation with Kōdō Chikyō. A serious social problem had obviously arisen with this exploitation of a loophole in the Religious Corporations Ordinance.

In 1948 a member of Kōdō Chikyō arrested for selling controlled foodstuffs on the black market in Kisarazu, Chiba Prefecture, accused the authorities of violating his freedom of religious belief. He was tried, found guilty, and punished with confiscation of the foodstuffs and a fine. Newspapers, magazines, and radio journalists made much of similar incidents, and public criticism increased. Kōdō Chikyō quickly faded from the scene. In April 1951 the Religious Corporations Law was enacted. Since it required not only registration but also certification, dubious religious organizations soon disappeared.

Striving for Legitimacy

Extreme methods of propagation also caused problems. The media raised a great outcry over such incidents as an ill person who was prevented from seeing a doctor and was subjected to exorcism and trampled to death as a victim of "possession by a fox." The media branded new religious movements as fraudulent, evil sects that arrested the development of a healthy society and fostered fanaticism. "New religion" became a synonym for fanaticism. Harsh public criticism continued as instances of misconduct made the headlines, for example, the excesses of Makoto Kyō-dan (now named Shinnyoen) in the summer of 1950 and the Reiyūkai Affair, consisting of a number of incidents between 1949, when Reiyūkai was accused of tax evasion, and 1953, when its president, Kotani Kimi (1901–71), was arrested on suspicion of embezzling donations to a community-chest fund and dealing in American dollars on the black market.

In 1956 Risshō Kōsei-kai came under suspicion for illegal land acquisition, and the influential daily newspaper *Yomiuri Shimbun* mounted a campaign against the organization unprecedented in its vigor and relentlessness. Risshō Kōsei-kai held firmly to its religious convictions, resisting what it called persecution, and retaliated by organizing a boycott of the newspaper. Risshō Kōsei-kai's ability to ward off attacks and criticism contributed to its growth into a major force among the new religious organizations.

Despite the harsh, sometimes vitriolic, attacks of the press and public criticism, by the autumn of 1951 twenty-four of the new religious organizations—including PL [Perfect Liberty] Kyōdan, Risshō Kōsei-kai, Sekai Kyūsei Kyō, and Seichō no Ie—had formed the Shin Nihon Shūkyō Dantai Rengō Kai (Union of New Religious Organizations of Japan), popularly called Shinshūren. In April the following year, the Shinshūren applied for formal affiliation with the Nihon Shūkyō Remmei (Japan Religions League), consisting of the Jinja Honchō (Association of Shintō Shrines), Kyōha Shintō Rengō Kai (Association of Shintō Sects), Zen Nihon Bukkyō Kai (All Japan Federation of Buddhist Sects), and Nihon Kirisutokyō Rengō Kai (Christian Liaison Committee in Japan). The Nihon Shūkyō Remmei, an association to protect mutual interests, served as a liaison organization for negotiations with government departments and the occupation authorities.

Deluged by the flood of public and media criticism, the new religions gradually began compiling the words of their founders and systematizing their doctrines, organizing themselves for further growth. From the outset, however, both Reiyūkai and Sōka Gakkai declined to join the Shinshūren, and Sekai Kyūsei Kyō, Seichō no Ie, and others later withdrew from it. Nevertheless, the Shinshūren is still an influential federation today, with eighty-six members.

Although the formation of the Shinshūren and its affiliation with the Nihon Shūkyō Remmei put the new religious organizations on an equal footing with the established religions, the established religions' antipathy toward and derision of the new religions did not end.

Worldly Benefits

In times of social change, people turn to religion for worldly benefits gained through direct contact with the divine. Almost all the founders of the new religions were known for their shamanic qualities, and people gathered around them in expectation of witnessing and sharing in their miraculous virtue. The founder of Sekai Kyūsei Kyō, Okada Mokichi, explained that poverty, conflict, and disease motivated people to join his sect. The new religions stated explicitly that they could offer prosperity, love, harmony, and health.

The religious rationale for gaining worldly benefits through the intervention of shamans is that calamity and disaster emanate from the spiritual realm. Underpinning that faith is the belief in ancestral spirits and the simple shamanism with which most Japanese are brought up. A good example of a religion incorporating all these beliefs is Reiyūkai, which is based on the Lotus Sutra. Seventy percent of the new religions were in fact based on the Lotus Sutra. More than a dozen of those that developed rapidly after World War II either were direct offshoots of Reiyūkai or were influenced by it. Those that broke away from it before the war include Nippon Keishin Sūso Jishūdan, Reishō-kai (later Sangai Kyōdan), Kōdō Kyōdan, Dai Nippon Risshō Kōsei-kai (now Risshō Kōsei-kai), and Shion-kai; among those that became independent after the war are Hakuai Dōshi-kai Kyōdan, Myōchi-kai Kyōdan, Bussho Gonen-kai Kyōdan, Hosshi-kai

Kyōdan, Myōhō-kyō, Seigi-kai Kyōdan, Myōdō-kai Kyōdan, Daiei-kai Kyōdan, and Daiji-kai.

The word "*reiyū*" in the name Reiyūkai refers to the links between the spirit of an individual and all the spirits of the three realms (desire, form, and formlessness). The cause of human unhappiness is traced directly to the ancestors, or rather to their restless spirits. Reiyūkai teaches veneration of the spirits of the universe and of the ancestors as the means of severing the causal connections between unhappy spirits and human suffering.

In his commentary on the Lotus Sutra Nishida Toshizō (1849–1918), the leader of Bussho Gonen-kai, interpreted the phrase *bussho gonen* (the buddhas watch over and keep in mind) as veneration and worship of the ancestral spirits and the spirits of the universe. The same thinking influenced Reiyūkai: a scroll bearing the characters for *reigan* (divine protection), the general posthumous name of the myriad spirits related to an individual's spirit, is dedicated at the believer's home altar and venerated by chanting the sacred title of the Lotus Sutra. The link between an individual's spirit and the myriad spirits implies that all wishes can be gratified by giving a religious name to the object of desire and venerating it. For example, a follower who wants to sell land at a high price gives the land a religious name and venerates it.

Similarly, the Tendai-derived Nempō Shinkyō teaches veneration of the *kami* and buddhas as the first of its "Five Holy Lessons." At the headquarters of Seichō no Ie a sect with no ties to Buddhism, Shintō, or Christianity that the Japanese government classifies among "other religions"—a scroll called the Spirit of Truth is enshrined in a receptacle before a scroll on which is inscribed the word "Truth." On the Spirit of Truth scroll are recorded the names and birth dates of the organization's leaders, who are called the Bodhisattva Holy Messengers. The president and members chant the "verse in praise of the Bodhisattva Holy Messengers" and pray for purification. Rites are also performed by groups of members to pray for the repose of the spirits of ancestors and deceased friends.

Ancestor Worship in Japan

Surveys conducted every five years since 1953 by the Ministry of Education's Institute of Statistical Mathematics support the contention that an emphasis on veneration based on ancestor worship has the power to attract believers. The first survey showed that approximately one in three Japanese was affiliated with a religion, principally Buddhism, and of these, 66 percent thought that the teachings of all religions were virtually the same. In response to the question "Do you revere your ancestors?," 77 percent replied yes and only 5 percent no. This suggests that ancestor worship is deeply rooted in the Japanese psyche.

Although in the past the ancestors were believed to mediate only within the family, a unique religious interpretation has emerged: the ancestors mediate with the individual and, through the individual, with the myriad spirits of the universe. With its focus on the causal relationship between the origin of suffering and the ancestral spirits, this interpretation has much in common with eighth- and ninth-century ideas about vengeful spirits. The established religions tended to concentrate on prayer for the repose of spirits (the function of *ekōji*, or memorial temples), and prayer for worldly benefits (the function of *kitōji*, or prayer temples) fell by the wayside. But the new religions combined the two functions, thus marking a new departure in the incorporation of the spiritual into everyday life.

The new religions' ultimate goal is to create an ideal realm on earth in which society is reformed and human beings make a fresh start as the mind of the individual is restored to its original purity. Tenshō Kōtai Jingūkyō (with its "through the salvation of the maggot comes the building of the country of the *kami*"), Sekai Kyūsei Kyō (with its aim to establish a "paradise on earth" free of disease, poverty, and strife), and Sōka Gakkai (with its goal of an ideal society free of distinction between the secular and the religious) are typical of the new religions in their determination to sweep away religion's negative image and emphasize its positive aspects.

Complex, Eclectic Doctrines

The various doctrinal strands noted above originate in folk beliefs deeply embedded in the fabric of Japanese culture. Belief in miracles and the efficacy of spiritual experience (that is, emphasis on human, worldly benefits), belief in vengeful spirits connected with ancestor worship, and belief in an "ideal community" (that is, the desire to build an earthly paradise) have combined, together with the borrowing and syncretizing of doctrines from the established sects, to contribute to eclectic beliefs. Most typical of such eclecticism and syncretism are the "other religions," those that are not considered offshoots of Buddhism, Shintō, or Christianity.

Seichō no Ie, for example, emerged from Ōmoto and developed as an ethically and socially oriented organization combining elements of all three of these religions. Moral training is a key element in its doctrines. Ekidō-kai and Nihon Ehoba [Jehovah] Kyōdan, which seek to improve fate, and Makoto no Michi, a moral-training organization derived from Shinrei Kenkyū-kai, all emphasize counseling and psychotherapy rather than religiosity. Seikōkyō, another sect that identifies itself as a religion but strongly emphasizes moral training, worships Makoto Ōkami, the companion deities Sanimasu Ōkami and Manimasu Ōkami, the world's five great sages (Zoroaster, Śākyamuni, Confucius, Jesus, and Muhammad), and Prince Shōtoku as emanations of the universal and ultimate god. Seikōkyō seeks to understand the true existence of the rules of causality, to elevate the human spirit, and to encourage "true" living based on daily gratitude.

All the new religions propagated by disseminating such eclectic doctrines. Since they focus on the problems of this world rather than the next, the new religions have concentrated on helping people lead worthwhile lives and on laying down rules for living. In many of the new religions, rules for living are scripture, for instance, the "Right Practice" of Reiyūkai; the "Five Holy Lessons," the "Nine Vows," and the "Counting Song" of Nempō Shinkyō; the "Founder's Admonitions" of Benten-shū; the "Lessons and Precepts for Members" of Ennōkyō; the "Essentials of Practice for Members" of Seichō no Ie, and the twenty-one "Rules for Faith and Life" of PL Kyōdan. Because such rules of conduct based on secular ethics chart a purpose in life, the new religions could attract believers from all walks of life.

Lay Participation

One characteristic of the new religions is lay participation in functions that are the domain of the clergy in established religions. While the established religions propagate via a vertical hierarchy, using a professional priesthood to perform ritual and preach, the new religions consider every member to be both a missionary and a priest. The Buddhist-influenced new religions tend to use small groups, which many call *hōza* (literally, Dharma circle), as the core of their activity.

The typical *hōza* is a circle of four to ten people who discuss the various problems and trials they face in daily life, opening their hearts and confessing all to the others. Talking about their problems in a *hōza* relieves their stress. The *hōza* leader sympathizes with the participants' troubles and analyzes and interprets them in the light of the Buddha's teachings, saying that participants' suffering will end if the sect's guidelines are followed. By baring their souls and sharing their problems, participants come to feel others' sufferings as their own. As a result, a strong group solidarity develops.

In those who were in the depths of despair and ready to clutch at any straw, the joy of salvation (or worldly benefit) arouses a sense of mission as they begin to feel the urge to share their joy with others. Membership grows as this broad-based missionary effort wins more and more believers. Propagation relies more on creating active small groups than on approaching people with a specific religious message. Consequently, doctrine is sometimes sacrificed to recruitment. The doctrinal message is often reduced to a sense of purpose and fellowship among members, which is to be expressed by further increasing the group's membership.

Establishing a Foundation

A final pattern is discerned in the nature of membership. Whereas the established religions have a stable membership, the new religions are still in the process of building a firm foundation. Parents' membership at a particular temple or shrine is passed on to children at birth. Infants automatically become parishioners of their local shrine and inherit their family's temple affiliation. The established religions are those to which commitment is made at birth. The new religions, on the other hand, are still building up their membership, recruiting people who decide to accept the founder's teachings.

The new religions that are growing with the help of members themselves are doing so in the context of the Japanese culture and tradition from which they emerged. Many of their elements are closely connected with the prewar family system. For example, although the new religions stress the importance of individual awakening to faith, members are registered together with their families, not as individuals. Shinnyoen calls its headquarters in Tachikawa, northern Tokyo, Oyasono (The Parents' Garden), and its founder and its leader are called "the two parents." Terminology employed by a large number of the new religions also stresses the family, for example, such words as *michibiki oya* (the "parent" in the faith, who offers religious guidance), *michibiki ko* (the "child" in the faith, who receives guidance), and *tedori* (the attention given by members leading others to the faith).

One doctrinal feature of the new religions, reverence for ancestors, is redolent of the traditions of the old agricultural communities. Though the new religions developed in the cities, most of their founders came from farming villages. The practice of *hōza*, derived from the community life of the countryside, is very popular among city dwellers, especially women. The new religions should be seen as a crystallization of the religious energy that lies at the very heart of the Japanese cultural and religious tradition.

MILESTONES IN THE DEVELOPMENT OF THE NEW RELIGIONS

Social Change and the Rise of New Religions

In modern times as in ages past, the birth and development of new popular cults in Japan have reflected social anxiety in periods of change. The last years of the Tokugawa shogunate, in the mid-nineteenth century, were a period of radical change, as Japan emerged from feudalism into the modern world. In the eighteenth century increased production through manual labor had contributed to growth in the number of wealthy merchants in the cities and to continuation of the social stratification of the farming population. On the whole, the standard of living rose and farmers accumulated profits, which enabled them to turn to manufacturing.

Middle- and upper-class landowners grew wealthy through manufacturing and became landed merchants. But farmers with only small holdings found themselves constantly short of ready cash, which they came to need as an infant market economy took root in the countryside. Trying to remedy their predicament, they mortgaged their land or sent family members into service. Despite their efforts, they often lost their land and became tenant farmers. Prosperous farmers who bought up the land became even wealthier, and clear class differences emerged in farming communities. Impoverished farmers, hard hit by heavy taxes and worn down by natural calamities and famine, gave vent to their anger in peasant uprisings.

As the shogunate continued to disintegrate, poor farmers found relief in the promises of world renewal and cures for illnesses made by a number of new religions. Typical of those promising such worldly benefits were two based on popular Shintō beliefs: Tenrikyō, found by Nakayama Miki in 1838, and Konkōkyō, begun by Kawate Bunjirō in 1859. Both religions offered emotional support to people buffeted by social unrest and won many converts. These religions aimed to establish an earthly paradise where relief from the sufferings of everyday existence would be found.

The Meiji Restoration of 1868 betrayed those who hoped to find true renewal in it. The new government's land-tax reform and education and conscription systems only increased people's burdens. Though popular protest found some expression in the Popular Rights Movement, the majority of people—the lower classes and the poor—were neglected by both the democratic ideology and the government-sponsored movement to achieve a civilization and enlightenment based closely on the European model.

One sect that attracted those ignored by the Meiji government was Maruyamakyō, which was based on the ethics of a traditional, feudal, agricultural society and advocated a world renewal that was the very opposite of the changes advocated by the government. The founder of Maruyamakyō, Itō Rokurōbei (1829–94), was born in Noborito, Kanagawa Prefecture, the son of a farming family that had for generations belonged to one of the Fuji Kō pilgrim associations. He married into the Itō family and became a Fuji Kō *sendatsu,* or pilgrim guide. In 1870, when his wife fell seriously ill, he claimed to have received a divine revelation; and in 1873 he set himself up as the leader of an independent sect, managing to avoid the control of the authorities.

When Shishino Nakaba (1844–84), the chief priest of Sengen Shrine in Fujinomiya, Shizuoka Prefecture, organized a large number of local Fuji Kō in 1875 as the Fuji Issan Kyōkai (Mount Fuji Association; renamed Fusōkyō in 1882), Itō affiliated his sect with the association. With its teachings of harmony and reverence for "the great ancestor deity," Itō's sect attracted a large following. When the police forced a group of Maruyamakyō adherents in Shizuoka Prefecture to disband in 1885 for advocating world renewal and peace, Maruyamakyō separated from Fusōkyō and accepted the supervision of Shintō Honkyoku, which was renamed Shintō Taikyō in 1940. At one point Maruyamakyō rivaled Tenrikyō in popularity, but it went into rapid decline.

Clearly, the establishment and development of new religions is related to economic and social unrest. In his book *Nihon Hyakunen no Shūkyō* (A

Hundred Years of Japanese Religion; 1966), Murakami Shigeyoshi divides the prewar history of popular religion into three main periods.

The first period is from around the 1840s to the 1890s, when such religions as Tenrikyō and Konkōkyō arose. The background to this period was the growing poverty of the poorer farmers and the difficulties that merchants and factory workers faced as a result of the social changes that preceded and followed the Meiji Restoration of 1868.

The second period is from around 1900 to the early 1920s. During this time, Japanese capitalism was being established and imperialism was becoming entrenched as a result of the industrial revolution, and poverty was widespread in both cities and villages, as were unrest and bankruptcy among the middle and lower classes. Ōmoto, Shintō Tokumitsukyō (the forerunner of Hito no Michi Kyōdan), and Nihonzan Myōhō-ji (which had been established in 1917, under Fujii Nittatsu), arose in these conditions, and Tenrikyō's influence expanded further.

The third period is the late 1920s and the 1930s, which saw the rise of Reiyūkai, Kokuchū-kai, and Seichō no Ie and further growth for Tenrikyō, Ōmoto, and Hito no Michi Kyōdan. This was an era of economic crisis, chronic depression, and panic resulting from basic inequities in Japanese capitalism.

Ōmoto

Ōmoto—the parent of such offshoots as Seichō no Ie, Sekai Kyūsei Kyō, Shintō Tenkōkyō, Jiukyō, Ananaikyō, and Makoto no Michi—was established in 1892, two years before the outbreak of the first Sino-Japanese War. The founder, Deguchi Nao (1837–1918), experienced divine possession when two of her daughters became mentally ill, one in 1890 and the other in 1891. In 1892, while possessed, she began writing her *Fudesaki*, in which she predicted the reconstruction and transformation of the world through the *kami* Konjin of the northeast.

Ōmoto resembled the popular-Shintō sects Konkōkyō and Tenrikyō in its advocacy of worldly benefits, practice of prophecy, and mass divine possession. Its prophecy of the attainment of the realm of Miroku Buddha (Maitreya, the buddha of the future) through reconstruction and transformation suggests that it is also an heir of those groups that, under the influence of the sixth Fuji Kō patriarch, Jikigyō Miroku (1671–1733), advocate the coming of Miroku's ideal world in the age of the Decay of the Law. With its doctrine of world renewal as restoration of the ideal agricultural community of the past—in opposition to the "new" culture of the Meiji period—Ōmoto shared the cultural tradition of Maruyamakyō.

Ōmoto came into being just three years after the promulgation of the Meiji Constitution, two years after the Imperial Rescript on Education, and two years before the outbreak of the first Sino-Japanese War. This was a critical period in the growth of Japanese imperialism and its ideological foundation of reverence for the emperor. The circumstances of Ōmoto's founding were very different from those of religions like Tenrikyō. Tenrikyō was based on popular Shintō, but to legalize its work, in 1880 it took the name Tenrin'ō Kōsha and declared itself a pietistic Buddhist association. It soon began to concentrate on revising its doctrine in order to win acceptance from State Shintō. In 1908 it gained official recognition and independence as one of the sects of Sectarian Shintō.

Deguchi Nao became a missionary for Konkōkyō (then known as Shintō Honkyoku Konkō Kyōkai), which had received official recognition in 1894. Besides legitimate propagation, she engaged in faith healing but left Konkōkyō after a dispute in 1897. In 1899 she invited Ueda Kisaburō (1871–1948), an Inari Kōsha missionary and a faith healer of high repute, to marry her daughter Sumi (1883–1952) and be adopted into the Deguchi family. In the same year she affiliated her sect, then called Kimmei Reigakkai, with Inari Kōsha. The articles of association stated that the group "esteemed the perfect imperial house and respectfully obeyed imperial commands," underscoring Nao's intention to base its teachings on the imperial system of that time.

The sect grew rapidly in the first decade of the twentieth century and rivaled Tenrikyō in size. In 1909 a sanctuary was completed in Ayabe, in western Kyoto Prefecture, but police harassment continued, and the sect affiliated itself with authorized religions, first Ontakekyō and then Taiseikyō and Izumo Ōyashirokyō in turn. In 1916 it changed its name to Kōdō Ōmoto (Great Fundamentals of the Imperial Way). After Nao's death in 1918 her daughter Sumi became the sect's second spiritual head, and her husband, now known as Deguchi Onisaburō, played a central role in the organization. In 1921, in what is known as the First Ōmoto Suppression, Ōmoto was charged with lèse-majesté and violation of the press laws by the authorities, who feared a popular uprising of people united by the rice riots that occurred in the panic after World War I. Nao's grave was ordered destroyed because it resembled an imperial tomb, and the sect's main facilities were demolished.

In the mid-1920s Onisaburō supported the Esperanto Propaganda Association and led the sect to renewed and unprecedented growth. Membership swelled when it was made public that Nao's *Fudesaki* had predicted the devastating Tokyo Earthquake of 1923. Newly released from prison, Onisaburō went to Mongolia in 1924 to pursue his plan to create an ideal religious state there. He was imprisoned again on returning to Japan, but his adventure had encouraged Japanese ambitions to conquer the Asian mainland, and his activities indirectly bolstered the military. When he was released after concerted efforts by Ōmoto to post bail, he devoted himself to creating a sacred center in Kameoka, Kyoto Prefecture, and to realizing his concept of a world federation of religions. Simultaneously with the inauguration of the World Religious Federated Association in Peking in 1925, he established the Jinrui Aizen-kai (Benevolence for Humankind Association). As a result, Ōmoto became better known outside Japan.

In December 1935—just two months before the February 26th Incident, an attempted coup d'état led by right-wing army officers in which several cabinet members were assassinated—amid an atmosphere of increasing fascism fed by State Shintō, Ōmoto was suppressed a second time by the authorities, who wanted to sever any connection between the right wing and revolutionary army elements. Charged with lèse-majesté and violations of the Peace Preservation Law, Ōmoto was dissolved and its facilities at Ayabe and Kameoka razed. Building materials for reconstruction were denied it. Onisaburō was again imprisoned, but he was released on bail in 1942. He died in despair in 1948.

Prewar Suppression of New Religions

Ōmoto did not reject the emperor system, and it had an auxiliary role in the State Shintō organization. Nevertheless, it was persecuted because it advocated a *kami* outside the imperial religious authority as the agent of the reconstructed and transformed world of Miroku. After the Second Ōmoto Suppression in 1935, all the new religions were classified as pseudo-religions (*ruiji shūkyō*) and subjected to increasing suppression.

In 1937 Hito no Michi Kyōdan, the predecessor of the present PL Kyōdan, was suppressed and dissolved for lèse-majesté and violation of the Peace Preservation Law. The sect had been founded in 1925 by Miki Tokuharu (1871–1938), a former Ōbaku Zen priest from Matsuyama, on Shikoku. Tokuharu, who went bankrupt and reverted to lay status, led an itinerant life for a time before being cured of chronic asthma by the faith healer Kanada Tokumitsu (1863–1919) and becoming a teacher in Kanada's sect, Shintō Tokumitsukyō. This group revered the Imperial Rescript on Education as a sacred text and practiced a magical rite called *ofurikae*, a method of faith healing based on the belief that the founder of a cult could absorb followers' illnesses.

After Kanada's death, Miki claimed to have received a divine revelation and in 1924 reestablished the cult as Jindō [Hito no Michi] Tokumitsukyō. The following year it received government recognition as an affiliate of Ontakekyō, and it later affiliated with Fusōkyō. The sect continued to teach the doctrines and techniques of Tokumitsukyō: reverence for the Imperial Rescript on Education, practice of *ofurikae*, practical religious training based on the unity of the human and the divine, and marital harmony. It grew rapidly, attracting the disaffected urban middle class in particular. Ironically, Hito no Michi's reverence for the Imperial Rescript became a pretext for government suppression. The sect's worship of the sun itself as Amaterasu Ōmikami was based on a folk belief in the sun as an agricultural deity. This was heresy to State Shintō, and in 1937 Hito no Michi, like Ōmoto, was accused of lèse-majesté and dissolved.

The Shinkō Bukkyō Seinen Dōmei (New Buddhist Youth Alliance), which had been established by Senoo Girō (1889–1961) and advocated a Buddhist revolution based on socialist principles, and Kirisutokyō Gakusei Shakai Undō (Student Christian Movement) were also suppressed in 1937. The following year Hommichi (then known as Tenri Kenkyūkai), a subsect of Tenrikyō, suffered its second suppression.

The founder of Hommichi, Ōnishi Aijirō (1881–1958), considered himself a living *kami* identical to the *kanrodai* of Tenrikyō. He abridged and amended his *Kenkyū Shiryō* (1926), the pamphlet setting out the aims of Hommichi that had been the object of the first suppression, in 1928, and, retitling it "Inspiration for Patriotic Warriors," made it the sixth work in the *Shoshin*, a collection of his pastoral letters published in 1938. He launched a movement to distribute the *Shoshin*. Fearful of the movement's influence, the government arrested Ōnishi and 373 of his followers in 1938, and the Home Ministry ordered the sect, then calling itself Tenri Hommichi, dissolved.

At the time of the 1928 suppression, Hommichi used the courtroom as a forum for denial of the emperor's divinity. After being convicted, Ōnishi appealed to the high court. Since the authorities did not want to dispute the emperor's divinity in court, they subjected Ōnishi to a psychiatric examination and had him acquitted by reason of insanity. At the time of the second suppression, in 1938, the authorities took Ōnishi and his followers into custody as political offenders but eventually released them after the war.

When the Religious Organizations Law went into effect, in 1940, government control over religions was intensified. Even some of the established religions were suppressed. The Jōdo Shin sect came under suspicion for lack of enthusiasm in its veneration of the Shintō deities, and the Nichiren sect was accused of disrespect toward Amaterasu Ōmikami because it considered her merely one of thirty-three guardian deities of the Lotus Sutra. The Kyūseigun (Salvation Army) and the Nihon Seikōkai (Anglican Episcopal Church) were also subjected to interference and suppression.

With the exception of Seichō no Ie and Reiyūkai, the new religions found their activities severely restricted and could do little but wait out the war. Seichō no Ie was founded by Taniguchi Masaharu (1893–1985). He had dropped out of Waseda University and, while working as a manual laborer, sought spiritual peace through Ōmoto and Ittōen, which had been founded in 1904 by Nishida Tenkō (1872–1968). However, Taniguchi was dissatisfied until 1929, when he claimed to have received divine instructions to "learn the truth of life." The following year he established his sect and began publishing prolifically, including the magazine *Seichō no Ie* (The House of Growth) and the first of the forty volumes of his *Seimei no Jissō* (The Truth of Life; 1932–67). Many joined the sect in the belief that their illnesses would be cured if they merely read Taniguchi's works. The sect's name was changed to Kyōke Dantai [Propagating Organization] Seichō no Ie in 1935 and to Shūkyō Kessha [Religious Association] Seichō no Ie Kyōdan in 1940. An army lieutenant-general was appointed chairman, and the sect glorified the war.

Reiyūkai had been organized in 1925 by Kubo Kakutarō (1892–1944) and his sister-in-law Kotani Kimi (1901–71). Its main doctrine—that the esoteric teaching of the Lotus Sutra is ancestor veneration—was formulated in 1930. Against the background of the Mukden Incident of 1931 and the rising tide of militarism in the 1930s, Reiyūkai established a governing board that was headed by Baron Nagayama Taketoshi and included Kubo as chairman and Kotani as honorary president. Faced with collapse because of the growing number of secessions by groups of members, Reiyūkai consolidated its organization and systematized its doctrine.

As persecution of the pseudoreligions became more severe, Reiyūkai invited Murakumo Nichiei to become its leader in 1937. Murakumo had been born into the noble Sengoku family, with whom Kubo Kakutarō had close connections, and had been adopted by the family of Prince Kujō. She had previously been the chief priest of Zuiryū-ji, an imperially connected Nichiren-sect temple in Kyoto. By enlisting well-connected supporters, and by praising the nation as a family, Reiyūkai managed to divert the attention of the authorities. Avoiding suppression, it attracted growing numbers of adherents.

Sōka Gakkai (Value-Creating Society), now a very large organization, was founded in 1930 as Sōka Kyōiku Gakkai (Value-Creating Education Society) by Makiguchi Tsunesabrō (1871–1944), a former elementary-school teacher and principal, and Toda Jōsei (1900–1958), a former elementary-school teacher. Makiguchi's theory of "value creation" is recorded in the second volume of his four-volume work *Sōka Kyōikugaku Taikei* (The System of Value-Creating Pedagogy; 1930–34), which he published with Toda's help. According to Makiguchi, the object of human life is happiness, that is, the attainment and creation of value. He defined the three greatest values as goodness, beauty, and gain and their antitheses as evil, ugliness, and loss. A value was to be judged by the extent of its practical and useful benefits.

Makiguchi had at that time already experienced the aggressive conversion methods of Nichiren Shōshū (True Nichiren sect) and undergone a religious awakening. When he was actively recruiting Sōka Kyōiku Gakkai members in 1936, he stipulated that prospective members be supporters of Nichiren Shōshū, the extreme sect of the Nichiren stream that had been known as the Fuji school until 1913 (founded by Nikkō [1246–1333], its headquarters are at Taiseki-ji in Fujinomiya, Shizuoka Prefecture). Makiguchi relied on Nichiren Shōshū teachings in trying to distinguish between relative and absolute values.

Sōka Kyōiku Gakkai was suppressed in 1943 because Nichiren Shōshū refused to merge with the Nichiren sect under the provisions of the Religious Organizations Law, because Sōka Kyōiku Gakkai laid too much emphasis on Nichiren's *Risshō Ankoku Ron* (On Establishing the Correct Teaching and Pacifying the Nation), and because Sōka Kyōiku Gakkai members refused to venerate the talismans from Ise Shrine that had been distributed to all households in the nation. Of those arrested for violating the Peace Preservation Law and for disrespect toward Shintō shrines, Makiguchi died the following year in prison, and all others except Toda and Yajima Shūhei recanted and were released. That was the end of Sōka Kyōiku Gakkai. Ironically, it was Toda's reading of Nichiren Shōshū works while in prison that prepared him for the organization's revival as Sōka Gakkai after the war.

Separation of Religion and the State

The postwar occupation policy on religion of the Supreme Commander for the Allied Powers (SCAP) was based on the Potsdam Declaration, which asserted that freedom of religion is a fundamental human right. All organizations and movements of an extreme nationalistic or militaristic character were banned, and freedom of religion was guaranteed. On October 4, 1945, shortly after the occupation began, SCAP authorities issued a directive requiring the Japanese government to "abrogate and immediately suspend all provisions of all laws, decrees, orders, ordinances, and regulations which: establish or maintain restrictions on freedom . . . of religion" and "by their terms or their application, operate unequally in favor of or against any person by reason of . . . creed." The Peace Preservation Law and the Religious Organizations Law, which abused the limitations set out in Article 28 of the Meiji Constitution and had been used to persecute many people, were also abrogated; and all those who had been imprisoned for their religious beliefs were released by October 15.

Various new religions came into existence immediately after the war, but they were ridiculed by the press and disdained by the public. Those with the most extraordinary growth were Reiyukai and Rissho Kosei-kai, both of which were in the Nichiren stream and stressed ancestor veneration. Reiyūkai, whose leader, Kubo Kakutarō, had died in 1944, was aided by the facts that it had evaded suppression and its organization had been left intact. Members who had been evacuated from Tokyo had taken its teachings to rural areas. Under the forceful leadership of Kotani Kimi, Reiyūkai membership grew to seven hundred thousand households, about two million individuals. It was the largest of the new religions.

Risshō Kōsei-kai was founded in Tokyo in 1938 by Niwano Nikkyō (1906–99) and Naganuma Myōkō (1889–1957), who broke away from Reiyūkai. Meetings of the organization, which had thirty-eight members in the beginning, were held above Niwano's milk shop. The combination of the medium Naganuma and the organizer and systematizer of doctrine Niwano was felicitous. They traveled about the town on Niwano's bicycle, Naganuma perched on the carrier behind him, and their slow but sure proselytization brought their prewar membership to eight hundred and ten. The number expanded rapidly after the war and in 1952 stood at a

million. The early Risshō Kōsei-kai teachings were a skillful blend of fa-
talistic philosophy (based on various forms of divination) and the doctrine
of the Lotus Sutra.

Deguchi Onisaburō of Ōmoto was released from prison at the end of
the war, but old age prevented him from actively directing the sect's revival. His son-in-law, Deguchi Isao, was central in its rebirth under the
name Aizen'en. The sect's name was later changed back to Ōmoto.

Under its second leader, Miki Tokuchika (1900–1983), Hito no Michi
reassembled former members and reemerged with a new image provided
by the name PL [Perfect Liberty] Kyōdan. Although PL Kyōdan was on
the way to becoming a large organization, it was weakened by severe public
criticism of its cooperation with the militarists during the war. Nevertheless, it could draw on reserves of energy that it had accumulated during
the war and expanded its propagation efforts.

Thus at the end of the war all the new religions stood at the same
starting line in the race to acquire members as they entered into a period
of growth.

Large Organizations

The year 1951 marks the beginning of the second phase in the growth of
the new religions, which had consolidated their organizations and were in
a position to expand. In 1951 the Religious Corporations Ordinance was
superseded by the Religious Corporations Law, which required organizations to obtain certification from the relevant authorities to incorporate
and register a new religion. Enactment of the new law was fateful for the
hundreds of religious groups that had sprung up after the war. The 1999
edition of the *Shūkyō Nenkan* (Religious Yearbook), compiled by the Ministry
of Education's Agency for Cultural Affairs, lists 386 registered religions.
This figure clearly reveals that some of the religions established in the period of turmoil after the war went on to become large organizations while
many others were short-lived and soon disappeared.

It was in 1951, too, that Risshō Kōsei-kai, PL Kyōdan, Sekai Kyūsei
Kyō, Seichō no Ie, and others banded together to form the Shinshūren
(Union of New Religious Organizations of Japan). The following year this
organization became formally affiliated with the Nihon Shūkyō Remmei
(Japan Religions League).

The same year also saw steady growth in the facilities of the new religions, despite frequent media attacks and public criticism. Risshō Kōsei-kai, for example, built its second training hall in Tokyo that year; and in 1952 Kōdō Kyōdan completed its main Buddha Hall in Yokohama, Risshō Kōsei-kai its hospital in Tokyo, and Sekai Kyūsei Kyō its Shinsen-kyō sacred grounds and Hakone Museum of Art in Hakone. In 1953 Myōchi-kai Kyōdan, which had seceded from Reiyūkai in 1949, built its main practice hall in Tokyo. In 1954 Seichō no Ie finished its chief meeting hall in Tokyo and its special instruction center in Uji, Kyoto; and in 1955 the Buddhist organization Gedatsukai completed its main training center in Kitamoto, Saitama Prefecture, and PL Kyōdan two halls in its headquarters complex in Tondabayashi, on the outskirts of Osaka.

Sōka Gakkai, the successor to Sōka Kyōiku Gakkai, was still a small, insignificant group in 1951 when Toda Jōsei was inaugurated as its president and proclaimed a major campaign of *shakubuku* (aggressive propagation). By the following year, Sōka Gakkai membership numbered ten thousand households, and it was legally incorporated as an independent religious juridical person. In 1956 it massed seventy thousand members for a rally in the Kansai region and saw three of its political candidates elected to the House of Councilors, the upper chamber of the Diet. Sōka Gakkai's influence on society at large had begun to be felt.

The tide of urbanization and industrialization accompanying Japan's economic recovery in the wake of the outbreak of the Korean War in 1950 contributed to the growth of the new religions. The modernization of production created a need for vast numbers of laborers and led to a population redistribution, from the country to the city: by 1960, 64 percent of the population lived in cities. Around 1946 and 1947 the ratio of rural and urban dwellers had been 7:3; by 1961, it was 3:7. The major influx of new urban dwellers resulted in a large uncommitted population with no religious affiliation. The new religions attracted these people to their folds, and those that attracted the greatest numbers soon grew into large organizations.

Growing Consolidation

By the 1970s the new religions had grown so huge that institutional changes were inevitable. Membership increased rapidly as members themselves recruited more members. As a result, executive boards were formed; the organizations were further systematized; and the personal ties between the founders and their followers diminished. As the new religions became more organized, they found it necessary to maintain and broaden their teachings.

In 1973 Risshō Kōsei-kai polled members between the ages of fifteen and twenty-four on their attitudes toward themselves and society, and their role in society as members of Risshō Kōsei-kai. The survey clearly indicated the shift that had occurred in the new religions. Second- and third-generation members made up 88.8 percent of the total, and 40 percent of the total were nonpracticing—members in name only. Risshō Kōsei-kai was becoming an established religion. New members joined "to train and improve myself spiritually" (54.4 percent), "to be of service to society" (37.1 percent), "to gain peace of mind" (38.5 percent), and "to have friends to confide in" (35.4 percent). These motives are very different from those of earlier first-generation followers, who sought escape from the poverty, disease, and conflict of the unstable postwar period.

The changing times affected all the new religions. A natural development for new religions intent on maintaining their public image as organized religions while responding to change was the adoption of distinctive slogans to establish group goals for their members and guide their behavior. Risshō Kōsei-kai, for example, had separated administration from religious instruction after thoroughly surveying its doctrine in 1961, and declared 1976 to be a year for manifesting the buddha-nature. Such goals took concrete form: visible goals were established and made part of religious training.

In 1957 Sōka Gakkai proclaimed Tokyo a bloc; and in 1961—under its third president, Ikeda Daisaku (b. 1928)—all of Japan was declared a bloc and the Kōmei Seiji Remmei (League for Clean Politics) was founded. This group was reorganized in 1964 as the full-fledged political party Kōmeitō (Clean Government Party). Religion had become politicized.

Through its Brighter Society Movement, Risshō Kōsei-kai made religion a social force. Following the death of Kotani Kimi in February 1971, Reiyūkai concentrated on recruiting young members under its second president, Kubo Tsugunari (b. 1936), who launched an "inner trip" campaign. Shinnyoen, on the other hand, turned increasingly to counseling. The new religions, while trying to maintain their early momentum and meet the needs of followers, were well on the road to becoming established.

23. The Established
Religions Today

EARLY POSTWAR UPHEAVAL

Shintō

Shintō and Buddhism were dealt severe blows during the early postwar period. The Shintō Directive deprived Shinto of its official position and rendered it just one of many religious corporations. In 1956 some eighty thousand of the country's roughly 110,000 shrines organized the Jinja Honchō (Association of Shintō Shrines), an umbrella organization headed by Ise Grand Shrine. Other umbrella organizations include the Jinja Honkyō (organized by more than one hundred shrines in the Kansai region) and the Hokkaidō Jinja Kyōkai (organized by more than seventy shrines in Hokkaido Prefecture). A number of shrines—such as Yasukuni Shrine in Tokyo, Hachiman Shrine in Kamakura, Fushimi Inari Shrine near Kyoto, Sumiyoshi Shrine in Osaka, Ōmiwa Shrine and Kasuga Shrine in Nara, and Kumano Nachi Shrine in Wakayama Prefecture—became independent religious corporations.

In the large cities the wartime destruction of shrines led to paralysis of their functions. The number of worshipers decreased greatly, and the shrines, which previously had been supported by local parishioners and neighborhood associations, found themselves forbidden by the Shintō Directive to accept any but voluntary donations. With the traditional parish system on the verge of collapse, some shrines began to look for new means of supporting themselves, such as conducting weddings and offering courses in traditional Japanese culture for prospective brides.

With the exception of Shintō Shūseiha, Izumo Ōyashirokyō, and Misogi-kyō, the religions that had constituted Sectarian Shintō ended their affiliation or splintered into subsects. With only one or two exceptions, the Shintō sects had made every effort to foster patriotism in their followers by focusing on devotion to the emperor. Many of these sects fell into disorder when they could not adapt their doctrine to the postwar situation. The sects based on folk Shintō—Konkōkyō, Tenrikyō, and Kurozumi-kyō—were free to resume their original activities. On May 1, 1947, Tenrikyō organized a daily volunteer service to clean up bomb damage in the cities. Five thousand believers participated in about sixty cities, a very small number compared with prewar membership figures. Tenrikyō, which had been forced to revise its doctrine to gain legal recognition from the Meiji government, revised its doctrine again, restoring the original content. It was not until after 1949, when the revised doctrine started to become familiar to believers, that Tenrikyō's influence began to grow.

Buddhism

The established Buddhist sects were seriously weakened during the war by the destruction of their temples in the cities and the evacuation of parishioners and immediately after the war by land reform, which redistributed their landholdings. Statistics in the February 1948 *Shūkyō Binran* (Religious Handbook), published by Jiji Tsūshin-sha in Tokyo, indicate that nationwide 4,609 temples had been destroyed by bombs, roughly 6 percent of all the temples in Japan. Compared with the 10 percent of Shintō shrines and 25 percent of Christian churches destroyed, Buddhist losses were light. Yet with destruction concentrated in the cities and with the high rate of dependence on parishioners for income, the evacuation of parishioners was a serious blow for temple finances. Postwar land reform resulted in the expropriation of temple lands; for example, 61.2 percent of Sōtō-sect temples, 61 percent of Kōyasan Shingon temples, 62 percent of Shingon-sect Chizan-school temples, and 54 percent of Shingon-sect Buzan-school temples lost land. Except for those at Jōdo Shin–sect temples, priests at small country temples were forced to take secular jobs to support themselves.

While the temples experienced financial difficulties, the organizations of which they were a part continued to be afflicted by schism and dispute, as well as internal and external problems. The fifty-six subsects of Buddhism, which had been combined into twenty-eight under the Religious

Organizations Law of 1939, quickly returned to their original groupings after the Religious Corporations Ordinance was promulgated, at the end of 1945. In addition, new schisms developed at an increasing pace, and soon two hundred and sixty Buddhist subsects, including new religions, were registered.

The subsects' return to their prewar affiliations was predictable, but religious conflicts also fed schism. In September 1946 the Jōdo-sect temple Konkaikōmyō-ji in Kurodani, Kyoto, declared its independence from the Jōdo ecclesiastical organization and formed the Kurodani Jōdo sect. The head temple of the Jōdo sect, Chion-in in Kyoto, seceded in 1947, taking with it a large number of branch temples and forming the Hompa Jōdo sect. The schism in the Jōdo sect persisted for fifteen years, until 1962, when splinter groups were reunited.

Similar schisms occurred in other sects, unsettling Buddhist circles throughout the country as powerful temples severed their traditional sectarian affiliations. On July 13, 1946, one hundred and twenty temples led by Sainan-ji in Takarazuka, Hyōgo Prefecture, seceded from the Kōyasan Shingon sect and formed the independent Shin Bukkyō Kūkai sect. In March 1946 the Nichiren-sect Nakayama-school temple Hokekyō-ji in Ichikawa, Chiba Prefecture, noted for its rigorous ascetic training, left the Nichiren sect and formed the Nakayama Myō sect. Lay supporters who declared the secession invalid were drawn into the dispute, and the resulting litigation continued for decades. In 1949 the Tendai sect also suffered a number of secessions: Kurama-dera in Kyoto formed Kurama Kōkyō, Shitennō-ji in Osaka formed the Wa sect, and Sensō-ji in Tokyo formed the Shō Kannon sect. In 1950 Hōryū-ji in Nara left the Hossō sect to form the independent Shōtoku sect.

Changes in the *ie* (household) institution continued to affect Buddhism. Since the Edo period (1603–1868) the *danka*, or parishioner, system had supported the temples. Though legally the *danka* system was discontinued after the Meiji Restoration of 1868, the *ie* system was strengthened, thus bolstering the *danka* system and allowing it to function unchanged.

In the wake of the postwar abolition of the *ie* system, together with other social changes, however, the nuclear family supplanted the extended family. As a result, the obligatory relationships between main and cadet families gave way to those based on emotional ties, and emphasis shifted from vertical, hierarchal relationships between parents, children, and grandchildren to horizontal, egalitarian relationships between spouses. These changes led to problems of succession in certain occupations and family businesses and to changes in social values, which began to reflect individual rather than group needs.

These changes were accelerated by the economic recovery stimulated by the outbreak of the Korean War in 1950, which resulted in a population shift as workers moved from the countryside to the cities. The newcomers had no sense of belonging to a specific temple and were a rootless population with no particular religious affiliation. The migration left many rural temples facing destitution, which contributed to a growing sense of crisis in various religious organizations.

Christianity

With Shintō and Buddhism weakened by internal conflicts and external troubles—and ignoring the new religions for the moment—it was the growth of Christianity that caused the greatest stir in the early postwar period. Christian churches, which had been concentrated in the cities, suffered from the dispersal of their congregations and from war damage. Their economic distress was acute, but the hostility, prejudice, and persecution to which Christianity had been subjected earlier came to an end, and Christianity was further aided by the arrival in Japan of foreign missionaries and of relief supplies from foreign churches. All in all, journalists reported favorably on Christianity—in contrast to their attitude toward the new religions.

The Religious Organizations Law had forced the thirty-four prewar Protestant denominations to merge as the Nihon Kirisuto Kyōdan (United Church of Christ in Japan). Postwar religious freedom coincided with a worldwide move toward ecumenism, and with some exceptions—the Lutheran Church, part of the Baptist Church, and the greater part of the Salvation Army—most Christian organizations remained united in the Nihon Kirisuto Kyōdan. Christianity was greatly strengthened by its minimal fragmentation. In June 1946 the Nihon Kirisuto Kyōdan organized a national Christian conference at Aoyama Gakuin University, a Christian institution in Tokyo. The conference proclaimed a three-year campaign to rebuild Japan and a nationwide mission to be led by the social reformer Kagawa Toyohiko (1888–1960). In three years the Protestant population grew from 170,000 to 200,000.

On the scorched earth of the destroyed cities, churches were established in Quonset huts donated by churches in America. In February 1947 the American Bible Society sent 2.4 million Bibles to Japan. Starved for books in a time of severe paper shortages, the intelligentsia fought for copies, and Christianity spread among intellectuals and young people. The Socialists won the general election of April 1947 and their leader, Katayama Tetsu (1887–1978), a Christian, became prime minister.

The Catholics also rebuilt their churches relatively quickly with aid from abroad. Father Edward J. Flanagan, founder of Boys Town in America, visited Japan in 1946; and in 1949, on the four hundredth anniversary of the arrival of Francis Xavier, the Vatican sent the relic of Xavier's right arm to Japan, and the services in Urakami Catholic Church in Nagasaki received prominent press coverage.

In 1949 an entire hamlet near Kyoto was converted to Catholicism. With the help of a powerful postwar convert, the Catholic church in Maizuru, Kyoto Prefecture, undertook missionary work in the hamlet of Hōonji, in present-day Ayabe. The villagers, suffering in a time of material shortages, were grateful for the relief goods they received and were eager for a Catholic school to be built in their district. A movement advocating conversion arose, and of the six hamlets that then constituted the village of Saga, Hōonji decided that it would convert en masse, an event that had a large impact in religious circles. Nonetheless, Catholic missionary activity was on the whole modest compared with that of the Protestants.

With the economic recovery of the early 1950s, the popularity of Christianity began to wane as established Buddhism and Shintō took on new life. Christians, counting both long-time followers and new converts, remained less than 1 percent of the population.

POSTWAR DEVELOPMENTS

Buddhist Prison Chaplains

In the late 1940s Buddhism and Shintō were at their nadir, and public attention focused on Christian missionary activities; yet the work of Buddhist prison chaplains attracted considerable attention. The press widely reported the work of the Buddhist scholar Hanayama Shinshō (b. 1898), a professor at the University of Tokyo and a priest of the Hongan-ji school of the Jōdo Shin sect, who was a chaplain to the class A war criminals, including General Tōjō Hideki, at Sugamo Prison, in Tokyo; as well as the work of the Buddhist scholar Tajima Ryūjun (1892–1958), a professor at Tokyo's Taisho University and a priest of the Buzan school of the Shingon sect, who brought relief to prisoners burdened with a sense of guilt and a fear of death. The prisoners revered him as a father. Newspaper articles also featured the activities of Kagao Shūnin (1901–77), a priest of the Kōyasan Shingon sect working in the prison at Montin Lupa on Luzon in the Philippines.

In 1960 some 1,303 chaplains were working in prisons, reformatories, and other correctional facilities. As of the end of 2,000, some 1,700 were doing so. Among them, 624 belonged to the Pure Land sects, 242 to Christian churches, 196 to Shintō denominations, 179 to the Zen sects, 138 to the Shingon sect, 135 to Tenrikyō, 132 to the Nichiren sect, and 34 to the Tendai sect. Appreciation for the work of prison chaplains has since grown since 1954. Now a national conference of chaplains is convened once every two years, and small conferences are held twice a year. Their work encourages many donations from commercial enterprises and private donors.

Resurgent Shintō and Buddhism

With Japan's economic recovery in the 1950s, the established religions began to rebound from their long period of decline. In view of the competition from the new religions, voices were raised in every sect for reform and modernization of sect administration and for open discussion of the role of religion in modern society. A forerunner of the Buddhist reform movement was the Shinri (Truth) movement, centering on the scholar-priest Tomomatsu Entai (1875–1973), founded in May 1946.

The Shinri movement, which seceded from the Jōdo sect, rejected narrow sectarianism and espoused a form of lay Buddhism. In 1947 it declared its newly built Kanda-dera in Tokyo's Kanda district a suprasectarian temple and an instrument for bringing Buddhism into everyday life. The temple's architectural style is modern; the main hall has chairs; and a choir leads the singing of Buddhist hymns at services, such as funerals. The temple also sponsors lectures on temple reform.

At the first World Fellowship of Buddhists, which met in Colombo, Sri Lanka, in 1950, it was decided to hold a conference every two years, with the next in Japan. That decision stimulated the nonsectarian Buddhist movement. In 1951 the Conference of Japanese Buddhists (Nihon Bukkyōto Kaigi) was inaugurated; and as a result of the second World Fellowship of Buddhists, the Zen Nihon Bukkyō Kai (All Japan Federation of

Buddhist Sects) was established in 1954 and a yearly conference inaugurated.

The revival of Shintō was apparent in October 1953, when the long-delayed ritual rebuilding of Ise Grand Shrine was completed at a cost of 700 million yen, collected by public subscription. The event marked both a return of public confidence after the trials of the war years and the deep-rooted strength of Shintō as a folk belief. With political support and financial support from the business sector, the Jingū Kōgakukan at Ise Grand Shrine, abolished under the Shintō Directive, was reestablished as a university; and Meiji Shrine in Tokyo and Atsuta Shrine in Nagoya, both of which had been severely damaged during the war, were rebuilt. Most ordinary shrines attracted supporters either by providing wedding facilities, or, like the Tenjin or Suitengū shrines, by stressing the efficacy of their enshrined *kami*.

Within Sectarian Shintō, in 1956 Tenrikyō commemorated the seventieth anniversary (by Japanese reckoning) of the death of its founder by completing the Oyasato Yakata at a cost of 2.3 billion yen, and Konkōkyō erected an ultramodern ceremonial center in Okayama Prefecture in 1959.

Sect Reform Movements

The Zen Nihon Bukkyō Kai was formed as an alliance to unite the Buddhist movement, but sectarian differences prevented it from becoming a springboard for federation. The year 1961 marked the divide between the new religions' periods of growth and of consolidation. In Buddhist circles, however, 1961 saw the strong bonds between Buddhism and its parishioners spotlighted—the bonds forged because of the custom of ancestor veneration and memorial services that dated to the Edo period.

By Japanese reckoning, 1961 was the seven hundred and fiftieth anniversary of the death of Hōnen, founder of the Jōdo sect, and the seven hundredth anniversary of the death of Shinran, founder of the Jōdo Shin sect. More than two million pilgrims visited the two sects' main temples in Kyoto: Chion-in (head temple of the Jōdo sect), Higashi Hongan-ji (head temple of the Ōtani branch of the Jōdo Shin sect), and Nishi Hongan-ji (head temple of the Hongan-ji branch of the Jōdo Shin sect). In commemoration that year, Chion-in built the Chion-in Shūgaku Kenkyūjo (an institute for doctrinal study of sects affiliated with Chion-in) in Kyoto and a public hall in the complex of Zōjō-ji in Tokyo.

In March 1962 the fifteen-year rift between the Hompa Jōdo sect and the Jōdo sect was mended. In the Ōtani branch of the Jōdo Shin sect, the memorial celebrations were the occasion for the establishment of an educational foundation and the building of a hall for Jōdo Shin believers. The stage was set for sectarian reform.

Right up till the splendid celebrations, Chion-in and the two Hongan-ji temples had been considering a return to their original role of teaching Buddhism. As mentioned earlier, family support was collapsing and rural temples were suffering financially from a population drain. The war had deprived urban temples of many of their usual parishioners, and urban temples were further unsettled by large numbers of newcomers. The influx of newcomers kept many temples too busy with funerals and memorial services to instruct the laity, and the situation reached the point that methods suitable for a new missionary effort in the cities had to be found. All the Buddhist sects began to concern themselves with modernization, particularly in terms of self-renewal as organizations of faith rather than of ritual, and with maintaining both temples and an effective missionary effort.

The Jōdo Shin sect, which had a strong rural base, suffered most from the flood of migrants to the cities. To strengthen ties between temples and parishioners, on the occasion of the 1961 celebrations the Hongan-ji branch of the Jōdo Shin sect inaugurated the Monshinto Kai (Followers Association) movement. The following year the Ōtani branch initiated a similar movement, the Dōbō Kai (Brotherhood) movement, concerned with sect reform based on individual faith rather than family religious affiliation. In 1962 the Jōdo sect Otetsugi (Join Hands) movement developed out of a temple-support association at Chion-in, and by 1966 it had spread to other Jōdo-sect temples and was functioning independently of Chion-in. Other sects established similar groups: the Nichiren sect set up its Gohō (Protection of the Law) movement, the Myōshin-ji school of the Rinzai sect its Hanazono Kai movement, the Sōtō sect its Goji Kai and Sanzon Butsu movements, the Seizan Zenrin-ji school of the Jōdo sect its Mikaeri movement, the Buzan school of Shingon its Kōmyō Mandara movement, the Kōyasan Shingon school its Gasshō movement, the Daikaku-ji school of Shingon its Shakyō (Sutra Copying) movement, the Chizan school of Shingon its Tsukushiai movement, and Tendai its Ichigū o Terasu movement.

All these movements were concerned with sect reform. Prompted by their shared perception of crisis, they stressed the faith of the individual rather than the household (*ie*) and undertook organizational reform to respond to people's real needs. The Ōtani Dōbō Kai movement was concerned less with strengthening the temples and the ecclesiastical organization than with propagating Buddhism through the efforts of the laity as well as the clergy, and it sought ways to make the faith of Shinran relevant in the spiritual stagnation of modern society. The purpose of the Jōdo Shin sect's Hongan-ji Monshinto Kai was to restore to temples the functions they originally filled at the time of the early Jōdo Shin movement. It sought to make temples places for sharing the teachings and to make priests the unifying nucleus for followers. This movement differed from other movements: its three chief aims were to build temples (restore branch temples), build character, and build society (take Buddhism to the world). Members met in small groups called *hōza* to discuss these aims.

Initially concentrating on the ideal of the unity of laity and clergy, the Ōtani Dōbō Kai movement aided in restoring Shinran's mausoleum and in special missionary work. Eventually, however, local bodies sought autonomy, and a sense of crisis developed as differences in goals became apparent: some groups sought more active lay control, and others sought to increase the material prosperity of the group.

In June 1969, during the implementation of the movement's second five-year plan, a confrontation between the reform faction and the forces of the aristocracy, centering on the Ōtani family, became public. The problem concerned the appointment of a new administrator. In an attempt at sect reform, the sect's deliberative assembly in June 1975 decided to transfer to the director of religious affairs all the rights of appointment held by the superintendent priest. The Ōtani family rejected this move as a violation of the sect's constitution, and the dispute was eventually taken to court. On the surface this was a largely predictable conflict arising from the development of a lay movement in a religious organization with an ordained clergy. It will be interesting to see how similar faith-centered movements that question the values of modern religion will develop in other sects.

Growing Cooperation

For religious organizations, freedom of belief means that they are completely free from government interference in either their internal organization or their religious activities. In other words, the 1951 Religious Corporations Law makes it clear that secular authorities can be concerned with the physical facilities of religious organizations but not with their doctrine. Whereas the prewar Religious Organizations Law considered religion a public affair, all legislation since the 1945 Religious Corporations Ordinance and the Religious Corporations Law has regarded it as a private affair. All religions are free to propagate, and all people are free to choose their faith. Old and new religions are equal under the law.

Since the end of World War II the secularization of religion has become a worldwide phenomenon. People of religion no longer confine their activities to religious matters but in ever growing numbers concern themselves with social issues. Religions have become politicized. In Japan religious circles' interest in politics, nonexistent before the war, was aroused by the shock of Sōka Gakkai's entry into politics. Its political arm, the Kōmei Seiji Remmei (League for Clean Politics), was reorganized as the Kōmeitō (Clean Government Party) in 1964 and won twenty-five seats in the lower house of the Diet in the elections of January 1967.

In September 1962, in response to the 1961 founding of the Kōmei Seiji Remmei, the Shinshūren (Union of New Religious Organization of Japan) formed its Assembly for the Study of Social and Political Problems. Individual religions quickly followed suit, founding quasi-political groups, for example, Risshō Kōsei-kai's Kōsei Konwa Kai (Kōsei Friendly Chat Association) in November 1962 and Seichō no Ie's Seichō no Ie Seiji Rengō (Seichō no Ie Political League) in September 1964. In 1966 interested people in Tokyo from a wide range of Shintō, Buddhist, and Christian organizations and new religious sects and denominations joined together out of their concern for safeguarding freedom of belief and established the Jikyoku Taisaku Shūkyōsha Kaigi (Conference of Religionists to Consider Emergency Strategy). In December that year, the Shinshūren formed the Shinshūren Seiji Rengō (Shinshūren Political League). The Hongan-ji subsect of the Jōdo Shin sect inaugurated its Nishi Hongan-ji Jiji Kyōkai (Nishi Hongan-ji Current Topics Association) in May 1967, and the Jinja Honchō organized the Shintō Seiji Remmei (Shintō Political Federation) in November 1969. Thus politics gave various religious groups a common forum for discussion.

Movements for world peace have also fostered interreligious cooperation. The peace movement in Japan began in December 1946 with the inauguration of a national conference on religion and peace by the Nihon Shūkyō Remmei (Japan Religions League), supported by the Shūkyō Bunka Kyōkai (Religion and Culture Association). The first conference was held in May the following year at Tsukiji Hongan-ji in Tokyo. In 1952 the Shinshūren joined the Nihon Shūkyō Remmei, and in 1970 the first World Conference on Religion and Peace was held in Kyoto under the auspices of the Nihon Shūkyō Remmei. Thereafter, the conference secretariat was maintained under the leadership of Risshō Kōsei-kai and the Shinshūren. At the time of the first conference, the cofounder of Risshō Kōsei-kai, Niwano Nikkyō, was a director of both the Shinshūren and the Nihon Shūkyō Remmei.

Within thirty years of the end of World War II, the new religions had overcome public distrust and become reconciled with the established religions, and a base for interreligious understanding and cooperation was being established. Yet the continuing controversy over the Yasukuni Shrine Bill (which would provide government funding for Tokyo's Yasukuni Shrine, the principal shrine for the nation's war dead) and the lingering controversy surrounding the Shintō ground-breaking ceremony for a municipal gymnasium in Tsu, Mie Prefecture, in January, 1965, reflect the growing involvement of religion in politics and secular affairs. Today religions are moving rapidly into an era of rivalry that is unrelated to whether they are old or new.

The Authors

Masao Fujii, a professor at Taisho University, wrote all of chapters 22 and 23.

Tatsuo Hagiwara, a former professor at Meiji University, wrote the first section of chapter 12 and the third section of chapter 13. Deceased, 1985.

Masatoshi Hasegawa, president of Shukutoku University, wrote the first section of chapter 14.

Eishun Ikeda, a professor at Hokkai Gakuen University, wrote all of chapter 21.

Aishin Imaeda, a former professor at the University of Tokyo, wrote all of chapter 9 and the third section of chapter 14.

Kazuo Kasahara, a former professor at the University of Tokyo, wrote the preface, the introduction, the first section of chapter 2, the fourth section of chapter 4, the first section of chapter 5, all of chapters 7 and 11, the first section of chapter 13, and the first section of chapter 18.

Hitoshi Miyake, a professor at Kokugakuin University and president of the Japanese Association for Religious Studies, wrote the second section of chapter 12 and the second section of chapter 17.

Noboru Miyata, a former professor at Kanagawa University, wrote the first section of chapter 17. Deceased, 2000.

Kiyomi Morioka, a professor emeritus at Seijo University, wrote the third section of chapter 19 and all of chapter 20.

Junko Oguri, a lecturer at the Chuo Academic Research Institute, wrote the second section of chapter 15 and the second and third sections of chapter 18.

Tetsuya Ōhama, a professor at Tsukuba University, wrote all of chapter 16 and the first two sections of chapter 19.

Toshio Ōhashi, a lecturer at the Japan Culture Institute, wrote the third section of chapter 3, the first section of chapter 4, all of chapters 6 and 8, and the second section of chapter 14.

Sekiyo Shimode, a former professor at Meiji University, wrote the second and third sections of chapter 2, the second section of chapter 3, and the second and third sections of chapter 4. Deceased, 1998.

Shigetsugu Sugiyama, a professor at the Institute for Japanese Culture and Classics affiliated with Kokugakuin University, wrote all of chapter 1.

Yutaka Takagi, a former professor at Rissho University, wrote the first section of chapter 3, the second section of chapter 5, all of chapter 10, and with Fumio Tamamuro the first section of chapter 15. Deceased, 1999.

Fumio Tamamuro, a professor at Meiji University, wrote the second section of chapter 13 and with Yutaka Takagi the first section of chapter 15.

Bibliography

Aiba Shin. *Fujufuse-ha Junkyō no Rekishi* (A History of the Martyrdom in the Fujufuse Subsect). Tokyo: Daizo Shuppan, 1976.

Akamatsu Toshihide. *Shinran* (Shinran). Tokyo: Yoshikawa Kobunkan, 1961.

Akamatsu Toshihide and Kasahara Kazuo, eds. *Shinshū Shi Gaisetsu* (A Survey of the Jōdo Shin Sect). Kyoto: Heirakuji Shoten, 1963.

Akamatsu Toshihide. *Kamakura Bukkyō no Kenkyū* (A Study of Kamakura Buddhism). 2 vols. Kyoto: Heirakuji Shoten, 1957, 1966.

Andō Toshio and Sonoda Kōyū, ed. *Saichō* (Saichō). Vol. 4 of *Nihon Shisō Taikei* (Systematized Japanese Thought). Tokyo: Iwanami Shoten, 1974.

Asai Endō. *Jōko Nihon Tendai Hommon Shisō Shi* (A History of Ancient Japanese Tendai Thought on the Realm of Origin). Kyoto: Heirakuji Shoten, 1973.

Bukkyō University, ed. *Hōnen Shōnin Kenkyū* (A Study of Hōnen Shōnin). Kyoto: Heirakuji Shoten, 1961.

Chiba Jōryū. *Chūbu Sanson Shakai no Shin Shū* (The Jōdo Shin Sect in Communities in Mountain Villages of the Chūbu Area). Tokyo: Yoshikawa Kobunkan, 1971.

Ebisawa Arimichi. *Nihon Kirishitan Shi* (A History of Japanese Christians). Tokyo: Hanawa Shobo, 1965.

Ebisawa Arimichi and Ōuchi Saburō. *Nihon Kirisutokyō Shi* (A History of Christianity in Japan). Tokyo: The Board of Publications of the United Church of Christ in Japan, 1970.

Fujii Manabu. "Hokke Ikki to Machi-gumi" (The Hokke Uprisings and the Townspeople). In *Kinsei no Taidō* (Signs of Forthcoming Activities in the Early Modern Period). Vol. 3 of *Kyōto no Rekishi* (A History of Kyoto) edited by Kyoto City. Kyoto: Gakugei Shorin, 1968.

———. "Saigoku o Chūshin toshita Hokke-kyōdan no Tenkai" (The Development of the Hokke Organizations Centering around Western Japan). In vol. 6-1 of *Bukkyō Shigaku* (Historical Study of Buddhism). 1957.

599

Fujii Masao. *Gendai-jin no Shinkō Kōzō* (Structure of the Faith of People Today). Tokyo: Hyoronsha, 1974.

Fukui Kōjun, ed. *Jikaku Daishi Kenkyū* (A Study of the Great Teacher Jikaku). Tokyo: Tendai Association of Buddhist Studies, 1964.

Furuno Kiyoto. *Kakure Kirishitan* (Hidden Christians). Tokyo: Shibundoh, 1959.

Furuta Takehiko. *Shinran* (Shinran). Tokyo: Shimizu-Shoin, 1970.

Futsū-sha, ed. *Shinran Zenshū* (Complete Collection of Shinran's Writings). Tokyo: Kodansha Ltd., 1958.

Gorai Shigeru. *Yama no Shūkyō—Shugendō* (Mountain Religion—Shugendō). Kyoto: Tankosha Publishing Co., Ltd., 1970.

———. *Yoshino/Kumano Shinkō no Kenkyū* (A Study of the Yoshino-Kumano Belief). Vol. 4 of *Sangaku Shūkyō Kenkyū Sōsho* (Series on the Study of Mountain Religion). Tokyo: Meicho Shuppan, 1975.

Haga Kōshirō. *Chūsei Zenrin no Gakumon oyobi Bungaku nikansuru Kenkyū* (A Study of the Learning and Literature of Medieval Zen Temples). Tokyo: Japan Society for the Promotion of Science, 1956.

Haga Noboru. *Bakumatsu Kokugaku no Tenkai* (The Development of National Learning Toward the End of the Edo Period). Tokyo: Hanawa Shobo, 1963.

———. *Kokugaku no Hitobito* (People Involved with National Learning). Tokyo: Hyoronsha, 1975.

Haga Noboru and Tahara Tsuguo, eds. *Hirata Atsutane / Ban Nobutomo / Ōkuni Takamasa* (Hirata Atsutane / Ban Nobutomo / Ōkuni Takamasa). Vol. 50 of *Nihon Shisō Taikei* (Systematized Japanese Thought). Tokyo: Iwanami Shoten, 1973.

Haga Noboru, Matsumoto Sannosuke, eds. *Kokugaku Undō no Shisō* (The Ideology of the Movement of National Learning). Vol. 51 of *Nihon Shisō Taikei* (Systematized Japanese Thought). Tokyo: Iwanami Shoten, 1971.

Hagiwara Tatsuo. *Chūsei Saishi Soshiki no Kenkyū* (A Study of Ceremonial and Ritual Organizations in the Middle Ages). Tokyo: Yoshikawa Kobunkan, 1962.

Hara Keigo. *Kurozumi Munetada* (Kurozumi Munetada). Tokyo: Yoshikawa Kobunkan, 1960.

Harada Toshiaki. *Jinja—Minzokugaku no Tachiba karamiru* (Shinto Shrines—From the Standpoint of Folklore). Tokyo: Shibundoh, 1961.

Hattori Shisō. *Rennyo* (Rennyo). Tokyo: Kokudo-sha, 1948.

———. *Shinran Nōto* (Shinran's Notes). 2 vols. Tokyo: Fukumura Shuppan Inc., 1948.

Hayami Tasuku. *Heian Kizoku Shakai to Bukkyō* (Buddhism and the Aristocratic Society of the Heian Period). Tokyo: Yoshikawa Kobunkan, 1975.

———. *Miroku Shinkō—Mōhitotsu no Jōdo Shinkō* (Faith in Maitreya—One More Pure Land Belief). Vol. 12 of *Nihonjin no Kōdo to Shisō* (Conduct and Thinking of the Japanese). Tokyo: Hyoronsha, 1973.

Hayashi Taiun. *Nihon Zen Shū Shi* (A History of Japanese Zen). Tokyo: Daito Publishing Co., Inc., 1938. Reprinted by Nihon Tosho Center, Tokyo, in 1977.

Hazama Jikō. *Nihon Bukkyō no Tenkai to Sono Kichō* (The Development of Japanese Buddhism and Its Keynote). 2 vols. Tokyo: Sanseido Co., Ltd., 1953.

———. *Tendai Shi Gaisetsu* (An Outline of the History of Tendai Buddhism). Tokyo: Daizo Shuppan, 1969.

Hikaku Shisō-shi Kenkyū-kai, ed. *Meiji Shisōka no Shūkyō Kan* (Meiji-Period Thinkers' Views on Religion). Tokyo: Daizo Shuppan, 1975.

Hirabayashi Moritoku *Ryōgen* (Ryōgen). Tokyo: Yoshikawa Kobunkan, 1976

Hori Ichirō. *Minkan Shinkō* (Popular Beliefs). Tokyo: Iwanami Shoten, 1977.

———. *Waga-kuni Minkan Shinkō Shi Kenkyū* (A Study of the History of Popular Beliefs of Our Country). Osaka: Sogensha, 1953.

Ide Katsumi, tr. *Jūrokuseiki Kirishitan Shijō no Senrei Shigan Ki* (The Application Term for Baptism in the Sixteenth-century Chiristian History). Translated from Jesús López-Gay's *El catecumenando en la mision del Japon del S. XVI* (Roma: Libreria dell'Universita Gregoriana, 1966). Tokyo: Association for the Study of Kirishitan Culture, 1968.

———. *Shoki Kirishitan Jidai ni okeru Jumbi Fukyō* (Preparatory Dissemination in the Early Christian Period). Translated from Jesús López-Gay's "La Preevangelización en las primeros años de la misión del Japón," published in *Missionalia Hispanica*, num. 19, Madrid, 1962. Tokyo: Association for the Study of Kirishitan Culture, 1968.

Ienaga Saburō, Akamatsu Toshihide, and Tamamuro Taijō, eds. *Nihon Bukkyō Shi* (A History of Japanese Buddhism). 3 vols. Kyoto: Hozokan, 1967.

———. *Chūsei Bukkyō Shisō Shi Kenkyū* (A Study of Buddhist Thought in the Middle Ages). Kyoto: Hozokan, 1947.

Ikeda Eishun. *Meiji no Bukkyō—Sono Kōdō to Shisō* (Buddhism of the Meiji Period—Its Activities and Doctrines). Vol. 31 of *Nihonjin no Kōdō to Shisō* (Conduct and Thinking of the Japanese). Tokyo: Hyoronsha, 1976.

———. *Meiji no Shin Bukkyō Undō* (New Buddhist Movements in the Meiji Period). Tokyo: Yoshikawa Kobunkan, 1976.

Ikeda Toshio. *Jimbutsu ni yoru Nihon Katorikku Kyōkai Shi* (A History of the Japanese Catholic Church Illustrated with Personal Examples). Tokyo: Chūō Shuppansha, 1968.

Ikoma Kanshichi. *Ontake no Rekishi* (A History of Mount Ontake). Nishichikuma-gun, Nagano Prefecture: Kiso Ontake Honkyō, 1966.

Imaeda Aishin. *Chūsei Zen Shū Shi no Kenkyū* (A Study of the History of the Zen Sect in the Middle Ages). Tokyo: University of Tokyo Press, 1970.

———. *Dōgen to Sono Deshi* (Dōgen and His Disciples). Tokyo: The Mainichi Newspapers Co., Ltd., 1972.

———. *Dōgen—Sono Kōdō to Shisō* (Dōgen—His Activities and Thought). Vol. 3

of *Nihonjin no Kōdō to Shisō* (Conduct and Thinking of the Japanese). Tokyo: Hyoronsha, 1970.

———. *Dōgen—Zazen Hitosuji no Shamon* (Dōgen—a Religious Mendicant Devoted Singlemindedly to Zazen). Tokyo: Japan Broadcast Publishing Co., Ltd., 1976.

———. *Zen Shū no Rekishi* (A History of the Zen Sect). Vol. 93 of *Nihon Rekishi Shinsho* (Paperback Series on Japanese History). Tokyo: Shibundoh, 1962.

Inagaki Shin'ei. *Heieki o Kyohishita Nihonjin—Tōdai-sha no Senjika Teikō* (Japanese Who Rejected Military Service—Todai-sha's Wartime Resistance). Tokyo: Iwanami Shoten, 1972.

Inobe Shigeo. *Fuji no Shinkō* (Beliefs in Mount Fuji). Vol. 3 of *Fuji no Kenkyū* (Studies of Mount Fuji). Tokyo: Meicho Shuppan, 1973.

Inoue Kaoru. *Gyōgi* (Gyōgi). Tokyo: Yoshikawa Kobunkan, 1959.

———. *Nara-chō Bukkyō Shi no Kenkyū* (A Study of Nara Buddhism). Tokyo: Yoshikawa Kobunkan, 1966.

Inoue Kozan. *Myōshin-ji Shi* (A History of the Temple Myōshin-ji). Kyoto: Myōshin-ji, 1917. Reprinted by Shibunkaku Shuppan, Kyoto, 1975.

Inoue Mitsusada. *Nihon Jōdo-kyō Seiritsu no Kenkyū* (A Study of the Establishment of Japanese Pure Land Buddhism). Tokyo: Yamakawa-Shuppan-Sha, 1956.

———. *Nihon Kodai Bukkyō no Tenkai* (The Development of Ancient Japanese Buddhism). Tokyo: Yoshikawa Kobunkan, 1975.

———. *Nihon Kodai no Kokka to Bukkyō* (The Nation and Buddhism in Ancient Japan). Tokyo: Iwanami Shoten, 1971.

Inoue Mitsusada and Ōsone Shōsuke, eds. *Ōjōden / Hokke Kenki* (Biographies of the Believers in Rebirth / Records of the Miracles of the Hokke Faith). Vol. 7 of *Nihon Shisō Taikei* (Systematized Japanese Thought). Tokyo: Iwanami Shoten, 1974

Inoue Toshio. *Hongan-ji* (The Temple Hongan-ji). Tokyo: Shibundoh, 1961.

———. *Ikkō Ikki no Kenkyū* (A Study of the Ikkō Uprisings). Tokyo: Yoshikawa Kobunkan, 1968.

Institute of Nichiren Buddhist Studies of Risshō University, ed. *Nichiren Kyōdan Zenshi* (The Complete History of Nichiren Sect Organizations). Kyoto: Heirakuji Shoten, 1964.

Ishida Mitsuyuki. *Kamakura Jōdokyō Seiritsu no Kiso Kenkyū—Hōnen-monryū Shoki Kyōgaku o Chūshin ni* (A Basic Study of the Establishment of Pure Land Buddhism in the Kamakura Period—Centering on the Early Doctrine of the Honen School). Kyoto: Hyakka-en, 1966.

Ishida Mizumaro. *Gokuraku Jōdo eno Izanai* (Invitation to the Paradise of the Pure Land). Vol. 35 of *Nihonjin no Kōdō to Shisō* (Conduct and Thinking of the Japanese). Tokyo: Hyoronsha, 1976.

———. *Nihon Bukkyō niokeru Kairitsu no Kenkyū* (A Study of the Precepts of Japanese Buddhism). Tokyo: Nakayama Shobō, 1976.

Ishida Mizumaro, ed. *Genshin* (Genshin). Vol. 6 of *Nihon Shisō Taikei* (Systematized Japanese Thought). Tokyo: Iwanami Shoten, 1970.

Ishihara Ken. *Kirisutokyō to Nihon* (Christianity and Japan). Tokyo: The Board of Publications of the United Church of Christ in Japan, 1976.

Itō Shintetsu. *Heian Jōdokyō Shinkō Shi no Kenkyū* (A Study of the Belief in Pure Land Buddhism in the Heian Period). Kyoto: Heirakuji Shoten, 1974.

Itō Tasaburō. *Sōmō no Kokugaku* (The National Learning of the Common People). Tokyo: Hata Shoten, 1945. Reprinted by Masago Shoten, Tokyo, 1966.

Iwasaki Toshio. *Hompō Shōshi no Kenkyū* (A Study of the Small Shirines of Japan). Tokyo: Meicho Shuppan, 1976.

Kadowaki Teiji, et al. *Nihonteki Seikatsu no Botai* (Matrix of the Japanese Lifestyle). Vol. 1 of *Nihon Seikatsu Bunkashi* (Cultural History of Japanese Life). Tokyo: Kawade Shobo Shinsha, 1975.

Kageyama Gyōō. *Nichiren Kyōdan Shi Gaisetsu* (A Survey of Nichiren Sect Organizations). Kyoto: Heirakuji Shoten, 1969.

Kageyama Gyōō, ed. *Nichiren Shū Fujufuseha no Kenkyū* (A Study of the Fujufuse Subsect of the Nichiren Sect). Kyoto: Heirakuji Shoten, 1972.

Kageyama Haruki. *Hiei-zan* (Mount Hiei). Tokyo: Kadokawa Shoten Publishing Co., Ltd., 1966.

Kasahara Kazuo. *Chūsei niokeru Shin Shū Kyōdan no Keisei* (The Formation of the Jōdo Shin Sect in the Middle Ages). Tokyo: Shin Jimbutsu Ōrai-sha, 1971.

————. *Gendai-jin to Bukkyo* (People Today and Buddhism). Tokyo: Hyoronsha, 1975.

————. *Ikkō Ikki no Kenkyū* (A Study of the Ikkō Uprisings). Tokyo: Yamakawa-Shuppan-Sha, 1962.

————. *Ikkō Ikki—Sono Kōdō to Shisō* (The Ikkō Uprisings—Their Conduct and Ideology). Vol. 5 of *Nihonjin no Kōdo to Shisō* (Conduct and Thinking of the Japanese). Tokyo: Hyoronsha, 1970.

————. *Nihon Shi ni Miru Jigoku to Gokuraku—Josei to Bukkyō* (Hell and Paradise as Seen in Japanese History—Women and Buddhism). Tokyo: Japan Broadcast Publishing Co., Ltd., 1976.

————. *Nyonin Ōjō Shisō no Keifu* (The Genealogy of Thought on Women's Rebirth). Tokyo: Yoshikawa Kobunkan, 1975.

————. *Rennyo* (Rennyo). Tokyo: Yoshikawa Kobunkan, 1963.

————. *Seiji to Shūkyō—Kiro nitatsu Sōkagakkai* (Politics and Religion—Soka Gakkai at a Turning Point). Tokyo: Asoka Shuppan-sha, 1965.

————. *Shin Shū Kyōdan Kaiten Shi* (A History of the Development of the Jōdo Shin Sect). Tokyo: Unebi Shobō, 1942.

————. *Shin Shū ni okeru Itan no Keifu* (The Genealogy of the Heresies of the Jōdo Shin Sect). Tokyo: University of Tokyo Press, 1962.

————. *Shinran Kenkyū Nōto* (Notes on the Study of Shinran). Tokyo: Tosho Shimbun, 1965.

————. *Shinran to Tōgoku Nōmin* (Shinran and the Peasants of Eastern Japan). Tokyo: Yamakawa-Shuppan-Sha, 1957.

————. *Shinran—Bonnō Gusoku no Hotoke* (Shinran—A Buddha with Defilements). Tokyo: Japan Broadcast Publishing Co., Ltd., 1973.

————. *Sōkagakkai to Hongan-ji Kyōdan* (Soka Gakkai and the Hongan-ji Organization). Tokyo: Shin Jimbutsu Ōrai-sha, 1970.

————. *Tenkan-ki no Shūkyō—Shin Shū, Tenrikyō, Sōkagakkai* (Religions of the Turning-Point Period—Jōdo Shin Sect, Tenrikyō, and Soka Gakkai). Tokyo: Japan Broadcast Publishing Co., Ltd., 1966.

Kasahara Kazuo, ed. *Nihon Shūkyō Shi Nempyō* (Chronology of Japanese Religion). Special vol. 2 in the series of *Nihonjin no Kōdo to Shisō* (Conduct and Thinking of the Japanese). Tokyo: Hyoronsha, 1974.

————. *Nihon Shūkyō Shi Nyūmon—Sengo no Seika to Kadai* (Gateway to the History of Japanese Religion—Post-war Achievements and Problems). Special vol. 1 of *Nihonjin no Kōdo to Shisō* (Conduct and Thinking of the Japanese) Tokyo: Hyoronsha, 1971.

Kasahara Kazuo and Oguri Junko. *Kyōso Tanjō* (Births of the Founders of Religions). Tokyo: Nihon Keizai Shimbun Inc., 1968.

Kasahara Kazuo, Inoue Toshio, et al., eds. *Rennyo / Ikkō Ikki* (Renyo / The Ikkō Uprisings) Vol. 17 of *Nihon Shisō Taikei* (Systematized Japanese Thought). Tokyo: Iwanami Shoten, 1972.

Kashiwahara Yūsen. *Kinsei Shomin Bukkyō no Kenkyū* (A Study of Popular Buddhism in the Edo Period). Kyoto: Hozokan, 1971.

————. *Nihon Kinsei Kindai Bukkyō Shi no Kenkyū* (Studies in the Buddhist History of Early Modern Japan and Modern Japan). Kyoto: Heirakuji Shoten, 1969.

Kashiwahara Yūsen and Fujii Manabu, eds. *Kinsei Bukkyō no Shisō* (Buddhist Thought in the Edo Period). Vol. 57 of *Nihon Shisō Taikei* (Systematized Japanese Thought). Tokyo: Iwanami Shoten, 1973.

Kataoka Yakichi, Tamamuro Fumio, and Oguri Junko. *Kinsei no Chika Shinkō* (Underground Faith in the Edo Period). Tokyo: Hyoronsha, 1974.

————. *Uragami Yomban Kuzure* (The Disbandment of the Uragami No. 4). Tokyo: Chikuma Shobo, 1963.

Katsuno Ryūshin. *Hiei-zan to Kōya-san* (Mount Hiei and Mount Koya). Tokyo: Shibundoh, 1955.

Kawaski Yōsuke and Kasahara Kazuo, eds. *Shūkyō Shi* (A History of Religion). Vol. 18 of *Taikei Nihonshi Sōsho* (Systematized Series on Japanese History). Tokyo: Yamakawa Shuppan, 1964.

Kawazoe Shōji. *Nichiren—Sono Shisō/Kōdō to Mōko Shūrai* (Nichiren—His Thought and Activities and the Mongolian Attacks). Tokyo: Shimizu-Shoin, 1971.

Kodama Shiki. *Kinsei Shin Shū no Tenkai Katei* (The Developmental Process of the Jōdo Shin Sect in the Edo Period). Tokyo: Yoshikawa Kobunkan, 1976.

Kondō Yoshihiro. *Shikoku Henro* (Pilgrimages in Shikoku). Tokyo: Ōfū-sha, 1971.

Kubota Osamu. *Chūsei Shintō no Kenkyū* (A Study of Medieval Shinto). Kyoto: Shintō Shigakkai, 1964.

————. *Shintō Shi no Kenkyū* (Studies in the History of Shinto). Ise: Kogakkan University Shuppan-bu, 1973.

Kuroda Toshio. *Nihon Chūsei no Kokka to Shūkyō* (The Nation and Religion in Medieval Japan). Tokyo: Iwanami Shoten, 1975.

Kushida Ryōkō. *Shingon Mikkyō Seiritsu Katei no Kenkyū* (A Study of the Formation Process of Shingon Esoteric Buddhism). Tokyo: Sankibo Busshorin, 1964.

Matsuda Kiichi, tr. *Nihon Junsatsu Ki* (Notes from an Inspection Tour of Japan). Translated from Alessandro Valignano's *Sumario de las cosas de Japón* (1583) and *Adiciones del sumario de Japón* (1592), published in *Monumenta Nipponica Monographs*, No. 9 (Sophia University, Tokyo, 1954). Tokyo: Heibonsha Ltd., 1973.

Matsuno Junkō. *Shinran—Sono Kōdo to Shisō* (Shinran—His Activies and Thought). Vol. 4 of *Nihonjin no Kōdo to Shisō* (Conduct and Thinking of the Japanese) Tokyo: Hyoronsha, 1971.

————. *Shinran—Sono Shōgai to Shisō no Tenkai Katei* (Shinran—His Life and the Development of His Thought). Tokyo: Sanseido Co., Ltd., 1959.

Miyaji Naokazu. *Shintō Shi* (A History of Shinto). 3 vols. Matsudo City: Riso-Sha, 1958-63.

Miyake Hitoshi. *Shugendō Girei no Kenkyū* (A Study of the Rituals of Shugendō). Tokyo: Shunju-Sha, 1970.

————. *Yamabushi—Sono Kōdō to Soshiki* (Yamabushi—Their Activities and Organization). Vol. 29 of *Nihonjin no Kōdō to Shisō* (Conduct and Thinking of the Japanese). Tokyo: Hyoronsha, 1973.

Miyata Noboru. *Ikigami Shinkō* (Beliefs in Living Gods). Tokyo: Hanawa Shobo, 1970.

————. *Kinsei no Hayari-gami* (Popular Deities in the Edo Period). Tokyo: Hyoronsha, 1972.

————. *Minzoku Shūkyō Ron no Kadai* (Problems in the Studies of Folk Religion) Tokyo: Mirai-Sha, 1977.

————. *Tsuchi no Shisō* (Thoughts of the Soil). Vol. 6 of *Sōsho Shintai no Shisō* (Series on Thoughts of the Body). Tokyo: Sobun-Sha, 1977.

Miyazaki Eishū. *Fujufuse-ha no Genryū to Tenkai* (The Origin and Development of the Fujufuse Subsect). Kyoto: Heirakuji Shoten, 1959.

————. *Fujufuse-ha no Genryū to Tenkai* (The Origin and Development of the Fujufuse Subsect). Kyoto: Heirakuji Shoten, 1969.

————. *Kinsei Fujufuse-ha no Kenkyū* (A Study of the Kinsei Fujufuse Subsect). Kyoto: Heirakuji Shoten, 1959.

————. *Nichiren to Sono Deshi* (Nichiren and His Disciples). Tokyo: The Mainichi Newspapers Co., Ltd., 1971.

————. *Nichiren Shū no Shugojin* (Guardian Deities of the Nichiren Sect). Heirakuji Shoten, 1958.

Miyazaki Enjun. *Shin Shū Shoshigaku no Kenkyū* (Bibliographical Study of the Jōdo Shin Sect). Kyoto: Nagata Bunshodo, 1949.

———. *Shinran to Sono Montei* (Shinran and His Disciples). Kyoto: Nagata Bunshodo, 1956.

Mochizuki Kankō. *Nichiren Kyōgaku no Kenkyū* (A Study of the Nichiren Teachings). Kyoto: Heirakuji Shoten, 1958.

Mori Ryūkichi. *Shinran—Sono Shisōshi* (Shinran—The History of His Thought). Tokyo: San-ichi Publishing Co., Ltd., 1961.

Mori Ryūkichi, Kashiwahara Yūsen, Kino Kazuyoshi, and Yoshida Kyūichi. *Gudō no Hitobito—Bukkyō Hyaku-nen no Ayumi* (People Seeking the Way—Modern Buddhism's Progress over One Hundred Years). Tokyo: Shunju-Sha, 1969.

Morioka Kiyomi. *Gendai Shakai no Minshū to Shūkyō* (People and Religion in Modern Society). Tokyo: Hyoronsha, 1975.

———. *Nihon no Kindai Shakai to Kirisutokyō* (Japan's Modern Society and Christianity). Tokyo: Hyoronsha, 1970.

Munakata Jinja Fukkō Kisei-kai, ed. *Okinoshima* (Oki Island). 2 vols. Fukuoka Prefecture: Munakata Jinja Fukkō Kisei-kai, 1958 and 1961.

Murakami Shigeyoshi. *Butsuryū Kaidō Nagamatsu Nissen* (The Leader of Butsuryū-kō: Nagamatsu Nissen). Tokyo: Kodansha Ltd., 1976.

———. *Irei to Shōkon—Yasukuni no Shisō* (The Consolation of Spirits and the Invocation of Souls—the Ideology of Yasukini). Tokyo: Iwanami Shoten, 1974.

———. *Kindai Minshū Shūkyō Shi no Kenkyū* (A Study of the History of Popular Religion in the Modern Age). Kyoto: Hozokan, 1963.

———. *Kokka Shintō* (State Shinto). Tokyo: Iwanami Shoten, 1970.

———. *Konkō Daijin no Shōgai* (The Entire Life of Konkō Daijin). Tokyo: Kodansha Ltd., 1972.

———. *Nihon Hyakunen no Shūkyō* (A Hundred Years of Japanese Religion). Tokyo: Kodansha Ltd., 1966.

———. *Tennō no Saishi* (Imperial Ceremonies and Rituals). Tokyo: Iwanami Shoten, 1977.

Murakami Shigeyoshi and Yasumaru Yoshio, eds. *Minshū Shūkyō no Shisō* (The Ideology of Popular Religions). Vol. 67 of *Nihon Shisō Taikei* (Systematized Japanese Thought). Tokyo: Iwanami Shoten, 1971.

Murakami Toshio. *Shugendō no Hattatsu* (The Development of Shugendō). Tokyo. Unebi Shobo, 1943. Reprinted by Meicho Shuppan, Tokyo, 1977.

Muraoka Noritsugu. *Norinaga to Atsutane* (Norinage and Atustane). Tokyo: Sobun-Sha, 1957.

———. *Shintō Shi* (A History of Shinto). Tokyo: Sobun-Sha, 1956.

Murayama Shūichi. *Hiei-zan* (Mount Hiei). Tokyo: Japan Broadcast Publishing Co., Ltd., 1970.

————. *Honji Suijaku* (A Manifestation of a Buddha or Bodhisattva in the Temporary Form of a Shinto Deity). Tokyo: Yoshikawa Kobunkan, 1974.

————. *Kodai Bukkyō no Chūseiteki Tenkai* (Ancient Buddhism's Development in the Medieval Period). Kyoto: Hozokan, 1976.

————. *Shimbutsu Shūgō Shichō* (The Trends of Thought in Shinto-Buddhist Syncretism). Kyoto: Heirakuji Shoten, 1957.

————. *Yamabushi no Rekishi* (A History of the Yamabushi). Tokyo: Hanawa Shobo, 1970.

Nakamura Hajime, Kasahara Kazuo, and Kanaoka Shūyū, eds. *Nihon-hen* (Series on Japan). 9 vols. In *Ajia Bukkyō Shi* (A History of Asian Buddhism). Tokyo: Kosei Publishing Co., 1975.

Nakao Takashi, ed. *Nichiren Shū no Sho-mondai* (Various Problems of the Nichiren Sect). Tokyo: Yuzankaku Shuppan, 1970.

————. *Nichiren Shū no Seiritsu to Tenkai* (The Establishment and Development of the Nichiren Sect). Tokyo: Yoshikawa Kobunkan, 1973.

————. *Nisshin—Sono Kōdō to Shisō* (Nisshin—His Activities and Thought). Vol. 15 of *Nihonjin no Kōdō to Shisō* (Conduct and Thinking of the Japanese). Tokyo: Hyoronsha, 1971.

Nakao Toshihiro. *Nihon Shoki Tendai no Kenkyū* (A Study of Early Japanese Tendai Buddhism). Kyoto: Nagata Bunshodo, 1973.

Nakazawa Kemmyo. *Shin Shū Genryū Shiron* (Theory of the History of the Origin of the Jōdo Shin Sect). Kyoto: Hozokan, 1951.

Nanto Bukkyō Kenkyū-kai, ed. *Jūgen Shōnin no Kenkyū* (A Study of Jūgen Shōnin). Nara: Nanto Bukkyō Kenkyū-kai, 1955.

Nishida Nagao. *Jinja no Rekishiteki Kenkyū* (A Historical Study of Shinto Shrines). Tokyo: Hanawa Shobo, 1966.

————. *Shintō Shi no Kenkyū* (Studies in the History of Shinto). 2 vols. Vol. 1, Tokyo: Yuzankaku Shuppan, 1943. Vol. 2, Matsudo City: Riso-Sha, 1957.

Nishimura Kengyō. *Kiyozawa Manshi Sensei* (Kiyozawa Manshi, Teacher). Kyoto: Hozokan, 1951.

Nishiyama Matsunosuke and Ogi Shinzō. *Edo Sambyaku-nen* (Three Hundred Years of Edo). Tokyo: Kodansha Ltd., 1976.

Ōba Iwao, ed. *Shintō Kōkogaku Kōza* (Lecture on Shinto Archaeology). Vols. 2, 4, 5, 6. Tokyo: Yuzankaku Shuppan, 1972-74.

Ogawa Keiji, ed. *Nihonjin to Kirisutokyō* (The Japanese and Christianity). Tokyo: Sanseido Co., Ltd., 1973.

Ogisu Jundō. *Nihon Chūsei Zen Shū Shi* (A History of Japanese Zen in the Middle Ages). Tokyo: Mokujisha, 1965.

Oguri Junko. *Myōkōnin to Kakure Nembutsu* (Myōkōnin and Hidden Nembutsu). Tokyo: Kodansha Ltd., 1975.

————. *Nakayama Miki—Tenrikyō* (Nakayama Miki—Tenrikyō). Tokyo: Shin Jimbutsu Ōrai-sha, 1970.

————. *Nihon no Kindai Shakai to Tenrikyō* (Modern Japanese Society and Tenri-kyō). Tokyo: Hyoronsha, 1969.

Ōhara Shōjitu. *Shin-shū Igi Ianjin no Kenkyū* (A Study of the Heresies of the Jōdo Shin Sect). Kyoto: Nagata Bunshodo, 1964.

Ōhashi Toshio. *Hōnen—Sono Kōdō to Shisō* (Hōnen—His Activities and Thought). Vol. 1 of *Nihonjin no Kōdō to Shisō* (Conduct and Thinking of the Japanese). Tokyo: Hyoronsha, 1970.

————. *Ippen—Sono Kōdō to Shisō* (Ippen—His Activities and Thought). Vol. 14 of *Nihonjin no Kōdō to Shisō* (Conduct and Thinking of the Japanese). Tokyo: Hyoronsha, 1971.

————. *Jishū no Seiritsu to Tenkai* (The Establishment and Development of the Ji Sect). Tokyo: Yoshikawa Kobunkan, 1973.

————. *Odori Nembutsu* (Dancing Nembutsu). Tokyo: Daizo Shuppan, 1974.

————. *Yugyō Hijiri—Shomin no Bukkyō Shiwa* (Wayfaring Holy Men—Historical Budddhist Tales for the People). Tokyo: Daizo Shuppan, 1971.

Ōhashi Toshio, ed. *Hōnen / Ippen* (Hōnen / Ippen) Vol. 10 of *Nihon Shisō Taikei* (Systematized Japanese Thought). Tokyo: Iwanami Shoten, 1971.

Ōkubo Dōshū. *Dōgen Zenji-den no Kenkyū* (A Study of the Biographies of Zen Master Dōgen). Tokyo: Iwanami Shoten, 1953.

Ōshima Taishin. *Jōdo Shū Shi* (A History of the Jōdo Sect). Vol. 20 of *Jōdo Shu Zensho* (Complete Documents of the Jōdo Sect). Kyoto: Jōdo Shū Kaishū Happyaku-nen Kinen Keisan Jumbi-kyoku, 1972.

Ōsumi Kazuo. *Shōbō—Rigen Daishi* (Shōbō—the Great Teacher Rigen). Kyoto: Daigo-ji, 1976.

Ōsumi Kazuo, ed. *Chūsei Shintō Ron* (Medieval Shinto Theories). Vol. 19 of *Nihon Shisō Taikei* (Systematized Japanese Thought). Tokyo: Iwanami Shoten, 1977.

Sakuma Tadashi, tr. *Pedoro Morehon Nihon Junkyō Roku* (Pedro Morejon's Record of Christian Martyrdom in Japan). 2 vols. Translated from *Relacion de la Persecvcion qve vvo en la Yglesia de Iapon: Y de los insignes Martyres, que gloriosamente dieron su vida en defensa de nra santa Fè, el Año de 1614; y 615. Mexico 1616.* Tokyo: Association for the Study of Kirishitan Culture, 1968–69.

Sakurai Kageo. *Nanzen-ji Shi* (A History of the Temple Nanzen-ji). 2 vols. Kyoto: Nanzen-ji, 1940, 1954. (Vol. 1, reprinted by Hozokan, Kyoto, 1977).

Sakurai Tokutarō. *Kō Shūdan Seiritsu Katei no Kenkyū* (A Study of the Establishment Process of the *Kō* Groups). Tokyo: Yoshikawa Kobunkan, 1962.

————. *Minkan Shinkō* (Popular Beliefs). Tokyo: Hanawa Shobo, 1966.

————. *Sangaku Shūkyō to Minkan Shinkō no Kenkyū* (A Study of Mountain Religion and Popular Beliefs). Vol. 6 of *Sangaku Shūkyō Kenkyū Sōsho* (Series on Studies of Mountain Religion). Tokyo: Meicho Shuppan, 1976.

Sakurai Tokutarō, et al., eds. *Jisha Engi* (Legends of the Founding of Temples and Shrines). Vol. 20 of *Nihon Shisō Taikei* (Systematized Japanese Thought). Tokyo: Iwanami Shoten, 1975.

Sawa Ryūken. *Daigo-ji* (The Temple Daigo). Tokyo: Tōyō Bunka Shuppan, 1976.

————. *Kūkai no Kiseki* (Traces of Kūkai). Tokyo: The Mainichi Newspapers Co., Ltd., 1973.

————. *Nihon Mikkyō—Sono Tenkai to Bijutsu* (Japanese Esoteric Buddhism—Its Development and Art). Tokyo: Japan Broadcast Publishing Co., Ltd., 1966.

SCAP's *Minkan Jōhō Kyōiku-bu Shūkyōbunka Shiryō-ka*, ed. and Ministry of Education's religious study group, tr. *Nihon no Shūkyō* (Religions in Japan). Tokyo: Kokumin Kyōiku Fukyū-kai/Daito Publishing Co., Inc., 1948.

Shigematsu Akihisa. *Nihon Jōdo-kyō Seiritsu Katei no Kenkyū* (A Study of the Formation Process of Japanese Pure Land Buddhism). Tokyo: Yoshikawa Kobunkan, 1964.

Shimizudani Kyōjun. *Tendai Mikkyō no Seiritsu ni kansuru Kenkyū* (A Study of the Establishment of Tendai Esoteric Buddhism). Tokyo: Bun-ichi Shuppan, 1972.

Shimode Sekiyo. *Dōkyō to Nihonjin* (Taoism and the Japanese). Tokyo: Kodansha Ltd., 1975.

————. *Nihon Kodai no Jingi to Dōkyō* (The Deities and Taoism of Ancient Japan). Tokyo: Yoshikawa Kobunkan, 1972.

Shingyō Norikazu. *Ikkō Ikki no Kiso Kōzō—Mikawa Ikki to Matsudaira-shi* (The Ikkō Uprisings and Their Basic Structure—the Mikawa Uprising and the Matsudaira Clan). Tokyo: Yoshikawa Kobunkan, 1975.

Shinjō Tsunezō. *Shaji Sankei no Shakai-keizaishi-teki Kenkyū* (A Socio-economic Historical Study of People's Visits to Shrines and Temples). Tokyo: Hanawa Shobo, 1964.

Shinshūren Chōsashitsu, ed. *Sengo Shūkyo Kaiso Roku* (Reflections on Religions in the Postwar Period). Tokyo: PL Shuppan-sha, 1963.

Shiraishi Kogetsu. *Tōfuku-ji Shi* (A History of the Temple Tōfuku-ji). Kyoto: Tōfuku-ji, 1930.

Sonoda Kōyū and Tamura Enchō. "Heian Bukkyō" (Heian Buddhism). In vol. 4 of *Iwanami Kōza Nihon Rekishi—Kodai* 4 (Iwanami Lecture: A History of Japan—the Ancient Period, vol. 4). Tokyo: Iwanami Shoten, 1962.

Sukeno Kentarō. *Kirishitan no Shinkō Seikatsu* (The Religious Life of Christians). Tokyo: Chuō Shuppan-sha, 1957.

Sumiya Mikio. *Kindai Nihon no Keisei to Kirisutokyō* (The Formation of Modern Japan and Christianity). Tokyo: Shinkyō Shuppan-sha, 1950.

————. *Nihon Shihon-shugi to Kirisutokyō* (Japanese Capitalism and Christianity). Tokyo: University of Tokyo Press, 1962.

Suzuki Munenori. *Nihon no Kindaika to On no Shisō* (The Modernization of Japan and the Ideology of On). Kyoto: Horitsu Bunka-Sha. 1964.

Suzuki Taizan. *Zenshū no Chihōteki Hatten* (The Development of the Zen Sect in Local Areas). Tokyo: Unebi Shobō, 1942.

Taga Sōjun. *Jien* (Jien). Tokyo: Yoshikawa Kobunkan, 1959.

Tahara Tsuguo. *Hirata Atsutane* (Hirata Atsutane). Tokyo: Yoshikawa Kobunkan, 1963.

Taira Shigemichi. *Kinsei Nihon Shisō Shi Kenkyū* (Studies in the History of Japanese Thought in the Edo Period). Tokyo: Yoshikawa Kobunkan, 1969.

———. *Yoshikawa Shintō no Kisoteki Kenkyū* (A Basic Study of Yoshikawa Shinto). Tokyo: Yoshikawa Kobunkan, 1966.

Taira Shigemichi and Abe Akio, eds. *Kinsei Shintō Ron / Zenki Kokugaku* (Shinto Doctrines in the Edo Period / National Learning in the Preceding Period). Vol. 39 of *Nihon Shisō Taikei* (Systematized Japanese Thought). Tokyo: Iwanami Shoten, 1972.

Takagi Hiroo. *Nihon no Shinkō Shūkyō—Taishū-undō no Seishi to Riron* (New Religions of Japan—Correct History and Theory of Mass Ideological Movements). Tokyo: Iwanami Shoten, 1959.

Takagi Yutaka. *Heian Jidai Hokke Bukkyō Shi Kenkyū* (A Study of the History of Hokke Buddhism in the Heian Period). Kyoto: Heirakuji Shoten, 1973.

———. *Nichiren to Sono Montei* (Nichiren and His Disciples). Tokyo: Kobundo, 1965.

———. *Nichiren—Sono Kōdō to Shisō* (Nichiren—His Activities and Thought). Vol. 4 of *Nihonjin no Kōdō to Shisō* (Conduct and Thinking of the Japanese). Tokyo: Hyoronsha, 1970.

Takahashi Bonsen. *Kakushi Nembutsu Kō* (Thoughts about the Hidden Nembutsu). Vol. 1–2. Tokyo: Japan Society for the Promotion of Science, 1956.

Takeda Chōshū. *Kinsei Sonraku no Shaji to Shimbutsu Shūgō* (Shinto Shrines and Buddhist Temples and Shinto-Buddhist Syncretism of Villages in the Edo Period). Kyoto: Hozokan, 1972.

———. *Nihonjin no Ie to Shūkyō* (The Homes and Religions of the Japanese). Tokyo: Hyoronsha, 1976.

Takeda Kiyoko. *Haikyō-sha no Keifu—Nihonjin to Kirisutokyō* (The Genealogy of Apostasy—the Japanese and Christianity). Tokyo: Iwanami Shoten, 1973.

Takeuchi Michio. *Nihon no Zen* (Japanese Zen). Tokyo: Shunju-Sha, 1976.

Tamamura Takeji. *Gozan Bungaku* (Literature of the Gozan School). Vol. 6 of *Nihon Rekishi Shinsho* (Paperback Series on Japanese History). Tokyo: Shibundoh, 1955.

———. *Musō Kokushi* (Teacher of the Nation, Musō). Kyoto: Heirakuji Shoten, 1958.

———. *Nihon Zen Shū Shi Ronjū* (Historical Anthology of the Japanese Zen Sect), vol. 1. Kyoto: Shibunkaku Shuppan, 1976.

Tamamura Takeji and Inoue Zenjō. *Engaku-ji Shi* (A History of the Temple Engaku-ji). Tokyo: Shunju-Sha, 1964.

Tamamuro Fumio. *Edo-bakufu no Shūkyō Tōsei* (The Edo Shogunate's Regulation of Religion). Tokyo: Hyoronsha, 1971.

———. *Shimbutsu Bunri* (Divisions Between Shinto and Buddhism). Vol. 113 of

Rekishi Shinsho (Paperback Series on Religious History). Tokyo: Kyōiku-sha, 1977.

Tamamuro Fumio and Miyata Noboru. *Shomin Shinkō no Gensō* (Illusions of Popular Beliefs). Tokyo: The Mainichi Newspapers Co., Ltd., 1977.

Tamayama Jōgen. *Fukō Kanchi Kokushi—Kinsei Shoki niokeru Jōdo Shū no Hatten* (The Teacher of the Nation, Fukō Kanchi—the Development of the Jōdo Sect in the Early Edo Period). Tokyo: Hakutei-Sha, 1970.

Tamura Enchō. *Asuka Bukkyō Shi Kenkyū* (A Study of Asuka Buddhism). Tokyo: Hanawa Shobō, 1969.

———. *Hōnen* (Hōnen). Tokyo: Yoshikawa Kobunkan, 1959.

Tamura Enchō and Kō Junchō, eds. *Shiragi to Asuka Hakuhō no Bukkyō Bunka* (Buddhist Culture of the Shiragi and Asuka/Hakuho Periods). Tokyo: Yoshikawa Kobunkan, 1975.

Tamura Yoshirō. *Kamakura Shin Bukkyō Shisō no Kenkyū* (A Study of the Thought of Kamakura New Buddhism). Kyoto: Heirakuji Shoten, 1965.

———. *Nichiren—Junkyō no Nyorai Shi* (Nichiren—a Martyr Sent by the Tathāgata). Tokyo: Japan Broadcast Publishing Co., Ltd., 1975.

Tamura Yoshirō, et al. *Nihon Kindai to Nichiren-shugi* (Modern Japan and Nichirenism). Vol. 4 of *Kōza Nichiren* (Lectures on Nichiren). Tokyo: Shunju-Sha, 1972.

Tamura Yoshirō, et al., eds. *Tendai Hongaku Ron* (The Theory of Original Enlightenment in Tendai Buddhism). Vol. 9 of *Nihon Shisō Taikei* (Systematized Japanese Thought). Tokyo: Iwanami Shoten, 1973.

Tanaka Hisao. *Myōe* (Myōe). Tokyo: Yoshikawa Kobunkan, 1961.

Tanaka Hisao and Kamata Shigeo, eds. *Kamakura Kyū Bukkyō* (Kamakura Old Buddhism). Vol. 15 of *Nihon Shisō Taikei* (Systematized Japanese Thought). Tokyo: Iwanami Shoten, 1971.

Tanishita Ichimu. *Shin Shū Shi no Sho-kenkyū* (Various Studies of the Jōdo Shin Sect). Kyoto: Heirakuji Shoten, 1941.

Tendai Association of Buddhist Studies, ed. *Dengyō Daishi Kenkyū* (A Study of the Great Teacher Dengyō). Tokyo: Waseda University Press, 1973.

The Mainichi Newspapers Co., Ltd., ed. *Umi no Shōsōin—Okinoshima* (Shōsō-in of the Sea: Oki Island). Tokyo: The Mainichi Newspapers Co., Ltd., 1972.

Togawa Anshō. *Dewa Sanzan Shugendō no Kenkyū* (A Study of Shugendō in the Dewa Three Mountains). Tokyo: Kosei Publishing Co., 1973.

Togoro Shigemoto. *Kindai Shakai to Nichiren-shugi* (Modern Society and Nichirenism). Vol. 18 of *Nihonjin no Kōdō to Shisō* (Conduct and Thinking of the Japanese). Tokyo: Hyoronsha, 1972.

———. *Nichiren no Shisō to Kamakura Bukkyō* (The Thought of Nichiren and Kamakura Buddhism). Tokyo: Fuzan-bō, 1965.

Togoro Shigemoto and Tagaki Yutaka, eds. *Nichiren* (Nichiren). Vol. 14 of *Nihon*

Shisō Taikei (Systematized Japanese Thought). Tokyo: Iwanami Shoten, 1970.

Tomura Masahiro, ed. *Jinja Mondai to Kirisutokyō* (The Shinto Shrine Issue and Christianity). Tokyo: Shinkyō Shuppan-sha, 1977.

Tsuda Sōkichi. *Nihon no Shintō* (Japanese Shinto). Tokyo: Iwanami Shoten, 1949.

Tsuji Zennosuke. *Nihon Bukkyō Shi* (A History of Japanese Buddhism). 10 vols. Tokyo: Iwanami Shoten, 1955.

Tsunemitsu Kōnen. *Meiji no Bukkyō-sha* (Buddhists of the Meiji Period). 2 vols. Tokyo: Shunju-Sha, 1968–69.

Umehara Ryūshō. *Kinsei Shin Shū Shi no Sho-mondai* (Various Problems in the History of the Jōdo Shin Sect in the Edo Period). Kyoto: Kenshin Gakuen Shuppan-bu, 1962.

————. *Shinran Den no Sho-mondai* (Various Questions in the Biographies of Shinran). Kyoto: Kenshin Gakuen, 1951.

Wajima Yoshio. *Eison / Ninshō* (Eison and Ninshō). Tokyo: Yoshikawa Kobunkan, 1970.

Wakamori Tarō. *Sangaku Shūkyō no Seiritsu to Tenkai* (The Establishment and Development of Mountain Religion). Vol. 1 of *Sangaku Shūkyō Kenkyū Sōsho* (Series on the Study of Mountain Religion). Tokyo: Meicho Shuppan, 1975.

————. *Shugendō Shi Kenkyū* (A Study of the History of Shugendō). Tokyo: Kawade Shobo, 1943. Reprinted by Heibonsha Ltd., Tokyo, 1972.

————. *Yamabushi—Nyūhō, Shugyō, Juhō* (Yamabushi—Entering the Mountain, Asceticism, and Mantra Rituals). Tokyo: Chuokoron-Sha, 1964.

Washio Junkyō. *Nihon Zen Shū Shi no Kenkyū* (A Study of the History of the Japanese Zen Sect). Vol. 1 of *Ranzan Zenshū* (Complete Collection of Washio Junkyō's Works). Kyoto: Kyōten Shuppan, 1945.

Watanabe Shōkō, ed. *Saichō/Kūkai Shū* (Anthology of Writings by Saichō and Kūkai). Vol. 1 of *Nihon no Shisō* (Thought in Japan). Tokyo: Chikuma Shobō, 1969.

White, James W., *The Soka Gakkai and Mass Society*. Stanford: Stanford University Press, 1970.

Yamada Bunshō. *Shinran to Sono Kyōdan* (Shinran and His Religious Organization). Kyoto: Hozokan, 1948.

Yamaguchi Kōen. *Tendai Jōdokyō Shi* (A History of Tendai Pure Land Buddhism). Kyoto: Hozokan, 1967.

Yokota Kenichi. *Dōkyō* (Taoism). Tokyo: Yoshikawa Kobunkan, 1959.

Yoshida Kogorō, tr. and Father Krischer, ed. *Reon Pajesu Nihon Kirishitan Shūmon Shi* (Léon Pagés's History of Japanese Christianity). 3 vols. Translated from *Histoire de la religion chrétienne au Japón depuis 1958 jusqu'a 1651, comprenant les faits relatifs aux deux cent cinq martyrs béatifiés le 7 juillet 1867* (2 vols. Paris: Charles Douniol, Libraire-éditeur, 1869). Tokyo: Iwanami Shoten, 1960.

Yoshida Kyūichi. *Kiyozawa Manshi* (Kiyozawa Manshi). Tokyo: Yoshikawa Kobunkan, 1971.

————. *Nihon Kindai Bukkyō Shakai Shi Kenkyū* (Studies in the History of Buddhist Society in Modern Japan). Tokyo: Yoshikawa Kobunkan, 1964.

————. *Nihon Kindai Bukkyō Shi Kenkyū* (Studies in the History of Buddhism in Modern Japan). Tokyo: Yoshikawa Kobunkan, 1959.

————. *Nihon no Kindai Shakai to Bukkyō* (Modern Japanese Society and Buddhism). Vol. 6 of *Nihonjin no Kōdō to Shisō* (Conduct and Thinking of the Japanese). Tokyo: Hyoronsha, 1970.

Index

Ōuchi Yoshihiro (大内義弘), 243
Ōuchi Yoshinaga (大内義長), 423
Ōuchi Yoshitaka (大内義隆), 422
Outer Shrine, dispute with Inner Shrine, 303–6
Outer Shrine Shintō, 305–6
Ōyama Tameoki (大山為起), 349
Ōyu site, stone circles at, 29–32

Paekche Buddhism: influence on Asuka Buddhism, 57, 58; rivalry with Silla Buddhism, 57–58
palaces, construction methods of, 55–57
Pao-yüeh (宝月), 81
parish system, 334
pastoral letter(s), 408; from Bukkō ji abbot, 412; from Gyōshū, 414–15; of Hongan-ji leaders, 409–10
patronage, under Tokugawa shogunate, 338–40
Pereira, Guilherme, 426
periods in Japanese history, 21–24. See also *individual periods*
Perpetual Lectures on the Lotus Sutra (Hokke Jōgō), 94, 95
Perry, Commodore Matthew C., 495
persecution/exile: of Buddhist clerics, 70; of Christians, 436–37, 499–500, 516–17; Eikyō Persecution, 273; of Fuju Fuse faction, 400–401; of Jōdo Shin believers, 199; Kumogaike Persecution, 550; Namekawa Persecution, 400; of Nichiren, 258–59, 260–64, 266; of Nichiren sect, 260–61, 265; Shimōsa Persecution, 400–401; Tatsunokuchi Persecution, 260–61; of Tenrikyō, 483–84
Petitjean, Bernard T., 497–99, 502
phallicism. See *dōsojin*
pilgrimages: to Ise Grand Shrine, 302–3; by *ko*, 471–73; to Kūkai's tomb, 165; to sacred sites, 138; Shikoku circuit, 473–74; to temples/shrines, 442, 473–74; to western Honshu, 329
pledge-book priests, 135, 344
PL Kyōdan, 582, 583
politics, poverty of, 23

popular Buddhism, 71–72
popular Shintō, 350–52
poverty, as starting point of salvation, 481, 482
practices: associated with rebirth, 155; exclusive/easy vs. rigorous, 158–59; Ten Realms practice, 324–26, 464; undertaken by women, 291. See also *daimoku* practice; meditation practice; *nembutsu*
precepts, Buddhist: bestowed in Sōtō sect, 253; conferring, as propagation method, 362; devised by Saichō, 78–79; dormancy of, 167–68; return to, 546–48
precepts, Meiji government's, 527
priests: battlefield, 222; bodhisattva, 79; of Fuke sect, 386; funerary role of, 335; Heian-period practices of, 49–50; integrated into Jōdo sect, 188; of Ju faction, 403–4; Nara-period practices of, 48, 49–50; offenses of Ji-sect, 218; persecution of, 70; pledge-book, 135, 344; popular, 150–54, 363–66; Pure Land subtemples and, 122–23; ranks for Zen, 235–36; ranks of Ji-sect, 373; ranks of Shugendō, 457; sham, 151–52; Shintō, 300, 301, 313–14, 530–32, 540–41; as shogunate public servants, 333–35; teaching duties of Jōdo-sect, 358–60; of Tendai sect, 79, 90; training of, 357–58, 374–75; wandering/mendicant Sōtō, 381–82; as warriors, 90, 126; women, 267, 295. *See also* clerics
prison chaplains, Buddhist, 589–90
protection of nation, Lotus Sutra and, 93–94
Protestantism: bands of converts, 514–16; consolidation of sects and denominations, 521–23; early missionaries/converts, 511–14; intellectual vs. spiritual belief, 519–21; in Meiji period (map), 512; other converts, 517–18; postwar, 588–89; recent survey of, 523; revolutionary nature of, 516–17; social factors in conversions, 518–19; society and, 520–21. See also *individual churches*